BEHOLD THE PROVERBS OF A PEOPLE

Behold the Proverbs of a People

Proverbial Wisdom in Culture, Literature, and Politics

WOLFGANG MIEDER

UNIVERSITY PRESS OF MISSISSIPPI • JACKSON

www.upress.state.ms.us

The University Press of Mississippi is a member of the Association of
American University Presses.

Copyright © 2014 by University Press of Mississippi
All rights reserved
Manufactured in the United States of America

First printing 2014
∞
Library of Congress Cataloging-in-Publication Data

Mieder, Wolfgang.
  Behold the proverbs of a people : proverbial wisdom in culture, literature,
and politics / Wolfgang Mieder.
      pages cm
  Includes bibliographical references and index.
  ISBN 978-1-62846-140-4 (hardback) — ISBN 978-1-62846-141-1 (ebook)
  1. Proverbs—History and criticism. I. Title.
  PN6401.M476 2014
  398.9′09—dc23

                    2014010121

British Library Cataloging-in-Publication Data available

published with a grant from

Jewish Federation of Greater Hartford

that truth be peopled

Contents

Proverbs in Literature

Proverbs in Culture

BEHOLD THE PROVERBS OF A PEOPLE

Introduction

It has been my good fortune to have had the welcome opportunity to present some of my articles that have appeared over the years in various journals and books in Europe and the United States in a number of essay volumes, to wit *The Politics of Proverbs: From Traditional Wisdom to Proverbial Stereotypes* (1997), *Strategies of Wisdom: Anglo-American and German Proverb Studies* (2000), *Proverbs Are the Best Policy: Folk Wisdom and American Politics* (2005), and *"Proverbs Speak Louder Than Words": Folk Wisdom in Art, Culture, Folklore, History, Literature, and Mass Media* (2008). About five years have passed since the appearance of the last book, and I am delighted to put forth this fifth volume entitled *Behold the Proverbs of a People: Proverbial Wisdom in Culture, Literature, and Politics,* whose thirteen chapters bear witness to my ongoing dedication to tilling the fascinating field of international paremiology. Its main title comes from Carl Sandburg's lengthy poem "Good Morning, America" (1928), in which he characterizes the United States as a country of immigrants and numerous ethnic groups by way of its multifaceted language. As an immigrant from Germany myself, I still remember when I came across this poem in 1970. I was so taken by its spirit of multicultural and linguistic diversity that it resulted in my first publication written in English: "'Behold the Proverbs of a People': A Florilegium of Proverbs in Carl Sandburg's Poem 'Good Morning, America,'" *Southern Folklore Quarterly* 35 (1971): 160–68. Two years later I followed this up with a more detailed analysis in the same journal of Sandburg's powerful epic poem *The People, Yes* (1936), still the perfect work to introduce people to the cultural and linguistic mix that characterizes this country. But be that as it may, there are two lines in the eleventh section of "Good Morning, America" that have stuck with me for over forty years, and they have surely become proverbial to me, as I enjoy citing them in my studies and at the beginning of my large lecture course on "'Big Fish Eat Little Fish': The Nature and Politics of Proverbs" that I teach every year at the University of Vermont:

A code arrives; language; lingo; slang;
behold the proverbs of a people, a nation:

This call is followed by dozens of slang terms, idioms, and proverbial expressions in addition to such proverbs as "It's the roving bee that gathers the honey," "Business is business," "Courtesy pays," "The customer is always right," "Figures don't lie but liars can figure," "The good die young," "The grass is higher in the back yard," "Let one hand wash the other," "The higher they go the farther they drop," "Honesty is the best policy," "What you don't know won't hurt you," "There are lies, damned lies, and statistics," "Life is what you make it," "Money isn't everything," "It's hell to be poor," "Speak softly and carry a big stick," "War is hell," and "It's all in the way you look at it." Many of these proverbs registered by Carl Sandburg reappear in the thirteen chapters presented here that illustrate the ubiquity of proverbs in the United States and Europe. They will certainly show that it behooves us to "behold the proverbs of a people" and that proverbs give us a lens into the worldview of the people who make use of them to underscore life's trials, tribulations, challenges, successes, fortunes, and joys.

It was not particularly difficult to divide my thirteen studies from 2007 until 2013 into four cohesive groups. The first is comprised of three chapters that deal with the field of paremiology in general, the spread of Anglo-American proverbs in Europe, and the phenomenon of modern proverbs. The second group consists of four chapters looking at the use of proverbs in the world of politics. Two of them analyze the effective employment of proverbs by Martin Luther King and President Barack Obama respectively. Next follows a chapter on proverbs as they relate to the concept of an interconnected world, and there is also an analysis of proverbs relating to war and peace. Another three chapters make up the group dedicated to literary topics: Ralph Waldo Emerson's engaged interest in proverbs, the use and function of proverbs in modern mini-poems, and Friedrich Nietzsche's philosophy expressed by way of his aphoristic reactions to proverbs. The last group is made up of three detailed cultural studies of the origin, history, dissemination, use, function, and meaning of the two proverbial expressions "The dog in the manger" and "To build castles in Spain," as well as the American proverb "Let George do it." Together the thirteen chapters comprise an intriguing and informative entry into the world of proverb scholarship, illustrating that proverbs always have been and continue to be in vogue today. I suppose I could say with proper humility that my book title *Proverbs Are Never Out of Season: Popular Wisdom in the Modern Ages* (1993) says it all when it comes to the omnipresence of proverbs with their multiple functions, contexts, and meanings. Proverbs are part and parcel of oral and written communication, and as so-called verbal and often metaphorically expressed *monumenta humana* they deserve to be studied from a multitude of viewpoints.

While the various chapters deal with a multitude of issues and approaches, they are connected by a rhetorical perspective that looks at proverbs as speech acts with text, texture, and context that have a noteworthy impact on oral and written communication within a culture and society. Whether proverbs appear in everyday speech, on the radio, on television, in films, on the pages of newspapers or magazines, in advertisements, in literary works of all types, or in political speeches, they are employed as formulaic verbal devices to add authoritative weight through tradition, convention, and wisdom. As communicative signs they also usually add metaphorical expressiveness to statements that otherwise might lack in rhetorical effectiveness. Proverbs certainly are not mere didactic bits of wisdom to be employed as generalized rules of life and behavior. Instead, they are communicative or rhetorical signs that put the entire human experience into formulaic and concise utterances to be repeated at the right moment as apparent truths. That does not mean that proverbs are universally true. In fact, they are as contradictory as life itself, but they are valid in certain situations. And, of course, proverbs can be manipulated to express a new insight or simply to make them fit into a novel context. Such anti-proverbs often have an additional rhetorical value in that they juxtapose the traditional wisdom with an innovative alternative. In any case, proverbs are invaluable social signs that have a great strategic influence on all types of communication.

All of this is developed further in the first chapter, "'The Wit of One, and the Wit of Many': Proverbs as Cultural Signs of Folklore," which serves as an introduction to proverb studies or paremiology as such. Its title cites Lord John Russell's by now proverbial definition of proverbs as "The wit of one, and the wisdom of many" from the mid-nineteenth century. It is my earnest attempt to survey the field of proverb studies, dealing with the vexing problem of the definition of proverbs, their varied meanings, and the empirical approaches toward ascertaining which proverbs of a given culture belong to the so-called paremiological minimum. This is followed by a look at proverbs as cultural signs that are performed in all kinds of communication, from spoken discourse to written texts and on to visual images. Proverbs certainly are part of culture, folklore, and history, and their careful analysis reveals that they are neither saccharine nor without their problems, to wit stereotypical proverbs against minorities and proverbs expressing a misogynous worldview. The chapter goes on to look at what the social sciences contribute to proverb studies, what role proverbs have played in religion and wisdom literature, and how they serve as didactic and pedagogical tools including foreign language teaching. The last section of this inclusive survey looks at the widespread use of proverbs in the mass media, including their appearance as newspaper headlines, advertisement slogans, cartoon captions, T-shirt inscriptions, greeting card messages, etc. Finally, mention is also made of proverbs in popular culture, including the use of proverbs in song lyrics, films, and, of course, the internet. A detailed bibliography, emphasizing scholarship written in English as the lingua franca of the modern age, rounds off this general treatise. In fact, every chapter of this book concludes with its own major bibliography, giving students and scholars the opportunity to copy individual chapters with their appropriate references.

Speaking of the predominance of the English language in an age of globalization, it should not be surprising that the next chapter, with its anti-proverbial title "'Many Roads Lead to Globalization': The Translation and Distribution of Anglo-American Proverbs in Europe," addresses the spread of English proverbs throughout the world. Classical antiquity, the Bible, and the Middle Ages were the three general times when many of the common proverbs known in Europe and the United States originated and then spread as translations into numerous languages and cultures. The fourth period is made up of the "Englishes" of the world, with British and American proverbs in particular being disseminated in English as the lingua franca or as loan translations. This chapter begins with a short survey of European paremiography, i.e., a review of major comparative proverb collections that list proverbs from various European languages and cultures. This is followed by a short overview of European phraseology and paremiology, showing that scholars are working on isolating those phraseologisms and proverbs that are known throughout Europe. The origin and dissemination of such common European proverbs is analyzed next, only to be followed by two sections on older and then modern loan translations of Anglo-American proverbs in Europe. As one might expect, the chapter concludes with a look at those proverbs that have been translated from the English into the German language, among them "It takes two to tango," "Good fences make good neighbors," "An apple a day keeps the doctor away", "The grass always looks greener on the other side of the fence," and "One picture is worth a thousand words." The chapter ends with a heartfelt plea for more work on the truly modern proverbs that are presently spreading from one European language to another, with many of them being of Anglo-American origin.

The third chapter, "'Think Outside the Box': Origin, Nature, and Meaning of Modern Anglo-American Proverbs," is based on the proverbs contained in the new *Dictionary of Modern Proverbs* (New Haven, Connecticut: Yale University Press, 2012) compiled by Charles Clay Doyle, Fred R. Shapiro, and me. It begins with a short history and description of this exciting project of collecting and presenting truly modern proverbs (no older than the year 1900) that took about four years to complete. This is followed by a survey of collections and studies that contain modern proverbs in the English language that, with the addition of proverbs that we identified by way of our own field research, became the actual corpus of our dictionary. Next I discuss the difficulty of choosing the appropriate lemmas, how to register variants, and the fact that modern proverbs, just as older ones, differ in length from a minimum of two to more than twenty words. Other sections deal with modern proverbs expressed as laws of life, the attribution of some of the proverbs to famous individuals, and advertising slogans, song lyrics, and films as sources of modern proverbs. Many of the proverbs refer to animals or body parts, but as expected, they also cover the world of business, sports, and technology. As far as frequent keywords are concerned, I note that "life," "man," "woman," "God," "friend," "time," "age," "love," and "beauty" are particularly productive in the formulation of new proverbs. The final section addresses the appearance of sexuality, obscenity, and scatology in modern proverbs. Such proverbs were usually excluded from proverb collections, but we felt that the time had surely come to register this modern wisdom couched in language that might be problematic to some readers. In any case, this chapter and *The Dictionary of Modern Proverbs* show that new Anglo-American proverbs are perhaps less metaphorical than traditional proverbs, that they tend to be shorter, and that they do at least in part reflect the mores and the worldview of the modern age.

With the fourth chapter, "'Life, Liberty, and the Pursuit of Happiness': Martin Luther King's Proverbial Struggle for Equality," my attention turns to political matters. King distinguished himself as one of the greatest social reformers of modern times, and he has been celebrated in a vast array of biographies and studies as a civil rights leader, a defender of nonviolence in the struggle for desegregation, a champion of the poor, an anti-war proponent, and a broad-minded visionary of an interrelated world of free people. His large amount of verbal and written communications in the form of sermons, speeches, interviews, letters, essays, and several books are replete with Bible proverbs as "Love your enemies," "He who lives by the sword shall perish by the sword," and "Man does not live by bread alone." Such proverbs are frequently employed in his sermons and his struggle for civil rights. But King also makes effective use of folk proverbs like "Time and tide wait for no man," "Last hired, first fired," and "No gain without pain" in his fight against prejudice and injustice. In addition, he also delights in citing quotations that have long become proverbs, to wit "No man is an island," "All men are created equal," and "No lie can live forever." He recycles these bits of traditional wisdom in various contexts, varying his proverbial messages as he addresses the multifaceted issues of his social agenda. His rhetorical prowess is thus informed to a considerable degree by his impressive repertoire of proverbs, which he frequently uses as leitmotifs or amasses into set pieces of fixed phrases. The analysis finishes with comments on King's use of the proverb "Making a way out of no way" and an analysis of the proverbial underpinnings of his "I have a dream" speeches.

There is no doubt that President Barack Obama has learned much from the sermonic and proverbial rhetoric of Martin Luther King. This became quite obvious during his campaign speeches and in particular in his first inaugural address. The fifth chapter, "'The Golden Rule as Political Imperative': President Barack Obama's Proverbial Worldview," presents a detailed analysis of this memorable speech, pointing out that Obama also created a number of formulaic statements in the form of pseudo-proverbs that might over time become proverbial, as for example "Greatness is never a given, it must be earned" or "People will judge you on what you can build, not what you can destroy." In addition, he employed a considerable amount of folk speech in the form of proverbial phrases like "To pick oneself up" and "To dust oneself off," with these emotive metaphors giving his speech a solid balance between intellectual formulations and traditional folk language. His rhetoric is clearly informed by practical wisdom and pragmatic judgment expressed at least in part by quotable and proverbial statements. And to be sure, President Obama uses similar rhetorical means when he addresses large crowds on his travels abroad. The use of proverbial language gives his speeches a colloquial and metaphorical expressiveness that enables him to communicate effectively with people of different ethnic, social, and linguistic backgrounds. On the world stage he has stressed the common humanity of people and used a number of national and international proverbs to bring his message of hope and moral values across in a world where globalization draws humanity ever closer together. As he strives for peace and for eradication of war, deprivation, and disease, he sees the guiding moral principle for an interconnected world in the universal proverb "Do unto others as you would have them do unto you," known by all religions and philosophies as the golden rule or the moral compass of humankind.

Proverbs in political rhetoric help grass-roots efforts to bring about human and social improvements regionally, nationally, and globally. The title of the sixth chapter, "'It Takes a Village to Change the World': Proverbial Politics and the Ethics of Place," plays with the modern proverb "It takes a village to raise a child" in order to show how local engagement can have considerable influence on the world scene. Drawing on the proverbial prowess of such historical and national figures as Abigail and John Adams, Abraham Lincoln, Frederick Douglass, Elizabeth Cady Stanton, Susan B. Anthony, Franklin Delano Roosevelt, John F. Kennedy, Martin Luther King, Barack Obama, and others, this chapter shows that they employed proverbs based on spatial metaphors or proverbs in general that help to bring into focus the ethics of place that is ever more concerned with global matters. In fact, it is amazing to see how deeply interested these historical figures were in overcoming their regional or national interests in favor of an encompassing view of the world. Their speeches, letters, essays, and books make it clear that proverbs like "No man liveth unto himself" (Romans 14:7) and "The world is a place" add up to a vision of a world in which people share the fruits of their labors, assist each other during natural catastrophes, take care of each other in sickness and health, and make certain that the globe remains an environmentally sustainable place. Doubtlessly proverbs—as tested wisdom with considerable authority—play a part in the ongoing struggle toward progress on many social and political fronts in an interconnected world. As traditional and also newly coined wisdom, to wit "Act locally, think globally," proverbs play a significant role in relating local and national issues to the global sphere of politics aimed at the equality of all people and their right to life, liberty, and the pursuit of happiness. As this chapter shows, the wisdom of Bible and folk proverbs is such that they can perfectly well add insight to the concept of ethics of place that has become a dominant theme in the politics of the world.

Unfortunately, that very world continues to be riddled by conflicts and wars, and so it should not be surprising that the seventh chapter, "'Beating Swords into Plowshares': Proverbial Wisdom about War and Peace," is concerned with what the folk has to say about this unfortunate situation. While numerous proverbs deal with the interrelationship of war and peace, they stress that it is peace that is being sought. Most of the older proverbs on this subject matter are not part of the frequently employed paremiological minimum any longer, but proverbs like "If you want peace, you must prepare for war," "All's fair in love and war," and "War is hell" remain quite current today. However, as the many textual examples from various languages and cultures show, the number of proverbs about war far outnumbers those referring to peace, an unfortunate reflection of the human condition over the centuries. There are, to be sure, two proverbs in particular that have found repetitive use in the verbal arguments against aggression and warfare, namely the Bible proverb "He who lives by the sword shall perish be the sword" (Matthew 26:52), with its clear warning against violent confrontation that might lead to war and self-destruction, and the Biblical proverbial expression "To beat swords into plowshares" (Isaiah 2:4) urging people to put aside dreadful weapons and concentrate on peaceful coexistence. These two secularized metaphors have been employed most ingeniously in the name of peace by such renowned public figures as George Washington, Abigail Adams, Abraham Lincoln, Frederick Douglass, Winston S. Churchill, Harry S. Truman, Dwight D. Eisenhower, Martin Luther King, and Ronald Reagan. Famous modern musicians like John Lennon and Michael Jackson have done their part in arguing for peace in their songs that are known throughout the world, as for example Lennon's proverbial "Give Peace a Chance" and Jackson's song "Heal the World" that expresses the hope that we might "See the nations turn / Their swords / Into plowshares." Little wonder that Bishop Desmond Tutu encouraged the world to work for peace with the request "Let us beat our swords into plowshares" during his Nobel Peace Prize lecture in 1984. And it must also not be forgotten that the phrase "Beating swords into plowshares" is the metaphorical motto for peace of the United Nations.

The section on proverbs in literature begins with the eighth chapter, "'The Poetry of the People': Proverbs in the Works of Ralph Waldo Emerson." Who would ever have thought that this prolific transcendentalist, preacher, lecturer, essayist, and pragmatist would prove to be a proverb scholar as well? His many volumes of speeches, sermons, essays, journals, poems, and letters are replete with proverbs, showing that this intellectual certainly did not consider it inappropriate to cite proverbs and proverbial expressions in his writings. In fact, not only did he make use of this traditional folk wisdom but he also theorized about its origin, nature, and meaning. Emerson clearly was a paremiographer in his own right, assembling small lists of proverbs and proverbial phrases in his journals that he found in written sources or registered from oral use. Polyglot that he was, he also noted down proverbs from other languages, obviously enjoying every new discovery. In addition,

Emerson was definitely one of the earliest paremiologists in America, giving much thought to the definition, use, function, language, and importance of proverbs. Altogether these theoretical comments amount to an impressive understanding of proverbs as verbal signs of human life and general experiences and observations. In his journals he often employs proverbs to underscore an observation or experience, but he also comments on the significance of proverbs as apparent truths expressed in colorful metaphorical language. The appearance of proverbs in his letters shows that Emerson enjoyed using them as ready-made wisdom that adds considerable folksiness and also humor to his intellectual prose. His sermons, essays, and lectures are informed by this folk wisdom that adds life and spice to his philosophical deliberations on any imaginable subject matter. At times he even amasses small collections of proverbs to prove a particular point, and it is indeed fascinating how this intellectual never shies away from traditional folk wisdom to underscore his innovative deliberations. Emerson is well aware of the fact that proverbs are employed analogically, and it is this semiotic nature of proverbs that make them so very suitable for explanatory summations of more complex ideas. In the end, Emerson even cites proverbs in his poetry, in which he moves from the discussion of everyday tribulations and trials on to an envisioned transcendence. Proverbs for Ralph Waldo Emerson are, then, if surprisingly perhaps, signposts on humankind's path to progressive transcendentalism that combine the prosaic world of folk wisdom with the poetic world of philosophical thought.

But speaking of poetry, there exists a long literary tradition of proverbs appearing in poems. While the poetry of the Middle Ages and that of later centuries has been looked at by literary and proverb scholars, relatively little attention has been paid to the appearance of proverbs, proverbial expressions, and proverbial comparisons in modern literature. Consequently, the ninth chapter, "'Proverbs and Poetry Are Like Two Peas in a Pod': The Proverbial Language of Modern Mini-Poems," looks at particularly short poems from two to ten lines in length, showing that epigrammatic poems by earlier poets like John Heywood, Thomas Wyatt, and John Mennes were continued by such later poets as John Gay, William Blake, Samuel Taylor Coleridge, and Emily Dickinson. The modern British and American poets Edgar Bogardus, Robert Creeley, Adrian Henri, Don Marquis, Seymour Mayne, Shel Silverstein, Raymond Souster, Mark Strand, Edward Thomas, Judith Viorst, and many others are continuing to integrate proverbial language into their mini-poems to add metaphorical expressiveness to their short texts. The many examples discussed in this chapter are presented in five groups:

1. poems with proverb titles, 2. poems with unchanged proverbs, 3. poems containing personalized proverbs, 4. poems with proverb allusions, and 5. poems with proverbs changed into anti-proverbs. Some of the proverbs are dealt with in a humorous, ironical, or satirical fashion and include such standard old wisdom as "Money talks," "The apple doesn't fall far from the tree," "Waste not, want not," "Home is where the heart is," "Big fish eat little fish," "Make hay while the sun shines," "Good fences make good neighbors," "The early bird catches the worm," "Familiarity breeds contempt," "Every cloud has a silver lining," and "Time heals all wounds." The discussion of the use, function, language, and meaning of the proverbs in these short and often contrary poems leaves no doubt that there exists a sub-genre of proverb poetry, with modern poets clearly excelling in the writing of proverbial mini-poems that range from the sublime to the ridiculous.

The tenth chapter, "'My Tongue—Is of the People': Friedrich Nietzsche's Proverbial Philosophy in *Thus Spoke Zarathustra*," might in and of itself be something of a surprise by illustrating that proverbs can play a significant role in a philosophical literary work. And yet, there can be no doubt that Friedrich Nietzsche repeatedly relies on elements of preformulated folk speech to add a certain metaphorical flavor to his thoughts and arguments, no matter whether they appear in aphorisms, fragments, poems, letters, essays or entire books. It is then surprising that the considerable secondary literature on *Thus Spoke Zarathustra* (1883–85) has been almost completely silent on its obvious proverbiality, and this even though Nietzsche occasionally refers with distinct introductory formulas to Bible and folk proverbs employed by him. This might well be due to the fact that Nietzsche seldom cites proverbs in their traditional wording because they would be far too didactic and moralistic for his insistence on the revaluation of all values. Thus he parodies, manipulates, alienates, and contradicts proverbs by changing them into innovative anti-proverbs, while at the same time also creating his own pseudo-proverbs to argue for a life free of antiquated rules and regulations, to wit "God is dead" and "Man is something that must be overcome." Often he only alludes to proverbs using their metaphors merely to enhance his expressive style without any agreement with their wisdom. After all, Nietzsche wants to show how everything is something becoming and not an end, and that the positive struggle with fate has to be undertaken in eternal repetition (return) without rigid guidelines as proverbs would be. In any case, proverbial matters accompany Zarathustra on his path toward self-recognition and the acceptance of life. The numerous proverbial expressions with their metaphors add much to the poetic style of *Thus Spoke Zarathustra*, including even such mundane texts as "To stick one's head in the sand" and "To be high time." And as expected, the usually varied Bible and folk proverbs are used to underscore the break with God, Christianity, and moral didacticism. There is no doubt that the message of this literary and philosophical work is to a considerable degree informed by the nuances of its proverbial language. This is proverbially and philosophically expressed at the end of this Nietzschean masterpiece by way of Zarathustra's proverbial stone of Sisyphus as a symbol of the eternal repetition of life.

The last three chapters are case studies that trace the origin, dissemination, meaning, and use of individual proverbs and proverbial expressions over time. The eleventh chapter, "'The Dog in the Manger': The Rise and Decline in Popularity of a Proverb and a Fable," begins with a discussion of the fact that the phrase "To be a dog in the manger" is much less known today due to the steady decrease in cultural literacy as far as ancient motifs and metaphors are concerned. The proverbial expression that has also been called a proverb has its roots in Greek antiquity and may even go as far back as Sumerian folk wisdom. As is the case with many Greek expressions, it was translated into Latin and centuries later it entered into the vernacular languages of Europe, with Erasmus of Rotterdam's widely distributed *Adagia* (1500ff.) having much to do with this process. Even though the claim has repeatedly been made that the phrase might well go back to an Aesopic fable, no ancient fable has yet been found as proof. In fact, the earliest connection of the proverbial expression with the narrative of a fable stems from an anonymous Latin manuscript of the fifteenth century. Once this fable was translated into other languages, a certain Aesopization took place, i.e., the short fable was added to collections of Aesop's fables. The English tradition begins with William Caxton's frequently reprinted *Aesop's Fables* (1484), and the short didactic narrative has been published in prose or verse innumerable times ever since. In addition, the older proverb or proverbial phrase upon which it is based has been included in many Anglo-American proverb collections, attesting to its spread as a folk metaphor. Over time, the phrase or the fable has found its way into literary works, political discourse, and the mass media. There is no doubt that "The dog in the manger" proverb is still alive today as an animal metaphor to describe those who refuse to let others have something for which they themselves have no use or need. However, with fables not playing much of a role in the education of today's children, the narrative and also the proverbial phrase are at times not understood any longer.

The twelfth chapter, "'To Build Castles in Spain': The Story of an English Proverbial Expression," explains that the phrase is known in a number of variants in numerous European languages. The idea or concept of building an imagined structure in the form of a house in the air might well go back to the church-father Saint Augustine. The meaning of the popular phrase is always that of making impracticable or unrealizable plans, of imagining unrealistic hopes, or of dreaming wishful thoughts without any chance that these pipe dreams might ever become a reality. The origin of the expression "To build castles in Spain" dates back to French literature of the Middle Ages, with the earliest reference thus far having been located in the medieval epic *Roman de la Rose* (1225/30) by Guillaume de Lorris in the wording of "faire des châteaux en Espagne." The first English reference of any variant of the proverbial expression is found in what is believed to be Geoffrey Chaucer's translation of the French *Roman de la Rose* during the last quarter of the fourteenth century. The fact that he kept the country designation of Spain was surely the key factor in establishing the phrase in the English language. Many contextualized references from such literary authors as Robert Burton, Alexander Pope, Charles Dickens, Ralph Waldo Emerson, Mark Twain, Eugene O'Neill, George Bernard Shaw, Aldous Huxley, and Martin Luther King show how the proverbial expression "To build castles in Spain" and its "air," "clouds," and "sky" variants remain very popular in the Anglo-American world. The proverbial expressions are also found in poems by John Godfrey Saxe, James Russell Lowell, and Florence Earle Coates as well as songs by Irving Berlin, Vernon Duke, Lorenz Hart, and Jimi Hendrix. Headlines, advertisements, and the mass media in general also feature the phrases, indicating that there is plenty of wishful thinking going around. From the dreams of lovers to the desires and wishes for a better existence and on to the highs of psychedelic hallucinogenic drugs, the phrase has served humanity as a metaphorical sign for the wonders of human existence.

The final chapter, "'Let George Do It': The Cultural History of a Problematic American Proverb," begins with a survey of what earlier scholars have been able to find out about this proverb from the late nineteenth century. This is followed by a detailed discussion of the French proverb "Laissez faire à Georges," which refers to the French minister of state Georges d'Amboise under King Louis XII, who at the end of the fifteenth century used it when handing difficult tasks over to his capable administrator. Many lexicographers and paremiographers continue to believe that the English proverb "Let George do it" is in fact nothing but a loan translation of the French text. However, while polygenesis appears to be a rare phenomenon with proverbs, the old French proverb and the new American proverb "Let George do it" actually do have two different origins. The two "Georges" of the proverbs have no relationship to each other, and it would have made little sense for the French proverb with its relationship to Georges d'Amboise to have been adopted by the Anglo-American world. The American proverb is based on another George, namely the generic name given to emancipated slaves who were employed as African American porters on George Pullman's railroad cars during the second half of the nineteenth century and beyond. They were called "George's boys" as an unfortunate slur by the white travelers, and in due time the proverb "Let George do it" was a verbal sign to let the porters do the heavy lifting and other services. Over time, the stereotypical proverb took on a more general meaning, especially in light of the fact that a number of American presidents were called George. Today the proverb is an innocuous statement that simply states that someone is pushing an undesirable or unpleasant task on to someone else. Numerous references from Anglo-American proverb collections, dictionaries, literary works, and the mass media show in considerable detail how the stereotypical proverb became a general proverb and how it survives with less frequent use in today's oral and written communication.

Together, the thirteen chapters of this book show that proverbs and proverbial expressions matter in culture, literature, and politics. Carl Sandburg was right when he underscored the importance of proverbial wisdom with the imperative "Behold the proverbs of a people," thereby signaling that they deserve to be studied as communicative signs of great relevance. As I present the fruits of my recent labors in this volume, I would like to express my appreciation to various editors for granting me the permission to reprint these studies here in a cohesive manner. I would also like to thank Craig Gill, Assistant Director and Editor-in-Chief of the University Press of Mississippi, for his interest in this book and for shepherding it through the publication process. As I researched these different topics and delivered shorter versions at conferences here at home and abroad, I benefitted greatly from the knowledge and help of four renowned scholars and special friends, who have tilled the rich field of folklore together with me. Their wisdom and friendship have meant so very much to me during the past decades, and it is with much gratitude and appreciation that I would like to dedicate this book to Simon J. Bronner (Pennsylvania State University at Harrisburg), Charles Clay Doyle (University of Georgia), Jay Mechling (University of California at Davis), and Patricia A. Turner (University of California at Los Angeles). For the five of us the proverb "Old friends are best" rings true and will hopefully tie us together in a scholarly circle for many more years.

FALL 2013   WOLFGANG MIEDER

Proverbial Wisdom

1. "THE WIT OF ONE, AND THE WISDOM OF MANY"
Proverbs as Cultural Signs of Folklore

Of the various verbal folklore genres like fairy tales, legends, tall tales, jokes, and riddles, proverbs are the most concise but not necessarily the simplest form. The vast scholarship on proverbs is ample proof that they are anything but mundane matters in human communication (Mieder 1982–2001; Mieder 1999). Proverbs fulfill the human need to summarize experiences and observations into nuggets of wisdom that provide ready-made comments on personal relationships and social affairs. There are proverbs for every imaginable context, and they are thus as contradictory as life itself. Proverb pairs like "Absence makes the heart grow fonder" and "Out of sight, out of mind" or "Look before you leap" and "He who hesitates is lost" make it abundantly clear that proverbs do not represent a logical philosophical system. But when the proper proverb is chosen for a particular situation, it is bound to fit perfectly, becoming an effective formulaic strategy of communication. Contrary to some isolated opinions, proverbs have not lost their usefulness in modern society. They serve people well in oral speech and the written word, coming to mind almost automatically as prefabricated verbal units. While the frequency of their employment might well vary among people and contexts, proverbs are a significant rhetorical force in various modes of communication, from friendly chats, powerful political speeches, and religious sermons to lyrical poetry, best-selling novels, and the influential mass media. Proverbs are in fact everywhere, and this ubiquity has led scholars from many disciplines to study them from classical times to the modern age (Mieder 1997a). The playful alteration of the proverb "If the shoe fits, wear it" to "If the proverb fits, use it" says it all!

Definition and Meaning

The definition of a proverb has caused scholars from many disciplines much chagrin over the centuries. Many attempts have been made from Aristotle to the present time (Kindstrand 1978; Russo 1983), ranging from philosophical considerations to cut-and-dry lexicographical definitions. The American paremiologist Bartlett Jere Whiting (1904–1995) reviewed many definitions, summarizing his findings in a lengthy conglomerate version of his own:

> A proverb is an expression which, owing its birth to the people, testifies to its origin in form and phrase. It expresses what is apparently a fundamental truth—that is, a truism,—in homely language, often adorned, however, with alliteration and rhyme. It is usually short, but need not be; it is usually true, but need not be. Some proverbs have both a literal and figurative meaning, either of which makes perfect sense; but more often they have but one of the two. A proverb must be venerable; it must bear the sign of antiquity, and, since such signs may be counterfeited by a clever literary man, it should be attested in different places at different times. This last requirement we must often waive in dealing with very early literature, where the material at our disposal is incomplete. (Whiting 1932: 302; also in Whiting 1994: 80)

That certainly is a useful summation, albeit not a very precise statement. It represents a reaction to a tongue-in-cheek statement that Whiting's friend Archer Taylor (1890–1973) had made a year earlier at the beginning of his classic study on *The Proverb* (1931; see also Taylor 1975):

> The definition of a proverb is too difficult to repay the undertaking; and should we fortunately combine in a single definition all the essential elements and give each the proper emphasis, we should not even then have a touchstone. An incommunicable quality tells us this sentence is proverbial and that one is not. Hence no definition will enable us to identify positively a sentence as proverbial. Those who do not speak a language can never recognize all its proverbs, and similarly much that is truly proverbial escapes us in Elizabethan and older English. Let us be content with recognizing that a proverb is a saying current among the folk. At least so much of a definition is indisputable. (Taylor 1931: 3)

In 1985 I put to the test Taylor's supposition that people in general know what a proverb is, and simply asked a cross section of fifty-five Vermont citizens how they would define a proverb. After all, the general folk uses proverbs all the time, and one would think that they know intuitively what a proverb represents. A frequency study of the words contained in the definition attempts made it possible to formulate the following general description:

"A proverb is a short, generally known sentence of the folk which contains wisdom, truth, morals, and traditional views in a metaphorical, fixed and memorizable form and which is handed down from generation to genera-tion" (Mieder 1985b: 119; also in Mieder 1993: 24). This summary definition mirrors that of Whiting, while the short conglomerate version "A proverb is a short sentence of wisdom" based on the words most often used in the fifty-odd definitions resembles Taylor's statement. People in general, not bo-thered by academic concerns and intricacies, thus have a good idea of what a proverb encompasses. This is also borne out by a number of proverbs about proverbs, representing folk definitions as it were: "Proverbs are the children of experience," "Proverbs are the wisdom of the streets," and "Proverbs are true words." Proverbs obviously contain a lot of common sense, experience, wisdom, and truth, and as such they represent ready-made traditional strate-gies in oral speech acts and writings from high literature to the mass media (Hasan-Rokem 1990).

But proverb scholars have, of course, not been satisfied with the vagaries of this type of definition. Again and again they have tried to approximate *the* definition (Arora 1984). Suffice it to cite two more general work-definitions, starting with Stuart A. Gallacher's short statement: "A proverb is a concise statement of an apparent truth which has [had, or will have] currency among the people" (1959: 47). The parenthetical modifications have been added by me to indicate that while some proverbs have been in use for hundreds of years, others have passed out of circulation and new ones will certainly be coined. One of my own attempts of defining proverbs precisely shows my indebtedness to my teacher Stuart A. Gallacher: "Proverbs [are] concise tra-ditional statements of apparent truths with currency among the folk. More elaborately stated, proverbs are short, generally known sentences of the folk that contain wisdom, truths, morals, and traditional views in a metaphorical, fixed, and memorizable form and that are handed down from generation to generation" (Mieder 1996b: 597).

One of the major concerns of paremiologists is to get to the bottom of that "incommunicable quality" of proverbiality. It is a fact that not even the most complex definition will be able to identify all proverbs. The crux of the matter lies in the concept of traditionality that includes aspects of both age and currency. In other words, a particular sentence might sound like a proverb—for example, "Where there is money, there is crime"—and yet not be one. This invented sentence is based on the common proverb pattern "Where there is X, there is Y" (Peukes 1977), and it appears to contain some perceived generalizations about wealth and legal matters. But that does not attest to its alleged proverbiality. This piece of created wisdom would have to be taken over by others and be used over a period of time to be considered a bona fide proverb. As it stands here on this page, it is nothing more than a "proverb-like" statement. Proverb definitions often include the term "traditional," but proving that a given text has gained traditionality is quite another matter. This makes it very difficult to decide what new statements have in fact gained proverbial status. Such modern American texts as "Been there, done that," "The camera doesn't lie," "No guts, no glory," and "There is no (such thing as a) free lunch" have made it (Doyle 1996). Why is this so? Simply stated, they have been registered numerous times over the years. The last example also shows the formation of variants. And it is exactly the requirement of all folklore, including proverbs, that various references and possibly also variants are found that attest to oral currency.

Stephen D. Winick has tried valiantly to break with the requirement of traditionality for new proverbs, arguing that a text becomes a proverb upon its creation (see also Honeck and Welge 1997). That would make the sentence "Where there is money, there is crime" a proverb! Most folklorists and paremiologists would disagree with this assessment. The fact that the sentence is "proverb-like" does not make it a folk proverb, putting in question Winick's convoluted definition:

> Proverbs are brief (sentence-length) entextualized utterances which derive a sense of wisdom, wit and authority from explicit and intentional intertextual reference to a tradition of previous similar wisdom utterances. This intertextual reference may take many forms, including replication (i.e., repetition of the text from previous contexts), imitation (i.e., modeling a new utterance after a previous utterance), or use of features (rhyme, alliteration, meter, ascription to the elders, etc.) associated with previous wisdom sayings. Finally, proverbs address recurrent social situations in a strategic way. (Winick 2003: 595)

The preference for metaphorical proverbs lies in the fact that they can be employed in a figurative or indirect way. Verbal folklore in general is based on indirection, and much can indeed be said or implied by the opportune use of such proverbs as "Don't look a gift horse in the mouth," "Don't count your chickens before they are hatched," "Every cloud has a silver lining," or "You can't teach an old dog new tricks." By associating an actual situation with a metaphorical proverb, the particular matter is generalized into a common occurrence of life. Instead of scolding someone directly for not behaving according to the cultural customs of a different social or cultural setting, one might indirectly comment that "When in Rome, do as the Romans do." Or if someone must be warned to be more careful with health issues, the proverb "An ounce of prevention is worth a pound of cure" might well serve the purpose to add some commonly accepted wisdom to the argument. Kenneth Burke has provided the following explanation of this effective use of metaphorical proverbs: "Proverbs are strategies for dealing with situations. In so far as situations are typical and recurrent in a given social structure, people develop names for them and strategies for handling them. Another name for strategies might be attitudes" (1941: 256). Proverbs in actual use refer to social situations, and this social context in turn gives them meaning (Seitel 1969). They act as signs for human behavior and social contexts and as such must be studied both from the structural and semiotic point of view (Kuusi 1957a; Grzybek 1987; Zholkovskii 1978).

The meaning of proverbs is thus very much dependent on the contexts in which they appear. Barbara Kirshenblatt-Gimblett has shown how a number of common proverbs have multiple meanings that come to light only in particular situations. For example, she asked about eighty students in Texas to explain the meaning of the proverb "A friend in need is a friend indeed." Here are the different explanations with comments on the various sources of the multiple meanings:

(1) Someone who feels close enough to you to be able to ask you for help when he is in need is really your friend—Syntactic ambiguity (is your friend in need or are you in need?).

(2) Someone who helps you when you are in need is really your friend—Lexical ambiguity (indeed or in deed).

(3) Someone who helps you by means of his actions (deeds) when you need him is a real friend as opposed to someone who just makes promises—Key meaning.

(4) Someone who is only your friend when he needs you is not a true friend— Does "a friend indeed" mean "a true friend" or "not a true friend"?

(Kirshenblatt-Gimblett 1973: 822; also in Mieder and Dundes 1981: 113–14)

Clearly only a specific context will reveal what the proverb really wants to say. The Estonian paremiologist Arvo Krikmann has spoken in this regard of the "semantic indefiniteness" of proverbs that results from their hetero-situativity, poly-functionality, and poly-semanticity (Krikmann 1974a, 1974b). The meaning of any proverb must therefore be analyzed in its distinctive context, be it social, literary, rhetorical, journalistic, or whatever.

Genesis and Evolution

Proverbs, like riddles, jokes or fairy tales, do not fall out of the sky and neither are they products of a mythical soul of the folk. Instead they are always
coined by an individual either intentionally or unintentionally, as expressed
in Lord John Russell's well-known one-line proverb definition that has taken
on a proverbial status of sorts: "A proverb is the wit of one, and the wisdom
of many" (1823). If the statement contains an element of truth or wisdom,
and if it exhibits one or more proverbial markers (such as alliteration, rhyme,
parallelism, ellipsis, etc.), it might "catch on" and be used first in a small family circle, and subsequently in a village, a city, a region, a country, a continent,
and eventually the world. The global spread of proverbs is not a pipe dream,
since certain ancient proverbs have spread to many parts of the world. Today,
with the incredible power of the mass media, a newly formulated proverb-
like statement might become a bona fide proverb relatively quickly by way
of the internet, radio, television, and print media. As with verbal folklore
in general, the original statement might well be varied a bit as it gets picked
up and becomes ever more an anonymous proverb whose wording, structure, style, and metaphor are such that it is memorable. Older literary sources
show very clearly that proverbs existed in such variants until one dominant
wording eventually became the standard, to wit the following three historical variants of a proverb of prudence: "It is good to be wise before the mischief" (1584), "After the business is over, every one is wise" (1666), and "It is
easy to be wise after the event" (1900), with the latter version having become
today's standard form (Wilson, 1970: 898).

It is usually quite difficult to trace the origin and history of a proverb in
a particular language. Such studies quickly take on major proportions, and
they get very involved if the proverb under investigation proves to go back to
medieval times or even further to classical antiquity. Any bilingual speaker or
translator will have noticed that there exist two types of proverbs. On the one
hand, there are those that mean the same but that have different structures,
vocabulary, and metaphors, and consequently have different origins in their
respective languages. Thus, English speakers since Shakespeare say "Brevity
is the soul of wit" while Germans utter "In der Kürze liegt die Würze" (In
brevity there is [lies] spice). Whoever needs to translate one of these texts
would have to know the quite different equivalent in the target language or
find it in a dictionary. Regional proverbs become especially difficult translation problems, since possible equivalents are often missing from dictionaries, which tend to include only the more common proverbs. On the other

hand, many proverbs are identical not only in German and English but in most Germanic, Romance, and Slavic languages of Europe, and these do not present any particular translation problem. In other words, there exist general European proverbs, i.e., proverbs that have been disseminated through precise loan translations throughout Europe. That is why Emanuel Strauss could publish his three-volume *Dictionary of European Proverbs* (1994) and why Gyula Paczolay could follow suit with his invaluable collection *European Proverbs in 55 Languages* (1997), to name but two of the many polyglot proverb collections.

Four sources for the distribution of European proverbs can be identified (similar processes have occurred in the dissemination of proverbs in Asian, African, and other linguistic and cultural groups). There is first of all Greek and Roman antiquity, whose proverbial wisdom found a broad geographical dissemination primarily through the Latin language. The scholarly study of proverbs begins with Aristotle, and many Greek proverbs have been found in the works of Plato, Sophocles, Homer, Aristophanes, Aeschylus, Euripides, etc. Many of them reappeared in Latin translation in Plautus, Terence, Cicero, Horace, and other Roman writers (see Mieder and Bryan 1996). Ancient writers also added new Latin proverbs, and many of these classical texts became part of a rich medieval Latin proverb tradition. More importantly, however, these common Latin texts were then translated into the many developing European languages. Erasmus of Rotterdam played a major role in spreading this classical and medieval wisdom throughout Europe by means of the many editions of his *Adagia* (1500ff.), which contains over four thousand explanatory notes and essays on classical proverbs and proverbial expressions (Phillips 1964). His works were read and translated, and he himself had also shown interest in early Dutch regional proverbs. The same is true for Martin Luther in Germany, who was a masterful translator of classical proverbs but who also employed many indigenous German proverbs in his writings (Cornette 1942). Latin proverbs were used in school translation exercises, and many of them entered the various languages through oral channels, thus spreading classical wisdom through the written and spoken word all over Europe. By way of English they travelled on to Australia, Canada, the United States, and the rest of the world, where English is used as a second language. Some of these proverbs have truly taken on an international and global currency, showing once again that they contain universal human experiences and insights.

There is then no doubt that a considerable corpus of common European proverbs can be traced back to classical times. Since they were loan translated from the same sources, they exist in the many languages of Europe in identical wordings and structures. Little wonder then that Gyula Paczolay was able to find exact equivalents of "Where there is smoke, there is fire" in 54 European languages. A few other popular proverbs from classical times that are still very much in use today in Europe and elsewhere are: "Barking dogs do not bite" (51 European languages), "One swallow does not make a summer" (49), "Walls have ears" (46), "One hand washes the other" (46), "Make haste slowly" (43), "Children and fools tell the truth" (41), "Still waters run deep" (38), and "Love is blind" (37). Their general use in present-day Europe and beyond indicates a strong intellectual, ethical, and human bond among people. All of these texts express general human wisdom without any specific national or ethnic references. And since they are basically identical in all languages, they are and will continue to be effective modes of metaphorical communication among Europeans, North Americans, and other peoples.

A second source of proverbs for the entire European continent and beyond is the Bible, whose proverbs date back to classical antiquity and early wisdom literature. As a widely translated book, the Bible had a major influence on the distribution of common proverbs, since the various translators were dealing with the same texts. Several dozen Biblical proverbs are thus current in identical wordings in many European languages, even though speakers might not remember that they are employing proverbs from the Bible. A few obvious examples are "As you sow, so you reap" (Paczolay lists 52 European references; see Galatians 6:7); "He who digs a pit for others, falls in himself" (48; Proverbs 26:27); "He that will not work, shall not eat" (43; 2 Thessalonians 3:10); "A prophet is not without honor save in his own country" (39; Matthew 13:57); "An eye for an eye, a tooth for a tooth" (38; 2 Moses 21:24); and "There is nothing new under the sun" (29; Ecclesiastes 1:9). It is important to note, however, that the number of Biblical proverbs in various European languages is not identical. Much depended on the linguistic skills of the translators. In the case of Martin Luther, quite a few of his German formulations have actually become proverbial without having been proverbs in the original text.

The third source for common European proverbs is medieval Latin. The Latin language of the Middle Ages had the status of a lingua franca, and as such it developed new proverbs that cannot be traced back to classical times. Hans Walther and Paul Gerhard Schmidt have put together thousands of medieval proverbs in their massive nine-volume collection of *Lateinische Sprichwörter und Sentenzen des Mittelalters* (1963–86), and the thirteen-volume *Lexikon der Sprichwörter des romanisch-germanischen Mittelalters*

(1995–2002) by Samuel Singer and Ricarda Liver shows the relationship of many of these Latin proverbs to those of the vulgate languages. Many medieval Latin proverbs in their exact translations have spread to European languages, and they certainly belong to some of the most popular proverbs today. A few well-known examples are: "Crows will not pick out crows' eyes" (Paczolay lists 48 European references); "Strike while the iron is hot" (48); "New brooms sweep clean" (47); "All that glitters is not gold" (47); "When the cat is away, the mice will play" (46); "The pitcher goes so long to the well until it breaks at last" (40); "No rose without thorns" (39); "At night all cats are grey" (38); and "Clothes do not make the man" (37). Of special interest is the Middle Latin proverb "Mille via ducunt hominem per secula ad Romam" from the twelfth century, for which Paczolay cites 33 European equivalents. In all these languages the direct loan translation of "All roads lead to Rome" exists. However, there are also variants that replace "Rome" with another city: in an Estonian proverb the city is St. Petersburg, a Finnish proverb refers to the old capital Turku, a Russian proverb mentions Moscow, and a Turkish proverb names Mecca. But these are variants one might well have expected in Europe, and perhaps one day the American version "All roads lead to Washington" will also appear in a proverb collection. It does exist, but has simply not been recorded yet. As for one speaker, I know that I have used this variant from time to time when discussing national politics.

The fourth source for common European proverbs reverses the historical move of proverbs from Europe to the United States. These are modern texts that have been disseminated since the middle of the twentieth century throughout Europe by means of the mass media. A few new proverbs, which are already spreading across the European continent either in the new lingua franca of English or in new loan translations, are such American proverbs as "A picture is worth a thousand words," "It takes two to tango," and "Garbage in, garbage out" (from the world of computers). Of special interest is also the "Europeanization" of the well-known American proverb "What's good for General Motors is good for America," which originated as a misquotation of a statement by the President of General Motors Charles Erwin Wilson during a Senate hearing on January 15, 1953. Willy Brandt, the renowned European politician, changed this proverb in a loan translation to fit the European context. Calling for European solidarity in a speech on November 18, 1971, he exclaimed: "Im übrigen könnte man jedoch in Abwandlung eines alten amerikanischen Sprichwortes sagen: Was gut ist für Europa, ist gut für die Vereinigten Staaten. Die Zeit des Feiertags-Europäertums ist vorbei, Europa ist unser Alltag" (All around one could say by changing an old

American proverb: What is good for Europe, is good for the United States. The time of holiday-Europeanness is over, Europe is our normal workday). One is inclined to change the sixteenth-century proverb "Handsome is as handsome does" to the new proverbial slogan "Europe is as Europe does" to fit the new European consciousness as the move toward unity continues (Mieder 2000c). In any case, the United States and its English language are not only spreading new words throughout Europe and the rest of the world; they are also disseminating new proverbs from popular culture (music, film, etc.) and the mass media (advertisements, cartoons, etc.) as bits of wisdom that fit the twenty-first century.

Empiricism and Paremiological Minima

As Peter Grzybek and Christoph Chlosta (1993) have shown, scholars must base their studies on demographic research methods utilizing questionnaires and sophisticated statistical analyses in order to establish lists of those proverbs that are actually known and continue to be in current use (Levin 1968–69; Mieder 1985a). This research methodology will also help establish the proverbiality of the new proverbs of the modern age (Doyle 1996). There is thus a definite need for increased global field research, from highly technological societies to those parts of the world where life continues to be based on traditional and rural life. Such empirical work will, of course, also help establish "paremiological minima" for many languages and cultures, as Grigorii L'vovich Permiakov (1919–1983), one of the greatest theoretical paremiologists of the twentieth century, suggested in the early 1970s.

Utilizing his paremiological experiment conducted in Moscow in 1970, Permiakov was able to establish the general currency of 1,494 phraseological units among modern inhabitants of that city. Included were 268 proper proverbs, and the rest of the texts were proverbial expressions, proverbial comparisons, wellerisms, fables, anecdotes, riddles, slogans, weather signs, superstitions, allusions to fairy tales, oaths, etc. Permiakov's list shows clearly that many long folk narratives have currency as short phraseological remnants (allusions). All of these texts are part of the general cultural literacy of Russians (Permiakov 1971). Native as well as foreign speakers of Russian need to know them in order to communicate effectively in that language. Permiakov subsequently established a so-called "paremiological minimum" of 300 such texts based on this experiment (Permiakov 1982 [1989]) and published it with an explanatory introduction and many notes as *300 obshcheupotrebitel'nykh russkikh poslovits i pogovorok* (1985; see Grzybek and

Eismann 1984: 351–58). German and Bulgarian translations have appeared that enable foreign language instructors to teach their students the most frequently used Russian proverbs, proverbial expressions, proverbial comparisons, etc.

Similar paremiological minima of such common phraseological units of other national languages are now being established by paremiographers, to wit the very useful results for Croatian, Czech, German, and Hungarian. Many proverbs of classical, Biblical, or medieval origin will belong to the paremiological minima of European languages. But there will still be room for national proverbs among a list of about 300 texts. Since these texts are identified by statistical frequency studies of actual use in oral and written communication, they become a useful list for foreign language instruction. After all, it is important to teach the most well-known and current proverbs to foreign language learners rather than obscure and seldom-used texts. The proverbs that belong to the paremiological minimum of a language are clearly part of the cultural literacy of native speakers, and it behooves foreign language teachers to include them in their instruction of language and culture (Mieder 1992; Tóthné Litovkina 1998). Demoscopic research will also finally give scholars a much better idea as to which of the thousands of proverbs listed in the older collections are still in actual use today. Paremiography cannot remain a science that looks primarily backwards and works only with texts of times gone by. Modern paremiographers can and should also assemble proverb collections that include the texts of the twentieth and twenty-first centuries, as is the case at least in part with Stewart A. Kingsbury's, Kelsie B. Harder's and my *Dictionary of American Proverbs* (1992).

Regarding the English language, no precise paremiological minimum has been established thus far. However, some empirically oriented work has been done (Mieder 1992a; Tóthné Litovkina 1994; Lau 1996), indicating that such proverbs as the following are certainly used with high frequency in the United States today: "Absence makes the heart grow fonder," "An apple a day keeps the doctor away," "Beauty is only skin deep," "The early bird catches the worm," "You can't judge a book by its cover," "First come, first served," "The grass is always greener on the other side of the fence," "Make hay while the sun shines," "Honesty is the best policy," "Practice makes perfect," "A stitch in time saves nine," "A rolling stone gathers no moss," "If at first you don't succeed, try, try again," "Time is money," etc.

Semiotics and Performance

Theoretical proverb scholarship has been influenced to a large degree by the semiotic studies of Grigorii L'vovich Permiakov (1970), Peter Grzybek and Wolfgang Eismann (1984), and Zoltán Kanyó (1981). Grzybek has summarized this linguistic approach to proverbs in his seminal article "Foundations of Semiotic Proverb Study" (1987; see also Grzybek 2000). As scholars investigate the hetero-situativity, poly-functionality, and poly-semanticity of proverbs as "einfache Formen" (simple forms), it is important that they pay attention to the paradigmatic, syntagmatic, logical, structural, pragmatic, and semantic aspects of these traditional utterances as communicative and strategic signs (Anscombre 2000). Structural analyses of texts will certainly gain in value if semiotic aspects of proverbs as linguistic and cultural signs are added to them with a special focus on actual proverb performance in speech acts (Goodwin and Wenzel 1979).

Linguists and folklorists have repeatedly attempted to explain the semantic ambiguity of proverbs, which results to a large degree from being used in various contexts with different functions (Jason 1971). But proverbs also act as analogies, which adds to the complexity of understanding their precise meaning in a particular speech act (Kirshenblatt-Gimblett 1973; Honeck and Kibler 1984; Lieber 1984; Suard and Buridant 1984). In fact, linguist Neal R. Norrick dedicated an entire book, *How Proverbs Mean: Semantic Studies in English Proverbs* (1985), to this problem. He deals primarily with both the literal and (more often) the figurative meaning of proverbs, emphasizing the ambiguity of metaphorical proverbs. In trying to understand the meaning of proverbs in certain contexts, one must keep in mind that they are usually employed to disambiguate complex situations and events. Yet they are paradoxically inherently ambiguous, because their meaning depends on analogy. Proverbs as devices of disambiguation, the paradox of analogic ambiguity in proverb usage, and the socio-cultural use of proverbs in oral and written communication still require further study by paremiologists as they map out the strategies used in the appropriate employment of seemingly simple and yet so complex proverbial utterances.

Clearly the meaning and purpose of proverbs are best revealed by strategic use in social situations (Seitel 1969; Barakat 1980). When one considers proverbs in context, it should not be surprising that there are such contradictory proverb pairs as "Birds of a feather flock together" and "Opposites attract." After all, proverbs are not universal truths but rather limited pieces of folk wisdom that are valid only in certain situations. The problem of contradictory proverbs exists primarily because people ignore their social context (Yankah 1984). If one deals with proverbs only as a concept of a cultural fact or truism, contradictions are easily found in any proverb repertoire. In contextual usage, however, proverbs function effectively as social strategies. Proverbs in normal discourse are not contradictory at all, and they usually make perfect sense to the speaker and listener. After all, people do not speak in proverb pairs, unless they are "dueling" with proverbs as a verbal contest (Yankah 1989).

Today it has almost become a cliché to point out that proverbs must be studied in context, but it took a long time for anthropologically oriented proverb collectors to go beyond mere texts and look at the use and function of the proverbial materials in actual speech acts. The noted anthropologist Edward Westermarck (1862–1939) began to look at proverbs from this contextual point of view in his *Wit and Wisdom in Morocco: A Study of Native Proverbs* (1930). Modern scholars trained in the theoretical aspects of speech acts or performance look at proverbs as part of active verbal communication. E. Ojo Arewa and Alan Dundes (1964) laid the groundwork for this type of analysis by looking at such questions as "What rules govern the use of proverbs? Who is using them and to whom? On what occasions? In what places?" (see also Penfield 1983; Fabian 1990). A study by anthropologist Charles L. Briggs (1985) on the pragmatics of proverb performances is exemplary in this respect. He conducted field research on the oral proverb performance in Córdova, a community of about 700 inhabitants located in the mountains of northern New Mexico in the United States. From transcriptions of recorded performances, Briggs isolates eight features of proverb use: tying phrase (i.e., introductory formula), identity of owner, quotation-framing verb, proverb text, special association, general meaning or hypothetical situation, relevance of context, and validation of the performance. Most speakers have never thought of all of this when expressing a proverb during an actual speech act, but these linguistic strategies definitely exist, as proverbs are cited as signs of commonly understood and accepted folk wisdom.

Culture, Folklore, and History

Folklorists, cultural historians, and philologists have occupied themselves for a long time with tracing the origin, history, dissemination, and meaning of individual proverbs and their variants. One could go so far as to say that there is a "story" behind every proverb, and it is usually a sizable task to deal with just one text in this diachronic and semantic fashion. About some proverbs entire books have been written (Kuusi 1957b), but there are also numerous lengthy articles and small notes on specific expressions (Mieder 1977). The German folklorist and paremiologist Lutz Röhrich has put together a three-volume *Das große Lexikon der sprichwörtlichen Redensarten* (1991–92), in which he discusses the history and meaning of hundreds of German texts. While there exist exemplary studies on such proverbs as "When Adam delved and Eve span, who was then the gentleman?" (Friedman 1974), "Don't throw the baby out with the bathwater" (Mieder 1993: 193–224), and "It is an ill bird that fouls its own nest" (Kunstmann 1939), much remains to be done for obscure regional and dialectical texts (Hain 1951; Ruef 1995) as well as for globally disseminated proverbs.

Folklorists and cultural historians are also interested in how proverbs were used in different historical periods. Proverbs do, at least to a degree, reflect the attitudes or worldview (mentality) of various social classes at different periods, for example in an English urban industrial region or in early modern French society (McKelvie 1965; Davis 1975). The African paremiologist J. O. J. Nwachukwu-Agbada (1990) has analyzed the origin, meaning, and value of Igbo historical proverbs, showing that they are significant keys for an understanding of the cultural history of Nigeria. Although the proverbs might not be precise history, they contain important information concerning the folk interpretation of colonialism, wars, and other events. The fact that these matters were crystallized into proverbial form brought about the remembrance and memorability of such historical facts in a primarily oral culture. Of major interest is also James Obelkevich's (1987) social investigation of the users and uses of proverbs in Europe during different historical periods. He deals with various meanings of proverbs in their historical and social context, emphasizing their significance as expressions of "mentalities" or worldview and socially relevant wisdom.

Another area of interest for folklorists and cultural historians is proverbs that belong to a particular group or that can be grouped together under a theme, showing, for example, the traditional wisdom about gender issues and misogyny over the centuries (Kerschen 1998; Rittersbacher 2002). At their best, studies of this type are comparatively oriented, i.e., they look at proverbs from different cultural and linguistic groups (Sabban and Wirrer 1991; Prahlad 1994 and 1996; Petrova 2003). A group can be just a family, and folklorists have been eager to find out how proverbs function in these small social units (Levy and Zumwalt 1990; Williams 2003). But the group studied can also be as complex as the multi-ethnic society of Israel. Galit-Hasan Rokem (1992) has dealt with the use and function of proverbs in Israeli discourse, showing that proverbs can take on an important role in conflict solutions. Finally, one might ask what the proverb repertoire of one particular person might be. In order to answer this question, Stanley Brandes (1974) interviewed an elderly Spanish widow. He compares her proverbs with the total inventory of proverbs collected in her village, examines how the proverb content may reflect or relate to her direct experience, evaluates whether her proverbs express consistent or contradictory notions, and determines the functions and goals of her proverb use. Above all, Brandes shows that there is always a selection process going on whereby each person seizes upon or rejects the proverbs he or she has heard, depending upon his or her momentary outlook, status, or life style. All of this is yet another indication that proverbs are no simple matter. Being acquainted with a number of proverbs is one thing; knowing when and how to use what proverb is quite another. Any person speaking a foreign language is well aware of this communicative difficulty with proverbs.

More than other scholars, folklorists and cultural historians are also interested in the content of proverbs, to wit what cultural realia are contained in individual proverbs and how they differ from culture to culture in proverbs that might mean the same. Many proverbs refer to old measurements, obscure professions, outdated weapons, unknown tools, plants, animals, names, and various other traditional matters. Often it is not clear any longer what exactly is meant by certain words in a proverb, even though its actual sense is understood, to wit "Many a mickle makes a muckle" or "Possession is nine points of the law" (Geise 1999). That is why people so often ask what a proverb really means, where it comes from, etc. Folklorists and cultural historians together with historically minded linguists are the ones who provide answers to these fascinating questions (Mieder 1978a; Röhrich and Mieder 1977; Seiler 1922).

Stereotypes and Worldview

Care must be taken, when looking at proverbs as expressing aspects of a certain worldview or mentality of a people, that no stereotypical conclusions about a so-called "national character" are drawn. There are so many popular proverbs from classical, Biblical, and medieval times current in various cultures that it would be foolish to think of them as reflecting some imagined national character, as for example Chinese or Finnish (Lister 1874–75; Kuusi 1967). Nevertheless, the frequent use of certain proverbs in a particular culture could be used together with other social and cultural indicators to

formulate valid generalizations. Thus, if the Germans really do use the proverbs "Morgenstunde hat Gold im Munde" (The morning hour has gold in its
mouth, i.e., "The early bird catches the worm") and "Ordnung ist das halbe
Leben" (Order is half of life) with high frequency, then they do mirror at
least to some degree the German attitude toward getting up early and keeping things in good order (Dundes 1984). Nevertheless, proverb studies looking for national character traits should be undertaken with much care.

Proverbs can be quite negative when they express, as many of them do,
slurs or stereotypes (Profantová 1997; Ronesi 2000). Such negative proverbial texts appear in the earliest proverb collections, and they are still used today
despite attempts to be open-minded toward ethnic, religious, sexual, national, and regional differences. Two special collections are Otto von Reinsberg-
Düringsfeld, *Internationale Titulaturen* (1863), and Abraham A. Roback, *A
Dictionary of International Slurs* (1944). Folklorist Alan Dundes (1975) has
studied the international scope of national slurs or *blasons populaires*, dealing with such topics as stereotypes, national character, ethnocentrism, and
prejudice. Shirley L. Arora (1994) has dealt with the proverbial stereotypes
that the Spanish colonizers invented against the native populations of Central and South America. I have described the use of anti-Semitic proverbs
by the National Socialists in their murderous campaign of the destruction
of the European Jews (Mieder 1982), and Nwachukwu-Agbada (1988) has
studied the historical and social background of proverbs against the white
colonizers. The sad story of hateful proverbs I have shown in my analyses
of the proverbs "The only good Indian is a dead Indian" (1993a) and "No
tickee, no washee" (1996a) as well as in my book-length study *"Call a Spade a
Spade": From Classical Phrase to Racial Slur* (2002). These proverbial stereotypes against Native Americans, Chinese Americans, and African Americans
respectively have done much harm in the American society, and they should
not be used any longer.

Finally, folklorists, historians, and political scientists have also looked
at the use of proverbs in politics as most effective rhetorical devices (Louis
2000). Shirley L. Arora (1989) scrutinized the intriguing role that the Greek
proverb "The fish rots from the head first" with its major variant "The fish
begins to stink at the head" played during the American presidential campaign in the summer of 1988 in the mass media. Politicians from classical
to modern times have deployed proverbs effectively in their rhetoric. Adolf Hitler, for example, used proverbs in his propagandistic and prophetic
book *Mein Kampf* (*My Battle*, 1925–26) to advocate the military and deadly
goals of Nazism (Mieder 1997: 9–38; Doerr 2000). Winston S. Churchill

employed proverbs in his speeches and letters to convince the British people and the rest of the world that Nazi Germany had to be overcome by all means (Mieder and Bryan 1995). And, as expected, the plain-speaking Harry S. Truman added many proverbs and proverbial expressions to his verbal messages in order to communicate in a language that the average folk could understand (Mieder and Bryan 1997).

But proverbs in political use are not without their problems. While they can do much good in creating solid communication based on generational wisdom, they can also be misused to manipulate people into following the wrong leaders. Nazi Germany is a warning of how proverbs, especially anti-Semitic proverbs, become dangerous verbal weapons. People followed such proverbial invectives blindly, forgetting that proverbs are not absolute truths. Proverbs can cut both ways in the political realm—as stereotypical invectives they can lead to tensions, but as metaphors of indirection they can in fact relax tensions (Raymond 1956). My investigation of the proverbs and political cartoons employed during the Cold War shows clearly that world leaders like Leonid Brezhnev, Mikhail Gorbachev, Margaret Thatcher, Helmut Kohl, François Mitterand, and Ronald Reagan as well as international journalists employed such proverbs as "Hear no evil, see no evil, speak no evil," "Big fish eat little fish," "The pen is mightier than the sword," and "It takes two to tango" to deal with serious political issues (Mieder 1987; Mieder 1997b: 99–137, 214–21 [notes]). As the world continues its struggle toward peace and democracy, people might well keep in mind the American proverb of democracy: "Government of the people, by the people, for the people" (Mieder 2003b).

Proverbs and the Social Sciences

Social scientists have contributed a wealth of scholarship about the multi-faceted characteristics, uses, functions, and meanings of proverbs (Mieder and Sobieski 2003). Some of the major areas of inquiry are abstraction, attitude, behavior, cognition, communication, community, ethnicity, experience, gender, intelligence, memory, mental health, perception, schizophrenia, socialization, transmission, validity, and wisdom. Anthropologist Ruth Finnegan (1970) has given a detailed survey of the concept of proverbs in African societies, especially among the Jabo, Zulu, and Azande peoples. While she deals in general with the language, style, content, use, and function of the proverbs as part of social life, there is also Samuel Gyasi Obeng's (1996) much more specific study on how proverbs are employed as a mitigating and politeness strategy in Akan discourse. He interprets the performance of proverbs in social contexts, showing that it is the indirection of the proverbial message that brings about a congenial communicative process that otherwise might have been confrontational.

While social anthropologists have dealt with proverbs since the nineteenth century, basing their studies on impressive field research, sociologists regrettably have had much less interest in proverbs. And yet, as they study the social organizations and the behavior of people in them, it would make eminent sense to take a look at how proverbs relate and participate in social structures and life. Some exciting new scholarship is available, as for example Paul Hernadi's and Francis Steen's (1999) cross-disciplinary look at proverbs as socially sanctioned advice. Marilyn A. Nippold, Linda D. Uhden, and Ilsa E. Schwarz (1997) have studied the ability of understanding and interpreting proverbs at different age stages, and Alyce McKenzie (1996a; see also Mieder 1989: 317–32) analyzed the American proverb "Different strokes for different folks," explaining that while this modern proverb does advocate the freedom of choice (especially in behavioral matters), it must not be interpreted from a relativistic point of view lacking any moral and social obligations. The liberating thoughts of this proverb regarding individual choices obviously should go only as far as they conform with ethical concepts of society at large.

Proverbs have also been studied and used by social psychologists to help people deal with various behavioral problems, including alcohol or drug addictions. Tim B. Rogers (1989) has shown that proverbs like "No pain, no gain" can be used on posters in treatment centers as a constant reminder that it is a worthwhile struggle to overcome an addiction in order to live a normal life. Such proverbs have also been used during discussions in group therapeutic sessions, where they help create a common ground for the addicts. But the therapeutic use of proverbs is not without its problems, and they should not be overused as simplistic remedies of folk speech (Whaley 1993).

Psychologists and psychiatrists have long been interested in proverbs for testing intelligence, attitudes, aptitudes, and various mental illnesses. Numerous so-called "proverbs tests" have been devised for this purpose, the best-known and most commonly used of which is the Gorham Proverbs Test. It was developed by Donald R. Gorham in 1956 as a tool for diagnosing schizophrenia, because schizophrenics have difficulty in understanding the metaphors of proverbs and tend to interpret them literally (Gorham 1956). Obviously, psycho- and sociolinguistic aspects of normal comprehension of metaphors by children vs. adults, native vs. foreign speakers, white-collar vs. blue-collar workers, etc., enter into this. Of greatest importance, however, is that proverbs tests usually exclude any contextualization of the proverbs, even though it has long been established that proverbs can only be understood properly in social contexts (Mieder 1978b; Rogers 1986).

But it is in the area of psycholinguistics that the true cutting-edge work is going on in theoretical paremiology. Psycholinguists have employed proverbs to study the mental development of children and the whole question of cognition and comprehension of metaphors (Mieder 2003a). Diana Van Lancker's seminal article "The Neurology of Proverbs" (1990) looks at the complex mental processes that must take place in the brain of healthy people to understand abstract (i.e., metaphorical) proverbs, and Raymond W. Gibbs and Dinara Beitel (1995) discuss various theories of metaphor understanding based on proverbs. The psycholinguist Richard P. Honeck has dedicated his entire scholarly career to finding solutions to the vexing problems of cognition and figurative (metaphorical) language. In his superb book *A Proverb in Mind: The Cognitive Science of Proverbial Wit and Wisdom* (1997), he reviews all relevant previous scholarship on metaphor comprehension and then examines proverbs in particular, looking at such matters as cognition, comprehension, communication, indirection, memory, and metaphor. As Honeck and his psycholinguistic colleagues have shown, proverbs might appear to be simple truths, but to be properly understood and effectively used they certainly demand complex brain transactions.

Use in Folk Narratives and Literature

The interrelationship of proverbs with other verbal folklore genres has been of great interest to folklorists in general and paremiologists in particular for a long time. Classical Greek and Latin writers commented on the obvious interrelationship between fables and proverbs, theorizing, as it were, about which of the genres came first (Carnes 1988). In other words, does the proverb that adds a bit of moralizing or ethical wisdom at the end of a fable summarize its content, or is the fable nothing but an explanatory comment on the original proverb? The use and function of proverbs in German fairy tales has been studied by Lothar Bluhm and Heinz Rölleke (1997), and I have shown that especially Wilhelm Grimm changed the style of the fairy tales that he and his brother Jacob had collected from oral sources to make them sound even more "folksy" and ready-made for children (Mieder 1986). Galit Hasan-Rokem's valuable study *Proverbs in Israeli Folk Narratives: A Structural Semantic Analysis* (1982) is also of much interest. The connections between proverbs and riddles, proverbs and jokes, and wellerisms and tall tales have also been studied in smaller articles and notes, and both Bartlett Jere Whiting and Richard Sweterlitsch have looked at the significance of proverbs in the narrative texts of ballads (Whiting 1934; Sweterlitsch 1985; see also Harris 1933). Much work remains to be done in this area, especially regarding etiological tales that serve the purpose of explaining the origin and meaning of proverbs and proverbial expressions (Taylor 1971–73; Röhrich 1991–92).

Much has also been accomplished regarding the use and function of proverbs in literature (Mieder and Bryan 1996). Early scholarship consists primarily of annotated lists of the proverbs found in literary works, while more recent publications address the problems of identification and interpretation of proverbial language in poetry, dramas, and prose. There are hundreds of literary proverb studies, primarily centering on European and American authors ranging from the Middle Ages through the nineteenth century (Abrahams and Babcock 1977), but there are now also investigations of the proverbs in modern writers of Africa, Asia, and elsewhere (Adéékó 1998). While the many monographs on famous writers like Goethe (Pfeffer 1948), Cervantes (Colombi 1989), Voltaire (Calvez 1989), Shakespeare (Donker 1992), Agatha Christie (Bryan 1993), and Frederick Douglass (Mieder 2001) are of importance, there are also more inclusive literary proverb studies of a national literature or a certain historical period, as on the use and function of proverbs in nineteenth-century German literature (Mieder 1976), medieval French literature (Schulze-Busacker 1985), African literature (Adéékó 1998), and Russian literature (McKenna 1998). Rather than writing yet another study on Chinua Achebe or William Shakespeare, more such inclusive investigations are in order to draw valid conclusions regarding the use and function of proverbs during different literary periods of various cultures and languages. The many specific analyses of literary works ought to add up to a better understanding of the poetics of proverbs in literature, also indicating, of course, what proverbs were in frequent use at what time.

Although authors differ in the frequency with which they employ proverbs, proverbial expressions, proverbial comparisons, and wellerisms, their works become important repositories of proverbial language. Whatever the number of proverbial texts in a literary work might be, locating them and interpreting their meaning can be a significant twofold task. Identification serves primarily paremiographical goals in that it deals with the texts. Since the oral use of proverbs in former centuries can no longer be investigated through field research, scholars depend on the written word as sources of them. Every literary investigation of proverbs should, ideally, include an index of all proverbial material with proper verification of their proverbiality (as far as this is possible) by means of standard proverb dictionaries. Such annotated proverb lists are of great importance for the preparation of both expanded and new historical proverb dictionaries.

However, this is only the paremiographical side of the coin. In addition to the identification of proverbial texts there should also be a detailed interpretation of their contextual function. Literary critics, folklorists, and paremiologists want to know when, why, how, by whom, and to whom proverbs are used in literary works. They will thus consider each example in its context to determine what effect it has on the style and message of the entire work. Of much interest is also whether introductory formulas are used to integrate the proverb into the text, whether the formulaic standard structure of the proverb has been changed for stylistic effect, whether a proverb is merely alluded to in an ironic twist, whether a proverb is intentionally parodied or questioned, etc. Ideally, a literary proverb investigation consists of a proverb index and an interpretive essay.

Religion and Wisdom Literature

Proverbs derived from the sacred writings of the world's religions have also gained wide circulation and have been collected as international expressions of wisdom (Champion 1945; Griffin 1991). A vast international scholarship centers on wisdom literature that has found its way into traditional proverbs in various languages and cultures (Plopper 1926; Thompson 1974; Fontaine 1988; Winton 1990; O'Connor 1993; Perry 1993; Westermann 1995; Brown 2000). But much more comparative work is needed to point out the similarities and dissimilarities of the proverbial wisdom of the various religions. There is also not enough known yet about the influence that Biblical proverbs had on the African or Asian population due to missionary work (see Nzambi 1992; Saayman 1997). Yet such indigenous studies as Gerald J. Wanjohi's *The Wisdom and the Philosophy of the Gikuyu Proverbs* (1997) are also of great value in understanding the religious and ethical value system of various peoples as expressed in folk proverbs.

Evidence of verbal wisdom, much of it in the form of proverbs, can be seen in religious writings and in everyday communication on all levels. Scholars from such diverse fields as theology, philosophy, medicine, psychology, and linguistics continue to look at the sources of this wisdom (ancient wisdom literature, cultural traditions, moral values), the science of wisdom (cognition, comprehension, psycholinguistics), and the learning of wisdom (pedagogy, memorization, communication). John Marks Templeton published an uplifting book, *Worldwide Laws of Life: Two Hundred Eternal Spiritual Principles* (1997), based on wisdom drawn from major sacred scriptures of the world and different philosophies. The book is intended to help people acquaint themselves with and hopefully to practice universally accepted moral truths, often expressed in the form of proverbs, as for example "Love your neighbor as yourself" (Matthew 19:19), "Hitch your wagon to a star" (Ralph Waldo Emerson), "A healthy mind in a healthy body," and, of course, the so-called golden rule "Do unto others, as you would have them do unto you" (Matthew 7:12).

There is also the ever-expanding area of "self-help" books that draw on the wisdom of religious and folk proverbs to assist people in coping with the many challenges of modern life. Such books are meant to be therapeutic both from a sociological and psychological point of view, being based to a considerable extent on such proverbs as "If at first you don't succeed, try, try again," "No pain, no gain," and "Don't put off until tomorrow what you can do today" (Arthurs 1994; Eret 2001). Some of the "gurus" of the self-help phenomenon also create their very own maxims in the style of proverbs to spread their message among their eager readers.

Finally, there is the long tradition of the sermonic use of proverbs. Preachers in all religions frequently base their sermons on religious as well as folk proverbs to teach moral values for an upright life. From the folk preachers of the Middle Ages through Martin Luther (Cornette 1942) to the nineteenth-century American preacher Henry Ward Beecher and on to internationally acclaimed preachers like Martin Luther King, proverbs have played a central role in their religious and social messages. At times the proverbs were simply used in an exegetic way to clarify certain Bible passages, but a much more important function of proverbs in sermons is to employ them as a sapiential leitmotif (McKenzie 1996b).

Pedagogy and Language Teaching

Proverbs have been used as teaching tools for centuries to teach moral values and social skills. In fact, there exist special proverbs that deal with such matters as the mind, wisdom, experience, learning, authority, and the teacher (Stanciu 1986). Proverbs contain much educational wisdom, and they have long been used as didactic tools in child rearing, in linguistic and religious instruction in schools, and in teaching about general human experiences. Such proverbs continue to play a major role as a pedagogical tool in modern societies, especially among family members and at school. They deserve to be taught as part of general education, and since they belong to the common knowledge of basically all native speakers, they are indeed very effective devices to communicate wisdom and knowledge about human nature and the world at large. The African educator Felix Boateng (1985) has called for a return to traditional education in Africa with an emphasis on the rich heritage of oral literature as expressed in fables, myths, legends, folk tales, and proverbs. Clearly the educational and communicative power of proverbs in African societies lies in their use as validators of traditional ethics, procedures, and beliefs in teaching children as well as adults. The value and power of proverbs as educational tools are also recognized in modern technological societies.

Proverbs have also been used in native language instruction and to bring cultural traditions to foreign language classes. Textbooks on the teaching of both native and foreign languages usually include at least some lists of proverbs and accompanying exercises. In Europe this began in the Middle Ages, when Latin proverbs were used for translation exercises and to teach children moral precepts. This tradition has by no means come to an end. In fact, the developmental stage of fourth graders might be the perfect time to confront students with the character-building values of proverbial laws of life. The fact that they learn proverbs, that they can employ them in meaningful contexts, and that they act according to their wisdom is proof that children aged nine to ten can cope with abstract and metaphorical proverbs as rules of moral conduct (Mieder and Holmes 2000).

Proverbs also play a major role in the teaching of English as a second language, where they are included as part of metaphorical and cultural learning. Obviously it behooves new speakers of English or any other language to be acquainted with proverbs and other phraseological units for effective communication. As instructors plan the curriculum and devise textbooks for teaching another language, they do well to choose those proverbs for inclusion that are part of the paremiological minimum. It is the proverbs that are in use today that need to be taught (Abadi 2000). All of this also holds true for foreign language instruction in general, where proverbs have always been included as fixed cultural expressions. There is much scholarship on how to integrate proverbs into the teaching of foreign languages (McKenna 1991; Nuessel 1999), but Anna Tóthné Litovkina's book *A Proverb a Day Keeps Boredom Away* (2000) is exemplary. While it is intended primarily for Hungarian students learning English, it could easily be adapted for other language classes. The aim of the book is to familiarize language students with over 450 Anglo-American proverbs by providing a series of activities and exercises that will help the learner discover what each proverb means and how to apply it in particular situations. The exercises bring the proverbs alive with short illustrative references from books, magazines, and newspapers, as well as from poems, fables, and folk narratives. The book also focuses on proverb humor, including anti-proverbs and wellerisms. The fact that the author has also provided sixty proverb illustrations from such well-known artists as Hieronymus Bosch and Pieter Bruegel the Elder as well as woodcuts, engravings, emblems, caricatures, cartoons, and advertisements (Jones 1989; Mieder and Sobieski 1999) makes it a most attractive and useful textbook for proverb acquisition in language classes.

Mass Media and Popular Culture

While it is perfectly appropriate for paremiologists to look backward for the use of proverbs, they must not forget to investigate their traditional and innovative use in modern times (see Koller 1977). With the growing interest in popular culture, the mass media, and cultural literacy, paremiologists look at which traditional proverbs survive today and which have actually been coined in the twentieth and twenty-first centuries (Rees 1984). I have dealt with the modern German scene (Mieder 1983, 1985c, 1992b, 1995a, 1995b, 2000a) and with Anglo-American materials (Mieder 1989, 1993b) in a number of books, showing that people do not necessarily consider proverbs to be sacrosanct. The fun of parodying, manipulating, and perverting traditional proverbs has become quite widespread. While such parodies might be humorous, they also often express serious socio-political satire in the form of slogans and graffiti (Nierenberg 1983). There is, of course, also the well-established tradition of intentionally rephrased anti-proverbs in all types of modern communication, from books of witticisms to T-shirt inscriptions to advertising slogans (Mieder 1989: 239–75; Valdaeva 2003). While such play is not absolutely new, humorous or satirical proverb parodies certainly abound in modern literature, the mass media, and the popular culture of television, film, and music. Anna Tóthné Litovkina and I have assembled over 3,000 parodied proverbs in *Twisted Wisdom: Modern Anti-Proverbs* (1999; see also Mieder 1998). Here I list but a few expressive anti-proverbs that include humor as well as social comments, the traditional proverb text cited first. It is, after all, the juxtaposition of the original proverb with the innovative variation that adds even more spice to this play with proverbial language:

Absence makes the heart grow fonder.
Absence makes the heart go wander.
An apple a day keeps the doctor away.
A condom a day keeps the doctor away.
Too many cooks spoil the broth.
Too many legislators spoil reform.
Experience is the best teacher.
Expedience is the best teacher.
A miss is as good as a mile.
A Ms. is as good as a male.
Nobody is perfect.
No body is perfect.
Different strokes for different folks.
Different Volks for different folks.

The last anti-proverb was a popular advertisement for various Volkswagen models in the 1970s.

Proverbs have been an intricate part of the persuasive if not manipulative tactics of advertisements for a long time. Copy writers noted decades ago that the authority and truth inherent in proverbs could easily be exploited as advertising headlines. In order to add even more convincing power to such proverbial slogans, they often use Biblical proverbs, thus putting an almost sacrosanct claim of high value on the advertised product (Mieder and Mieder 1977). While such traditional use of proverbs continues in advertisements to the present day, the modern proverbial slogans tend to be based on different strategies. Proverbs are more often than not twisted into innovative formulations based on puns that act as attention-getters. An eye-catching picture and relatively little precise information do the rest to push the reader and viewer into a purchasing decision (Mieder 1989: 293–315; Winick 1998: 163–216).

Much work has also been accomplished on the manipulative use of proverbs in the mass media as well as their (mis)use in political discourse. Journalists long ago discovered the usefulness and effectiveness of proverbial headlines. Placed at the beginning of an article in large and bold print, they summarize the content of a newspaper or magazine article into an interpretive and emotionalized image. As with advertising slogans, traditional proverbs or their innovative variations serve as attention-getters to get readers to stop and actually read the following article. While the proverb of the headline does not deal with specifics, the subtitle usually zeroes in on the actual topic. Journalists obviously delight in citing traditional proverbs that are short enough to fit into a one-line headline. If they exceed the limited space, they are quickly shortened into mere allusions that will be understood by most readers. Above all, journalists enjoy "playing" with proverbs, creating revealing anti-proverbs that will get the readers' attention who then want to read the entire article. Such proverbial headlines can be found in all sections of newspapers and magazines, from politics and economics to sports and entertainment. This play with proverbial language can go so far that up to three headlines based on proverbs and proverbial expressions can be found on just one page, including sophisticated newspapers like the *New York Times* and the *Wall Street Journal* (McKenna 1996, 2002).

The use of proverbs as satirical caricatures or humorous cartoons goes back at least to the seventeenth century, and certainly by the beginning of the nineteenth century sequences of framed images based on proverbs foreshadow the comic strips of today. This tradition of illustrating proverbs for the purpose of humorous, ironical, or satirical commentaries on the sociopolitical life has been maintained by modern artists (Mieder 1989: 277–92). For some proverbs there exists an iconographic history from medieval to modern times that comprises dozens of woodcuts, misericords, emblems, paintings, caricatures, cartoons, and comic strips, including also various types of illustrated greeting cards (Röhrich 1991–92). Usually the modern illustrations have captions to assure meaningful communication, but there are also proverb depictions that merely allude to the proverb or that exclude any caption whatsoever. In the latter case the cartoonist expects viewers to understand the proverbial message from the picture alone, something that is perfectly possible if the proverb is in fact well known. It is not difficult to find such proverb depictions in magazines and newspapers, commenting as it were with image and text on literally all social issues. While caricatures in newspapers usually refer to social and political problems, proverb illustrations in the comics section stress the humorous side of life. Single-frame series like *Family Circus, Dennis, the Menace*, and *The Far Side* abound with proverbs (Winick 1998: 217–83), and comic strips like *Peanuts, Hi and Lois*, and *Beetle Bailey* are frequently based on more than one proverb. There is no doubt that proverbs are very much alive in this visual type of communication. However, their wisdom is often put into question, resulting in innovative anti-proverbs.

The appearance and function of proverbs in film and music have received only little attention thus far. Donald Haase (1990) has looked at the use of proverbs in Angela Carter's and Neil Jordan's film version of her tale *The Company of Wolves* (1979), based on the fairy tale *Little Red Riding Hood*. Of special value is also an analysis of proverbial statements in the film *Forrest Gump* (1994), including such "Gumpisms" as "Life is like a box of chocolates: you never know what you're gonna get," which has become a proverb due to the incredible popularity of this Hollywood film (Winick 1998: 83–162). In the area of music, George B. Bryan (1999) uncovered the pervasive use of proverbs in the popular music of Gilbert and Sullivan; Steven Folsom (1993) has done the same for the hits of American country music (1993); and I have discussed the inclusion of proverbs (Mieder 1989: 195–221) in such hits as Bob Dylan's "Like a Rolling Stone" (1965), Cher's "Apples Don't Fall Far from the Tree" (1973), and the Beatles' song "[Money] Can't Buy Me Love" (1964).

This review of scholarship and approaches with an emphasis on publications in English shows that ubiquitous proverbs enable and empower paremiologists and scholars from other disciplines to study them everywhere at any time. Modern paremiology is an absolutely open-ended phenomenon with many new challenges lying ahead. There is no doubt that proverbs, those old gems of generationally tested wisdom, help people in everyday life and communication cope with the complexities of the modern human condition. The traditional proverbs and their value system provide some basic structure, and if their worldview does not fit a particular situation, they are quickly changed into revealing and liberating anti-proverbs. And there are, of course, the new proverbs of modern times, such as "Different strokes for different folks," that express a liberated worldview. Proverbs do not always have to be didactic and prescriptive; they can also be full of satire, irony, and humor. As such, the thousands of proverbs that make up the stock of proverbial wisdom of all cultures represent not a universally valid but certainly a pragmatically useful treasure. In retrospect, paremiologists have amassed a truly impressive body of proverb scholarship upon which prospective paremiology can build in good faith. Modern theoretical and empirical paremiology doubtlessly will lead to new insights about human behavior and communication, and by comparing these research results on an international basis, paremiologists might add their bit to a humane and enlightened world order based on common sense and experienced wisdom.

BIBLIOGRAPHY (EMPHASIS ON ENGLISH-LANGUAGE PUBLICATIONS)

This chapter first appeared as "Proverbs as Cultural Units or Items of Folklore." *Phraseology. An International Handbook of Contemporary Research*. Harald Burger, Dmitrij Dobrovol'skij, Peter Kühn, and Neal R. Norrick, eds. 2 vols. Berlin: Walter de Gruyter, 2007. I, 394–414.

Abadi, Michael Cyrus. 2000. "Proverbs as ESL [English as Second Language] Curriculum." *Proverbium* 17: 1–22.

Abrahams, Roger, and Barbara Babcock. 1977. "The Literary Use of Proverbs." *Journal of American Folklore* 90: 414–29. Also in *Wise Words: Essays on the Proverb*. Wolfgang Mieder, ed. New York: Garland, 1994. 415–37.

Adéèkó, Adélékè. 1998. *Proverbs, Textuality, and Nativism in African Literature*. Gainesville, Florida: University Press of Florida.

Anscombre, Jean-Claude. 2000. *La parole proverbiale*. Paris: Larousse.

Arewa, E. Ojo, and Alan Dundes. 1964. "[Yoruba] Proverbs and the Ethnography of Speaking Folklore." *American Anthropologist* 66, part 2: 70–85.

Arora, Shirley L. 1984. "The Perception of Proverbiality." *Proverbium* 1: 1–38. Also in *Wise Words: Essays on the Proverb*. Wolfgang Mieder, ed. New York: Garland, 1994. 3–29.

———. 1989. "On the Importance of Rotting Fish: A Proverb and Its Audience." *Western Folklore* 48: 271–88.

———. 1994. "Proverbs and Prejudice: *El Indio* in Hispanic Proverbial Speech." *Proverbium* 11: 27–46. Also in *Cognition, Comprehension, and Communication: A Decade of North American Proverb Studies (1990–2000)*. Wolfgang Mieder, ed. Baltmannsweiler: Schneider Verlag Hohengehren. 17–36.

Arthurs, Jeffrey D. 1994. "Proverbs in Inspirational Literature: Sanctioning the American Dream." *Journal of Communication and Religion* 17: 1–15. Also in *Cognition, Comprehension, and Communication: A Decade of North American Proverb Studies (1990–2000)*. Wolfgang Mieder, ed. Baltmannsweiler: Schneider Verlag Hohengehren. 37–52.

Barakat, Robert A. *A Contextual Study of Arabic Proverbs*. Helsinki: Suomalainen Tiedeakatemia.

Bluhm, Lothar, and Heinz Rölleke. 1997. *Redensarten des Volkes, auf die ich immer horche: Märchen, Sprichwort, Redensart. Zur volkspoetischen Ausgestaltung der Kinder- und Hausmärchen durch die Brüder Grimm*. Stuttgart: S. Hirzel.

Boateng, Felix. 1985. "African Traditional Education: A [Proverb] Tool for Intergenerational Communication." *African Culture: The Rhythms of Unity*. Molefi Kete Asante and Kariamu Welsh Asante, eds. Westport, Connecticut: Greenwood. 109–22.

Brandes, Stanley H. 1974. "The Selection Process in Proverb Use: A Spanish Example." *Southern Folklore Quarterly* 38: 167–86.

Briggs, Charles L. 1985. "The Pragmatics of Proverb Performances in New Mexican Spanish." *American Anthropologist* 87: 793–810. Also in *Wise Words: Essays on the Proverb*. Wolfgang Mieder, ed. New York: Garland, 1994. 317–49.

Brown, Warren S., ed. 2000. *Understanding Wisdom: Sources, Science, and Society*. Philadelphia, Pennsylvania: Templeton Foundation Press.

Bryan, George B. 1993. *Black Sheep, Red Herrings, and Blue Murder: The Proverbial Agatha Christie*. Bern: Peter Lang.

———. 1999. "The Proverbial W. S. Gilbert: An Index to Proverbs in the Works of Gilbert and Sullivan." *Proverbium* 16: 21–35.

Burke, Kenneth. 1941. "Literature [i.e., proverbs] as Equipment for Living." In Kenneth Burke, *The Philosophy of Literary Form: Studies in Symbolic Action*. Baton Rouge, Louisiana: Louisiana University Press. 253–62.

Calvez, Daniel Jean. 1989. *Le langage proverbial de Voltaire dans sa correspondance (1704–1769)*. New York: Peter Lang.

Carnes, Pack, ed. 1988. *Proverbia in Fabula: Essays on the Relationship of the Fable and the Proverb*. Bern: Peter Lang.

Champion, Selwyn Gurney. 1945. *The Eleven Religions and Their Proverbial Lore*. New York: E.P. Dutton.

Colombi, Maria Cecilia. 1989. *Los refranes en el Quijote: Texto y contexto*. Potomac, Maryland: Scripta Humanistica.

Cornette, James C. 1942. *Proverbs and Proverbial Expressions in the German Works of Martin Luther*. Diss., University of North Carolina at Chapel Hill. Posthumously ed. by Wolfgang Mieder and Dorothee Racette. Bern: Peter Lang, 1997.

Davis, Natalie Zemon. 1975. "Proverbial Wisdom and Popular Error." In Natalie Zemon Davis, *Society and Culture in Early Modern France*. Stanford, California: Stanford University Press. 227–67, 336–46 (notes).

Doerr, Karin. 2000. "'To Each His Own' (*Jedem das Seine*): The (Mis-)Use of German Proverbs in Concentration Camps and Beyond." *Proverbium* 17: 71–90.

Donker, Marjorie. 1992. *Shakespeare's Proverbial Themes: A Rhetorical Context for the "Sententia" as "Res."* Westport, Connecticut: Greenwood.

Doyle, Charles Clay. 1996. "On 'New' Proverbs and the Conservativeness of Proverb Collections." *Proverbium* 13: 69–84. Also in *Cognition, Comprehension, and Communication: A Decade of North American Proverb Studies (1990–2000)*. Wolfgang Mieder, ed. Baltmannsweiler: Schneider Verlag Hohengehren. 85–98.

Dundes, Alan. 1975. "Slurs International: Folk Comparisons of Ethnicity and National Character." *Southern Folklore Quarterly* 39: 15–38. Also in *Wise Words: Essays on the Proverb*. Wolfgang Mieder, ed. New York: Garland, 1994. 183–209.

———. 1984. *Life is Like a Chicken Coop Ladder: A Portrait of German Culture Through Folklore*. New York: Columbia University Press. Rpt. Detroit, Michigan: Wayne State University Press, 1989.

Eret, Dylan. 2001. "'The Past Does Not Equal the Future': Anthony Robbins' Self-Help Maxims as Therapeutic Forms of Proverbial Rhetoric." *Proverbium* 18: 77–103.

Fabian, Johannes. 1990. *Power and Performance: Ethnographic Explorations through Proverbial Wisdom and Theater in Shaba, Zaire*. Madison, Wisconsin: University of Wisconsin Press.

Finnegan, Ruth. 1970. "Proverbs. The Significance and Concept of the Proverb. Form and Style. Content. Occasions and Functions." In Ruth Finnegan, *Oral Literature in Africa*. Oxford: Clarendon. 389–425. Also in *The Wisdom of Many: Essays on the Proverb*. Wolfgang Mieder and Alan Dundes, eds. New York: Garland, 1981. 10–42.

Folsom, Steven. 1993. "Proverbs in Recent American Country Music: Form and Function in the Hits of 1986–87." *Proverbium* 10: 65–88.

Fontaine, Carole R. 1982. *Traditional Sayings in the Old Testament: A Contextual Study*. Sheffield, UK: Almond.

Friedman, Albert B. 1974. "'When Adam Delved . . .': Contexts of an Historic Proverb." *Harvard English Studies* 4: 213–30. Also in *Wise Words: Essays on the Proverb*. Wolfgang Mieder, ed. New York: Garland, 1994. 495–513.

Gallacher, Stuart A. 1959. "Frauenlob's Bits of Wisdom: Fruits of His Environment." *Middle Ages, Reformation, Volkskunde. Festschrift for John G. Kunstmann*. Frederic E. Coenen et al, eds. Chapel Hill, North Carolina: University of North Carolina Press. 45–58.

Geise, Nancy M. 1999. "'Possession Is Nine-Tenths of the Law': History and Meaning of a Legal Proverb." *Proverbium* 16: 105–24.

Gibbs, Raymond W., and Dinara Beitel. 1995. "What Proverb Understanding Reveals about How People Think." *Psychological Bulletin* 118: 133–54. Also in *Cognition, Comprehension, and Communication: A Decade of North American Proverb Studies (1990–2000)*. Wolfgang Mieder, ed. Baltmannsweiler: Schneider Verlag Hohengehren. 109–62.

Goodwin, Paul D., and Joseph W. Wenzel. 1979. "Proverbs and Practical Reasoning: A Study in Socio-Logic." *Quarterly Journal of Speech* 65: 289–302. Also in *The Wisdom of Many: Essays on the Proverb*. Wolfgang Mieder and Alan Dundes, eds. New York: Garland, 1981. 140–60.

Gorham, Donald R. 1956. "A Proverbs Test for Clinical and Experimental Use." *Psychological Reports* 2: 1–12.

Griffin, Albert Kirby. 1991. *Religious Proverbs: Over 1600 Adages from 18 Faiths Worldwide.* Jefferson, North Carolina: McFarland.

Grzybek, Peter. 1987. "Foundations of Semiotic Proverb Study." *Proverbium* 4: 39–85. Also in *Wise Words: Essays on the Proverb.* Wolfgang Mieder, ed. New York: Garland, 1994. 31–71.

———, ed. 2000. *Die Grammatik der sprichwörtlichen Weisheit von G. L. Permjakov. Mit einer Analyse allgemein bekannter deutscher Sprichwörter.* Baltmannsweiler: Schneider Verlag Hohengehren.

Grzybek, Peter, and Christoph Chlosta. 1993. "Grundlagen der empirischen Sprichwortforschung." *Proverbium* 10: 89–128.

Grzybek, Peter, and Wolfgang Eismann, eds. 1984. *Semiotische Studien zum Sprichwort. Simple Forms Reconsidered I.* Tübingen: Gunter Narr.

Haase, Donald. 1990. "Is Seeing Believing? Proverbs and the Film Adaptation of a Fairy Tale." *Proverbium* 7: 89–104.

Hain, Mathilde. 1951. *Sprichwort und Volkssprache: Eine volkskundlich-soziologische Dorfuntersuchung.* Gießen: Wilhelm Schmitz.

Harris, Clement A. 1933. "Music in the World's Proverbs." *Musical Quarterly* 19: 382–92.

Hasan-Rokem, Galit. 1982. *Proverbs in Israeli Folk Narratives: A Structural Semantic Analysis.* Helsinki: Suomalainen Tiedeakatemia.

———. 1990. "The Aesthetics of the Proverb: Dialogue of Discourses from Genesis to Glasnost." *Proverbium* 7: 105–16.

———. 1992. "Proverbs as Inter-Ethnic Dialogue in Israel." *Jewish Folklore and Ethnology Review* 14: 52–55.

Hernadi, Paul, and Francis Steen. 1999. "The Tropical Landscapes of Proverbia: A Crossdisciplinary Travelogue." *Style* 33: 1–20. Also in *Cognition, Comprehension, and Communication: A Decade of North American Proverb Studies (1990–2000).* Wolfgang Mieder, ed. Baltmannsweiler: Schneider Verlag Hohengehren. 185–204.

Honeck, Richard P. 1997. *A Proverb in Mind: The Cognitive Science of Proverbial Wit and Wisdom.* Mahwah, New Jersey: Lawrence Erlbaum.

Honeck, Richard P., and Clare T. Kibler. 1984. "The Role of Imagery, Analogy, and Instantiation in Proverb Comprehension." *Journal of Psycholinguistic Research* 13: 393–414.

Honeck, Richard P., and Jeffrey Welge. 1997. "Creation of Proverbial Wisdom in the Laboratory." *Journal of Psycholinguistic Research* 26: 605–29. Also in *Cognition, Comprehension, and Communication: A Decade of North American Proverb Studies (1990–2000).* Wolfgang Mieder, ed. Baltmannsweiler: Schneider Verlag Hohengehren. 205–30.

Jason, Heda. 1971. "Proverbs in Society: The Problem of Meaning and Function." *Proverbium* 17: 617–23.

Jones, Malcolm. 1989. "The Depiction of Proverbs in Late Medieval Art." *Europhras 88: Phraséologie contrastive.* Gertrud Gréciano, ed. Strasbourg: Université des Sciences Humaines. 205–23.

Kanyó, Zoltán. 1981. *Sprichwörter—Analyse einer Einfachen Form: Ein Beitrag zur generativen Poetik.* The Hague: Mouton.

Kerschen, Lois. 1998. *American Proverbs about Women: A Reference Guide.* Westport, Connecticut: Greenwood.

Kindstrand, Jan Fredrik. 1978. "The Greek Concept of Proverbs." *Eranos* 76: 71–85. Also in *Proverbia in Fabula: Essays on the Relationship of the Fable and the Proverb.* Pack Carnes, ed. Bern: Peter Lang, 1988. 233–53.

Kirshenblatt-Gimblett, Barbara. 1973. "Toward a Theory of Proverb Meaning." *Proverbium* 22: 821–27. Also in *The Wisdom of Many: Essays on the Proverb.* Wolfgang Mieder and Alan Dundes, eds. New York: Garland, 1981. 111–21.

Koller, Werner. 1977. *Redensarten: Linguistische Aspekte, Vorkommensanlysen, Sprachspiel*. Tübingen: Max Niemeyer.

Krikmann, Arvo. 1974a. *On Denotative Indefiniteness of Proverbs*. Tallinn: Academy of Sciences of the Estonian SSR, Institute of Language and Literature; also in *Proverbium* 1 (1984): 47–91.

———. 1974b. *Some Additional Aspects of Semantic Indefiniteness of Proverbs*. Tallinn: Academy of Sciences of the Estonian SSR, Institute of Language and Literature; also in *Proverbium* 2 (1985): 58–85.

Kunstmann, John G. 1939. "The Bird that Fouls Its Nest." *Southern Folklore Quarterly* 3: 75–91. Also in *The Wisdom of Many: Essays on the Proverb*. Wolfgang Mieder and Alan Dundes, eds. New York: Garland, 1981. 190–210.

Kuusi, Matti. 1957a. *Parömiologische Betrachtungen*. Helsinki: Suomalainen Tiedeakatemia.

———. 1957b. *Regen bei Sonnenschein: Zur Weltgeschichte einer Redensart*. Helsinki: Suomalainen Tiedeakatemia.

———. 1967. "Fatalistic Traits in Finnish Proverbs." *Fatalistic Beliefs in Religion, Folklore and Literature*. Helmer Ringgren, ed. Stockholm: Almqvist & Wiksell. 89–96. Also in *The Wisdom of Many: Essays on the Proverb*. Wolfgang Mieder and Alan Dundes, eds. New York: Garland, 1981. 275–83.

Lau, Kimberly J. 1996. "'It's about Time': The Ten Proverbs Most Frequently Used in Newspapers and Their Relation to American Values." *Proverbium* 13: 135–59.

Levin, Isidor. 1968–69. "Überlegungen zur demoskopischen Parömiologie." *Proverbium* 11: 289–93 and 13: 361–66.

Lévy, Isaac Jack, and Rosemary Lévy Zumwalt. 1990. "A Conversation in Proverbs: Judeo-Spanish *Refranes* in Context." *Proverbium* 7: 117–32. Also in *Cognition, Comprehension, and Communication: A Decade of North American Proverb Studies (1990–2000)*. Wolfgang Mieder, ed. Baltmannsweiler: Schneider Verlag Hohengehren. 255–69.

Lieber, Michael D. 1984. "Analogic Ambiguity: A Paradox of Proverb Usage." *Journal of American Folklore* 97: 423–41. Also in *Wise Words: Essays on the Proverb*. Wolfgang Mieder, ed. New York: Garland, 1994. 99–126.

Lister, Alfred. 1874–75. "Chinese Proverbs and Their Lessons." *China Review* 3: 129–38. Also in *The Wisdom of Many: Essays on the Proverb*. Wolfgang Mieder and Alan Dundes, eds. New York: Garland, 1981. 242–56.

Louis, Cameron. 2000. "Proverbs and the Politics of Language." *Proverbium* 17: 173–94. Also in *Cognition, Comprehension, and Communication: A Decade of North American Proverb Studies (1990–2000)*. Wolfgang Mieder, ed. Baltmannsweiler: Schneider Verlag Hohengehren. 271–92.

McKelvie, Donald. 1965. "Proverbial Elements in the Oral Tradition of an English Urban Industrial Region." *Journal of the Folklore Institute* 2: 244–61.

McKenna, Kevin J. 1991. "'Na poslovitsu ni suda ni raspravy': The Role of Proverbs in the Russian Language Curriculum." *Russian Language Journal* 45: 17–37.

———. 1996. "Proverbs and *Perestroika*: An Analysis of *Pravda* Headlines, 1988–1991." *Proverbium* 13: 215–33. Also in *Cognition, Comprehension, and Communication: A Decade of North American Proverb Studies (1990–2000)*. Wolfgang Mieder, ed. Baltmannsweiler: Schneider Verlag Hohengehren. 293–310.

———, ed. 1998. *Proverbs in Russian Literature: From Catherine the Great to Alexander Solzhenitsyn*. Burlington, Vermont: University of Vermont Press.

———. 2002. "Politics and the Russian Proverb: A Retrospective of *Pravda* Political Cartoons in the 1990s." *Proverbium* 19: 225–52.

McKenzie, Alyce M. 1996a. "'Different Strokes for Different Folks': America's Quintessential Postmodern Proverb." *Theology Today* 53: 201–12. Also in *Cognition, Comprehension, and Communication: A Decade of North American Proverb Studies (1990–2000)*. Wolfgang Mieder, ed. Baltmannsweiler: Schneider Verlag Hohengehren. 311–24.

———. 1996b. *Preaching Proverbs: Wisdom for the Pulpit.* Louisville, Kentucky: Westminster John Knox Press.

Mieder, Barbara, and Wolfgang Mieder. 1977. "Tradition and Innovation: Proverbs in Advertising." *Journal of Popular Culture* 11: 308–19. Also in *The Wisdom of Many: Essays on the Proverb.* Wolfgang Mieder and Alan Dundes, eds. New York: Garland, 1981. 309–22.

Mieder, Wolfgang. 1976. *Das Sprichwort in der deutschen Prosaliteratur des neunzehnten Jahrhunderts.* München: Wilhelm Fink.

———. 1977. *International Bibliography of Explanatory Essays on Individual Proverbs and Proverbial Expressions.* Bern: Herbert Lang.

———, ed. 1978a. *Ergebnisse der Sprichwörterforschung.* Bern: Peter Lang.

———. 1978b. "The Use of Proverbs in Psychological Testing." *Journal of the Folklore Institute* 15: 45–55.

———. 1982. "Proverbs in Nazi Germany: The Promulgation of Anti-Semitism and Stereotypes through Folklore." *Journal of American Folklore* 95: 435–64. Also in Wolfgang Mieder, *Proverbs Are Never Out of Season: Popular Wisdom in the Modern Age.* New York: Oxford University Press, 1993. 225–55.

———. 1982–2001. *International Proverb Scholarship: An Annotated Bibliography,* 4 vols. New York: Garland. New York: Peter Lang (vol. 4).

———. 1983. *Deutsche Sprichwörter in Literatur, Politik, Presse und Werbung.* Hamburg: Helmut Buske.

———. 1985a. "Neues zur demoskopischen Sprichwortforschung." *Proverbium* 2: 307–28.

———. 1985b. "Popular Views of the Proverb." *Proverbium* 2: 109–43; also in Mieder 1993b, 18–40.

———. 1985c. *Sprichwort, Redensart, Zitat: Tradierte Formelsprache in der Moderne.* Bern: Peter Lang.

———. 1986. "Wilhelm Grimm's Proverbial Additions in the Fairy Tales." *Proverbium* 3: 59–83.

———. 1987. *Tradition and Innovation in Folk Literature.* Hanover, New Hampshire: University Press of New England.

———. 1989. *American Proverbs: A Study of Texts and Contexts.* Bern: Peter Lang.

———. 1992a. "Paremiological Minimum and Cultural Literacy." *Creativity and Tradition in Folklore: New Directions.* Simon J. Bronner, ed. Logan, Utah: Utah State University Press. 185–203; also in Mieder 1993b, 41–47 and Mieder 1994, 297–316.

———. 1992b. *Sprichwort—Wahrwort!? Studien zur Geschichte, Bedeutung und Funktion deutscher Sprichwörter.* Frankfurt am Main: Peter Lang.

———. 1993a. "'The Only Good Indian Is a Dead Indian': History and Meaning of a Proverbial Stereotype." *Journal of American Folklore* 106: 38–60. Also in Wolfgang Mieder, *The Politics of Proverbs: From Traditional Wisdom to Proverbial Stereotypes.* Madison: University of Wisconsin Press, 1997. 138–59, 221–27 (notes).

———. 1993b. *Proverbs Are Never Out of Season: Popular Wisdom in the Modern Age.* New York: Oxford University Press. Rpt. New York: Peter Lang, 2012.

———, ed. 1994. *Wise Words: Essays on the Proverb.* New York: Garland.

———. 1995a. *Deutsche Redensarten, Sprichwörter und Zitate: Studien zu ihrer Herkunft, Überlieferung und Verwendung.* Wien: Edition Praesens.

———. 1995b. *Sprichwörtliches und Geflügeltes: Sprachstudien von Martin Luther bis Karl Marx.* Bochum: Norbert Brockmeyer.

———. 1996a. "'No Tickee, No Washee': Subtleties of a Proverbial Slur." *Western Folklore* 55: 1–40. Also in Wolfgang Mieder, *The Politics of Proverbs: From Traditional Wisdom to Proverbial Stereotypes.* Madison: University of Wisconsin Press, 1997. 160–89, 227–35 (notes).

———. 1996b. "Proverbs." *American Folklore: An Encyclopedia.* Jan Harold Brunvand, ed. New York: Garland. 597–601.

———. 1997a. "Modern Paremiology in Retrospect and Prospect." *Embracing the Baobab Tree: The African Proverb in the 21st Century.* Willem Saayman, ed. Pretoria: Unisa Press. 3–36. Also in Wolfgang

Mieder, *Strategies of Wisdom: Anglo-American and German Proverb Studies*. Baltmannsweiler: Schneider Verlag Hohengehren, 2000. 7–36.

———. 1997b. *The Politics of Proverbs: From Traditional Wisdom to Proverbial Stereotypes*. Madison, Wisconsin: University of Wisconsin Press.

———. 1998. *Verdrehte Weisheiten: Antisprichwörter aus Literatur und Medien*. Wiesbaden: Quelle & Meyer.

———. 1999. *Sprichwörter/Redensarten—Parömiologie*. Heidelberg: Julius Groos.

———. 2000a. *Aphorismen, Sprichwörter, Zitate: Von Goethe und Schiller bis Victor Klemperer*. Bern: Peter Lang.

———. 2000b. *Strategies of Wisdom: Anglo-American and German Proverb Studies*. Baltmannsweiler: Schneider Verlag Hohengehren.

———. 2000c. "The History and Future of Common Proverbs in Europe." *Folklore in 2000. Voces amicorum Guilhelmo Voigt sexagenario*. Ilona Nagy and Kincsö Verebélyi, eds. Budapest: Universitas Scientarium de Rolando Eötvös nominata. 300–314.

———. 2001. *"No Struggle, No Progress": Frederick Douglass and His Proverbial Rhetoric for Civil Rights*. New York: Peter Lang.

———. 2002. *"Call a Spade a Spade": From Classical Phrase to Racial Slur*. New York: Peter Lang.

———, ed. 2003a. *Cognition, Comprehension, and Communication: A Decade of North American Proverb Studies (1990–2000)*. Baltmannsweiler: Schneider Verlag Hohengehren.

———. 2003b. "'Government of the People, by the People, for the People': The Making and Meaning of an American Proverb of Democracy." *Proverbium* 20: 259–308.

Mieder, Wolfgang, and George B. Bryan. 1995. *The Proverbial Winston S. Churchill: An Index to Proverbs in the Works of Sir Winston Churchill*. Westport, Connecticut: Greenwood.

———. 1996. *Proverbs in World Literature: A Bibliography*. New York: Peter Lang.

———. 1997. *The Proverbial Harry S. Truman: An Index to Proverbs in the Works of Harry S. Truman*. New York: Peter Lang.

Mieder, Wolfgang, and Alan Dundes, eds. 1981. *The Wisdom of Many: Essays on the Proverb*. New York: Garland. Rpt. Madison, Wisconsin: University of Wisconsin Press, 1994.

Mieder, Wolfgang, and Deborah Holmes. 2000. *Children and Proverbs Speak the Truth: Teaching Proverbial Wisdom to Fourth Graders*. Burlington, Vermont: University of Vermont.

Mieder, Wolfgang, Stewart A. Kingsbury, and Kelsie B. Harder, eds. 1992. *A Dictionary of American Proverbs*. New York: Oxford University Press.

Mieder, Wolfgang, and Janet Sobieski. 1999. *Proverb Iconography: An International Bibliography*. New York: Peter Lang.

———. 2003. *Proverbs and the Social Sciences: An Annotated International Bibliography*. Baltmannsweiler: Schneider Verlag Hohengehren.

Mieder, Wolfgang, and Anna Tóthné Litovkina. 1999. *Twisted Wisdom: Modern Anti-Proverbs*. Burlington, Vermont: University of Vermont Press.

Moll, Otto. 1958. *Sprichwörterbibliographie*. Frankfurt am Main: Vittorio Klostermann.

Nierenberg, Jess. 1983. "Proverbs in Graffiti: Taunting Traditional Wisdom." *Maledicta* 7: 41–58. Also in *Wise Words: Essays on the Proverb*. Wolfgang Mieder, ed. New York: Garland, 1994. 543–61.

Nippold, Marilyn A., Linda D. Uhden, and Ilsa E. Schwarz. 1997. "Proverb Explanation Through the Lifespan: A Developmental Study of Adolescents and Adults." *Journal of Speech, Language, and Hearing Research* 40: 245–53. Also in *Cognition, Comprehension, and Communication: A Decade of North American Proverb Studies (1990–2000)*. Wolfgang Mieder, ed. Baltmannsweiler: Schneider Verlag Hohengehren. 367–83.

Norrick, Neal R. 1985. *How Proverbs Mean: Semantic Studies in English Proverbs*. Amsterdam: Mouton.

Nuessel, Frank H. 1999. "Proverbs and Metaphoric Language in Second-Language Acquisition." *Studies in Applied Psychosemiotics* 16: 157–78. Also in *Cognition, Comprehension, and Communication: A Decade of North American Proverb Studies (1990–2000)*. Wolfgang Mieder, ed. Baltmannsweiler: Schneider Verlag Hohengehren. 395–412.

Nwachukwu-Agbada, J. O. J. 1988. "'Bèkeè' [the white man] in Igbo Proverbial Lore." *Proverbium* 5: 137–44.

———. 1990. "Origin, Meaning and Value of Igbo Historical Proverbs." *Proverbium* 7: 185–206.

Nzambi, Philippe D. 1992. *Proverbes bibliques et proverbes kongo: Étude comparative de Proverbia 25-29 et de quelques proverbes kongo*. Frankfurt am Main: Peter Lang.

Obelkevich, James. 1987. "Proverbs and Social History." *The Social History of Language*. Peter Burke and Roy Porter, eds. Cambridge: Cambridge University Press. 43–72. Also in *Wise Words: Essays on the Proverb*. Wolfgang Mieder, ed. New York: Garland, 1994. 211–52.

Obeng, Samuel G. 1996. "The Proverb as a Mitigating and Politeness Strategy in Akan Discourse." *Anthropological Linguistics* 38: 521–49. Also in *Cognition, Comprehension, and Communication: A Decade of North American Proverb Studies (1990–2000)*. Wolfgang Mieder, ed. Baltmannsweiler: Schneider Verlag Hohengehren. 413–42.

O'Connor, Kathleen M. 1993. *The Wisdom Literature*. Collegeville, Minnesota: Liturgical Press.

Paczolay, Gyula. 1997. *European Proverbs in 55 Languages with Equivalents in Arabic, Persian, Sanskrit, Chinese and Japanese*. Veszprém, Hungary: Veszprémi Nyomda.

Penfield, Joyce. 1983. *Communicating with Quotes: The Igbo Case*. Westport, Connecticut: Greenwood.

Permiakov, Grigorii L'vovich. 1970. *Ot pogovorki do skazki: Zametki po obshchei teorii klishe*. Moskva: Nauka. Also in English translation by Y. N. Filippov. *From Proverb to Folk-Tale: Notes on the General Theory of Cliché*. Moscow: Nauka, 1979.

———. 1971. *Paremiologicheskie eksperiment. Materialy dlia paremiologicheskogo minimuma*. Moskva: Nauka.

———. 1982. "K voprosu o russkom paremiologicheskom minimume." *Slovari i lingvostranovedenie*. E. M. Vereshchagina, ed. Moskva: Russkii iazyk. 131–37. Translated into English by Kevin J. McKenna as "On the Question of a Russian Paremiological Minimum." *Proverbium* 6 (1989): 91–102.

———. 1985. *300 obshcheupotrebitel'nykh russkikh poslovits i pogovorok*. Moskva: Russkii iazyk.

Perry, Theodore A. 1993. *Wisdom Literature and the Structure of Proverbs*. University Park, Pennsylvania: Pennsylvania State University Press.

Petrova, Roumyana. 2003. "Comparing Proverbs as Cultural Texts." *Proverbium* 20: 331–44.

Peukes, Gerhard. 1977. *Untersuchungen zum Sprichwort im Deutschen: Semantik, Syntax, Typen*. Berlin: Erich Schmidt.

Pfeffer, J. Alan. 1948. *The Proverb in Goethe*. New York: Columbia University Press.

Phillips, Margaret M. 1964. *The Adages of Erasmus: A Study with Translations*. Cambridge: Cambridge University Press.

Plopper, Clifford H. 1926. *Chinese Religion Seen Through the Proverb*. Shanghai: China Press. Rpt. New York: Paragon, 1969.

Prahlad, Sw. Anand. 1994. "'No Guts, No Glory': Proverbs, Values and Image among Anglo-American University Students." *Southern Folklore* 51: 285–98. Also in *Cognition, Comprehension, and Communication: A Decade of North American Proverb Studies (1990–2000)*. Wolfgang Mieder, ed. Baltmannsweiler: Schneider Verlag Hohengehren. 443–58.

———. 1996. *African-American Proverbs in Context*. Jackson, Mississippi: University Press of Mississippi.

Profantová, Zuzana. 1997. *"Little Fish Are Sweet": Selected Writings on Proverbs*. Bratislava: Ustav etnológie SAV.

Raymond, Joseph. 1956. "Tensions in Proverbs: More Light on International Understanding." *Western Folklore* 15: 153–58. Also in *The Wisdom of Many: Essays on the Proverb*. Wolfgang Mieder and Alan Dundes, eds. New York: Garland, 1981. 300–308.

Rees, Nigel. 1984. *Sayings of the Century: The Stories Behind the Twentieth Century's Quotable Sayings.* London: George Allen & Unwin.

Reinsberg-Düringsfeld, Otto von. 1863. *Internationale Titulaturen.* 2 vols. Leipzig: Hermann Fries. Rpt. ed. by Wolfgang Mieder. Hildesheim: Georg Olms, 1992.

Rittersbacher, Christa. 2002. *Frau und Mann im Sprichwort: Einblicke in die sprichwörtliche Weltanschauung Großbritanniens und Amerikas.* Heidelberg: Das Wunderhorn.

Roback, Abraham A. 1944. *A Dictionary of International Slurs.* Cambridge, Massachusetts: Sci-Art Publishers. Rpt. Waukesha, Wisconsin: Maledicta Press, 1979.

Rogers, Tim B. 1986. "Psychological Approaches to Proverbs: A Treatise on the Import of Context." *Canadian Folklore Canadien* 8: 87–104. Also in *Wise Words: Essays on the Proverb.* Wolfgang Mieder, ed. New York: Garland, 1994. 159–81.

———. 1989. "The Use of Slogans, Colloquialisms, and Proverbs in the Treatment of Substance Addiction: A Psychological Application of Proverbs." *Proverbium* 6: 103–12.

Röhrich, Lutz. 1991–92. *Das große Lexikon der sprichwörtlichen Redensarten.* 3 vols. Freiburg: Herder.

Röhrich, Lutz, and Wolfgang Mieder. 1977. *Sprichwort.* Stuttgart: Metzler.

Ronesi, Lynne. 2000. "'Mightier than the Sword': A Look at Proverbial Prejudice." *Proverbium* 17: 329–47.

Ruef, Hans. 1995. *Sprichwort und Sprache: Am Beispiel des Sprichworts im Schweizerdeutschen.* Berlin: Walter de Gruyter.

Russo, Joseph. 1983. "The Poetics of the Ancient Greek Proverb." *Journal of Folklore Research* 20: 121–30.

Saayman, Willem, ed. 1997. *Embracing the Baobab Tree: The African Proverb in the 21st Century.* Pretoria: Unisa Press.

Sabban, Annette, and Jan Wirrer, eds. 1991. *Sprichwörter und Redensarten im interkulturellen Vergleich.* Opladen: Westdeutscher Verlag.

Schulze-Busacker, Elisabeth. 1985. *Proverbes et expressions proverbiales dans la littérature narrative du moyen âge français: Recueil et analyse.* Paris: Honoré Champion.

Seiler, Friedrich. 1922. *Deutsche Sprichwörterkunde.* München: C.H. Beck. Rpt. München: C.H. Beck, 1967.

Seitel, Peter. 1969. "Proverbs: A Social Use of Metaphor." *Genre* 2: 143–61. Also in *The Wisdom of Many: Essays on the Proverb.* Wolfgang Mieder and Alan Dundes, eds. New York: Garland, 1981. 122–39.

Singer, Samuel, and Ricarda Liver, eds. 1995–2002. *Thesaurus proverbiorum medii aevi. Lexikon der Sprichwörter des romanisch-germanischen Mittelalters.* 13 vols. Berlin: Walter de Gruyter.

Stanciu, Dumitru. 1986. "The Proverb and the Problems of Education." *Proverbium* 3: 153–78.

Strauss, Emanuel. 1994. *Dictionary of European Proverbs.* 3 vols. London: Routledge.

Suard, François, and Claude Buridant, eds. 1984. *Richesse du proverbe.* 2 vols. Lille: Université de Lille.

Sweterlitsch, Richard. 1985. "Reexamining the Proverb in the Child Ballads." *Proverbium* 2: 233–56.

Taylor, Archer. 1931. *The Proverb.* Cambridge, Massachusetts: Harvard University Press. Rpt. as *The Proverb and An Index to The Proverb.* Hatboro, Pennsylvania: Folklore Associates, 1962. Rpt. again with an introduction and bibliography by Wolfgang Mieder. Bern: Peter Lang, 1985.

———. 1971–73. "The Collection and Study of Tales and Proverbs." *Béaloideas* 39–41: 320–28.

———. 1975. *Selected Writings on Proverbs.* Wolfgang Mieder, ed. Helsinki: Suomalainen Tiedeakatemia.

Templeton, John Marks. 1997. *Worldwide Laws of Life.* Philadelphia, Pennsylvania: Templeton Foundation Press.

———. 1974. *The Form and Function of Proverbs in Ancient Israel.* The Hague: Mouton.

Tóthné Litovkina, Anna. 1994. "The Most Powerful Markers of Proverbiality: Perception of Proverbs and Familiarity with Them among 40 Americans." *Semiotische Berichte* 1–4: 227–353.

———. 1998. "An Analysis of Popular American Proverbs and Their Use in Language Teaching." *Die heutige Bedeutung oraler Tradition: Ihre Archivierung, Publikation und Index-Erschließung.* Walther Heissig and Rüdiger Schott, eds. Opladen: Westdeutscher Verlag. 131–58.

———. 2000. *A Proverb a Day Keeps Boredom Away*. Pécs-Szekszárd: IPF-Könyvek.

Valdaeva, Tatiana. 2003. "Anti-Proverbs or New Proverbs: The Use of English Anti-Proverbs and Their Stylistic Analysis." *Proverbium* 20: 379–90.

Van Lancker, Diana. 1990. "The Neurology of Proverbs." *Behavioural Neurology* 3: 169–87. Also in *Cognition, Comprehension, and Communication: A Decade of North American Proverb Studies (1990–2000)*. Wolfgang Mieder, ed. Baltmannsweiler: Schneider Verlag Hohengehren. 531–54.

Walther, Hans, and Paul Gerhard Schmidt, eds. 1963–86. *Proverbia sententiaeque latinitatis medii aevi. Lateinische Sprichwörter und Sentenzen des Mittelalters*. 9 vols. Göttingen: Vandenhoeck & Ruprecht.

Wanjohi, Gerald J. 1997. *The Wisdom and the Philosophy of the Gikuyu Proverbs*. Nairobi: Paulines Publications Africa.

Westermann, Claus. 1995. *Roots of Wisdom: The Oldest Proverbs of Israel and Other Peoples*. Louisville, Kentucky: Westminster John Knox Press.

Westermarck, Edward. 1931. *Wit and Wisdom in Morocco: A Study of Native Proverbs*. New York: Horace Liveright. Rpt. New York: AMS Press, 1980.

Whaley, Bryan B. 1993. "When 'Try, Try Again' Turns to 'You're Beating a Dead Horse': The Rhetorical Characteristics of Proverbs and Their Potential for Influencing Therapeutic Change." *Metaphor and Symbolic Action* 8: 127–39. Also in *Cognition, Comprehension, and Communication: A Decade of North American Proverb Studies (1990–2000)*. Wolfgang Mieder, ed. Baltmannsweiler: Schneider Verlag Hohengehren. 555–70.

Whiting, Bartlett Jere. 1932. "The Nature of the Proverb." *Harvard Studies and Notes in Philology and Literature* 14: 273–307. Also in *"When Evensong and Morrowsong Accord": Three Essays on the Proverb*. Joseph Harris and Wolfgang Mieder, eds. Cambridge, Massachusetts: Department of English and American Literature and Language, Harvard University, 1994. 51–85.

———. 1934. "Proverbial Material in the Popular Ballad." *Journal of American Folklore* 47: 22–44.

———. 1994. *"When Evensong and Morrowsong Accord": Three Essays on the Proverb*. Joseph Harris and Wolfgang Mieder, eds. Cambridge, Massachusetts: Department of English and American Literature and Language, Harvard University.

Williams, Derek A. 2003. "'Everything that Shine Ain't Gold': A Preliminary Ethnography of a Proverb in an African American Family." *Proverbium* 20: 391–406.

Wilson, F. P. 1970. *The Oxford Dictionary of English Proverbs*. Oxford: Clarendon.

Winick, Stephen D. 1998. *The Proverb Process: Intertextuality and Proverbial Innovation in Popular Culture*. Diss., University of Pennsylvania.

———. 2003. "Intertextuality and Innovation in a Definition of the Proverb Genre." *Cognition, Comprehension, and Communication: A Decade of North American Proverb Studies (1990–2000)*. Wolfgang Mieder, ed. Baltmannsweiler: Schneider Verlag Hohengehren. 571–601.

Winton, Alan P. 1990. *The Proverbs of Jesus: Issues of History and Rhetoric*. Sheffield, UK: Sheffield Academic Press.

Yankah, Kwesi. 1984. "Do Proverbs Contradict?" *Folklore Forum* 17: 2–19. Also in *Wise Words: Essays on the Proverb*. Wolfgang Mieder, ed. New York: Garland, 1994. 127–42.

———. 1989. *The Proverb in the Context of Akan Rhetoric: A Theory of Proverb Praxis*. Bern: Peter Lang.

Zholkovskii, Aleksandr K. 1978. "At the Intersection of Linguistics, Paremiology and Poetics." *Poetics* 7: 309–32.

2. "MANY ROADS LEAD TO GLOBALIZATION"
The Translation and Distribution of Anglo-American Proverbs
in Europe

More than forty years ago, the renowned Finnish paremiologist Matti
Kuusi delivered and published a significant lecture in his native Finnish language that was finally published in English translation in 1994 with
the intriguing title "Research Problems in Loan-Proverbs" in a major collection of his essays entitled *Mind and Form in Folklore*. As is characteristically
true for this doyen of twentieth-century proverb studies, there is a profound,
terse statement in this article that might well serve as a starting point and
motto for the present deliberations. Having discussed how proverbs from
other European languages entered or failed to enter the non-Indo-European
language of Finnish in the form of loan translations, he very wisely made the
following observation:

> From a consideration of Finland and Europe, it is, I believe, necessary before
> long to move to a global examination of proverbs. . . . Tens of thousands of
> publications now make it at least theoretically possible to determine to what
> extent the peoples of Eurasia, Africa and Polynesia have proverbs in common.
> (Kuusi 1969 [1994]: 129)

As someone who assembled one of the largest libraries of proverb collec-
tions from around the world in the Folklore Archive of the Finnish Literature
Society in Helsinki, Kuusi was obviously aware of hundreds of comparative
proverb collections that shed much light on the international dissemination of proverbs, including his own magisterial *Proverbia septentrionalia. 900
Balto-Finnic Proverb Types with Russian, Baltic, German and Scandinavian
Parallels* (1985) that he painstakingly assembled with the help of a number of
Nordic paremiographers. Of course, this untiring scholar had also completed
the groundwork *Towards an International Type-System of Proverbs* (1972) on
which he labored, together with his daughter Outi Lauhakangas, for over

twenty-five years. She has now published her own book on *The Matti Kuu-si International Type-System of Proverbs* (2001), which describes this giant paremiographical database that is accessible to students and scholars world-wide via the internet.

European Paremiography

There is no need to review the rich accomplishments of comparative pare-miography before and after Matti Kuusi's efforts (Mieder 1982–2001), but a few publications regarding the European scene should be mentioned as they relate to the issues of the present discussion. There is first of all O. J. Tallgren-Tuulio's fundamental essay, "Locutions figurées calquées [loan translated] et non calquées. Essai de classification pour une série de langues littéraires" (1932), which has undeservedly been ignored far too long. While it deals with proverbial expressions and not bona fide proverbs, it is concerned with their origin and chronological distribution into other languages through the process of loan translations. The author presents twenty-seven groups of possible borrowings from Greek antiquity to the Latin, French, German, Swedish, and Finnish languages and cultures. He shows, for example, that a certain Greek expression might have been translated into various European languages including Finnish in the North, but then there might also be a Latin phrase which has no Greek parallel and which only was translated into French and German. Of special importance is also Tallgren-Tuulio's willing-ness to include the possibility of polygenesis into his paradigm: "Il semble nécessaire en effet d'admettre la vraisemblance théorique de l'existence d'une polygenèse européenne (et facultativement, extra-europénne) de locutions figurées; mais il n'est pas toujours facile de l'étayer de preuves matérielles" (1932: 292). Indeed, proving the possibility of polygenesis is difficult, show-ing clearly that diachronic and synchronic considerations must at all times be part of comparative proverb studies. As Kuusi's American friend Archer Taylor quite correctly also pointed out in his chapter on "Translated Pro-verbs" in his celebrated book *The Proverb*, "We must be on our guard lest we compare analogous proverbs which are nevertheless of entirely indepen-dent origin" (1931: 46). In light of the fact that basically any comparatively informed collection or study of proverbs will at least touch on the matter of direct or translated borrowing among languages (Röhrich and Mieder 1977: 37–40), it is surprising that the invaluable two-volume *Phraseology: International Handbook of Contemporary Research* (Burger, Dobrovol'skij, Kühn, and Norrick 2007) does not offer a separate article on these linguistic and cultural processes for all types of phraseologisms. Regarding proverbs of Europe, I have dealt with this matter in the section "Genesis and Evolution" in my essay on "Proverbs as Cultural Units and Items of Folklore" (2007b: 396–99) in this very handbook (see also Mieder 2004e: 10–13).

To be sure, much is known about the centuries of interlinguistic and intercultural give-and-take of proverbs, albeit at the expense of this process in Africa, Asia, and other parts of the world. Numerous bi- or multilingual collections have appeared, of which I will mention but two here. There is the three-volume multilingual *Dictionary of European Proverbs* (1994) by Emanuel Strauss, with its 1,804 English proverbs and complete or partial equivalents from most European languages (including variants). Even though this massive collection was subsequently also published as a one-volume *Concise Dictionary of European Proverbs* (1998), it has received relative little attention in international paremiology. This is most likely due to its high price and also because Strauss did not supply any sources for his vast materials. Things are quite different with Gyula Paczolay's magisterial and unsurpassed *European Proverbs in 55 Languages with Equivalents in Arabic, Persian, Sanskrit, Chinese and Japanese* (1997), which registers the direct European equivalents for 106 proverbs, citing all references in their original languages and with precise bibliographical information. But the truly polyglot Paczolay goes far beyond Europe with his unique compilation, and no paremiologist or paremiographer with international interests can possibly work without this invaluable publication (see also Paczolay 2005). Alas, his compilation includes only proverbs that originated in classical, Biblical, or medieval times with their respective loan translations, without giving any answers for the European dissemination of proverbs from later centuries.

Fortunately for Europeanists with interests beyond that continent, Elisabeth Piirainen, with similar polyglot abilities that include Japanese, is now hard at work on the international dissemination of what she calls "widespread idioms" that include traditional proverbial expressions but not proverbs. Her fascinating paper "*Europeanism, Internationalism* or Something Else? Proposal for a Cross-Linguistic and Cross-Cultural Research Project on Widespread Idioms in Europe and Beyond" (2005; see also Piirainen 2006) presents multilingual references for such phraseologisms as "To shed crocodile tears," "To be within one's four walls," and "To tear one's hair out." Where possible she lists Arabic, Chinese, Japanese, and Korean direct equivalents, asking the penultimate question: "Common source or independent origin?" (2005: 68–70). Her work contains diachronic and synchronic considerations, and also includes geographic mapping attempts of the linguistic distribution of idioms or phraseologisms throughout Europe and to a lesser extent beyond that continent. In fact, most recently she expanded my dia-chronic and literary study on the proverbial expression "To tilt at wind-mills" (2006) into the linguistic and geographical realm in her paper "Gegen Windmühlen käpmfen'—ein weit verbreitetes europäisches Idiom" (2008). Teaming up with Dmitrij Dobrovol'skij and his polyglot abilities, they have now published an unparalleled study, *Figurative Language: Cross-Cultural and Cross-Linguistic Perspectives* (2005). This book features multilingual idioms and proverbial expressions relating to fear, house, numbers, and ele-ments, citing dozens of references from Indo-European and non-Indo-Eu-ropean languages and quite often from the Japanese. While Piirainen and Dobrovol'skij are linguists, they definitely emphasize cultural, geographical, and historical aspects, also including folkloristic concerns. All of this adds up to an encouraging revitalization and extension of the geographic-historical research method that was pioneered by such renowned Finnish folklorists as Kaarle Krohn, Antti Aarne, and many other well-known folklorists, in-cluding, of course, Matti Kuusi's exemplary study *Regen bei Sonnenschein: Zur Weltgeschichte einer Redensart* (1957), based on this comparative and diachronic paradigm. This 420-page study appeared in the renowned Finn-ish FFC series (*Folklore Fellows Communications*, published by the Finnish Academy of Science and Letters), with its by now almost 300 volumes based in large degree on this established method. And I might add here that my own student, Olga V. Trokhimenko, followed in Kuusi's footsteps some forty years later with her monograph, *"Wie ein Elefant im Porzellandladen": Zur Weltgeschichte einer Redensart* (1999), which discusses the origin, history, and worldwide dissemination of the proverbial comparison "Like a bull in a china shop" and its variants in numerous languages.

European Phraseology and Paremiology

Looking at Europe with American eyes, I have to admit that, phraseologi-cally speaking, "Europe is where it's at," i.e., phraseology is doubtlessly blos-soming on that continent, with paremiology playing a somewhat smaller role. But these two fields work "hand in glove," and what can be said for one is often at least in part also true for the other. With the European Common Market and the European Union steadily growing in cultural, economic, and political importance, it should not be surprising that scholars of many fields look to the European continent. In the area of phraseology and paremiol-ogy, we have the well-established European Society of Phraseology with its meetings every two years somewhere in Europe. The results have been voluminous proceedings that often have the neologism "Europhras" and the year of the international conference as part of their title, as for example the 821-page volume edited by Wolfgang Eismann entield *EUROPHRAS 95. Europäische Phraseologie im Vergleich: Gemeinsames Erbe und kulturelle Vielfalt* (1998). Similar essay volumes with a definite European bent are, for example, Gloria Corpas Pastor, ed., *Las lenguas de Europa: Estudios de fraseología, fraseografía y traducción* (2000), and Harry Walter, Valerii M. Mokienko, and Michael Alekseenko, eds., *Neue Phraseologie im neuen Europa* (2001). Among new individually published articles let me mention at least the following: Antica Menac, "Gemeinsame semantische Gruppen in der Phraseologie der europäischen Sprachen" (1987); Peter Braun and Dieter Krallmann, "Inter-Phraseologismen in europäischen Sprachen" (1990); Mario Wandruszka, "Sprache [in Europa] aus Bildern" (1990); Andreas Musolff, "'Dampfer', 'Boote' und 'Fregatten': Metaphern als Signale im 'Geleitzug' der Europäischen Union" (1996); Valerii M. Mokienko, "Phraseologisierung von Europäismen oder Europäisierung von Phraseologismen? Divergente und konvergente Prozesse in phraseologischen Systemen europäischer Sprachen" (1998); Gyula Paczolay, "European Proverbs" (1998); Liudmila Stepanova, "On the Problem of International [European] Idioms in Related Languages" (1998); Wolfgang Mieder, "Sprichwörter des [europäischen] Kontinents" (1999a); Maria Isabel González Rey, "A fraseodidáctica e o Marco europeo común de referencia para as linguas" (2006); Pasi Pirttisaari, "Phraseologie im 'Gemeinsamen europäischen Referenzrahmen für Sprachen'" (2006); and Elisabeth Piirainen, "Phraseologie in europäischen Bezügen: zu einem Forschungsprojekt" (2007). In addition, Gertrud Gréciano from Strasbourg has dealt with a number of European phraseological issues, including "Europaphraseologie im Vergleich" (1998); "Europhraseologie. Zur Findung und Verbreitung der Begriffe über Bilder" (2002); "Fachtextphraseologie aus europäischer Perspektive" (2004a); and "L'Europe sous un seul toit / Europa unter einem Dach / Europe under a single roof / [. . .]: phraséologie des textes européens" (2004b). The spread of these investigations goes from linguistic to cultural and political issues, with Valerii Mokienko's following statement adding up to a generally applicable summation:

> The convergence of the processes of the internationalization of the phraseological basis of European languages is especially intensive today. The opposition of "Europeanization : phraseologization" as well as the closely related opposition of "universality : idiomaticity" and "universality : individuality"

generate a special dynamics, which supports the richness of European language systems. Phraseological universality, however, does not destroy the national
specifics of idioms, because even the universal and the international might
achieve individual, national features under concrete lingual and culturological
conditions. (1998: 539 [English abstract])

This observation acutely encompasses the possibility of linguistic variation as
phraseologisms enter other languages. But alas, the investigations mentioned
here deal primarily with phraseologism that include proverbial expressions
but leave proverbs as such out of consideration.

Be that as it may, many of the findings of these publications about phraseologisms (including proverbial expressions or proverbial comparisons) are
transferable to full-fledged proverbs. Piirainen's large research project on
"widespread idioms" of Europe and beyond can easily be broadened to include actual proverbs, and Mokienko's contrast of phraseologization of Euro-
peanisms and Europeanization of phraseologisms can most certainly include
the proverbialization of direct borrowings or loan translations of proverbs
in Europe. In fact, this process is absolutely nothing new, no matter whether
one speaks of individual words, clichés, idioms, binary (twin) or routine formulas, phraseologisms, proverbial expressions or comparisons, quotations, or
whatever. And, as paremiologists have shown for folk proverbs for centuries,
proverbs do indeed travel in their original language or as loan translations
and may become proverbial in another culture in either form or both. Today,
with many Europeans speaking English as a foreign language, it should not
be surprising that English proverbs in particular are accepted into other linguistic cultures in English first, with their translation gaining currency later.

Origin and Dissemination of Common European Proverbs

But before looking more specifically at the modern dissemination of Anglo-
American proverbs in Europe with an emphasis on English-German developments, it will be good to make just a few general historical remarks on
these loan processes in Europe (Mieder 1996). Many paremiologists and
others, with scholarly prowess since the time of Erasmus of Rotterdam, have
dealt with this phenomenon, including, for example, such pleasurable compilations as Walter K. Kelly's *A Collection of the Proverbs of All [European]
Nations* (1859) or Baron Louis Benas's readable essay "On the Proverbs of
European Nations" (1877–78). Hundreds of diachronic and comparative
proverb collections and investigations have shown that there were basically

three major sources and waves of dissemination of those proverbs and proverbial expressions that belong to the common and identical European stock.
For example, Friedrich Seiler's four-volume investigation *Das deutsche Lehnsprichwort* (1921–24) remains a classic investigation, with hundreds of diachronically presented examples of how many proverbs entered the German
language by these loan processes. In general terms, I have described this
process in my article on "The History and Future of Common Proverbs in
Europe" (2000b), dealing with the three historical periods and importantly
adding a modern or even futuristic fourth step to it.

As is well known, many common European proverbs stem from Greek
and Roman antiquity and were spread via the Latin lingua franca and humanists like Erasmus of Rotterdam throughout Europe, where they gained
acceptance and currency as loan translations. Such proverbs as "Barking dogs
do not bite," "One swallow does not make a summer," "One hand washes
the other," "Love is blind," or "Let the cobbler stick to his last" found their
way into most European languages (and beyond); as I have shown for the
classical proverb "Big fish eat little fish" and its path from Hesiod to its
use in modern German (Mieder 2003a), they present a major philological
challenge to those scholars who wish to trace their path diachronically and
comparatively using the Finnish geographic-historical method. The same is
true for the many proverbial expressions that date back to classical times, as
can be seen from my monograph on *"Call a Spade a Spade": From Classical
Phrase to Racial Slur. A Case Study* (2002). In this case I was also able to trace
the semantic shift of an innocuous expression of calling a garden tool (or a
thing) what it is to an ethnic slur against African Americans. In addition,
the originally Greek phrase has in modern times been loan translated into
German from the English as "Einen Spaten einen Spaten nennen" with the
meaning of the German equivalent expression "Das Kind bei seinem Namen
nennen" (Mieder 1978).

The Bible represents the second major source for common European
proverbs, delivering such still widely used translated proverbs as "An eye for
an eye, a tooth for a tooth" (2 Moses 21:24), "He who digs a pit for others, falls in himself" (Prophets 26:27), "There is nothing new under the sun"
(Ecclesiastes 1:9), "A prophet is not without honor save in his own country"
(Matthew 13:57), and the so important golden rule "Do unto others as you
would have them do unto you" (Matthew 7:12). The third source consists of
the many proverbs that were coined during the Middle Ages in Latin and
then subsequently translated into the vernacular languages, including such
gems as "Strike while the iron is hot," "New brooms sweep clean," "All that

glitters is not gold," "The pitcher goes so long to the well until it breaks at last," "No rose without thorns," and the popular "All roads lead to Rome," which perhaps surprisingly does not refer to imperial but rather to papal Rome. While these three strands of loan translation processes had considerable influence on the common repertoire of European proverbs, it must not be forgotten that proverbs have also been borrowed and translated from one language to another at later times, especially in the case of linguistically related languages or those that share a geographical border. As Europe in the modern age grows ever more together in business, communication, mass media, travel, etc., both old and new proverbs will be disseminated by way of borrowed loan translations. And, as has always been the case, in due time native speakers of the receiving culture will not even be aware of the fact that certain proverbs were originally not at all indigenous to their language.

It must, however, be said that the diachronic and comparative study of the loan translation of proverbs has primarily dealt with the three classical, Biblical, and medieval sources, with regrettably little attention having been paid to how traditional and above all modern proverbs have entered or are conquering the diverse linguistic market of the European languages. Regarding modern proverbs as such, it is equally deplorable that paremiologists and paremiographers have paid so little attention to modern proverbs, i.e., those proverbs that were coined after the year 1900 as a somewhat arbitrary date of departure. The descriptive words "new" or "modern" appear relatively seldom in titles of publications on proverbs, with Charles Clay Doyle's seminal article "On 'New' Proverbs and the Conservativeness of Proverb Dictionaries" (1996; see also Doyle 2007: 193–95) being a welcome exception, especially since it lists several dozen modern Anglo-American proverbs with a dating attempt. It was thus a very encouraging sign when a large conference took place in 2001 in Szczecin, Poland, of which at least the abstracts were published by Harry Walter, Valerii M .Mokienko, and Michael Alekseenko with the title *Neue Phraseologie im neuen Europa* (2001). Mokienko also put together the fascinating collection *Novaia russkaia frazeologiia* (2003), registering new Russian phraseologisms with important contextual and dating annotations.

It should also be mentioned that Elisabeth Piirainen is including some modern texts in her impressive research project into the most common so-called widespread idioms, to wit the geographical and linguistic distribution of "To be on the same wavelength" (Piirainen 2005: 65–66) and "To give somebody the green light" (Piirainen 2006: 158–59). And I have described a joint project with Charles Clay Doyle and Fred Shapiro in my article "'New

Proverbs Run Deep': Prolegomena to a Dictionary of Modern Anglo-American Proverbs" (2008), which includes a bibliography of what has been done on modern proverbs thus far. The result of our labors is *The Dictionary of Modern Proverbs* (2012), which includes approximately 1,500 modern Anglo-American proverbs with their earliest contextualized citations, including such popular new-age folk wisdom as "There is no such thing as a free lunch," "Money can't buy you love," "You snooze, you lose," "What goes around comes around," "Last hired, first fired," and "Been there, done that."

Anglo-American Proverbs on the European Scene

Turning now to what role traditional and innovative Anglo-American proverbs have played in the intercultural and interlinguistic loan processes, it is indeed disappointing to see how little attention has been paid to the considerable influence of modern English as a lingua franca with its European, Asian, and African, in short global significance. For example, Friedrich Seiler includes but four English loan translations into German in his major treatise, namely the phraseologisms "ein Gesetz einbringen" (to introduce a bill), "die oberen Zehntausend" (the upper ten thousand), "ein selbstgemachter Mann" (a self-made man), and "sein Steckenpferd reiten" (to ride one's hobby horse) (Seiler 1921: I, 83). But this is not the place or time to review the sporadic discussions of phraseological borrowings of English phraseologisms into other European languages. Suffice it to say that three articles have recently appeared that deal with this phenomenon as found in German, Russian, and Polish. They cite a few examples of Anglo-American proverbs that have entered these three languages as loan translations, including "The early bird gets the worm," "You cannot make an omelette without breaking eggs" (Fiedler 2006: 456), "There is no such thing as a free lunch" (Stepanova 2007: 603), "Diamonds are a girl's best friend," and "It takes two to tango" (Rozumko 2007: 39–40). Regarding the influence of English phraseology on the German language, Sabine Fiedler has recently published her welcome overview entitled "'Willkommen zurück!'—Der Einfluss des Englischen auf die Phraseologie der deutschen Gegenwartssprache" (2006). As she points out, English and German are closely related Germanic languages, and linguists have labored for quite some time showing that hundreds or thousands of English words have been borrowed or translated into the German language, as summarized in Broder Carstensen's and Ulrich Busse's invaluable and richly documented three-volume *Anglizismen-Wörterbuch* (1993–96). Carstensen, as Germany's leading scholar on Anglo-Americanisms, referred repeatedly to the borrowing and translation of English phraseologisms in his many publications, but always just in passing, with the exception of his specific article on "Rund um 'rund um die Uhr'" (1977). Here he showed that the American expression "(A)round the clock" goes back to the middle of the nineteenth century and argued that it appeared as the German loan translation "Rund um die Uhr" about one hundred years later. The popular song "Rock Around the Clock" (1954) by Bill Haley doubtlessly helped popularize the phrase. But be that as it may, as I have shown, Carstensen and other comparative linguists concentrated on individual words, mentioning basically the same few phraseologisms to show that multi-word expressions were borrowed and translated as well, among them "das Beste aus etwas machen" (to make the best of something), "im gleichen Boot sitzen" (to be in the same boat), "grünes Licht geben/bekommen" (to give/get the green light), "die Schau stehlen" (to steal the show), and "eine gute Zeit haben" (to have a good time) (Mieder 2004b: 193). Anglo-American proverbs, however, were simply no part of the discussion as far as their appearance in English or as loan translations in the German language or other European languages were concerned. Citing an English expression, one might well state with a bit of proverbial irony that these scholars missed the boat!

But speaking of boats, let me say a few words about the proverbial expression "to be in the same boat" just mentioned, because it represents a perfect example of the complexity of the history and international dissemination of phraseologisms of all types. Some years ago I traced its origin, history, use, and function back to classical Roman times. It was first used in Latin as "In eadeam es navi" in a letter from the year 53 B.C. by Marcus Tullius Cicero, appearing in numerous other publications ever since until it was included by Erasmus of Rotterdam in his *Adagia* (1500ff.). I then show by way of many diachronically arranged and contextualized references how the phrase was loan translated into English during the late sixteenth century, eventually reaching the United States with the many immigrants who settled there. Interestingly enough, the expression did not gain any currency as a translation from Erasmus into Dutch, German, or French. These languages adopted it as a loan translation only after 1945 through the influence of the Anglo-American language and culture. In fact, the German language had the equivalent expression "am gleichen Strang ziehen" (to pull on the same rope), but since the 1950s it has slowly but surely been pushed aside by the German loan translation of Cicero's formulation (Mieder 1990b; Peil 1986). In the meantime Valerii Mokienko (1997) has followed my request and published an article on the phrase, indicating that it also entered the

Russian language by way of the Anglo-American route, and the Canadian phraseologist Elizabeth Dawes (2007) took up the challenge in her detailed survey outlining the modern loan translation of the phrase into French and Italian (also mentioning the English and German situation once again) and stressing the polysemanticity of it in contextualized references. This wealth of materials for several European languages makes clear that there is not always a direct geographical and historical borrowing route. In this case, it took Cicero's Latin phrase about two thousand years to make the jump from its Anglo-American tradition across the Atlantic and the English Channel to mainland Europe. I am sure that it exists in other European languages as well, and I am certain that Elisabeth Piirainen will want to include it in her survey of widespread idioms.

In any case, during the past decade or so I have attempted to set the record straight, as it were, at least for a few proverbs of English or American origin. In these studies, I have usually also indicated whether the proverb might also have appeared as loan translations in languages other than German. I will here concentrate on the English-German relationship, expressing the hope that other scholars might investigate the twelve proverbs that I will mention to see whether they could by now be considered "widespread European proverbs," to adapt Elisabeth Piirainen's concept of "widespread idioms" to proverbs. It would be my conjecture, in part based on actual findings, that some of them have indeed entered other languages. After all, as I have tried to show in my article "American Proverbs as an International, National, and Global Phenomenon" (2005a), the Englishes of the world have a tremendous influence on most languages.

Older European Loan Translations of Anglo-American Proverbs

Due to the fact that the Anglo-American language has gained an incredible international dominance since the end of World War II, it should not come as a surprise that many loan translations have occurred during the past six decades. A particularly interesting case in point is the Biblical proverb "A house divided against itself cannot stand" (Mark 3:25). This is the way the masterfully translated King James Bible rendered the original that soon reached proverbial status. Martin Luther, who is known for his masterful Bible translation with many of his texts becoming proverbial, did not succeed in this case. His "Wenn ein Haus mit sich selbst uneins wird, kann es nicht bestehen" did not gain any traditional currency among the folk. But things were quite different in the religious United States, where the Bible reference underwent an effective secularization in that it was used as a meta-phor for social and political issues. Famous Americans like Thomas Paine and Daniel Webster employed it, and Abraham Lincoln elevated the prov-erb to a national slogan in his famous "House divided" speech that he de-livered on June 18, 1858, in Springfield, Illinois. He used it again and again as a rallying leitmotif for maintaining the young American Union as it was slithering into civil war. Since then, Lincoln's name has become attached to the proverb, and many Americans think of Lincoln as the originator of this wisdom. When Willy Brandt, as the mayor of Berlin, was invited in 1959 to present a lecture at the sesquicentennial celebration of Abraham Lincoln's birthday on April 12th, he mentioned that Lincoln had "quoted the passage from the Bible about the house divided against itself" (Mieder 1998: 117) in his English language speech, obviously alluding to his divided city and coun-try. He used it subsequently in English and German, and when at the time of German reunification Brandt traveled to various German cities supporting this move, he closed his speeches in 1990 with references to Lincoln, quoting the proverb "A house divided against itself cannot stand" together with his German translation "Ein in sich gespaltenes Haus hat keinen Bestand." His repeated use of this successful translation of Lincoln's Bible proverb caught on. After all, thousands of people saw and heard Brandt on television or the radio, while newspapers printed parts of his speeches. The mass media carried the message to the population, and in this wording the Bible text has now become a German proverb by way of Abraham Lincoln and Willy Brandt. Many references can be found in the mass media and on the internet attesting to this fact, proving that the proverb is solidly established in the German language. Whether Mark 3:25 has become proverbial beyond the Anglo-American and German languages still needs to be checked. My con-jecture is that this is not the case, in that the German loan translation owes its existence to a specific historical occurrence (see Mieder 1998: 115–25 and 2000a: 84–90).

Another proverb falsely attributed to Lincoln has, however, gained a much broader European acceptance as a loan translation. The American president had used the proverb in a remark on June 9, 1864, as he was getting ready to run for reelection: "I have not permitted myself to conclude that I am the best man in the country; but I am reminded, in this connection, of a story of an old Dutch farmer, who remarked to a companion once that 'it was not best to swap horses when crossing streams'" (Mieder 2007a: 4). The earliest American reference found thus far stems from 1840 and proves the fact that Lincoln did not originate the proverb, which in its standard variant is today usually cited as "Don't swap horses in the middle of the stream." Of course, Lincoln never claimed to have done so, and yet, his name is attached to the proverb to this very day. This can be seen even in many of the German references where the loan translated proverb "Mitten im Strom soll man die Pferde nicht wechseln" has been frequently cited as a statement by Lincoln since the middle of the twentieth century both in quotation and phraseology dictionaries as well as in multiple occurrences in the mass media (see Mieder 2005b). By now definite Europeanization of the loan proverb has occurred, as can be seen from French, Swedish, Russian, Polish, and Czech loan translations. Beyond that, a globalization of the proverb in English has taken place, with references being found in Canada, England, Ireland, New Zealand, and doubtlessly many other countries (Mieder 2007a: 27–34).

Modern Loan Translations of Anglo-American Proverbs

Regarding more modern times, I can report yet another example of how a politician was instrumental in establishing an English language proverb as a German loan translation. This time it was President Ronald Reagan who helped the modern American proverb "It takes two to tango" make the jump to Germany. The proverb comes from the song "Takes Two to Tango" (1952), with lyrics by Al Hoffman and melody by Dick Manning, that became very popular by way of the African American singer Pearl Bailey. Reagan clearly knew the song and the proverb, and when, upon Leonid Brezhnev's death, he was asked whether US-Soviet relations might improve with Yuri Andropov at the helm, he stated on November 11, 1982: "For ten years détente was based on words from them [the Russians] and not any deeds to back those words up. And we need some action that they—it takes two to tango—that they want to tango also" (Mieder 1997b: 125). About a week later, on November 19, 1982, the well-known German journalist Theo Sommer cited this Reagan statement in a lead article with the effectively formulated headline "Zum Tango gehören immer zwei" (Mieder and Bryan 1983: 100). By now this loan translation in the shortened form of "Zum Tango gehören zwei" has established itself very well as a loan translation in German, and this is also true to some extent for other European languages. There are, however, also times that the proverb is cited in English, clearly attesting to English as the lingua franca of Europe.

Things are, however, not always so clear-cut in loan processes, and it is usually quite difficult or impossible to find the precise translation date of any given proverb. In any case, it takes time for the loan translation to gain currency, familiarity, and traditionality to be considered a new proverb in the receiving language. All of this needs to be proven by way of numerous contextualized examples. This has been done for the proverbs stated thus far, and it is also true for those that will be discussed now. Of special interest is doubtlessly the English proverb "The early bird gets the worm," which goes back to the early seventeenth century. In all bilingual English-German dictionaries and collections of proverbs, it has always been considered to be the equivalent of the German proverb "Morgenstunde hat Gold im Munde." However, primarily due to the power of the Anglo-American mass media of film, television, radio, music, newspaper, advertisement, cartoon, comics, etc., and the necessity of translation, the English proverb has now found its way into the German language in the form of the literal translation "Der frühe Vogel fängt den Wurm." Since the early 1980s this text has become solidly established, and lexicographers, phraseographers, and paremiographers would do well to include it in their dictionaries and collections as a new loan proverb of the German language (Mieder 2004b). It is hard to believe, but this proverb is actually competing well with the old sixteenth-century German "Morgenstunde" proverb, which, according to empirical scholarship, is one of the most popular German proverbs (Mieder 1997a). Germans don't just use it as a translation of the English original any longer, but they employ it clearly as a proverb in place of the older German text. This might psycholinguistically have something to do with the overuse of the traditional proverb and the appealing metaphor of the new bit of wisdom.

Another English proverb from the early seventeenth century that has been picked up by the German language is "Don't put all of your eggs into one basket." Even though Karl Friedrich Wilhelm Wander included the German translation "Man muss nicht alle Eier in einen Korb tun" in 1867 in his celebrated five-volume *Deutsches Sprichwörter-Lexikon* (1867–80: I, col. 756, no. 139), he cited it without references and might simply have listed it as a proverb that he encountered during his one-year stay in the United States during 1850/51. At least no texts have been found thus far before the early 1980s that include a German version. Since that time, however, the loan translation "Man muß (soll) nicht alle Eier in einen Korb legen (tun)" has steadily gained in currency and familiarity so that it can justifiably be considered a proverb in German (Mieder 2004d). Dmitrij Dobrovol'skij, in his revealing article "On Cultural Component in the Semantic Structure of Idioms" (1998), has shown that the English proverb also exists as a word-forword translation in Russian, and he cites a convincing argument why Russians and by extension Germans and other Europeans might be so quick in accepting such loan translations:

The [Russian] idiom *klast' vse jajca v odnu korzinu* that is a word-by-word translation of the English idiom *put all one's eggs into one basket* was taken over by current Russian so easily probably because it goes back to two conceptual metaphors which are well-known in Russian, namely MEANS OF ACHIEVING GOALS ARE PHYSICAL ENTITIES [. . .] and DOMAINS OF ACHIEVING GOALS ARE CONTAINERS [. . .]. (Dobrovol'skij 1998: 58)

In a longer German version of this article, Dobrovol'skij includes several contextualized Russian references that show the acceptance of the loan translation into Russian (Dobrovol'skij 1999: 49–51). The fact that he speaks of an idiom and not of a proverb is simply due to the fact that, as so often in folk speech, the text can be cited as the proverbial expression "to put all one's eggs into one basket" or as a proverb "Don't put all of your eggs into one basket." One might add that the actual realia of the idiom/proverb are also easily transferable from one country and culture to the other. This is, to be sure, the case with all of the loan translations under discussion.

New German Loan Translations of American Proverbs

Turning now to a few proverbs of American origin (see also Mieder 2004a: 423–26), I have been able to show by way of numerous German references found in literature, the mass media, and the internet that they have caught on as loan translations in Germany, where they are also at times cited in English or in English followed with a German translation. When cited in German, they are frequently preceded by such introductory formulas as "according to the old proverb" or even "as the German proverb says," indicating that they are considered German proverbs by many native speakers. This is the case for the mid-nineteenth-century American proverb "Good fences make good neighbors" (Mieder 2003b) that became very popular in part because of its inclusion in Robert Frost's celebrated poem "Mending Wall" (1914). The earliest German translation I have found thus far was a graffito in slightly incorrect German on the Berlin Wall from the beginning of the 1980s: "Gute Zaune machen gute Nachbaren?" One can well imagine that an American student of German visiting Berlin might have tried out his or her linguistic abilities here. But be that as it may, during the past twenty-five years the proverb has become well established in its German form as "Gute Zäune machen gute Nachbarn" (Mieder 2004c: 145–47), especially in the journalistic contexts reporting on the many border conflicts in the world.

Unfortunately, the United States is also the source of a German loan proverb that would better not have been borrowed. As is well known, there are many proverbs and proverbial expressions that contain ethnic stereotypes or slurs. Minorities are seen as bothersome outsiders, foreign citizens are judged to be inferior, members of other religions are demonized, and in extreme cases such verbal aggressions lead to actual genocide. In the United States, such hatred and bigotry resulted in the misguided coinage of the proverb "The only good Indian is a dead Indian." It was first recorded in 1868 at the time when the United States Army persecuted Native Americans by forcing them onto reservations or, in worse cases, killing them. The invective gained acceptance and became a stereotypical slogan to dehumanize the native American population, and over time the proverb turned into a metaphor against any undesirable person, animal, or thing. In addition, the proverb was reduced to the structural formula "The only good X is a dead X," where the variable could easily be filled with such terms as "Nigger," "Jew," "German," "Serb," "rat," "teacher," etc. I have recorded dozens of Anglo-American variations of this phenomenon (Mieder 1993c), but I was amazed to find that this despicable proverb has been translated into German as "Nur ein toter Indianer ist ein guter Indianer." References have been found from about 1980 on, both in the actual German wording and also in variants (Mieder 1993a). It appears that this loan translation is here to stay, and I wonder whether the American original has also established itself in other European languages. Stereotypes, especially in easily adapted structural formulas of proverbs, have long been part of the European scene—and the rest of the world, as numerous major collections of them attest, to wit Otto von Reinsberg-Düringsfeld's two-volumes *Internationale Titulaturen* (1863), Abraham Aaron Roback's *A Dictionary of International Slurs* (1944), and more recently José Esteban's *Refranero contra Europa* (1996). In my article "Viele Wege führen nach Europa: Sprichwörtliche Stereotypen und interkultureller Ausgleich" (2004), I have also reviewed these stereotypical preconceptions among Europeans, arguing that such divergence needs to be overcome by new proverbs that emphasize the convergence of European nations, stressing similarities of culture and purpose rather than differences. Varying the English proverb "Handsome is as handsome does," I put forth the proverbial slogan "Europe is as Europe does!" (Mieder 2004f: 295).

Fortunately, much more positive American proverbs also have found their way to Europe. One of them is the surprisingly young proverb "A dog is man's best friend" from the last quarter of the nineteenth century. With dogs since that time for the most part not being working animals any longer but rather treasured family members, the proverb could gain a place among the most popular English proverbs. Even though the German loan translation "Der Hund ist des Menschen bester Freund" has not yet appeared in a

German proverb collection, I have in my proverb archives numerous references starting in the mid-1970s. This proverb also brings to mind the somewhat ironic "Diamonds are a girl's best friend," which originated as the title of a song written by Leo Rubin and set to music by Jule Styne in 1949. It was a big success in the Broadway musical *Gentlemen Prefer Blondes* of the same year that in turn was based on Anita Loos's best-selling novel (1926) of the same name. At first "Diamonds are a girl's best friend(s)" was nothing but a clever variation or anti-proverb of "A dog is man's best friend," but it too became popular and eventually a new proverb in its own right, often with the name of Marilyn Monroe attached to it as having coined it. This proverb too has grown roots in German and gained considerable currency at least since around 1990, as for example in the variants of "Diamanten sind eines Girls bester Freund," "Diamanten sind eines Mädchens beste Freunde," "Diamanten sind die besten Freunde der Frau," "Diamanten sind der Frauen beste Freunde," "Diamanten sind die besten Freunde einer Frau," "Diamanten sind die besten Freunde eines Mädchens," "Diamanten sind der Mädchen liebste Freunde," etc. This shows that it can take time for loan translations to find a standard proverbial formulation that might eventually also make it into dictionaries and collections.

Another case in point is the German loan translation of the American proverb "An apple a day keeps the doctor away," which appeared on the American scene during the first quarter of the twentieth century and might itself be based on the related and longer English proverb "Eat an apple on going to bed, and you'll keep the doctor from earning his bread" from the seventeenth century (Mieder 1991: 96–103). It has become quite established in Germany at least since the early 1990s, but again in variants: "Ein Apfel pro Tag erspart uns den Doktor," "Ein Apfel am Tag hält den Arzt fern," "Ein Apfel pro Tag hält den Doktor fern," "Ein Apfel täglich erspart den Doktor," "Einen Apfel am Tag verzehr'n hält den Doktor fern," etc. When I reported on this particular loan process, I reached the conclusion that the variant "Ein Apfel pro Tag hält den Arzt fern" might be considered the standard form, but time will tell (Mieder 2004c: 140–44). Some lexicographer or paremiographer will have to decide on this, once this loan proverb makes it into a compendium that includes modern texts. This also holds true for the American proverb "The grass is always greener on the other side of the fence," which was coined around 1913 and gained popularity by way of the song "The Grass Is Always Greener (In the Other Fellow's Yard)," written by Raymond B. Egan and set to music by Richard A. Whiting in 1924. It has long become America's favorite proverb of discontent (Mieder 1993b; Doyle et al. 2012: 110–11), and is now establishing itself in its standard loan

translation of "Das Gras auf der anderen Seite des Zaunes ist immer grüner"
in German as well (Mieder 2004c: 147–49).

Let me close these deliberations with an American proverb that has gained
much acceptance in various European languages. Coined around 1911, it began its world conquest with Fred R. Barnard's advertising slogan "One Look
Is Worth a Thousand Words," used as a headline in the American advertising
journal *Printers' Ink* on December 8, 1921. Barnard repeated it in another advertisement in the same magazine on March 10, 1927, in the somewhat varied
wording of "One picture is worth ten thousand words." The rest is history, as
one might well say. The slogan caught on quickly, soon to reach the standard
form of "A (One) picture is worth a thousand words" (Mieder 1990; Doyle
et al. 2012: 196). As a German loan translation it made its debut no later than
1975, when it appeared in a television advertisement in the magazine *Stern*
as "Ein Bild ersetzt tausend Worte." By 1984 it had found its standard form
in German as "Ein Bild sagt mehr als tausend Worte" in another magazine
advertisement, and in the meantime I have collected literary dozens of references of the new German proverb and its variations as anti-proverbs in literature and the mass media (Mieder 1989a). I have also heard it used orally on
numerous occasions, and it exists as a loan translation in other European languages as well, with numerous multilingual references on the internet. Once
again it must be stated that this and other proverbs have not yet found their
way into modern mono- and bilingual dictionaries or collections (Mieder
2003c: 422–23; Mieder 1999b: 25–29). This is indeed a poor state of affairs
that clearly calls for correction, as Charles Doyle, Fred Shapiro, and I have attempted to do with our *Dictionary of Modern Proverbs* (2012).

A Plea for Modern European Paremiography

With a sincere plea for new collections of modern proverbs, I can bring this
short overview of European loan proverbs from the Anglo-American language to a close. I am well aware that I have emphasized primarily how a few
English and American proverbs entered the modern German language, but I
was able at least in some cases to state that a proverb has also been loan translated into other European languages. But that is obviously not good enough,
and in order to get a better picture, I would like to make the following sug-
gestion to my fellow European paremiologists of various mother tongues:
Let's have some scholarly fun and embark on a project to see how the twelve
proverbs that I have touched upon here have fared in other European cultures and languages. As I have suggested, I know or suspect that at least some

of them have been adapted as widespread European proverbs, but let us do some serious investigation and publish the results in *Proverbium*! Here are the dozen proverbs to be studied:

A house divided against itself cannot stand.
Don't swap horses in the middle of the stream.
It takes two to tango.
The early bird gets the worm.
Don't put all your eggs into one basket.
Good fences make good neighbors.
The only good Indian is a dead Indian.
A dog is man's best friend.
Diamonds are a girl's best friend.
An apple a day keeps the doctor away.
The grass is always greener on the other side of the fence.
A picture is worth a thousand words.

The diachronic range of the Anglo-American proverbs under consideration reaches from the 1611 King James Bible proverb "A house divided against itself cannot stand" to the "Diamonds are a girl's best friend" from 1949 (see Wilson 1970; Mieder, Kingsbury, and Harder 1992; Speake 2003). It does not include some of the most recent Anglo-American proverbs like "No good deed goes unpunished," "There is safety in numbers," "No guts, no glory," "The best things in life are free," "You can't have it both ways," and many others that are part of *The Dictionary of Modern Proverbs*. Time and research, especially using various databases and the internet, will tell whether they are already being loan translated or not. Of course, not all new proverbs come only from the Anglo-American world. Of greatest importance is also the question of what modern proverbs of other European languages have been spread as loan translations in Europe. We know a great deal about the earlier processes, and so I want to stress once again that it is the modern proverb repertoire that needs our undivided attention (see Mieder 1989b). Otherwise paremiology and paremiography will not progress much, and nobody would want that!

BIBLIOGRAPHY

This chapter appeared first with the same title in *Phraseologie: global—areal—regional. Akten der Konferenz EUROPHRAS 2008 vom 13.–16.8.2008 in Helsinki*. Jarmo Korhonen, Wolfgang Mieder, Elisabeth Piirainen, and Rosa Piñel, eds. Tübingen: Gunter Narr, 2010. 43–59.

Benas, Baron Louis. 1877–78. "On the Proverbs of European Nations." *Proceedings of the Literary and Philosophical Society of Liverpool* 32: 291–332.

Braun, Peter, and Dieter Krallmann. 1990. "Inter-Phraseologismen in europäischen Sprachen." *Internationalismen. Studien zur interlingualen Lexikologie und Lexikographie.* Peter Braun, Burkhard Schaeder, and Johannes Volmert, eds. Tübingen: Max Niemeyer. 74–86.

Burger, Harald, Dmitrij Dobrovol'skij, Peter Kühn, and Neal R. Norrick, eds. 2007. *Phraseologie. Ein internationales Handbuch zeitgenössischer Forschung / Phraseology. An International Handbook of Contemporary Research.* 2 vols. Berlin: Walter de Gruyter.

Carstensen, Broder. 1977. "Rund um 'rund um die Uhr.'" *Der Sprachdienst* 21: 81–85.

Carstensen, Broder, and Ulrich Busse. 1993–96. *Anglizismen-Wörterbuch. Der Einfluss des Englischen auf den deutschen Wortschatz nach 1945.* 3 vols. Berlin: Walter de Gruyter.

Corpas Pastor, Gloria, ed. 2000. *Las lenguas de Europa: Estudios de fraseología, fraseografía y traducción.* Albolote (Granada): Comares.

Dawes, Elizabeth. 2007. "'Être dans le même bateau' en italien, anglais, français et allemande: Étude contrastive d'une locution polysémique." *Proverbium* 24: 51–108.

Dobrovol'skij, Dmitrij. 1998. "On Cultural Component in the Semantic Structure of Idioms." *EUROPHRAS 97: Phraseology and Paremiology.* Peter Ďurčo, ed. Bratislava: Akadémia PZ. 55–61.

———. 1999. "Kulturelle Spezifik in der Phraseologie: Allgemeine Probleme und kontrastive Aspekte." *Phraseologie und Übersetzen. Phrasemata II.* Annette Sabban, ed. Bielefeld: Aisthesis Verlag. 41–58.

Dobrovol'skij, Dmitrij, and Elisabeth Piirainen. 2005. *Figurative Language: Cross-Cultural and Cross-Linguistic Perspectives.* Amsterdam: Elsevier.

Doyle, Charles Clay. 1996. "On 'New' Proverbs and the Conservativeness of Proverb Dictionaries." *Proverbium* 13: 69–84. Also in *Cognition, Comprehension, and Communication: A Decade of North American Proverb Studies (1990–2000).* Wolfgang Mieder, ed. Baltmannsweiler: Schneider Verlag Hohengehren, 2003. 85–98.

———. 2007. "Collections of Proverbs and Proverb Dictionaries: Some Historical Observations on What's in Them and What's Not (With a Note on Current 'Gendered' Proverbs)." *Phraseology and Culture in English.* Paul Skandera, ed. Berlin: Walter de Gruyter. 181–203.

Doyle, Charles Clay, Wolfgang Mieder, and Fred R. Shapiro, eds. 2012. *The Dictionary of Modern Proverbs.* New Haven, Connecticut: Yale University Press.

Eismann, Wolfgang, ed. 1998. *EUROPHRAS 95: Europäische Phraseologie im Vergleich: Gemeinsames Erbe und kulturelle Vielfalt.* Bochum: Norbert Brockmeyer.

Esteban, José. 1996. *Refranero contra Europa.* Madrid: Ollero & Ramos.

Fiedler, Sabine. 2006. "'Willkommen zurück!'—Der Einfluss des Englischen auf die Phraseologie der deutschen Gegenwartssprache." *Phraseology in Motion I. Methoden und Kritik. Akten der Internationalen Tagung zur Phraseologie (Basel, 2004).* Annelies Häcki Buhofer and Harald Burger, eds. Baltmannsweiler: Schneider Verlag Hohengehren. 451–65.

González Rey, María Isabel. 2006. "A fraseodidáctica e o Marco europeo común de referencia para as linguas." *Cadernos de fraseoloxía galega* 8: 123–45.

Gréciano, Gertrud. 1998. "Europaphraseologie im Vergleich." *EUROPHRAS 95: Europäische Phraseologie im Vergleich: Gemeinsames Erbe und kulturelle Vielfalt.* Wolfgang Eismann, ed. Bochum: Norbert Brockmeyer. 247–62.

———. 2002. "Europhraseologie. Zur Findung und Verbreitung der Begriffe über Bilder." *Ansichten der deutschen Sprache. Festschrift für Gerhard Stickel.* Ulrike Haß-Zumkehr, Werner Kallmeyer, and Gisela Zifonun, eds. Tübingen: Gunter Narr. 305–23.

———. 2004a. "Fachtextphraseologie aus europäischer Perspektive." *Wortverbindungen—mehr oder weniger fest.* Kathrin Steyer, ed. Berlin: Walter de Gruyter. 394–414.

————. 2004b. "L'Europe sous un seul toit / Europa unter einem Dach / Europe under a single roof / [. . .]: phraséologie des textes européens." *L'espace euro-méditerranéen: Une idiomaticité partagée. Actes du colloque international, Hammamet, les 19–21 septembre 2003.* Salah Mejri, ed. 2 vols. Tunis: Université de Tunis. II, 127–40.

Kelly, Walter K. 1859. *A Collection of the Proverbs of All Nations.* London: W. Kent, 1859. Rpt. Andover, Massachusetts: Warren F. Draper, 1869. Rpt. again with an introduction by Wolfgang Mieder. Burlington, Vermont: University of Vermont, 2002.

Kuusi, Matti. 1957. *Regen bei Sonnenschein. Zur Weltgeschichte einer Redensart.* Helsinki: Suomalainen Tiedeakatemia. Italian translation by Maria Teresa Bizzarri. *La pioggia con il sole. Storia di un modo di dire nel mondo.* Bologna: Società editrice il Mulino, 1992-1994. Also in *Quaderni di Semantica,* 13, no. 2 [1992]: 279–327; 14, no. 1 [1993]: 79–152; 14, no. 2 [1993]: 249–331; 15, no. 1 [1994]: 123–79; 15, no. 2 [1994]: 273–320.

————. 1969. "Lainasananlaskujen tutkimusongelmia." *Esitelmät ja Pöytäkirjat 1968.* Esko Suomalainen, ed. Helsinki: Suomalaisen Kirjallisuuden Kirjapaino Oy. 169–81. Also in English as "Research Problems in Loan-Proverbs" in Matti Kuusi, *Mind and Form in Folklore: Selected Articles.* Henni Ilomäki, ed. Helsinki: Suomalaisen Kirjallisuuden Seura, 1994. 123–30.

————. 1972. *Towards an International Type-System of Proverbs.* Helsinki: Suomalainen Tiedeakatemia. Also in *Proverbium* 19 (1972): 699–736.

Kuusi, Matti (in cooperation with Marje Joalaid, Elsa Kokare, Arvo Krikmann , Kari Laukkanen, Pentti Leino, Vaina Mälk, and Ingrid Sarv). 1985. *Proverbia septentrionalia. 900 Balto-Finnic Proverb Types with Russian, Baltic, German and Scandinavian Parallels.* Helsinki: Suomalainen Tiedeakatemia.

Lauhakangas, Outi. 2001. *The Matti Kuusi International Type System of Proverbs.* Helsinki: Suomalainen Tiedeakatemia.

Menac, Antica. 1987. "Gemeinsame semantische Gruppen in der Phraseologie der europäischen Sprachen." *Aktuelle Probleme der Phraseologie.* Harald Burger and Robert Zett, eds. Bern: Peter Lang. 269–90.

Mieder, Wolfgang. 1978. "'Einen Spaten einen Spaten nennen.'" *Der Sprachdienst* 22: 121–22.

————. 1982–2001. *International Proverb Scholarship. An Annotated Bibliography.* 4 vols. New York: Garland. New York: Peter Lang (volume 4).

————. 1989a. "'Ein Bild sagt mehr als tausend Worte.' Ursprung und Überlieferung eines amerikanischen Lehnsprichworts." *Proverbium* 6: 25–37. Also in Wolfgang Mieder, *Sprichwort—Wahrwort!? Studien zur Geschichte, Bedeutung und Funktion deutscher Sprichwörter.* Frankfurt am Main: Peter Lang, 1992. 191–201.

————. 1989b. "Moderne Sprichwörterforschung zwischen Mündlichkeit und Schriftlichkeit." *Volksdichtung zwischen Mündlichkeit und Schriftlichkeit.* Lutz Röhrich and Erika Lindig, eds. Tübingen: Gunter Narr, 1989. 187–208. Also in Wolfgang Mieder, *Sprichwort—Wahrwort!? Studien zur Geschichte, Bedeutung und Funktion deutscher Sprichwörter.* Frankfurt am Main: Peter Lang, 1992. 13–36.

————. 1990a. "'A Picture is Worth a Thousand Words': From Advertising Slogan to American Proverb." *Southern Folklore* 47: 207–25. Also in Wolfgang Mieder, *Proverbs Are Never Out of Season: Popular Wisdom in the Modern Age.* New York: Oxford University Press, 1993. 135–51.

————. 1990b. "'Wir sitzen alle in einem Boot.' Herkunft, Geschichte und Verwendung einer neueren deutschen Redensart." *Muttersprache* 100: 18–37. Also in Wolfgang Mieder, *Deutsche Redensarten, Sprichwörter und Zitate. Studien zu ihrer Herkunft, Überlieferung und Verwendung.* Wien: Edition Praesens, 1995. 140–59.

————. 1991. "'An Apple a Day Keeps the Doctor Away': Traditional and Modern Aspects of English Medical Proverbs." *Proverbium* 8: 77–106. Also in Wolfgang Mieder, *Proverbs Are Never Out of Season: Popular Wisdom in the Modern Age.* New York: Oxford University Press, 1993. 152–72.

————. 1993a. "'Nur ein toter Indianer ist ein guter Indianer': Zur Geschichte eines nicht nur amerikanischen Sprichwortes." *Der Sprachdienst* 37: 137–42. Also in Wolfgang Mieder, *Sprichwörtliches und Geflügeltes. Sprachstudien von Martin Luther bis Karl Marx.* Bochum: Norbert Brockmeyer, 1995. 165–74.

————. 1993b. "'The Grass Is Always Greener on the Other Side of the Fence': An American Proverb of Discontent." *Proverbium* 10: 151–84. Also in *Wise Words: Essays on the Proverb.* Wolfgang Mieder, ed. New York: Garland, 1994. 515–42.

————. 1993c. "'The Only Good Indian Is a Dead Indian': History and Meaning of a Proverbial Stereotype." *Journal of American Folklore* 106: 38–60. Also in Wolfgang Mieder, *The Politics of Proverbs: From Traditional Wisdom to Proverbial Stereotypes.* Madison, Wisconsin: University of Wisconsin Press, 1997. 138–59, 221–27 (notes).

————. 1996. "Geschichte des Sprichwortes und der Redensart im Deutschen." *Proverbium* 13: 235–52. Also as "Grundzüge einer Geschichte des Sprichwortes und der Redensart" in *Sprachgeschichte. Ein Handbuch zur Geschichte der deutschen Sprache und ihrer Erforschung.* Werner Besch, Anne Betten, Oskar Reichmann, and Stefan Sonderegger, eds. 2nd ed. 3 vols. Berlin: Walter de Gruyter, 2003. III, 2559–69.

————. 1997a. *"Morgenstunde hat Gold im Munde": Studien und Belege zum populärsten deutschsprachigen Sprichwort.* Wien: Edition Praesens.

————. 1997b. "'Raising the Iron Curtain': Proverbs and Political Cartoons of the Cold War." In Wolfgang Mieder, *The Politics of Proverbs: From Traditional Wisdom to Proverbial Stereotypes.* Madison, Wisconsin: University of Wisconsin Press. 99–137, 214–21 (notes).

————. 1998. *"A House Divided": From Biblical Proverb to Lincoln and Beyond.* Burlington, Vermont: University of Vermont.

————. 1999a. "Sprichwörter des Kontinents." *Das gemeinsame Haus Europa. Handbuch zur europäischen Kulturgeschichte.* Wulf Köpke and Bernd Schmelz, eds. München: Deutscher Taschenbuch Verlag. 956–65.

————. 1999b. "Sprichwörter in den größeren allgemeinen und phraseologischen Wörterbüchern Deutsch-Englisch/Englisch-Deutsch." *Studien zur zweisprachigen Lexikographie mit Deutsch.* Herbert Ernst Wiegand, ed. 4 vols. Hildesheim: Georg Olms. IV, 1–40. Also in *Germanistische Linguistik*, 143–44 [1999]: 1–40. Also in Wolfgang Mieder, *"Andere Zeiten, andere Lehren." Sprichwörter zwischen Tradition und Innovation.* Baltmannsweiler: Schneider Verlag Hohengehren, 2006. 261–303.

————. 2000a. "'A House Divided': From Biblical Proverb to Lincoln and Beyond." *Understanding Wisdom: Sources, Science, & Society.* Warren S. Brown, ed. Philadelphia: Templeton Foundation Press. 57–102. Also in Wolfgang Mieder, *Strategies of Wisdom: Anglo-American and German Proverb Studies.* Baltmannsweiler: Schneider Verlag Hohengehren, 2000. 171–203. Also in Wolfgang Mieder, *Proverbs Are the Best Policy: Folk Wisdom and American Politics.* Logan, Utah: Utah State University Press, 2005. 90–117, 264–71 (notes).

————. 2000b. "The History and Future of Common Proverbs in Europe." *Folklore in 2000: Voces amicorum Guilhelmo Voigt sexagenario.* Ilona Nagy and Kincsö Verebélyi, eds. Budapest: Universitas Scientiarium de Rolando Eötvös nominata. 300–314.

————. 2002. *"Call a Spade a Spade": From Classical Phrase to Racial Slur: A Case Study.* New York: Peter Lang.

————. 2003a. *"Die großen Fische fressen die kleinen": Ein Sprichwort über die menschliche Natur in Literatur, Medien und Karikaturen.* Wien: Edition Praesens.

————. 2003b. "'Good Fences Make Good Neighbors': History and Significance of an Ambiguous Proverb." *Folklore* (London) 114: 155–79. Also longer version in Wolfgang Mieder, *Proverbs Are the Best*

Policy: Folk Wisdom and American Politics. Logan, Utah: Utah State University Press, 2005. 210–43, 287–96 (notes).

——. 2003c. "Sprichwörter im GWDS [*Das große Wörterbuch der deutschen Sprache*]." *Untersuchungen zur kommerziellen Lexikographie der deutschen Gegenwartssprache.* Herbert Ernst Wiegand, ed. 2 vols. Tübingen: Max Niemeyer. I, 413–36.

——. 2004a. "'Andere Zeiten, andere Lehren': Sprach- und kulturgeschichtliche Betrachtungen zum Sprichwort." *Wortverbindungen—mehr oder weniger fest.* Kathrin Steyer, ed. Berlin: Walter de Gruyter. 415–38. Also in Wolfgang Mieder, *"Andere Zeiten, andere Lehren": Sprichwörter zwischen Tradition und Innovation.* Baltmannsweiler: Schneider Verlag Hohengehren, 2006. 39–64.

——. 2004b. "Der frühe Vogel und die goldene Morgenstunde. Zu einer deutschen Sprichwortenlehnung aus dem Angloamerikanischen." *Etymologie, Entlehnungen und Entwicklungen. Festschrift für Jorma Koivulehto.* Irma Hyvärinen, Petri Kallio, and Jarmo Korhonen, eds. Helsinki: Société Néophilologique. 193–206. Also in Wolfgang Mieder, *"Andere Zeiten, andere Lehren": Sprichwörter zwischen Tradition und Innovation.* Baltmannsweiler: Schneider Verlag Hohengehren, 2006. 247–59.

——. 2004c. "'Ein Apfel pro Tag hält den Arzt fern': Zu einigen amerikanischen Lehnsprichwörtern im Deutschen." *Revista de Filología Alemana* 12: 135–49.

——. 2004d. "'Man soll nicht alle Eier in einen Korb legen': Zur deutschsprachigen Entlehnung eines anglo-amerikanischen Sprichwortes." *Nauchnyi vestnik. Seriia: Sovremennye lingvisticheskie metodiko-didakticheskie issledovaniia* 1: 21–31. Also with minor changes in *Der Sprachdienst* 50 (2006): 178–85.

——. 2004e. *Proverbs: A Handbook.* Westport, Connecticut: Greenwood.

——. 2004f. "Viele Wege führen nach Europa: Sprichwörtliche Stereotypen und interkultureller Ausgleich." *Erzählen zwischen den Kulturen.* Sabine Wienker-Piepho and Klaus Roth, eds. Münster: Waxmann. 275–304. Also in Wolfgang Mieder, *"Andere Zeiten, andere Lehren": Sprichwörter zwischen Tradition und Innovation.* Baltmannsweiler: Schneider Verlag Hohengehren, 2006. 65–94.

——. 2005a. "American Proverbs as an International, National, and Global Phenomenon." *Tautosakos Darbai / Folklore Studies* (Vilnius) 30: 57–72. Also with minor changes in Wolfgang Mieder, *Proverbs Are the Best Policy: Folk Wisdom and American Politics.* Logan, Utah: Utah State University Press, 2005. 1–14, 244–48 (notes).

——. 2005b. "'Mitten im Strom soll man die Pferde nicht wechseln': Zur Geschichte eines deutschamerikanischen Sprichworts." *Zeitschrift für germanistische Linguistik* 33: 106–24.

——. 2006. *"Tilting at Windmills": History and Meaning of a Proverbial Allusion to Cervantes' "Don Quixote."* Burlington, Vermont: University of Vermont.

——. 2007a. "'Don't Swap Horses in the Middle of the Stream': An Intercultural and Historical Study of Abraham Lincoln's Apocryphal Proverb." *Folklore Historian* 24: 3–40. Also a shorter version as "'Don't Swap Horses in the Middle of the Stream': An Intercultural and Interdisciplinary Study of an International Proverb." *Estudos sobre Património Oral.* Gabriela Funk, ed. Ponta Delgada, Azores: Câmara Municipal de Ponta Delgada, 2007. 243–70.

——. 2007b. "Proverbs as Cultural Units or Items of Folklore." *Phraseologie. Ein internationales Handbuch zeitgenössischer Forschung.* Harald Burger, Dmitrij Dobrovol'skij, Peter Kühn, and Neal R. Norrick, eds. 2 vols. Berlin: Walter de Gruyter. I, 394–414.

——. 2008. "'New Proverbs Run Deep': Prolegomena to a Dictionary of Modern Anglo-American Proverbs." *Proceedings of the First Interdisciplinary Colloquium on Proverbs, 5th to 12th November 2007, at Tavira, Portugal.* Rui J. B. Soares and Outi Lauhakangas, eds. Tavira: Tipografia Tavirense. 69–87.

Mieder, Wolfgang, and George B. Bryan. 1983. "'Zum Tango gehören zwei.'" *Der Sprachdienst* 27: 100–102, 181. Also in Wolfgang Mieder, *Sprichwort, Redensart, Zitat. Tradierte Formelsprache in der Moderne.* Bern: Peter Lang, 1985. 151–54.

Mieder, Wolfgang, Stewart A. Kingsbury, and Kelsie B. Harder, eds. 1992. *A Dictionary of American Proverbs*. New York: Oxford University Press.

Mokienko, Valerii M. 1997. "Die russische Geschichte des Amerikanismus 'Wir sitzen alle in einem Boot.'" *Proverbium* 14: 231–45.

———. 1998. "Phraseologisierung von Europäismen oder Europäisierung von Phraseologismen? Divergente und konvergente Prozesse in phraseologischen Systemen europäischer Sprachen." *EUROPHRAS 95: Europäische Phraseologie im Vergleich: Gemeinsames Erbe und kulturelle Vielfalt.* Wolfgang Eismann, ed. Bochum: Norbert Brockmeyer. 539–55.

Musolff, Andreas. 1996. "'Dampfer,' 'Boote' und 'Fregatten': Metaphern als Signale im 'Geleitzug' der Europäischen Union." *Öffentlicher Sprachgebrauch: Praktische, theoretische und historische Perspektiven.* Karin Böke, Matthias Jung, and Martin Wengeler, eds. Opladen: Westdeutscher Verlag. 180–89.

Paczolay, Gyula. 1997. *European Proverbs in 55 Languages with Equivalents in Arabic, Persian, Sanskrit, Chinese and Japanese.* Veszprém, Hungary: Veszprémi Nyomda.

———. 1998. "European Proverbs." *EUROPHRAS 95: Europäische Phraseologie im Vergleich: Gemeinsames Erbe und kulturelle Vielfalt.* Wolfgang Eismann, ed. Bochum: Norbert Brockmeyer. 605–18.

———. 2005. "Universal, Regional, Sub-Regional, and Local Proverbs." *Tautosakos Darbai/Folklore Studies* (Vilnius) 30: 73–85.

Peil, Dietmar. 1986. "'Im selben Boot': Variationen über ein metaphorisches Argument." *Archiv für Kulturgeschichte* 68: 269–93.

Piirainen, Elisabeth. 2005. *"Europeanism, Internationalism* or Something Else? Proposal for a Cross-Linguistic and Cross-Cultural Research Project on Widespread Idioms in Europe and Beyond." *Hermes: Journal of Linguistics* 35: 45–75.

———. 2006. "Widespread Idioms: Cross-linguistic and Cross-cultural Approaches." *Phraseology in Motion I. Methoden und Kritik. Akten der Internationalen Tagung zur Phraseologie (Basel, 2004).* Annelies Häcki Buhofer and Harald Burger, eds. Baltmannsweiler: Schneider Verlag Hohengehren. 155–73.

———. 2007. "Phraseologie in europäischen Bezügen: zu einem Forschungsprojekt." *Europhras Slovenija 2005. Phraseology in Linguistics and Other Branches of Science.* Erika Kržišnik and Wolfgang Eismann, eds. Ljubljana: Univerza v Ljubljani. 533–51.

———. 2008. "'Gegen Windmühlen kämpfen'—ein weit verbreitetes europäisches Idiom." *Proverbium* 25: 353–66.

Pirttisaari, Pasi. 2006. "Phraseologie im 'Gemeinsamen europäischen Referenzrahmen für Sprachen.'" *Wörter-Verbindungen: Festschrift für Jarmo Korhonen.* Ulrich Breuer and Irma Hyvärinen, eds. Frankfurt am Main: Peter Lang. 247–57.

Reinsberg-Düringsfeld, Otto von. 1863. *Internationale Titulaturen.* 2 vols. Leipzig: Hermann Fries. Rpt. in one volume with an introduction and bibliography by Wolfgang Mieder. Hildesheim: Georg Olms, 1992.

Roback, Abraham Aaron. 1944. *A Dictionary of International Slurs (Ethnophaulisms) with a Supplementary Essay on Aspects of Ethnic Prejudice.* Cambridge, Massachusetts: Sci-Art. Rpt. Waukesha, Wisconsin: Maledicta Press, 1979.

Röhrich, Lutz, and Wolfgang Mieder. 1977. *Sprichwort.* Stuttgart: Metzler.

Rozumko, Agata. 2007. "Skrzydlate słowa 'twory przysłowiopodobne' czy przysłowia? Nowe przysłowia angielski we współczesnej polszczyźnie." *Poradnik Językowy* 10: 34–45.

Seiler, Friedrich. 1921–24. *Das deutsche Lehnsprichwort.* 4 vols. Halle: Verlag der Buchhandlung des Waisenhauses. Rpt. ed. by Wolfgang Mieder. Hildesheim: Georg Olms, 2007. Also in F. Seiler. *Die Entwicklung der deutschen Kultur im Spiegel des deutschen Lehnworts,* vols. 5–8.

Speake, Jennifer, ed. 2003. *The Oxford Dictionary of Proverbs*. New edition, previously co-edited with John A. Simpson. Oxford: Oxford University Press.

Stepanova, Liudmila. 1998. "On the Problem of International Idioms in Related Languages." *EURO-PHRAS 95: Europäische Phraseologie im Vergleich: Gemeinsames Erbe und kulturelle Vielfalt*. Wolfgang Eismann, ed. Bochum: Norbert Brockmeyer. 765–71.

———. 2007. "Frazeologicheskie zaimstvovaniia v russkom i cheshskom iazykakh: staroe i novoe." *Kritik und Phrase. Festschrift für Wolfgang Eismann*. Peter Deutschmann, ed. Wien: Praesens. 597–610.

Strauss, Emanuel. 1994. *Dictionary of European Proverbs*. 3 vols. London: Routledge.

———. 1998. *Concise Dictionary of European Proverbs*. London: Routledge.

Tallgren-Tuulio, O. J. 1932. "Locutions figurées calquées et non calquées. Essai de classification pour une série de langues littéraires." *Mémoires de la société néo-philologique de Helsingfors* 9: 279–324.

Taylor, Archer. 1931. *The Proverb*. Cambridge, Massachusetts: Harvard University Press. Rpt. as *The Proverb and an Index to The Proverb*. Hatboro, Pennsylvania: Folklore Associates, 1962. Rpt. again with an introduction and a bibliography by Wolfgang Mieder. Bern: Peter Lang, 1985.

Trokhimenko, Olga V. 1999. *"Wie ein Elefant im Porzellanladen": Zur Weltgeschichte einer Redensart*. Burlington, Vermont: University of Vermont.

Walter, Harry, Valerii M. Mokienko, and Michael Alekseenko, eds. 2001. *Neue Phraseologie im neuen Europa. Thesen der gemeinsamen wissenschaftlichen Konferenz der Universität Szczecin und der Ernst-Moritz-Arndt-Universität Greifswald, 6–9.9.2001*. Greifswald: Ernst-Moritz-Arndt-Universität.

Wander, Karl Friedrich Wilhelm. 1867–80. *Deutsches Sprichwörter-Lexikon*. 5 vols. Leipzig: F.A. Brockhaus. Rpt. Darmstadt: Wissenschaftliche Buchgesellschaft, 1964.

Wandruszka, Mario. 1990. "Sprache aus Bildern." In Mario Wandruszka, *Die europäische Sprachengemeinschaft: Deutsch-Französisch-English-Italienisch-Spanisch im Vergleich*. Tübingen: A. Francke. 51–76.

Wilson, F. P. 1970. *The Oxford Dictionary of English Proverbs*. 3rd ed. Oxford: Clarendon.

3. "THINK OUTSIDE THE BOX"

Origin, Nature, and Meaning of Modern Anglo-American Proverbs

Among modern proverb scholars it has become almost proverbial to call for the collection and study of proverbs that have been coined in more recent times. For too long have paremiologists and paremiographers looked backwards at traditional proverbs without paying much attention to what modernity has contributed to the treasure trove of proverbial wisdom. Archer Taylor, the doyen of twentieth-century paremiology, lamented this unfortunate situation in an invaluable article on "The Study of Proverbs" (1939), calling for new collections that would be "made as complete as humanly possible, showing not only old proverbs and variations of old ones that are still current, but also new ones that have come into use, thus giving a complete cross-section of the proverbs of our time" (1939 [1975]: 62–63 [46]; see also Taylor 1969). Following my revered mentor in this plea, I observed some fifty years later in my "Prolegomena to Prospective Paremiography" that "paremiography cannot remain a science that looks primarily backwards and works only with texts of times gone by. Modern paremiographers can and should also assemble proverb collections that include the texts of the twentieth century [and beyond]" (1990b: 142; see also 2000: 16). Such calls have not remained unheeded for English language proverbs, as my survey "'New Proverbs Run Deep': Prolegomena to a Dictionary of Modern Anglo-American Proverbs" (2009a; see also Sevilla Muñoz 2009) has shown.

Collections and Studies Containing Modern Proverbs

The overview just mentioned was a direct result of a contract for a new *Dictionary of Modern Proverbs* that my friends Charles Clay Doyle, Fred R. Shapiro, and I signed on September 21, 2007, with the prestigious Yale University Press. Even before signing the contract, we had already more or less independently begun to assemble modern Anglo-American proverbs, i.e., proverbs for which no references before the year 1900 can be found. Doyle had published about 200 such texts in his invaluable compilation "On 'New' Proverbs and the Conservativeness of Proverb Dictionaries" (1996 [2003]; see also Doyle 2001 and 2007b), Shapiro had included a list of 104 "Modern Proverbs" in his magisterial *The Yale Book of Quotations* (2006: 526–30), and I had amassed about 300 texts that qualified as modern proverbs during the four decades of establishing my International Proverb Archives. After combining these three sets of modern proverbs, of which many quite expectedly proved to be duplicates, we examined six major and eighteen minor proverb collections published during the past few decades for possible modern proverbs, among them Nigel Rees, *Sayings of the Century: The Stories Behind the Twentieth Century's Quotable Sayings* (1984); Bartlett Jere Whiting, *Modern Proverbs and Proverbial Sayings* (1989); Nigel Rees, *Bloomsbury Dictionary of Phrase & Allusion* (1991); Wolfgang Mieder, Stewart A. Kingsbury, and Kelsie B. Harder, *A Dictionary of American Proverbs* (1992); David Pickering, Alan Isaacs, and Elizabeth Martin, *Brewer's Dictionary of 20th-Century Phrase and Fable* (1992); Anne Bertram and Richard Spears, *NTC's Dictionary of Proverbs and Clichés* (1993); Linda and Roger Flavell, *Dictionary of Proverbs and Their Origins* (1993); Nigel Rees, *Phrases & Sayings* (1995); Anna T. Litovkina, *A Proverb a Day Keeps Boredom Away* (2000); Adrian Room, *Brewer's Dictionary of Modern Phrase & Fable* (2000); David Pickering, *Cassell's Dictionary of Proverbs* (2001); Gregory Titelman, *Random House Dictionary of Popular Proverbs and Sayings* (2000); Martin H. Manser, *Facts on File Dictionary of Proverbs* (2002); Wolfgang Mieder, *English Proverbs* (2003); George B. Bryan and Wolfgang Mieder, *A Dictionary of Anglo-American Proverbs & Proverbial Phrases Found in Literary Sources of the Nineteenth and Twentieth Centuries* (2005); Stan Nussbaum, *American Cultural Baggage [i.e., Proverbs]: How to Recognize and Deal with It* (2005); Susan Ratcliffe, *Oxford Dictionary of Phrase, Saying, and Quotation* (2006); Nigel Rees, *A Word in Your Shell-Like: 6,000 Curious and Everyday Phrases Explained* (2006); and Jennifer Speake, *The Oxford Dictionary of Proverbs* (2008). In addition, we looked through about seventy publications that in one way or another also cite modern proverbs, for example Richard Jente, "The American Proverb" (1931–32); Frances M. Barbour, "Some Uncommon Sources of Proverbs" (1963); Kenneth L. Higbee and Richard J. Millard, "Visual Imagery and Familiarity Ratings for 203 Sayings" (1983); Jess Nierenberg, "Proverbs in Graffiti: Taunting Traditional Wisdom" (1983 [1994]); Robert R. Hoffman and Richard P. Honeck, "Proverbs, Pragmatics, and the Ecology of Abstract Categories" (1987); Wolfgang Mieder, *American Proverbs: A Study of Texts and Contexts* (1989a); Wolfgang Mieder, *Proverbs Are*

Never Out of Season: Popular Wisdom in the Modern Ages (1993a); Christoph Chlosta and Peter Grzybek, "Empirical and Folkloristic Paremiology: Two to Quarrel or to Tango?" (1995); Kimberly Lau, "'It's about Time': The Ten Proverbs Most Frequently Used in Newspapers and Their Relation to American Values" (1996 [2003]); Roumyana Petrova, "Language and Culture: One Step Further in the Search for Common Ground (A Study of Modern English Proverbs)" (1996); Sw. Anand Prahlad, *African-American Proverbs in Context* (1996); Stephen D. Winick, *The Proverb Process: Intertextuality and Proverbial Innovation in Popular Culture* (1998); Anna Tóthné Litovkina, "An Analysis of Popular American Proverbs [found in the Folklore Archive at UC Berkeley] and Their Use in Language Teaching" (1998); Paul Hernadi and Francis Steen, "The Tropical Landscape of Proverbia: A Crossdisciplinary Travelogue" (1999 [2003]); George B. Bryan, "An Unfinished List of Anglo-American Proverb Songs" (2001); and Charles Clay Doyle, "Collections of Proverbs and Proverb Dictionaries: Some Historical Observations on What's in Them and What's Not" (2007b). After pooling all of these references, we eventually had the impressive database of not quite 700 modern Anglo-American proverbs (for more details see Mieder 2009a).

Establishing a Corpus of Modern Proverbs

For all the proverbs found we undertook the laborious task to prove that they in fact were not older than the 1900 cutoff year. Many of our sources did not provide any dates of occurrences, and we consequently had to use various databases (Google, Google Books, Google News, ProQuest Historical Newspapers, Newspaperarchive, America's Historical Newspapers, 19th Century U.S. Newspapers, LexisNexis Academic, JSTOR, etc.) to find the earliest citation possible (Chlosta and Ostermann 2002; Colson 2007; Kleinberger Günther 2006; Lauhakangas 2001; Rittersbacher and Mösch 2005; Umorova 2005; Winick 2001). But not just that, for as I have said in my earlier description of this vexing and time-consuming task: "Texts alone no proverbs make, and as with all folklore genres, it takes currency and traditionality, usually also variants, . . . to decide whether a text is in fact in more or less general use beyond being a mere one-day wonder!" (2009a: 257). In other words, we felt compelled to establish the proverbiality of each and every text, thus going far beyond all previous background material accumulated on these proverbs. But our work did not stop there, for we clearly were not satisfied with only about 700 modern proverbs! Many contenders eventually had to be dropped because we were able to establish that they were already in use before 1900 (Stevenson 1948; Wilson 1970), among them such surprises as the following (our dictionary includes a much longer appendix with additional texts):

Business before pleasure.
Buy low, sell high.
The *camera* cannot lie.
You are what you *eat*.
An *elephant* never forgets.
The *future* is already here.
Behind every great *man* there's a great woman.
The second *million* (dollars) is always easier (than the first).
Money isn't everything.
There is nothing to fear but *fear* itself.
It pays to *advertise*.
Records are set to be broken.
Safety first.
You can prove anything with *statistics*.
First *things* first.
The best *things* (in life) are free.
No *tickee*, no washee (shirtee). (Arora 1988; Mieder 1996 [1997])
Use it or lose it. (Doyle 2009)

But the sixty-four thousand dollar question was and remains: How do we find ever more modern proverbs? Our own reading, relatives, friends, colleagues, and above all our students were of great help. We also continued gathering possible proverbs from literature, the mass media, films, songs, advertisements, speeches, and oral communications of all types (Mieder and Sobieski 2006), and for our *Dictionary of Modern Proverbs* (published in April 2012 by Yale University Press) we submitted a final manuscript of 1,422 modern proverbs, of which 731 had not been registered before! The voluminous e-mail correspondence among the three of us, living relatively far apart in Athens, Georgia (Charles Doyle), New Haven, Connecticut (Fred Shapiro), and Burlington, Vermont (myself), is a telling testimony for the wondrous excitement in discovering one proverb after another during about four years of enthusiastic and rewarding work on this fascinating project.

We have done our very best throughout to establish the earliest possible reference for each proverb, citing this reference in its context with precise bibliographical information. We also include variants and, where necessary, explanatory comments regarding linguistic, cultural, and semantic matters. We checked every proverb for its currency and frequency, with most proverbs garnering tens of thousands of raw Google hits (we are obviously aware of duplications and errors in these electronic searches). The hits in Google Books and Google News are significantly less "raw," but even there the results are not always reliable. Of course, Google also shows deceptively low numbers for proverbs that became obsolete by mid-century, or that are extremely recent in their coinage.

Have we found and included all possible modern Anglo-American proverbs in our *Dictionary of Modern Proverbs*? Of course not. We will have missed plenty of new proverbs and also those that are presently being created (Honeck and Welge 1997 [2003]), and for this reason we have included the address of a website so that readers can hopefully draw our attention to numerous additional texts. Obviously this project will be ongoing, and we hope in due time to bring out an updated and expanded version of our proverb dictionary. But we do want to stress once again that the identification of modern proverbs is extremely difficult and is in need of as much help as possible from people interested in the proverbial wisdom of the modern age.

Having completed our task for the time being, we can now draw some conclusions about the nature, origin, and meaning of these modern Anglo-American proverbs. What follows is my attempt to draw some general conclusions from our 1,422 truly modern proverbs regarding such matters as variants, form, syntax, structure, length, poetics, metaphor, origin (authorship, attribution, anonymity), and semantics. I will also comment on how these proverbs reflect on modern social, political, economic, psychological, and sexual matters, showing that some of the major sources of the proverbs are advertising slogans, so-called "laws" of modernity, songs, motion pictures, the world of business, sports, technology, and sexuality (also obscenity and scatology). It will also be shown that animal and somatic metaphors are quite prevalent, but clearly there are also numerous proverbs concerned with religion (God), beauty, love, success, and other matters. As has always been the case with traditional wisdom, modern proverbs also show themselves to be observations and generalizations about basic human behavior and the trials and trepidations of human life (Mieder 1987 [1993], 2004).

Lemmas, Variants, Structures, and Length of Modern Proverbs

Following the lead of some of the major proverb collections already mentioned, we have alphabetized the proverb entries according to the first noun in each proverb. If the text has no noun, then the first finite verb serves as the keyword, using italics in both cases to mark the keywords. For cases in which variants of a given proverb have differing keywords, cross-references are included with a "See" indicator followed by the standard variant of the proverb showing the user where to find more information about it. Each entry begins with the proverb itself, with principal variants shown in parentheses. Then follows the earliest contextualized reference, introduced by its date, with precise bibliographical information. Further dated examples of the text in context usually follow, especially if the earliest reference cited leaves some doubt as to its proverbiality, if the proverb is not well known or has not been recorded in any proverb collection before, if important variants need to be illustrated in actual use, or if additional textual references shed further light on the origin, attribution, evolution, or meaning of the proverb. Where it seemed necessary to us, we have also added further brief comments. Finally, all of this is augmented by precise references to those proverb collections and other sources in which 691 of the 1,422 proverbs have been registered before.

As all paremiographers know, it is at times quite difficult to decide on the precise wording of the lemma for a particular proverb, especially since many proverbs are current in degrees of variation. For this reason quite a large number of lemmas contain principal variants in parentheses, as for example:

Free *advice* is worth (exactly) what you pay for it.
No matter how (thin) you slice (cut) it, it's still *baloney*.
Don't take (tear) down a *fence* (wall) unless you are sure why it was put up.
Flattery will get you everywhere (anywhere).
If *life* hands (gives, throws) you scraps, make a quilt.
You are only as good as your last (latest) *mistake*.
It is (is always, must be) five (six) *o'clock* somewhere (in the world).
There are no *problems*, only opportunities (challenges).
Tough (Hard, Difficult) *times* call for tough (hard, difficult) decisions (choices).
Tragedy (Every tragedy) is an opportunity.
Trust is (must be) earned.

In those cases where the variants are more substantial (i.e., having a different keyword), we do list the variant as a separate entry followed with a "See" and the standard proverb lemma where the variant is to be found. Scholarly proverb dictionaries need to include such cross-references so that their users do not miss those proverbs that, like all verbal folklore, exist in considerable variants:

Almost doesn't count. See "Close doesn't count."
Never trust a skinny *cook*. See "Never trust a skinny chef."
Grow where you are planted. See "Bloom where you are planted."
Never ask (You don't want to know) what's in a *hotdog*. See "Never ask what's in a sausage."
When all else fails, read the *instructions*. See "When all else fails, read the directions."
If *life* isn't one thing, it's another. See "If it isn't one thing, it's another."
Nearly is not good enough. See "Almost is not good enough."
There will always be another *streetcar*. See "There will always be another bus."
Think big *thoughts*. See "Think big."
The older the *violin*, the sweeter the tune. See "The older the fiddle, the sweeter the tune."

Turning to syntactical matters, it can be stated that most modern proverbs are straightforward indicative sentences, with 61 of 1,422 or 4.4% following the "A(n) / noun / verb / . . ." pattern, as for example:

A *boy* cannot do a man's work.
A *candle* loses nothing by lighting another candle.
A *chip* on the shoulder is a good indication of wood higher up.
A *crisis* is an opportunity.
A *diamond* is (Diamonds are) forever.
An *expert* is only a fool a long way from home.
A *handicap* is what you make it.
A *man* is no better than his horse.
A *woman's* place is any place she wants to be.

Another 33 proverbs or 2.3% expand the pattern by a descriptive adjective, i.e., "A(n) / adjective / noun / verb . . . ," as can be seen from the following examples:

A clear *conscience* is (usually) a sign of (usually comes from) a bad memory.
An old *dog* barks sitting down.
A boiled (fried, cooked) *egg* won't hatch.
A wise *head* is better than a pretty face.
An empty *pot* does not boil over.
A live *soldier* is better than a dead hero.
A good *start* often means a bad finish.

A kind *thought* is never lost.
A rising *tide* lifts all boats (ships).

As one would expect, quite a few proverbs (67 or 4.7%) follow the indicative pattern "The / noun / verb . . .":

The *future* is not (is no longer) what it used to be.
The *hand* will not reach for what the heart does not long for.
The *joy* is in the journey.
The *life* you save may (could) be your own.
The *mountains* are calm even in a tempest.
The *nail* that sticks out gets pounded (hammered down).
The *rush* (Sometimes the rush) is worth the risk.
The *sun* will come out tomorrow.
The *world* (Everyone) hates a quitter.

The same pattern expanded by a modifying adjective is not quite as prevalent, but the collection does contain 39 (2.7%) texts based on "The / adjective / noun / verb . . . ":

The unaimed *arrow* never misses.
The first *casualty* of war is truth (Truth is the first casualty of war).
The same *knife* cuts the sheep and the goat.
The longest *mile* is the last mile home.
The second *mouse* gets the cheese.
The best (easiest, safest) *place* to hide is in plain sight.
The worst (kind of) *ride* is better than the best (kind of) walk.
The best *way* to kill time is to work it to death.
The squeaking (squeaky) *wheel* gets the grease.

In addition to these quite similar syntactical patterns totaling 200 (14.1%) texts, a considerable number of proverbs, 57 or 4.0% to be precise, follow the "You can't (cannot) / verb . . ." pattern, thereby continuing an established proverbial way of expressing the impossibility of a situation or action:

You can't put the *bullet* back in the gun.
You cannot herd *cats*.
You cannot tell the *depth* of the well by the length of the handle on the pump.
You can't unscramble *eggs*.

You can't go *home* again.
You can't *know* where you're going unless you know where you've been.
You can't be (There is no such thing as) a little (bit) *pregnant*.
You can't fix *stupid*.
You can't put *toothpaste* back in the tube.

Somewhat related to the sentiment expressed by way of the "You can't" impossibility marker are proverbs (68 or 4.8%) that state their messages by way of the "Don't (Do not) / verb . . ." imperative, which certainly is a well-established proverbial formula:

Do not (You cannot) compare *apples* and oranges.
Don't *believe* everything you think.
Don't *fall* before you're pushed.
Don't draw a *gun* unless you're going to use it.
Don't *judge* yourself by others.
Don't *knock* it till you've tried it.
Don't get caught with your *pants* (trousers, britches) down.
Don't *try* to be someone you are not.
Don't *worry*, be happy.

Another 30 (2.1%) proverbs follow the "Never / verb . . ." formula, once again expressing their advice in the form of an imperative:

Never miss a *chance* to sit down and rest your feet.
Never work with *children* or animals.
Never *give* anything away that you can sell (Why give something away when you can sell it?).
Never argue with a *fool*; people might not know the difference.
Never (You don't) bring (take) a *knife* to a gunfight.
Never play *leapfrog* with a unicorn.
Never (Don't) *let* them see you sweat.
Never try to teach a *pig* to sing; it wastes your time, and it annoys the pig.

All together, 98 (6.9%) proverbs state their message in the form of an imperative, not a particularly high number to be sure. Perhaps this is due the fact that people today are less willing to be told directly what to do or not to do. In other words, the obviously didactic nature of many traditional proverbs appears to be on the decline.

Proverbs in the form of humorous, ironic, or sarcastic questions have never been especially numerous, and this is also true for modern proverbs. In fact, in some of the 14 (1%) texts the interrogative is merely a variant of the standard proverb. Nevertheless, these proverbs in the form of a question add rhetorical spice to the intended message:

A *bird* may love a fish, but where would they live (build a home, build a nest)?
Birds sing after a storm (so why shouldn't we?).
Who cares if a *cat* is black or white as long as it catches mice?
Never *give* anything away that you can sell (Why give something away when you can sell it?).
Where does a 500-pound (800-pound, etc.) *gorilla* sit?
Why go out for *hamburger* (for a hamburger, for fast food) when you can get steak at home?
Nobody ever said *life* is fair (Who ever said life is fair?).
Other than that, Mrs. *Lincoln*, how did you like the play?

Concerning prevalent structures, it comes as a surprise that the well-established pattern of "Where there is X, there is Y" does not at all appear among these modern proverbs. This can perhaps be taken as a sign that some of the traditional structures are not necessarily of great importance in the formulation of new proverbs. The most dominant structure in our corpus is "If you X, (you) Y" with 62 (4.4%) proverbs, as for example:

If you don't believe in *cooperation*, watch what happens to a wagon (car) when one wheel comes off.
If you can *dream* it, you can do it (be it, have it).
If you can't be *good*, be careful.
If you can't stand (don't like) the *heat*, get out of the kitchen. (Mieder and Bryan 1997: 59–61)
If you can't ride two *horses* at once, you shouldn't be in the circus.
If you (can) *make* it here, you can make it anywhere.
If you keep your *mouth* shut, you won't put your foot in it.
If you want something done, ask a busy *person*.
If you are not at the *table*, you may be on the menu.

But this is really the only structure that has at least something of a claim for being of considerable frequency. The number of texts based on other structures falls off rather drastically, showing once again that by far the majority of modern proverbs are rather straightforward indicative sentences with few formulaic or poetic characteristics. Here then are the examples for eleven structures, with nine groups of texts not even reaching 1% of the corpus:

"X is Y" (24, 1.7%; definitional proverbs)
>*Age* is just a number.
>Old *age* is hell.
>*Beauty* is only skin.
>*Black* is beautiful.
>*History* is bunk.
>*Life* is a funny (strange) old dog.
>*Politics* (All politics) is local.
>The *sky* is the limit.
>The *world* is a place. (Mieder 2009b: 56–57, 2010c, 2011: 24–26)

"X is better than Y" (16, 1.1%)
>The *chase* (hunt) is better than the kill.
>*Fame* is better than fortune (Better fame than fortune)
>A *friend's* frown is better than a foe's smile.
>A wise *head* is better than a pretty face.
>A bad *professional* is better than a good amateur.
>The worst (kind of) *ride* is better than the best (kind of) walk.
>*Second best* is better than nothing (at all).
>A live *soldier* is better than a dead hero.
>Once seen is better than a hundred *times* heard.

"It's not X, it's (but) Y" (9, 0.63%)
>It's not the *crime* but the cover-up.
>It's not what you've *got*, it's what you do with it.
>It's not how many *times* you get knocked down that matters but how many times you get back up.
>It's not the *years*, it's the mileage (miles).

"When you X, (you) X(Y)" (9, 0.63%)
>When you pray, move your *feet*.
>When you're *good*, you're good.
>When you are in a *hole*, stop digging.
>When you're *hot*, you're hot (and when you're not, you're not).
>When you have *nothing*, you have nothing to lose.

"Better X than Y" (8, 0.56%)

> Better to *cheat* than repeat.
>
> Better a good *cow* than a cow of a good kind.
>
> Better a big *fish* in a little pond (puddle, pool) than a little fish in a big pond (mighty ocean).
>
> Better *red* than dead. (Barrick 1979)
>
> Better to burp (belch) and bear the *shame* than swallow the burp (belch) and bear the pain.

"No X, no Y" (8, 0.56%)

> No *brain*, no pain.
>
> No *guts*, no glory. (Prahlad 1994 [2003])
>
> No *harm*, no foul.
>
> No *pass*, no play.
>
> No *victim*, no crime.

"X is (are) X" (7, 0.49%, tautologies)

> *Bosses* are (will be) bosses.
>
> A *deadline* is a deadline.
>
> *Good enough* is good enough.
>
> A *kiss* is just a kiss.

"There is no such thing as X" (7, 0.49%)

> There is no such *thing* as a definitive study (text, edition, etc.).
>
> There is no such *thing* as a free lunch (There is no free lunch).
>
> There is no such *thing* as bad publicity (press, P.R., ink).
>
> There is no such *thing* as bad weather, only the wrong clothes.

"He who Xs, Ys" (6, 0.42%)

> He who has the *gold* makes the rules (Whoever has the gold rules).
>
> He who marries for *money* earns it.
>
> He who dies with the most *toys* still dies.

"There are no X, only (just) Y" (6, 0.42%)

> There are no bad *children*, only bad parents.
>
> There are no bad *dogs*, only bad owners.
>
> There are no *problems*, only opportunities (challenges).
>
> There are no bad *students*, just bad teachers.

"One man's X, is another man's Y" (4, 0.28%)
 One *man's* floor is another man's ceiling.
 One *man's* terrorist is another man's freedom fighter (One man's freedom
     fighter is another man's terrorist).
 One *man's* trash is another man's treasure.

From this dearth of proverbs based on repeated structures we move on to an analysis of the length of proverbs. Taking all 1,422 proverbs without variants, the total word count is 10,225 words, resulting in an average length of 7.2 words per proverb. This corresponds very much to the length of traditional Anglo-American proverbs in general (Grzybek 2000). As one would expect, our corpus includes texts that consist of the minimum of two words required for a *bona fide* proverb (Dundes 1975 [1981]). Old proverbs like "Time flies" and "Money talks" (Kirshenblatt-Gimblett 1973 [1981]) easily come to mind, but considering the predisposition of modern speakers for short sound bites, it is surprising that our collection contains but 11 (0.77%) two-word proverbs. The range of messages clearly goes from the didactic boy-scout motto "Be prepared" to the slang proverb "Life sucks" all the way to proverbs based on scatological and sexual images:

 Question *authority*.
 Life sucks.
 Manners matter (much).
 Be *prepared*.
 Sex sells.
 Shit (Stuff) happens.
 Speed kills.

The group of proverbs consisting of three words comprises 39 (2.7%) texts, of which about a fifth are definitional proverbs of the structure "X is Y" already listed above. Some texts are simple imperatives like "Just do it" or "Just say no," while others are very short statements expressing some basic generalizations about modern life and behavior:

 Everyone *finds* someone.
 Gentlemen prefer blondes.
 Just *do* it.
 Just say *no*.

Money never sleeps.
Nothing grows forever.
Publish or perish.
Signs don't vote.

The group of proverbs consisting of four words is expectedly much larger with 150 (10.5%) texts. There is a predominance of monosyllabic words in these texts, making them very short pieces of rather directly expressed insights that often lack any metaphorical element. Many of them follow a parallel structure with or without rhyme. However, regarding rhyme, it should be noted that this proverbial marker does not play a major role in modern proverbs (about 51 texts or 3.6%), among them "Your ego is not your amigo," "Move your *feet*, lose your seat," "Drive for *show*, put for dough," "If you don't *speculate*, you can't accumulate," and "Different *ways* for (on) different days." A few more rhymed proverbs are included in this list of four-word proverbs:

Get your *act* together.
No *beauty* (There is no beauty) without pain.
No *brain*, no pain.
Think outside the *box*.
The *buck* stops here. (Mieder and Bryan 1997: 62–65)
Close but no *cigar*. (Cohen 1989)
Been there, *done* that.
Everyone can't be *first*.
Go with the *flow*.
Garbage in, garbage out. (Winick 2001)
Last *hired*, first fired.
Make *love*, not war.
You can't fix *stupid*.

Of course, there are also proverbs of a much greater length, reaching as many as 23 words. Some have parallel structures; others begin with a statement that is elaborated in the second part (often beginning with the conjunction "but"); and there are also those texts that simply state a truism in a somewhat wordy way. Owing to their length and perhaps to the problem of memorability, these texts do not belong to those of frequent use. If they are used, they are most likely only cited partially, assuming that people will be able to complete them in their own minds:

15 words:

If you always *do* what you've always done, you'll always get what you've always gotten.

Men are only good for one thing—and sometimes they aren't even good for that.

16 words:

Be nice to *people* on your way up because you'll meet them on your way down.

17 words:

The *toes* you step on today may be attached (connected) to the ass you have to kiss tomorrow.

Worry is like a rocking chair: it gives you something to do but doesn't get you anywhere.

18 words:

When you're up to your *ass* in alligators, it's hard to remember you're there to drain the swamp (it's too late to start figuring out how to drain the swamp). (Dundes and Pagter 1987)

A *government* big enough to give you everything you want is big enough to take everything you have.

19 words:

You can take a *boy* (man, girl, etc.) out of the country, but you can't take the country out of a boy (man, girl).

It is better to be thought a *fool* than to open your mouth and let the world know it.

20 words:

It is better to be a big *duck* in a little puddle (pond) than a little duck in a big puddle (pond).

21 words:

You can't keep *birds* (crows) from flying over your head, but you can keep them from building a nest in your hair (on your head).

It's not the *size* of the dog in the fight that matters; it's the size of the fight in the dog.

23 words:

When a *lady* says *no*, she means 'perhaps'; when she says *perhaps*, she means 'yes'; when she says *yes*, she is no lady.

The *caribou* and the wolf are one; for the caribou feeds the wolf, but it is the wolf who keeps the caribou strong.

Counter-Proverbs, Anti-Proverbs, and Reincarnated Proverbs

As has been shown, a considerable number of modern proverbs are based on traditional structures, giving them a familiar appearance albeit with new contents. This is also the case with two special types of new proverbs, namely so-called counter-proverbs and anti-proverbs. According to Charles Doyle, who coined the term *counter-proverb* in 1972,

> a *counter-proverb* is simply an overt negation or sententious-sounding rebuttal of a proverb, an explicit denial of the proverb's asserted truth. A counter-pro-verb does not typically aim for any ironic effect, other than calling into doubt whatever wisdom it is that proverbs are supposed to encapsulate. For examp-le, in the twentieth century we find, with some frequency, "One rotten apple does not spoil the whole barrel," rebutting the very old proverb "One rotten apple will spoil the whole barrel." Sometimes [especially when both texts are modern] it is impossible to determine which is the original proverb and which the counter-proverb: "Good enough is not good enough" seems to be about the same age as "Good enough is good enough"; the sayings "Life is just a bowl of cherries" and "Life is not a bowl of cherries" are contemporaneous. (quoted from the introduction of our collection)

Just as such traditional contrasting proverb pairs as "Absence makes the heart grow fonder" and "Out of sight, out of mind," these counter-proverb pairs mirror the contradictions of life itself. Since proverbs are not a logical sys-tem, such opposing bits of wisdom are perfectly legitimate. But be that as it may, our collection only includes 11 (0.77%) counter-proverbs. In the follow-ing list the counter-proverb is cited with the date of its earliest recording but without contextualized references. After that I cite the original proverb on which the new counter-proverb is based:

Bigger is not always (necessarily) better. 1928. [. . .] The proverb perhaps origi-nated as counter-proverb responding to "The bigger the better."

You cannot fight *fire* with fire. 1917. [. . .] The proverb perhaps originated as a counter-proverb rebutting the very old "Fight fire with fire" or "You've got to fight fire with fire."

Flattery will get you everywhere (anywhere). 1926. [. . .] The proverb probably originated as a counter-proverb rebutting "Flattery will get you nowhere"—or else "Flattery will get you nowhere" rebuts "Flattery will get you everywhere."

Life is not a bowl of cherries. 1931. [. . .] Presumably the proverb originated as a counter-proverb rebutting "Life is a bowl of cherries"—or vice versa.

The *plural* of *anecdote* is not *data* (*evidence*). 1982. [. . .] Presumably the proverb originated as a counter-proverb responding to the waggish "The plural of *anecdote* is *data*"—or vice versa.

Not all *publicity* (press) is good (publicity). 1915. [. . .] The proverb perhaps originated as a counter-proverb rebutting "Any publicity is good publicity"—or vice versa.

Size does matter. 1964. [. . .] The proverb, with the emphatic auxiliary verb *does*, probably originated as a counter-proverb rebutting the proverb "Size doesn't matter."

Our collection also includes a considerably larger number of anti-proverbs (Litovkina and Lindahl 2007; Litovkina and Mieder 2006), namely 118 (8.3%). I coined the term *anti-proverb* in 1982, with the definition being

> an allusive distortion, parody, misapplication, or unexpected contextualization of a recognized proverb, usually for comic or satiric effect. Anti-proverbs occur frequently in commercial advertising, on greeting cards, in the captions of cartoons, and as the punch lines of "shaggy dog" jokes. Sometimes they pass into oral tradition as proverbs in their own right (Valdaeva 2003): for example, "Absence makes the heart go wander"; "Beauty is only skin"; "No body is perfect"; "Do unto others before they can do unto you"; "Dynamite comes in small packages." (cited from the introduction of our collection)

In the following selection of examples, I cite first the anti-proverb with the date of its earliest recording, once again leaving out all contextualized references. This is followed by the traditional proverb upon which the anti-proverb was formulated:

> Don't *believe* everything you think. 1948. [. . .] The proverb originated as an anti-proverb based on "Don't believe everything you hear (read, see)."

You *booze*, you lose. 1986. [. . .] The rhyming proverb may have originated as an anti-proverb based on "You snooze, you lose."

Do unto others before they (can) do unto you (before they do you). [. . .] The proverb originated as an anti-proverb based on the golden rule (Matthew 7:12) "Do unto others as you would have them do unto you" (Mieder 2010b).

Expedience is the best teacher. 1966. [. . .] The proverb originated as an anti-proverb based on "Experience is the best teacher."

A *ms.* (miss) is as good as a male. 1942. [. . .] The proverb originated as an anti-proverb based on "A miss is as good as a mile."

Love thy *neighbor*, but don't get caught. 1967. [. . .] The proverb is an anti-proverb based on Jesus's advice to "love thy neighbor as thyself."

People who live in glass houses should (always) wear clothes. 1904. [. . .] The proverb originated as an anti-proverb based on "People who live in glass houses shouldn't throw stones."

Somewhat related to counter-proverbs and anti-proverbs are what we have called reincarnations of older proverbs, i.e., modern proverbs based on the general wording, metaphor (if there is one), and meaning of an older proverb. Such pairs of texts may coexist, of course, but usually the more modern one will win out in the struggle for dominance. A few truncated examples will illustrate this phenomenon:

You *break* it, you buy (bought, own) it (If you break it, it's yours). 1957. [. . .] Sometimes, in recent years, the proverb is called "the Pottery Barn rule." Cf. the older proverb (and legal maxim) "He who breaks pays."

You never get a second *chance* to make a first impression. 1952. [. . .] Cf. the older proverb "First impressions are lasting."

Don't shit on your own *doorstep*. 1967. [. . .] Cf. "Don't shit where you eat [sit]" and the older "A bird does not foul its own nest."

The older the *fiddle* (violin), the sweeter (finer) the tune (melody, sound). 1909. [. . .] Cf. the older proverb "There's many a good tune played on an old fiddle."

Only dead *fish* go with the flow. 1989. [. . .] Cf. the older proverb "A dead fish can float downstream, but it takes a live one to swim upstream." The modern variant (among other implications) satirizes—and sometimes retorts to—the proverbial advice "Go with the flow."

Nobody ever said *life* is easy (Who ever said life is easy?). 1965. [. . .] Cf. the older proverb—from which this one perhaps evolved—"Life is not meant to be easy."

A good *man* is hard to find. 1918. [. . .] The proverb is the twentieth-century incarnation (or equivalent) of the older proverb "Good men are scarce" (Doyle 2007a).

Modern Proverbs Expressed as Laws of Life

Modern proverbs also are consciously created by individuals as so-called "laws" summarizing life's trials and tribulations that appear to repeat themselves. Usually these insights have the name of their originator attached to them, and there are entire books on such (in)famous laws. Some of them have clearly become proverbial, and our collection includes 15 (1.1%) of them (Bloch 1979, 1982a, 1982b). A few are listed here with their date and the name of the person who (supposedly) coined them. Our actual entries provide much more material, as can be seen from this one complete text for perhaps the most famous of these laws:

If anything can *go wrong*, it will (Anything that can go wrong, will go wrong; Anything that can possibly go wrong usually does). 1908 Nevil Maskelyne, "The Art in Magic," *The Magic Circular* (June) 25: "It is an experience common to all men to find that, on any special occasion, such as the production of a magical effect for the first time in public, everything that *can* go wrong *will* go wrong. Whether we must attribute this to the malignity of matter or to the total depravity of inanimate things, whether the exciting cause is hurry, worry, or what not, the fact remains" (italics as shown). 1951 Anne Roe, "Child Behavior, Animal Behavior, and Comparative Psychology," *Genetic Psychology Monographs* 43 (May) 204: "As for himself he realized that this was the inexorable working of the second law of the thermodynamics which stated Murphy's law 'If anything can go wrong it will.' I always liked Murphy's law." 1955 Lee Corey, "Design Flaw," *Astounding Science Fiction* 54 (Feb.) 54: "'Reilly's Law,'

Guy Barclay said cryptically. 'Huh?' 'Reilly's Law,' Guy repeated. 'It states that in any scientific or engineering endeavor, anything that can go wrong *will* go wrong" (italics as shown). [References to collections are deleted here and elsewhere.] In popular legend, Murphy's Law originated in 1949 at Edwards Air Force Base in California, coined by project manager George E. Nichols after hearing Edward A. Murphy, Jr., complain about a wrongly-wired rokket-sled experiment. However, there is no documentation of that connection until 1955. The idea embodied in Murphy's Law (less often, "Reilly's Law" or "O'Reilly's Law") has appeared in numerous forms, in reference to a variety of activities, from antiquity forward (see the cross-references at the *YBQ* entry). For example: 1878 Alfred Holt, "Review of the Progress of Steam Shipping during the Last Quarter of a Century," *Minutes of Proceedings of the Institution of Civil Engineers*, 51: 8: "It is found that anything that can go wrong at sea generally does go wrong sooner or later." 1941 George Orwell, "War-Time Diaries," in *Collected Essays, Journalism and Letters*, edited by Sonia Orwell and Ian Angus (New York: Harcourt, Brace & World, 1968) 2: 400–401: "Iraq, Syria, Morocco, Spain, Darlan, Stalin, Raschid Ali, Franco—sensation of utter helplessness. If there is a wrong thing to do, it will be done, infallibly. One has come to believe in that as if it were a law of nature." The term "Murphy's law" has come to designate a range of seemingly reasonable but often paradoxical or absurd-sounding propositions.

Here are a few more laws in much truncated form to save space. They make clear that at times they are simply attributed to a person, with Edward A. Murphy winning the prize as the supposed coiner of such laws of which but a few have become proverbial:

> When you are in a *hole*, stop digging. 1911. *Washington Post* 25 Oct.: "Nor would a wise man, seeing that he was in a hole, go to work and blindly dig it deeper, as [William Jennings] Bryan did when he shifted ground and assailed the integrity of the President and the Judges." [. . .] 1984. *New York Times* 11 Sep.: "There is a Law of Holes that says, when you are in one, stop digging. That is a law Congress finds it almost impossible to observe." [. . .] In British publications, the "Law of Holes" is often referred to as "Healey's Law," after the statesman Denis Healey, a popularizer of the expression in the later 1980s.

> Everything (always) *takes* longer than it should (it does, it takes, you expect). 1900. Florence Converse, *The Burden of Christopher* (Boston: Houghton, Mifflin) 139: "To be sure, we're still profit sharing, we haven't gone into real

coöperation yet; but then, things always take longer than you think they will
…" […] Especially in absurdly worded forms like "Everything takes longer
than it takes," the proverb is often given as one of "Murphy's Laws."

You can never do merely (just, only) one *thing*. 1963. Garrett Hardin, "The
Cybernetics of Competition," *Perspectives in Biology and Medicine* 7, no. 4
(Autumn) 80: "The moral of the myth [a narrative of the magically-granted
three wishes] can be put in various ways. One: wishing won't make it so. Two:
every change has its price. Three (and this one I like the best): we can never
do merely one thing. Wishing to kill insects, we may put an end to the singing
of birds. Wishing to 'get there faster,' we insult our lungs with smog." […] In
Living within Limits (New York: Oxford UP, 1993) 199–201, Hardin traces
the tradition and background of the principle that the proverb encapsulates,
which came to be called "Hardin's Law"—but Hardin himself prefers to think
of it as the "First Law of Ecology."

Work expands to fill the available (allotted) time. 1955. "Parkinson's Law," the
Economist 177: 633 (the reference is to C. Northcote Parkinson): "It is a commonplace observation that work expands so as to fill the time available for its
completion … Before the discovery of a new scientific law—herewith presented to the public for the first time, and to be called Parkinson's Law—there
has, however, been insufficient recognition of the implications of this fact in
the field of public administration."

These examples show that the actual authorship of some of these proverbial
laws is not at all certain. This is quite naturally also the case with the other
proverbs in our corpus. To be sure, some modern proverbs have simply been
attributed to certain well-known persons, just as this has been done in previous times (Taylor 1931: 34–43). Detailed research on our part has shown that
such attributions can usually not be proven, even though people will cling to
these claims when citing such proverbs.

Attribution of Modern Proverbs to Certain Individuals

What it takes to come to terms with such attributions can best be seen from
our discussion of the internationally disseminated modern proverb "A woman without a man is like a fish without a bicycle" (Mieder 1982):

A *woman* without a man is like a fish without a bicycle (A woman needs a
man like a fish needs a bicycle). *1976 Corpus Christi* [Texas] *Times* 5 May

(quoting Barbara Hower): "... [A] feminist said recently an independent woman needs a man like a fish needs a bicycle. That's horse feathers, at least for
me. I like what I'm doing but I'd like someone to scratch and giggle with" (credited to *Chicago Daily News*). 1976 *Seattle Times* 5 June: "Sign in a (feminist?)
dress shop in Seattle, Wash.: 'A woman without a man is like a fish without a
bicycle.'" 1976 *People* 6, no. 4 (26 July) 20 (photo caption): "Gloria Steinem
(left) planned to wear a shirt that said, 'A woman without a man is like a fish
without a bicycle,' but, like Candy Bergen, arrived unlettered at a [Democra-
tic Party] women's fund raiser." 1976 Mary Murphy, "Superstar Women and
Their Marriages," *New York Magazine* 9, no. 32 (9 Aug.) 26: "[Gloria] Steinem
sums it up: 'Today a woman without a man is like a fish without a bicycle.'"
1979 Deborah Goleman Wolf, *The Lesbian Community* (Berkeley: U of California P) [vi] (epigraph): "'*A woman without a man is like a fish without a
bicycle.*' (Graffito in the women's lavatory, Student Union, University of California Berkeley, 1975, attributed to Flo Kennedy)" (italics as shown). 1976
Seattle Times 5 June: "Sign seen in a (feminist?) dress shop in Seattle, Wash.:
'A woman without a man is like a fish without a bicycle.' [...] The proverb
perhaps originated as an anti-proverb patterned after "A woman without a
man is like a handle without a pan" (or other old similes suggesting uselessness
or absurdity). Steinem, in *Time* 156, no. 15 (9 Oct. 2000) 20, disclaimed credit
for originating the feminist expression: "Irina Dunn, a distinguished Australi-
an educator, journalist and politician, coined the phrase back in 1970 ..." The
image of a fish without (or not needing) a bicycle has had a life of its own. Cf.
"A man without faith is like a fish without a bicycle" and "A man without a
woman is like a fish without a bicycle" and "A woman without a man is like a
fish without a net."

Here are but a few more examples of this phenomenon, once again stripped
of many additional contextualized references:

Old *age* is not for sissies. 1969 Eugene P. Bertin, "Ravelin's: Threads Detached
from Texture," *Pennsylvania School Journal* 17: 546 (in a series of witty sayings
commemorating Senior Citizen Month, May): "Old age is not for sissies."
[...] The proverb's origin is often attributed to the actress Bette Davis.

Float like a *butterfly*, sting like a bee. 1964 *New York Times* 19 Feb.: "'Put the
poison on him,' yelled Drew (Budini) Brown, Clay's spiritual adviser and assistant trainer. 'Float like a butterfly, sting like a bee. Oh, beautiful, Cassius,
you should see yourself.'" [...] The saying has generally been attributed to
Muhammad Ali (*né* Cassius Clay) himself.

It's (The game is) not *over* till it's over. 1921 Roy Sahm, "It Is Believed Rotarians Won," *The Delta of Sigma Nu Fraternity* 38: 667: "It is said the score was 23 to 21 in favor of Rotary, they having tied the score in the seventh. They passed Kiwanis in the eighth and held Kiwanis in the ninth. All of which goes to prove that a ball game's never over until it's over" (credited to the *Indianapolis News*). [. . .] Often, the saying is apocryphally attributed to Yogi Berra. Cf. the older expression "When it's over, it's over," which has a different meaning.

Trust but verify. 1966 Michel Tatu, "Soviet Reforms: The Debate Goes On," *Problems in Communism* 15, no. 1 (Jan.-Feb.) 31: "Supplemented by the Khrushchevian motto, 'Trust but verify' (*dovierat no provierat*), this attitude leaves agricultural producers [in the USSR] very little freedom of action." [. . .] Ironically, the proverb is often attributed to Ronald Reagan, even though Reagan himself stated that he had learned it (as a Russian proverb) from Mikhail Gorbachev.

A *week* is a long time in politics. 1961 Richard Cox, "Nyerere Sees a Middle Way for Africa," *New York Times Magazine* (3 Dec.) 121: "He [Prime Minister Julius Nyerere] will undoubtedly find it difficult to negotiate federation when it comes to the details, but as the weeks pass—and a week is a long time in African politics—it seems more and more likely that he will succeed." [. . .] The proverb is commonly attributed to Prime Minister Harold Wilson; however, no record of his using it can be found from earlier than 1968, and Wilson himself is on record saying he cannot remember when he first uttered it.

All of this is not to say that our collection does not contain modern proverbs about which we know precisely who originated them when and where. Such original citations by known persons begin basically as statements in books, articles, speeches, motion pictures, songs, etc. As they are repeated they become quotations, and with ever more frequent use, often without any awareness of the originator, these memorable texts can become proverbs. Sometimes quite similar statements precede such a quotation that for various reasons caught on and became proverbial. This is well illustrated by one of John F. Kennedy's most famous statements:

Ask not what your *country* can do for you—ask what you can do for your country. 1961. The saying (often slightly misquoted) entered oral tradition as a proverb from President John F. Kennedy's inaugural address, 20 Jan. 1961. An 1884 speech by Oliver Wendell Holmes, Jr., is sometimes cited as a prototype of Kennedy's wording, since it anticipates the (commonplace) idea and the parallel phrasing, the chiasmus: "...[W]e pause...to recall what our country has done for each of us, and to ask ourselves what we can do for our country in return." A closer prior analog: 1922 Isaac Doughton, *Preparing for the World's Work* (New York: Charles Scribner's Sons) 4: "But as good citizens you are not so anxious to know what your country does for you as you are to know what you can do for your country." The eeriest anticipator of both Holmes's and Kennedy's wording occurred in 1858—except that the writer, one Rev. M. Thomson, was engaging in satire, proffering ironic advice—and thus inverting the clauses—in "Our Youth: Their Principles and Prospects," *Ladies' Repository* 18: 285: "Fetter the noblest powers and impulses of the soul; turn all your genius into cunning; prefer your wages to your work; study not what you can do for your country, but what your country can do for you." (Mieder 2005c: 172–73)

Here are a few shortened examples from our collection that are in fact rather straightforward regarding their first appearance in a written or oral communication by a known person of considerable consequence:

He who *can* does; he who can't teaches (Those who can do; those who can't teach). 1903. The saying entered oral tradition as a proverb from George Bernard Shaw's *Man and Superman* (the appended "Maxims for Revolutionists"). [...] The proverb has acquired various codas: "...he who can't teach teaches others to teach"; "...he who can't teach, administrates"; etc.

If it (If the glove) doesn't *fit*, you must acquit. 1995. The saying entered oral tradition as a proverb from its use as a mantra by the defense lawyer Johnnie Cochran, Jr., in his closing argument at the murder trial of O. J. Simpson (27 Sep.). [...] The proverb means "You must reject, abandon, or discard a belief or plan that does not 'fit' with realities, goals, or purposes." The proverb is less commonly applied jurisprudentially. (Winick 2003: 587–88; Prahlad 2006: II, 1026)

You can't go *home* again. 1940. The saying probably entered oral tradition as a proverb from the title of Thomas Wolfe's novel, published posthumously (Wolfe died in 1938). [...]

Love means never having to say you're sorry. 1970. The saying entered oral tradition as a proverb from Erich Segal's best-selling novel *Love Story* (New

York: Harper & Row), which first appeared (somewhat condensed) in *Ladies Home Journal* 87, no. 2 (Feb.) 124: "She cut off my apology, then said very quietly, 'Love means not ever having to say you're sorry.'" In the popular motion picture, "never" replaces "not ever." The novel was written after Segal's screenplay but published before the release of the movie in Dec. 1970. [...]

Pain is (Tough times are) temporary; failure (quitting) is forever. 2003. Lance Armstrong (with Sally Jenkins), *Every Second Counts* (New York: Random House) 3–4: "But the fact is I wouldn't have won a single Tour de France without the lesson of illness. What it teaches is this: pain is temporary. Quitting lasts forever." [...]

Speak (Talk, Walk) softly and carry a big stick. 1900. Theodore Roosevelt, letter to Henry Sprague (26 Jan.): "I have always been fond of the West African proverb: 'Speak softly and carry a big stick; you will go far.' If I had not carried the big stick the organization would not have gotten behind me . . ."; *Letters*, edited by Elting E. Morison (Cambridge, MA: Harvard UP, 1951–54) 2: 1141. On several occasions Roosevelt uttered the saying, without the last clause and without the West African connection. In oral tradition, the proverb often varies the first verb. [...] An interesting prior analog: 1882 C. H. Spurgeon, "Colportage a Want of the Age," in *Booksellers and Bookbuyers*, by Spurgeon et al. (London: Passmore and Alabaster) 12: "Amid abundant laughter, our friend [an evangelist] declared that he had not fought wild beasts at Ephesis, but . . . he had found it well to trust in God *and carry a big stick*" (italics as shown).

War will cease when men refuse to fight. 1933. Albert Einstein, *The Fight against War*, edited by Alfred Lief (New York: John Day) 37 (excerpted from Einstein's interview with George Sylvester Viereck, Jan. 1931): "I am not only a pacifist but a militant pacifist. I am willing to fight for peace. Nothing will end war unless the peoples themselves refuse to war [*sic*]." [...] Cf. "Some day they will give a war and nobody will come."

Advertising Slogans as Sources of Modern Proverbs

It has long been established that advertising slogans have given rise to new proverbs (Mieder and Mieder 1977 [1981]; Prahlad 2004; Winick 2011), but the 17 (1.2%) texts in our collection are certainly not an overwhelming number. Many slogans are simply too specifically oriented toward a certain product to take on the nature of a general proverb. In addition, over time the association with the original advertising campaign is lost, making it difficult to establish clear-cut connections. In other words, proverbs starting as advertising slogans have a tendency to become anonymous traditional sayings, as is, of course, the very nature of real proverbs. The complexity of all of this, including variants building on such slogans, can readily be seen from this one reference from our collections cited in its entirety:

What happens (goes on) in *Las Vegas* stays in Las Vegas. 2002 *Las Vegas Review-Journal* 25 Nov.: "The Las Vegas Visitors and Convention Authority, meanwhile, continued its saucy come-to-Vegas-baby advertising campaign with six new spots filmed over a three-day period last week. Depicting the theme 'what happens in Las Vegas stays in Las Vegas,' the national commercials, produced by Hungry Man Productions, feature Vegas visitors indulging fantasies in locations ranging from a limousine to a tattoo parlor." 2002 Kellye M. Garrett et al., "Everything the Top Football Stars Can't Live Without," *Vibe* 62 (Nov.) (quoting the football player Adam Archuleta): "Favorite city: Las Vegas . . . You party and have a good time with your friends. What happens in Vegas stays in Vegas." Whether the advertising campaign originated the saying or merely employed an existing proverb, "What happens in Las Vegas stays in Las Vegas" has become, by far, the most common of the popular sayings that follow the formula; it is widely assumed to be the prototypical version, and currently it can be uttered (figuratively) in reference to any site of conduct that calls for non-disclosure. However, it was anticipated—at least as early as the 1970s—by parallel sayings about secrecy or discretion of various sorts: "What's said (What happens) at home stays at home," an expression sometimes used to lament the secrecy of child abuse or spousal abuse; the clinical or psychotherapeutic adage "What happens in the group (at the meeting, at the session) stays . . ."; the professional baseball maxim "What happens in the clubhouse stays . . ." Even in the dissipated-vacation usage, other versions are apparently older: 1996 *San Antonio Express-News* 13 Nov.: "But there was one condition. Drill sergeants told them repeatedly: 'Whatever happens in Mexico stays in Mexico.'" 1998 *Orlando Sentinel* 30 Mar.: "'What happens in Daytona, stays in Daytona,' he tells the others."

Here are a few shortened examples of advertising slogans turned proverb, with only one text actually maintaining the name of a company (Delta Airlines). Nevertheless, a certain amount of cultural literacy and knowledge about the commercial world belong at least in part to the proper understanding of some of these texts (Mieder 1992 [1994]; see also Haas 2008):

> Where is the *beef*? 1984. The saying entered oral tradition as a proverb from an advertising slogan for Wendy's hamburgers. [. . .] In the proverb, the word *beef* is understood to mean "substance" in various senses. (Barrick 1986)

> It's what's up front that *counts*. c1957. The saying entered oral tradition as a proverb from an advertising slogan for Winston cigarettes—playing on the older proverb "It's what inside that counts." [. . .]

> Say it with *flowers*. 1917. The saying entered oral tradition as a proverb from an advertising slogan of the Society of American Florists. [. . .]

> *Number two* tries harder (When you're number two, you try harder). 1962. The proverb probably entered oral tradition from an advertising campaign for Avis: "We're Number Two. We try harder" (Avis was second to Hertz in the car-rental business).

> *Reach* out and touch someone. 1970. Eliot Tiegel, "Reach Out and Touch Someone," *Billboard* (15 Aug.) 26; the title of the review of a live performance by Diana Ross presumably alludes to Ross's song "Reach Out and Touch Somebody's Hand." [. . .] Beginning in 1978 the proverb was featured in an advertising campaign for AT&T's long-distance phone service. [. . .]

> Have it your *way*. 1973. The saying entered oral tradition as a proverb from the advertising slogan of Burger King. It asserts that a consumer should demand to be accommodated by commercial establishments or agents. [. . .] The invention of the slogan—or its popularity as a proverb—might have been influenced by Frank Sinatra's famous song "My Way" (1969; lyrics by Paul Anka), with the refrain "I did it my way."

> You've come a long *way*, baby. 1968. The saying probably entered oral tradition as a proverb from an advertising campaign for Philip Morris cigarettes, which promoted the liberating effects of smoking for women. [. . .] A 1978 Hallmark greeting card (purchased in Burlington, VT): [front] "You've come a long way, baby . . ." [inside] ". . . from Adam's rib to 'Women Lib'" (ellipsis dots as shown). [. . .]

As can be seen from two of these examples, proverb-like one-liners from the world of advertising and popular music can actually work hand in hand in creating and spreading new proverbs.

Songs and Films as Sources of Modern Proverbs

With music playing such a large role on the modern entertainment scene, it should not be surprising that songs have given rise to ample modern proverbs, with our collection containing 65 (4.6%) texts. It should be noted, however, that this is nothing new as far as the creation of proverbs is concerned (Bryan 2001; Mieder 1988). Religious hymns, anonymous folksongs, operettas, and musicals have long given rise to proverbs, with the song texts of Gilbert and Sullivan being prime examples in the nineteenth and early twentieth centuries (Bryan 1999). Nothing in this regard has changed on the modern scene, as can be seen by country songs, blues, reggae, or rap music (Folsom 1993; Prahlad 2001; Taft 1994). In fact, songs by famous lyricists and musicians like the Beatles, Bob Dylan, and Bruce Springsteen have led to new proverbs. But in order to illustrate once again the complexity of locating the earliest recording of a proverb in a song, its subsequent use, and its later incorrect attribution to a famous person, let me cite one entry from our collection almost in its entirety:

> Old *soldiers* never die (they just fade away). 1916 Bruce Bairnsfather, *Bullets & Billets* (London: Grant Richards) 52–53: "Occasionally, in the silent, still, foggy mornings, a voice from somewhere in the alluvial depths of a miserable trench, would suddenly burst into a scrap of song, such as—Old soldiers never die, / They simply fade away.—a voice full of 'fed-upness,' steeped in determination." In the same book (202) appears a drawing of a singing "Tommy" in a trench, holding a raised umbrella; over the umbrella appears a line of music with the words "old soldiers never die, they simply fades [*sic*] a-way." Snippets of the song (said to be to the tune of "Kind Words Can Never Die") appear in other reminiscences of World War I, with slight variations ("they fade away"; "they always fade away"). In 1920 the song was copyrighted by one J. Foley, but there is no good evidence that he was the actual author. The proverb is now popularly associated with its use by General Douglas McArthur in his farewell address to Congress in 1951. The proverb has given rise to a cycle of parodic jokes, which are anti-proverbs ("Old doctors never die, they just lose their patients"; "Old golfers never die, they just lose their balls"). [. . .]

But here are at least a few examples from the treasure trove of proverbs stemming from popular songs. Of course, let me also state for the record that lyric poets also employ traditional proverbs and formulate lines that later become proverbs, as can be seen from many such proverb poems (Sobieski and Mieder 2005):

There's no *business* like show business. 1946. The saying entered oral tradition as a proverb from the title and first line of a song by Irving Berlin. [. . .]

Diamonds are (A diamond is) a girl's best friend. 1949. The saying entered oral tradition as a proverb from the title and refrain of a song by Leo Robin. [. . .]

It's not *easy* being green. 1970. The saying entered oral tradition as a proverb from a song by Joe Raposo, sung by the character Kermit the Frog of the Muppets. The proverb laments the pain of being "different"—perhaps including differences in color or race. Eventually it came to apply to the difficulty of efforts to save the environment and perhaps to other kinds of figurative "greenness."

Everybody wants to go to *heaven*, but nobody wants to die. 1950. The proverb originated with—or gained popularity from—the title of Tommy Dorsey's song "Everybody Wants to Go to Heaven (But No One Wants to Die)."

A *kiss* is just a kiss. 1931. The song "As Time Goes By," lyrics by Herman Hupfeld (in the musical *Everybody's Welcome*), contained the lines "A kiss is still a kiss, / A sigh is just a sigh"; the saying entered oral tradition (and many performances of the song itself) with the lines conflated: "A kiss is just a kiss." [. . .] More recently, the song has been featured in the BBC television series *As Time Goes By* (1992–2005). [. . .]

Life is (just) a cabaret. 1966. The saying entered oral tradition as a proverb from the featured song in the musical *Cabaret*, lyrics by Fred Ebb (music by John Kander). [. . .] The proverb updates the venerable Elizabethan commonplace of the world as a stage (and men and women merely players).

All you need is *love*. 1967. The saying passed into oral tradition as a proverb from the title and refrain of the Beatles' song (lyrics by John Lennon).

It takes *two* to tango. 1952. The saying entered oral tradition as a proverb from the song "It Takes Two to Tango," by Al Hoffman and Dick Manning. [. . .]

The proverb may have originated as an anti-proverb based on "It takes two to quarrel." (Mieder and Bryan 1983; Mieder 1985: 151–54)

Motion pictures are not surprisingly also a fruitful ground for spreading gnomic insights to large segments of the population, who in turn help distribute them by frequent repetition as new proverbs of the folk. Our collection assembles 19 (1.3%) such proverbs whose origin can be traced back to popular films:

If you *build* it, they will come (Build it and they will come). 1979. The saying probably entered oral tradition as a proverb—or at least gained popularity—from W. P. Kinsella's story "Shoeless Joe Jackson Comes to Iowa" and the motion picture based on it, *Field of Dreams* (1989). [...]

Keep your *friends* close and (but) your enemies closer. 1974. The proverb probably entered oral tradition from a speech in the motion picture *The Godfather, Part II*: "There are many things my father taught me here in this room. He taught me: Keep your friends close, but your enemies closer." Occasionally it is referred to as an ancient Chinese proverb.

If (When) you've *got* it, flaunt it. 1968. The saying may have entered oral tradition as a proverb from the motion picture *The Producers*: "That's it, baby! When you got it, flaunt it!" (or the character in the movie may have been uttering a proverb). Most frequently the proverb refers to the display of an individual's sexuality.

Life is like (is just) a box of chocolates (chocolate). 1994. The saying entered oral tradition as adapted from the motion picture *Forrest Gump*: "Life is a box of chocolates, Forrest. You never know what you're going to get." The proverb sometimes intends to *satirize* the sententious utterance of Forest Gump's mother.

Life is too short (to wait) for *someday*. 1969. *On Her Majesty's Secret Service* (motion picture). "[Father:] 'Bond—he's in love with you?' [Daughter:] 'That may come too, someday.' [Father:] 'Life's too short for someday, Tereza.'" [...] (Krummenacher 2007: 145).

There are no *rules* in a knife fight. 1969. The proverb entered oral tradition as a proverb, garbled, from dialogue in the motion picture *Butch Cassidy and the Sundance Kid*: "[Butch:] 'No, no, not yet. Not until me and Harvey get the

rules straightened out.' [Harvey Logan:] 'Rules? In a knife fight? No rules!'"
(at which instant Butch kicks Harvey in the groin). [...]

Animals, Body Parts, Business, Sports, Technology, America

Turning now to the realia of modern proverbs, it is perhaps surprising that
various animals continue to appear with considerable frequency. Obviously
the modern age still relates well to animals, especially such domesticated
animals as cats, cows, dogs, horses, and pigs. But wild animals like birds, elephants, fish, frogs, monkeys, and others are also employed to express human behavior and attitudes via metaphors. There is, of course, also the telling
modern proverb "All animals are (created) equal, but some are more equal
than others" that entered oral tradition from George Orwell's *Animal Farm*
(1945), expressing in metaphorical wording an unfortunate aspect of human
life. In any case, our proverb collection contains 116 (8.2%) so-called animal
proverbs, among them:

> A *bird* may love a fish, but where would they live (build a home, build a nest)?
> *Cats* look down on you, dogs look up at you, pigs look at you as equals.
> If you can't run with the big *dogs*, stay on (under) the porch.
> If it looks like a *duck*, walks like a duck, and quacks like a duck, it's a duck.
> It is possible to swallow (You can eat) an *elephant*—one bite at a time.
> You have to kiss a lot of *frogs* (toads) to find a prince.
> When you hear *hoofbeats*, think horses, not zebras (When you hear hoofbeats,
>   don't look for zebras). (Dundes, Streiff, and Dundes 1999)
> Always ride the (your) *horse* in the direction it's going (it wants to go).
> You can put *lipstick* on a pig but it's still a pig (A pig wearing lipstick is still a pig).
> Only *monkeys* work for peanuts (If you pay peanuts, you get monkeys).
> The second *mouse* gets the cheese.
> Old *rats* like cheese too.

Just as animal metaphors have not disappeared from modern proverbs,
the same is also true for somatisms, with such nouns as ass (behind), eye,
hand, head, heart, mouth, and nose being the most frequent among the 49
(3.4%) texts.

> Your *arms* are too short (not long enough) to box (fight, spar) with God.
> If you're too open-minded, your *brains* will fall out.
> Every shut *eye* is not asleep.

It is better to die on your *feet* than to live on your knees.
If you want *food*, your nose must run.
Busy *hands* are happy hands.
You can't measure *heart*.
Never take more on your *heels* than you can kick off with your toes.
A *moment* (minute) on the lips, a lifetime (forever) on the hips.
A closed (shut) *mouth* gathers (catches) no feet.
Keep your *nose* clean.
Everyone puts his (All men put their) *pants* on one leg at a time (the same way).
The *toes* you step on today may be attached (connected) to the ass you have to
   kiss tomorrow.

Today's preoccupation with business, finance, and money has left its mark
on modern proverbs as well, with 47 (3.3%) texts showing up in our corpus.
They all reflect the pecuniary aspects of modern life, stressing the importance of business, the power of money, the rights and expectations of cus-
tomers, the hope for prosperity, etc.:

Buy the *best* and you only cry once (If you buy quality, you only cry once).
Business goes where it is invited and stays where it is well-treated.
The *customer* is always right. (Taylor 1958)
Another *day*, another dollar.
Never *give* anything away that you can sell (Why give something away when you
   can sell it?).
Put your *money* where your mouth is.
You *pay* now (You can pay) or pay later (with interest).
If you have to ask the *price* (the cost, how much it costs), you can't afford it.
No one ever went bankrupt (went broke, lost money) taking (making) a *profit*.
Prosperity is always just around the corner.
The best *way* to make money is to save it (is not to lose it).

Speaking of modern preoccupations, it comes as no surprise that at least
39 (2.7%) proverbs relate to the ever-present and fascinating world of sports.
There are several more general proverbs referring to games as such or balls,
but it is indeed striking that the majority of sports proverbs are based on the
American national sport of baseball (Frank 1983). While these proverbs relate literally to that very sport, their figurative meanings are, of course, much
broader and can be applied to situations far removed from the actual game of
baseball. Yet popular as these proverbs might be especially in American folk

language, they are also the ones that will give people not acquainted with the lingo of this sport certain comprehension difficulties. But here are a few striking examples:

> You can't hit the *ball* (get a hit) if you don't swing (the bat).
> You can't score unless you have the *ball*.
> Nobody *bats* 1000.
> You can't steal *first base*.
> It isn't whether you win or lose (that counts); it's how you play the *game* (It's not winning that counts, it's playing the game).
> You can't hit a *home run* every time.
> Don't hate the *player*, hate the game.
> If you have two *quarterbacks*, you don't have one (any).
> You can't *score* if you don't shoot.
> You can't steal *second base* while your foot is on first base (if you keep one foot on first).
> You miss 100 per cent of the *shots* you don't take.
> Three *strikes* and you're out.

In comparison to the importance of sports for the origin of modern proverbs, it is surprising that our corpus includes but 24 (1.7%) texts that exhibit at least some relationship to technology by way of certain words. It is here where we might want to look for new proverbs in the future. Of course, there are some modern proverbs like "Garbage in, garbage out" that come from the world of computers, but they do not show by the choice of words any immediate relationship to technology. Our entry with its contextualized references makes this connection clear:

> *Garbage* in, garbage out. (Often abbreviated with the acronym *GIGO.*) 1957 Ernest E. Blanche, "Applying New Electronic Computers to Traffic and Highway Problems," *Traffic Quarterly* 11: 411: "When the basic data to be used by a computer are of questionable accuracy or validity, our personnel have an unusual expression—GIGO—to characterize such information and the answers the computer produces. It simply means 'garbage in—garbage out.'" 1959 B. A. Wilson, "Operations Research and Management," *Business Quarterly* 24, no. 4 (Winter): 215: "The attempt to use existing records and data in O.R. studies may eventually indicate the inadequacy or inconsistency of existing data, but any results derived from using such data can be no better than the basic data. As one consultant puts it, 'Garbage in, Garbage out.'" [...]

In any case, here are some additional proverbs that indicate that technology is playing at least a small role in the creation of modern proverbs, with more to be found or to come in the foreseeable future:

You never forget how to ride a *bicycle*.
There will always be another *bus* (streetcar).
Nobody washes (We don't wash) a rental (rented) *car*.
You can't judge a *car* by its paint (job).
Dot-com, dot-bomb.
Drinking and driving do not mix.
Dynamite comes in small packages.
Gasoline and whiskey (Alcohol and gasoline, etc.) do not mix.
A *ring* on the finger is worth two on the phone.
Speed kills.
You cannot tell which way the *train* went (is going) by looking at the tracks.
Sometimes (Some days) you're the *windshield*, and sometimes you're the bug (bird).

Even though our collection has no texts that indicate by certain word choices that they were coined in Australia, Great Britain, or elsewhere where English is spoken, there are 16 (1.1%) modern proverbs in our collection that refer explicitly to American matters, with a text like "What is good for General Motors is good for America" needing an explanatory comment:

What is good for *General Motors* is good for America (the country). 1953. The proverb originated as a misquotation from US Senate testimony of Charles E. Wilson (former president of General Motors): "For years I thought what was good for our country was good for General Motors, and vice versa. The difference did not exist." [. . .] The proverb most often satirizes the concept that the well-being of giant corporations is inextricably and benevolently connected with the welfare of the nation and its populace.

Such comments are also added to some of the following proverbs that might not necessarily be clear to non-native speakers of American English:

Never (Don't) sell *America* short.
The *business* of America is business.
As *California* goes, so goes the nation.
There is no *law* west of the Pecos.

Other than that, Mrs. *Lincoln*, how did you like the play?
Only *Nixon* could go to China.
Don't mess with *Texas*.

The meager number of proverbs referring to American matters is a clear sign that our collection is in many ways a compilation of texts that are in general use in the United States, Great Britain, Canada, and elsewhere.

Life, Man, Woman, God, Friend, Time, Age, Love, Beauty

This general distribution is, of course, also true for those proverbs that have very common keywords. The most popular word is "life," and it is hardly surprising that modern humankind has much wisdom about existence. Altogether 46 (3.2%) proverbs contain "life" as a keyword, with most of them following the structural and definitional pattern "Life is X." While some of them in two or four words refer to life being problematic, e.g., "Life sucks" and "Life is a bitch," others look at life much more positively, as for example "Life begins at forty" and "If life hands you lemons, make lemonade." Additional representative examples:

> *Life* comes at you fast.
> *Life* deals us each a hand.
> *Life* is a journey, not a destination.
> *Life* is a party.
> *Life* is a picture; paint it well.
> *Life* is not a spectator sport.
> *Life* is what happens while you are making other plans.
> To lengthen your *life*, lessen your meals.
> You get out of *life* (the world, something, anything) what you put into it.

Next in high-frequency keywords is "man/men," with 34 (2.3%) dealing positively or negatively with the male species. Some texts also contrast men with women, of course, and some use this keyword in its generic meaning, thus somewhat inflating this group of "male" proverbs:

> A *man* who kicks his dog will beat his wife.
> Every *man* to his own poison (To every man his own poison).
> *Men* are from Mars, women are from Venus.
> No *man* is above the law, and no man is below it.

Old *men* make wars, and young men fight them (pay the price).
Stand by your *man*.
The best *man* for the job may be a woman.
The bigger a *man's* head gets, the easier it is to fill his shoes.
The *man* most down on a thing is he who is least up on it.
The *man* who reads is the man who leads (He who reads leads).

Proverbs with "woman/women" as the keyword are smaller in number, with but 8 (not even 0.56%), but notice that none of them refer to men. As wisdom about women, they are pretty much split between positive and negative characterizations, quite in keeping with traditional proverbs that often express misogynous generalizations (Kerschen 1998; Schipper 2003):

A *woman* should be (kept) barefoot and pregnant (barefoot, pregnant, and in the kitchen).
A *woman* without a man is like a fish without a net (A woman needs a man like a fish needs a net).
A *woman's* place is any place she wants to be.
Never run after a *woman* or a streetcar (Girls are like buses); if you miss one, another will come along soon.
Well-behaved *women* rarely (seldom) make history.
Women and elephants never forget.

Here are a few more lists for relatively high-frequency keywords, with "God" proverbs perhaps reflecting the religious preoccupation of parts of the American society. Proverbs about friends, time, age, love, beauty, knowing, pain, success, children, luck, and winning are nothing new as far as Anglo-American proverbs and those of other languages and cultures are concerned, but there are now texts that contain references that identify them as proverbs that could only have originated in more recent times, such as the drug-related "A friend with weed is a friend indeed" as an anti-proverb based on the traditional "A friend in need is a friend indeed," or "Act your age, not your IQ" with its reference to the score of an intelligence test. Above all, it should be noticed that most of these modern proverbs are rather literal statements of basic truths of modern life without couching them into expressive metaphors. Folklorists obviously will delight in the proverb "Every beauty needs her beast," a proverbial allusion to the fairy tale of "The Beauty and the Beast."

God (19)

 God can make a way out of no way. (Mieder 2010a: 171–86)
 God doesn't love ugly.
 God doesn't make junk (trash).
 God doesn't play dice.
 God is good, but don't dance in a small boat.
 God is in the details.
 God sends no cross that you cannot bear.
 Kill them all, and let *God* sort them out. (Russell 1999)
 Let go; let *God*.

friend (15)

 A (true, good) *friend* walks in when (all) others walk out.
 A *friend* with weed is a friend indeed.
 A *friend's* frown is better than a foe's smile.
 A true *friend* is one who knows all your faults and still loves (likes) you.
 Fast pay (payment) makes (for) fast *friends*.
 If you want a *friend*, get (buy) a dog.
 Little *friends* may prove (become) great friends.
 Make *friends* when you don't need them (before you need them).
 You cannot use your *friends* and have them too.

time (11)

 It's not how many *times* you get knocked down that matters but how many times you get back up.
 Once seen is better than a hundred *times* heard.
 Time flies when you're having fun.
 Time spent wishing is time wasted.
 Time you enjoy wasting is not (always) wasted time.
 To win, you only have to get up one more *time* than you fall down.
 Tough (Hard, Difficult) *times* call for tough (hard, difficult) decisions (choices).

age (8)

 Act your *age*, not your IQ.
 Act your *age*, not your shoe size.
 Age (Old age) is a high price (too high a price) to pay for maturity (Maturity is a high price to pay for growing up).
 Age is just a number.

Old *age* (Getting old) is better than the alternative (Old age sucks, but it's better than the alternative).
Old *age* is hell.

love (8)
If you *love* something, let it go (set it free); if it comes back to you, it is yours.
Love is where you find it.
Love it or leave it.
Make *love*, not war.
The *love* you take is equal to the love you make.

beauty (7)
Beauty does not buy happiness.
Beauty is pain.
Beauty may open doors but only virtue (strength, etc.) enters.
Every *beauty* needs her (a) beast.

know (7)
If you don't *know* what it is, (then) don't mess with (fool with, touch, eat) it.
You can't *know* where you're going unless you know where you've been.
You have to *know* when to hold them [cards] and know when to fold them.
You never *know* what you have till it's gone.

pain (7)
Don't tell me about the *pain* (labor pains); just show me the baby.
Pain (Fatigue) is nature's way of telling you to slow down (you need a rest).
Pain is the price of glory.

success (7)
Success (Victory) has many (a hundred) fathers, but failure (defeat) is an orphan.
Success is always preceded by preparation.
Success is never final (and failure is never fatal).

children (5)
Children (Our children, The children) are our future.
Children should be seen and not had.
Teach your (Parents must teach their) *children* to walk, then to walk away.

luck (5)
> *Luck* (Good luck, Bad luck) does not just happen.
> *Luck* is when (what happens when) preparation meets opportunity.
> You can't trust *luck*.

win (5)
> You can't *win* if you don't play.
> You can't *win* them all if you don't (unless you) win the first one.
> You have to be (get) in it to *win* it (You can't win it unless you are in it).

Proverbs from these groups organized according to various dominant keywords show at least in a generalized way some of the preoccupations of modern society. People at times appear to be obsessed with matters of age, beauty, love, luck, success, winning, and of course also the element of time (Lau 1996 [2003]). While it is problematic to deduce the worldview of masses of people from different countries by way of a corpus of proverbs (Dundes 1972 [2007]; White 1987), there is no denying that some themes permit us to draw tentative conclusions about the nature of modern proverbs. Continuing along these lines, it can also be said that people are concerned about pain and anxieties of various types, that they look for friendships in an ever more segmented and chaotic modern life, and that they continue to find solace in knowing that God might assist them in coping with modernity.

Sexuality, Obscenity, and Scatology in Modern Proverbs

With this said, we can turn to one last major group of 83 (5.8%) proverbs that belong to the realms of sexuality, obscenity, and scatology. Looking at earlier proverb collections, one might well get the impression that the folk has no so-called "dirty" proverbs. Even though paremiographers usually have included at least some such proverbs, they have in general been reluctant to collect them, or their publishers did not consent to publish them. And yet, some specialized collections have been published along these lines separately from major collections. Thus Ignace Bernstein in Poland followed his massive collection *Jüdische Sprichwörter und Redensarten* (1908 [1969]) up with a published manuscript of *Proverbia Judaeorum Erotica et Turpia. Jüdische Sprichwörter erotischen und rustikalen Inhalts* (1918 [1971]). And Edwin Miller Fogel augmented his important collection *Proverbs of the Pennsylvania Germans* (1929 [1995]) with a privately distributed *Supplement to Proverbs of the Pennsylvania Germans* (1929), which I had the audacity to include in the reprint of the major collection in 1995. Numerous smaller collections of obscene proverbs have been published in books, journals, and above all in three serial publications dedicated explicitly to taboo folkloric matters: *Anthropophyteia* (1904–13), *Kryptadia* (1883–1911 [1970]), and *Maledicta* (1977–2004). Today, with a more open attitude, popular collections of erotic proverbs and proverbial expressions are more readily available, to wit Marinus A. van den Broek's *Erotisch Spreekwoordenboek. Spreekwoorden en zegswijzen* (2002).

In any case, we have not shied away from including suggestive or obscene proverbs. Some are rather explicit and literal, while others are metaphorical and figurative to the point that many native speakers might have difficulty understanding them. But the fact remains that these proverbs exist, and they are part and parcel of the proverbial speech among the initiated, as our Google searches have proven beyond any doubt. They are part of the world of slang, graffiti, latrinalia (Dundes 1966 [2007]), and the so-called "vulgar tongue," with Francis Grose's *A Classical Dictionary of the Vulgar Tongue* (1785 [1931, 1992]) in the eighteenth century having set the stage for a rich tradition of compendia dealing with obscenities of the underworld and "upperworld." Proverbs deal with all aspects of life, and they certainly have always commented on such basic issues as sexuality. It should not be surprising, in an age that deals quite openly with sex in particular, that proverbs will be involved as well. Of course, it is exactly the way that proverbs comment on sexuality in a metaphorical way that makes these texts especially interesting.

The word "shit," less taboo in fine society than in former times, is quite prevalent in this type of proverb. But in most of these proverbs this scatological term does not refer to feces as such but rather to something bad or unpleasant. This is also the case for the slang term "bullshit" (often cited in its abbreviated form, "B.S."), with the meaning of "nonsense, lies, or exaggeration." A few examples, with the short proverb "Shit happens" (Rees 2005) and its clean variant "Stuff happens" being very popular indeed, will illustrate this:

If you can't dazzle them with *brilliance*, baffle (blind) them with bullshit (B.S.).
Bullshit can get you to the top, but it won't keep you there.
Life is a shit sandwich: the more bread you have, the less shit you eat.
Shit (Piss) or get off the *pot*.
Don't *shit* where you eat.
If you stir (up) *shit*, it will stink (you raise a stink).
Shit flows (runs, rolls) downhill.

Shit (Stuff) happens.
Shit rubs off.
You can't kill *shit* (Shit never dies). (Winick 2004)
You can't sprinkle *sugar* on shit (bullshit) and make (call) it candy (dessert, a
   treat, etc.).

A few other proverbs dealing with urination, flatulence, and feces (i.e.,
turds) are clear indications that people at times rely on this crassly expressed wisdom as a summary of some of the unpleasant aspects of human
interaction:

When you've got to *go*, you've got to go [reference to defecation].
The *one* who smelt it dealt it.
It's better to be *pissed* off than pissed on.
Opinions are like assholes (armpits)—everybody's got one (and they all stink).
Nobody minds the *smell* of his own farts (Everyone likes to smell his own farts).
Don't eat yellow *snow* [reference to urine].
Don't kick a (fresh) *turd* on a hot day.
You can't polish (gild) a *turd*.

Male genitalia, i.e., testicles and the penis, appear in various slang trans-
mutations, with "balls" in the two proverbs listed below usually not being
thought of as testicles by speakers. In other words, the metaphorical proverb
legitimizes a slang word so that the proverb "Take the bull by the balls" with
the meaning of taking charge of a situation becomes quite innocuous.

Grab them (If you've got them) by the *balls*, their hearts and minds will follow.
Take (Grab) the *bull* (life, the world) by the balls.
Big *car*, small dick (prick).
Chicks [girls] before dicks.
Don't let your *meat* loaf (meatloaf).
Big *mouth*, small pecker (dick, prick).
All *prick* and no pence.

As can be seen from these texts, males showing off with big cars or a big
mouth are quickly ridiculed by the claim that their apparent wealth and bois-
terousness is but a psychological coverup for a small penis size, which in this
case serves as a weakening of their masculinity. The proverb "All prick and no

pence" expresses the reverse, i.e., the macho man with his big penis has nothing else to show in the way of money or brains. But only the proverb "Don't
let your meat loaf" actually has a sexual meaning in that it gives the advice
that a man ought not to let his meat (penis) be inactive. Of course, it is a
well-known fact that males as well as females have had their ideas about the
matter of penis size, and this concern has found its way into modern proverbs as well. As sex surveys have shown, the feeling about the importance of
penis size for sexual satisfaction differs considerably, and this is mirrored in
the conflicting proverbs about this topic as well:

> It's not the *meat*, it's the motion.
> It's not the *size* of the boat (ship) but the motion of the ocean (that matters).
> *Size* does matter.
> *Size* doesn't matter (it's what you do with it, it's how you use it).

In any case, sexual intercourse appears to be the talk of the town everywhere, with some of the proverbs dealing with this matter being quite crude.
But they also show that their male originators unfortunately at times express
an aggressive or even violent attitude toward women, who are seen as mere
sex objects:

> Old enough to *bleed*, old enough to breed (butcher, stick, etc.).
> Close (Shut) your *eyes* and think of England (the Empire, the queen, Old Glory,
>   etc.).
> You don't fuck the *face*.
> *Fuck* them (Find them, fuck them) and forget them.
> If there's *grass* on the field [woman's pubic area], (you can) play ball.
> *Hit* it and quit it [short sexual act or relationship].
> Wham (Slam), bam—thank you, *ma'am*.
> If she *smokes*, she pokes [fornicates].
> Won't *tell*, won't swell [get pregnant], grateful as hell [regarding "older" women].

Much more positive are the two related proverbs "The blacker the berry
(meat), the sweeter the juice" and "The blacker the *meat*, the sweeter the
bone (piece)" that are part of the rich African American proverb tradition
(Daniel, Smitherman-Donaldson, and Jeremiah 1987; Prahlad 1996). While
they are clearly sexual metaphors, they do look positively at black women, as
we documented in the following entry:

The blacker the *berry* (meat), the sweeter the juice. 1929 *Chicago Defender* 2 Mar.: "They tell me that 'The blacker the berry, the sweeter the Juice:' is that so?" 1929 Wallace Thurman, *The Blacker the Berry* (New York: Macaulay) [3]; an epigraph to the novel gives the full form, presented as verse: "The blacker the berry / The sweeter the juice"—identifying it as a "Negro folk saying." 1934 Zora Neale Hurston, *Jonah's Gourd Vine* (Philadelphia: J. B. Lippincott) 234: "Ah could uh married one uh dem French women but shucks, gimme uh brown skin eve'y time. Blacker de berry sweeter de juice." [. . .] Cf. "The blakker the MEAT, the sweeter the bone." The proverb praises blackness, usually in regard to sexual desirability. (Prahlad 1996: 209–10)

Little wonder that modern Anglo-American proverbs also include cautionary texts that warn against sex at an early age, advocate safe sex, and also declare that people have the right to refuse a sexual encounter:

Keep your *dress* down and your panties (drawers) up.
No glove [condom], no *love*.
No means "no."

And what is the proverbial wisdom on sex in general, with the short word "sex" finally also appearing in a proverb collection? Once again we have conflicting attitudes, and the proverb "Everybody lies about sex" most likely has a solid truth claim to it:

If it exists, there is *porn* of it.
Bad *sex* is better than no sex (Any sex is better than no sex, The only bad sex is no sex).
Everybody lies about *sex*.
No *sex* is better than bad sex.
Sex sells.
There is no such *thing* as bad sex (a bad fuck, a bad piece).

As the extremely short proverb "Sex sells" states, sexuality has become an inducement to buying in the modern world obsessed with this topic. These sexual games have little to do with love, about which many traditional proverbs comment much more positively, without forgetting that love has its problems, too (Mieder 1989b).

When Dealing with Modern Proverbs: "Think Outside the Box"

In conclusion, let me reiterate that Charles Doyle, Fred Shapiro, and I have done our level best to register as many modern Anglo-American proverbs as possible. We have assembled 1,422 richly annotated proverbs, of which 731 (51.4%) have never been recorded in paremiographical or paremiological publications before. The other 691 (48.6%) proverbs were located text by text in numerous collections and scholarly books and articles. We have thus unearthed and registered an impressive proverbial corpus for the first time in one place in our *Dictionary of Modern Proverbs* (published in April 2012), and we hope that other proverb scholars will follow suit by compiling collections of modern proverbs for their languages and cultures. Regarding our collection, I can offer two more statistics that might be of considerable interest. Regarding the distribution of our 1,422 texts over the eleven decades from 1900 to 2010, it can be stated that the number of new proverbs appearing on the scene is quite constant, albeit with a noticeable drop-off during the two most recent decades:

1900–1909:	155 proverbs
1910–1919:	169
1920–1929:	152
1930–1939:	149
1940–1949:	124
1950–1959:	139
1960–1969:	154
1970–1979:	152
1980–1989:	116
1990–1999:	86
2000–2009	26
total	1,422

With time and more research, more proverbs will be identified for the period from 1990–2010, and since proverbs will surely be created as time goes on, the immediate presence will also yield proverbs that will be discovered in due time. And here then is the last statistical information, with the caveat that it is at times difficult to decide whether a certain proverb is metaphorical or not. But keeping such questionable cases in mind, 676 (47.5%) of our 1,422 proverbs are clearly metaphorical, with slightly more than half of our corpus (746, 52.5%) being literal statements. In order to draw definitive conclusions from this data, statistical information concerning the metaphorical/ non-metaphorical dichotomy of traditional proverbs would have to be obtained. For now, it is reasonable to state that modern Anglo-American proverbs might well be less metaphorical than the proverbs from earlier periods. But that is not to say that such eminently American proverbs as "Different strokes for different folks" (McKenzie 1996; Mieder 1989a: 317–32, 2006), "The grass is always greener on the other side of the fence" (Mieder 1993b [1994]), and "A picture is worth a thousand words" (Mieder 1990a [1993a], 2005a) with their international dissemination in English or loan translations are not as metaphorical as proverbs usually come (Mieder 2005b, 2005c)! One thing is for certain: proverbs are alive and well in the modern age (Mieder 1993a), and as folk wisdom they express the attitudes, beliefs, mores, and values of the people who use them. As such they are indeed "monumenta humana" (Kuusi 1957: 52), and warrant the attention of paremiographers and paremiologists throughout the world who, in order to identify and interpret them, must, to speak proverbially, "think outside the box."

BIBLIOGRAPHY

This chapter was first published with the same title in *Proverbium: Yearbook of International Proverb Scholarship* 29 (2012): 137–96.

Anthropophyteia. 1904–13. *Anthropophyteia. Jahrbuch für ethnologische, folkloristische und kulturgeschichtliche Sexualforschungen.* Friedrich S. Krauss, ed. 10 vols. Leipzig: Ethnologischer Verlag.

Arora, Shirley L. 1988. "'No Tickee, No Shirtee': Proverbial Speech and Leadership in Academe." *Inside Organizations: Understanding the Human Dimension.* Michael Owen Jones, Michael Dane Moore, and Richard Christopher Snyder, eds. Newbury Park, California: Sage. 179–89.

Barbour, Frances M. 1963. "Some Uncommon Sources of Proverbs." *Midwest Folklore* 13: 97–100.

Barrick, Mac E. 1979. "Better Red than Dead." *American Notes and Queries* 17: 143–44.

———. 1986. "Where's the Beef?" *Midwestern Journal of Language and Folklore* 12: 43–46.

Bernstein, Ignace. 1908 (1969, 1988). *Jüdische Sprichwörter und Redensarten.* Warschau: Kauffmann, 1908. Rpt. ed. Hans Peter Althaus. Hildesheim: Georg Olms, 1969; rpt. Wiesbaden: Fourier, 1988.

Bernstein, Ignace. 1918 (1971). *Proverbia Judaeorum Erotica et Turpia. Jüdische Sprichwörter erotischen und rustikalen Inhalts.* Als Manuskript gedruckt. Wien and Berlin: R. Löwit, 1918; rpt. Haifa: "Renaissance" Publishing, 1971.

Bertram, Anne, and Richard Spears. 1993. *NTC's Dictionary of Proverbs and Clichés.* Lincolnwood, Illinois: National Textbook.

Bloch, Arthur. 1979. *Murphy's Law and Other Reasons Why Things Go Wrong.* Los Angeles, California: Price, Stern, Sloan.

———. 1982a. *Murphy's Law: Book Two: More Reasons Why Things Go Wrong.* Los Angeles: Price, Stern, Sloan.

———. 1982b. *Murphy's Law: Book Three: Wrong Reasons Why Things Go More.* Los Angeles: Price, Stern, Sloan.

Broek, Marinus A. van den. 2002. *Erotisch Spreekwoordenboek. Spreekwoorden en zegswijzen.* Antwerpen: L.J. Veen.

Bryan, George B. 1999. "The Proverbial W. S. Gilbert: An Index to Proverbs in the Works of Gilbert and Sullivan." *Proverbium* 16: 21–35.

———. 2001. "An Unfinished List of Anglo-American Proverb Songs." *Proverbium* 18: 15–56.

Bryan, George B., and Wolfgang Mieder. 2005. *A Dictionary of Anglo-American Proverbs and Proverbial Phrases Found in Literary Sources of the Nineteenth and Twentieth Centuries.* New York: Peter Lang.

Chlosta, Christoph, and Peter Grzybek. 1995. "Empirical and Folkloristic Paremiology: Two to Quarrel or to Tango?" *Proverbium* 12: 67–85.

Chlosta, Christoph, and Torsten Ostermann. 2002. "Suche *Apfel* Finde *Stamm*. Überlegungen zur Nutzung des Internats in der Sprichwortforschung." *"Wer A sägt, muss auch B sägen": Beiträge zur Phraseologie und Sprichwortforschung aus dem Westfälischen Arbeitskreis.* Dietrich Hartmann and Jan Wirrer, eds. Baltmannsweiler: Schneider Verlag Hohengehren. 39–56.

Cohen, Gerald Leonard. 1989. "'Close But No Cigar.'" *Studies in Slang* 2: 100–102.

Colson, Jean-Pierre. 2007. "The World Wide Web as a Corpus for Set Phrases." *Phraseology: An International Handbook of Contemporary Research.* Harald Burger, Dmitrij Dobrovol'skij, Peter Kühn, and Neal R. Norrick, eds. 2 vols. Berlin: Walter de Gruyter. II, 1071–77.

Daniel, Jack L., Geneva Smitherman-Donaldson, and Milford A. Jeremiah. 1987. "Makin' a Way Outa No Way: The Proverb Tradition in Black Experience." *Journal of Black Studies* 17: 482–508.

Doyle, Charles Clay. 1996 (2003). "On 'New' Proverbs and the Conservativeness of Proverb Dictionaries." *Proverbium* 13: 69–84. Also in *Cognition, Comprehension, and Communication: A Decade of North American Proverb Studies (1990–2000).* Wolfgang Mieder, ed. Baltmannsweiler: Schneider Verlag Hohengehren, 2003. 85–98.

———. 2001. "Is the Third Time a Charm? A Review of *The Concise Oxford Dictionary of Proverbs*." *Proverbium* 18: 453–68.

———. 2007a. "A Good Man Is Hard to Find: The Proverb." *Flannery O'Connor Review* 5: 5–22.

———. 2007b. "Collections of Proverbs and Proverb Dictionaries: Some Historical Observations on What's in Them and What's Not (with a Note on Current 'Gendered' Proverbs)." *Phraseology and Culture in English.* Paul Skandera, ed. Berlin: Mouton de Gruyter. 181–203.

———. 2009. "'Use It or Lose It': The Proverb, Its Pronoun, and Their Antecedents." *Proverbium* 26: 105–18.

Doyle, Charles Clay, Wolfgang Mieder, and Fred R. Shapiro. 2012. *The Dictionary of Modern Proverbs.* New Haven, Connecticut: Yale University Press.

Dundes, Alan. 1966 (2007). "Here I Sit—A Study of American Latrinalia." *The Kroeber Anthropological Society Papers* 34: 91–105. Also in Alan Dundes, *The Meaning of Folklore: The Analytical Essays of Alan Dundes.* Simon J. Bronner, ed. Logan: Utah State University Press, 2007. 360–74.

———. 1972 (2007). "Folk Ideas as Units of Worldview." *Towards New Perspectives in Folklore.* Américo Paredes and Richard Bauman, eds. Austin: University of Texas Press. 93–103. Also in Alan Dundes, *The Meaning of Folklore: The Analytical Essays of Alan Dundes.* Simon J. Bronner, ed. Logan: Utah State University Press, 2007. 179–92.

———. 1975 (1981). "On the Structure of the Proverb." *Proverbium* 25: 961–73. Also in *The Wisdom of Many: Essays on the Proverb.* Wolfgang Mieder and Alan Dundes, eds. New York: Garland. 43–64.

Dundes, Alan, and Carl R. Pagter. 1987. *When You're Up to Your Ass in Alligators: More Urban Folklore from the Paperwork Empire.* Detroit, Michigan: Wayne State University Press.

Dundes, Lauren, Michael Streiff, and Alan Dundes. 1999 (2003). "'When You Hear Hoofbeats, Think Horses, Not Zebras': A Folk Medical Diagnostic Proverb." *Proverbium* 16: 95-103. Also in *Cognition,*

Comprehension, and Communication: A Decade of North American Proverb Studies (1990–2000)*. Wolfgang Mieder, ed. Baltmannsweiler: Schneider Verlag Hohengehren, 2003. 99–107.

Flavell, Linda, and Roger Flavell. 1993. *Dictionary of Proverbs and Their Origins*. London: Kyle Cathie.

Fogel, Edwin Miller. 1929 (1995). *Proverbs of the Pennsylvania Germans*. Lancaster, Pennsylvania: Lancaster Press; rpt. ed. Wolfgang Mieder. Bern: Peter Lang, 1995.

———. 1929. *Supplement to Proverbs of the Pennsylvania Germans*. Fogelsville, Pennsylvania: Americana Germanica Press.

Folsom, Steven. 1993. "A Discography of American Country Music Hits Employing Proverbs: Covering the Years 1986–1992." *Proceedings for the 1993 Annual Conference of the Southwest-Texas Popular Culture Association*. Sue Poor, ed. Stillwater, Oklahoma: Southwest-Texas Popular Culture Association. 31–42.

Frank, Lawrence. 1983. *Playing Hardball: The Dynamics of Baseball Folk Speech*. New York: Peter Lang.

Grose, Francis. 1785 (1931, 1992). *A Classical Dictionary of the Vulgar Tongue*. London: S. Hooper, 1785; rpt. ed. Eric Partridge. London: Scholartis, 1931; rpt. New York: Dorset, 1992.

Grzybek, Peter. "Zum Status der Untersuchung von Satzlängen in der Sprichwortforschung: Methodologische Vor-Bemerkungen." *Slovo vo vremeni i prostranstve. K 60-letiiu professora V. M. Mokienko*. G. A. Lilich, A. K. Birikh, and E. K. Nikolaeva, eds. Sankt-Peterburg: Folio-Press, 2000. 430–57.

Haas, Heather H. 2008. "Proverb Familiarity in the United States: Cross-Regional Comparisons of the Paremiological Minimum." *Journal of American Folklore* 121: 319–47.

Hernadi, Paul, and Francis Steen. 1999 (2003). "The Tropical Landscape of Proverbia: A Crossdisciplinary Travelogue." *Style* 33: 1–20. Also in *Cognition, Comprehension, and Communication: A Decade of North American Proverb Studies (1990–2000)*. Wolfgang Mieder, ed. Baltmannsweiler: Schneider Verlag Hohengehren, 2003. 185–204.

Higbee, Kenneth L., and Richard J. Millard. 1983. "Visual Imagery and Familiarity Ratings for 203 Sayings." *American Journal of Psychology* 96: 211–22.

Hoffman, Robert R., and Richard P. Honeck. 1987. "Proverbs, Pragmatics, and the Ecology of Abstract Categories." *Cognition and Symbolic Structures: The Psychology of Metaphoric Transformation*. Robert E. Haskell, ed. Norwood, NJ: Ablex. 121–40.

Honeck, Richard P., and Jeffrey Welge. 1997 (2003). "Creation of Proverbial Wisdom in the Laboratory." *Journal of Psycholinguistic Research* 26: 605–29. Also in *Cognition, Comprehension, and Communication: A Decade of North American Proverb Studies (1990–2000)*. Wolfgang Mieder, ed. Baltmannsweiler: Schneider Verlag Hohengehren, 2003. 205–30.

Jente, Richard. 1931–32. "The American Proverb." *American Speech* 7: 342–48.

Kerschen, Lois. 1998. *American Proverbs about Women: A Reference Guide*. Westport, CT: Greenwood.

Kirshenblatt-Gimblett, Barbara. 1973 (1981). "Toward a Theory of Proverb Meaning." *Proverbium* 22: 821–27. Also in *The Wisdom of Many: Essays on the Proverb*. Wolfgang Mieder and Alan Dundes, eds. New York: Garland. 111–21.

Kleinberger Günther, Ulla. 2006. "Phraseologie und Sprichwörter in der digitalen Öffentlichkeit—am Beispiel von Chats." *Phraseology in Motion I. Methoden und Kritik. Akten der Internationalen Tagung zur Phraseologie (Basel, 2004)*. Annelies Häcki Buhofer and Harald Burger, eds. Baltmannsweiler: Schneider Verlag Hohengehren. 229–43.

Krummenacher, Adrian. 2007. "'To Live and Let Die': Sprichwörter, Redensarten und Zitate in den James-Bond-Filmen." *Sprichwörter sind Goldes wert. Parömiologische Studien zu Kultur, Literatur und Medien*. Wolfgang Mieder, ed. Burlington, Vermont: University of Vermont. 127–52.

Kryptadia. 1883–1911 (1970). No editor given. *Kryptadia. Recueil de documents pour servir à l'étude des traditions populaires*, 12 vols. Paris: H. Welter; rpt. Darmstadt: J.G. Bläschke, 1970.

Kuusi, Matti. 1957. *Parömiologische Betrachtungen*. Helsinki: Suomalainen Tiedeakatemia.

Lau, Kimberly J. 1996 (2003). "'It's about Time': The Ten Proverbs Most Frequently Used in Newspapers and Their Relation to American Values." *Proverbium* 13: 135–59. Also in *Cognition, Comprehension, and Communication: A Decade of North American Proverb Studies (1990–2000)*. Wolfgang Mieder, ed. Baltmannsweiler: Schneider Verlag Hohengehren, 2003. 231–54.

Lau, Kimberly J., Peter Tokofsky, and Stephen D. Winick, eds. 2004. *What Goes Around Comes Around: The Circulation of Proverbs in Contemporary Life: Essays in Honor of Wolfgang Mieder*. Logan, Utah: Utah State University Press.

Lauhakangas, Outi. 2001. "How to Avoid Losing a Needle in a Haystack. Challenges and Problems of Compiling Paremiological Databases." *Tautosakos Darbai / Folklore Studies* (Vilnius, Lithuania) 22: 93–102.

Litovkina, Anna T. 2000. *A Proverb a Day Keeps Boredom Away*. Pécs-Szekszárd, Hungary: IPF-Könyek.

Litovkina, Anna T., and Carl Lindahl, eds. 2007. *Anti-Proverbs in Contemporary Societies*. Budapest: Akadémiai Kiadó. (*Acta Ethnographica Hungarica* 52).

Litovkina, Anna T., and Wolfgang Mieder. 2006. *Old Proverbs Never Die, They Just Diversify: A Collection of Anti-Proverbs*. Burlington, Vermont: University of Vermont; Veszprém, Hungary: Pannonian University of Veszprém.

Maledicta. 1977–2004. *Maledicta. The International Journal of Verbal Aggression*. Reinhold Aman, ed. 13 vols. Waukesha, Wisconsin: Maledicta.

Manser, Martin H. 2002. *Facts on File Dictionary of Proverbs*. New York: Facts on File.

McKenzie, Alyce M. 1996. "'Different Strokes for Different Folks': America's Quintessential Postmodern Proverb." *Theology Today* 53: 201–12.

Mieder, Barbara, and Wolfgang Mieder. 1977 (1981). "Tradition and Innovation: Proverbs in Advertising." *Journal of Popular Culture* 11: 308–19. Also in *The Wisdom of Many: Essays on the Proverb*. Wolfgang Mieder and Alan Dundes, eds. New York: Garland, 1981. 309–22.

Mieder, Wolfgang. 1982. "'Eine Frau ohne Mann ist wie ein Fisch ohne Velo.'" *Sprachspiegel* 38: 141–42.

———. 1985. *Sprichwort, Redensart, Zitat. Tradierte Formelsprache in der Moderne*. Bern: Peter Lang.

———. 1987 (1993). "The Proverb in the Modern Age: Old Wisdom in New Clothing." In Wolfgang Mieder, *Tradition and Innovation in Folk Literature*. Hanover, NH: University Press of New England. 118–56, 248–55 (notes). Also in Wolfgang Mieder, *Proverbs Are Never Out of Season: Popular Wisdom in the Modern Age*. New York: Oxford University Press, 1993. 58–96.

———. 1988. "Proverbs in American Popular Songs." *Proverbium* 5: 85–101.

———. 1989a. *American Proverbs: A Study of Texts and Contexts*. Bern: Peter Lang.

———. 1989b. *Love: Proverbs of the Heart*. Shelburne, Vermont: New England Press.

———. 1990a (1993). "'A Picture Is Worth a Thousand Words': From Advertising Slogan to American Proverb." *Southern Folklore* 47: 207–25. Also in Wolfgang Mieder, *Proverbs Are Never Out of Season: Popular Wisdom in the Modern Age*. New York: Oxford University Press, 1993. 135–51.

———. 1990b. "Prolegomena to Prospective Paremiography." *Proverbium* 7: 133–44.

———. 1992 (1994). "Paremiological Minimum and Cultural Literacy." *Creativity and Tradition in Folklore*. Simon J. Bronner, ed. Logan, Utah: Utah State University Press. 185–203. Also in *Wise Words: Essays on the Proverb*. Wolfgang Mieder, ed. New York: Garland, 1994. 297–316.

———. 1993a. *Proverbs Are Never Out of Season: Popular Wisdom in the Modern Age*. New York: Oxford University Press.

———. 1993b (1994). "'The Grass Is Always Greener on the Other Side of the Fence.'" *Proverbium* 10: 151–84. Also in *Wise Words: Essays on the Proverb*. Wolfgang Mieder, ed. New York: Garland, 1994. 515–42.

———, ed. 1994. *Wise Words: Essays on the Proverb*. New York: Garland.

———. 1996. "'No Tickee, No Washee': Subtleties of a Proverbial Slur." *Western Folklore* 55: 1–40. Also in Wolfgang Mieder, *The Politics of Proverbs: From Traditional Wisdom to Proverbial Stereotypes*. Madison, Wisconsin: University of Wisconsin Press, 1997. 160–89, 227–35 (notes).

———. 1997. *The Politics of Proverbs: From Traditional Wisdom to Proverbial Stereotypes*. Madison, Wisconsin: University of Wisconsin Press.

———. 2000. "'Proverbs Bring It to Light': Modern Paremiology in Retrospect and Prospect." In Wolfgang Mieder, *Strategies of Wisdom: Anglo-American and German Proverb Studies*. Baltmannsweiler: Schneider Verlag Hohengehren. 7–36.

———, ed. 2003a. *Cognition, Comprehension, and Communication: A Decade of North American Proverb Studies (1990–2000)*. Baltmannsweiler: Schneider Verlag Hohengehren.

———. 2003b. *English Proverbs*. Stuttgart: Phillip Reclam.

———. 2004. *Proverbs: A Handbook*. Westport, Connecticut: Greenwood.

———. 2005a. "'A Proverb Is Worth a Thousand Words': Folk Wisdom in the Modern Mass Media." *Proverbium* 22: 167–233.

———. 2005b (2005c). "American Proverbs as an International, National, and Global Phenomenon." *Tautosakos Darbai/Folklore Studies* (Vilnius, Lithuania) 30: 57–72. Also in Wolfgang Mieder, *Proverbs Are the Best Policy: Folk Wisdom and American Politics*. Logan, Utah: Utah State University Press, 2005. 1–14, 244–48 (notes).

———. 2005c. *Proverbs Are the Best Policy: Folk Wisdom and American Politics*. Logan, Utah: Utah State University Press.

———. 2006. "'Different Strokes for Different Folks.'" *Encyclopedia of African American Folklore*. Sw. Anand Prahlad, ed. 3 vols. Westport, Connecticut: Greenwood. I: 324–27.

———. 2009a. "New Proverbs Run Deep: Prolegomena to a Dictionary of Modern Anglo-American Proverbs." *Proverbium* 26: 237–74.

———. 2009b. *"Yes We Can": Barack Obama's Proverbial Rhetoric*. New York: Peter Lang.

———. 2010a. *Making a Way Out of No Way: Martin Luther King's Sermonic Proverbial Rhetoric*. New York: Peter Lang.

———. 2010b. "The Golden Rule as a Political Imperative for the World: President Barack Obama's Proverbial Messages Abroad." *Millî Folklor* 22: 26–35.

———. 2010c. "'The World is a Place': Barack Obama's Proverbial View of an Interconnected Globe." *Sopostavitel'naia filologiia i polilingvizm*. A. A. Aminova and N. N. Fattakhova, eds. Kazan', Tatarstan (Russia): G. Ibragimova An RT. 192–96.

———. 2011. "'It Takes a Village to Change the World': Proverbial Politics and the Ethics of Place." *Journal of American Folklore* 124: 4–28.

Mieder, Wolfgang, and George B. Bryan. 1983 (1985). "'Zum Tango gehören zwei.'" *Der Sprachdienst* 27: 100–102, 181. Also in Wolfgang Mieder, *Sprichwort, Redensart, Zitat. Tradierte Formelsprache in der Moderne*. Bern: Peter Lang, 1985. 151–54.

———. 1997. *The Proverbial Harry S. Truman: An Index to Proverbs in the Works of Harry S. Truman*. New York: Peter Lang.

Mieder, Wolfgang, and Alan Dundes, eds. 1981. *The Wisdom of Many: Essays on the Proverb*. New York: Garland.

Mieder, Wolfgang, Stewart A. Kingsbury, and Kelsie B. Harder, eds. 1992. *A Dictionary of American Proverbs*. New York: Oxford University Press.

Mieder, Wolfgang, and Janet Sobieski, eds. 2006. *"Gold Nuggets or Fool's Gold?" Magazine and Newspaper Articles on the (Ir)relevance of Proverbs and Proverbial Phrases*. Burlington, Vermont: University of Vermont.

Nierenberg, Jess. 1983 (1994). "Proverbs in Graffiti: Taunting Traditional Wisdom." *Maledicta* 7: 41–58. Also in *Wise Words: Essays on the Proverb.* Wolfgang Mieder, ed. New York: Garland. 543–61.

Nussbaum, Stan. 2005. *American Cultural Baggage [i.e., Proverbs]: How to Recognize and Deal with It.* Maryknoll, New York: Orbis.

Petrova, Roumyana. 1996. "Language and Culture: One Step Further in the Search for Common Ground." *Europe from East to West: Proceedings of the First International European Studies Conference.* Martin Dangerfield, Glyn Hambrook, and Ludmilla Kostova, eds. Varna, Bulgaria: PIC. 237–48.

Pickering, David. 2001. *Cassell's Dictionary of Proverbs.* 2nd ed. London: Cassell.

Pickering, David, Alan Isaacs, and Elizabeth Martin. 1992. *Brewer's Dictionary of 20th-Century Phrase and Fable.* Boston: Houghton Mifflin.

Prahlad, Sw. Anand. 1994 (2003). "'No Guts, No Glory': Proverbs, Values and Image among Anglo-American University Students." *Southern Folklore* 51: 285–98. Also in *Cognition, Comprehension, and Communication: A Decade of North American Proverb Studies (1990–2000).* Wolfgang Mieder, ed. Baltmannsweiler: Schneider Verlag Hohengehren, 2003. 443–58.

———. 1996. *African-American Proverbs in Context.* Jackson, Mississippi: University Press of Mississippi.

———. 2001. *Reggae Wisdom: Proverbs in Jamaican Music.* Jackson, Mississippi: University Press of Mississippi.

———. 2004. "The Proverb and Fetishism in American Advertisements." *What Goes Around Comes Around: The Circulation of Proverbs in Contemporary Life: Essays in Honor of Wolfgang Mieder.* Kimberly J. Lau, Peter Tokofsky, and Stephen D. Winick, eds. Logan, Utah: Utah State University Press. 127–51.

———, ed. 2006. *Encyclopedia of African American Folklore.* 3 vols. Westport, Connecticut: Greenwood.

Ratcliffe, Susan. 2006. *Oxford Dictionary of Phrase, Saying, and Quotation.* 3rd ed. Oxford: Oxford University Press.

Rees, Nigel. 1984. *Sayings of the Century: The Stories Behind the Twentieth Century's Quotable Sayings.* London: Allen & Unwin.

———. 1991. *Bloomsbury Dictionary of Phrase & Allusion.* London: Bloomsbury.

———. 1995. *Phrases & Sayings.* London: Bloomsbury.

———. 2005. "'Shit Happens.'" *"Quote . . . Unquote" Newsletter* 14, no. 2: 6.

———. 2006. *A Word in Your Shell-Like: 6,000 Curious and Everyday Phrases Explained.* London: HarperCollins.

Rittersbacher, Christa, and Matthias Mösch. 2005. "A Haystack Full of Precious Needles—The Internet and Its Utility for Paremiologists." *Proverbium* 22: 337–62.

Room, Adrian. 2000. *Brewer's Dictionary of Modern Phrase & Fable.* London: Cassell.

Russell, Melissa Anne. 1999. "Kill 'Em All and Let God Sort 'Em Out: The Proverb as an Expression of Verbal Aggression." *Proverbium* 16: 287–302.

Schipper, Mineke. 2003. *"Never Marry a Woman with Big Feet": Women in Proverbs from Around the World.* New Haven, Connecticut: Yale University Press.

Sevilla Muñoz, Julia. 2009. "The Challenges of Paremiology in the XXI. Century." *Proceedings of the Second Interdisciplinary Colloquium on Proverbs, 9th to 16th November 2008.* Rui J. B. Soares and Outi Lauhakangas, eds. Tavira, Portugal: Tipografia Tavirense. 438–48.

Shapiro, Fred. 2006. *Yale Book of Quotations.* New Haven, Connecticut: Yale University Press.

Sobieski, Janet, and Wolfgang Mieder, eds. 2005. *"So Many Heads, So Many Wits": An Anthology of English Proverb Poetry.* Burlington, Vermont: University of Vermont.

Speake, Jennifer. 2008. *The Oxford Dictionary of Proverbs.* 5th ed. Oxford: Oxford University Press.

Stevenson, Burton. 1948. *Home Book of Proverbs, Maxims and Familiar Phrases.* New York: Macmillan.

Taft, Michael. 1994. "Proverbs in the Blues: How Frequent is Frequent?" *Proverbium* 11: 227–58.

Taylor, Archer. 1931 (1985). *The Proverb*. Cambridge, Massachusetts: Harvard University Press; rpt. ed. Wolfgang Mieder. Bern: Peter Lang, 1985.

———. 1939 (1975). "The Study of Proverbs." *Modern Language Forum* 24: 57–83. Also in Archer Taylor, *Selected Writings on Proverbs*. Wolfgang Mieder, ed. Helsinki: Suomalainen Tiedeakatemia. 40–47 (co-authored with Bartlett Jere Whiting, Francis W. Bradley, Richard Jente, and Morris Palmer Tilley).

———. 1958. "'The Customer Is Always Right.'" *Western Folklore* 17: 54–55.

———. 1969. "How Nearly Complete Are the Collections of Proverbs?" *Proverbium* 14: 369–71.

Titelman, Gregory. 2000. *Random House Dictionary of America's Popular Proverbs and Sayings*. 2nd ed. New York: Random House.

Tóthné Litovkina, Anna. 1998. "An Analysis of Popular American Proverbs [found in the Folklore Archive at UC Berkeley] and Their Use in Language Teaching." *Die heutige Bedeutung oraler Tradition: Ihre Archivierung, Publikation und Index-Erschließung*. Walther Heissig and Rüdiger Schott, eds. Opladen: Westdeutscher Verlag. 131–58.

Umurova, Gulnas. 2005. *Was der Volksmund in einem Sprichwort verpackt . . . Moderne Aspekte des Sprichwortgebrauchs—anhand von Beispielen aus dem Internet*. Bern: Peter Lang.

Valdaeva, Tatiana. 2003. "Anti-Proverbs or New Proverbs: The Use of English Anti-Proverbs and Their Stylistic Analysis." *Proverbium* 20: 379–90.

White, Geoffrey M. 1987. "Proverbs and Cultural Models: An American Psychology of Problem Solving." *Cultural Models in Language and Thought*. Dorothy Holland and Naomi Quinn, eds. Cambridge, UK: Cambridge University Press. 151–72.

Whiting, Bartlett Jere. 1989. *Modern Proverbs and Proverbial Sayings*. Cambridge, Massachusetts: Harvard University Press.

Wilson, F. P. 1970. *Oxford Dictionary of English Proverbs*. 3rd ed. Oxford: Clarendon.

Winick, Stephen D. 1998. *The Proverb Process: Intertextuality and Proverbial Innovation in Popular Culture*. Diss., University of Pennsylvania.

———. 2001. "'Garbage In, Garbage Out,' and Other Dangers: Using Computer Databases to Study Proverbs." *Proverbium* 18: 354–64.

———. 2003. "Intertextuality and Innovation in a Definition of the Proverb Genre." *Cognition, Comprehension, and Communication: A Decade of North American Proverb Studies (1990–2000)*. Wolfgang Mieder, ed. Baltmannsweiler: Schneider Verlag Hohengehren. 571–601.

———. 2004. "'You Can't Kill Shit': Occupational Proverb and Metaphorical System Among Young Medical Professionals." *What Goes Around Comes Around: The Circulation of Proverbs in Contemporary Life: Essays in Honor of Wolfgang Mieder*. Kimberly J. Lau, Peter Tokofsky, and Stephen D. Winick, eds. Logan, Utah: Utah State University Press. 86–106.

Proverbs in Politics

4. "LIFE, LIBERTY, AND THE PURSUIT OF HAPPINESS"
Martin Luther King's Proverbial Struggle for Equality

A vast array of biographies and studies have celebrated Martin Luther King (1929–1968) as a civil rights leader, a defender of nonviolence in the struggle for desegregation, a champion for the poor, an anti-war proponent, and a broad-minded visionary of an interrelated world of free people. The proverbial truths expressed in the beginning of the Declaration of Independence that "All men are created equal" and that they have the right to "life, liberty, and the pursuit of happiness" form the basis of King's engaged and heartfelt fight for freedom, universal suffrage, anti-racism, and socioeconomic improvements for minorities. As a communicator *par excellence*, he made ample use of fixed phrases as leitmotifs in his effective oral and written rhetoric in the service of a plethora of topics and causes. Even though the term "proverb" does not belong to King's active vocabulary, he most certainly delights in using folk and Bible proverbs, famous quotations (of which some have taken on a definite claim to proverbiality), and a wealth of proverbial phrases.

Lack of Research on Martin Luther King's Formulaic Rhetoric

It is incomprehensible that the vast scholarship on King's magisterial use of the English language has hardly commented on the proverbial nature of his multifaceted communications. It is as if the study of rhetoric as a discipline, by not stressing phraseological matters, has prevented any attention being paid to such preformulated language. As the massive two-volume collection of recent essays entitled *Phraseology: An International Handbook of Contemporary Research* (Burger et al. 2007) shows, this picture is slowly changing; rhetorical scholars are now more eager to include the disciplines of phraseology in general and paremiology (the study of proverbs) in particular (Mieder 2009a). Nevertheless, regarding the proverbial language of Martin Luther King, the studies dedicated to his highly expressive and emotive language have almost completely ignored his reliance on proverbs and proverbial expressions, the exceptions being my former student Dženeta Karabegović's revealing short essay "'No Lie Can Live Forever': Zur sprich-wörtlichen Rhetorik von Martin Luther King" (2007), and my own book *"Making a Way Out of No Way": Martin Luther King's Sermonic Proverbial Rhetoric* (2010).

Having surveyed the extant secondary literature on King's sermonic and sociopolitical language, there is little to report. Mervyn A. Warren deals with the "vividness and imagery" as well as the "figures of speech" (Warren 1966: 201; also in Warren 2001: 145) in King's style, but no mention is made of pro-verbial matters in the discussion of alliteration, anaphora, comparison, me-taphor, repetition, and simile (See Warren 1966: 201–8; also in Warren 2001: 145–51). Other scholars speak of King's "figures of speech—similes, meta-phors, allegories, and personifications" (Boulware 1969: 254), his "metapho-ricality" (Spillers 1971: 17 [1989: 879]), and his stylistic preoccupation with metaphors, repetition, parallelism, and antithesis (Ensslin 1990: 120–22), with Lewis V. Baldwin referring in passing to "King's eloquence and brilliant use of imagery and the folk idiom [that] help explain the ease with which he found a route to the hearts and eventually to the heads of his people" (Bald-win 1991: 296). Jonathan Rieder makes the keen observation that

> A King [sermonic or rhetorical] performance was a collective act [. . .]: his [. . .] sermons and speeches were collage compositions. [. . .] If he was able to provoke assorted audiences, it was because his life lay at the junction of diver-se lines of affiliation that taught him to speak in many tongues. Those net-works formed a transmission belt through which the raw materials of song, argument, homily, citation, inflection, philosophy, sermon, rhythm, examples, authors, theology, and ideas flowed. (Rieder 2008: 10–11)

All of these remarks are perfectly fitting, but why are proverbs and proverbial phrases missing in these enumerations of King's elements of style?

Scholars who have pointed out that King's language is very much infor-med by orally transmitted speech patterns might especially have been expec-ted to make a point of his reliance on fixed phrases. They discuss the sense of community during sermons that often included call-response or testifying between King as the preacher and his audience (Harrison and Harrison 1993: 169; Baldwin 1988: 81–82 [1989: 41–42]). This give and take of the sermonic practice in African American churches (see Daniel and Smitherman 1976: 33–39; Daniel 1979) requires a language filled with formulaic expressions that help the audience react as a group to statements made in the pulpit. Bruce Rosenberg has shown that repetition of familiar words, phrases, and stories from the Bible enhance the comprehensibility and effectiveness of orally delivered sermons (Rosenberg 1970: 105), and Walter J. Ong has pointed out that traditional and formulaic phrases take on an extremely important communicative role in sermons and speeches that address audiences orally:

> Formulas help implement rhythmic discourse and also act as mnemonic aids in their own right, as set expressions circulating through the mouths and ears of all. "Red in the morning, the sailor's warning; red in the night, the sailor's delight." "Divide and conquer." "To err is human, to forgive is divine." [. . .] "Chase off nature and she returns at a gallop." Fixed, often rhythmically balanced, expressions of this sort and of other sorts can be found occasionally in print, indeed can be "looked up" in books of sayings, but in oral cultures they are not occasional. They are incessant. They form the substance of thought itself. Thought in any extended form is impossible without them, for it consists in them. (Ong 1982: 35)

Referring to Ong's findings, Keith D. Miller, as the undeniable expert on King's differentiated rhetoric, has characterized his discursive use of formulaic language as "shared treasure, voice merging, and self-making" (Miller 1990: 77; see also Farrell 1991; Miller 1991b). Miller also observed:

> In the folk pulpit, one gains an authoritative voice by adopting the persona of previous speakers as one adapts the sermons and formulaic expressions of a sanctified tradition. Like generations of folk preachers before him, King often borrowed, modified, and synthesized themes, analogies, metaphors, quotations, illustrations, arrangements, and forms of argument used by other preachers. Like other folk preachers, King typically ended his oral sermons (and almost every major speech) by merging his voice with the lyrics of a spiritual, hymn, or gospel song. (Miller 1991a: 121)

In other words, while many of his powerful formulaic statements are not his own, it is the "blending" (Rieder 2008: 160) of them with his own voice that assures the discursive powers of Martin Luther King as a speaker and writer.

David Fleer has spoken in this regard of King's impressive and innovative "reformation" of his vast amount of sources, reminding scholars and others that by 1957 King gave at least two hundred sermons and speeches a year (in later years one or two a day!). It should not be surprising that he had to rely on voice merging and certain sets of materials that he could easily intersperse into his sermons and speeches. This voice merging is part and parcel of his compelling and persuasive oral and written rhetoric, with his creative transformation or reformation of his sources making King a rhetorical artist (see Fleet 1995: 158–60). Similar thoughts and arguments were also presented by Keith D. Miller, arguing that King borrowed from many sources of which a considerable amount "are highly familiar—the modern equivalents of the commonplaces of classical rhetoric" (Miller 1986: 249 [1989: 643]).

Rosa Louise Parks (1913–2005), the seamstress and civil rights champion who precipitated the successful bus boycott in Montgomery, Alabama, by her refusal on December 1, 1955, to adhere to the segregated bus-seating policies in that city, has perhaps characterized King's proverbially informed oratory the best: "But let us remember that what gave his speeches and sermons legitimacy was that Dr. King didn't just talk the talk; he walked the walk from Montgomery to Memphis, enduring jails, beatings, abuse, threats, the bombing of his home, and the highest sacrifice a person can make for a righteous cause" (Carson and Shepard 2001: 4). Yes, indeed, Martin Luther King is the epitome of the black folk wisdom of "talking the talk and walking the walk." He breathed, talked, and walked civil rights by word and deed, setting an example for millions of African Americans in particular and Americans in general. In his nonviolent but compassionate and unbending struggle for "life, liberty and the pursuit of happiness" he left no proverbial stone unturned, making ample use of Bible and folk proverbs as well as proverbial expressions and proverb-like quotations to add metaphorical and emotive expressiveness to his oral and written messages (see Mieder 2010).

Martin Luther King's Sermonic Use of Proverbs

Even though King was not prone to use the term "proverb," he certainly based a number of sermonic outlines and actual sermons on the explication of proverbs, citing them at times as leitmotifs but not explicitly referring to them as Bible or folk proverbs. Always being the preacher and teacher, he would call on such proverbial wisdom as a base of his religious and social messages. An early example can be seen from a minuscule sermon introduction with the proverb "Life is what you make it" as a title:

Life Is What You Make It

INTRODUCTION

Many people wander into the world, and they pick up everything they can get their hands upon looking for life. They never get it. What they get is existence. Existence is what you find; life is what you create. Therefore, if life ever seems worth while to you, it is not because you found it that way, but because you made it so. (VI, 83–84; Nov. 30, 1948–Feb. 16, 1949; all Roman numerals refer to the six volumes edited by Clayborne Carson et al., *The Papers of Martin Luther King, Jr.* [1992–2007])

Always having yet another sermon in mind, King also wrote down short sermon conclusions that might come in handy when another text needed to be composed in a hurry. These introductions and conclusions were kept in folders for ready reference. The following example is once again of special interest, since King uses the introductory formula "there is an old saying" to indicate that he is citing a folk proverb. The "saying"-designation implies a proverb, of course, but even this term appears very seldom in King's communications:

Success In Life

There is an old saying, "If wishes were horses beggars would ride." Friends, the great highroad of success lies along the old high-way of steadfast well-doing; and they who are the most industrious and the most persistent, and work in the truest spirit, will invariably be the most successful. Success treads on the heels of every right effort. (VI, 85; Nov. 30, 1948–Feb. 16, 1949)

While such paragraphs are mere rudiments, King also has left us with complete sermons with proverbial titles and an ensuing explication of the texts. The quintessential example is King's preoccupation with the Bible proverb "Love your enemies" (Matt. 5:44), which he explicated in a number of related "Loving Your Enemies" sermons. In fact, King used the proverb "Love your enemies" a total of 53 times, and it will surprise no one that it is his favorite proverb as an expression of his Christian-based "fundamental concept of nonviolence" (Hedgepeth 1984: 81 [1989: 543]). In his "Loving Your Enemies" sermon delivered on November 17, 1957, at the Dexter Avenue Baptist Church in Montgomery, King points out that the idea of nonviolence is perfectly expressed in the "Love your enemies" proverb of the New Testament:

So I want to turn your attention to this subject: "Loving Your Enemies." It's so basic to me because it is a part of my basic philosophical and theological orientation: the whole idea of love, the whole philosophy of love. In the fifth chapter of the gospel as recorded by Saint Matthew, we read these very arresting words, flowing from the lips of our Lord and Master: "Ye have heard that it has been said, 'Thou shall love thy neighbor, and hate thine enemy.' But I say unto you, love your enemies, bless them that curse you, do good to them that hate you, and pray for them that despitefully use you, that ye may be the children of your Father which is in heaven" [Matt. 5:43–45]. (IV, 3126; Nov. 17, 1957)

When he gave another version of this sermon on March 7, 1961, in Detroit, his words and the Bible verses were quite similar, but they show that he usually does not quote himself verbatim. In this later paragraph he argues from a much more personal vantage point, and also connects the idea of loving one's enemies with civil rights issues:

Now this afternoon I would like to have you think with me on a passage of scripture that has been a great influence in my life and a passage that I have sought to bring to bear on the whole struggle for racial justice, which is taking place in our nation. The words are found in the fifth chapter of the gospel as recorded by Saint Matthew. And these words flow from the lips of our Lord and Master: "Ye have heard it said of old that thou shall love thy neighbor and hate thine enemy. But I say unto you, love your enemies. Bless them that curse you. Do good to them that hate you, and pray for them that despitefully use you, that ye may be the children of your Father which is in heaven" [Matt. 5:43–45]. (VI, 422; March 7, 1961)

Additional references to this all-pervasive proverb in these and other sermons all illustrate the many mutations of King's basic argument that love is the key element in a world of nonviolence. Adding the folk proverb "Hate begets hate" as a warning to his emphasis on the Bible proverb "Love your enemies," he makes the following strong statement in yet another restatement of this sermon in his book *Strength to Love* (1963):

Why should we love our enemies? The first reason is fairly obvious. Returning hate for hate multiplies hate, adding deeper darkness to a night already devoid of stars. Darkness cannot drive out darkness; only light can do that. Hate cannot drive out hate; only love can do that. Hate multiplies hate, violence multiplies violence, and toughness multiplies toughness in a descending spiral of destruction. So when Jesus says "Love your enemies" [Matt. 5:44], he is setting forth a profound and ultimately inescapable admonition. Have we not come to such an impasse in the modern world that we must love our enemies—or else? The chain reaction of evil—hate begetting hate, wars producing more wars—must be broken, or we shall be plunged into the dark abyss of annihilation. (King 1963: 37)

This paragraph becomes a proverbial cautionary tale, as in fact many of King's sermons might well be classified. Of course, despite all of this anxiety, gloom, and despair, King always has the audacity of hope for a better world. The purpose of his sermonic explications of proverbs is thus an uplifting attempt of finding a better way for humankind to struggle for freedom and peace throughout the world. His favorite Bible proverb "Love your enemies" is the wisdom that can lead us there.

Bible Proverbs in the Fight for Desegregation and Civil Rights

Martin Luther King was above all a preacher whose "rhetoric was of the *Biblical vernacular*" (Marbury 1971: 4 [1989: 626]). He knew his Bible, and he spoke and wrote with the Holy Book always on his mind. He could quote entire passages from the Bible, and he used its well-known phrasings to add authority to his views and arguments (Calloway-Thomas and Lucaites 1993). The scriptures were always with him, but as he quoted them, he also was perfectly capable of applying them to the sociopolitical issues of his time. While he was steeped in the Bible and believed in the word of God, he most certainly used its language and wisdom to help along the cause of desegregation and civil rights. There is thus hardly a page in King's oeuvre that does not at least contain a reference to the Bible (Stevenson 1949; Mieder 1990). At times he retells Biblical parables or quotes entire verses; more often than not he restricts himself to but a sentence or two from the Bible. Sometimes he explains the specific meaning that they might have for the modern world, and in other instances he employs them to add argumentative weight to his religious and social rhetoric. Since he is a social reformer wearing the preacher's robe, he is clearly also a moral teacher relying heavily on Bible proverbs to spread the good word. Preachers have always made use of Biblical proverbs (McKenzie 1996 and 2002), with his namesake Martin Luther having been a champion of Bible and folk proverbs in Germany during the Reformation (Cornette 1942 [1997]).

When King delivered a version of his well-known sermon "The Three Dimensions of a Complete Life" on April 9, 1967, at New Covenant Church in Chicago, he included the proverb "Love your neighbor as you love yourself" (Gal. 5:14) as an expression of reciprocal love, and two additional proverbial Bible passages from Amos and Isaiah. Above all, he summarizes the three dimensions of a complete life by way of the golden rule "Do unto others as you would have them do unto you" (Matt. 7:12). This proverb, which is known in various forms in the world's religions, could easily have become King's proverbial leitmotif for his nonviolent struggle for human rights (Hertzler 1933–34; Griffin 1991: 67–69; Templeton 1997: 8–12), but he chose the shorter and more direct proverb "Love your enemies" (Matt. 5:44) instead.

Here then is King's rhetorical masterpiece that amasses four Bible proverbs into a powerful statement of love, justice, peace, and morality:

> Go out this morning. Love yourself, and that means rational and healthy self-interest. You are commanded to do that. That's the length of life. Then follow that: Love your neighbor as you love yourself [Gal. 5:14]. You are commanded to do that. That's the breadth of life. And I'm going to take my seat now by letting you know that there's a first and even greater commandment: "Love the Lord thy God with all thy heart, [*Yeah*] with all thy soul, with all thy strength" [Deut. 6:5]. I think the psychologist would just say "with all thy personality." And when you do that, you've got the breadth [King meant to say: height] of life.
>
> And when you get all three of these together, you can walk and never get weary [Isaiah 40:31]. You can look up and see the morning stars singing together, and the sons of God shouting for joy [Job 38:7]. When you get all of these working together in your very life, judgment will roll down like waters, and righteousness like a mighty stream [Amos 5:24].
>
> When you get all the three of these together, the lamb will lie down with the lion [Isaiah 11:6]. [. . .]
>
> When you get all three of these working together, you will do unto others as you'd have them do unto you [Matt. 7:12].
>
> When you get all three of these together, you will recognize that out of one blood God made all men to dwell upon the face of the earth. (Carson and Holloran 1998: 139; April 9, 1967)

And yet, despite its grand Biblical and moral rhetoric, this passage says nothing about racial and social matters. But such exclusion is relatively rare. In fact, the many sermons and the various versions of one and the same basic message offer valuable opportunities to illustrate Martin Luther King's *modus operandi* with the religious *and* sociopolitical implications of the proverbial wisdom included in them. A fine example involves the widely known Bible proverb "Man does not live by bread alone" (Deut. 8:3, Matt. 4:4) that appears in both the Old and New Testaments. King used it in a sermon on "The Christian Doctrine of Man" on March 12, 1958, at the Council of Churches Noon Lenten Services in Detroit, stating that he as a minister had a moral and social obligation to his parishioners and the world at large. But there is also an extremely important interpretive twist of the proverb in this text when King states that the word "alone" in the proverb implies that Jesus was very well aware that man cannot live without bread nor by it alone (Turner 1977: 52 [1989: 1000]; Rieder 2008: 289). And this in turn gives King the proverbial argument that poverty must be combated in the United States and throughout the world:

> And so in Christianity the body is sacred. The body is significant. This means that in any Christian doctrine of man we must forever be concerned about man's physical well-being. Jesus was concerned about that. He realized that men had to have certain physical necessities. One day he said, "Man cannot live by bread alone" [Deut. 8:3, Matt. 4:4]. [*Yeah*] But the mere fact that the "alone" was added means that Jesus realized that man could not live without bread. [*Yes*] So as a minister of the gospel, I must not only preach to men and women to be good, but I must be concerned about the social conditions that often make them bad. [*Yeah*] It's not enough for me to tell men to be honest, but I must be concerned about the economic conditions that make them dishonest. [*Amen*] I must be concerned about the poverty in the world. I must be concerned about the ignorance in the world. I must be concerned about the slums in the world. (VI, 332; March 12, 1958)

Usually relying on the proverbial wisdom of Jesus (Winton 1990), King found the perfect metaphor for his social agenda in the New Testament proverb "He who lives by the sword shall perish by the sword" (Matt. 26:52). It became *the* symbolic argument against all the ills of violent mistreatment of others. In his address on "The Montgomery Story" at the Annual NAACP Convention on June 27, 1956, in San Francisco, he cites the Bible proverb as a metaphorical sign of violence that must be overcome by a philosophy of nonviolence:

From the beginning there has been a basic philosophy undergirding our movement. It is a philosophy of nonviolent resistance. It is a philosophy which simply says we will refuse on a nonviolent basis, to cooperate with the evil of segregation. In our struggle in America we cannot fret with the idea of retaliatory violence. To use the method of violence would be both impractical and immoral. We have neither the instruments nor the techniques of violence, and even if we had it, it would be morally wrong. There is the voice crying [*applause*], there is a voice crying through the vista of time, saying: "He who lives by the sword will perish by the sword" [Matt. 26:52]. [*applause*] History is replete with the bleached bones of nations who failed to hear these words of truth, and so we decided to use the method of nonviolence, feeling that violence would not do the job. (III, 305; June 27, 1956)

Many other passages with this "sword" proverb could be cited, but suffice it to quote this one additional text from an address on "Some Things We Must Do" that King gave on December 5, 1957, at the Second Annual Institute on Nonviolence and Social Change in Montgomery. It is once again a rather general statement on the opposition of violence and nonviolence, with such statements as "Violence solves no social problems" and "Violence is not the way" taking on the role of quotational slogans by Martin Luther King, even though they have not been recorded in books of King's famous utterances (see Hoskins 1968; Ayres 1993):

We must plunge deeper into the whole philosophy of nonviolence as we continue to move on in our quest for freedom. As I look at our situation and the situation of oppressed peoples all over the world, it seems to me that there are three ways that oppressed people can deal with their oppression. One is to rise up in armed revolt, one is to rise up with violence, and many people have used that method. It seems that violence has become something of the inseparable twin of western materialism. It's even become the hallmark of its grandeur. Violence nevertheless solves no social problems. It only creates new and more complicated ones. Yes, violence often brings about temporary victory, but never permanent peace. This evening as I stand before you, it seems that I can hear the voice crying through the vista of time, still saying to men in this generation: "He who lives by the sword, will perish by the sword" [Matt. 26:52]. [*All right*] History is cluttered with the wreckage of nations and communities that failed to hear that command. Violence is not the way. [...] It seems to me there is a third way. There is a third way that is more powerful and enduring and lasting than the first two: that is the way of nonviolent resistance. (IV, 340–41; Dec. 5, 1957)

Folk Proverbs in the Struggle against Prejudice and Injustice

While Martin Luther King has numerous favorite Bible proverbs and literary quotations that he cites on numerous occasions as rhetorical leitmotifs, he does not show this great fascination with any particular folk proverb. This does not mean that he shies away from using such folk wisdom when it suits him, but as a preacher he is clearly more steeped in Biblical truths. As has been pointed out already, King does not even use the term "proverb" when citing proverbs from traditional folk speech. If he uses introductory formulas at all, he prefers such designations as "truism" or "saying," but usually he simply integrates folk proverbs without calling special attention to them. He might well have thought that they are so well known that they need no label. After all, he assumes the same with many of the Bible proverbs that he also often does not identify as such. In any case, the fact remains that the frequency of Bible proverbs outweighs that of folk proverbs (there are plenty of proverbial expressions from folk speech!), and this might in part be due to his pride in having obtained a Ph.D. degree. That does not automatically need to result in a lesser emphasis on folk speech in the form of proverbs, but it is a known fact that King used a rather elevated style in his oral and written communications. While the transcriptions of sermons in his home church include some colloquial speech, he usually speaks and writes in an uplifting style that is intended to reach audiences of varied racial, social, economic, and intellectual levels. His sermonic and agitating rhetoric is based on a conscious attempt to address his listeners and readers on a demanding linguistic and intellectual level. But, of course, that by no means excludes the significant integration of proverbs and proverbial expressions in his highly emotional and argumentative language. As preformulated or ready-made linguistic units, they flow quite naturally into his messages and add considerable wisdom and expressiveness to them. Even though King does not overemphasize folk proverbs by using them as sapiential leitmotifs, he uses numerous proverbs with much rhetorical skill. Actually, just as Abraham Lincoln and Frederick Douglass did before him and as Barack Obama is doing now, the combined emphasis on Bible and folk proverbs makes these sociopolitical statements so effective (Mieder 2000, 2001, 2009c). People then and now could easily identify with this wisdom (see Mieder 1993) and subsequently marched along with their champions in the struggle for equality and freedom. There certainly is no doubt that proverbs have played a significant role in political discourse over the centuries, and they continue to be of considerable effectiveness in (inter)national politics today (see Nichols 1996; Mieder 1997, 2005, 2008a/b; Louis 2000).

King utilizes various proverbs and proverbial expressions in his depictions of segregation and the necessary fight against it. There is in fact a most fitting proverb that King found to describe how African Americans have fought segregation in a nonviolent way by, proverbially speaking, straightening up their backs and thereby validating the proverb "You can't ride a man's back unless it is bent." The passage that includes the proverbial phrase and the proverb in tandem appears in the published version of an interview in the January 1965 issue of *Playboy*. In this statement King also reflects on the best way of protesting against segregation, arguing that more specific approaches in certain locales are better than general arguments against segregation as a whole:

> The mistake I made there [at Albany, Georgia] was to protest against segregation generally rather than against a single and distinct facet of it. Our protest was so vague that we got nothing, and the people were left very depressed and in despair. It would have been much better to have concentrated upon integrating the buses or the lunch counters. One victory of this kind would have been symbolic, would have galvanized support and boosted morale. But I don't mean that our work in Albany ended in failure. The Negro people there straightened up their bent backs; you can't ride a man's back unless it's bent. Also, thousands of Negroes registered to vote who never had voted before, and because of the expanded Negro vote in the next election for governor of Georgia —which pitted a moderate candidate against a rabid segregationist—Georgia elected its first governor who had pledged to respect and enforce the law impartially. And what we learned from our mistakes in Albany helped our later campaigns in other cities to be more effective. We have never since scattered our efforts in a general attack on segregation, but have focused upon specific, symbolic objectives. (Washington 1986: 344; Jan. 1965)

In his stirring address of June 23, 1963, at the Freedom Rally in Cobo Hall in Detroit, King cites the modern proverb "Last hired, first fired" as an unfortunate truism regarding the employment injustice that African Americans face in light of racial discrimination:

We've been pushed around so long; we've been the victims of lynching mobs so long; we've been the victims of economic injustice so long—still the last hired and the first fired all over this nation. And I know the temptation. I can understand from a psychological point of view why some caught up in the clutches of the injustices surrounding them almost respond with bitterness and come to the conclusion that the problem can't be solved within, and they talk about getting away from it in terms of racial separation. But even though I can understand it psychologically, I must say to you this afternoon that this isn't the way. Black supremacy is as dangerous as white supremacy. [*Applause*] And oh, I hope you will allow me to say to you this afternoon that God is not interested merely in the freedom of black men and brown men and yellow men. God is interested in the freedom of the whole human race. [*Applause*] And I believe that with this philosophy and this determined struggle we will be able to go on in the days ahead and transform the jangling discords of our nation into a beautiful symphony of brotherhood. (Carson and Shepard 2001: 68–69; June 23, 1963)

The element of time in eradicating such racial injustice wore heavily on Martin Luther King's mind. In his chapter on "The Dilemma of Negro Americans" of his book *Where Do We Go from Here: Chaos or Community?* (1967), he alludes negatively to the two folk proverbs "Time heals all wounds" and "Time and tide wait for no man," with the first alteration implying that the evils of segregation will not be forgotten and the second variation stating that the time has surely come to rid the country of this racial injustice once and for all:

The challenge we face is to unite around powerful action programs to eradicate the last vestiges of racial injustice. We will be greatly misled if we feel that the problem will work itself out. Structures of evil do not crumble by passive waiting. If history teaches anything, it is that evil is recalcitrant and determined, and never voluntarily relinquishes its hold short of an almost fanatical resistance. Evil must be attacked by a counteracting persistence, by the day-to-day assault of the battering rams of justice.

We must get rid of the false notion that there is some miraculous quality in the flow of time that inevitably heals all evils. There is only one thing certain about time, and that is that it waits for no one. If it is not used constructively, it passes you by. (King 1967a: 128)

In his constant concern for the progress in the fight for civil rights, King found another proverb to express that there is no easy way or quick fix, namely "No pain, no gain." He cites the less frequent variant "No gain without pain" in his already mentioned address at the "Freedom Rally in Cobo Hall" (1963) to explain that there is a heavy price to pay (an additional proverbial phrase) for social advancement:

> And I do not want to give you the impression that it's going to be easy [to get civil rights]. There can be no great social gain without individual pain. And before the victory for brotherhood is won, some will have to get scarred up a bit. Before the victory is won, some more will be thrown into jail. Before the victory is won, some, like Medgar Evers, may have to face physical death. But if physical death is the price that some must pay to free their children and their white brothers from an eternal psychological death, then nothing can be more redemptive. Before the victory is won, some will be misunderstood and called bad names, but we must go on with a determination and with a faith that this problem can be solved. [*Yeah*] [*Applause*] (Carson and Shepard 2001: 70–71; June 23, 1963)

One thing for certain in King's socially conscious mind and heart, however, is that something must be done against the incredible poverty among citizens of all races in the richest country of the world. In the chapter on "Nonviolence and Social Change" in his book *The Trumpet of Conscience* (1967), he describes a planned march on Washington in support of the poor to his listeners. And he is quick in modifying the proverb "Beware the man who has nothing to lose" to include the word "revolutionary." Since he supplies the information that "people say" this, he acknowledges, albeit indirectly, the proverbiality of the statement:

> The only real revolutionary, people say, is a man who has nothing to lose. There are millions of poor people in this country who have very little, or even nothing, to lose. If they can be helped to take action together, they will do so with a freedom and a power that will be a new and unsettling force in our complacent national life. Beginning in the New Year, we will be recruiting three thousand of the poorest citizens from ten different urban and rural areas to initiate and lead a sustained, massive, direct-action movement in Washington. Those who choose to join this initial three thousand, this nonviolent army, this "freedom church" of the poor, will work with us for three months

to develop nonviolent action skills. Then we will move on Washington, determined to stay there until the legislative and executive branches of the government take serious and adequate action on jobs and income. (King 1967b: 60)

Despite his constant struggle against violence and injustice, King also had a good sense of humor. This can also be seen from his retelling of an occasion where a student hit the proverbial nail on the head when he cited the folk proverb "If rabbits could throw rocks, there would be fewer hunters in the forest." Readers of King's essay "The Time for Freedom Has Come" in the *New York Times Magazine* of September 16, 1961, must have enjoyed this relatively little-known animal proverb. But as King is quick to point out in his explication of this piece of wisdom, there is much more to this witticism than meets the eye:

It is not a solemn life, for all of its seriousness. During a vigorous debate among a group of students discussing the moral and practical soundness of nonviolence, a majority rejected the employment of force. As the minority dwindled to a single student, he finally declared, "All I know is that, if rabbits could throw rocks, there would be fewer hunters in the forest."

This is more than a witty remark to relieve the tensions of serious and even grim discussion. It expresses some of the pent-up impatience, some of the discontent and some of the despair produced by minute corrections in the face of enormous evil. Students necessarily have conflicting reactions. It is understandable that violence presents itself as a quick, effective answer for a few.

For the large majority, however, nonviolent, direct action has emerged as the better and more successful way out. It does not require that they abandon their discontent. This discontent is a sound, healthy social response to the injustice and brutality they see around them. Nonviolence offers a method by which they can fight the evil with which they cannot live. It offers a unique weapon which, without firing a single bullet, disarms the adversary. It exposes his moral defenses, weakens his morale, and at the same time works on his conscience. (Washington 1986: 163–64; Sept. 10, 1961)

The one thing that these young people and everybody need to remember is that all of life and existence is interconnected, and King found the perfect quotation, long turned proverb, to express this idea on numerous occasions.

"No Man Is an Island" and Human Interconnectedness

Martin Luther King began referring in the early 1950s to the first line, "No man is an island" (1624), of John Donne's meditation, citing much more of the actual text in his address on "Facing the Challenge of a New Age" at the First Annual Institute on Nonviolence and Social Change on December 3, 1956, in Montgomery. Even at this early date, King already speaks of an absolutely interconnected world, where people must try to find ways to interrelate in a humane fashion. Everybody's very existence depends on other people, and the bell of accountability rings for all, as Donne exclaims. This statement has long become a proverbial phrase as well, and King often uses both proverbial lines from Donne's poem together to point to this common fate of people throughout the world:

> This says [. . .] to us that our world is geographically one. Now we are faced with the challenge of making it spiritually one. Through our scientific genius we have made of the world a neighborhood; now through our moral and spiritual genius we must make of it a brotherhood. We are all involved in the single process. Whatever affects one directly affects all indirectly. We are all links in the great chain of humanity. This is what John Doane [*sic*] meant when he said years ago:
>
> > "No man is an island, entire of it selfe; every man
> > is a peece of the Continent, a part of the maine;
> >   [. . .]; any mans death
> > diminishes me, because I am involved in Mankinde;
> > And therefore never send to know for whom the bell tolls;
> > it tolls for thee."
> > (III, 456–57; Dec. 3, 1956; also in Washington 1986: 138; April, 1957)

Typical for Martin Luther King, this statement went through several mutations in a number of sermons and speeches (Boesak 1976: 28 [1989: 86]); Lischer 1995: 43), with the last one appearing in his sermon "Remaining Awake Through a Great Revolution" at the National Cathedral (Episcopal) on March 31, 1968, in Washington, D.C., once again including "John Donne's famous dictum 'No man is an island' to reinforce his argument about America's interrelationship with the rest of the world and therefore its need to be concerned about all citizens not just its own" (Sharman 1999: 98):

Through our scientific and technological genius, we have made of this world a neighborhood and yet . . . we have not had the ethical commitment to make of it a brotherhood. But somehow, and in some way, we have got to do this. We must all learn to live together as brothers. Or we will all perish together as fools. We are tied together in the single garment of destiny, caught in an inescapable network of mutuality. And whatever affects one directly affects all indirectly. For some strange reason I can never be what I ought to be until you are what you ought to be. And you can never be what you ought to be until I am what I ought to be. This is the way God's universe is made; this is the way it is structured.

John Donne caught it years ago and placed it in graphic terms—"No man is an island entire of itself. Every man is a piece of the continent—a part of the main." And he goes on toward the end to say, "Any man's death diminishes me because I am involved in mankind. Therefore never send to know for whom the bell tolls; it tolls for thee." We must see this, believe this, and live by it . . . if we are to remain awake through a great revolution. (Washington 1986: 269–70; March 31, 1968)

In his book *Where Do We Go from Here: Chaos or Community?* (1967), King included a chapter on "The World House," arguing that "We have inherited a large house, a great 'world house' in which we have to live together—black and white, Easterner and Westerner, Gentile and Jews, Catholic and Protestant, Moslem and Hindu—a family unduly separated in ideas, culture and interest, who, because we can never again live apart, must learn somehow to live with each other in peace" (King 1967a: 167). And here, in this uplifting passage from his sermon, he speaks of a brotherhood (sisterhood is implied) that is poetically "tied together in the single garment of destiny, caught in an inescapable network of mutuality." As we speak today of globalization and an interconnected world, it behooves us to remember such passages from Martin Luther King to appreciate what a great visionary he really was not only for civil rights in the United States but for justice, equality, and freedom all over the globe.

New Mousetraps and Bright Stars as Proverbial Signs of Change

After such a spirited call for a united world connected by basic human rights, it might come as quite a surprise that the well-educated and sophisticated orator King would turn with all seriousness to such a mundane American proverb as "If you build (make) a better mousetrap, the world will beat a path to your door" (Mieder et al. 1992: 420). Actually, considerable scholarly work has been done on the origin of this text (Stevenson 1935: 343–81), and even though King always credits Ralph Waldo Emerson with having coined it in his eight citations of it between 1956 and 1963, matters are not quite as definite about Emerson's coinage of the proverbial metaphor (regarding such questionable attributions, see Taylor 1931: 34–43). As Fred Shapiro and other quotation sleuths before him have pointed out, what Emerson actually wrote down and which might have given rise to the proverb as it is known today appears in a journal entry by Emerson from 1855: "I trust a good deal to common fame, as we all must. If a man has good corn, or wood, or boards, or pigs, to sell, or can make better chairs or knives, crucibles or church organs, than anybody else, you will find a broad hard-beaten road to his house, though it be in the woods" (Shapiro 2006: 244–45; see also Stevenson 1935: 343–81, 1948: 1633). But be that as it may, King used it repeatedly as an Emerson quotation; he might well have simply used it as a proverb, but probably liked the quotational authority—as for example in his lecture "The Rising Tide of Racial Consciousness" on September 6, 1960, when he talked to the National Urban League in New York City:

> We must constantly stimulate our youth to rise above the stagnant level of mediocrity, and seek to achieve excellence in their various fields of endeavor. Doors are opening now that were not open in the past, and the great challenge facing minority groups is to be ready to enter these doors as they open. No greater tragedy could befall us at this hour but that of allowing new opportunities to emerge without the concomitant preparedness to meet them. Ralph Waldo Emerson said in a lecture back in 1871 that "if a man can write a better book, or preach a better sermon, or make a better mousetrap than his neighbor, even if he builds his house in the woods the world will make a beaten path to his door." This has not always been true. But I have reason to believe that because of the shape of the world today and the fact that we cannot afford the luxury of an anemic democracy, this affirmation will become increasingly true. We must make it clear to our young people that this is an age in which they will be forced to compete with people of all races and nationalities. We cannot aim merely to be good Negro teachers, good Negro doctors, or good Negro skilled laborers. We must set out to do a good job irrespective of race. We must seek to do our life's work so well that nobody could do it better. The Negro who seeks to be merely a good Negro, whatever he is, has already

flunked his matriculation examination for entrance into the university of integration. (V, 506; Sept. 6, 1960)

There is one more quotation-turned-proverb that needs to be mentioned, namely the historian Charles A. Beard's insight based on the natural phenomenon that "When it gets dark enough you can see the stars" that King cites for the last time in his sermon "I See the Promised Land" on April 3, 1968, just one day before his assassination in Memphis, Tennessee:

> I know, somehow, that only when it is dark enough, can you see the stars. And I see God working in this period of the twentieth century in a way that men, in some strange way, are responding—something is happening in our world. The masses of people are rising up. And wherever they are assembled today, whether they are in Johannesburg, South Africa; Nairobi, Kenya; Accra, Ghana; New York City; Atlanta, Georgia; Jackson, Mississippi; or Memphis, Tennessee—the cry is always the same—"We want to be free." (Washington 1986: 279–80; April 3, 1968)

Yes, indeed, stars of hope were everywhere when Martin Luther King spoke of freedom with his typical eloquence, which was at least in part informed by his perfect utilization of quotations with a certain claim of proverbiality.

Proverbs and Quotations as Rhetorical "Set Pieces"

It should not be surprising that someone so inclined to the use of proverbial quotations and proverbs would also amass them into paragraphs of utmost rhetorical authority. Once King found a certain combination of quotations and proverbs that he liked as "set pieces," he usually kept them in the same order when making use of these ready-made collages in his sermons and speeches (Miller 1992: 153–55; Lischer 1995: 104–5). Whenever appropriate, he could simply call on this impressive repertoire that he basically had memorized and could employ to add Biblical, literary, or folkloric authority to his often quite spontaneous remarks.

His preference of stringing together two or more quotations and proverbs to express a certain belief or conviction can clearly be seen by his frequent reliance on two famous statements from the Declaration of Independence. By citing the proverb "All men are created equal" and the proverbial triad "Life, liberty, and the pursuit of happiness" in tandem as they appear originally in this American creed (Aron 2008: 91–96), King knows that his listeners and readers will identify positively with the fundamental ideas of equality and freedom expressed in them. And while King always cites this wisdom with positive conviction, it gives him the rhetorical opportunity to show that the ideal expressed in them has not been achieved regarding the African American citizens, to wit the following paragraph from his stirring sermon "The Christian Doctrine of Man," delivered on March 12, 1958, in Detroit. Judging by the responses of the audience, people must have been quite taken by King's sermonic stroke of genius of letting God talk to them through their preacher:

> The God of the universe stands there in all of His love and forgiving power saying, "Come home. [*Yeah, Amen, Amen*] Western civilization, you have strayed away into the far country of colonialism and imperialism. You have taken one billion six hundred million of your brothers in Asia and Africa, dominated them politically, exploited them economically, segregated and humiliated them. You have trampled over them. But western civilization, if you will rise up now and come out of this far country of imperialism and colonialism and come on back to your true home, which is freedom and justice, I'll take you in. [*Yeah, Oh amen*] America, I had great intentions for you. I had planned for you to be this great nation where all men would live together as brothers—a nation of religious freedom, a nation of racial freedom. And America, you wrote it in your Declaration of Independence. You meant well, for you cried out, 'All men are created equal and endowed by their creator with certain unalienable rights. [*Yeah*] Among these are life, liberty, and the pursuit of happiness.' [*Preach*] But in the midst of your creed, America, you've strayed away to the far country of segregation and discrimination. [*Say it, Amen*] You've taken sixteen million of your brothers, trampled over them, mistreated them, inflicted them with tragic injustices and indignities. But America, I'm not going to give you up. If you will rise up out of the far country of segregation and discrimination [*Amen*], I will take you in, America. [*Amen, Amen*] And I will bring you back to your true home." (VI, 337; March 12, 1958)

As can be imagined, Martin Luther King was not always satisfied just citing his favorite proverb "All men are created equal" and the proverbial triad "Life, liberty, and the pursuit of happiness." To add even more rhetorical credence to his arguments, he expands this double dose of authority by one, two, or even three additional quotations or proverbs in the same paragraph. And in order to add a somewhat satirical twist to these phrase collages, he constructs them around the idea of a responsible person having to be "maladjusted."

Employing the anaphora "as maladjusted as" and other uses of the word "maladjusted," King claims that it takes maladjusted people to bring about equality, justice, and freedom. In his speech of September 2, 1957, in Monteagle, Tennessee, on "A Look to the Future," King, the stylistic tinkerer and "mix-master, blending and layering different elements of talk" (Rieder 2008: 104), augments Jefferson's proverbial words with three Bible proverbs, namely "Let judgment run down like waters and righteousness like a mighty stream" (Amos 5:24), "He who lives by the sword will perish by the sword" (Matt. 26:52), and "Love your enemies" (Matt. 5:44). With that anaphoral tour de force he has indeed found an authoritative statement for the future in which people will be courageously "maladjusted" to bring about social change:

> But there are some things in our social system to which I am proud to be maladjusted and to which I suggest that you too ought to be maladjusted. I never intend to adjust myself to the viciousness of mob rule. I never intend to adjust myself to the evils of segregation and the crippling effects of discrimination. I never intend to adjust myself to the tragic inequalities of an economic system which takes necessities from the masses to give luxuries to the classes. I never intend to become adjusted to the madness of militarism and the self-defeating method of physical violence. I call upon you to be maladjusted. Well you see, it may be that the salvation of the world lies in the hands of the maladjusted. The challenge to you this morning as I leave you is to be maladjusted—as maladjusted as the prophet Amos, who in the midst of the injustices of his day, could cry out in terms that echo across the centuries, "Let judgment run down like waters and righteousness like a mighty stream" [Amos 5:24]; as maladjusted as Lincoln, who had the vision to see that this nation could not survive half slave and half free; as maladjusted as Jefferson, who in the midst of an age amazingly adjusted to slavery could cry out in words lifted to cosmic proportions, "All men are created equal, and are endowed by their creator with certain inalienable rights, that among these are life, liberty and the pursuit of happiness." Yes, as maladjusted as Jesus of Nazareth who dared to dream a dream of the fatherhood of God and the brotherhood of man. He looked at men amid the intricate and fascinating military machinery of the Roman Empire, and could say to them, "He who lives by the sword will perish by the sword" [Matt. 26:52]. Jesus, who could look at men in the midst of their tendencies for tragic hate and say to them, "Love thy enemies. Bless them that curse you. Pray for them that despitefully use you" [Matt. 5:44]. The world is in desperate need of such maladjustment. Through such maladjustment we

will be able to emerge from the bleak and desolate midnight of man's inhu-
manity to man into the bright and glittering daybreak of freedom and justice.
(IV, 276; Sept. 2, 1957)

While this rhetorical set piece in its various mutations can be found several
times in King's sermons, speeches, and books, mention should also be made
of a similar often repeated and reformulated paragraph that begins with two
at first unidentified quotations and eventually is expanded to include a third
quotation and a Bible proverb. In his "Statement on Ending the Bus Boycott" on December 20, 1956, in Montgomery, King quotes the abolitionist
Theodore Parker and the poet William Cullen Bryant in support of his argument that justice had indeed prevailed:

> These twelve months [in Montgomery] have not at all been easy. Our feet
> have often been tired. We have struggle[d] against tremendous odds to
> maintain alternative transportation. There have been moments when roaring
> waters of disappointment poured upon us in staggering torrents. We can re-
> member days when unfavorable court decisions came upon us like tidal waves,
> leaving us treading in the deep and confused waters of despair. But amid all of
> this we have kept going with the faith that as we struggle, God struggles with
> us, and that the arc of the moral universe, although long, is bending toward
> justice [a statement from the abolitionist Theodore Parker that became a leit-
> motif in King's oratory]. We have lived under the agony and darkness of Good
> Friday with the conviction that one day the heightening glow of Easter would
> emerge on the horizon. We have seen truth crucified and goodness buried, but
> we have kept going with the conviction that truth crushed to earth will rise
> again [line from the poet William Cullen Bryant]. (III, 486; Dec. 20, 1956)

By the time King gives his emotionally charged speech "Our God is Marching On!" on March 25, 1965, in Montgomery, he adds Thomas Carlyle's "No
lie can live forever" and the Bible proverb "As you sow, so shall you reap"
(Gal. 6:7) to this set piece of "messianic discourse" (Charteris-Black 2005:
64) and reverses the order of the other two in this peroration of merged quotations and proverbs (Luker 2003: 41–43). This might well be yet another
example of how King works from memory as he calls on his repertoire of
such proverbial collages at the spur of the moment:

> Our aim must never be to defeat or humiliate the white man but to win his
> friendship and understanding. We must come to see that the end we seek is

a society at peace with itself, a society that can live with its conscience. That will be a day not of the white man, not of the black man. That will be the day of man as man.

I know you are asking today, "How long will it take?" [Psalms 6:3, Rev. 6:10] I come to say to you this afternoon however difficult the moment, however frustrating the hour, it will not be long, because truth pressed to earth will rise again.

How long? Not long, because no lie can live forever.

How long? Not long, because you still reap what you sow [Gal. 6:7].

How long? Not long. Because the arm [*sic*, arc] of the moral universe is long but it bends toward justice.

How long? Not long, 'cause mine eyes have seen the glory of the coming of the Lord, trampling out the vintage where the grapes of wrath are stored. He has loosed the fateful lightning of his terrible swift sword. His truth is marching on.

He has sounded forth the trumpets that shall never call retreat. He is lifting up the hearts of man before His judgment seat. Oh, be swift, my soul, to answer Him. Be jubilant, my feet. Our God is marching on. (Washington 1986: 230; March 25, 1965)

According to fellow civil rights advocate and now U.S. Representative John Lewis, "this is poetry" (Carson and Shepard 2001: 116), and it would have been absolutely ridiculous if King had in fact included the names of Bryant, Carlyle, and Parker or the precise Bible reference in his powerful anaphora "How long? Not long, because . . ." (Lischer 1995: 128; see Carter 1996: 128, 141, who mistakenly thinks Parker's statement to be King's "own metaphor"). Jonathan Rieder, referring to this set piece, very appropriately speaks of King's "theology of hope" (Rieder 2008: 322) that it expresses, calling to mind Barack Obama's more secularly stated "audacity of hope" (Obama 2006) for humankind.

"Making a Way Out of No Way"

Martin Luther King's struggle for freedom and equality moved forward in many different ways, and as he spoke about the various paths taken, he frequently used proverbs and proverbial phrases that have the noun "way" in them. They are by their very nature usually future oriented and are thus perfectly suited as metaphors to describe and reflect upon the way to progress. There is no doubt that King himself never tired of going out of his way for the civil and human rights movement, giving his energy and time for the cause of justice and equality in the United States and far beyond. With all the setbacks and defeats, he never faltered, citing the proverbial phrase "to have come a long way" to emphasize the progress that had been made, while at the same time stressing with the proverbial phrase "to have a long way to go" that much work still lies ahead. He connects these two phrases for the first time in his philosophically informed article "The 'New Negro' of the South" that appeared in the June 1956 journal the *Socialist Call*:

> Like the synthesis of Hegelian philosophy, the realistic attitude seeks to reconcile the truths of two opposites and avoid the extremes of both. So the realist in race relations would agree with the optimist in saying, we have come a long way, but he would balance that by agreeing with the pessimist that we have a long long way to go. It is this realistic position that I would like to set forth: We have come a long long way, and we have a long long way to go. (III, 282; June 1956)

By citing both proverbial phrases twice together, King presents a convincing realistic argument that finds a synthesis between the optimistic and pessimistic assessment concerning the progress of race relations. Clearly he is always more interested in looking to the future, realizing that the end of the road toward racial justice is still far off. King exhibits an incredible faith in the future, with his strong belief in a benevolent God giving him the strength to continue on the long and treacherous way that lies ahead.

But there is one speech with the title "A Long Way to Go" that wins the proverbial prize, so to speak. King delivered it on April 27, 1965, on the campus of the University of California at Los Angeles, and it was published six years later in Arthur L. Smith's and Stephen Robb's edited volume *The Voice of Black Rhetoric: Selections* (1971), with the editors commenting very briefly that "'A Long Way to Go' demonstrates King's mastery of the classical canons of style and arrangement. Clearly delineating introduction, body and conclusion in this speech, King's rhetorical organization is presented at its best. While there is little that is creative about the two-section arrangement (it has been used by many speakers), King's content allows suspense to be a key factor in this speech" (Smith and Robb 1971: 183). Agreed, but what would have been wrong in also saying that the speech has a proverbial title and that both the proverbial expressions "to have come a long way" and "to have a long way to go" as individual and combined leitmotifs (always with the emphatic double use of "long") inform the structural and rhetorical mastery of this address? As it is, the two folk metaphors are part of the dual structure of the lecture, and it cannot be a surprise to learn that this rhetorical genius begins his speech with a juxtaposition of them to set the stage:

> Many of you want to know, are we making any progress? That is the desperate question, a poignant question on the lips of millions of people all over our nation and all over the world. I get it almost every day. It is a question of whether we are making any real progress in the area of race relations. And so I'm going to try to answer that question and deal with many of the issues involved using as a subject from which to speak, the future of integration.
>
> Now there are some people who feel that we aren't making any progress; there are some people who feel that we're making overwhelming progress. I would like to take what I consider a realistic position and say that we have come a long, long way in the struggle to make justice and freedom a reality in our nation, but we still have a long, long way to go. And it is this realistic position that I would like to use as a basis for our thinking together. (Smith and Robb 1971: 188–89; April 27, 1965)

Having said this, the realistic King is ready to present a short history lesson regarding the progress in racial relations, couching this optimistic view into the proverbial leitmotif "to have come a long way." In the second half of the speech King gives an overview of what still remains to be done, now using the proverbial phrase "to have a long, long way to go" as his hopeful leitmotif. Altogether, the speech becomes a prophetic vision of the future.

But in addition to these proverbial expressions commenting on the "long way" of the civil rights movement, there is also Martin Luther King's ingenious use of the spiritual (faith) and secular (hope) proverb "God can (will) make a way out of no way." It grew out of the African American experience of searching to carve out a life of equality and dignity. Strange as it might seem, very little is known about the actual origin, history, and dissemination of this hopeful piece of folk wisdom. It does not appear in any of the standard proverb collections that are notoriously slow in registering new proverbs (Doyle 1996; Mieder 2009b; Mieder et al. 2011). But there is no doubt that it is indeed a folk proverb with considerable amounts of recorded references. Its original version "God can (will) make a way out of no way" yields 2,950 Google hits, with its truncated and secular variant "Making a way out of no way" easily reaching 84,300 references in Google. The proverb has not been found in print before 1900, which does not mean that it might not have been in oral use prior to that date.

Certainly Jack L. Daniel, Geneva Smitherman-Donaldson, and Milford A, Jeremiah, who have studied the rich proverb lore of African Americans, know this text, as can be seen from the title of their article "Makin' a Way out of No Way: The Proverb Tradition in the Black Experience" (1987). However, strangely enough, they do not present the proverb in their list of fifty proverbs collected from African Americans. All that their article does include is the statement "that the essence of the Black Experience is: to make a way out of no way" (Daniel et al. 1987: 494; see also Daniel 1973; Smitherman 1977: 245–46; Barnes-Harden 1980: 57–80; Folly 1982; Mieder 1989: 111–28; Smitherman 1994; Prahlad 1996). This, however, is proof positive that these scholars consider this proverb to reflect the African American worldview of trying to cope and advance with God's help in a world that is not exactly supportive of their efforts.

Among King scholars, it is Jonathan Rieder who has recognized that Martin Luther King did not only cite the proverb but that his entire life and work is the epitome of its basic idea. In fact, his book *The Word of the Lord Is Upon Me: The Righteous Performance of Martin Luther King, Jr.* (2008) contains a short section entitled "The Lord will make a way out of no way" (Rieder 2008: 152–57); but while he refers to King's use of the Bible proverb "Justice will run down like water, and righteousness like a mighty stream" as well as to King's "grandiloquence" and "mobilization talk" (Rieder 2008: 154, 155, 157), he does not mention the folk proverb itself. However, later in his book, Rieder does have this to say: "Like a cheerleader, King offered counter-depressive aphorisms to rouse the spirit: love will not go unredeemed; God will make a way out of no way; my God is a good God; my God is marching on. Such phrases echoed the theology of hope King preached to his congregation, to whom he offered balm that would 'make the wounded whole'" (Rieder 2008: 207).

With this background we can turn to Martin Luther King's obvious knowledge and multiple use of this proverb. For example, in the chapter "Desegregation at Last" of his book *Stride Toward Freedom: The Montgomery Story* (1958), King speaks of God being part of the struggle during the bus boycott and that it is the faith in His power that will give African Americans the strength to carry on. So when King writes "We must believe that a way will be made out of no way," the hidden subject of this passive sentence is in fact God who can find a way out of no way, as the original proverb has it:

The evening came, and I mustered up enough courage to tell them the truth. I tried, however, to end on a note of hope. "This may well be," I said, "the darkest hour just before dawn. We have moved all of these months with the daring faith that God was with us in our struggle. The many experiences of days gone by have vindicated that faith in a most unexpected manner. We must go out with the same faith, the same conviction. We must believe that a way will be made out of no way." But in spite of these words, I could feel the cold breeze of pessimism passing through the audience. It was a dark night—darker than a thousand midnights. It was a night in which the light of hope was about to fade away and the lamp of faith about to flicker. We went home with nothing before us but a cloud of uncertainty. (King 1958: 158–59)

This is, of course, a typically optimistic statement by King that is much enhanced by the inclusion of the folk proverb "The darkest hour is just before dawn." Later, during his interview with *Playboy* editors that appeared in the January 1965 issue, he recounted what he had said to the people involved in the Montgomery bus boycott. And while his memory is quite correct, he now states the proverb with God as its clear subject: "God will make a way for us when there seems no way." By expanding its text slightly, King does in fact explicate its meaning to the editors, who, most likely as whites, might not have known the African American proverb at that time:

There was one dark moment when we doubted it [to be successful with the bus boycott]. We had been struggling to make the boycott a success when the city of Montgomery successfully obtained an injunction from the court to stop our car pool. I didn't know what to say to our people. They had backed us up, and we had let them down. It was a desolate moment. I saw, all of us saw, that the court was leaning against us. I remember telling a group of those working closest with me to spread in the Negro community the message, "We must have the faith that things will work out somehow, that God will make a way for us when there seems no way." It was about noontime, I remember, when Rex Thomas of the Associated Press rushed over to where I was sitting and told me of the news flash that the U.S. Supreme Court had declared that bus segregation in Montgomery was unconstitutional. It had literally been the darkest hour before the dawn. (Washington 1986: 343–44; Jan. 1965)

On August 16, 1967, King cites the proverb once again in his last address as president of the Southern Christian Leadership Conference, entitling his remarks with the question "Where Do We Go from Here?" Almost as expected by now, the proverb is found in the last paragraph of the entire speech, in which King looks with much hope to a better future. While the two quotational proverbs "The arc of the moral universe is long, but it bends towards justice" and "Truth crushed to earth will rise again" together with the Bible proverb "As you sow, so shall you reap" (Gal. 6:7) imply that morality, honesty, and diligence will be rewarded, it is also made clear that there is "a power [i.e., God] that is able to make a way out of no way" for the African American people:

> When our days become dreary with low-hovering clouds of despair, and when our nights become darker than a thousand midnights, let us remember that there is a creative force in this universe, working to pull down the gigantic mountains of evil, a power that is able to make a way out of no way and transform dark yesterdays into bright tomorrows. Let us realize the arc of the moral universe is long but it bends toward justice [Theodore Parker].
>
> Let us realize that William Cullen Bryant is right: "Truth crushed to earth will rise again." Let us go out realizing that the Bible is right: "Be not deceived, God is not mocked. Whatsoever a man soweth, that shall he also reap" [Gal. 6:7]. This is for [*sic*] hope for the future, and with this faith we will be able to sing in some not too distant tomorrow with a cosmic past tense, "We have overcome, we have overcome, deep in my heart, I did believe we would overcome." (Washington 1986: 252; Aug. 16, 1967)

The fact that Martin Luther King quotes the proverb in these variants is an indication that he could rely on his audience knowing it in its basic wording. More importantly, its encouraging wisdom and orientation to the future made it the perfect proverb for King's religious and secular messages filled with faith, hope, and love for a world house of peace and freedom. Against all odds and obstacles, Martin Luther King, as a servant of God and humanity, was indeed a man who believed in and succeeded in "making a way out of no way" in words and deeds. There is then no doubt that this proverb epitomizes the entire civil and human rights movement in the United States and throughout the world, and as such it is the perfect verbal sign for unwavering hope and courageous action. But there is one more fact that deserves to be registered at this point: Martin Luther King's oral and written rhetoric would perhaps not have held people's attention to the degree it did without its proverbial language adding life, spice, and wisdom to it by way of traditional and innovative metaphors.

Proverbial Underpinnings of the "I Have a Dream" Speeches

Finally, one more metaphor needs to be addressed that goes hand in hand with the proverb "Making a way out of no way." In order to look for the ways of social improvements, humankind needs to have a visionary and prophetic dream that promises that a solid faith and unwavering hope in the struggle for civil and human rights will eventually lead to progress. King himself adhered to this dream of equality and justice for all during his entire life. King and the many participants of the civil rights movement fortunately had the audacity to dream of making a way out of no way, and it should thus not be surprising that dreams of an interconnected new world house for all of humanity are a leitmotif in many of King's sermons and speeches, with the very word "dream" repeatedly appearing in their titles.

A passage from an NAACP address "The Negro and the American Dream" that King delivered on September 25, 1960, in Charlotte, North Carolina, shows this very convincingly in the first three paragraphs (Sundquist 2009: 27). It begins with a quotable statement, "America is essentially a dream—a dream yet unfulfilled" (see Kelly-Gangi 2009: 52), and almost predictably includes the two proverbial claims from the Declaration of Independence. But as always, dreaming the dream is not enough for King with the challenge of changing America's dream into reality demanding that all people are willing to pay a high price, as King concludes with yet another one of his favorite proverbial expressions:

> This afternoon I would like to speak from the subject, "The Negro and the American Dream." In a real sense America is essentially a dream—a dream yet unfilfilled [sic]. It is the dream of a land where men of all races, colors and creeds will live together as brothers. The substance of the dream is expressed in these sublime words: "We hold these truths to be self-evident, that all men are created equal, that they are endowed by their creator with certain unalienable rights, that among these are life, liberty and the pursuit of happiness." This is the dream. It is a profound, eloquent and unequivocal expression of the dignity and worth of all human personality.
>
> But ever since the founding fathers of our nation dreamed this dream, America has manifested a schizophrenic personality. She has been torn between [two] selves—a self in which she has proudly professed democracy and a self in which she has sadly practiced the antithesis of democracy. Slavery and segregation have been strange paradoxes in a nation founded on the principle that all men are created equal.

> Now more than ever before America is challenged to bring her noble
> dream into reality. The shape of the world today does not permit America
> the luxury of exploiting the Negro and other minority groups. The price that
> America must pay for the continued opression [*sic*] of the Negro is the price
> of its own destruction. (V, 508–9; Sept. 25, 1960)

This is indeed a memorable paragraph, of which there can be found so many
in King's oeuvre. But it should once again be noted that while this great orator takes his audience to lofty heights regarding the American ideals of democracy, he is quick to point out that they are still far from having been
achieved. Democracy, equality, freedom, etc. demand work and struggle, and
the best way to verbalize these demands is by way of proverbial language.

To a certain degree, these "dream" speeches foreshadow King's famous
"I Have a Dream" oration of August 28, 1963 (Carson and Holloran 1998:
xvi–xvii). But before turning to that address with its unforgettable "I have a
dream" anaphora, at least one of several precursors needs to be mentioned,
for it has been established that "in the spring and summer of 1963, 'I have
a dream' became one of King's most frequently delivered set pieces" (Hansen 2003: 111). On June 23, 1963, King delivered his major "Address at the
Freedom Rally in Cobo Hall" in Detroit. This speech, a mere two months
before the one in Washington, is an excellent example of how King integrates certain rhetorical set pieces with some variations again and again into
his speeches. This version of the "I have a dream" speech includes such fixed
phrases as "If a man has not discovered something that he will die for, he isn't
fit to live"; "Injustice anywhere is a threat to justice everywhere"; "Love your
enemies"; "Love or perish"; "Last hired, first fired"; "No gain without pain";
"to put on the brakes"; "to be called names"; "to have clean hands"; and "to
pay the price for something." But here is the actual "I have a dream" sequence
that adds the proverbs and phrases "to join hands with someone"; "to be
judged by the content of one's character and not by the color of one's skin";
"Let justice roll down like waters, and righteousness like a mighty stream"
(Amos 5:24); "All men are created equal"; "Life, liberty, and the pursuit of
happiness"; and a repetition of "to join hands with someone." This is indeed
a powerful collage of preformulated language, with the "I have a dream"
anaphora adding a contagious rhythm to it, as can be heard from the almost
sermonic testifying by the Detroit audience:

> And so this afternoon, I have a dream. [*Go ahead*] It is a dream deeply rooted
> in the American dream.

I have a dream that one day, right down in Georgia and Mississippi and Alabama, the sons of former slaves and the sons of former slave owners will be able to live together as brothers.

I have a dream this afternoon [*I have a dream*] that one day [*Applause*], one day little white children and little Negro children will be able to join hands as brothers and sisters.

[...]

I have a dream this afternoon [*Yeah*] that my four little children, that my four little children will not come up in the same young days that I came up within, but they will be judged on the basis of the content of their character, and not the color of their skin. [*Applause*]

I have a dream this afternoon that one day right here in Detroit, Negroes will be able to buy a house or rent a house anywhere that their money will carry them and they will be able to get a job. [*Applause*] [*That's right*]

Yes, I have a dream this afternoon that one day in this land the words of Amos will become real and justice will roll down like waters, and righteousness like a mighty stream [Amos 5:24].

I have a dream this evening that one day we will recognize the words of Jefferson that "all men are created equal, that they are endowed by their Creator with certain unalienable Rights, that among these are Life, Liberty and the pursuit of Happiness." I have a dream this afternoon. [*Applause*]

[...]

I have a dream this afternoon that the brotherhood of man will become a reality in this day.

And with this faith I will go out and carve a tunnel of hope through the mountain of despair. With this faith, I will go out with you and transform dark yesterdays into bright tomorrows. With this faith, we will be able to achieve this new day when all of God's children, black men and white men, Jews and Gentiles, Protestants and Catholics, will be able to join hands and sing with the Negroes in the spiritual of old:

Free at last! Free at last!

Thank God Almighty, we are free at last! [*Applause*].

(Carson and Shepard 2001: 71–73; June 23, 1963)

Had this address in Detroit drawn as large a crowd and as much (inter)national attention by the press, it might well have become the most treasured speech by Martin Luther King, giving Detroit (my first home when I arrived in the United States as a German immigrant in August of 1960) a much needed boost as a city that is struggling to this day with racism, poverty, un-employment, and many other social problems.

By the time King delivered his "I have a dream" speech with its set of quo-tational and proverbial statements at the Lincoln Memorial on August 28, 1963, it was billed as the keynote address of the March on Washington, D.C., for Civil Rights. The press from here and abroad was present, a quarter mil-lion people had assembled, and Martin Luther King found himself at the largest public event of the civil rights movement. It gave him and his idea of nonviolent struggle for equality, justice, and freedom a national and sub-sequently an international forum, never to be forgotten by those who were fortunate enough to be present at this momentous occasion, who witnessed the speech on television or listened to it on the radio, read it in the papers the following day, or have come across it on film or in print ever since. Not surprisingly, then, much scholarly attention has been directed to this very speech (see Solomon 1993; Bobbit 2004; Vail 2006; Sayenko 2008), includ-ing two invaluable books, by Drew D. Hansen, *The Dream: Martin Luther King, Jr., and the Speech that Inspired a Nation* (2003), and by Eric J. Sund-quist, *King's Dream* (2009).

As is well known, King began his speech reading from a carefully pre-pared manuscript but, sensing that it prevented him from reaching the large crowd, he spontaneously switched to his "I have a dream" sequence, as Drew D. Hansen has shown in a revealing side-by-side comparison of the written manuscript with the actual oral delivery (Hansen 2003: 71–86). As was his custom, he now relied on his "repertoire of oratorical fragments" or "his own storehouse of oratory" (Hansen 2003: 70), knowing intuitively that his "dream" set piece, spoken as an orally performed conclusion (Patton 1993: 114–16), would give him the desired conclusion that he had not been able to compose during his work on this all-important address the days and night before its delivery. Here then is the "I have a dream" peroration with but three proverbial statements, i.e. "All men are created equal" and the prover-bial phrases "to be judged by the content of one's character and not by the color of one's skin" and "to join hands with someone," with the latter being cited twice as a verbal sign of true brother- and sisterhood in an America of equality, justice, and freedom:

> So I say to you, my friends, that even though we must face the difficulties of today and tomorrow, I still have a dream. It is a dream deeply rooted in the American dream that one day this nation will rise up and live out the true

meaning of its creed—we hold these truths to be self-evident, that all men are created equal.

I have a dream that one day on the red hills of Georgia, sons of former slaves and sons of former slave-owners will be able to sit down together at the table of brotherhood.

I have a dream that one day, even the state of Mississippi, a state sweltering with the heat of injustice, sweltering with the heat of oppression, will be transformed into an oasis of freedom and justice.

I have a dream my four little children will one day live in a nation where they will not be judged by the color of their skin but by content of their character. I have a dream today!

I have a dream that one day, down in Alabama, with its vicious racists, with its governor having his lips dripping with the words of interposition and nullification, that one day, right there in Alabama, little black boys and black girls will be able to join hands with the little white boys and white girls as sisters and brothers. I have a dream today! [...]

With this faith we will be able to hear [*sic*, i.e. hew] out of the mountain of despair a stone of hope. With this faith we will be able to transform the jangling discords of our nation into a beautiful symphony of brotherhood.

With this faith we will be able to work together, to pray together, to struggle together, to go to jail together, to stand up for freedom together, knowing that we will be free one day. This will be the day when all of God's children will be able to sing with new meaning— "my country 'tis of thee: sweet land of liberty; of thee I sing; land where my fathers died, land of the pilgrim's pride; from every mountain side, let freedom ring"—and if America is to be a great nation, this must become true.

So let freedom ring [...]

And when we allow freedom to ring, when we let it ring from every village and hamlet, from every state and city, we will be able to speed up that day when all of God's children—black men and white men, Jews and Gentiles, Catholics and Protestants—will be able to join hands and to sing in the words of the old Negro spiritual, "Free at last, free at last; thank God Almighty, we are free at last."
(Washington 1986: 219–20; August 28, 1963)

It goes to Eric J. Sundquist's credit that he draws attention to King's formulaic "Not by the Color of Their Skin" statement at the beginning of his long chapter with that title in his book *King's Dream* (2009: 194–228):

Even though it does not provide the Dream speech's most famous phrase, one sentence stands alone for the philosophy it appeared to announce and the contentious use to which it has since been put: "I have a dream that my four little children will one day live in a nation where they will not be judged by the color of their skin but by the content of their character." If King's dream began to be realized with passage of the Civil Rights Act of 1964, his apparently clear elevation of character over color proved central to subsequent arguments about the reach and consequences of that landmark legislation. Those thirty-five spontaneous words have done more than any politician's polemic, any sociologist's theory, or any court's ruling to frame public discussion of affirmative action over the past four decades. (Sundquist 2009: 194)

Regarding the use of the "phrase" (he comes close to calling it a proverbial phrase), Sundquist is correct in referring to its "spontaneous" use in the context of this particular speech. It was in fact not included in the original manuscript and King added it during his extemporaneous peroration: "'I started out reading the speech,' recalled Martin Luther King, Jr., then 'all of a sudden this thing came out of me that I have used—I'd used it many times before, that thing about 'I have a dream'—and I just felt that I wanted to use it here. I don't know why, I hadn't thought about it before the speech'" (Sundquist 2009: 14). King was thus obviously aware of his recycling of the "I have a dream" sequence in a number of variants, and I would assume that he also knew about his previous use of the "character/skin" phrase in his "dream" peroration of the address in Detroit two months earlier. If Sundquist, with his reference to "spontaneous words," means to imply that the use of the phrase was new in the Washington speech, then he would be mistaken. In fact, as it were, King quite liked its metaphor and meaning, citing it three more times in sermons and speeches during 1967, thereby effectively helping his formulation along the path of becoming a proverbial expression.

By the end of 1967, the "I have a dream" anaphora, modified to "I still have a dream" after its (inter)national exposure at the Lincoln Memorial on August 28, 1963, had doubtlessly become King's rhetorical signature phrase. Of course, it represents but one of his quotational and proverbial leitmotifs that made his sermons, speeches, letters essays, and books such effective and memorable statements in the cause of civil and human rights. Quotations turned proverbs, Bible proverbs, folk proverbs, and a plethora of proverbial expressions are an intrinsic part of King's rhetorical prowess, providing his messages with colorful metaphors and authoritative strength. His noble dream of an America and a world interconnected by equality, justice, freedom, love, and hope had to be expressed through language so that the nonviolent movement for civil and human rights could march forward. Individual words and sentences were needed to bring these dignified ideals across, and there can be no doubt that proverbs and proverbial phrases as ready-made expressions served King extremely well in adding imagery and expressiveness to his numerous oral and written communications. His dream needed words and deeds, and being a master of both, Martin Luther King was and remains the visionary champion of making a way out of no way for all of humanity that due to him has come a long way but still has a long way to go. Moving on with an adherence to the Biblical triad of "faith, hope, and love" and the acceptance of the African American proverb "Making a way out of no way" will keep Martin Luther King's proverbial dream alive for future generations as they confront their fate in the world house of brotherly and sisterly mutuality.

BIBLIOGRAPHY

This chapter was first published with the same title in *Proverbium: Yearbook of International Proverb Scholarship* 28 (2011): 147–92.

Aron, Paul. 2008. *We Hold These Truths . . . And Other Words that Made America*. Lanham, Maryland: Rowman & Littlefield.

Ayres, Alex, ed. 1993. *The Wisdom of Martin Luther King, Jr.* New York: Meridian.

Baldwin, Lewis V. 1988 (1989). "The Minister as Preacher, Pastor, and Prophet: The Thinking of Martin Luther King, Jr." *American Baptist Quarterly* 7: 79–97. Also in *Martin Luther King, Jr.: Civil Rights Leader, Theologian, Orator*. David J. Garrow, ed. 3 vols. Brooklyn, New York: Carlson, 1989. I, 39–57.

———. 1991. *There Is a Balm in Gilead: The Cultural Roots of Martin Luther King, Jr.* Minneapolis, Minnesota: Augsburg Fortress.

Barnes-Harden, Alene L. 1980. "Proverbs, Folk Expressions, and Superstitions." In A. L. Barnes Harden, ed., *African American Verbal Arts: Their Nature and Communicative interpretation (A Thematic Analysis)*. Diss., State University of New York at Buffalo. 57–80.

Bobbitt, David A. 2004. *The Rhetoric of Redemption: Kenneth Burke's Redemption Drama and Martin Luther King, Jr.'s "I Have a Dream" Speech*. Lanham, Maryland: Rowman & Littlefield.

Boesak, Allan. 1976 (1989). *Coming in out of the Wilderness: A Comparative Interpretation of the Ethics of Martin Luther King, Jr. and Malcolm X*. Kampen, Nederland: Theologische Hogeschool der Gereformeerde Kerken. Also in *Martin Luther King, Jr.: Civil Rights Leader, Theologian, Orator*. David J. Garrow, ed. 3 vols. Brooklyn, New York: Carlson, 1989. I, 59–126.

Boulware, Marcus H. 1969. *The Oratory of Negro Leaders: 1900–1968*. Westport, Connecticut: Negro Universities Press.

Burger, Harald, Dmitrij Dobrovol'skij, Peter Kühn, and Neal R. Norrick, eds. 2007. *Phraseology: An International Handbook of Contemporary Research*. 2 vols. Berlin: Walter de Gruyter.

Calloway-Thomas, Carolyn, and John Louis Lucaites, eds. 1993. *Martin Luther King, Jr., and the Sermonic Power of Public Discourse*. Tuscaloosa, Alabama: University of Alabama Press.

Carson, Clayborne, et al., eds. 1992–2007. *The Papers of Martin Luther King, Jr.* 6 vols. Berkeley, California: University of California Press.

Carson, Clayborne, and Peter Holloran, eds. 1998. *A Knock at Midnight: Inspiration from the Great Sermons of Reverend Martin Luther King, Jr.* New York: Warner.

Carson, Clayborne, and Kris Shepard, eds. 2001. *A Call to Conscience: The Landmark Speeches of Dr. Martin Luther King, Jr.* New York: Grand Central.

Carter, Dale. 1996. "Bending Towards Justice: Martin Luther King, Jr. and the Assessment of History." *American Studies in Scandinavia* 29: 128–41.

Charteris-Black, Jonathan. 2005. "Martin Luther King: Messianic Myth." *Politicians and Rhetoric: The Persuasive Power of Metaphor.* J. Charteris-Black, ed. New York: Palgrave Macmillan. 58–85, 214–17 (appendix).

Cornette, James C. 1942 (1997). *Proverbs and Proverbial Expressions in the German Works of Martin Luther.* Diss., University of North Carolina at Chapel Hill. Posthumously edited and published by Wolfgang Mieder and Dorothee Racette. Bern: Peter Lang, 1997.

Daniel, Jack L. 1973. "Towards an Ethnography of Afroamerican Proverbial Usage." *Black Lines* 2: 3–12.

———. 1979. *The Wisdom of Sixth Mount Zion [Church] from the Members of the Sixth Mount Zion and Those Who Begot Them.* Pittsburgh, Pennsylvania: University of Pittsburgh College of Arts and Sciences.

Daniel, Jack L., and Geneva Smitherman. 1976. "How I Got Over: Communication Dynamics in the Black Community." *Quarterly Journal of Speech* 62: 26–39.

Daniel, Jack L., Geneva Smitherman-Donaldson, and Milford A. Jeremiah. 1987. "Makin' a Way out of no Way: The Proverb Tradition in the Black Experience." *Journal of Black Studies* 17: 482–508.

Doyle, Charles Clay. 1996. "On 'New' Proverbs and the Conservativeness of Proverb Dictionaries." *Proverbium* 13: 69–84.

Doyle, Charles Clay, Wolfgang Mieder, and Fred R. Shapiro, eds. 2012. *The Dictionary of Modern Proverbs.* New Haven, Connecticut: Yale University Press.

Ensslin, Birgit. 1990. "'I Have a Dream'—Martin Luther King und die Bürgerrechtsbewegung in den USA. Eine rhetorische Analyse ausgewählter Texte von Martin Luther King." *Lebende Sprachen* 35: 118–23.

Farrell, Thomas J. 1991. "The Antecedents of King's Message." *Publications of the Modern Language Association* 106: 529–30.

Fleer, David. 1995. *Martin Luther King, Jr.'s Reformation of Sources: A Close Rhetorical Reading of His Compositional Strategies and Arrangement.* Diss., University of Washington.

Folly, Dennis Wilson (Sw. Anand Prahlad). 1982. "'Getting the Butter from the Duck': Proverbs and Proverbial Expressions in an Afro-American Family." *A Celebration of American Family Folklore: Tales and Traditions from the Smithsonian Collection.* Steven J. Zeitlin, Amy J. Kotkin, and Holly Cutting Baker, eds. New York: Pantheon. 232–41, 290–91 (notes).

Garrow, David J., ed. 1989. *Martin Luther King, Jr.: Civil Rights Leader, Theologian, Orator.* 3 vols. Brooklyn, New York: Carlson.

Griffin, Albert Kirby. 1991. *Religious Proverbs: Over 1600 Adages from 18 Faiths Worldwide.* Jefferson, North Carolina: McFarland.

Hansen, Drew D. 2003. *The Dream: Martin Luther King, Jr., and the Speech that Inspired a Nation.* New York: HarperCollins.

Harrison, Robert D., and Linda K. Harrison. 1993. "The Call from the Mountaintop: Call-Response and the Oratory of Martin Luther King, Jr." *Martin Luther King, Jr., and the Sermonic Power of Public Discourse.* Carolyn Calloway-Thomas and John Louis Lucaites, eds. Tuscaloosa, Alabama: University of Alabama Press. 162–78.

Hedgepeth, Chester M. 1984 (1989). "Philosophical Eclecticism in the Writings of Martin Luther King, Jr." *Western Journal of Black Studies* 8: 79–86. Also in *Martin Luther King, Jr.: Civil Rights Leader, Theologian, Orator.* David J. Garrow, ed. 3 vols. Brooklyn, New York: Carlson, 1989. II, 541–48.

Hertzler, Joyce O. 1933–34. "On Golden Rules." *International Journal of Ethics* 44: 418–36.

Hoskins, Lotte, ed. 1968. *"I Have a Dream": The Quotations of Martin Luther King Jr.* New York: Grosset & Dunlap.

Karabegović, Dženeta. 2007. "'No Lie Can Live Forever': Zur sprichwörtlichen Rhetorik von Martin Luther King." *Sprichwörter sind Goldes wert: Parömiologische Studien zu Kultur, Literatur und Medien.* Wolfgang Mieder, ed. Burlington, Vermont: University of Vermont. 223–40.

Kelly-Gangi, Carol. 2009. *Essential African American Wisdom.* New York: Fall River Press.

King, Martin Luther. 1958. *Stride Toward Freedom: The Montgomery Story.* New York: Harper & Row.

———. 1963. *Strength to Love.* New York: Harper & Row.

———. 1964. *Why We Can't Wait.* New York: Harper & Row.

———. 1967a. *Where Do We Go from Here: Chaos or Community?* New York: Harper & Row.

———. 1967b. *The Trumpet of Conscience.* New York: Harper & Row.

Lischer, Richard. 1995. *The Preacher King: Martin Luther King, Jr. and the Word that Moved America.* New York: Oxford University Press.

Louis, Cameron. 2000. "Proverbs and the Politics of Language." *Proverbium* 17: 173–94.

Luker, Ralph E. 2003. "Quoting, Merging, and Sampling the Dream: Martin Luther King and Vernon Johns." *Southern Cultures* 9: 28–48.

Marbury, Carl H. 1971 (1989). "An Excursus on the Biblical and Theological Rhetoric of Martin Luther King." *Essays in Honor of Martin Luther King, Jr.* John H. Cartwright, ed. Evanston, Illinois: Garrett Evangelical Theological Seminary. 14–28. Also in *Martin Luther King, Jr.: Civil Rights Leader, Theologian, Orator.* David J. Garrow, ed. 3 vols. Brooklyn, New York: Carlson, 1989. III, 623–34.

McKenzie, Alyce M. 1996. *Preaching Proverbs: Wisdom for the Pulpit.* Louisville, Kentucky: Westminster John Knox Press.

———. 2002. *Preaching Biblical Wisdom in a Self-Help Society.* Nashville, Tennessee: Abingdon Press.

Mieder, Wolfgang. 1989. *American Proverbs: A Study of Texts and Contexts.* Bern: Peter Lang.

———. 1990. *Not by Bread Alone: Proverbs of the Bible.* Shelburne, Vermont: New England Press.

———. 1993. *Proverbs Are Never Out of Season: Popular Wisdom in the Modern Ages.* New York: Oxford University Press.

———. 1997. *The Politics of Proverbs: From Traditional Wisdom to Proverbial Stereotypes.* Madison, Wisconsin: University of Wisconsin Press.

———. 2000. *The Proverbial Abraham Lincoln: An Index to Proverbs in the Works of Abraham Lincoln.* New York: Peter Lang.

———. 2001. *"No Struggle, No Progress": Frederick Douglass and His Proverbial Rhetoric for Civil Rights.* New York: Peter Lang.

———. 2004. *Proverbs: A Handbook.* Westport, Connecticut: Greenwood.

———. 2005. *Proverbs Are the Best Policy: Folk Wisdom and American Politics.* Logan, Utah: Utah State University Press.

———. 2008a. "'Let Us Have Faith that Right Makes Might': Proverbial Rhetoric in Decisive Moments of American Politics." *Proverbium* 25: 319–52.

———. 2008b. *"Proverbs Speak Louder Than Words": Folk Wisdom in Art, Culture, Folklore, History, Literature, and Mass Media.* New York: Peter Lang.

———. 2009a. *International Bibliography of Paremiology and Phraseology.* 2 vols. Berlin: Walter de Gruyter.

———. 2009b. "'New Proverbs Run Deep': Prolegomena to a Dictionary of Modern Anglo-American Proverbs." *Proverbium* 26: 237–74.

———. 2009c. *"Yes We Can": Barack Obama's Proverbial Rhetoric.* New York: Peter Lang.

———. 2010. *"Making a Way out of No Way": Martin Luther King's Sermonic Proverbial Rhetoric.* New York: Peter Lang.

Mieder, Wolfgang, Stewart A. Kingsbury, and Kelsie B. Harder, eds. 1992. *A Dictionary of American Proverbs.* New York: Oxford University Press.

Miller, Keith D. 1986 (1989). "Martin Luther King, Jr. Borrows a Revolution: Argument, Audience, and Implications of a Secondhand Universe." *College English* 48: 249–65. Also in *Martin Luther King, Jr.: Civil Rights Leader, Theologian, Orator.* David J. Garrow, ed. 3 vols. Brooklyn, New York: Carlson, 1989. III, 643–59.

———. 1990. "Composing Martin Luther King, Jr." *Publications of the Modern Language Association* 105: 70–82.

———. 1991a. "Martin Luther King, Jr., and the Black Folk Pulpit." *Journal of American History* 78: 120–23.

———. 1991b. "Reply [to Thomas J. Farrell, 'The Antecedents of King's Message']." *Publications of the Modern Language Association* 106: 530–31.

———. 1992. *Voice of Deliverance: The Language of Martin Luther King, Jr. and Its Sources.* New York: Free Press.

Nichols, Ray. 1996. "Maxims, 'Practical Wisdom,' and the Language of Action." *Political Theory* 24: 687–705.

Obama, Barack. 2006. *The Audacity of Hope: Thoughts on Reclaiming the American Dream.* New York: Three Rivers Press.

Ong. Walter J. 1982. *Orality and Literacy: The Technologizing of the Word.* New York: Methuen.

Patton, John H. 1993. "'I Have a Dream': The Performance of Theology Fused with the Power of Orality." *Martin Luther King, Jr., and the Sermonic Power of Public Discourse.* Carolyn Calloway-Thomas and John Louis Lucaites, eds. Tuscaloosa, Alabama: University of Alabama Press. 104–26.

Prahlad, Sw. Anand. 1996. *African-American Proverbs in Context.* Jackson, Mississippi: University Press of Mississippi.

Rieder, Jonathan. 2008. *The Word of the Lord Is Upon Me: The Righteous Performance of Martin Luther King, Jr.* Cambridge, Massachusetts: Harvard University Press.

Rosenberg, Bruce. 1970. *The Art of the American Folk Preacher.* New York: Oxford University Press.

Sayenko, Tetyana. 2008. "On the Pragmatic and Prosodic Structure of an Inspirational Political Address [i.e., Martin Luther King's 'I Have a Dream']." *Rhetorical Aspects of Discourses in Present-Day Society.* Lotte Dam, Liese-Lotte Holmgreen, and Jeanne Strunck, eds. Newcastle upon Tyne: Cambridge Scholars Publishing. 129–53.

Shapiro, Fred, ed. 2006. *The Yale Book of Quotations.* New Haven, Connecticut: Yale University Press (21 references by King on pp. 427–29).

Sharman, Nick. 1999. "'Remaining Awake Through a Great Revolution': The Rhetorical Strategies of Martin Luther King Jr." *Social Semiotics* 9: 85–105.

Smith, Arthur L., and Stephen Robb, eds. 1971. *The Voice of Black Rhetoric: Selections.* Boston: Allyn and Bacon.

Smitherman, Geneva. 1977. *Talkin and Testifyin: The Language of Black America.* Detroit, Michigan: Wayne State University Press.

———. 1994. *Black Talk: Words and Phrases from the Hood to the Amen Corner.* Boston: Houghton Mifflin.

Solomon, Martha. 1993. "Covenanted Rights: The Metaphoric Matrix of 'I Have a Dream.'" *Martin Luther King, Jr., and the Sermonic Power of Public Discourse.* Carolyn Calloway-Thomas and John Louis Lucaites, eds. Tuscaloosa, Alabama: University of Alabama Press. 68–84.

Spillers, Hortense J. 1971 (1989). "Martin Luther King and the Style of the Black Sermon." *Black Scholar* 3: 14–27. Also in *Martin Luther King, Jr.: Civil Rights Leader, Theologian, Orator.* David J. Garrow, ed. 3 vols. Brooklyn, New York: Carlson, 1989. III, 876–89.

Stevenson, Burton. 1935. "The Mouse-Trap [and] More about the Mouse-Trap." In Burton Stevenson, *Famous Single Poems and the Controversies which Have Raged around Them.* New York: Dodd, Mead. 343–81.

——. 1948. *The Home Book of Proverbs, Maxims, and Famous Phrases.* New York: Macmillan.

——. 1949. *The Home Book of Bible Quotations.* New York: Harper & Brothers.

Sundquist, Eric J. 2009. *King's Dream.* New Haven, Connecticut: Yale University Press.

Taylor, Archer. 1931 (1985). *The Proverb.* Cambridge, Massachusetts: Harvard University Press. Rpt. with an introduction and bibliography by Wolfgang Mieder. Bern: Peter Lang, 1985.

Templeton, John Marks. 1997. *Worldwide Laws of Life.* Philadelphia, Pennsylvania: Templeton Foundation Press.

Turner, Otis. 1977 (1989). "Nonviolence and the Politics of Liberation." *Journal of the Interdenominational Theological Center* 4: 49–60. Also in *Martin Luther King, Jr.: Civil Rights Leader, Theologian, Orator.* David J. Garrow, ed. 3 vols. Brooklyn, New York: Carlson, 1989. III, 997–1008.

Vail, Mark. 2006. "The 'Integrative' Rhetoric of Martin Luther King Jr.'s 'I Have a Dream' Speech." *Rhetoric & Public Affairs* 9: 51–78.

Warren, Mervyn A. 1966. *A Rhetorical Study of the Preaching of Doctor Martin Luther King, Jr., Pastor and Pulpit Orator.* Diss., Michigan State University.

——. 2001. *King Came Preaching: The Pulpit Power of Dr. Martin Luther King Jr.* Downers Grove, Illinois: InterVarsity Press (revised version of the previous entry).

Washington, James M., ed. 1986. *A Testament of Hope: The Essential Writings of Martin Luther King, Jr.* San Francisco, California: Harper & Row.

Winton, Alan P. 1990. *The Proverbs of Jesus: Issues of History and Rhetoric.* Sheffield, UK: Sheffield Academic Press.

5. "THE GOLDEN RULE AS POLITICAL IMPERATIVE"
President Barack Obama's Proverbial Worldview

On January 20, 2009, the brand-new President of the United States Barack Obama delivered his eagerly awaited inaugural address to the American people and the rest of the world. Of course, the pressures and expectations for Obama to give a most memorable speech were exceedingly high, and there was much talk and speculation about what he would include and how he would verbalize this address. This also led to a series of reviews of previous inaugural addresses, with Jill Lepore's essay of January 12, 2009, on "The Speech: Have Inaugural Addresses Been Getting Worse?" in *The New Yorker* standing out as a solid piece of historical scholarship. It begins with the statement that "Barack Obama has been studying up, reading Abraham Lincoln's speeches, raising everyone's expectations for what just might be the most eagerly awaited inaugural" (Lepore 2009: 49). The author goes on to explain how previous presidents received plenty of help from friends and speechwriters in the formulation of their inaugurals, with James Garfield and Jimmy Carter most likely being the only presidents who wrote this particular address completely on their own. As has been pointed out repeatedly by presidential historians and rhetorical studies (see Denton and Woodward 1998; Lim 2008), the ritual of the inauguration of the president has turned the speech into a somewhat formulaic event, making it very difficult to deviate from various traditional expectations:

> From a generic perspective, then, a presidential inaugural reconstitutes the people as an audience that can witness the rite of investiture, rehearses communal values from the past, sets forth the political principles that will guide the new administration, and demonstrates that the president can enact the presidential persona appropriately. Still more generally, the presidential inaugural address is an epideictic [rhetorically demonstrative] ritual that is formal, unifying, abstract, and eloquent. At the core of this ritual lies epideictic timelessness—the fusion of the past and future of the nation in an eternal

present in which we reaffirm what Franklin Roosevelt called "our covenant with ourselves," a covenant between the executive and the nation that is the essence of democratic government. (Campbell and Jamieson 2008: 56)

Having looked at previous inaugural addresses that are easily accessible in a number of anthologies (see Hunt 1997; Lott 1961; Remini and Golway 2008), Barack Obama was well aware of the uplifting purpose that is certainly different from speeches given during political campaigns. So Obama, the impressive rhetorician and orator, did well to decide to write his speech himself (see Newton-Small 2008), receiving only minor editorial or factual help, as reported by Mary Kate Cary, former speechwriter for President George H. W. Bush:

Earlier this morning [January 20, 2009], aides to Mr. Obama told reporters that the president-elect had consulted historian David McCullough (presumably to double-check the references to Valley Forge); Lincoln biographer Doris Kearns Goodwin (he mentioned the Gettysburg address, and his homage to those who endured the "lash of the whip" was a reference to a line in Lincoln's second inaugural) and the dean of the White House speechwriters, Kennedy speechwriter Ted Sorensen. I'm sure Mr. Sorensen liked the litany "To the Muslim world . . . To those leaders around the globe . . . To those who cling to power through corruption . . . To the people of poor nations . . ." which clearly echoed a similar litany in Kennedy's inaugural address. (Cary 2009)

An Inaugural Address without Famous Quotations

One of the big surprises of the inaugural speech was in fact that Obama, breaking with his own predilection for doing so, did not include any well-known quotations by such great Americans as Abraham Lincoln, Franklin D. Roosevelt, John F. Kennedy, and others. Gerard Baker put it somewhat negatively in his comments on "The Speech That Failed to Fly" one day after its delivery in the London *Times*:

There were few truly memorable pieces of phraseology—no Kennedyesque, or Rooseveltian quotations for the ages.

He [Obama] laboured hard to echo the tone and cadence of his biggest campaign performances. And there was more than a hint of a self-conscious echo—distractingly—of the speeches of his hero and fellow Illinoisan, Abraham Lincoln.

The language in particular sounded decidedly 19th century in parts—all those commands to "know" some or other intent of US policy, all those glancing biblical references.

But it wasn't up to Lincoln's standards—which perhaps is asking too much. In fact, it may not have been really memorable at all. It's unlikely that most people will remember a phrase from it a few weeks from now, let alone a century.

In fairness it was a speech more obviously measured to the practical immensity of the immediate challenges. It was directed at two audiences: a hopeful but anxious one at home, and an uncertain but hopeful one overseas. (Baker 2009)

I must admit that at first I was also a little disappointed by Obama not having employed any of his "favorite" quotations, many of which have turned into proverbs, to wit Abraham Lincoln's use of "A house divided against itself cannot stand" and "Government of the people, by the people, and for the people"; Frederick Douglass's "Power never concedes without a demand"; Franklin D. Roosevelt's "We have nothing to fear but fear itself"; John F. Kennedy's "Don't ask what your country can do for you, ask what you can do for your country"; etc. (see Mieder 1997: 99–137, 1998, 2000, 2001, 2005d). Of course, I liked Obama's allusion to Winston S. Churchill's title *The Gathering Storm* (1948) of the first volume of his celebrated six-volume history of *The Second World War* (1948–54) by speaking of the fact that "every so often, the [presidential] oath is taken amidst gathering clouds and raging storms" (see Mieder and Bryan 1995; Sanger 2009). His variation, at the end of the inaugural address, of William Shakespeare's proverbial line "Now is the winter of our discontent" (1594, *Richard III*), further popularized by John Steinbeck's last novel *The Winter of Our Discontent* (1961), was clearly also very effective as a follow-up comment to the unexpected and little-known quotation of a statement made by George Washington at Valley Forge:

In the year of America's birth, in the coldest of months, a small band of patriots huddled by dying campfires on the shores of an icy river. The capital was abandoned. The enemy was advancing. The snow was stained with blood. At a moment when the outcome of our revolution was most in doubt, the father of our nation ordered these words to be read to the people:

"Let it be told to the future world . . . that in the depth of winter, when nothing but hope and virtue could survive . . . that the city and the country, alarmed at one common danger, came forth to meet [it]."

America. In the face of our common dangers, in this winter of our hardship, let us remember these timeless words. With hope and virtue, let us brave once more the icy currents, and endure what storms may come. (For references from Barack Obama's speeches see www.obamaspeeches.com/)

This quotation from the father of the American nation marks the beginning of Obama's emotional peroration of his magisterial address, which speaks not of the "discontent" of the American people but rather of the "hardship" that they can and will conquer: "Let it be said by our children's children that when we were tested, we refused to let this journey end, that we did not turn back, nor did we falter; and with the eyes fixed on the horizon and God's grace upon us, we carried forth that great gift of freedom and delivered it safely to future generations." This is inaugural speech at its best at the end, and upon reflection I am thoroughly convinced that Barack Obama was wise to finish with Washington's insistence on hope, virtue, and freedom couched not in a quotable phrase but rather in a verbal image of striving toward a better future.

Immediate Journalistic Reactions to the Inaugural Address

Before moving on to an analysis of the proverbial language of Obama's inaugural address, let me present a few additional comments by journalists and former presidential speechwriters concerning the relationship between rhetoric and content in his remarks. Michael Gerson, who basically wrote George W. Bush's first inaugural address in 2001, was quite harsh in his criticism, claiming that "too many of his [Obama's] words were platitudes" and that "heading into this inaugural address, many expected the speech to be rhetorically masterful but perhaps ideologically shallow. Instead, we heard a speech that was rhetorically flat and substantively interesting. On his first day in office, President Obama has managed to surprise." Gerson goes on to argue that "like Lincoln or Martin Luther King Jr. [see Karabegović 2007; Mieder 2010], Obama positioned himself as a conservative revolutionary— attempting to re-create our country by reasserting the traditional moral principles that gave it birth" (Gerson 2009). I am not certain whether all of these leaders would agree with the "conservative revolutionary" label, but, to look at it positively, it might help Obama bring more Republican conservatives on board of the changing ship of state.

Tom Brune, writing in *Newsday*, is a bit more balanced in his analysis of the epideictic nature of Obama's speech, stressing in all fairness that the address had to be somewhat anti-climatic in view of all the incredible "noise" that the media had created around this event:

> Barack Obama didn't always soar in his inaugural address yesterday, but he scored the points he needed to satisfy the legion of hopeful supporters eagerly listening to the new president here and around the world.
>
> Looking out over a sea of people from the Capitol's west steps on a cold, sunny midday, Obama delivered a confident, almost somber speech, rooted in history and aimed at the future, with the primary themes of responsibility and change.
>
> After all the hype leading up to the ceremony yesterday, Obama's address almost seemed anti-climatic, but it still hit every marker he needed to hit in a strong speech that lasted just about 20 minutes. (Brune 2009)

And here is a third view, this time from abroad, by Fintan O'Toole of *The Irish Times*, who to my way of thinking hits the proverbial nail on the head with his analysis. Yes, there definitely was a change from Obama's rallying campaign rhetoric, with its use of preformulated language based on emotive expressiveness, to a more sober and content-rich communicative approach. On January 20, 2009, with the oath of office and the inaugural speech, the candidate and President-elect Barack Obama changed to President Barack Obama, and this giant step is, appropriately so, reflected in a noticeable change of language:

> The shift from candidate to president was obvious to a degree that may have disappointed some of his hearers.
>
> It was not just that Obama's eloquence was less fluent, less dazzling, less of a performance, than the electrifying speeches that previously defined him, the address to the Democratic Party convention in 2004 that marked him out [see Frank and McPhail 2005], or the brilliant discourse on race that saved his candidacy last year [see Wills 2008].
>
> His body language was certainly more constrained, his cadences less dramatic, his rhythms less mesmeric. (O'Toole 2009)

From a purely rhetorical point of view I also was at first a bit disappointed with the inaugural address by the absence of quotations, pseudo-proverbs, proverbs, proverbial phrases and twin formulas that had been the trademark of Obama's writings and speeches. Upon reflection, I came around to thinking that Obama, wanting this speech to be his very own, must have consciously decided to stay away from some of those expected quotations by former presidents and time-worn proverbs (see Harnsberger 1964; Jay 1996; Miller 1989).

Lack of President Obama's Earlier Quotable Creations

However, I am still wondering why he did not use some of his own phraseological creations from previous speeches that by their structures and metaphors have a good chance to become quotable or proverbial (see Mieder 2004: xii–xiii, 132–33):

"America prospers when all Americans prosper." (June 28, 2008, Washington, and in five subsequent speeches)

"If you invest in America, America will invest in you." (June 16, 2008, Flint, Michigan, and in nine subsequent speeches)

"In America, separate can never be equal." (May 1, 2005, Detroit, Michigan, and in three subsequent speeches)

"Ballot boxes don't make a democracy." (March 21, 2007, Washington, and in one subsequent speech)

"Countries that out-teach us today will out-compete us tomorrow." (September 3, 2007, Manchester, New Hampshire, and in one subsequent speech)

"You can't change direction with a new driver who follows the same old map." (September 18, 2008, Espanola, New Mexico, and in one subsequent speech)

"The government that people count on most is the one that's closest to the people." (June 21, 2008, Miami, Florida)

"One man cannot make a movement." (September 28, 2007, Washington)

"Opportunity doesn't come easy." (September 18, 2007, Washington)

"A new politics for a new time." (August 28, 2008, Denver, Colorado)

"We cannot have a thriving Wall Street and a struggling Main Street (while Main Street suffers)." (July 30, 2008, Springfield, Missouri, and in seven subsequent speeches)

Obviously not every one of these quotable creations, in the form of pseudo-proverbs (i.e., proverb-like), by Barack Obama would have been suitable for the inaugural address, but his formulation "A new politics for a new time" would have fit, at least in my opinion. He had used it in his acceptance speech on "The American Promise" at the Democratic National Convention on August 28, 2008, in Denver, Colorado, with millions of Americans witnessing its creation as they watched and heard Obama on television. Strangely enough, he never used this pseudo-proverb again, and he missed the opportunity to make it into a truly memorable phrase at the time of his inauguration when he said:

> That we are in the midst of crisis is now well understood. Our nation is at war, against a far-reaching network of violence and hatred. Our economy is badly weakened, a consequence of greed and irresponsibility on the part of some, but also our collective failure to make hard choices and prepare the nation for a new age. Homes have been lost; jobs shed; businesses shuttered. Our health care is too costly; our schools fail too many; and each day brings further evidence that the ways we use energy strengthen our adversaries and threaten our planet.

At the end of this enumeration, I believe that Barack Obama might well have interspersed his quotable, memorable, and proverb-like invention "A new politics for a new time." I am convinced that critics of the inaugural address would have interpreted its use positively.

No Direct Reference to the Proverbs of American Democracy

Instead, Obama moved on with a short but powerful paragraph, employing the first of eighteen proverbs, pseudo-proverbs, and proverbial phrases that are part of this speech:

These are the indicators of crisis, subject to data and statistics. Less measurable but no less profound is a sapping of confidence across our land—a nagging fear that America's decline is inevitable, and that the next generation must lower its sights. Today I say to you that the challenges we face are real. They are serious and they are many. They will not be met easily or in a short span of time. But know this, America: They will be met.

This is vintage Obama rhetoric, with first applying the negative proverbial phrase "To lower one's sights" and then immediately pushing it aside in favor of meeting the challenges facing the country with courage, hope, and optimism. By now Obama is on a proverbial roll, even though his use of the Biblical phrase "To set aside childish things" (I Corinthians 13:11; Stevenson 1949: 290) and the allusion to the proverb "All men are created equal" and the triad "Life, liberty, and the pursuit of happiness" from the Declaration of Independence are much more subtle than their employment during the campaign:

We remain a young nation, but in the words of Scripture, the time has come to set aside childish things. The time has come to reaffirm our enduring spirit; to choose our better history; to carry forward that precious gift, that noble idea, passed on from generation to generation: the God-given promise that all are equal, all are free, and all deserve a chance to pursue their full measure of happiness.

Here I can show that Barack Obama consciously tuned down his use of quotations and proverbs as he was gearing up for his inaugural address. It will be remembered that three days before his inauguration, on Saturday, January 17, 2009, Barack Obama and Joe Biden and their families embarked on a whistle-stop train trip from Philadelphia to Washington, in part retracing the trip that Abraham Lincoln had taken to his inauguration. In two basically identical speeches in Philadelphia and Baltimore on that day Obama said:

And yet, they [early patriots] were willing to put all they were and all they had on the line—their lives, their fortunes and their sacred honor—for a set of ideals that continue to light the world. That we are equal. That our rights to life, liberty and the pursuit of happiness come not from our laws, but from our maker. And that government of, by and for the people can endure. It was these ideals that led us to declare independence and craft our constitution, producing documents that were imperfect but had within them, like our nation itself, the capacity to be made more perfect.

Already here he has changed the proverb "All men are created equal" to the shorter and gender-free statement "We are all equal." However, he still maintains the proverbial triad "Life, liberty, and the pursuit of happiness," and also at least alludes to the proverbial definition of democracy by stating that "government of, by and for the people can endure" (see Mieder 2005b; Wills 1992). Personally, I wish he had not dropped this proverb in its shortened form. In fact, I think this entire paragraph, with its reference to making the union more perfect, is better formulated than its counterpart in the inaugural address. But I can also understand Barack Obama's predicament. He clearly was working on his whistle-stop and inaugural speech at the same time, and he did not want to have them be identical! So he edited a bit more, weakening his key address ever so slightly from a rhetorical and proverbial vantage point.

"We Must Pick Ourselves up, Dust Ourselves off"

To return to the inaugural speech, Obama next turns to a major theme of his, the basic greatness of the American nation. Here he includes the statement "Greatness is never a given. It must be earned," which in its wording, form, and structure is memorable and consequently might, in due time, find its way into quotation dictionaries:

> In reaffirming the greatness of our nation, we understand that greatness is never a given. It must be earned. Our journey has never been one of shortcuts or settling for less. It has not been the path for the fainthearted—for those who prefer leisure over work, or seek only the pleasures of riches and fame. Rather it has been the risk-takers, the doers, the makers of things—some celebrated, but more often men and women obscure in their labor—who have carried us up the long, rugged path toward prosperity and freedom.

Using such favorite words as "struggle" and "work," Obama continues to argue that America and its people need to be steadfast in dealing with the socioeconomic crisis at hand, once again amassing three proverbial phrases, namely "To stand pat," "To pick oneself up," and "To dust oneself off," thereby adding some colloquial color to his plea:

This is the journey we continue today. We remain the most prosperous, powerful nation on Earth. Our workers are no less productive than when this
crisis began. Our minds are no less inventive, our goods and services no less
needed than they were last week or last month or last year. Our capacity
remains undiminished. But our time of standing pat, of protecting narrow
interests and putting off unpleasant decisions—that time has surely passed.
Starting today, we must pick ourselves up, dust ourselves off, and begin again
the work of remaking America.

Not being a poker player, I did not know the phrase "To stand pat" with
the meaning of "to stick by a decision, to refuse to budge" (Wilkinson 1993:
486). Obama, on the other hand, appears to be well versed in the phrases
relating to this card game, as can be seen from his use of the expression "To
maintain a poker face" in his autobiography *Dreams from My Father* (1995):
"Roy maintained a poker face, as if the conversation didn't concern him.
Both he and Amy had the sheen of too many beers, and I saw Jane sneak an
anxious look at Kezia. I decided to change the subject, and asked Zeituni
if she'd been to Garden Square before" (Obama 2004: 363). The *New York
Times* columnist and former speechwriter for President Richard Nixon, William Safire, in his quite negative review of this speech—"[it] fell short of
the anticipated immortality"—includes a fascinating comment regarding the
idea of standing pat that plays off the first name of Nixon's wife Pat:

> He [Obama] got into good rhythm with a cheer-up paragraph, reminding us
> of America's productive workers and inventive minds, our capacity undimi-
> nished, setting up his warning against "standing pat." (I once wrote a line for
> Nixon, "America cannot stand pat," which got a glare from the First Lady—we
> never used the phrase again.) Obama topped that passage with a warmly fami-
> liar metaphor: "Starting today, we must pick ourselves up, dust ourselves off,
> and begin again the work of remaking America." That worked. (Safire 2009)

Great comment by the acute language observer William Safire! Yet, he does
not know everything, for that "warmly familiar metaphor," which I had
identified as a combination of the two proverbial phrases "To pick oneself
up" and "To dust oneself off," can actually be found in print as early as 1915
(Doyle et al. 2012: 196). However, Barack Obama most likely borrowed his
wording from two lines of "a Hollywood musical" as the unsigned editorial "Inaugural Address Sounds Notes of Optimism and Reality" in the *Los*

Angeles Times reminded its readers ("Inaugural Address" 2009). When I asked our administrative assistant Janet Sobieski of the Department of German and Russian at the University of Vermont about these lines and a possible song, she recalled it instantly and subsequently located it by way of a Google search. The song "Pick Yourself Up" (lyrics by Dorothy Fields, music by Jerome Kern) was part of the film *Swing Time* (1936), staring Fred Astaire and Ginger Rogers. The following stanza appears twice in the popular song:

> Don't lose your confidence if you slip,
> Be grateful for a pleasure trip,
> And pick yourself up,
> Dust yourself off,
> Start all over again.

For the record, there was also Jeff Shesol, deputy speechwriter for President Bill Clinton, who should have done a bit more checking before writing the following comment a few hours after President Obama finished his address:

> The speech was well written, structured and paced. To the credit of Mr. Obama and his speechwriters [he basically wrote it himself!], there was no swinging for the rhetorical fences. They did not yield to temptation. They did not strain to etch a new line in granite somewhere or in Bartlett's [*Familiar Quotations*] or the collective memory. Perhaps as a result, there were memorable passages but few memorable phrases. What appears (at least for now) to be the most quoted line was one of the most colloquial: "pick ourselves up, dust ourselves off" may not be poetry, but it well describes a nation that's been knocked to the ground and kicked around for eight years. (Shesol 2009)

These well-known lines by the American songwriter Dorothy Fields (1905–1974), who also wrote lyrics to such famous songs as "On the Sunny Side of the Street" (1930) and "I'm in the Mood for Love" (1935), have still not made it into the most recent edition of John Bartlett's *Familiar Quotations* (2002); but Fred Shapiro's exquisite *Yale Book of Quotations* (2006) does include several memorable lines from four of her songs—alas not yet from the "Pick Yourself Up" lyrics (Shapiro 2006: 255–56). Now that Barack Obama has revitalized the lines by changing "yourself" to the more inclusive "ourselves," new editions of Bartlett, Shapiro, and other quotation dictionaries are bound to list them. The new "proverb" might even become associated with Barack Obama, just as the "Government of, by, and for the people" will forever be linked with Abraham Lincoln. Jeff Shesol is certainly correct in claiming that Obama's slightly modified lines from Dorothy Fields are already the most frequently cited from his inaugural address (see Brune 2009; Cary 2009; Stewart 2009).

Barack Obama's Attempts at New Quotable Formulations

Speaking of quotable passages in President Obama's inaugural address, I would think that his statement "[It] is not whether our government is too big or too small, but whether it works" might reach a certain currency, even though it appears to be something of an allusion to President Ronald Reagan's famous maxim that Obama quotes in *The Audacity of Hope* (2006): "Or, as Ronald Reagan succinctly put it: 'Government is not the solution to our problem; government is the problem'" (Obama 2006: 147). In any case, here is Obama's own formulation in context:

> What the cynics fail to understand is that the ground has shifted beneath them—that the stale political arguments that have consumed us for so long no longer apply. The question we ask today is not whether our government is too big or too small, but whether it works—whether it helps families find jobs at a decent wage, care they can afford, a retirement that is dignified. Where the answer is yes, we intend to move forward. Where the answer is no, programs will end. And those of us who manage the public's dollars will be held to account—to spend wisely, reform bad habits, and do our business in the light of day—because only then can we restore the vital trust between a people and their government.

It is interesting to note that Obama adds the proverbial metaphor "To do something in the light of day" at the end of this paragraph to underscore his intent of conducting the nation's business in a fair and open fashion. No matter how pragmatic or philosophical his remarks might be, he usually resorts to some fixed phrase to add an easily understood image to his rhetoric.

And he strikes an impressive balance between quotable statements in the form of his own pseudo-proverbs and traditional folk expressions. Consequently, he continues with a well-formulated paragraph that includes yet another statement that could catch on in common political parlance, namely "A nation cannot prosper long when it favors only the prosperous":

Nor is the question before us whether the market is a force for good or ill. Its power to generate wealth and expand freedom is unmatched, but this crisis has reminded us that without a watchful eye, the market can spin out of control—and that a nation cannot prosper long when it favors only the prosperous. The success of our economy has always depended not just on the size of our gross domestic product, but on the reach of our prosperity; on our ability to extend opportunity to every willing heart—not out of charity, but because it is the surest route to our common good.

Let me here return one more time to William Safire, who agrees with my assessment of this quotable statement, and who also mentions a number of other proverbial utterances by Obama that I wish to comment upon as well:

> To his oratorical credit, the president did not strain for quotable quotes. "A nation cannot prosper when it favors only the prosperous" was a nice insertion with an eye toward Bartlett's, and I liked "the lines of tribe shall soon dissolve," though it is not in the league with "the mystic chords of memory" [in the last paragraph of Lincoln's first inaugural address of March 4, 1861]. Obama's "know that you are on the wrong side of history" message to Muslim extremists concluded with "we will extend a hand if you are willing to unclench your fist"; that is quotable if it is original, but I think I've seen it before. His "this winter of our hardship" is a well-turned phrase about discontent, even if not as Shakespeare punned it, "made glorious summer by this sun of York." (Safire 2009)

First of all, I actually think that President Obama strained at least a bit "for quotable quotes," especially since he knew very well that his entire audience—from general citizen to erudite scholar—wanted him to deliver at least two or three memorable phrases! For example, Safire misses an incredibly important statement in the very paragraph that he is discussing, namely "People will judge you on what you can build, not what you can destroy." The audience liked this pseudo-proverb, and they also could relate to Obama's extension of the proverbial phrase "To be on the wrong side" to include human history in general:

> To the Muslim world, we seek a new way forward, based on mutual interest and mutual respect. To those leaders around the globe who seek to sow conflict, or blame their society's ills on the West: Know that your people will judge you on what you can build, not what you destroy. To those who cling to

power through corruption and deceit and the silencing of dissent, know that you are on the wrong side of history; but that we will extend a hand if you are willing to unclench your fist.

Regarding the other memorable sentence in this "loaded" proverbial paragraph, "We will extend a hand if you are willing to unclench your fist," I have to admit that my comprehensive search in numerous dictionaries of quotations and also on the internet have not resulted in any identification of an earlier use. Thus my conclusion is that Obama has simply taken the proverbial phrase "To extend a hand to someone" (see this phrase in his speech of July 24, 2008, in Berlin and in two subsequent speeches, in Mieder 2009: 229–30) and expanded it with the somatic image of an "unclenched fist" into a memorable statement.

And how about Obama's sententious "The world has changed, and we must change with it" that summarizes his entire presidential campaign for change in one sentence that he had not used before? This formulaic phrase might also be remembered:

To the people of poor nations, we pledge to work alongside you to make your farms flourish and let clean waters flow; to nourish starved bodies and feed hungry minds. And to those nations like ours that enjoy relative plenty, we say we can no longer afford indifference to suffering outside our borders; nor can we consume the world's resources without regard to effect. For the world has changed, and we must change with it.

Of course, the necessity for change is always just one side of the equation in the struggle for progress, as far as Obama is concerned. The other side is clearly the return to a solid value system based on rigorous work ethics, where all Americans give their proverbial all to perfect the union and by extension the world:

Our challenges might be new. The instruments with which we meet them may be new. But those values upon which our success depends—hard work and honesty, courage and fair play, tolerance and curiosity, loyalty and patriotism—these things are old. These things are true. They have been the quiet force of progress throughout our history. What is demanded then is a return to these truths. What is required of us now is a new era of responsibility—a recognition, on the part of every American, that we have duties to ourselves, our nation and the world; duties that we do not grudgingly accept but rather seize gladly, firm in the knowledge that there is nothing so satisfying to the spirit, so defining of our character, than giving our all to a difficult task. This is the price and the promise of citizenship.

That last sentence is a fitting reminiscence of Barack Obama's frequent use of that seemingly mundane proverbial expression "To pay a (the) price for something" that he uses twenty-nine times in his books and speeches. In his book *The Audacity of Hope*, Obama uses the phrase in connection with his hero Abraham Lincoln having done his utmost to save a house divided and to perfect the union through ethical struggle: "Lincoln, and those buried at Gettysburg, remind us that we should pursue our own absolute truths only if we acknowledge that there may be a terrible price to pay" (Obama 2006: 98). This severe statement would not have been in the spirit of an epideictic inaugural address, in which the new President of the United States wants to be positive and optimistic.

By relying on quotable new pseudo-proverbs of his own and traditional proverbs as well as proverbial phrases, Obama followed in the footsteps of previous presidents, as I have shown in my study "'It's Not a President's Business to Catch Flies': Proverbial Rhetoric in Presidential Inaugural Addresses" (Mieder 2005c). And uplifting as this speech and other major addresses might have been in language and content, Obama's political rhetoric is characterized by such important ingredients as "'practical wisdom,' 'practical knowledge,' 'practical reason,' [and] 'practical judgment'" that are part of quotations and proverbs in particular (Nichols 1996: 687; see also Louis 2000). With his most closely watched address behind him, President Barack Obama has once again illustrated that proverbial language is a significant part of the inauguration of the presidents of the United States. Quotations, pseudo-proverbs, proverbs, and proverbial phrases certainly do their metaphorical part in making the inaugural addresses "timeless words," to use two final words from President Barack Obama's memorable inaugural address. But such folk speech together with innovative variations and new formulations assures colorful, meaningful, and comprehensible communication with the American people.

From Inaugural Speech to the World Stage

When Obama presents a speech, he must by necessity be aware of the cultural and linguistic background of his audience, i.e., he has to find a solid common denominator that binds his audience together. Even if he addresses only people within the United States, he has to realize that there are numerous citizens and aliens who might have considerable difficulty in following his remarks. This is also the case when he speaks more generally to the entire world, in which case he has to be especially careful to couch his thoughts in English words and phrases that people who speak and understand English as a second language can comprehend. From the way Obama does relate linguistically to Americans and to peoples of the world, it appears that he is cognizant of the cultural literacy of the people he happens to be addressing at any given time (Mieder 1992). And since proverbs in particular and proverbial expressions and proverbial comparisons in general are without doubt part of this general knowledge, such language serves him extremely well in bringing across his political, social, and ethical points. By now he has proven himself to be a magisterial communicator, elevating the American political discourse to new rhetorical heights after it had declined considerably since John F. Kennedy's pride in language (Denton and Woodward 1998; Campbell and Jamieson 2008; Lim 2008).

My book "Yes We Can": Barack Obama's Proverbial Rhetoric (2009) shows that this modern politician knows how to engage all the registers of the rich English language and that he is especially gifted in adding a folkloric touch to his political rhetoric that helps make his utterances appealing to people everywhere. His two books Dreams from My Father (1995) and The Audacity of Hope (2006) are filled with proverbial language, and his approximately three hundred speeches during his steady move toward the presidency bear convincing witness to his proverbial prowess. There can be no doubt that Obama's ability to find linguistic common ground with a broad spectrum of the American population helped him get the nomination to become a presidential candidate and subsequently to be elected to that coveted office. It is now also of considerable interest to take a look at how Barack Obama as president of the United States is communicating with the world at large. After all, as the head of one of the world powers, he is in constant communication with the leaders and the people of countries throughout the world.

The question then arises: how does his proverbial arsenal serve him to communicate on the world stage of international politics? The quick and superficial answer is that he uses proverbial language less frequently when he speaks to audiences abroad, and that does in fact make perfect sense. After all, people who have learned English as a second language are not as fluent in proverbial language as native speakers would be. In order to be understood by foreign audiences, Obama does well in avoiding highly metaphorical or idiomatic language. But that does not mean that he excludes proverbs and proverbial expressions completely. Linguistically aware as he happens to be, Obama is careful in choosing such internationally disseminated proverbs and proverbial phrases where he can basically count on the fact that his audience will know them by way of their native languages. Or he chooses such preformulated phrases whose metaphors are relatively accessible, thus assuring solid communication while adding some expressive flavor to his speeches in foreign countries.

In his political and personal manifesto *The Audacity of Hope*, Obama states unequivocally that he is guided by the proverb "Do unto others as you would have them do unto you" (Matthew 7:12), commonly referred to as the "golden rule" for human conduct. In fact, he can rest assured that people everywhere and no matter of what faith will know what this moral code signifies, since it is part of all religions and has found its philosophical expression in Immanuel Kant's categorical imperative "Act as if the maxim of your action were to become by your will a universal law" (Hertzler 1933–34). The various ways in which this fundamental law of humanity is expressed in the holy books of the world's religions have been conveniently listed in a special section on the "Golden Rule" in Albert K. Griffin's *Religious Proverbs: Over 1600 Adages from 18 Faiths Worldwide* (1991: 67–69; see also Champion 1945: xviii; Burrell 1997: 13–27; Templeton 1997: 8–12). Being well aware of the general knowledge and currency of the law of life expressed either in its longer proverbial form or simply its "golden rule" designation, Barack Obama can assume that his readers or audience will be able to understand and hopefully identify with his subjective statement that "a sense of empathy [. . .] is at the heart of my moral code, and it is how I understand the Golden Rule—not simply as a call to sympathy or charity, but as something more demanding, a call to stand in somebody else's shoes and see through their eyes" (2006: 66). Always the proverbialist, he is quick to add the two proverbial expressions "to put oneself into somebody else's shoes" and "to see through someone else's eyes" to the not directly stated proverbial law, thereby stressing that this golden rule will only be fulfilled if people have understanding and compassion for each other. Later in this book, he reiterates his personal commitment to this high moral principle: "There are some things that I'm absolutely sure about—the Golden Rule, the need to battle cruelty in all its forms, the value of love and charity, humility and grace" (2006: 224).

Turkish Proverb: "You Cannot Put out Fire with Flames"

Barack Obama knows only too well that his country is but one player on this globe, and that as its leader he must be concerned with the "world" at large. Having made his views as possible peacemaker and humble servant of humankind known at his inaugural event that was broadcast to every corner of the world, Obama got to work and soon had to realize that his refreshing idealism and courageous hope for a better world would face considerable obstacles at home and abroad. But the youthful and energetic president appears to be unshakable in his vision of carving out a better America and an improved world order. He certainly never tires of repeating his call for steady improvement, ever mindful that progress will only take place by way of struggle.

He took the opportunity to repeat this fundamental belief when he traveled to Ankara, Turkey, where he was given the honor of addressing the Turkish Parliament on April 6, 2009. His hosts obviously were pleased when he said: "Turkey's democracy is your own achievement. It was not forced upon you by any outside power, nor did it come without struggle and sacrifice. Turkey draws strength from both the successes of the past, and from the efforts of each generation of Turks that makes new progress for your people." Then, stressing cooperation between Turkey and the United States, he returned to his "lending a hand" proverbial metaphor to underscore the good will among the industrialized nations:

> Already, America and Turkey are working with the G20 on an unprecedented response to an unprecedented economic crisis. Now, this past week, we came together to ensure that the world's largest economies take strong and coordinated action to stimulate growth and restore the flow of credit; to reject the pressures of protectionism, and to extend a hand to developing countries and the people hit hardest by this downturn; and to dramatically reform our regulatory system so that the world never faces a crisis like this again.

This proverbial leitmotif appears two more times in this important first speech on foreign ground by the new American president. Praising Turkey for its diplomatic role in the Near Eastern conflict, he argues that "We must extend a hand to those Palestinians who are in need, while helping to strengthen their own institutions. We must reject the use of terror, and recognize that Israel's security concerns are legitimate." And then, toward the end of his major foreign policy address, he once again uses the same proverbial phrase to tell the Turkish Parliament that "Our focus will be on what we can do, in partnership with people across the Muslim world, to advance our common hopes and our common dreams. And when people look back on this time, let it be said that of America that we extended the hand of friendship to all people."

Following this statement at the end of his speech, Obama with a rhetorical stroke of genius quoted a Turkish proverb in English translation that definitely touched a folkloric nerve in an audience that had listened with obvious delight to the words of the new president who had chosen Turkey for his foreign debut as a world leader:

> There's an old Turkish proverb: "You cannot put out fire with flames." America knows this. Turkey knows this. There's some who must be met by force, they will not compromise. But force alone cannot solve our problems, and it is no alternative to extremism. The future must belong to those who create, not those who destroy. That is the future we must work for, and we must work for it together.

It is not clear where President Obama found this proverb (most likely with the help of his young speech writer Jon Favreau), but I assume the Turkish original is "Ates atesle söndürülmez," which usually is rendered into English as "Fire cannot be extinguished with fire," with a possible English equivalent being "Revenge is a dish that should be eaten cold" (Yurtbasi 1993: 313). Of course, there is now also the modern American proverb "You cannot fight fire with fire" (Doyle et al. 2012: 77) that should be given as an equivalent in Turkish-English proverb dictionaries. In any case, while Obama states that at times force might be necessary to solve a particular conflict (in his Nobel Peace Prize speech discussed below, he speaks of a "just war"), he wants to emphasize with this proverbial wisdom from Turkey that it is best to deal with the problems of the world by negotiation and bridge-building rather than armed conflict. As he had observed in his inaugural address in a pseudo-proverbial way, "People will judge you on what you can build, not what you can destroy," he now states quite similarly "The future must belong to those who create, not those who destroy." From a paremiologist point of view, I might comment here that Obama might want to zero in on the most quotable form of this observation and stick to it. With his exposure to the mass media of the world, he might get his utterance into quotation dictionaries and ultimately perhaps even into proverb dictionaries.

The "Golden Rule" Proverb as Moral Compass for the World

Two months later President Obama undertook his second trip abroad, this time to Egypt, Germany, and France. It was on June 4, 2009, at Cairo University, where he gave his major address reaching out to the Muslim world as no modern American president had done before. Arguing for a better understanding among people of different religions, he cites proverbial wisdom from the Koran, with the audience applauding his willingness to quote from this holy book:

> There must be sustained effort to listen to each other; to learn from each other; to respect one another; and to seek common ground. As the Holy Koran tells us, "Be conscious of God and speak always the truth." (Applause.) That is what I will try to do today—to speak the truth as best I can, humbled by the task before us, and firm in my belief that the interests we share as human beings are far more powerful than the forces that drive us apart.
>
> The Holy Koran teaches that whoever kills an innocent is as—it is as if he has killed all mankind. (Applause.) And the Holy Koran also says whoever saves a person, it is as if he has saved all mankind. (Applause.) The enduring faith of over a billion people is so much bigger than the narrow hatred of a few. Islam is not part of the problem in combating violent extremism—it is an important part of promoting peace.

Throughout the speech Obama stresses "our common humanity," claiming the "simple truth: that violence is a dead end." I have not been able to establish the proverbiality of this statement, but certainly the idea that "Violence is a dead end" could well advance from the status of a pseudo-proverb to an actual proverb.

During this speech Obama argues forcefully "against negative stereotypes of Islam," but he is quick to point out that eradicating the world of stereotypes must involve people everywhere, who, after all, were all created equal, as Obama never tires of pointing out proverbially:

> Just as Muslims do not fit a crude stereotype, America is not the crude stereotype of a self-interested empire. The United States has been one of the greatest sources of progress that the world has ever known. We were born out of revolution against an empire. We were founded upon the ideal that all [men] are created equal, and we have shed blood and struggled for centuries to give meaning to those words—within our borders, and around the world. We are

shaped by every culture, drawn from every end of the Earth, and dedicated to a simple concept: E pluribus unum—"Out of many, one."

The old classical proverb "E pluribus unum," which is part of the American seal, embodies Obama's vision of a world in which people emphasize their similarities rather than stress their differences (Fields 1996: 1–25; Aron 2008: 23–25). And this view includes a democratic form of government, of course, as Obama stresses by citing part of the proverbial triad of a "government of the people, by the people, for the people" that was popularized as the shortest definition of democracy by way of Abraham Lincoln's Gettysburg Address of November 19, 1863, when he had said at the end of his oration: "[...] that this nation, under God, shall have a new birth of freedom—and that government of the people, by the people, for the people, shall not perish from the earth" (Mieder 2005b: 29). But here is what Obama said about democracy in Cairo:

> There are some who advocate for democracy only when they're out of power; once in power, they are ruthless in suppressing the rights of others. (Applause.) So no matter where it takes hold, government of the people and by the people sets a single standard for all who would hold power: You must maintain your power through consent, not coercion; you must respect the rights of minorities, and participate with a spirit of tolerance and compromise; you must place the interests of your people and the legitimate workings of the political process above your party. Without these ingredients, elections alone do not make a true democracy.

It is not clear why Obama does not cite the third element "for the people" of this proverbial definition, but what he does say surely refers to the fact that the government is there for the people whom it serves. And then, close to the end of this moving and inspiring speech to thousands of Arabic students, he asked them "to reimagine the world, to remake this world." Little wonder that there were repeated applause and calls of the type "Barack Obama, we love you!" during the speech. The climax of the speech was reached when the President called for a new world of brother- and sisterhood informed by empathy and mutual respect, with the center of his powerful statement once again being occupied by the proverbial golden rule:

> All of us share this world for but a brief moment in time. The question is whether we spend that time focused on what pushes us apart, or whether we

commit ourselves to an effort—a sustained effort—to find common ground, to focus on the future we seek for our children, and to respect the dignity of all human beings.

It's easier to start wars than to end them. It's easier to blame others than to look inward. It's easier to see what is different about someone than to find the things we share. But we should choose the right path, not just the easy path. There's one rule that lies at the heart of every religion—that we do unto others as we would have them do unto us. (Applause.) This truth transcends nations and peoples—a belief that isn't new; that isn't black or white or brown; that isn't Christian or Muslim or Jew. It's a belief that pulsed in the cradle of civilization, and that still beats in the hearts of billions around the world. It's a faith in other people, and it's what brought me here today.

That is rational and emotional rhetoric, coming both from the mind and the heart, as it calls for a new world based on ethical values that bind humankind together. One certainly can hear echoes of Abraham Lincoln, Frederick Douglass, and Martin Luther King in this deeply moral worldview.

Of course, as one would expect, Barack Obama conjured up the spirit of nonviolence espoused by Martin Luther King when he followed in the footsteps of that great preacher and civil rights champion who had received the Nobel Peace Prize before him in 1964 for his valiant efforts. Who would have thought that forty-five years later an African American president of the United States would travel to Oslo, Norway, to receive the same coveted prize on December 10, 2009? The acceptance speech was no easy task for Barack Obama, as he was trying to wind down the war in Iraq while escalating the war in Afghanistan. As he received the prize for peace, he waged war, a "just war," as he tried to explain. There were plenty of critics, not just about some parts of this well-crafted speech, but also because of a general feeling—shared by Obama himself—that he was being honored too early. But the prize committee wanted to recognize him for his sincere attempt of changing the status quo of the world order, for his vision of creating a better world, and for his sincere conviction that humankind can find peace on this earth. In his acceptance speech he emphasized the fact that in a world that constantly grows smaller, people should realize that we are actually quite similar and basically want the same things out of life. And yet, at times we appear to be moving backwards into religious and sectarian confrontation. This unfortunate situation is visible especially in the misguided use and interpretation of religion, even though they all preach the golden rule, as Obama once again points out with this basic law of life:

Most dangerously, we see it [the political and social disintegration] in the way that religion is used to justify the murder of innocents by those who have distorted and defiled the great religion of Islam, and who attacked my country from Afghanistan. These extremists are not the first to kill in the name of God; the cruelties of the Crusades are amply recorded. But they remind us that no Holy War can ever be a just war. For if you truly believe that you are carrying out divine will, then there is no need for restraint—no need to spare the pregnant mother, or the medic, or even a person of one's own faith. Such a warped view of religion is not just incompatible with the concept of peace, but the purpose of faith—for the one rule that lies at the heart of every major religion is that we do unto others as we would have them do unto us.

Adhering to this law of love has always been the core struggle of human nature. We are fallible. We make mistakes, and fall victim to the temptation of pride, power, and sometimes evil. Even those of us with the best intentions will at times fail to right the wrongs before us.

But we do not have to think human nature is perfect for us to still believe that the human condition can be perfected. We do not have to live in an idealized world to still reach for those ideals that will make it a better place.

The "moral compass," as Barack Obama sees it, that can guide us in improving our problematic world riddled by war, disease, poverty, and many other ills, is the very basic law of life that is known as the golden rule. And, as a modern politician and concerned citizen of the world, Barack Obama has the audacity of hope for people everywhere as globalization draws humanity ever closer together. He wants to strive for peace and for the eradication of war, deprivation, and disease, and if his guiding principle can remain the proverb "Do unto others as you would have them do unto you," he will continue to have his chance to follow in the footsteps of his heroes Lincoln, Douglass, and King (in the Nobel Peace Prize speech he also mentions Albert Schweitzer, Woodrow Wilson, Mahatma Gandhi, George Marshall, and Nelson Mandela), who tried their level best to improve the human condition. His proverbial rhetoric will doubtlessly continue to serve him well in his valiant struggle for progress on all possible fronts.

BIBLIOGRAPHY

This chapter combines parts of two smaller publications: "'We Must Pick Ourselves Up, Dust Ourselves Off': President Barack Obama's Proverbial Inaugural Address," *Paremia* 18 (2009): 31–42; and "The Golden Rule as a Political Imperative for the World: President Barack Obama's Proverbial Messages Abroad," *Milli Folklor* 85 (2010): 26–35.

Aron, Paul. 2008. *We Hold These Truths . . . And Other Words that Made America*. Lanham, Maryland: Rowman & Littlefield.

Baker, Gerard. 2009. "The Speech That Failed to Fly [Barack Obama]." *The Times* January 21: 3.

Bartlett, John. 2002. *Familiar Quotations*. Justin Kaplan, ed. 17th ed. Boston: Little, Brown.

Brune, Tom. 2009. "Confident, Somber, Historic [Barack Obama]." *Newsday* January 21: W8.

Burrell, Brian. 1997. *The Words We Live By: The Creeds, Mottoes, and Pledges that Have Shaped America*. New York: Free Press.

Campbell, Karlyn K., and Kathleen H. Jamieson. 2008. *Presidents Creating the Presidency: Deeds Done in Words*. Chicago: University of Chicago Press.

Cary, Mary K. 2009. "Hungry for Words [Barack Obama]." *New York Times* January 21: online. roomfordebate.blogs.nytimes.com/2009/01/20/the-speech-the-experts-critique/.

Champion, Selwyn Gurney. 1945. *The Eleven Religions and Their Proverbial Lore*. New York: E.P. Dutton.

Denton, Robert E., and Gary C. Woodward. 1998. *Political Communication in America*. 3rd ed. Westport, Connecticut: Praeger.

Doyle, Charles Clay, Wolfgang Mieder, and Fred R. Shapiro, eds. 2012. *The Dictionary of Modern Proverbs*. New Haven, Connecticut: Yale University Press.

Fields, Wayne. 1996. *Union of Words: A History of Presidential Eloquence*. New York: Free Press.

Gerson, Michael. 2009. "The Conservative Revolutionary [Barack Obama]." *Washington Post* January 21: A11.

Griffin, Albert Kirby. 1991. *Religious Proverbs: Over 1600 Adages from 18 Faiths Worldwide*. Jefferson, North Carolina: McFarland.

Harnsberger, Thomas, ed. 1964. *Treasury of Presidential Quotations*. Chicago: Follett.

Hertzler, Joyce. 1933–34. "On Golden Rules." *International Journal of Ethics* 44: 418–36.

Hunt, John G., ed. 1997. *The Inaugural Addresses of the Presidents*. New York: Gramercy.

"Inaugural Address Sounds Notes of Optimism and Reality [Barack Obama]" (editorial). 2009. *Los Angeles Times* January 21: A16.

Jay, Antony, ed. 1996. *The Oxford Dictionary of Political Quotations*. Oxford: Oxford University Press.

Karabegović, Dženeta. 2007. "'No Lie Can Live Forever': Zur sprichwörtlichen Rhetorik von Martin Luther King." *Sprichwörter sind Goldes wert: Parömiologische Studien zu Kultur, Literatur und Medien*. Wolfgang Mieder, ed. Burlington, Vermont: University of Vermont. 223–40.

Lepore, Jill. 2009: "The Speech: Have Inaugural Addresses Been Getting Worse?" *New Yorker* January 12: 49–53.

Lim, Elvin T. 2008. *The Anti-Intellectual Presidency: The Decline of Presidential Rhetoric from George Washington to George W. Bush*. New York: Oxford University Press.

Lott, David N., ed. 1961: *The Inaugural Addresses of the American Presidents from Washington to Kennedy*. New York: Holt, Rinehart and Winston.

Louis, Cameron. 2000. "Proverbs and the Politics of Language." *Proverbium* 17: 173–94. Also in *Cognition, Comprehension, and Communication: A Decade of North American Proverb Studies (1990–2000)*. Wolfgang Mieder, ed. Baltmannsweiler: Schneider Verlag Hohengehren, 2003. 271–92.

Mieder, Wolfgang. 1992. "Paremiological Minimum and Cultural Literacy." *Creativity and Tradition in Folklore: New Directions*. Simon J. Bronner, ed. Logan, Utah: Utah State University Press. 185–203. Also in Wolfgang Mieder, *Proverbs Are Never Out of Season: Popular Wisdom in the Modern Age*. New York: Oxford University Press, 1993. 41–57.

———. 1997. *The Politics of Proverbs: From Traditional Wisdom to Proverbial Stereotypes*. Madison, Wisconsin: University of Wisconsin Press.

———. 1998. *"A House Divided": From Biblical Proverb to Lincoln and Beyond*. Burlington, Vermont: University of Vermont.

——. 2000. *The Proverbial Abraham Lincoln: An Index to Proverbs in the Works of Abraham Lincoln*. New York: Peter Lang.

——. 2001. *"No Struggle, No Progress": Frederick Douglass and His Proverbial Rhetoric for Civil Rights*. New York: Peter Lang.

——. 2004. *Proverbs: A Handbook*. Westport, Connecticut: Greenwood.

——. 2005a. "'Do Unto Others as You Would Have them Do Unto You': Frederick Douglass's Proverbial Struggle for Civil Rights." In Wolfgang Mieder, *Proverbs Are the Best Policy: Folk Wisdom and American Politics*. Logan, Utah: Utah State University Press, 2005. 118–46.

——. 2005b. "'Government of the People, by the People, for the People': The Making and Meaning of an American Proverb about Democracy." In Wolfgang Mieder, *Proverbs Are the Best Policy: Folk Wisdom and American Politics*. Logan, Utah: Utah State University Press, 2005. 15–55.

——. 2005c. "'It's Not a President's Business to Catch Flies': Proverbial Rhetoric in Presidential Inaugural Addresses." In Wolfgang Mieder, *Proverbs Are the Best Policy: Folk Wisdom and American Politics*. Logan, Utah: Utah State University Press, 2005. 147–86.

——. 2005d. "'We Are All in the Same Boat Now': Proverbial Discourse in the Churchill-Roosevelt Correspondence." In Wolfgang Mieder, *Proverbs Are the Best Policy: Folk Wisdom and American Politics*. Logan, Utah: Utah State University Press, 2005. 187–209.

——. 2009. *"Yes We Can": Barack Obama's Proverbial Rhetoric*. New York: Peter Lang.

——. 2010. *"Making a Way Out of No Way": Martin Luther King's Sermonic Proverbial Rhetoric*. New York: Peter Lang.

Mieder, Wolfgang, and George B. Bryan. 1995. *The Proverbial Winston S. Churchill: An Index to Proverbs in the Works of Sir Winston Churchill*. Westport, Connecticut: Greenwood.

Miller, Donald L., ed. 1989. *From George . . . to George: 200 Years of Presidential Quotations*. Washington, DC: Braddock Communications.

Newton-Small, Jay. 2008. "How Obama Writes His Speeches." *Time* August 28: online. www.time.com/time/politics/article/0,8599,1837368,00.html.

Nichols, Ray. 1996. "Maxims, 'Practical Wisdom,' and the Language of Action." *Political Theory* 24: 687–705.

Obama, Barack. 2002–2009. Speeches: www.obamaspeeches.com/.

——. 1995. *Dreams from My Father: A Story of Race and Inheritance*. New York: Three Rivers.

——. 2006. *The Audacity of Hope: Thoughts on Reclaiming the American Dream*. New York: Three Rivers.

O'Toole, Fintan. 2009. "A Rhetoric That Made Newness Threaten Less [Barack Obama]." *Irish Times* January 21: 3.

Remini, Robert V., and Terry Golway, eds. 2008. *Fellow Citizens: The Penguin Book of U.S. Presidential Inaugural Addresses*. New York: Penguin.

Safire, William. 2009. "No Memorable Theme [Barack Obama]." *New York Times* January 21: online. roomfordebate.blogs.nytimes.com/2009/01/20/the-speech-the-experts-critique/.

Sanger, David E. 2009. "[Inaugural] Speech Spanned History and Confronted Bush." *New York Times* January 21: online. www.nytimes.com/2009/01/21/us/politics/w21assessS2.html.

Shapiro, Fred R. 2006. *The Yale Book of Quotations*. New Haven, Connecticut: Yale University Press.

Shesol, Jeff. 2009. "Powerful Words [Barack Obama]." *New York Times* January 21: online. www.nytimes .com/2009/01/21/us/politics/w21assessS2.html.

Stevenson, Burton. 1949. *The Home Book of Bible Quotations*. New York: Harper & Brothers.

Stewart, Gordon. 2009. "Giving No Offense [Barack Obama]." *New York Times* January 21: online. www .nytimes.com/2009/01/21/us/politics/w21assessS2.html.

Templeton, John Mark. 1997. *Worldwide Laws of Life*. Philadelphia: Templeton Foundation Press.

Wilkinson, P. R. 1993. *Thesaurus of Traditional English Metaphors*. London: Routledge.

Wills, Garry. 1992. *Lincoln at Gettysburg: The Words That Remade America*. New York: Touchstone.

Yurtbasi, Metin. 1993. *A Dictionary of Turkish Proverbs*. Ankara: Turkish Daily News.

6. "IT TAKES A VILLAGE TO CHANGE THE WORLD"
Proverbial Politics and the Ethics of Place

Let me begin with an ancient proverbial expression that contains what the geographer D. W. Meinig has called "a personal sense of place" (1979: 3). I am referring to the traditional metaphor of "standing on the shoulders of giants" (Deutscher 2006) that places me as a scholar in the intellectual space of great proverb scholars who have come before me and who are no longer with us. From abroad I might mention Matti Kuusi, Grigorii L'vovich Permiakov, Lutz Röhrich, and Démétrios Loukatos, and from this country I would mention Alan Dundes, Pack Carnes, Herbert Halpert, Wayland Hand, Archer Taylor, and Bartlett Jere Whiting. These great folklorists and paremiologists have lent me their shoulders. Let us not forget them as we stake out our own intellectual territory by having learned from them. The ethics of place in this very narrow sense should help us in recognizing that we are indebted to scholars of previous generations on whose shoulders we stand and whose names and works we should treasure and perpetuate. Of course, this spatially expressed recognition of great heroes does not hold true solely for folklorists, as President Ronald Reagan reminded us in his first inaugural address of January 20, 1981:

> At the end of this open mall [in front of the Capitol] are those shrines to the giants, on whose shoulders we stand. Directly in front of me, the monument to a monumental man: George Washington, Father of Our Country. A man of humility who came to greatness reluctantly. He led America out of revolutionary victory into infant nationhood. Off to one side, the stately memorial to Thomas Jefferson. The Declaration of Independence flames with his eloquence. And then beyond the Reflecting Pool the dignified columns of the Lincoln Memorial. Whoever would understand in his heart the meaning of America will find it in the life of Abraham Lincoln. (Hunt 1997: 477)

From standing on the shoulders of American giants, Reagan takes his metaphors to the heart as the place for emotive understanding and on to the nation as a place of national pride. The more subjective identification with the country brings to mind such proverbs as "Home is home, be it ever so homely"; "Home is where you hang your hat"; "East or west, home is best"; "There is no place like home"; and "Home is where the heart is."

Proverbial Wisdom about House, Home, and Other Places

Yet the folk does not only romanticize the house as a warm and comfortable abode. Looking at such a structure as a safe haven that protects against unwanted or violent intruders, it has long claimed proverbially "A man's home is his castle" (Taylor 1965). Other proverbs about houses also go well beyond the home as hearth by stressing socio-political issues: "A house divided against itself cannot stand"; "A house that is built on sand will surely fall"; "If everyone swept in front of his house, the whole town would be clean"; and "People who live in glass houses shouldn't throw stones." In certain contexts these proverbs and their metaphors can signify places other than the domicile. To be sure, there are plenty of proverbs referring quite generally to places as such, as for example the early-sixteenth-century wisdom "There is a time and place for everything" (based on the shorter Bible proverb "There is a time for everything" [Ecclesiastes 3:1]) and the well-known "A place for everything and everything in its place" (Taylor 1968). And since a fitting proverb can be found for almost any subject, it should not be surprising that some of them refer to entire nations as "Different countries, different customs"; "My country, right or wrong"; "A prophet is without honor in his own country"; and "It's a free country." Quite expectedly, then, there are also proverbs looking at the entire world as a global place, to wit "All the world's a stage"; "It's a small world"; "One half of the world does not know how the other half lives"; "The world is your cow, but you have to do the milking"; "The world is what people make it"; and "It takes all kinds of people to make a world." Of course the proverb "Every home is a world in itself" describes the integrity of the family home with its customs and traditions, but thousands of such social microcosms make up the global and interconnected macrocosm, as the relatively new proverb "The world is a place" makes clear (see Mieder, Kingsbury, and Harder 1992). Adding human ethics to this insight, the musical group Rhythm in 1976 came out with the following short lyrics with the proverb introducing the call for a better world:

The world is a place
for the whole human race
to live and relate
as brothers.
(www.youtube.com/watch?v=XXILWhNqe6M)

A few years earlier, another group of singers, Sly and the Family Stone, popularized the quintessential American proverb "Different strokes for different
folks" (Mieder 1989: 317–32; McKenzie 2003; Mieder 2006) in their song
"Everyday People" (1968), emphasizing the same point of all people living
together in harmony in this country:

We've got to live together.
I am no better and neither are you.
We are the same in whatever we do.
[…]
I am everyday people.
[…]
Different strokes for different folks.
(Mieder 1989: 325)

But let us also not forget our previously discussed lines from Carl Sandburg's
poem "Good Morning, America" (1928):

A code arrives; language; lingo; slang;
behold the proverbs of a people, a nation:
(Sandburg 1950: 328)

Even though he speaks about the American people, Sandburg thinks of all
of humanity as exemplified by this nation of immigrants of all ethnicities
and nationalities. This is even more apparent in his masterfully scripted epic
American poem *The People, Yes* (1936), replete with literally hundreds of
proverbs, proverbial expressions, proverbial comparisons, and other forms of
folk speech. In that work he cites the proverb "It takes all kinds of people to
make a world" (1936: 57), connecting everyday people in their homes with
the world at large, and explaining in over two hundred pages of a phraseological *tour de force* that basic ethical values tie humanity together (Mieder 1971,
1973; Bryan and Mieder 2003). At no time should there be any place on this
earth without ethical underpinnings, as Benn Burroughs has pointed out in

his poem "Time and Place" (1957), which is based on the proverb "There's a time and place for everything":

> There's a time and place for everything
> [...]
> ... it's experience that helps us ... to
> gain joy and detour care ... but there are
> some things I know of ... like kindness and
> love's embrace ... that will live throughout
> the ages ... without need of time or place.
> (Burroughs 1957: 87–88)

Robert David Sack, in his intriguing book *Homo Geographicus: A Framework for Action, Awareness, and Moral Concern* (1997), transposes this poetic interpretation of time and place into the real world by bringing the proverb "A place for everything and everything in its place" into play:

> We are now linked globally. Human actions here affect another person, another culture, and a natural system a continent away. [...] This new level of interrelatedness is a consequence of human activity that we acknowledge by saying we are now participating in a world culture and global system, although we may also wistfully call it a global village, and thereby hope to shrink the process to a single shared local experience. This interconnectedness now takes place (and I mean that word quite literally) in innumerable and fragmented units of space. There is virtually a place for everything and everything is supposed to be in its place. (Sack 1997: 8)

These comments bring to mind that relatively new proverb "Think globally, act locally" which has been traced back to the year 1942 (Speake 2008: 316–17; Doyle et al. 2012: 256). By now it has developed into a generally accepted slogan for globalization, but there is also the modern proverb "It takes a village to raise a child" that has become quite popular.

"It Takes a Village to Raise a Child"

It does not appear to be of Nigerian origin, notwithstanding common allegations, and most likely it is not African at all, even though some parallels exist, like the Swahili proverb "One hand cannot bring up a child," meaning that child upbringing is a communal effort (Scheven 1981: 123, note 474).

It probably is of American coinage, with Toni Morrison's related statement during a 1981 interview hardly qualifying as the first use of the actual proverb: "I don't think one parent can raise a child. I don't think two parents can raise a child. You really need the whole village" (Wilson 1981: 86). It is, however, of interest that the next appearance of the proverb in 1984 relates back to this very interview: "As author Toni Morrison has said, it takes a village to raise a child, not one parent, not two parents, but the whole village" (Meriwether 1984: 151; for later references see Speake 2008: 336). It was popularized by way of Jane Cowen-Fletcher's young adult novel *It Takes a Village* (1993), where Yemi tries to watch her little brother Kokou on market day in a small village in Benin and finds that the entire village is watching out for him as well. But there is also Hillary Rodham Clinton's acclaimed book *It Takes a Village and Other Lessons Children Teach Us* (1996), which helped spread this wisdom throughout the United States and beyond. In her first chapter with the truncated proverbial title "It Takes a Village," she includes a revealing explanation for her interest in this text, albeit once again claiming its African origin:

> Children exist in the world as well as in the family. From the moment they are born, they depend on a host of other "grown-ups"—grandparents, neighbors, teachers, ministers, employers, political leaders, and untold others who touch their lives directly and indirectly. [...] It takes a village to raise a child.
>
> I chose that old African proverb to title this book because it offers a timeless reminder that children will thrive only if their families thrive and if the whole of society cares enough to provide for them.
>
> [...] In earlier times and places—and until recently in our own culture—the "village" meant an actual geographic place where individuals and families lived and worked together. [...] For most of us, though, the village doesn't look like that anymore. [...] The horizons of the contemporary village extend well beyond the town line. From the moment we are born, we are exposed to vast numbers of other people and influences through radio, television, newspapers, books, movies, computers, compact discs, cellular phones, and fax machines. Technology connects us to the impersonal global village it has created. [...] The village can no longer be defined as a place on the map, or a list of people or organizations, but its essence remains the same: it is the network of values and relationships that support and affect our lives. (Clinton 1996: 11–13)

This being said, the title of this chapter begins to make sense. Of course "It takes a village to raise a child," but Hillary Clinton very astutely incorporates the village with its familial and social structures, traditions, and values as a small place into the nation as a whole, and beyond that into the world. After all, the child of today is a citizen not only of a particular country but of the entire interconnected world. The ethical values with which any child grows up are and should be informed not only from the home but also from the ethics that govern the globe. The anti-proverb "It takes a village to change the world"—formulated by me as a title to reflect on the proverbial rhetoric that takes us from the local and national sphere to global considerations—might just express in a formulaic way how humanity can get from local or national actions based on solid ethics to thinking, and better yet behaving, globally in a responsible fashion in a world committed to the safeguarding of the environment, human rights, and world peace.

The Ethics of Place in a Global Worldview

But is all of this really that new when we look at the history of the sociopolitical endeavors of a country like the United States and its ethics of place? In his seminal study of the small Ulster community of Ballymenone, folklorist Henry Glassie concludes a chapter on "The Idea of Place" with the insightful observation that "Inescapably inscribed in the land, history is intrinsic to the idea of place that forces people to be human" (1995: 665). Yet what is true for a small place in Northern Ireland can also be observed on a larger scale by an historical glance at the solid commitment by major American socio-political figures to the idea of ethics of place that goes beyond the local and encompasses all of humanity throughout the world with "a global or universal view of morality" (Sack 1997: 23).

Much has in fact been made of the idea of "ethics of place" lately, linking history, geography (place and space), ecology, humanity, and ethics into a holistic understanding of modernity. As Chenxi Tang put it in his study on *The Geographic Imagination of Modernity* (2008), the moment "society came to deem historicity to be a fundamental mode of being in the world, it also realized that to be in the world necessarily meant to inhabit the earth and that geographic space was every bit as constitutive of human existence as historical time. Modernity, therefore, has an intrinsic spatial dimension" (2008: 1) with a multitude of cultural and traditional landscapes and an understanding, as the American Studies scholar Yi-Fu Tuan has put it in one of his many studies on modern society, that "the sphere of moral concern is enlarged so that it now embraces the whole world" (1989: 170). In his significant investigation of *Space and Place: The Perspective of Experience* (1977), he reminds

204 *Proverbs in Politics*

us that there are three fundamental places that in various degrees define human existence in space: "Place exists at different scales. At one extreme a favorite armchair is a place, the other extreme the whole earth. Homeland is an important type of place at the medium scale" (Tuan 1977: 149). What is needed is that the rootedness in one's home country does not become the beginning and end all of existence, but that personal and national concerns include global issues. Or as Anna L. Peterson expresses it in her anthropological study *Being Human: Ethics, Environment, and Our Place in the World* (2001), "the human community is fully embedded in and committed to a particular place, and, through that specific relationship, to the earth more generally" (2001: 197). And finally, Tuan summarizes the multilayered levels of spatial belonging as "Home is a house and, in the larger sense, a neighborhood, hometown, country—and ultimately, the earth. Our identity expands and is enriched as the places in which we feel at home—if only temporarily—are multiplied" (2004: 12).

Home, country, and world: that is the spatial triad of human existence, and what should be of major concern is how these "complex cultural worlds that have points in common" (Tuan 1993: 161) can be brought into ethical harmony. Doubtlessly a good start would be an adherence to the fundamental ethical principle of the religions and philosophies of the world, the so-called proverbial golden rule: "Do unto others as you would have them do unto you" (Hertzler 1933–34; Griffin 1991: 67–69, nos. 656–79; Burrell 1997: 11–27; Templeton 1997: 8–12). Such altruistic and all-inclusive ethics of being and place could lead from "spatial segmentation" (Tuan 1982: 3) on various levels to a holistic view of the world.

At a conference on "Rethinking Progress" in Leh, India in September 1992, the American poet and ecologist Gary Snyder delivered a lecture very appropriately entitled "A Village Council of All Beings: Community, Place, and the Awakening of Compassion," arguing that "a consequence of our human interdependence should be a social ethic of mutual respect and a commitment to solving conflict as peacefully as possible" (Snyder 1995: 77). He suggests that humankind should be going after the spiritual and political implications of ecology in its widest sense "place by place" through the regional community politics of "village councils" that will feed into national and global organizations charged with saving life on earth.

Mick Smith, in his invaluable book *An Ethics of Place: Radical Ecology, Postmodernity, and Social Theory* (2001), speaks of a *"sensus communis* that can be inclusive of humans and nonhumans" (2001: 216), arguing convincingly that "an 'ethics of place' (i.e., of environments) reconnects moral and physical spaces in such a way as to subvert our present ethical agendas" (2001: 152). He understands "modernity as a process of metamorphosis, as a transformative restructuring and reorganizing of the world according to new principles, interests and needs" (2001: 154). And finally, Smith sums up his call for an inclusive ethics with the observation that "this heartfelt ethics cannot be learnt by rote or dictated by rules but depends crucially on the development of a 'feeling for life' and our place within it, that is, on the development of what might be termed an ecological *habitus* and an ethics of place" (2001: 168).

Such calls for taking the ethics of place to the global level have become quite widespread, emphasizing "the spatial extent of moral responsibilities to care for others" and directing humankind "towards universal benevolence" (Smith 1999: 277). Of course, scholars are aware of the tensions "between general and specific moralities, between universalism and particularism, between global and local, space and place, between essentialism and individualism or difference, between the natural and the socially constructed, between ethical thought and moral practice, and between is and ought" (Smith 1999: 275). Nevertheless, as American scholars from various disciplines reflect on the ethics to govern the multifaceted aspects of the modern American society and landscape, it is of utmost importance "to define ethical principles not just for this continent but for all times and all places" (Borgmann 2006: 3).

Clearly what is needed is a global ethics, and it behooves Americans to keep this in mind as American culture, politics, business, etc., are spreading around the globe more than ever before. Albert Borgmann has made this argument in his fascinating study on *Real American Ethics: Taking Responsibility for Our Country* (2006), but as with many other studies along this line, he argues primarily from the stance of modernity. I would like to add an historical, folkloric, and yes, paremiological component to this by showing, by means of a number of contextual references, that at least to some extent this emphasis on a common ethics of responsibility for the world has been a leitmotif among some of the greatest Americans (politicians and social reformers) over the past three centuries (Louis 2000; Mieder 2008a). The world has changed, of course, but the thought of making some of the true ethical treasures of America available throughout the world is nothing new. The Bible proverb "There is nothing new under the sun" (Ecclesiastes 1:9) still holds much truth when it comes to such matters as the golden rule, for example, as a universal guide for humankind in this complex world.

Ralph Waldo Emerson's View of Proverbs and the World

Let us take a look at what some of the greats of this country have had to say proverbially about the wisdom that "The world is a place." And not to give politicians the first word, we will let that universalist and transcendentalist Ralph Waldo Emerson, who was quite the early paremiologist as well, set the tone for the following historical and paremiological comments on an ethics that moves from the local to the global. Proverbs permeate all of Emerson's notes, sermons, lectures, and essays, which are informed by his vast knowledge and keen interest in the humanities and sciences and which usually progress from the specific or local to the general or global (see Mieder 1989: 147–69; Mieder 2007). For example, in a sermon of October 18, 1829, he asked his listeners to

> [. . .] consider how much practical wisdom passes current in the world in the shape of vulgar proverbs. These little maxims of worldly prudence are a part of the inheritance that have come down to this age from all the past generations of men. They have given us their institutions, their inventions, their books, and, by means of conversation, have transmitted their commentary upon all the parts of life in these proverbs. They were originally doubtless the happy thoughts of sagacious men in very distant times and countries, in every employment and of every character. No single individual, with whatever penetration, could have attained by himself to that accurate knowledge of human life, which now floats through the conversation of all society, by means of these pithy sentences. We are all of us the wiser for them. They govern us in all our traffic,—in all our judgments of men,—in all our gravest actions. (McGiffert 1968: 62–63)

And to prove his point that proverbs are current throughout the world as expressions of common experiences of humankind, Emerson included small collections of them, many in foreign languages, in his journals. But what Emerson sees in proverbs on the world scale, he also observes in a journal entry of August 2, 1857, as he describes his visit at Flint's Pond:

> The pond was in its summer glory, the chestnuts in flower, two fishermen in a boat, thundertops in the sky, and the whole picture a study of all the secrets of landscape. "A place for everything, and everything in its place"; "no waste and no want"; "each minds his own part, and none overdo and none interfere,"— these and the like rules of good housekeeping are kept here in nature. The

great afternoon spends like fireworks, or festival of the gods, with a tranquil
exultation, as of a boy that has launched his first boat, or his little balloon, and
the experiment succeeds. (Emerson and Forbes 1913: IX, 110)

Always the pragmatist philosopher, Emerson in his essay on *Montaigne: or,
the Skeptic* (1850) even moves from a well-known Anglo-American animal
proverb to the world of humankind by way of a fascinating anti-proverb that
calls for solid work ethics here and everywhere: "Let us have a robust, manly
life; let us know what we know, for certain; what we have, let it be solid and
seasonable and our own. A world in the hand is worth two in the bush. Let
us have to do with real men and women, and not with skipping ghosts" (Emerson 1903: IV, 159).

The Small and Large World of John and Abigail Adams

This passage is somewhat reminiscent of the sentiments that Abigail Adams
expressed eighty years earlier in a letter of May 1, 1780, to her husband John
Adams, who spent years of governmental service in France and England pri-
or to becoming the second president of the United States. Hoping to get
John to come home, she wrote proverbially: "I have a Castle in the air which
I shall write to you upon by the next opportunity, either for you to laugh
at and reject, or to think of it practicable" (Butterfield 1963: III, 335). This
imaginary "castle in the air" (Gallacher 1963; Mieder 2008b) actually was an
indirect reference to a haven in Vermont, where the couple could retire from
the politics of Massachusetts and the federal government; in her letter of December 9, 1781: "Two years my dearest Friend have passed since you left your
Native land. Will you return e'er the close of an other year? I will purchase
you a retreat in the woods of Virmont and retire with you from the vexa-
tions, toils and hazards of publick Life. Do you not sometimes sigh for such
a Seclusion—publick peace and domestick happiness?" (Butterfield 1963: IV,
257). And sure enough, this strong lady, the intellectual equal of some of the
famous founding fathers of this nation, purchased the land, writing to her
husband on July 18, 1782: "My favorite Virmont is a delightfull Country. I
cannot tell why, but I feel a great fondness for the prosperity of that State.
[. . .] I recollected the old adage Nothing venture nothing have; and [. . .] I
paid for [the land]" (Butterfield 1963: IV, 345). The use of the folk proverb
was indeed a shrewd way for Abigail to justify her purchase to John, who
was, however, not interested in early retirement from national and world
politics, as a brief comment in his letter of June 17, 1782, to James Warren

indicates: "God willing, I will not go to Vermont. I must be within the scent of the sea" (Adams 1854: IX, 513). And they didn't go, even though they now owned some 1,500 acres of beautiful and natural Vermont. John wanted and needed to be in the public sector. In fact, they were both early public servants par excellence, and their commitment to making a success of the young United States kept them from secluding themselves in quiet Vermont, which remained a mere proverbial castle in the air place after all.

John and Abigail Adams certainly represent an early example of an American lifestyle rooted in the landscape of a small town in Massachusetts but also embracing the nation and the world with an ethical commitment to making it a better place for all of humanity (see Mieder 2005: 56–89). In fact, in a letter of March 13, 1813, the old John Adams summarizes human life with all humility as being like a bubble, most likely thinking of that ancient Latin proverb "Homo bulla" (Mori 1996):

> They [his two granddaughters] fill the air of the room with their [soap] bubbles, their air balloons, which roll and shine reflecting the light of the fire and candles, and are very beautiful. There can be no more perfect emblem of the physical and political and theological scenes of human life. Morality only is eternal. All the rest is balloon and bubble from the cradle to the grave. (McCullough 2001: 611)

By adding the proverbial expression "From the cradle to the grave" to this paragraph, John Adams reduces the human life to two extremely small places symbolically standing for the beginning and the end of life. And yet, it is in between these two places that all human beings must find their place, reminding us of William Shakespeare's proverbial lines in his *As You Like it* (1600; ii, 7, 139):

> All the world's a stage,
> And all the men and women merely players:
> They have their exits and their entrances;
> And one man in his time plays many parts.

Abraham Lincoln's View of a Better World

The concept of the world as a place for all humanity has preoccupied American presidents and other major public figures ever since, with Abraham

Lincoln helping transform the Bible proverb "And if a house be divided against itself, that house cannot stand" (Mark 3:25) into the folk proverb "A house divided against itself cannot stand" with his famous "House Divided" speech of June 16, 1858. He delivered it in Springfield, Illinois, shortly before the famous debates with Senator Stephen A. Douglas over the issue of slavery in which the proverb was used repeatedly as an argument to save the union all the way up to the outbreak of the Civil War (Mieder 2000: 124–27). But here is what Lincoln said on that eventful evening in his home state:

> [Slavery] *will* not cease, until a *crisis* shall have been reached, and passed.
> "A house divided against itself cannot stand."
> I believe this government cannot endure, permanently half *slave* and half *free*.
> I do not expect the Union to be *dissolved*—*I do not expect the house to* fall—but I
>   *do* expect it will cease to be divided.
> It will become *all* one thing, or *all* the other.
> (Basler 1953: II, 461–62)

This speech is still a far cry from the Emancipation Proclamation of January 1, 1863, but Lincoln's use of the house metaphor to stand for the nation as such was a definite stroke of genius. It symbolized not only the division over slavery within the Union, but in a narrower sense also the rift that this issue caused in the homes of families. The proverb thus encompasses local places as well as the entire country, clearly stating that slavery was tearing apart the moral fibers of the young nation. This is not the place to look at the use of this proverb for various sociopolitical issues before and after Lincoln all the way to the present day (see Mieder 1998; Mieder 2005: 90–117), but it has certainly been employed again and again as a metaphorical and ethical call for keeping the United States politically and spatially intact.

Instead, let us look at yet another memorable address which Lincoln, the great orator whose speeches are usually informed by proverbs and proverbial phrases (Mieder 2000), delivered at the height of the Civil War. There was a time when many Americans learned the Gettysburg Address of November 19, 1863, by heart, but even today it can be argued that parts of it and certainly the concluding paragraph are a hallmark of cultural literacy. This is especially true for the proverbial and triadic definition of democracy at the end of his speech, which has a considerable history with several variants by such major political figures as John Adams, John Marshall, Daniel Webster, and especially the abolitionist Theodore Parker (Mieder 2005: 15–55), before Abraham Lincoln made it into a national motto:

The world will little note, nor long remember what we say here, but it can never forget what they [all the brave dead soldiers] did here. It is for us the living, rather, to be dedicated here to the unfinished work which they who fought here have thus far so nobly advanced. It is rather for us to be here dedicated to the great task remaining before us—that from these honored dead we take increased devotion to that cause for which they gave the last full measure of devotion—that we here highly resolve that these dead shall not have died in vain—that this nation, under God, shall have a new birth of freedom—and that government of the people, by the people, for the people, shall not perish from the earth. (Basler 1953: VIII, 23)

Of course, not only Americans but also citizens of the world did take note of these remarks delivered with sincere humility, with Garry Wills having provided a detailed study, *Lincoln at Gettysburg: The Words That Remade America* (1992). However, Wills says nothing in his rhetorical analysis about Lincoln's use of the words "world" and "earth" at the end of the speech. And yet, it would be my conjecture that Lincoln was at least metaphorically placing the tragic conflict over freedom for all inhabitants of the American landscape into the realm of humankind on earth. To be sure, he starts his address by speaking of only this nation, but then he continues his unforgettable sentence with the proverbial statement of the equality of all humankind from the Declaration of Independence:

Four score and seven years ago our fathers brought forth on this continent, a new nation, conceived in Liberty, and dedicated to the proposition that all men are created equal" (Basler 1953: VII, 23)

Clearly Lincoln is inclusive with this call for equality, freedom, and democracy. That this is not mere speculation, can be seen among other instances in a senatorial campaign speech of August 17, 1858, in Lewistown, Illinois. There he placed the claims of the "equality" proverb and the proverbial triad of "Life, liberty and the pursuit of happiness" squarely in the larger space of the world and beyond that the universe:

These communities [from the states in 1776], by their representatives in old Independence Hall, said to the whole world of men: "We hold these truths to be self evident: that all men are created equal; that they are endowed by their Creator with certain unalienable rights; that among these are life, liberty and the pursuit of happiness." This was their majestic interpretation of the

economy of the Universe. This was their lofty, and wise, and noble understanding of the justice of the creator to His creatures. Yes, gentlemen, to *all*
His creatures, to the whole great family of man. [. . .] They grasped not only
the whole race of man then living, but they reached forward and seized upon
the farthest posterity. They erected a beacon to guide their children and their
children's children, and the countless myriads who should inhabit the earth in
other ages. (Basler 1953: II, 546)

As might be expected, later presidents and political figures have continued
using the proverbs "All men are created equal" and "Government of the
people, by the people, [and] for the people" in at times even more direct
ways to encompass citizens of the world. The two proverbs did in fact not
only remake America but set the stage for the continued democratic struggle
throughout the world.

Frederick Douglass and "No Man Liveth unto Himself"

Frederick Douglass, former slave and then major abolitionist and also friend
of Abraham Lincoln, also incorporated the "government–people" triad into
a global vision in an address of May 30, 1882, in Rochester, New York, indicating that he went far beyond the purely American interpretation of its
wisdom. The breadth and depth of Douglass's thoughts on race, gender, and
politics are indeed revolutionary and most impressive at the end of the nineteenth century:

> The suppression of our rebellion [by the South] by force was not only a thing
> right and proper in itself but an immense and immeasurable gain to our coun-
> try and the world. Had that rebellion succeeded with all its malign purposes,
> what then would have become of our grand example of free institutions, of
> what value then would have been our government of the people by the people
> and for the people? What ray of light would have been left above the horizon,
> to kindle the first hope for the toiling millions in Europe? Every despot in the
> Old World would have seen in our manifest instability of government, a new
> and powerful argument in favor of despotic power. (Blassingame 1985: V, 48)

While this statement refers primarily to the American Civil War, Douglass
connects it with the struggles for freedom in Europe and other parts of the
world. In fact, in a speech exactly one year earlier on May 30, 1881, in Harpers
Ferry, Virginia, he had made a similar but more general statement, alluding

to two Biblical proverbs to underscore his important point that the world is interconnected and governed by ethical rules:

> To the broad vision of a true philosophy, nothing in this world stands alone. Everything is a necessary part of everything else. The margin of chance is narrowed by every extension of reason and knowledge, and nothing comes unbidden to the feat of human experience. The universe, of which we are part, is continually proving itself a stupendous whole, a system of law and order, eternal and perfect. Every seed bears fruit after its kind [see Matthew 7:17–20], and nothing is reaped which was not sowed [see Galatians 6:7]. (Blassingame 1985: V, 11)

Frederick Douglass, this champion for freedom and human rights, summarized his struggle for progress in this country and elsewhere in the final version of his autobiography *Life and Times* (1893) with yet another Bible proverb that expresses a worldview for humankind based on interconnectedness and interdependence:

> No man liveth unto himself, or ought to live unto himself [Romans 14:7]. My life has conformed to this Bible saying, for, more than most men, I have been the thin edge of the wedge to open for my people a way in many directions and places never before occupied by them. It has been mine, in some degree, to stand as their defense in moral battle against the shafts of detraction, calumny and persecution, and to labor in removing and overcoming those obstacles which, in the shape of erroneous ideas and customs, have blocked the way to their progress. (Douglass 1994: 941)

By extending the proverb "No man liveth unto himself" from a statement of fact into an imperative ("or ought to live unto himself"), he points to a moral obligation of humankind to improve the lot of others. Employing numerous proverbs in his powerful rhetoric (Mieder 2001), he dedicated his life to this effort, especially in his work for African Americans, summarizing his efforts in a speech of August 3, 1857, with his formulation of "If there is no struggle, there is no progress" (Blassingame 1985: III, 204) that might well or ought to become a proverb as "No struggle, no progress" (Mieder 2005: 118–46).

The Place of Women According to Stanton and Anthony

Two of his close friends, Elizabeth Cady Stanton and Susan B. Anthony, drew on Douglass's help as they struggled for women's rights. Like their friend, they traveled throughout this country as well as Europe, thus gaining a vision of equality for women not only in the United States but in the entire world. Once again, a more or less local and then national effort eventually encompasses the world at large, showing clearly that there must be no borders when it comes to the engaged struggle for freedom and equality. One might even go so far as to say that these two early feminists took a good lesson from Douglass in using moral suasion in the pursuit of their goals. On March 26, 1888, most likely in the presence of Douglass, Stanton delivered her "Address of Welcome to the International Council of Women" in Washington, D.C.:

> Here, under the shadow of the Capitol of this great nation, whose dome is crowned with the Goddess of Liberty, the women from many lands have assembled at last to claim their rightful place, as equal factors, in the great movements of the nineteenth century, so we bid our distinguished guests welcome, thrice welcome to our triumphant democracy. I hope they will be able to stay long enough to take a bird's eye view of our vast possessions, to see what can be done in a moral, as well as material point of view, in a government of the people. In the Old World they have governments and people; here we have a government of the people, by the people, for the people; that is, we soon shall have when that important half, called women, are enfranchised, and the laboring masses know how to use the power they possess. (Gordon 2009: V, 99)

This is most certainly effective rhetoric, quoting the "government of the people" proverb reminiscent of Lincoln and Douglass in a positive way and then adding an unexpected ironic twist to it that places it right in the middle of women's rights and the whole problem of voting by women and the masses in general. And, as Stanton addresses women from many lands, she quite consciously also employs the proverbial phrase "To claim one's place," which in this case deals with not a spatial but rather a social position, with the ethics involved in finding an equal place for women in sociopolitical issues being discussed in the speech as such.

About a year earlier, in a letter to her granddaughter Nora S. Blatch, Stanton had employed another play with a proverb to express her worldview when it came to equal rights for women: "It comprizes the globe, my motto being, 'the world is my country & all mankind my countrywomen'" (Gordon 2009: V, 23). The proverb "The world is my country" has been traced back to a maxim by Theodorus (ca. 312 B.C.), but there is also William Lloyd Garrison's motto for his journal *The Liberator* from 1830: "My country is the world; my countrymen are (all) mankind" (Stevenson 1948: 427, no. 3). Clearly Stanton has a bit of sociolinguistic fun with her motto, but it is nevertheless apparent that she looks at these women's issues not from a local or national point of view only but as matters of global concern. And her close friend Susan B. Anthony also understood her energetic work for women's equality and voting rights as being not only of American concern, coming up with the proverb-like motto "Give women the ballot for a fulcrum, and she will move the moral world" (Gordon 2003: III, 168) in a speech on "Moral Purity" on April 12, 1875, in St. Louis. Obviously she is alluding to Archimedes's (ca. 220 B.C.) declaration: "Give me a place to stand on and I will move the world [with a big enough lever]" (Stevenson 1948: 2627, no.[?] 6). But while the Greek is speaking of the physical world, the American is concerned with the ethics on that very globe.

The Proverbial Worldview of Twentieth-Century Presidents

President Theodore Roosevelt, contemporary of both Elizabeth Cady Stanton and Susan B. Anthony, might not have been a big champion for women's rights, but he certainly shared the views of the two grand old ladies that the United States cannot be an island in itself in the world. In his inaugural speech of March 5, 1905, he makes this quite clear, adding an allusion to the proverb "Deeds, not words" to his argument for America being a responsible player on the international scene:

> Much has been given us, and much will rightfully be expected from us. We have duties to others and duties to ourselves; we can shirk neither. We have become a great nation, forced by the fact of its greatness into relations with other nations of the earth, and we must behave as beseems a people with such responsibilities. Towards all other nations, large and small, our attitude must be one of cordial and sincere friendship. We must show not only in our words, but in our deeds, that we are earnestly desirous of securing their goodwill by acting toward them in a spirit of just and generous recognition of all their rights. (Hunt 1997: 300)

What an incredible statement, arguing that the United States has been forced into a central place in the world because of its ethical commitment to basic rights for all people! The ideals of this country, put forth in such magnificent documents as the Declaration of Independence, the Constitution, and the Bill of Rights that were created at a time when the United States consisted of but small communities, should be a moral beacon for its interrelationship with other nations of the world. And, as Roosevelt is quick to point out, this role of responsibility must not consist only of words but of deeds, as the proverb allusion makes perfectly clear.

While it is truly remarkable that America's earlier public figures were apt to move from local and national considerations to a more inclusive global commitment to human rights, it is perhaps not surprising that American leaders broadened this vision even further in light of the fact that America has become a dominant world power. As the United States has struggled with this responsibility, it was fortunate to have had civic leaders and presidents who tried to keep the country on an ethical course in world affairs. Franklin Delano Roosevelt's extremely short fourth inaugural speech (barely a page and a half) of January 20, 1945, delivered at the height of World War II, is a case in point. With the war hopefully drawing to an end, Roosevelt cited two proverbial expressions and a proverb to remind the American people of the necessity to find peace in the world by being a player on the world scene. Isolation then or after the war was clearly not a choice for a world power like the United States:

> Today, in this year of war, 1945, we have learned lessons—at a fearful cost— and we shall profit from them. We have learned that we cannot live alone, at peace; that our own well-being is dependent on the well-being of other nations far away. We have learned that we must live as men, not as ostriches, not as dogs in the manger. We have learned the simple truth, as Emerson said, that "the only way to have a friend is to be one." We can gain no lasting peace if we approach it with suspicion and mistrust or with fear. We can gain it only if we proceed with the understanding, the confidence, and the courage which flow from conviction. (Hunt 1997: 396)

The metaphors of the proverbial expressions "To be an ostrich" and "to be a dog in the manger" (Moravcsik 1964; Priest 1985) are perfect to express the two convictions that America cannot afford to turn a blind eye to world events and that it cannot retreat selfishly on its own territory. Local, regional, and national isolation are in Roosevelt's worldview no options, since the

United States has a responsible place to fill in the world at large. Being a global partner, the United States should rather be a fair and helpful friend to other nations, as Roosevelt explains by citing the wisdom "The only way to have a friend is to be one" from Ralph Waldo Emerson's essay on "Friendship" (1841), which has long since become a proverb (Stevenson 1948: 896, no. 3; Mieder, Kingsbury, and Harder 1992: 239).

Harry S. Truman, quite a contrast to the tall and well-educated Roosevelt, took over the presidency after Roosevelt's death, doing his "damned" best to fill his predecessor's shoes and continue in the footsteps of this giant of world politics. He might have been a little man lacking a college education, but he sure knew how to give such greats as Josef Stalin and Winston S. Churchill a bit of hell as they dealt with reshaping the world after the war. He also deserves credit for participating in the creation of the Marshall Plan, the North Atlantic Treaty Organization, and the United Nations.

When he continued his presidency on January 20, 1949, after having won the election against considerable odds, he uttered the following important words, perhaps consciously staying away from his normal plain speaking filled with proverbs and proverbial phrases at this historic moment (Mieder 1997: 67–98; Mieder and Bryan 1997). But as so many presidents before and after him, he did include Thomas Jefferson's sentence-turned-proverb "All men are created equal" in his inaugural speech, to encompass all of humanity in his deliberations of the ethical place of America in the world:

> The American people stand firm in the faith which has inspired this nation from the beginning. We believe that all men have a right to equal justice under law and equal opportunity to share the common good. We believe that all men have the right to freedom of thought and expression. We believe that all men are created equal because they are created in the image of God. From this faith we will not be moved. The American people desire, and are determined to work for, a world in which all nations and all peoples are free to govern themselves as they see fit and to achieve a decent and satisfying life. Above all else, our people desire, and are determined to work for, peace on earth—a just and lasting peace—based on a genuine agreement freely arrived at by equals. (Hunt 1997: 402–3)

This noble rhetoric can stand next to that of other great American presidents, and to be sure, Truman meant what he said, to wit the creation of the humanitarian Marshall Plan that helped undernourished youngsters like me to get fed. I was but five years old at the time, but my earliest childhood memories are my mother mixing powdered milk (perhaps from my beloved Vermont) with water or making scrambled eggs from dried eggs for me, and my father adding a bit of sugar to condensed milk so that I could enjoy something sweet. All of this came from America, including my favorite shoes, jacket, and pants. And then there were those little care packages. You should have seen my little legs carrying me to the small grocery store at the corner of the street to get one of them when a new shipment from America had arrived! A small treasure of peanut butter crackers, candied fruit, chewing gum (which we were not allowed to eat at school and did nevertheless), a candy bar, of course, and many other things. Perhaps this is why I longed to come to America from my childhood on, and at the age of sixteen, only fifteen years after America defeated the menace and the horrors of Nazi Germany, I had the opportunity of a lifetime. I will always be thankful to President Truman and General Marshall for what they did for us kids and to the hundreds of Americans who helped me find the ethics of place in my village of Williston, the state of Vermont, the United States, and other parts of the world.

As John F. Kennedy struggled to keep this peace at the height of the Cold War, he made the pledge to help people everywhere during his inaugural speech of January 20, 1961, appropriately replacing the reference to God in the proverb "God helps them who help themselves" by the pronoun "we" that stands for the United States and its citizens:

> To those people in the huts and villages across the globe struggling to break the bonds of mass misery, we pledge our best efforts to help them help themselves, for whatever period is required—not because the Communists may be doing it, not because we seek their votes, but because it is right. If a free society cannot help the many who are poor, it cannot save the few who are rich. (Hunt 1997: 429)

It is interesting to note how the president takes his moral message to the smallest "huts and villages across the globe," obviously wanting to reach people wherever possible with his message of humanitarian aid and the idea of freedom. And when Jimmy Carter took over the governmental reins on January 20, 1977, he picked up this same theme but added the proverbial phrase of a "place in the sun" to it:

> The world itself is now dominated by a new spirit. Peoples more numerous and more politically aware are craving and now demanding their place in the sun—not just for the benefit of their physical condition, but for basic human

rights. The passion for freedom is on the rise. Tapping this new spirit, there can be no nobler nor more ambitious task for America to undertake on this [inauguration] day of a new beginning than to help shape a just and peaceful world that is truly humane. (Hunt 1997: 465)

The phrase "a place in the sun" was coined by the German Chancellor Bernard von Bülow in a Reichstag speech of December 6, 1897, as he explained and tried to justify Germany's colonial ambitions: "In a word, we desire to throw no one into the shade, but we also demand our own place in the sun [Platz an der Sonne]" (Rees 1995: 382). Quite typical for Carter, he pushed aside the political and territorial claims of the phrase and employed it as an expression of a place governed by the light of human rights. The popularity of the expression in America probably results from the well-known song "A Place in the Sun" ("Where there's hope for everyone") by Ronald Miller and Bryan Wells—a hit song recorded by Stevie Wonder in 1966 and subsequently by numerous other pop singers.

Proverbs and Martin Luther King's Struggle for a Free World

Perhaps Jimmy Carter had Martin Luther King in mind as he uttered these words. With his rhetorical power and social commitment, King fought for human rights for all people in all places, from the smallest hamlet in the deep South to the city of Birmingham, from Alabama on to the entire United States, and finally throughout the world. Doubtlessly his many speeches and writings have a lasting influence throughout the land and beyond, and his poetic, sermonic, and at times proverbial style together with his demands for racial and social justice continue to be models in the struggle for better communities and nations around the globe. There is no doubt that Martin Luther King embodies the inclusive idea of ethics of place linguistically, intellectually, and socially through word and deed!

King's struggle for justice and equality began as a grass roots movement in the deep South in cities like Atlanta, Birmingham, Montgomery, and Selma, with protests and marches for civil rights that have entered the annals of American history forever. Eventually this nonviolent movement for improving the lot of African Americans and other minorities as well as women reached the national stage in Washington, D.C. The unforgettable climax came with Martin Luther King's "I Have a Dream" speech before the Lincoln Memorial on August 28, 1963, that stirred the nation. And when King received the Nobel Peace Prize in Oslo, Norway, on December 10, 1964, he had indeed conquered the moral world with his nonviolent struggle for universal civil rights. While he obviously started as a champion of justice and equality for African Americans in the region of his activities as a minister, he actually was concerned with larger goals that included not only the entire nation but the whole world. In a speech on "Facing the Challenge of a New Age," delivered in December 1956 in Montgomery, he declared: "The new world is a world of geographical togetherness. This means that no individual or nation can live alone. We must all learn to live together, or we will be forced to die together" (Washington 1986: 138). In his book *Stride Toward Freedom* (1958), which served as a handbook of this nonviolent movement, he argued that "in a real sense the racial crisis in America is a part of the larger world crisis" (Washington 1986: 469). But his commitment to taking his struggle for civil rights beyond the local and national to the international scene is best expressed through his metaphor of "the world house" in his book *Where Do We Go from Here: Chaos or Community?* (1967): "We have inherited a large house, a great 'world house' in which we have to live together—black and white, Easterner and Westerner, Gentile and Jew, Catholic and Protestant, Moslem and Hindu—a family unduly separated in ideas, culture and interest, who, because we can never again live apart, must learn to live with each other in peace" (Washington 1986: 617). As King expounds on this all-encompassing idea, he observes that "all inhabitants of the globe are now neighbors" and that "the large house in which we live demands that we transform this worldwide neighborhood into a world-wide brotherhood" (Washington 1986: 617, 620). And of course, typical for the moral preacher, King adds an ethical component to his vision of this geographical interconnectedness:

> Our hope for creative living in this world house that we have inherited lies in our ability to reestablish the moral ends of our lives in personal character and social justice. Without this spiritual and moral reawakening we shall destroy ourselves in the misuse of our own instruments.
>
> [. . .] The stability of the large world house which is ours will involve a revolution of values to accompany the scientific and freedom revolutions engulfing the earth. (Washington 1986: 621, 629)

To this ethics of humanity and space, King the preacher appends a few comments regarding the necessity for hopeful action and then closes with a powerful Bible verse of proverbial imagery:

Our only hope today lies in our ability to recapture our revolutionary spirit and go out into a sometimes hostile world declaring eternal opposition to poverty, racism and militarism. With this powerful commitment we shall boldly challenge the status quo and unjust mores and thereby speed the day when "every valley shall be exalted, and every mountain and hill shall be made low: and the crooked shall be made straight and the rough places plain." (Washington 1986: 632)

Waiting or standing by idly is no option for this moral activist, who would most certainly have argued against the passive proverb "Everything comes to him who waits." Instead he formulates the proverb-like statement "Wait has almost always meant never" in his famed "Letter from a Birmingham Jail" (1963), obviously pushing for change brought about by nonviolent action, for, as the true proverb says "Justice delayed is justice denied":

> This "Wait" has almost always meant "Never." It has been a tranquilizing thalidomide, relieving the emotional stress for a moment, only to give birth to an ill-formed infant of frustration. We must come to see with the distinguished jurist of yesterday that "justice too long delayed is justice denied." We have waited for more than 340 years for our constitutional and God-given rights. The nations of Asia and Africa are moving with jet-like speed toward the goal of political independence, and we still creep at horse and buggy pace toward the gaining of a cup of coffee at a lunch counter. (Washington 1986: 292)

Clearly proverbs are part of the rhetorical style of King, whose sermons, lectures, and books are replete with folk and Biblical wisdom (Karabegović 2007). In this he follows a strong phraseological tradition in African American parlance (Mieder 1989: 111–28; Prahlad 1996), taking his listeners and readers to verbal and ethical heights that are moving if not overwhelming in their expressive power. This is definitely the case in the following paragraph from his speech about "The American Dream" (1961) that he gave on June 6, 1961, at Lincoln University in Pennsylvania. He speaks of human interrelatedness both morally and spatially, using the proverb "No man is an island entire of itself" to argue that the American dream about freedom and justice must include the whole world:

> All [. . .] life is interrelated. We are caught in an inescapable network of mutuality; tied in a single garment of destiny. Whatever affects one directly, affects all indirectly. [. . .] This is the way the world is made. I didn't make it

that way, but this is the interrelated structure of reality. John Donne caught it a few centuries ago and could cry out, "No man is an island entire of itself; every man is a piece of the continent, a part of the main . . . any man's death diminishes me, because I am involved in mankind, and therefore never send to know for whom the bell tolls; it tolls for thee." If we are to realize the American dream we must cultivate this world perspective. (Washington 1986: 210)

Before concluding these deliberations with a look at Barack Obama's humane ethics of place, there is one more paragraph from Martin Luther King's book *Where Do We Go from Here: Chaos or Community?* (1967) that deserves to be cited. It is framed by two proverbial expressions: "To be in the red" is used to express the indebtedness of all people to one another, and "To be one's brother's keeper" is employed to remind people of the message of the Bible that people should take care of each other. And this ethics, as King makes perfectly clear, is to encompass the earth, or as the modern proverb song has it: "The world is a place, for the whole human race, to live and relate, as brothers":

All men are interdependent. Every nation is an heir of a vast treasury of ideas and labor to which both the living and the dead of all nations have contributed. Whether we realize it or not, each of us lives eternally "in the red." We are everlasting debtors to known and unknown men and women. When we arise in the morning, we go into the bathroom where we reach for a sponge which is provided for us by a Pacific islander. We reach for soap that is created for us by a European. Then at the table we drink coffee which is provided for us by a South American, or tea by a Chinese or cocoa by a west African. Before we leave for our jobs we are already beholden to more than half the world.

In a real sense, all life is interrelated. The agony of the poor impoverishes the rich; the betterment of the poor enriches the rich. We are inevitably our brother's keeper because we are our brother's brother. Whatever affects one directly affects all indirectly. (Washington 1986: 626)

A "world house"—based on ethics of place and a keen recognition of what King calls the "inescapable network of mutuality" among everyone and everything—is what it is all about, to use a modern turn of phrase.

President Barack Obama's Concept of "The World Is a Place"

Barack Obama is well aware of the ideals expressed by the admired Martin Luther King. Little wonder that he is fond of the proverbial expression "To stand on the shoulders of giants," with which he acknowledges the debt he owes especially to civil rights leaders and many others who helped him occupy the place that we call the White House as the first African American. As he said in a speech on July 14, 2008, in Cincinnati, Ohio: "It is always humbling to speak before the NAACP. It is a powerful reminder of the debt we all owe to those who marched for us and stood up on our behalf; of the sacrifices that were made for us by those we never knew, and of the giants whose shoulders I stand on here today" (Mieder 2009: 306). It cannot possibly then come as a surprise that Barack Obama also shares with Martin Luther King his predisposition for the proverbial interrogative "Am I my brother's keeper?" from the Bible. Both used it numerous times, with Obama very consciously expanding the proverb to include women (Mieder 2009: 180–81). The following remark from his speech on "A More Perfect Union" delivered on March 18, 2008, in Philadelphia is particularly telling, since it shows in but a few sentences the interconnectedness of the world as a place through the ethics of the golden rule:

> In the end then, what is called for is nothing more, and nothing less, than what all the world's great religions demand—that we do unto others as we would have them do unto us. Let us be our brother's keeper, Scripture tells us. Let us be our sister's keeper. Let us find the common stake we all have in one another, and let our politics reflect that spirit as well. (Mieder 2009: 180)

This short paragraph exemplifies Obama's rhetorical gift, which parallels that of the great orator Martin Luther King. It is especially noteworthy that he does add "sisters" to be inclusive, but it is also of great importance that he has changed the phrasing of the Bible text from a question to an imperative. In other words, we have a moral obligation to keep each other safe as a fundamental obligation in an interconnected world.

When Barack Obama gave his speech on "A World That Stands as One" on July 24, 2008, in Berlin, he won the hearts and minds of Germans and Europeans alike when he began with the personal comment: "I come to Berlin as so many of my countrymen have come before. Tonight, I speak to you not as a candidate for President, but as a citizen—a proud citizen of the United States, and a fellow citizen of the world" (Mieder 2009: 121). And then, reminiscent of tearing down the Berlin Wall, he made the significant point that globalization means tearing down walls and fences of all types throughout the world:

> The burdens of global citizenship continue to bind us together. [. . .] Partner-ship and cooperation among nations is not a choice; it is the one way, the only way, to protect our common security and advance our common humanity.
>
> That is why the greatest danger of all is to allow new walls to divide us from one another.
>
> The walls between old allies on either side of the Atlantic cannot stand. The walls between the countries with the most and those with the least can-not stand. The walls between races and tribes; natives and immigrants; Chri-stian and Muslim and Jew cannot stand. These now are the walls we must tear down. (Mieder 2009: 121–22)

This surely is a rhetorical masterpiece with the folkloric three-time repeti-tion of the proverbial formulation "The walls between [. . .] cannot stand" that will surely have brought to mind Lincoln's use of the Bible proverb "A house divided against itself cannot stand." Toward the end of the speech, Obama brings the United States back into focus, reminding his German and European audience that his country remains dedicated to the idea of self-improvement (perfecting the union!) as it serves others:

> I know that for more than two centuries, we [Americans] have strived—at great cost and great sacrifice—to form a more perfect union; to seek, with other nations, a more hopeful world. Our allegiance has never been to any particular tribe or kingdom—indeed, every language is spoken in our coun-try; every culture has left its imprint on ours; every point of view is expressed in our public squares. What has always united us—what has always driven our people; what drew my father to America's shores—is a set of ideals that speak to aspirations shared by all people: that we can live free from fear and free from want; that we can speak our minds and assemble with whomever we choose and worship as we please. (Mieder 2009: 123)

This nation of immigrants, the melting pot or tossed salad of the languages and cultures of the world, could well be a guidepost for the world. Obama expressed this thought in his formidable speech on race with the apt title "A More Perfect Union" on March 18, 2008, in Philadelphia: "I believe deeply that we cannot solve the challenges of our time unless we solve them together—unless we perfect our union by understanding that we may have different stories, but we hold common hopes; that we may not look the same and we may not have come from the same place, but we all want to move in the same direction—towards a better future for our children and grand-children" (Mieder 2009: 11). With his typical audacity of hope, epitomized by the proverbial slogan "Yes we can," Obama projects a typically American forward-looking vision, as Alan Dundes describes and interprets it in his article "'As the Crow Flies': A Straightforward Study of Lineal Worldview in American Folk Speech" (2004). Little wonder that an euphoric Barack Obama, in his victory speech on November 4, 2008, in Chicago, drew on the universal proverb "All things are possible," claiming its truth factor for himself as the first African American having been elected president and also for the entire United States: "America is a place where all things are possible" (Mieder 2009: 129).

Of course, Obama could simply have said "In America all things are possible," but he chose to stress America as a unique "place." The concept of place in its many ramifications is something with which Barack Obama has been quite preoccupied, and I do not mean only the natural question of what his "place in history" as president will be. It is finding his own place, his identity as it were, that might well serve as a conclusion of this short survey of the use and function of proverbial language in the ethics of place. As Obama reports and reflects on his quest for place, he proves himself to be quite the folklor-ist and ethnographer, as for example when he tells about his early work as a community organizer in Chicago in his celebrated autobiography *Dreams from My Father* (1995), for which he probably quite consciously chose the subtitle *A Story of Race and Inheritance* to stress its narrative character, in-cluding a plethora of stories, proverbs, proverbial phrases, and other folk-loric references based on a considerable amount of field research. He stresses the importance of listening to the personal narratives that people had to tell (Dolby 2008): "Stories full of terror and wonder, studded with events that still haunted or inspired them. Sacred stories" (Obama 2004: 190). As he explains that these stories helped him find his place with the common people of the South end of Chicago, he felt uplifted and part of a larger social net-work: "Then they'd offer a story to match or confound mine, a knot to bind our experiences together—a lost father, an adolescent brush with crime, a wandering heart, a moment of simple grace. As time passed, I found that these stories, taken together, had helped me bind my world together, that they gave me the sense of place and purpose I'd been looking for" (Obama 2004: 190). This certainly qualifies as a bit of psychological folklore work,

with the phrase "to bind one's world together" showing that Obama's sensi-
tive and effective rhetoric is informed by empathy for the place of others, as
he is searching himself for the place that gives him a social anchor.

Having found his place or identity in a small village in Africa, Obama,
the cosmopolitan, who could not possibly return to that setting in earnest,
is ready to continue his life's struggle in the service of others. Home, village,
and country are "no longer a construct of words" but rather places for responsible and engaged action (Nichols 1996). For Obama then, it took his
African village to change his world. That this is not solely a personal matter
might also be gleaned from this final use of a proverb by the intriguing proverbialist Obama that I had not known before reading his moving autobiography. The proverb in question appears in an interchange between Obama
and a friend who initiates it on a street in Chicago:

> "I'm telling you, man, the world's a *place*."
> "Say, the world is a place, huh."
> "That's just what I'm saying." (Obama 2004: 249)

As if to reinforce the message of this proverb describing the world as a place
where all kinds of things can happen, the friend follows up with an account
of a recent suicide of a young white girl ("one of these punk rock types, with
blue hair and a ring through her nose") who had jumped from a high building. The friend, stamping out his cigarette on the sidewalk, concludes his
story in solid street slang that shows Obama's ability to play the entire register of language, from the sublime to the scatological:

> "So that's what I'm saying, Barack. Whole panorama of life out there. Crazy
> shit going on. You got to ask yourself, is this kinda stuff happening elsewhere?
> Is there a precedent for all of this shit? You ever ask yourself that?"
> "The world's a place," I repeated.
> "See there! It's serious, man." (Obama 2004: 251)

Perhaps the proverb "The world is a place" is a modern variant of the traditional wisdom "The world is a stage" that is not so much an anti-proverb
(Litovkina and Mieder 200) but rather a semantic expansion of the original
proverb. It expresses the idea that all kinds of things take place in this world,
some of which are beyond our control and comprehension. But that should
not be cause for despair, for those "stubborn ideas—survival, and freedom,
and hope" (Obama 2004: 273), as Obama is quick to point out, will persist

and make the struggle for change and progress go on. Our global mutuality on all fronts clearly calls for a commitment to the universal concept of ethics of place, from village to nation and on to the world, with the golden rule being a guiding principle. The short proverb "The world is a place" might be too ambiguous in its simplistic message in order to serve as another ethical motto for humanity. But its longer variant "The world is a place for the whole human race" represents a perfect moral guidepost. Citing the first stanza of the song that it comes from once again, and also expanding the last line by a significant addition, we have a proverb for humanity that encapsulates the concept of an ethics of place that stretches from the individual to all humankind and from the village to the entire world:

> The world is a place
> For the whole human race
> To live and relate
> As brothers and sisters!

BIBLIOGRAPHY

This chapter first appeared with the same title in *Journal of American Folklore* 124 (2011): 4–28.

Adams, Charles Francis, ed. 1854. *The Works of John Adams*. Boston: Little, Brown.
Basler, Roy P., ed. 1953. *The Collected Works of Abraham Lincoln*. New Brunswick, New Jersey: Rutgers University Press.
Blassingame, John, ed. 1985. *The Frederick Douglass Papers*. New Haven, Connecticut: Yale University Press.
Borgmann, Albert. 2006. *Real American Ethics: Taking Responsibility for Our Country*. Chicago: University of Chicago Press.
Bryan, George B., and Wolfgang Mieder. 2003. "The Proverbial Carl Sandburg (1878–1967): An Index of the Folk Speech in His American Poetry." *Proverbium* 20: 15–49.
Burrell, Brian. 1997. *The Words We Live By: The Creeds, Mottoes, and Pledges that Have Shaped America*. New York: Free Press.
Burroughs, Ben. 1957. *Sketches*. New York: Fleet Press.
Butterfield, L. H., ed. 1963. *Adams Family Correspondence (1761–1785)*. Cambridge, Massachusetts: Harvard University Press.
Clinton, Hillary Rodham. 1996. *It Takes a Village and Other Lessons Children Teach Us*. New York: Simon & Schuster.
Cowen-Fletcher, Jane. 1993. *It Takes a Village*. New York: Scholastic.
Deutscher, Guy. 2005 (2006). "Standing on the Shoulders of Clichés—A Key Milestone on the Way to Ordinary Language." *New York Times* June 18: A13. Also in *"Gold Nuggets or Fool's Gold?": Magazine and Newspaper Articles on the (Ir)relevance of Proverbs and Proverbial Phrases*. Wolfgang Mieder and Janet Sobieski, eds. Burlington, Vermont: University of Vermont, 2006. 223–44.
Dolby, Sandra K. 2008. *Literary Folkloristics and the Personal Narrative*. Bloomington, Indiana: Trickster.

Douglass, Frederick. 1994. *Autobiographies: Narrative of the Life of Frederick Douglass* [1845], *My Bondage and My Freedom* [1855], *Life and Times of Frederick Douglass* [1893]. New York: Library of America.

Doyle, Charles Clay, Wolfgang Mieder, and Fred R. Shapiro, eds. 2012. *The Dictionary of Modern Proverbs*. New Haven, Connecticut: Yale University Press.

Dundes, Alan. 2004. "'As the Crow Flies': A Straightforward Study of Lineal Worldview in American Folk Speech." *What Goes Around Comes Around: The Circulation of Proverbs in Contemporary Life. Essays in Honor of Wolfgang Mieder.* Kimberly J. Lau, Peter Tokofsky, and Stephen D. Winick, eds. Logan, Utah: Utah State University Press. 171–87.

Emerson, Edward Waldo, ed. 1903. *The Complete Works of Ralph Waldo Emerson.* Boston: Houghton, Mifflin.

Emerson, Edward Waldo, and Waldo Emerson Forbes, eds. 1913. *Journals of Ralph Waldo Emerson.* Boston: Houghton, Mifflin.

Gallacher, Stuart A. 1963. "Castles in Spain." *Journal of American Folklore* 76: 324–29.

Glassie, Henry. 1995. *Passing the Time in Ballymenone: Culture and History of an Ulster Community.* Bloomington, Indiana: Indiana University Press.

Gordon, Ann D., ed. 2003. *The Selected Papers of Elizabeth Cady Stanton and Susan B. Anthony.* Volume III: *National Protection for National Citizens 1873 to 1880.* New Brunswick, New Jersey: Rutgers University Press.

——, ed. 2009. *The Selected Papers of Elizabeth Cady Stanton and Susan B. Anthony.* Volume V: *Their Place Inside the Body-Politic 1887 to 1895.* New Brunswick, New Jersey: Rutgers University Press.

Griffin, Albert Kirby. 1991. *Religious Proverbs: Over 1600 Adages from 18 Faiths Worldwide.* Jefferson, North Carolina: McFarland.

Hertzler, Joyce O. 1933–34. "On Golden Rules." *International Journal of Ethics* 44: 313–25.

Hunt, John Gabriel, ed. 1997. *The Inaugural Addresses of the Presidents.* New York: Gramercy.

Karabegović, Dženeta. 2007. "'No Lie Can Live Forever': Zur sprichwörtlichen Rhetorik von Martin Luther King. *Sprichwörter sind Goldes wert. Parömiologische Studien zu Kultur, Literatur und Medien.* Wolfgang Mieder, ed. Burlington, Vermont: University of Vermont. 223–40.

Litovkina, Anna T., and Wolfgang Mieder. 2006. *Old Proverbs Never Die, They Just Diversify: A Collection of Anti-Proverbs.* Burlington, Vermont: University of Vermont. Veszprém: Pannonian University of Veszprém.

Louis, Cameron. 2000. "Proverbs and the Politics of Language." *Proverbium* 17: 173–94.

McCullough, David. 2001. *John Adams.* New York: Simon & Schuster.

McGiffert, A. C., ed. 1968. *Young Emerson Speaks: Unpublished Discourses on Many Subjects by Ralph Waldo Emerson.* Port Washington, New York: Kennikat.

McKenzie, Alyce M. 2003. "'Different Strokes for Different Folks': America's Quintessential Postmodern Proverb." *Cognition, Comprehension, and Communication: A Decade of North American Proverb Studies (1990–2000).* Wolfgang Mieder, ed. Baltmannsweiler: Schneider Verlag Hohengehren. 311–24.

Meinig, D. W. 1979. "Introduction." *The Interpretation of Ordinary Landscapes: Geographical Essays.* D. W. Meinig, ed. New York: Oxford University Press. 1–7.

Meriwether, Louise. 1984. Teenage Pregnancy. *Essence* 14 (April): 151.

Mieder, Wolfgang. 1971. "'Behold the Proverbs of a People': A Florilegium of Proverbs in Carl Sandburg's Poem 'Good Morning, America.'" *Southern Folklore Quarterly* 35: 160–68.

——. 1973. "Proverbs in Carl Sandburg's *The People, Yes.*" *Southern Folklore Quarterly* 37: 15–36.

——. 1989. *American Proverbs: A Study of Texts and Contexts.* Bern: Peter Lang.

——. 1997. *The Politics of Proverbs: From Traditional Wisdom to Proverbial Stereotypes.* Madison, Wisconsin: University of Wisconsin Press.

———. 1998. *"A House Divided": From Biblical Proverb to Lincoln and Beyond*. Burlington, Vermont: University of Vermont.

———. 2000. *The Proverbial Abraham Lincoln: An Index to Proverbs in the Works of Abraham Lincoln*. New York: Peter Lang.

———. 2001. *"No Struggle, No Progress": Frederick Douglass and His Proverbial Rhetoric for Civil Rights*. New York: Peter Lang.

———. 2005. *Proverbs Are the Best Policy: Folk Wisdom and American Politics*. Logan, Utah: Utah State University Press.

———. 2006. "Different Strokes for Different Folks." *The Greenwood Encyclopedia of African American Folklore*. Anand Prahlad, ed. Westport, Connecticut: Greenwood. I, 324–27.

———. 2007. "Proverbs in the Works of Ralph Waldo Emerson." *Phraseology: An International Handbook of Contemporary Research*. Harald Burger, Dmitrij Dobrovol'skij, Peter Kühn, and Neal R. Norrick, eds. Berlin: Walter de Gruyter. I, 337–48.

———. 2008a. "'Let Us Have Faith that Right Makes Might': Proverbial Rhetoric in Decisive Moments of American Politics." *Proverbium* 25: 319–52.

———. 2008b. "Luftschlösser (bauen). Traditionelle und innovative Funktion eines Wunschsymbols." *Burgen, Länder, Orte*. Ulrich Müller and Werner Wunderlich, eds. Konstanz: UVK Verlagsgesellschaft. 511–27.

———. 2009. *"Yes We Can": Barack Obama's Proverbial Rhetoric*. New York: Peter Lang.

Mieder, Wolfgang, and George B. Bryan. 1997. *The Proverbial Harry S. Truman: An Index to Proverbs in the Works of Harry S. Truman*. New York: Peter Lang.

Mieder, Wolfgang, Stewart A. Kingsbury, and Kelsie B. Harder, eds. 1992. *A Dictionary of American Proverbs*. New York: Oxford University Press.

Moravcsik, Gyula. 1964. "'Hund in der Krippe.' Zur Geschichte eines griechischen Sprichwortes." *Acta Antiqua Academiae Scientiarum Hungaricae* 12: 77–86.

Mori, Yoko. 1996. "The Iconography of 'homo bulla' in Northern Art from the Sixteenth to the Nineteenth Centuries." *Homo Ludens: Der spielende Mensch* 6: 149–76.

Nichols, Ray. 1996. "Maxims, 'Practical Wisdom,' and the Language of Action: Beyond Grand Theory." *Political Theory* 24: 687–705.

Obama, Barack. [1995] 2004. *Dreams from My Father: A Story of Race and Inheritance*. New York: Three Rivers.

Peterson, Anna L. 2001. *Being Human: Ethics, Environment, and Our Place in the World*. Berkeley, California: University of California Press.

Prahlad, Sw. Anand. 1996. *African American Proverbs in Context*. Jackson, Mississippi: University Press of Mississippi.

Priest, John F. 1985. "'The Dog in the Manger': In Quest of a Fable." *Classical Journal* 81: 49–58.

Rees, Nigel. 1995. *Phrases & Sayings*. London: Bloomsbury.

Sack, Robert David. 1997. *Homo Geographicus: A Framework for Action, Awareness, and Moral Concern*. Baltimore, Maryland: Johns Hopkins University Press.

Sandburg, Carl. 1936. *The People, Yes*. New York: Harcourt, Brace.

———. 1950. *Complete Poems*. New York: Harcourt, Brace.

Scheven, Albert. 1981. *Swahili Proverbs*. Washington, DC: University Press of America.

Smith, David M. 1999. "Towards a Context-Sensitive Ethics." *Geography and Ethics: Journeys in a Moral Terrain*. James D. Proctor and David M. Smith, eds. London: Routledge. 275–90.

Smith, Mick. 2001. *An Ethics of Place: Radical Ecology, Postmodernity, and Social Theory*. Albany, New York: State University of New York.

Snyder, Gary. 1995. "A Village Council of All Beings: Community, Place, and the Awakening of Compassion." In Gary Snyder, *A Place in Space: Ethics, Aesthetics, and Watersheds*. Berkeley, California: Counterpoint. 74–81.

Speake, Jennifer. 2008. *The Oxford Dictionary of Proverbs*. 5th ed. Oxford: Oxford University Press.

Stevenson, Burton. 1948. *The Home Book of Proverbs, Maxims, and Familiar Phrases*. New York: Macmillan.

Tang, Chenxi. 2008. *The Geographic Imagination of Modernity: Geography, Literature, and Philosophy in German Romanticism*. Stanford, California: Stanford University Press.

Taylor, Archer. 1965. "The Road to 'An Englishman's House . . .'" *Romance Philology* 19: 279–85.

———. 1968. "Method in the History and Interpretation of a Proverb: 'A Place for Everything and Everything in Its Place.'" *Proverbium* 10: 235–38. Also in *Selected Writings on Proverbs by Archer Taylor*. Wolfgang Mieder, ed. Helsinki: Suomalainen Tiedeakatemia, 1975. 129–32.

Templeton, John Marks. 1997. *Worldwide Laws of Life: 200 Eternal Spiritual Principles*. Philadelphia: Templeton Foundation Press.

Tuan, Yi-Fu. 1977. *Space and Place: The Perspective of Experience*. Minneapolis, Minnesota: University of Minnesota Press.

———. 1982. *Segmented Worlds and Self: Group Life and Individual Consciousness*. Minneapolis, Minnesota: University of Minnesota Press.

———. 1989. *Morality and Imagination: Paradoxes of Progress*. Madison, Wisconsin: University of Wisconsin Press.

———. 1993. *Passing Strange and Wonderful: Aesthetics, Nature, and Culture*. Washington, DC: Island Press.

———. 2004. *Place, Art, and Self*. Santa Fe, New Mexico: Center for American Places.

Washington, James Melvin, ed. 1986. *A Testament of Hope: The Essential Writings of Martin Luther King, Jr.* New York: Harper & Row.

Wills, Garry. 1992. *Lincoln at Gettysburg: The Words That Remade America*. New York: Touchstone.

Wilson, Judith. 1981. "A Conversation with Toni Morrison." *Essence* 12 (July): 86.

7. "BEATING SWORDS INTO PLOWSHARES"
Proverbial Wisdom about War and Peace

Proverbs are not only ubiquitous but also all-inclusive in their comments on the multifaceted aspects of the human condition, so it should not be surprising that the massive treasure trove of the world's proverbs contains much proverbial wisdom on the interrelationship of war and peace. In fact, the short binary formula "war and peace" exists in most languages, to wit the French "guerre et paix," the German "Krieg und Frieden," the Russian "voina i mir," the Spanish "guerra y paz," etc. Of course, there are ample proverbs that comment on the symbiotic relationship of these two fundamental aspects of regional, national, and international coexistence. In fact, there are even small specialized collections for certain languages, including Selwyn Gurney Champion, *War Proverbs and Maxims East and West* (1945); Ursula Eichberger, *Über Krieg und Frieden. Sentenzen aus zweieinhalb Jahrtausenden* (1986); and Paul Dickson, *War Slang: Fighting Words and Phrases of Americans from the Civil War to the Gulf War* (1994). In general, they stress that while war and peace have always been interlinked in the experiences and minds of humankind, it is clearly peace that is being sought. This can also be seen in the many proverbs about war and peace from around the world that Lt. Col. Victor S. M. de Guinzbourg solicited from various ambassadors and delegates to the United Nations in his two privately printed and thus rare and unique books, *Wit and Wisdom of the United Nations: Proverbs and Apothegms on Diplomacy* (1961) and *The Eternal Machiavelli in the United Nations World* (1969).

The proverbial wisdom of the world is well aware of the interrelationship of war and peace over the centuries, and proverbs have long been employed during times of international tension or aggression (Raymond 1956; Russell 1999). But while the distinction between these two states of existence might have been rather clear in former times, matters have become blurred in the modern age. Wars are now not always declared, they are termed military actions or preventive measures, and they are not necessarily terminated by traditional peace treaties. It is thus not surprising that, in the middle of the twentieth century, Fritz Grob could already write his intriguing book, *The Relativity of War and Peace: A Study in Law, History, and Politics* (1949). The word "war" has been expanded semantically to such a degree that there are so-called wars against terrorism, crime, drugs, poverty, cancer, AIDS, obesity, etc. being fought in modern societies. While these wars might have their modern slogans to bring about change, they have little to do with the traditional concepts of war and peace.

Proverbs about the Relationship of War and Peace

As would be expected, a plethora of proverbs relating to war and peace can easily be found in hundreds of proverb collections from around the world. While many proverbs refer either to war or peace separately, there are also numerous international texts that stress the obvious link between war and peace, as the following small florilegium of such wisdom in English translation exemplifies:

A bad peace is better than a good war. (Russian)
Better an unjust peace than a just war. (German)
Better to have bread in peace than a fat calf in war. (Hungarian)
Even if you have the strength of an elephant and the courage of a lion, peace is better than war. (Iranian)
Fame will be won in peace as well as in war. (Latin)
He that makes a good war makes a good peace. (Italian)
He who excels in war will excel in peace. (Welsh)
In peace do not forget war. (Japanese)
Of all wars peace is the end. (Scottish)
Peace feeds, war wastes; peace breeds, war consumes. (Danish)
Peace is more powerful than war. (Latin)
Peace pays what war gains. (Serbo-Croatian)
Peace with a cudgel in hand is war. (Portuguese)
The greatest war had peace at last. (Irish)
War brings peace. (German)
War makes thieves, and peace hangs them. (Italian)
(Champion 1945: 54–59; Cordry 1997: 274–75; Mieder 1986: 365, 512–13)

Naturally, every language has numerous proverbs that deal with this obvious relationship, emphasizing social, political, economic, and basic human matters that play into the ever-evolving cycle of war and peace (Wölfflin 1888; Zouogbo 2004). Regarding the Anglo-American proverbial tradition that is the major thrust of this discussion, consider the following proverbs with their earliest registered occurrences. It should be noted, however, that none of these texts belongs to the paremiological minimum of Anglo-American proverbs, i.e., they are not much used or have basically been dropped altogether (Lau 1996; Haas 2008). As one would expect, a few texts correspond to the proverbs from other languages just cited, due to the fact that they go back to Latin sources that were loan translated into various European languages. Of interest is also that there are contradictory proverbs, as for example "A just war is better than an unjust peace" and "An unjust peace is preferred to a just war" from the sixteenth century. As with all proverbial wisdom, such contradictory proverb pairs signify the relativity of proverbial insights that do not conform to a logical philosophical system but rather reflect the ambiguities and ambivalences of life's experiences:

> After war peace is good. (1338)
> Of all war peace is the end. (1399)
> Peace is better than war. (1440)
> War is dreadful, virtuous peace is good. (1449)
> A just war is better than an unjust peace. (1545)
> An unjust peace is preferred to a just war. (1555)
> He that makes a good war, makes a good peace. (1590)
> War makes thieves, and peace hangs them. (1594)
> Clothe thee in war, arm thee in peace. (1640)
> He that will not have peace, God gives him war. (1640)
> Peace has her victories no less renowned than war. (1652)
> There never was a good war or a bad peace. (1775)
> Fiercer (hotter) war, sooner peace. (1820)
> The object of war is peace. (1826)
> The real and lasting victories are those of peace and not of war. (1860)
> The sooner the war, the quicker the peace. (20th cent.)
>
> (Mieder et al. 1992: 455–56, 639–40; Pickering 1997: 282; Tilley 1950: 528, 703; Whiting 1968: 449, 625–26; Whiting 1977: 469; Wilson 1970: 128, 416, 502, 616, 866)

The last text was collected in Ontario, Canada, between 1945 and 1985, and since no earlier references have been found, it might well reflect an attitude shortly before World War II, when Winston Churchill argued on behalf of the British Empire that the menace of Adolf Hitler's Nazi Germany had to be brought to a stop.

It should not be surprising that the proverb "If you want peace, you must prepare for war" is the proverb that gained the largest distribution and currency over time, since people have been and always will be concerned about the possibility of war. It has been attributed to the Roman historian Cornelius Nepos (ca. 94–24 B.C.) and was used most effectively by the Roman military strategist and writer Flavius Vegetius (4th cent. A.D.) in the introduction to his *Epitoma Institutionum Rei Militaris* as *Qui desiderat pacem, praeparet bellum* (He who desires peace must prepare for war) (Speake 2008: 246; Titelman 1996: 162). The Latin proverb (also quoted as *Si vis pacem, para bellum*) was translated into numerous European languages, and it has been registered in the English language since the sixteenth century in such variants as "In time of peace provide for war" (1548); "Into peace, you should provide for wars" (1552); "He that desires peace, he must prepare for wars" (1593); "Happy is that city which in time of peace thinks of war" (1624; mentioned in Robert Burton's *Anatomy of Melancholy* as an inscription in Venice); "The only best time to prepare for war is in time of peace" (1755); "If you want peace, you must prepare for war" (1885); and "We should provide in peace what we need in war," with the last text having been recorded in mid-twentieth century (Mieder et al. 1992: 455; Pickering 1997: 208; Speake 2008: 245; Whiting 1977: 329–30; Whiting 1989: 477; Wilson 1970: 616).

The wisdom of this particular proverb has played a significant role in American politics from early times until the present day, reaching almost absurd proportions during the arms race between the United States and the Soviet Union during the Cold War period when the Iron Curtain divided Europe (Mieder 1989, 1997). A fine example is a pre–Revolutionary War use of the proverb in a letter of September 22, 1774, by Abigail Adams to her husband John Adams, who later became the second president of the United States:

> I will not despair, but will believe that our cause being good we shall finally prevail [over the British]. The Maxim in time of peace prepair for war, (if this may be call'd a time of peace) resounds throughout the Country. Next tuesday they are warned at Braintree all above 15 and under 60 to attend with their arms, and to train once a fortnight from that time, is a Scheme which lays much at heart with many. (Butterfield 1963: I, 161; Mieder 2005: 80–81)

During the Revolutionary War, John Jay, early statesman and first chief justice of the United States, employed the proverb in a September 8, 1781, letter from St. Ildefonso, Spain, to observe that America must ever be vigilant and ready for war if it wants to assure a lasting peace:

> Peace and negotiations for it are the prevailing topics of conversation here, and perhaps in America also. I hope, however, that our countrymen will not suffer themselves to be too much influenced by prospects which may prove no less delusive than they are pleasing. To prepare vigorously for war is the only sure way of preparing for a speedy and valuable peace. (Johnston 1891: II, 67)

George Washington, general and later first president of the United States, not surprisingly was quite fond of this proverb of preparedness against any possible aggression against his young country. For example, in a letter of September 16, 1782, to one John Mitchell, he makes the following allusion to the proverb that doubtlessly came immediately to the mind of its recipient:

> I heartily wish that the general prevailing ideas of Peace may not be injurious to us; the appearances, in my opinion, are very equivocal; but one thing we are sure of, and that is that being in a state of perfect preparation for war, is the only sure and infallible means of producing Peace. How far the necessities of great Britain may compel her to grant unconditional Independence to this Country, I shall not take upon me to determine; but I have no doubt on my Mind of the Kings wishes to prosecute the War (in order to avert this measure) as long as the Nation will vote Men or Money to carry it on. (Fitzpatrick 1938: 25, 166)

This proverb has been used as a justification for ever-increasing military budgets ever since, and it is admittedly difficult to argue against its message of prepared vigilance. This mentality did, however, lead to the modern arms race with its long-range missiles carrying nuclear warheads. Fortunately this life-threatening weaponry is now controlled by arms reduction treaties, and perhaps the American poet Frank H. Woodstrike was not really off the mark when he juxtaposed this proverb with a contradictory proverb in one of the two-line stanzas of his poem "Paradoxical Proverbs" (1937):

> In peace prepare for war.
> Never cross a bridge until you come to it.
> (Sobieski and Mieder 2005: 239)

Proverbial Wisdom about War

This being said, the time has come to look at proverbs that deal only with war as such, with a discussion of peace proverbs following right behind. To begin with, here is a small international group of proverbs on the theme of war:

> A word has caused more than one war. (German)
> After the war, aid. (Greek)
> After the war many heroes present themselves. (Romanian)
> He who cannot stand the smell of gunpowder should not engage in war.
> (Yiddish)
> In war all suffer defeat, even the victors. (Swedish)
> In war it is not permitted twice to err. (Latin)
> Let him who does not know what war is go to war. (Spanish)
> Many futilities in war. (Greek) (Wheeler 1988)
> One war is worse than three swarms of locusts. (Chinese)
> There have been few wars which did not originate through priests or women.
> (Czech)
> War among grasshoppers delights the crows. (African)
> War begets no good offspring. (African)
> War begun, hell let loose. (Italian)
> War is brother to no one. (Serbian)
> War is deceit. (Lebanese)
> What is gained in war is eaten in war. (Finnish)
> (Champion 1945: 54–59; Cordry 1997: 274–75; Mieder 1986: 512–13)

Clearly all of these proverbs point to war as an ill-conceived exercise that brings with it depravation, pain, destruction, and death (Álvarez Díaz 2001; Ayers 1991; Kuchmann 1987; Seiler 1916). This is also the case for a large number of Anglo-American proverbs—most of which are no longer very prevalent. Note again that some of them go back to classical antiquity or to the Latin of the Middle Ages and thus exist in translation in other languages as well:

> In war some win and some lose. (1300)
> Many cry "War! war!" who know little to what war amounts. (1390)
> War at the beginning has a great entering but it is hard to know how it will end.
> (1390)

All may begin a war, few can end it. (1548)
In war it is not permitted twice to err. (1550)
Who has land has war. (1579)
Money is the sinews of love as well as of war. (1581)
That war is just which is necessary. (1597)
War is death's feast. (1611)
No war without a woman. (1639)
Wars bring scars. (1639)
Advise none to marry or go to war. (1640)
War, hunting, and law (love) are as full of trouble as pleasure. (1640)
When war begins hell opens (1642)
In wars, laws have no authority. (1651)
He who preaches up war is a fit chaplain of the devil. (1659)
War is the sport of kings. (1691)
War's chance (fortune) is uncertain. (1740)
In war beware of repeating a mistake. (1811)
Councils of war never fight. (1863)

(Mieder et al. 1992: 359, 417, 639–40; Pickering 1997: 55–56, 282; Speake 2008: 62; Tilley 1950: 528, 703; Whiting 1968: 625–26; Whiting 1977: 469–70; Wilson 1970: 4, 645, 866–67)

It is a shame that early proverbs like "War at the beginning has a great entering but it is hard to know how it will end" and "All may begin a war, few can end it" are not heard any longer today, for their advice might well be heeded before entering yet another military contest let alone a real war.

Note should also be taken of the fact that proverbs like "Money is the sinews of love as well as of war," "No war without a woman," and "Advise none to marry or go to war" bring love and gender politics to the war stage. While the first text with the somewhat antiquated noun "sinews," meaning strength and power, is still heard today, it is doubtlessly the proverb "All's fair in love and war" that continues to be quite popular. Precursors might date back to 1578, but it took the English translation of Miguel de Cervantes Saavedra's *Don Quixote* in 1620 for it to get close to its common formulation: "Love and warre are all one . . . It is lawfull to use sleights and stratagems to attaine the wished end" (Speake 2008: 108). In a modern translation of *Don Quixote* the passage reads as follows:

> Hold, Señores, hold, for it is not right to take revenge for the offenses that love commits; you should know that love and war are the same, and just as in war it is legitimate and customary to make use of the tricks and stratagems to

conquer the enemy, so in the contests and rivalries of love the lies and false-hoods used to achieve a desired end are considered fair, as long as they do not discredit or dishonor the beloved. (Grossman 2003: 595)

More to the point is this variant from the 1630 revised version of Francis Beaumont's and John Fletcher's play *Lovers' Progress* (1623): "All stratagems in love, and that [being] the sharpest war, are lawful." By 1801 the proverb still speaks of permissible strategies to be employed: "In love and war all stratagems are allowable." By at latest 1845 the less precise adjective "fair" is employed, but since the noun "stratagems" is maintained, there is no problem understanding the proverb properly. Then in 1884 the variant "All things are fair in love and war" appears, which subsequently is shortened to "All's fair in love and war" (Flavell 1993: 158–59; Mieder et al. 1992; Pickering 1998: 90; 14; Taylor and Whiting 1958: 5; Titelman 1996: 9; Whiting 1989: 8; Wilson 1970: 239). For non-native speakers and some native alike, it is quite a stretch to understand "fair" in this proverb not so much as being "fair game" but rather as meaning that all strategies are forgivable or that no restrictive rules govern behavior or actions when it comes to love or war. Be that as it may, E. D. Hirsch and his co-authors of the *Dictionary of Cultural Literacy* (1988) have included it in their list of 265 proverbs that all Anglo-American speakers ought to know: "All's fair in love and war. People in love and soldiers in wartime are not bound by the rules of fair play" (Hirsch et al. 1988: 47; Mieder 1994: 308–9). Of course, one senses the immediate danger of this proverb in those cases when soldiers have perhaps used this proverb to justify atrocities during wartime, arguing that the end justifies inhumane means. The following 1903 transformation of the proverb into an anti-proverb by the American humorist George Ade is in contrast rather harmless: "All's fair in love—an' war—an' politics" (Flavell 1993: 158).

But there is a second "war" proverb that by way of English as the lingua franca of the world has attained global distribution. The proverb "War is hell" has long been thought of as having originated with the American General William Tecumseh Sherman of Civil War fame. He did in fact utter the words "There is many a boy here to-day who looks on war as all glory, but, boys, it is all hell" during a speech at a reunion of war veterans on August 11, 1880, in Columbus, Ohio. But as the magisterial quotation sleuth Fred R. Shapiro has shown, the proverb was already known twenty years earlier, when it appeared on February 1, 1860, in the *Zion's Herald and Wesleyan Journal* as "War is hell" (Shapiro 2006: 708, 546). But as so often is the case, once a proverb is attributed to an (in)famous person, that association is hard to eradicate (Hirsch et al. 1988: 284; Mieder et al. 1992: 640; Royle 1989: 58; Stevenson 1948: 2449; Titelman 1996: 353–54). Since the proverb was already current around 1860, it is quite possible that President Abraham Lincoln was alluding to it during his speech of June 16, 1864, in Philadelphia. He might simply not have wanted to use the word "hell" at this dramatic state of the Civil War:

> War, at the best, is terrible, and this war of ours, in its magnitude and its duration, is one of the most terrible. It has deranged business, totally in many localities, and partially in all localities. It has destroyed property, and ruined homes; it has produced a national debt and taxation unprecedented, at least in this country. It has carried mourning to almost every home, until it can almost be said that the "heavens are hung in black." (Basler 1953: 7, 394; Mieder 2000: 203)

Five months later, Lincoln's friend and abolitionist, the freed slave Frederick Douglass, chose quite similar words during an address delivered on November 13, 1864, in Rochester, New York. Again, he might well have had the word "hell" in mind but chose to suppress it because of the seriousness of the dire situation that the Civil War had brought to people:

> We look and long for peace. It is natural and credible that such is the fact. War is an evil—a terrible evil. It has planted agony at a million hearthstones in our land, and mantled our country allover with the shadow of death. We would stop this terrible havoc and dreadful effusion of blood; but we know, as [the American politician] Henry Winter Davis has expressed it, peace is to be found only at the other side of the battle-field. (Blassingame and McKivigan 1991: 4, 37; Mieder 2001: 503)

Eight decades later, things looked quite different for that warhorse Winston S. Churchill, who as one of the greatest orators and writers of the twentieth century saw no problem at all in quoting the proverb "War is hell," citing, albeit erroneously, General Sherman. In his political radio broadcast of August 16, 1947, entitled "No Easy Passage," he addressed the terrible economic plight into which his victorious country had fallen two years after the war:

> I am shocked that two years after all the fighting has stopped the Socialist Government tell us we must have these various forms of industrial conscription.

"War is hell," said the American General Sherman, many years ago, but surely peace is supposed to be somewhat different? I am astounded that the trade unions with whom I have often worked in great matters, in peace and war, should be willing to countenance such a degradation of the fundamental rights and status of the labouring man or woman. I must make it absolutely clear that I will not support it as part of our peace-time system. (James 1974: 7, 7519; Mieder and Bryan 1995: 412)

In his book *The Great Democracies* (1958), the fourth volume of his acclaimed *History of the English-Speaking Peoples* (1956–58), Churchill returns to the proverb quite naturally in a chapter on "The Victory of the Union" during the American Civil War. After all, he is speaking of General Sherman specifically, whose infamous Civil War march across the state of Georgia embodies the idea that war is hell:

Georgia was full of food in this dark winter. Sherman set himself to march through it on a wide front, living on the country, devouring and destroying all farms, villages, towns, railroads, and public works which lay within his wide-ranging reach. He left behind him a blackened trail, and hatreds which pursue his memory to this day. "War is hell," he said, and certainly he made it so. But no one must suppose that his depredations and pillage were comparable to the atrocities which were committed during the World Wars of the twentieth century or to the barbarities of the Middle Ages. Searching investigation has discovered hardly a case of murder or rape. None the less a dark shadow lies upon this part of the map of the United States. (Churchill 1958: 4, 258–59; Mieder and Bryan 1995: 412)

Much more recently, President Barack Obama employed the proverb in his celebrated book *The Audacity of Hope* (2006) in which then Senator Obama set forth his political vision for America:

When I ponder the work of a George Kennan or a George Marshall, when I read the speeches of a Bobby Kennedy or an Everett Dirksen, I can't help feeling that the politics of today suffers from a case of arrested development. For these men, the issues America faced were never abstract and hence never simple. War might be hell and still the right thing to do. Economics could collapse despite the best-laid plans. People could work hard all their lives and still lose everything. (Obama 2006: 36; Mieder 2009: 336)

Surely the proverb "War is hell" will survive, and so it should as a clear metaphor for the horrors of war. But surely the question must arise whether there are any new or modern proverbs that comment on the horrid nature of war. The *Dictionary of American Proverbs* (1992), which registers proverbs recorded in the United States and Canada between 1945–85, lists the following proverbs for which no earlier references could be found. Their geographical distribution is usually very limited, sometimes to but one state, and so they most likely are not very well known and might well be older than 1945. In any case, they include the following texts:

> All delays are dangerous in war.
> Don't win the war before it's won.
> The fear of war is worse than war itself.
> War is a business that ruins those who succeed in it.
> War is the sink of all injustice.
> (Mieder et al. 1992: 143, 639–40)

In addition, *The Dictionary of Modern Proverbs* (2012) lists the following "war" proverbs from the twentieth century that have gained enough currency that they rightfully can be considered new proverbial wisdom about war. The following list presents the proverbs in chronological order according to the earliest reference that was found by way of numerous electronic databases:

> Wars are fought one battle at a time. (1903)
> Truth is the first casualty of war. (1915; Mieder et al. 1992: 86; Rees 2011: 73–74; Speake 2008: 328)
> You can lose a battle and (still) win the war. (1918)
> No one (ever) wins a war. (1928)
> There is no second place in battle (war). (1929)
> In war there is no substitute for victory. (1932) (Titelman 1996: 167–68)
> War will cease when men refuse to fight. (1933)
> Generals (Soldiers, etc.) always fight (prepare to fight) the last war. (1934)
> Someday they will give a war and nobody will come. (1936) (Bryan and Mieder 2005: 818; Bülow 1983; Roche 1983)
> Make love, not war. (1965)
> (Doyle, Mieder, and Shapiro 2012: 152–53)

It is comforting to see that at least some of these proverbs are clearly statements against war, with the newest proverb "Make love, not war" getting its start from the peace movement of the sixties. By now it has long traveled around the world, with its wisdom going well beyond its sexual implications to a broader understanding of peace among all people of the world.

In this regard it is a shame that the Latin proverb *Dulce bellum inexpertis*, about which Erasmus of Rotterdam wrote an illuminating essay in 1515 (Erasmus 2005; Hannemann 1987), is no longer current. It was translated into several European languages and has been known in English since 1539 as the proverb "War is sweet to them that know it not" (Mieder et al. 1992: 640; Stevenson 1948: 2448; Wilson 1970: 866). Since the nineteenth century it has basically been forgotten, even though it would make an excellent argument against those who are quick to call for war when they themselves have not experienced and will not have to endure its horrors. Two years later Erasmus also wrote one of the early treatises against war, entitling his essay "Querela pacis" (1517), "A Complaint of Peace" (Erasmus 1990). Great proverbialist that he was, it is surprising that he did not choose a proverb for the title of his plea for peace. Might he not have been able to locate a fitting proverb? He also does not integrate a peace proverb into the essay; this might be due to the smaller number of proverbs about peace in comparison to the many war proverbs. This imbalance might in itself tell quite a story about the history of humankind that has been plagued by war.

Proverbial Wisdom about Peace

But be that as it may, it is time to take a glance at some of the proverbs about peace:

A meager peace is better than a fat quarrel. (Latvian)
He who holds a sword will maintain peace. (Polish)
He who wants to love in peace should not disturb it. (Danish)
If you like peace don't contradict anybody. (Hungarian)
One peace is better than ten victories. (German)
Peace forever only lasts till the first fight. (Russian)
Peace is liberty in tranquility. (Latin)
Peace is more fattening than food. (African)
Peace is more valuable than gold. (Finnish)
Peace is the most profitable of things. (Greek)
Peace would be universal if there were neither "mine" nor "thine." (Italian)

The cudgel brings peace. (French)
The garment of peace never fades. (Syrian)
There is no peace until after enmity. (Egyptian)
Where there is peace there is blessing. (Yiddish)
Without peace there can be no national prosperity. (Filipino)
(Champion 1945: 38–41; Cordry 1997: 199–200; Mieder 1986: 365–66)

Traditional Anglo-American proverbs about peace mirror some of these texts, as was the case with international "war" proverbs, but there are also some indigenous English language proverbs, which are cited here in chronological order according to their first recorded references:

A bad peace is better than a good quarrel. (1545)
Better a lean peace than a fat victory. (1605)
By wisdom peace, by peace plenty. (1611)
A disarmed peace is weak. (1640)
Peace is better than victory. (1642)
Peace at any price. (1839)
(Mieder et al. 1992: 455–56; Tilley 1950: 528; Wilson 1970: 50, 189, 898)

While this is indeed a small harvest of "peace" proverbs that imply the opposite of war and not inner peace or peace in one's home, at least two additional proverbs were collected between 1945 and 1985 for which no earlier references have been located: "Better keep peace than make peace" and "Peace flourishes when reason rules" (Mieder et al. 1992: 455–56). They were registered in oral use in a few American states and might well be no older than the twentieth century. But *The Dictionary of Modern Proverbs* lists at least one more relatively new proverb. The earliest reference of the modern proverb "Give peace a chance" has been found in the *Christian Science Monitor* of November 14, 1923: "Editorial titled (in a box) 'Give Peace a Chance': 'He [Prime Minister David Lloyd George] believes, and many others believe with him, that Great Britain and America might give peace its needed chance" (Doyle, Mieder, and Shapiro 2012: 92–93). Of course, even though the proverb established itself during the following decades, it gained significant prominence primarily by way of John Lennon's song "Give Peace a Chance" (1969). It carried the message that any temporary peace initiative may eventually lead to a lasting peace by way of the international peace movement around the world:

Let me tell you now
Revolution, evolution, masturbation, flagellation,
regulations, integrations,
meditations, United Nations,
Congratulations.
All we are saying is give peace a chance.
(Brautigan 1975: 178)

The proverb has become a rallying cry for peace movements throughout the world with at times adding the word "real" to it for emphasis, i.e. "Give peace a real chance" (Titelman 1996: 115). This proverbial peace slogan, together with the proverbial anti-war slogan "Make love, not war" from the sixties, have certainly not lost any of their expressive prowess. Nigel Rees has discussed other slogans in his book *Don't You Know There's a War On? Words and Phrases from the World Wars* (2011), as for example "No more war" (1762), "The war to end wars" (1914), "The war to make the world safe for democracy" (1917), "No more bloody wars, no more bloody medals!" (from World War I), and "Don't you know there's a war on?" (from World War II) (Rees 2011: 143, 59, 143–44, 207–8). But while these are not proverbs as such, he does also list the proverbs "There are no atheists in the foxholes" (1942), "Praise the Lord and pass the ammunition" (1941), and "Old soldiers never die, they simply fade away" (1916) (Rees 2011: 141–42, 161, 153–54). They are also registered in *The Dictionary of Modern Proverbs* (2012), with the "soldier" proverb also having been documented in a number of earlier proverb collections as part of a soldier song from World War I that later became attributed to the American general Douglas McArthur, who had cited it in his farewell address to the Congress of the United States in 1951 (Hirsch et al. 1988: 53; Pickering 1997: 101; Speake 2008: 237; Titelman 1996: 259–60; Whiting 1989: 581). Of course, there are also such earlier "soldier" proverbs as "Soldiers in peace are like chimneys in summer" (1595) (Pickering 1997: 247; Wilson 1970: 750); "The bravest soldiers are the most civil to prisoners" (1736) (Whiting 1977: 405); "Soldiers must not complain" (1777) (Whiting 1977: 405); "What the soldier said isn't evidence" (1837) (Speake 2008: 292; Whiting 1989: 581–82); "The first duty of a soldier is obedience" (1847) (Speake 2008: 116); and "A live soldier is better than a dead hero" (1904) (Doyle, Mieder, and Shapiro 2012: 236).

Other languages have their "soldier" proverbs (Álvarez Díaz 2005–6; Champion 1945: 45–46; Mieder 1986: 445; Seiler 1917), but a more detailed discussion of proverbs about soldiers or the military in all of its aspects would go far beyond the scope of the present deliberations (see Álvarez Díaz 2000; Anonymous 2002; Donald 2008; Krebs 1892, 1895; Priest 2000; Shafritz 1990). Suffice it here to cite the mini-poem "Old Soldiers" (1977) by the American poet Raymond Souster, which will serve well as a transition to the discussion of two ancient proverbial utterances that argue against war and for peace:

Old Soldiers
Old soldiers never die—
they live on to send their sons off
to other wars.
(Sobieski and Mieder 2005: 214)

Clearly, wars of various types and proportions continue to plague human-kind, and so it appears strange that proverbs of war and peace are not part of the paremiological minimum with its claim of frequent employment. If politicians, diplomats, and the general population do not use proverbs with explicit comments on war and peace with any special frequency, the question quite naturally arises what proverbs are in fact employed repeatedly to combat the evil effects of the destructive and murderous nature of war. Two texts from the worldwide scene of proverbs come to mind that have found repetitive use in the verbal arguments against aggression and warfare. There is first of all the Bible proverb "He who lives by the sword shall perish by the sword" (Matt. 26:52), with its all-too-clear warning against violent confrontation that might lead to war and self-destruction. Related to this wisdom and employing once again the "sword" metonymy is the Biblical proverbial expression "To beat swords into plowshares" (Isaiah 2:4, Micah 4:3), urging people to put aside the weapons of destruction and concentrate on peaceful coexistence. Both of these proverbial statements lie at the basis of the United Nations, and the proverb and the proverbial expression, with or without reference to the Bible, have become secular metaphors to argue vehemently against the menace of war and its weaponry, urging people everywhere to lay down their weapons and strive instead for peace. After all, as the proverb says, "The real and lasting victories are those of peace and not of war."

"He Who Lives by the Sword Shall Perish by the Sword"

To zero in on the use of these two texts by a few renowned political figures, here are first several contextualized references from the past two centuries for the proverb "He who lives by the sword shall perish by the sword," which also exists in such variants as "All they that take the sword shall perish by the sword," "He who lives by the sword dies by the sword," "He that raises the sword shall die by the sword," "He that takes the sword shall perish by the sword," "If you draw the sword you will perish by the sword," "Those who live by the sword die by the sword," and "Who takes the sword shall perish by the sword" (Mieder et al. 1992: 577; Pickering 1997: 165; Speake 2008: 190–91; Stevenson 1948: 2265; Taylor and Whiting 1958: 363; Titelman 1996: 131–32; Whiting 1968: 573; Whiting 1977: 427; Whiting 1989: 608–9). The American abolitionist Frederick Douglass used it as a prophetic insight in a short essay of July 21, 1848, on the suppression of the liberal revolution in France:

> Could the prayers of the friends of freedom and humanity have availed, France might have escaped this most terrific and bloody baptism. But he that taketh the sword shall perish by the sword, remains the law of the living God, and is sure to execute itself. For the sake of Freedom and Progress, we lament this sad result. Superficial men will charge its evils upon Liberty and Democracy, just as the malpractice of churches and professed ministers of the gospel are too often charged upon Christianity; and for a time the cause of righteous Liberty, must bear up under a heavy load of reproach and infamy. [...] We say, God reigns, and will yet vindicate the right. He is now teaching the world, by French example, the folly of injustice, oppression and wrong, and of the foolishness of relying upon the sword for that which can only be accomplished by preaching. (Foner 1975: 5, 85–86; Mieder 2001: 462)

Almost a hundred years later, then Senator Harry S. Truman employed the proverb most effectively in a speech of March 6, 1944, in which he accurately declares that a turning point of World War II had been reached due to America's valiant participation:

> We are now in the third year of this terrible war. We are spurred by the grim determination to wage this war relentlessly on all fronts and on all seas until all those who have chosen to live by the sword have perished by it. We now have neither the time nor the inclination for self-appraisal. But when the time comes for the historians to write the record of our participation in this great struggle they will doubtlessly state that at this present period we had reached the turning point of the war. (Truman 1944: A1156; Mieder and Bryan 1997: 39–40)

As a deeply religious man, Truman drew frequently on his rich repertoire of Biblical proverbs to explain political issues. Although the King James Bible says "All they that take the sword shall perish with the sword," Truman varies the text to fit his syntax while at the same time obviously being aware of the fact that this passage of the Bible is usually cited as a folk proverb in the form of "He who lives by the sword shall perish by the sword." His audience doubtlessly understood very well his message that the war could be and had to be won if the world was to be saved from the menace of the Axis powers.

Not surprisingly Martin Luther King, a preacher by training and profession, relied repeatedly on Bible proverbs, with the proverb "He who lives by the sword shall perish by the sword" becoming a leitmotif for his message of nonviolence in all affairs of humankind (Mieder 2009: 73–85, 492–500). Thus, in a major address that King gave on December 5, 1957, at the Second Annual Institute on Nonviolence and Social Change in Montgomery, Alabama, he conjures up this Bible proverb as a universal law on the destructive nature of violence that stands in the way of peace on earth:

> We must plunge deeper into the whole philosophy of nonviolence as we continue to move on in our quest for freedom. As I look at our situation and the situation of oppressed peoples all over the world, it seems to me that there are three ways that oppressed people can deal with their oppression. One is to rise up in armed revolt, one is to rise up with violence, and many people have used that method. It seems that violence has become something of the inseparable twin of western materialism. It's even become the hallmark of its grandeur. Violence nevertheless solves no social problems. It only creates new and more complicated ones. Yes, violence often brings about temporary victory, but never permanent peace. This evening as I stand before you, it seems that I can hear the voice crying through the vista of time, still saying to men in this generation: "He who lives by the sword, will perish by the sword." History is cluttered with the wreckage of nations and communities that failed to hear that command. Violence is not the way. [. . .] It seems to me there is a third way. There is a third way that is more powerful and enduring and lasting than the first two: that is the way of nonviolent resistance. (Carson 1992–2007: 4, 340–41; Mieder 2010: 82–83)

From numerous other passages in which King employs this cautionary proverb against violence and war, the following, from his speech of March 9, 1959, stands out, since it shows his sincere admiration for Mahatma Gandhi as the embodiment of nonviolence and because it is a clear statement of

King's belief that with arsenals of modern weaponry "no nation can win a war" any longer:

> Mahatma Gandhi may well be God's appeal to this generation, a generation drifting again to its doom. This eternal appeal is in the form of a warning: "They that live by the sword shall perish by the sword." We must come to see in the world today that what he taught and his method throughout revealed to us that there is an alternative to violence and that if we fail to follow this we will perish in our individual and in our collective lives. For in a day when Sputniks and Explorers dash through outer space and guided ballistic missiles are carving highways of death through the stratosphere, no nation can win a war. (Carson 1992–2007: 5, 36; Mieder 2010: 497–98)

The proverb "He who lives by the sword shall perish by the sword" is thus the ultimate warning against starting a nuclear war that would destroy the world.

"To Beat Swords into Plowshares"

The Bible offers a truly magnificent proverbial metaphor to illustrate what could be done to overcome the seemingly eternal cycle of wars. The proverbial expression "To beat swords into plowshares" (Ichikawa 1964: 664; Royle 112; Stevenson 2264) is a most appropriate image for world peace, where all military arms will be transformed into useful tools to feed and sustain the world's population. For example, reflecting on the allied victory of World War I and its aftermath in his six-volume *The World Crisis* (1923–31), Winston Churchill was well aware of the difficulty of shutting down the war industry:

> My mind mechanically persisted in exploring the problems of demobilisation. What was to happen to our three million Munition workers? What would they make now? How would the roaring factories be converted? How in fact are swords beaten into ploughshares? How long would it take to bring the Armies home? What would they do when they got home? We had of course a demobilisation plan for the Ministry of Munitions. It had been carefully worked out, but it had played no part in our thoughts. Now it must be put into operation. (Churchill 1923–31: 4, 273–74; Mieder and Bryan 1995: 388)

While Churchill wondered how swords are beaten into ploughshares after a terrible war, President Harry S. Truman looked quite confidently into the future during his address at the "Lighting of the National Community Christmas Tree" on the White House grounds on December 24, 1945. A way to stop the production of life-threatening nuclear weapons must have been very much on his mind since he had authorized the dropping of two atomic bombs over Hiroshima and Nagasaki on August 6 and 9, 1945:

> It is well in this solemn hour that we bow to Washington, Jefferson, Jackson, and Lincoln [Truman had mentioned their memorial monuments in Washington, D.C.] as we face our destiny with its hopes and fears—its burdens and its responsibilities. Out of the past we shall gather wisdom and inspiration to chart our future course.
>
> With our enemies vanquished we must gird ourselves for the work that lies ahead. Peace has its victories no less hard won than success at arms. We must not fail or falter. We must strive without ceasing to make real the prophecy of Isaiah: "They shall beat their swords into plowshares and their spears into pruning-hooks: nation shall not lift up sword against nation, neither shall they learn war any more."
>
> In this day, whether it be far or near, the Kingdoms of this world shall become indeed the Kingdom of God and He will reign forever and ever, Lord of Lords and King of Kings. With that message I wish my countrymen a Merry Christmas and joyous days in the New Year. (Truman 1961: 585; Mieder and Bryan 1997: 219)

This certainly is a serious commitment by the president to world peace at Christmas time, and he did well to cite the entire Bible passage with its reference to not learning war anymore. But in hindsight one wonders why there was not at least a small reference to the nuclear holocaust that the United States had inflicted on Japan in its desperate drive to bring the war to an end. Truman also ignored these catastrophic events exactly one year later, when he once again delivered a religiously inspired message to the American nation at the ritualistic occasion of lighting the national Christmas tree on December 24, 1946. By this time he could look back at his invaluable accomplishment of establishing the United Nations in 1945 with its purpose of promoting international peace, security, and cooperation among the nations of the world. One can sense, however, his disappointment that peace by the end of 1946 was indeed a very fragile state. And yet, Truman the eternal optimist, returns to the proverbial expression of beating swords into plowshares as a metaphor for a peaceful America (racial strife had returned) and world that had already become divided by the Iron Curtain and the beginning of the Cold War:

I am very sorry to say all is not harmony in the world today. We have found that it is easier for men to die together on the field of battle than it is for them to live together at home in peace. But those who died have died in vain if in some measure, at least, we shall not preserve for the peace that spiritual unity in which we won the war.

The problems facing the United Nations—the world's hope for peace—would overwhelm faint hearts. But, as we continue to labor for an enduring peace through that great organization, we must remember that the world was not created in a day. We shall find strength and courage at this Christmas time because so brave a beginning has been made. So with faith and courage we shall work to hasten the day when the sword is replaced by the plowshare and nations do not "learn war any more." (Truman 1962: 511–12; Mieder and Bryan 1997: 219)

Fifteen years later President Dwight D. Eisenhower, in his farewell radio and television address to the American people of January 17, 1961, had to admit that despite all efforts by the United Nations, the arms race between East and West was accelerating at an alarming speed. He used his last speech as president to warn about the growing "military-industrial complex" that the struggle for world dominance between the United States and the Soviet Union was bringing about. And yet, as a former renowned general, he was only too aware that the country had no choice but to prepare for a possible war with the hope that it might be avoided. With a heavy heart, Eisenhower had to explain that American workers were now, in glaring contradiction to the proverbial expression in the Bible, turning plowshares into swords, i.e. turning valuable materials into weapons:

Until the latest of our world conflicts, the United States had no armaments industry. American makers of plowshares could, with time and as required, make swords as well. But now we can no longer risk emergency improvisation of national defense; we have been compelled to create a permanent armaments industry of vast proportions. Added to this, three and a half million men and women are directly engaged in the defense establishment. We annually spend on military security more than the net income of all United States corporations.

This conjunction of an immense military establishment and a large arms industry is new in the American experience. The total influence—economic, political, even spiritual—is felt in every city, every State house, every office of the Federal government. We recognize the imperative need for this development, yet we must not fail to comprehend its grave implications. Our toil, resources and livelihood are all involved; so is the very structure of our society.

In the councils of government, we must guard against the acquisition of unwarranted influence, whether sought or unsought, by the military-industrial complex. The potential for the disastrous rise of misplaced power exists and will persist.

We must never let the weight of this combination endanger our liberties or democratic processes. We should take nothing for granted. Only an alert and knowledgeable citizenry can compel the proper meshing of the huge industrial and military machinery of defense with our peaceful methods and goals, so that security and liberty may prosper together. (Eisenhower 1961: 1038)

Eisenhower's final speech proved to be full of prophetic wisdom by an experienced general and revered world leader, who might not have had the religious prowess of Martin Luther King, but who doubtlessly would have seconded the preacher's remarks in his speech of December 5, 1957, in which he had used the already cited proverb "He that lives by the sword shall perish by the sword." But now King expresses the hope, obviously shared by Eisenhower, that Americans and all people might succeed in beating swords into plowshares instead of the other way around:

God grant that right [to choose one's way] here in America and all over this world, we will choose the high way: a way in which men will live together as brothers. A way in which the nations of the world will beat their swords into plowshares, and their spears into pruning hooks. A way in which every man will respect the dignity and worth of all human personality. A way in which every nation will allow justice to run down like waters, and righteousness like a mighty stream [Amos 5:24]. A way in which men will do justly, love mercy, and walk humbly with God. A way in which men will be able to stand up, and in the midst of oppression, in the midst of darkness and agony, they will be able to stand there and love their enemies, bless those persons that curse them, pray for those individuals that despitefully use them [Matt. 5:44]. And this is the way that will bring us once more into that society which we think of as the brotherhood of man. This will be that day when white people, colored people, whether they are brown or whether they are yellow or whether they are black, will all join together and stretch out with their arms and be able to cry out: "Free at last! Free at last! Great God Almighty! We are free at last!" (Carson 1992–2007: 4, 342–43; Mieder 2010: 501)

What an incredible vision of peace and freedom for humankind throughout the world! And just like Harry S. Truman, Martin Luther King returned one final time to this Biblical metaphor in a Christmas address of December 24, 1967, just a few months before his assassination:

> I still have a dream today that one day justice will roll down like water, and righteousness like a mighty stream [Amos 5:24]. I still have a dream today that in all of our state houses and city halls men will be elected to go there who will do justly and love mercy and walk humbly with their God [Micah 6:8]. I still have a dream today that one day war will come to an end, that men will beat their swords into plowshares and their spears into pruning hooks, that nations will no longer rise up against nations, neither will they study war any more. I still have a dream today that one day the lamb and the lion will lie down together [cf. Isaiah 11:6] and every man will sit under his own vine and fig tree and none shall be afraid [Micah 4:4]. I still have a dream today that one day every valley shall be exalted and every mountain and hill will be made low, the rough places will be made smooth and the crooked places straight [Isaiah 40:4], and the glory of the Lord shall be revealed, and all flesh shall see it together. I still have a dream that with this faith we will be able to adjourn the councils of despair and bring new light into the dark chambers of pessimism. With this faith we will be able to speed up the day when there will be peace on earth and goodwill toward men [Luke 2:14]. It will be a glorious day, the morning stars will sing together, and the sons of God will shout for joy [Job 38:7]. (King 1967: 77–78; Mieder 2010: 502)

Twenty years later, it fell on the world leaders Mikhail Gorbachev, Ronald Reagan, Margaret Thatcher, and François Mitterand to help bring about the reunification of Germany and the lifting of the Iron Curtain in Europe. President Reagan had proclaimed the following challenge to Gorbachev during a speech on June 12, 1987, at the Brandenburg Gate in West Berlin: "Come here to this gate! Mr. Gorbachev, open this gate! Mr. Gorbachev, tear down this wall!" (Reagan 1989a: 635; Mieder 1997: 100–101). As is well known, about two years later, November 9, 1989, the Berlin Wall was opened and the Iron Curtain was lifted, ushering in a new and more peaceful relationship between the two superpowers of East and West. President Reagan had pushed for this earth-shaking event for at least two and a half years, to wit his fascinating address on September 21, 1987, to the 42nd Session of the United Nations General Assembly in New York. With a stroke of rhetorical genius Reagan referred to Alexis de Tocqueville's early study of *Democracy in America* (1835), which had juxtaposed the future of the United States and Russia in a most uncanny fashion, differentiating between the two nations by way of dividing the proverbial expression "To beat swords into plowshares" into two halves; it seems appropriate to cite this passage before turning to President Reagan's remarks:

> There are, at the present time, two great nations in the world, which seem to tend toward the same end, although they started from different points; I allude to the Russians and the Americans. Both of them have grown up unnoticed; and while the attention of mankind was directed elsewhere, they have suddenly assumed a most prominent place among the nations; and the world learned their existence and their greatness at almost the same time.
>
> All other nations seem to have nearly reached their natural limits, and only to be charged with the maintenance of their power: but these are still in the act of growth; all the others are stopped, or continue to advance with extreme difficulty; these are proceeding with ease and with celerity along a path to which the human eye can assign no term.
>
> The American struggles against the natural obstacles which oppose him; the adversaries of the Russian are men: the former combats the wilderness and savage life; the latter, civilization with all its weapons and its arts; the conquests of the one are therefore gained by the ploughshare; those of the other, by the sword. The Anglo-American relies upon personal interest to accomplish his ends, and gives free scope to the unguided exertions and common sense of the citizens; the Russian centres all the authority of society in a single arm: the principal instrument of the former is freedom; of the latter, servitude. Their starting-point is different, and their courses are not the same; yet each of them seems to be marked out by the will of Heaven to sway the destinies of half the globe. (Tocqueville 2007: 351–52 [end of volume one])

Admittedly, Tocqueville's comments might be a bit too general and stereotypical, but they certainly foreshadow some of the later developments that made adversaries out of these two great powers. In any case, President Reagan did well to recall this passage from Tocqueville and then very appropriately ask whether the world order really has to be divided into plowshares and swords:

> I have spoken today of a vision and the obstacles to its realization. More than a century ago a young Frenchman, Alexis de Tocqueville, visited America. After that visit he predicted that the two great powers of the future world would

be, on one hand, the United States, which would be built, as he said, "by the plowshare," and, on the other, Russia, which would go forward, again, as he said, "by the sword." Yet need it be so? Cannot swords be turned to plowshares? Can we and all nations not live in peace? In our obsession with antagonisms of the moment, we often forget how much unites all the members of humanity. Perhaps we need some outside, universal threat to make us recognize this common bond. I occasionally think how quickly our differences worldwide would vanish if we were facing an alien threat from outside this world. And yet, I ask you, is not an alien force already among us? What could be more alien to the universal aspirations of our peoples than war and the threat of war?

Two centuries ago, in a hall much smaller than this one, in Philadelphia, Americans met to draft a Constitution. In the course of their debates, one of them said that the new government, if it was to rise high, must be built on the broadest base: the will and consent of the people. And so it was, and so it has been.

My message today is that the dreams of ordinary people reach to astonishing heights. If we diplomatic pilgrims are to achieve equal altitudes, we must build all we do on the full breadth of humanity's will and consent and the full expanse of the human heart. Thank you, and God bless you all. (Reagan 1989b: 1063)

Of course, the major goal of the United Nations is to bring peace to the people of the world, as Reagan is emphasizing in this speech to its General Assembly. The proverbial expression "To beat swords into plowshares" has long become the metaphor for peace on earth, as can also be seen from a succinct statement by Bishop Desmond Tutu in his Nobel Peace Prize lecture on December 11, 1984: "Let us work to be peacemakers, those given a wonderful share in Our Lord's ministry of reconciliation. If we want peace, so we have been told, let us work for justice. Let us beat our swords into plowshares" (Tutu 1994: 94). And to take it from the sublime comments by a Nobel laureate to the vast influence of modern popular culture, here are the partial lyrics of Michael Jackson's celebrated song "Heal the World" (1991) that carried the message of love, peace, and turning swords into plowshares to young people around the world:

Heal the world
Make it a better place
For you and for me

And the entire human race

[. . .]

See the nations turn

Their swords

Into plowshares

(<www.azlyrics.com/lyrics/michaeljackson/healtheworld.html 9/5/2011>)

But to return one more time to the United Nations and its mission of beating swords into plowshares throughout the world, it should be noted that a large sculpture with the title "Let Us Beat Swords into Plowshares" by Evgeniy Vuchetich was presented to the United Nations by the officially atheistic Soviet Union in 1959. It stands on the grounds of the United Nations in front of the East River in New York, turning the verbal metaphor into a most telling piece of art to be observed by the world (en.wikipedia.org/wiki/File:Swords-Plowshares.jpg, 9/5/2011). There is yet another place in New York City where this proverbial message is inscribed for all to see and read and descant upon. Across First Avenue from the United Nations building is the small Ralph Bunche Park with the so-called "Isaiah Wall" that was inscribed with the proverbial message in 1975 (en.wikipedia.org/wiki/Ralph_Bunche_Park, 9/5/2011). Since the words of the prophet Isaiah (2:4) represent the ultimate proverbial expression for turning war into peace, they are the appropriate wisdom to bring these deliberations about proverbs on war and peace to a conclusion:

THEY SHALL BEAT THEIR SWORDS INTO
PLOWSHARES. AND THEIR SPEARS INTO
PRUNING HOOKS. NATION SHALL NOT LIFT
UP SWORD AGAINST NATION. NEITHER
SHALL THEY LEARN WAR ANY MORE.

BIBLIOGRAPHY

This chapter was first published with this title in *Proceedings of the Fifth Interdisciplinary Colloquium on Proverbs, 6th to 13th November 2011, at Tavira, Portugal*. Rui J. B. Soares and Outi Lauhakangas, eds. Tavira: Tipografia Tavirense, 2012. 92–120.

Álvarez Díaz, Juan José. 2000. *El Ejército, las armas y la guerra en el lenguaje coloquial: Modismos, locuciones, frases proverbiales, adagios, refranes y algunos vocablos*. Madrid: Ministerio de Defensa.

———. 2001. "Los refranes de la guerra." *Paremia* 10: 31–39.

———. 2005–6. "El soldado en el refranero." *Paremia* 14: 61–69 and 15: 41–49.

Anonymous. 2002. *Swinging the Lead & Spiking His Guns: Military & Naval Expressions and Their Origins*. Edison, New Jersey: Castle.

Ayers, Edward L., ed. 1997. *"A House Divided . . .": A Century of Great Civil War Quotations*. New York: John Wiley & Sons.

Basler, Roy P. 1953. *The Collected Works of Abraham Lincoln*. 8 vols. New Brunswick, New Jersey: Rutgers University Press.

Blassingame, John W., and John R. McKivigan, eds. 1991. *The Frederick Douglass Papers*. 5 vols. New Haven, Connecticut: Yale University Press.

Brautigan, Richard, ed. 1975. *The Beatles Lyrics Illustrated*. New York: Dell.

Bryan, George B., and Wolfgang Mieder. 2005. *A Dictionary of Anglo-American Proverbs & Proverbial Phrases Found in Literary Sources of the Nineteenth and Twentieth Centuries*. New York: Peter Lang.

Bülow, Ralf. 1983. "Stell dir vor, es gibt einen Spruch . . ." *Der Sprachdienst* 27: 97–100.

Butterfield, L. H., ed. 1963. *Adams Family Correspondence. Volume 1: December 1761–May 1776*. Cambridge, Massachusetts: Harvard University Press.

Carson, Clayborne. 1992–2007. *The Papers of Martin Luther King, Jr.* 6 vols. Berkeley, California: University of California Press.

Champion, Selwyn Gurney. 1945. *War Proverbs and Maxims East and West*. London: Arthur Probsthain.

Churchill, Winston S. 1923–31. *The World Crisis*. 6 vols. New York: Charles Scribner's Sons.

———. 1958. *The Great Democracies*. Volume four of *A History of the English-Speaking Peoples*. New York: Dodd, Mead.

Dickson, Paul. 1994. *War Slang: Fighting Words and Phrases of Americans from the Civil War to the Gulf War*. New York: Pocket Books.

Donald, Graeme. 2008. *Sticklers, Sideburns & Bikinis: The Military Origins of Everyday Words and Phrases*. Oxford: Osprey.

Doyle, Charles Clay, Wolfgang Mieder, and Fred R. Shapiro, eds. 2012. *The Dictionary of Modern Proverbs*. New Haven, Connecticut: Yale University Press.

Eichelberger, Ursula. 1986. *Über Krieg und Frieden. Sentenzen aus zweieinhalb Jahrtausenden*. Berlin: Militärverlag der DDR.

Eisenhower, Dwight D. 1961. *Public Papers of the Presidents of the United States. Dwight D. Eisenhower. January 1, 1960, to January 20, 1961*. Washington, DC: U.S. Government Printing Office.

Erasmus of Rotterdam, Desiderius. 1990. "A Complaint of Peace/*Querela pacis*." *The Erasmus Reader*. Erika Rummel, ed. Toronto: University of Toronto Press. 288–314.

———. 2005. *"Dulce bellum inexpertis*/War Is a Treat [Sweet] for Those Who Have Not Tried It." *Adages IIIiv1 to IVii100. (Collected Works of Erasmus*, vol. 35). Translated and annotated by Denis L. Drysdall, edited by John N. Grant. Toronto: University of Toronto Press. 399–440.

Fitzpatrick, John C., ed. 1938. *The Writings of George Washington from the Original Manuscript Sources 1745–1799*. Washington, DC: United States Government Printing Office.

Flavell, Linda, and Roger Flavell. 1992. *Dictionary of Idioms and Their Origins*. London: Kyle Cathie.

Foner, Philip S. 1975. *The Life and Writings of Frederick Douglass. Supplementary Volume*. New York: International Publishers.

Gopienko, J. 1990. "Der Begriff 'Frieden' in den deutschen idiomatischen Wendungen." *Pro pace mundi. Sprache des Friedens*. Helmut Metzler and Christine Römer, eds. Jena: Friedrich-Schiller-Universität. 103–15.

Grob, Fritz. 1949. *The Relativity of War and Peace: A Study in Law, History, and Politics*. New Haven, Connecticut: Yale University Press.

Grossman, Edith, transl. 2003. *Miguel de Cervantes: Don Quixote*. New York: HarperCollins.

Guinzbourg, Lt. Col. Victor S. M. de. 1961. *Wit and Wisdom of the United Nations: Proverbs and Apothegms on Diplomacy.* 2 vols. New York: Privately printed.

———. 1969. *The Eternal Machiavelli in the United Nations World.* New York: Privately printed.

Haas, Heather A. 2008. "Proverb Familiarity in the United States: Cross-Regional Comparisons of the Paremiological Minimum." *Journal of American Folklore* 212: 319–47.

Hannemann, Brigitte, ed. 1987. *Erasmus von Rotterdam. "Süß scheint der Krieg den Unerfahrenen"— "Dulce bellum inexpertis."* München: Chr. Kaiser.

Hargrave, Basil. 1925 (1968). *Origins and Meanings of Popular Phrases and Names. Including Those which Came into Use During the Great War.* London: T. Werner Laurie; rpt. Detroit: Gale Research.

Hirsch, E. D., Joseph Kett, and James Trefil. 1988. *The Dictionary of Cultural Literacy: What Every American Needs to Know.* Boston: Houghton Mifflin. 46–57 (proverbs), 58–80 (idioms).

Ichikawa, Sanki, Takuji Mine, Ryoichi Inui, Kenzo Kihara, and Shiro Takaha, eds. 1964. *The Kenkyusha Dictionary of Current English Idioms.* Tokyo: Kenkyusha.

James, Robert Rhodes, ed. 1974. *Winston S. Churchill: His Complete Speeches, 1897–1963.* 8 vols. New York: Chelsea House.

Johnston, Henry P., ed. 1891. *The Correspondence and Public Papers of John Jay.* New York: G.P. Putnam's Sons.

King, Martin Luther. 1967. *The Trumpet of Conscience.* New York: Harper & Row.

Krebs, Gotthold. 1892. *Militärische Redensarten und Kunst-Ausdrücke.* Wien: L.W. Seidel.

———. 1895. *Militärische Sprichwörter und Redensarten.* Wien: L.W. Seidel.

Kuchmann, Dieter, ed. 1987. *Rauh sind des Soldaten Wege. Zitate, Sprichwörter und Aphorismen aus Memoiren über den Großen Vaterländischen Krieg.* Berlin: Militärverlag der Deutschen Demokratischen Republik.

Lau, Kimberly J. 1996 (2003). "'It's about Time': The Ten Proverbs Most Frequently Used in Newspapers and Their Relation to American Values." *Proverbium* 13: 135–59. Also in *Cognition, Comprehension, and Communication: A Decade of North American Proverb Studies (1990–2000).* Wolfgang Mieder, ed. Baltmannsweiler: Schneider Verlag Hohengehren. 231–54.

Mieder, Wolfgang. 1986. *The Prentice-Hall Encyclopedia of World Proverbs.* Englewood Cliffs, New Jersey: Prentice-Hall; rpt. New York: MJF Books, 1996.

———. 1989. "'It's Five Minutes to Twelve': Folklore and Saving Life on Earth." *International Folklore Review* 7: 10–21.

———. 1994. "Paremiological Minimum and Cultural Literacy." *Wise Words: Essays on the Proverb.* Wolfgang Mieder, ed. New York: Garland. 297–316.

———. 1997. *The Politics of Proverbs: From Traditional Wisdom to Proverbial Stereotypes.* Madison, Wisconsin: University of Wisconsin Press.

———. 2000. *The Proverbial Wisdom of Abraham Lincoln: An Index to Proverbs in the Works of Abraham Lincoln.* New York: Peter Lang.

———. 2001. *"No Struggle, No Progress": Frederick Douglass and His Proverbial Rhetoric for Civil Rights.* New York: Peter Lang.

———. 2005. *Proverbs Are the Best Policy: Folk Wisdom and American Politics.* Logan, Utah: Utah State University Press.

———. 2009. *"Yes We Can": Barack Obama's Proverbial Rhetoric.* New York: Peter Lang.

———. 2010. *"Making a Way Out of No Way": Martin Luther King's Sermonic Proverbial Rhetoric.* New York: Peter Lang.

Mieder, Wolfgang, and George B. Bryan. 1995. *The Proverbial Winston S. Churchill: An Index to Proverbs in the Works of Sir Winston Churchill.* Westport, Connecticut: Greenwood.

————. 1997. *The Proverbial Harry S. Truman: An Index to Proverbs in the Works of Harry S. Truman*. New York: Peter Lang.

Mieder, Wolfgang, Stewart A. Kingsbury, and Kelsie B. Harder, eds. 1992. *A Dictionary of American Proverbs*. New York: Oxford University Press.

Obama, Barack. 2006. *The Audacity of Hope: Thoughts on Reclaiming the American Dream*. New York: Three Rivers.

Pickering, David. 1997. *Dictionary of Proverbs*. London: Cassell.

Priest, William L. 2000. *"Swear Like a Trooper": A Dictionary of Military Terms and Phrases*. Charlottesville, Virginia: Rockbridge.

Raymond, Joseph. 1953. "The Role of Proverbs in Tensions and Crises." *Central States Speech Journal* 4: 6–10.

————. 1956. "Tensions in Proverbs: More Light on International Understanding." *Western Folklore* 15: 153–58. Also in *The Wisdom of Many: Essays on the Proverb*. Wolfgang Mieder and Alan Dundes, eds. New York: Garland, 1981. 300–308.

Reagan, Ronald. 1989a. *Public Papers of the Presidents of the United States. Ronald Reagan. January 1 to July 3, 1987*. Washington, DC: U.S. Government Printing Office.

————. 1989b. *Public Papers of the Presidents of the United States. Ronald Reagan. July 4 to December 31, 1987*. Washington, DC: U.S. Government Printing Office.

Rees, Nigel. 2011. *Don't You Know There's a War Going On? Words and Phrases from the World Wars*. London: Batsford.

Roche, Reinhard. 1983. "'Stell dir vor . . .'" *Der Sprachdienst* 27: 158–60.

Royle, Trevor. 1989. *A Dictionary of Military Quotations*. New York: Simon & Schuster.

Russell, Melissa Anne. 1999. "'Kill 'em All and Let God Sort 'em Out': The Proverb as an Expression of Verbal Aggression." *Proverbium* 16: 287–302.

Seiler, Friedrich. 1916. "Der Krieg im deutschen Sprichwort." *Zeitschrift für deutschen Unterricht* 30: 507–16.

Seiler, Friedrich. 1917. "Soldatenleben im deutschen Sprichwort." *Zeitschrift für deutschen Unterricht* 31: 14–17.

Shafritz, Jay M. 1990. *Words on War: Military Quotations from Ancient Times to the Present*. New York: Prentice Hall.

Shapiro, Fred R. 2006. *The Yale Book of Quotations*. New Haven, Connecticut: Yale University Press.

Sobieski, Janet, and Wolfgang Mieder, eds. 2005. *So Many Heads, So Many Wits": An Anthology of English Proverb Poetry*. Burlington, Vermont: University of Vermont.

Speake, Jennifer, ed. 2008. *The Oxford Dictionary of Proverbs*. 5th ed. Oxford: Oxford University Press.

Stevenson, Burton Egbert. 1948. *The Home Book of Proverbs, Maxims and Familiar Phrases*. New York: Macmillan.

Taylor, Archer, and Bartlett Jere Whiting. 1958. *A Dictionary of American Proverbs and Proverbial Phrases, 1820–1880*. Cambridge, Massachusetts: Harvard University Press.

Tilley, Morris Palmer. 1950. *A Dictionary of the Proverbs in England in the Sixteenth and Seventeenth Centuries*. Ann Arbor, Michigan: University of Michigan Press.

Titelman, Gregory Y. 1996. *Random House Dictionary of Popular Proverbs and Sayings: Over 1,500 Proverbs and Sayings with 10,000 Illustrative Citations*. New York: Random House.

Tocqueville, Alexis de. 2007. *Democracy in America*. Isaac Kramnick, ed. New York: W.W. Norton.

Truman, Harry S. 1944. "Speech Before Women's National Democratic Club, March 6, 1944." *Congressional Record*, XC, 8: A1156–58.

————. 1961. *Public Papers of the Presidents of the United States. Harry S. Truman. April 12 to December 31, 1945*. Washington, DC: U.S. Government Printing Office.

———. 1962. *Public Papers of the Presidents of the United States. Harry S. Truman. January 1 to December 31, 1946.* Washington, DC: U.S. Government Printing Office.

Tutu, Desmond. 1994. *The Rainbow People of God: The Making of a Peaceful Revolution.* New York: Doubleday.

Wheeler, Everett L. 1988. "'Polla kena tou polemou' [Many futilities in war]—The History of a Greek Proverb." *Greek, Roman and Byzantine Studies* 29: 153–84.

Whiting, Bartlett Jere. 1968. *Proverbs, Sentences, and Proverbial Phrases from English Writings Mainly Before 1500.* Cambridge, Massachusetts: Harvard University Press.

———. 1977. *Early American Proverbs and Proverbial Phrases.* Cambridge, Massachusetts: Harvard University Press.

———. 1989. *Modern Proverbs and Proverbial Sayings.* Cambridge, Massachusetts: Harvard University Press.

Wilson, F. P. 1970. *The Oxford Dictionary of English Proverbs.* 3rd ed. Oxford: Clarendon.

Wölfflin, F. 1888. "Krieg und Frieden im Sprichworte der Römer." *Sitzungsberichte der philosophisch-philologischen und historischen Classe der k. b. Akademie der Wissenschaften zu München* 18: 197–215.

Zouogbo, Jean-Philippe. 2004 (2004). "Guerre et paix: Analyse parémiologique de la presse ivoirienne." *Proverbium* 21: 371–86. Also in *L'espace euro-méditerranéen: Une idiomaticité partagée. Actes du colloque international, Hammamet, les 19-21 septembre 2003.* Salah Mejri, ed. Tunis: Université de Tunis. II, 449–61.

Proverbs in Literature

8. "THE POETRY OF THE PEOPLE"
Proverbs in the Works of Ralph Waldo Emerson

Of the many American authors who delight in employing proverbs in their writings, Ralph Waldo Emerson (1803–1882) lends himself particularly well to illustrating how proverbs are effectively used in various forms of literature (Abrahams and Babcock 1977; Grzybek 1991; Mieder 1974a, 1974b; Taylor 1931: 171–83). This prolific nineteenth-century preacher, rhetorician, lecturer, essayist, transcendentalist, philosopher, pragmatist, humanist, and early paremiologist was intrigued by the wisdom expressed in proverbs throughout his long and active life. As one combs through the dozens of volumes of notes, letters, sermons, lectures, essays, and poems, it becomes clear that he was an early American proverb scholar of sorts. The many comments he made on proverbs throughout his voluminous writings add up to an impressive knowledge of this folklore genre (La Rosa 1969; Mieder 1989b). He went so far as to assemble small proverb collections, and theorized about the nature and meaning of proverbs. More importantly and perhaps somewhat surprisingly, this remarkable intellectual never shied away from using proverbs to underscore a particular observation or generalization. Even though he was fond of these ready-made bits of traditional wisdom, he saw their limitations and was well aware of the fact that proverbs are not universal truths. But metaphorical proverbs served him well, giving his demanding lectures and essays a refreshing and colorful style based on easily accessible elements of folk speech (Anderson 1953).

Emerson as Paremiographer

Emerson filled dozens of notebooks with thoughts and observations that might best be described as literary or philosophical fragments or aphorisms. Everything he found worthy of being remembered or reflected upon, he untiringly jotted down without any logical or thematic order. One is reminded of the notebooks of such other great eighteenth- and nineteenth-century authors as Georg Christoph Lichtenberg, Goethe (whom Emerson admired greatly), Novalis, Friedrich Schlegel, Arthur Schopenhauer (Mieder and Bryan 1996), and, of course, Emerson's Transcendentalist companion Henry David Thoreau (Loomis 1957; Moldenhauer 1967; Reaver 1967; Willis 1966).

In one of these fascinating notebooks, appropriately entitled *Encyclopedia* (1824–36), Emerson assembled hundreds of quotations from a multitude of sources and covering any subject imaginable. His encyclopedic mind was simply intrigued with everything, including philosophical reflections and folk wisdom (Loomis 1958; Taylor and Whiting 1958). While individual proverbs are registered throughout the notebooks and in the *Encyclopedia* in particular, Emerson also amassed them on occasion into his own small collections:

> *Proverbs*
> Vinegar is the Son of Wine.
> The rolling stone gathers no moss.
> Fling no stones from a glass house.
> Malum vas non frangitur.
> The last ounce broke the camel's back.
> "Man has been to man a wolf." Hobbes.
> Bygones be bygones.
> None so homely but likes a looking glass.
> Stercus cuique suum bene olet.
> Years know more than books.
> "Whilst the grass grows the steed starves."
> "Let well alone."
> Need breaks iron.
> (Journals VI: 138–41)

This considerably abbreviated list shows the polyglot interests of Emerson, who often cites proverbs in foreign languages (primarily Latin and French) or in translation, as for example "The apple does not fall far from the stem. German" (Journals VI, 224; part of another small proverb collection in Emerson's *Encyclopedia*, 224–25; see Mieder 1993). Some of Emerson's major sources for proverbs were Vicesimus Knox, *Elegant Extracts . . . in Prose* (1797); John Ray, *A Complete Collection of English Proverbs* (6th ed., 1817); and Thomas Fielding, *Select Proverbs of All Nations* (1825). For example, the following slightly shortened list of Italian and Spanish proverbs in English translation was copied from Knox (Cameron 1957), indicating his interest in the wisdom of other languages and cultures:

Proverbs
God comes to see us without a bell.
A wall between both, best preserves friendship.
God doth the cure, & the Physician takes the money for it.
Make the night night, & the day day.
The wise hand doth not all which the foolish tongue saith.
There's no fool like a learned fool.
(May 12, 1832; Journals IV: 16–17)

But Emerson's keen interest in proverbs also led him to create his own proverb-like statements based on proverbial structures and employing such markers as rhyme, parallelism, rhythm, etc. (Arora 1984; La Rosa 1972):

My Proverbs
The chief mourner does not always attend the funeral.
A fine day is not a weather breeder but a fine day.
All men are every moment growing wiser.
Look at the mark not at your arrow.
Knowledge is the best insurance.
'Tis as hard to tame a fly as a hyena.
God hides things by putting them near us.
A little praise / Goes a great ways.
(Journals VI: 197–98; abbreviated)

The last text has made it into *A Dictionary of American Proverbs* (Mieder, Kingsbury, and Harder 1992: 479), and so has Emerson's creation "Hitch your wagon to a star" (Journals VI: 637). He had used it in his lecture on *Civilization* in 1862 as a bit of uplifting advice: "Hitch your wagon to a star. Let us not fag in paltry works which serve our pot and bag alone. Let us not lie and steal. [. . .] Work rather for those interests which the divinities honor and promote,—justice, love, freedom, knowledge, utility" (January 1862; Complete Works VII: 30).

Such mini-proverb collections are, however, rather the exception in Emerson's work as a paremiographer. Most of the time he simply registers a single proverb without any context or explanation whatsoever. He must have heard or read the particular proverb, noting it down as yet one further example of life's experiences and observations distilled into a gem of folk wisdom:

> There is always less money, less wisdom, & less honesty than people imagine. Ital. Proverb.
>
> (1826; Journals VI: 28)
>
> Non est planeta Israeli—a Jewish proverb.
>
> (1827; Journals VI: 70)
>
> It is an Arabian Proverb—Darken five windows that the house may shine.
>
> (1929; Journals VI: 90)
>
> "Welcome is the best cheer." Proverb.
>
> (April 2, 1832; Journals IV: 9)
>
> "The barber learns his art on the orphan's face." Arabian Proverb.
>
> (February 12, 1834; Journals IV: 264; see Cameron 1958)
>
> Moreover saith the world "Nothing venture, nothing have."
>
> (September 15, 1834; Journals IV: 322)
>
> In vino veritas.
>
> (April 20, 1837; Journals V: 299)
>
> What just theology is in the popular proverb, "Every man for himself & the Lord for us all."
>
> (November 17, 1839; Journals VII: 307)
>
> "The saugh kens the basketmaker's thumb." Scottish proverb.
>
> (October 14, 1840; Journals VII: 407)
>
> Il n'y /a/est/ que le matin en toutes choses.
>
> (1863; Journals XV: 27, 114)
>
> We all know the rule of umbrellas,—if you take your umbrella, it will not rain; if you leave it, it will (rain).
>
> (1873; Journals XVI: 293)

This last somewhat longer example shows clearly what delight Emerson took in locating new proverbs. While he enjoyed their wisdom, his intellect could perfectly well see their inherent contradictions:

> Two proverbs I found lately; one; "He who would bring home the wealth of the Indies, must carry out the wealth of the Indies" [Spanish proverb]. The other may serve as foil to this magnificent sentence, "Small pot, soon hot." Then again I found in the "Phenix" [*A Collection of Old and Rare Fragments*, 1835], the Persian sentence, "Remember always that the gods are good" which for genius equals any other golden saying. (July 17, 1837; Journals V: 342)

The actual Persian piece of wisdom is "Not knowing that every god is good, you are fruitlessly vigilant," making it clear that Emerson has a bit of "fun" with the juxtaposition of these three sapiential sayings. He obviously also enjoyed a bit of paremiographical field research, when he entered this reference in his journal: "'When people are going to die their faults come out' was one of [his aunt] Mary Moody Emerson's old sayings" (November 19, 1839; Journals VII: 312). Doubtlessly proverbs fascinated Emerson during all of his encounters with others and his readings.

Emerson as Paremiologist

It should not be surprising that a person as interested in registering proverbs as Emerson would also reflect upon the definition and nature of this concise and traditional wisdom literature of the folk. As early as 1822, at the young age of nineteen, Emerson wrote these keen remarks into a notebook appropriately titled *Wide World* since it was meant to include old ideas and new thoughts on an all-encompassing and global scope:

> [. . .] the proverbs and familiar sayings of all nations [. . .] are the first generalizations of the mind and have been repeated by the mouth of the million. As the peculiar language of experience, altogether independent of other purposes than as tried guides of life, proverbs demand notice. It was early found that there were a few principles which controlled society; that the mother of all the arts, the nurse of social feelings, the impeller of individual energies— was Necessity [allusion to the proverb "Necessity is the mother of invention"]. These truths, ascertained by the progress of society, and corroborated by the observation of each succeeding generation, were incorporated into these short maxims as rules for youth which maturity would establish. (February 16, 1822; Journals I: 87)

Certainly Emerson is aware of the fact that proverbs are generalizations, that they are repeated over time by the folk, and that they usually serve as truthful and moral rules of life. He also sees "the value of Proverbs or the significance of every trivial speech as of a blacksmith or teamster concerning his tools or his beasts, Namely, that the same thing is found to hold true throughout Nature" (March 11, 1836; Journals V: 137). Naturally he is aware of contradictory proverbs, as they comment on life's many contradictions: "There is no concealment. There is no truth in the proverb that if you get up your name you may safely play the rogue. Thence the balancing proverb that in every wit is a grain of fool. You are known" (September 24, 1836; Journals V: 204). And, of course, not all proverbs are uplifting, since they comment on all aspects of life, including vulgar matters:

> Of proverbs, although the greater part have so the smell of current bank-bills that one seems to get the savor of all the marketmen's pockets, and no lady's mouth may they soil, yet are some so beautiful that they may be spoken by fairest lips unblamed; and this is certain,—that they give comfort and encouragement, aid and abetting to daily action. For example: "There are as good fish in the sea as ever came out of it," is a piece of trust in the riches of nature and God, which helps all men always. (September 5, 1838; Journals VII: 64–65)

The wisdom and value of proverbs can thus not be denied, as Emerson points out only two weeks after these comments, returning among others to the "fish" proverb that he had cited:

> Every homely proverb covers a single and grand fact. Two of these are often in my head lately: "Every dog his day," which covers this fact of Otherism, or rotation of merits; and "There are as many good fish in the sea as ever came out of it"; which was Nelson's adage of *merit*, and all men's of *marriage*. My third proverb is as deficient in superficial melody as either of the others: "The Devil is an ass." The seamen use another which has much true divinity: "Every man for himself and God for us all." (September 20, 1838; Journals VII: 82)

Thus, according to Emerson, proverbs might be homely and express rather obvious facts about life, but they are basically true and to be reckoned with as appropriate expressions of folk wisdom. They were originally coined by an individual, and by their repeated use the most fitting variant eventually became the standard form that survived decades if not centuries. This is what Emerson might have had in mind when he wrote that "Proverbs are boulders & get the roundness of boulders" (February 1847; Journals X: 10), i.e., they are well worn and have stood the test of time. Reflecting on his long interest in proverbs, Emerson becomes quite poetic in their praise: "Proverbs are the poetry, the Solomon, the Socrates of the people. What comfort & strength we have all owed once & again & often to 'There are as (many) good fish in the sea as ever came out of it.' And, 'Well, 'tis as broad as it is long'" (1862; Journals XV: 160).

Late in his life he returned to this laudation: "Proverbs are the poetry & literature of unreading nations. Books the immense advantage of the civilized" (1875; Journals XVI: 335). However, there was no need to restrict the value of proverbs to illiterate people. After all, that other great American admirer of proverbs, Benjamin Franklin (1707–1790), had shown a hundred years earlier that proverbs were a most welcome part of his incredibly successful *Poor Richard's Almanack*, which he published for twenty-five years between 1733 and 1758 (Newcomb 1957; Barbour 1974; Mieder 1989a: 129–42). Besides, Emerson's own preoccupation with proverbs throughout his life is ample proof that they are part and parcel of human communication both in its oral and written expression.

Proverbs in the Journals

In addition to including individual proverbs without context, several mini-collections of proverbs, and insightful observations on the nature of proverbs in his journals and notebooks, Emerson also repeatedly cites well-known proverbs in his short prose fragments. Here the proverbs serve him well to underscore an observation or explanation; but he also comments on the significance of traditional proverbs, observing again and again that these apparent truths couched in colorful folk speech have a definite purpose in both philosophical reflection and in everyday discourse.

Often Emerson starts one of his reflective fragments with a proverb, quickly turning from its folk wisdom to a comment on human behavior or social matters, as for example in his remarks on the proverb "Everything has its price":

> Then every thing has its price. Little goods are lightly gained, but the rich sweets of tilings are in the ribs of the mountain, and months and years must dig for them. For example, a jest or a glass of wine a man can procure without much pains to relieve his trouble for a moment; but a *habit of Patience*, which is the perfect (cordial) medicine, he cannot procure in a moment or a week or a month. It will cost thought and strife and mortification and prayer. (December 7, 1829; Journals III: 169)

Even when the sermonic Emerson wants to elaborate on humankind's need to make a commitment to social involvement, he begins his short statement with a traditional proverb, citing it in a dialect variant to boot:

One man may lead a horse to water, but ten canna gar him drink. It is so in the order of Providence with man. Heaven guards his freedom so carefully that nothing compels him to enter into the spirit of the festival to which he is invited. He may pout in the corner, if he will, and suck his thumbs. But the loss is his own. The company is large and can easily spare him; but he would do more wisely to conform himself to circumstances intended kindly, and carry forward the brilliant game. (April 23, 1831; Journals III: 250)

In addition to arguing for a *vita activa*, Emerson also points out by means of the proverb "Half is more (better) than the whole" that in life it is often better to be satisfied with half what one can acquire with safety than the whole that cannot be obtained without danger. In other words, he argues for the golden mean or moderation in all things:

A man is a method; a progressive arrangement; a selecting principle gathering his like to him wherever he goes. "Half is more than the whole." Yes, let the man of taste be the selector & Half is a good deal better than the whole or an infinitesimal part becomes a just representative of the Infinite. A man of taste sent to Italy shall bring me a few objects that shall give me more lively & permanent pleasure than galleries, cities, & mountain chains. A man is a choice. (January 22, 1836; Journals V: 114–15)

The following aphoristic observation starts with the mundane proverbial wisdom of "It never rains but it pours" and, in a matter of two sentences, moves on to the insight that humankind has a tendency of feeling overwhelmed by the nature of things: "It never rains but it pours. If you see pyrola you see nothing else but varieties of pyrola. To that one thing which man has in his head all nature seems an illustration[,] all men martyrs" (July 5, 1836; Journals V: 185).

Even the proverb "Love will creep where it cannot go," employed effectively by Shakespeare in his play *The Two Gentlemen of Verona*, is used by Emerson not to reflect on love's mysterious ways but rather as a statement of the strength of the will to live:

"Love will creep where it cannot go," will accomplish that by imperceptible original incalculable methods, being his own lever, fulcrum, & moving power, which force could never achieve. Have you not seen in the woods in a late autumn morning a poor little fungus, an agaric, a plant without any solidity, nay, that seemed nothing but a soft mush or jelly, yet by its constant, total, &

inconceivably gentle pushing had managed to break its way up through the frosty ground & actually to lift a pretty hard crust on its head? (September 19, 1840; Journals VII: 398)

But speaking of "love," Emerson also does not relate the proverb "Faint heart never won fair lady" to courtship issues. Instead, he shortens the proverb to "Faint heart never won" in the middle of a paragraph for once and relates it to a proclamation for the value of the work of the mind:

> The mason, the carpenter hold up their trowel & saw with honest pride[;] the Scholar thrusts his book into his pocket, (&) drops the nose gay he has gathered in his walk into the fields, & in conversation with the grocer & farmer affects to talk of business & farms. Faint heart never won. Other professions thrive because they who drive them do that one thing with a single & entire mind. Feel that fair weather or foul weather, good for grass or bad for grass, scarcity or plenty is all nothing to you: that your plough may go every day; and leave to God the care of the world. (May 30, 1836; Journals V: 164–65)

Finally, the journal entry with the title "Each dog" alludes to the proverb "Every dog has his day, and every man has his hour," indicating that Emerson knew how to play with proverbs as catchy titles as journalists do so often in the media. In his remarks he points out that all people are different, but that every person has his vocation, be he a recluse or a president:

> One thing experience teaches, the variety of men. The recluse thinks of men as having his manner or not having his manner; and as having degrees of it, more & less. But when he comes into a public assembly [and notices John Quincy Adams] then he sees with surprise that men have very different manners from his own & in their way admirable. [. . .] A steady mind[,] a believing mind wins the world. (May 7, 1837; Journals V: 325)

These examples from the journals suffice to illustrate Emerson's engrossment with proverbs (La Rosa 1976). He looks at them as truthful generalizations and employs them as analogies of human conduct and social rules as he experiences them in his day. Above all, proverbs lead Emerson to his transcendental thoughts that look for a meaningful and ethical purpose of human life. In fact, in his essay *Circles* (1841), Emerson established a clear link between certain proverbs and transcendentalism:

[. . .] I suppose that the highest prudence is the lowest prudence. Is this too sudden a rushing from the centre to the verge of our orbit? Think how many times we shall fall back into pitiful calculations before we take up our rest in the great sentiment, or make the verge of today the new centre. Besides, your bravest sentiment is familiar to the humblest men. The poor and the low have their way of expressing the last facts of philosophy as well as you. "Blessed be nothing" and "The worse things are, the better they are" are proverbs which express the transcendentalism of common life. (1841; Collected Works II: 186–87)

With "Blessed be nothing" Emerson appears to be referring in a truncated fashion to the proverb "Blessed are they who expect nothing, for they shall not be disappointed." In any case, these proverbs refer to the "law of eternal procession" (II: 186) that transcends objective reality.

Epistolary Use of Proverbs

Proverbs informed all kinds of Emerson's writings, as he saw the wisdom of generations distilled in them. They also quite naturally flowed into his numerous letters, where they are part of his style of successfully combining folk language with intellectual argumentation. This can be seen in a marvelous tongue-in-cheek letter that the fifteen-year-old Emerson wrote to his brother Edward (Ned):

[. . .] when I want to scribble I know not why, & care not what, & moreover have leisure & rhyme at command, and peradventure want to amuse myself, then as now the pen flies over the lines to my semi-Andover semi-Boston brother Ned. In short I write to you when I am in a serio-ludrico tragico-comico miscellany of feelings. If the paper is filled it matters not how. The old proverb is "Circumstances alter cases"; & now that your horizon is so essentially changed; from the dark murky clouds of misanthropy, fanaticism, & error that encircle Andover to the careless noisy scenes of Boston (two equally dreaded extremes) I suppose I must begin to vary my epistolary efforts [. . .] . (September 1818; Letters I: 70)

A letter to his brother William is particularly revealing as to Emerson's pervasive use of proverbs in his epistolary musings with family members. Rather than citing the two proverbs "Give him an inch and he'll take an ell" and "The rolling stone gathers no moss" in their traditional didactic wording, he varies the first to suit his purpose and merely alludes to the second. Both varied texts show that proverbs in context are not at all always cited precisely, i.e., proverbs are not as rigidly fixed as has been assumed:

> I know I ought, according to all rules, to have answered your letter enclosing $65, which I duly received. But I tho't you would leave me more inches of line than a better merchant & of course I took some ells. Your account agrees perfectly with mine. If I should succeed in selling my Mill-dam shares, I can better wait your convenience in paying the balance. [. . .] I am never a dollar in advance of my wants & if it were not for an expedient once or twice in a twelvemonth like Lecturing or an auction of my great *stock*, I should be flat on my back. But let me hope that my rotations are ended & that now I shall sit still & gather moss. (June 28, 1836; Letters II: 26)

It should be noted that Emerson also included the proverbial expression "To be flat on one's back" in this letter, but such metaphorical verbal phrases are not particularly common in his writings. In any case, Emerson certainly is fond of the English loan translation of the German proverb "Der Apfel fällt nicht weit vom Stamm," as can be seen in this letter to his aunt Mary Moody Emerson:

> [. . .] We have learned through Uncle Samuel R. the death of Mrs. Ripley [daughter of Rev. William Emerson]. She loved all her blood so well, and had from nature so much dignity of manners & of form, that though I have never spent but a few hours in her company, I feel as if I had lost a great deal of my family, in her death. [. . .] Her departure will cut one of your own ties to your present abode, and as men say the apple never falls far from the stem, I shall hope that another year will draw your eyes & steps to this old dear odious haunt of the race. (December 22, 1839; Letters II: 243)

A letter from Manchester, England, to his wife Lidian is also quite revealing in its use of the proverb "To each his own," since Emerson includes comments regarding his thoughts on various rhetorical styles:

> [. . .] Last night I heard a lecture from Mr. Cameron whom I have heretofore mentioned on some poetic & literary matters. [. . .] He talked without note or card or compass, for his hour, on Readers & Reading, very manly, very gaily, not quite deeply enough,—it did not cost him enough—yet what would I not do or suffer to buy that ability? "To each his own." A manly ability, a general

sufficiency, is the genius of the English. They have not, I think, the special and acute fitness to their employment that Americans have, but a man is a man here,—a quite costly & respectable production in his own & in all other eyes. [. . .] (January 26, 1848; Letters IV: 9)

Even though Emerson travelled to Europe a number of times to meet the intellectual elite of Great Britain and the continent, one finds some arguments against such so-called "grand-tours" to Europe in a letter to Caroline Wilson: "[. . .] I do not know how it [the travelling to Europe] is to be hindered. We all talk against it, but all go. We preach America, but practise Europe. It is a mild epidemic insanity, & nothing but indulgence & a cloying operates a cure. [People] must go to gaze at vicious Europe, & its tarnished wormy magnificence [. . .]" (May 8, 1854; Letters IV: 441). Once again the proverb in these few lines is barely discernible, but behind the statement "We preach America, but practise Europe" surely is hidden the proverb "Practice what you preach." Emerson simply decided to create his own slogan against the European craze of his compatriots, changing the general proverb to the specific phenomenon that was annoying him.

Emerson takes considerable liberties with traditional proverbs in his letters, but his readers most assuredly sensed the humor, irony, and satire in these proverb variations by one of the great minds of nineteenth-century America. And always the proverbialist, Emerson inserts proverbs in his letters whenever he can, and he certainly does not restrict himself to those of the English language. In yet another letter to his brother William dealing with pecuniary matters, he cites an Arabic proverb for good measure (Cameron 1958):

I received yesterday at Concord your letter & the cheque inclosed, on the Massachusetts Bank for $139.38 (I believe) at all events I had the money & the account,—in every way satisfactory. It seems that you also have experience of the delays of carpenters. Well, the work will be the better done. "Haste" say the Mahometans "is of the devil; delay is from the All-giving." (October 2, 1847; Letters III: 419)

But this proverb from the Islam religion is also handled with considerable liberty, its actual wording being "Deliberation in undertaking is pleasing to God, and haste is pleasing to the devil."

Proverbs in Lectures and Essays

Proverbs permeate all of Emerson's notes, sermons, lectures, and essays (Reaver 1963). His religious sermons actually were lectures on very diverse subjects, and they and his secular lectures were sooner or later published in polished and often expanded essays. They are all informed by his vast knowledge and keen interest in the humanities and sciences and, interestingly enough for such an inquisitive and philosophical mind, repeatedly return to proverbial matters. For example, in an early sermon on the value of *Conversation*, he included a paragraph on the origin and meaning of proverbs that play an important role in human communication:

> [. . .] consider how much practical wisdom passes current in the world in the shape of vulgar proverbs. These little maxims of worldly prudence are a part of the inheritance that have come down to this age from all the past generations of men. They have given us their institutions, their inventions, their books, and, by means of conversation, have transmitted their commentary upon all the parts of life in these proverbs. They were originally doubtless the happy thoughts of sagacious men in very distant times and countries, in every employment and of every character. No single individual, with whatever penetration, could have attained by himself to that accurate knowledge of human life, which now floats through the conversation of all society, by means of these pithy sentences. We are all of us the wiser for them. They govern us in all our traffic,—in all our judgments of men,—in all our gravest actions. (October 18, 1829; Emerson Speaks: 62–63)

Emerson certainly is aware of the fact that proverbs are handed on from one generation to another, especially in oral communication. He repeats this observation in yet another sermon on *The Authority of Jesus*, arguing that proverbial wisdom in its simplicity contains much authoritative truth:

> [. . .] Every one will remember how often he heard in youth without heeding it any one of the common proverbs that pass from mouth to mouth and the lively satisfaction he derived from the perception of its truth the first time that his own experience led him to express the same fact in similar language. And he smiled at saying anew so trite a sentence. (March 30, 1830; Emerson Speaks: 93)

Such comments reveal Emerson as a scholar with considerable interest in the deeper meanings of proverbs (Norrick 1985). His own paremiological progression is truly remarkable, though, as indicated in yet another short comment in a lecture on *The Uses of Natural History*:

> [...] every common proverb is only one of these facts in nature used as a picture or parable of a more extensive truth; as when we say, "A bird in the hand is worth two in the bush." "A rolling stone gathers no moss." "'Tis hard to carry a full cup even." "Whilst the grass grows the steed starves."—In themselves these are insignificant facts but we repeat them because they are symbolical of moral truths. These are only trivial instances designed to show the principle. (November 4, 1833; Lectures I: 25)

Two years later Emerson returned to these thoughts in his first lecture on *Shakspear* [*sic*]. While repeating some of the proverbs, he adds some others and speaks of proverbs as "pictures" and of "the value of their analogical import." These comments foreshadow the modern theoretical interpretation of proverbs as signs (see Grzybek 1987). One could indeed speak of Emerson as a precursor to paremiological semiotics:

> In like manner the memorable words of history and the proverbs of nations consist usually of a natural fact selected as a picture or parable of moral truth. Thus, "A rolling stone gathers no moss;" "A bird in the hand is worth two in the bush;" "A cripple in the right way will beat a racer in the wrong;" "'Tis hard to carry a full cup even;" "Vinegar is the son of wine;" "The last ounce broke the camel's back;" "Long lived trees make roots first;" and the like. In their primary sense these are trivial facts but we repeat them for the value of their analogical import. (December 10, 1835; Lectures I: 290)

With the addition of the proverb "Make hay whilst the sun shines," Emerson also included this paragraph in his significant chapter on "Language" in his book *Nature* (1836; see La Rosa 1970), explaining that "the world is emblematic. Parts of speech are metaphors because the whole of nature is a metaphor of the human mind" (1836; Collected Works I: 21–22). Clearly, Emerson looks at proverbs as emblematic or analogic signs for nature in general and humanity in particular.

It is interesting to note that, in his lectures and essays, Emerson likes to amass proverbs into mini-collections as examples. He does so again in his important lecture on *Ethics* (see February 16, 1837; Lectures II: 152–53), repeating his many examples and comments more or less verbatim in his essay on *Compensation* four years later:

> Proverbs, like the sacred books of each nation, are the sanctuary of the intuitions. That which the droning world, chained to appearances, will not allow the realist to say in his own words, it will suffer him to say in proverbs without contradiction. And this law of laws, which the pulpit, the senate and the college deny, is hourly preached in all markets and workshops by flights of proverbs, whose teaching is as true and as omnipresent as that of birds and flies.
>
> All things are double, one against another.—Tit for tat; an eye for an eye; a tooth for a tooth; blood for blood; measure for measure; love for love. Give, and it shall be given you. He that watereth shall be watered himself.—What will you have? quoth God; pay for it and take it.—Nothing venture, nothing have.—Thou shalt be paid exactly for what thou hast done, no more, no less.—Who doth not work shall not eat.—Harm watch, harm catch.—Curses always recoil on the head of him who imprecates them.—If you put a chain around the neck of a slave, the other end fastens itself around your own.—Bad counsel confounds the adviser.—The Devil is an ass.
>
> It is thus written, because it is thus in life. Our action is overmastered and characterized above our will by the law of nature. We aim at a petty end quite aside from the public good, but our act arranges itself by irresistible magnetism in a line with the poles of the world. (1841; Collected Works II: 63–64)

Emerson thus points out that proverbs reflect the binary structure of the world and that they play their important role in finding a balance or compensation between life's extremities. Above all, when Emerson argues that proverbs allow people to express matters metaphorically that they would not dare to state directly, he is in fact alluding to one of the major purposes of proverbs, i.e., communication through indirection.

To be sure, Emerson does not always theorize about proverbs. But he certainly is aware of the fact that Shakespeare was particularly adept at integrating proverbs into his plays, stating in his second lecture on *Shakspear* [*sic*] that "his wise sentences make in fact a large part of that treasury of proverbial wisdom which floats in the daily speech of all who use the English tongue being long ago so familiar that they who use them do not know their author" (December 17, 1835; Lectures I: 313). But besides mentioning that many proverbs found their way into literary works, he also quite appropriately points out in his lecture on *Trades and Professions* that there are a "multitude of proverbs which circulate in men's mouths teaching moral precepts in the form of some nautical, agricultural, or mechanical process" (February 2, 1837; Lectures II: 126). A few months later he states along these lines in his lecture on *Doctrine of the Hands* that "It is from the work of the smith, the mason, and the joiner that they [people] have drawn the proverbs of prudence and the words for the laws of life" (December 13, 1837; Lectures II: 232–33; see Templeton 1997). Yet such general comments on the appearance of proverbs in literature and their content (realia from all walks of life) are frequently superseded by the actual use of a particular proverb as a ready-made piece of wisdom to explain an argument or to underscore a point. In his lecture on *Trades and Professions*, for example, he argues for a solid work ethic and emphasizes his didactic comments by the fitting proverb "Idleness is the mother of all mischief":

> [...] this universal labor makes the globe a workshop wherein every man, every woman drives his or her own trade in companies or apart, teaches the other law of human nature, virtue. It not only gives man knowledge, and power which is the fruit of knowledge, but it gives man virtue, and love which is the fruit of virtue. The sense of all men expressed in innumerable proverbs brands idleness as the mother of all mischief [...]. (February 2, 1837; Lectures II: 124)

While Emerson does not explicitly point to the "idleness" proverb as such, he usually employs introductory formulas to signal his use of a proverb. This is especially the case in those instances where the erudite and polyglot Emerson cites proverbs from other languages and cultures. In the discussion on the art of reading in his lecture *The American Scholar*, he shows his own scholarly prowess by quoting an Arabic proverb:

> Undoubtedly there is a right way of reading,—so it be sternly subordinated. Man Thinking must not be subdued by his instruments. Books are for the scholar's idle times. When he can read God directly, the hour is too precious to be wasted in other men's transcripts of their readings. But when the intervals of darkness come, as come they must,—when the soul seeth not, when the sun is hid, and the stars withdraw their shine,—we repair to the lamps which were kindled by their ray to guide our steps to the East again, where the dawn is. We hear that we may speak. The Arabian proverb says, "A fig tree looking on a fig tree, becometh fruitful." (August 31, 1837; Collected Works I: 57)

But here are three contextualized passages from Emerson's significant lecture on *Prudence* that show the linguistic and rhetorical ingenuity with which this admirer of proverbs integrated them into his demanding prose. The first two references both include two proverbs in just a few lines:

> Bravery is the best panoply. Touch the nettle and it stings you; grasp it strongly and it hurts not. The Latin proverb says that "in battle the eye is first overcome." The eye is daunted and vastly exaggerates the real perils of the hour. Entire self-possession may make a battle very little more dangerous to life than a game of football. (January 17, 1838; Lectures II: 319–20)

> It is a proverb that Courtesy costs nothing; but more is true than this, that the best calculation would be a hearty love of men. Love is fabled to be blind but kindness is necessary to perception; love is not a hood but an eyewater. (January 17, 1838; Lectures II: 320)

> A worthy neighbor of mine who follows the business of teaming does not average more than Justinian's allowance [of but four hours a night]. And as he informed me it sometimes happens travelling all night that he is so overcome with drowsiness on the road that he cannot proceed. Then he stops his team, turns into a bush at the roadside, and sleeps for five minutes. This satisfies him and he goes on as wakeful as after a night's sleep. There is a fine old French proverb, God works in moments—
> En peu d'heure
> Dieu labeure—
> which is true also of the instinctive parts of our constitution. (January 17, 1838; Lectures II: 323)

It is truly amazing how Emerson recalls a rather prosaic account of a neighbor's sleeping habits, only to comment on it with a French proverb, and then taking all of this into the general realm of human behavior. Emerson the transcendentalist is at work here, going from the mundane to the sublime, as it were.

This can also be seen in one of the paragraphs that Emerson added to this lecture on *Prudence* when he published it as a considerably lengthened essay with the same title in 1841. Referring even to "the [proverbial] wisdom of Poor Richard," as Benjamin Franklin had recorded it in his almanacks, Emerson shows the same progression from everyday prudent behavior to a prudence of a higher realm, concluding his comments with the appropriate Bible proverb "As you sow, so shall you reap" (Galatians 6:7):

[. . .] The eye of prudence may never shut. Iron, if kept at the ironmonger's, will rust; beer, if not brewed in the right state of the atmosphere, will sour; timber of ships will rot at sea, or if laid up high and dry, will strain, warp and dry-rot; money, if kept by us, yields no rent and is liable to loss; if invested, is liable to depreciation of the particular kind of stock. Strike, says the smith, the iron is white; keep the rake, says the haymaker, as nigh the scythe as you can, and the cart as nigh the rake. [. . .] Let him [man] learn a prudence of a higher strain. Let him learn that every thing in nature, even motes and feathers, go by law and not by luck, and that what he sows he reaps. [. . .] Let him practice the minor virtues. (1841; Complete Works II: 234–35)

Even though he merely alludes to the proverb "Strike while the iron is hot," readers will certainly have understood the proverbial message. And seeing an agricultural economy around them, they would also have recognized the somewhat expanded variant of the proverb "Keep the rake near the scythe, and the cart near the rake."

Always the moralist, Emerson in his famous lecture on *Ethics* (1837) called for a detailed treatise "to unfold a part of philosophy very little treated in formal systems, and only treated in the proverbs of all nations, [. . .] which for want of a more exact title may stand under the title of Ethics" (February 16, 1837; Lectures II: 144). Using the classical proverbial expression "To call a spade a spade" that in more recent times has turned into a proverbial stereotype against African Americans (Mieder 2002), he calls for a comprehensive analysis of social norms in his lecture on *The Present Age*: "We call a spade a spade. We have great contempt for the superstitions and nonsense which blinded the eyes of all foregoing generations" (February 23, 1837; Lectures II: 169). And in his essay on *Montaigne; or, the Skeptic* (1850), Emerson once again called for a solid grasp of reality, changing the traditional proverb "A bird in the hand is worth two in the bush" slightly to point directly to worldly matters: "Let us have a robust, manly life; let us know what we know, for certain; what we have, let it be solid and seasonable and our own. A world in the hand is worth two in the bush. Let us have to do with real men and women, and not with skipping ghosts" (1850; Complete Works IV: 159).

But while Emerson the pragmatist is quite willing to look realistically at the prosaic world of technology and science, he emphasizes in a lecture provocatively entitled *Humanity and Science* that science must be linked to the philosophical and ethical realm: "As the proverb says, 'he counts without his host who leaves God out of his reckoning,' so science is bankrupt which attempts to cut the knot which always spirit must untie" (December 22, 1836;

Lectures II: 30). It is of importance to note that Emerson has expanded the folk proverb "He that reckons without his host must reckon again" to include the spiritual world of God. And in a lecture on *Religion*, Emerson simply cites the English translation of a Spanish proverb to point to the omnipresence of God in this world: "A wise old proverb says, 'God comes to see us without [a] bell': that is, as there is no screen or ceiling between our heads and the infinite heavens, so is there no bar or wall in the Soul, where man the effect ceases, and God the cause begins" (January 19, 1837; Lectures II: 85). Who would ever have thought that Emerson as a transcendentalist would use a folk proverb to express analogically the idea of a deep interconnectedness of the prosaic and poetic worlds of humankind with a steady progression towards the spiritual realm?

The Poetic World of Proverbs

While Emerson is not considered to be a major poet, it should not be surprising that he also used at least some proverbs to expound on his transcendentalist thoughts in his poems (D'Avanzo 1969). Similar to the uncontextualized citations of proverbs in the journals, Emerson also cites proverbial couplets in his poetry notebooks without any elaboration. For example, he took the translated Spanish proverb "There is no ill thing in Spain but that which can speak," varied it slightly, and added a variant of the English proverb "It's the wheel that squeaks that gets the oil" to it to create a proverbial couplet:

> There is no evil but can speak,
> If the wheel want oil t'will creak.
> (ca. 1839; Poetry: 47)

Another proverbial two-liner works quite similarly, contrasting two proverbs as it were:

> He who has a thousand friends has not a friend to spare,
> And he who has one enemy will meet him everywhere.
> (c. 1855; Poetry: 464)

He also played with the two contradictory sixteenth-century proverbs "Right makes might" and "Might makes right" by combining them into one sentence that expresses the duality of life (see Burke 1941), where, as Emerson had stated (see above), everything comes in doubles: "Men believe in right of might but also in the might of right" (ca. 1857–68; Poetry 528).

There is also an epigrammatic verse that begins with an old English proverb not much in use anymore today:

> Love creeps where else it cannot go
> And eats its way thro Alps of wo[e]
> Where way is none twill creep & wind
> And eat thro Alps its home to find.
>
> (ca. 1841; Poetry: 265)

This is not a particularly lyrical text, but it changes the idea of love conquering everything between two lovers to include love of the world. Emerson always returns to a reality check, i.e., he vacillates between the prosaic (secular) and the poetic (spiritual) realms. A short poem with a Latin proverb as a title shows the realistic world:

> *Suum cuique.*
> The rain has spoiled the farmer's day;
> Shall sorrow put my books away?
> Thereby are two days lost.
> Nature shall mind her own affairs,
> I will attend my proper cares,
> In rain, or sun, or frost.
>
> (1834; Poetry: 18)

The last stanza of the poem "To J.W." (i.e., Rev. John Weiss) also begins with a proverb; but here Emerson moves from everyday tribulations on to an envisioned transcendence:

> Life is too short to waste
> In critic peep or cynic bark,
> Quarrel or reprimand:
> 'Twill soon be dark;
> Up! mind thine own aim, and
> God speed the mark!
>
> (ca. 1842; Poems: 44)

Thus life is indeed based on the law of balance and compensation, and this "wisdom" is, according to Emerson's repeated observations, contained in the many proverbs of the world. In the right context, proverbs represent bits of folk wisdom on humankind's path towards progressive transcendentalism. All of this is well expressed in four lines of Emerson's "classical" poem "The Divine & The Celestial Love" that can serve as a summary of his transcendental philosophy and the significance of proverbs in the progressive way of things:

> Pan's Paths are wonderful,
> Who seeks to be wise shall not be.
> Subtle his counsel
> Wisdom needs circumstance
> Many concomitants.
>
> (ca. 1845; Poetry: 200)

Indeed, proverbs do need contexts and are applicable in a multitude of ways. Ralph Waldo Emerson's reflections on and uses of proverbs are ample proof that they fit into all types of literature. When it comes to the varied employment of proverbs in literary works, the proverb "The sky is the limit" tells it all.

BIBLIOGRAPHY

This chapter first appeared as "Proverbs in the Works of Ralph Waldo Emerson." *Phraseology: An International Handbook of Contemporary Research*. Harald Burger, Dmitrij Dobrovol'skij, Peter Kühn, and Neal R. Norrick, eds. 2 vols. Berlin: Walter de Gruyter, 2007. I, 337–48.

PRIMARY SOURCES

Collected Works: Ferguson, Alfred R., and Joseph Slater, eds. 1971–94. *The Collected Works of Ralph Waldo Emerson*. 5 vols. Cambridge, Massachusetts: Harvard University Press.

Complete Works: Emerson, Edward Waldo, ed. 1903. *The Complete Works of Ralph Waldo Emerson*. 8 vols. Boston, Massachusetts: Houghton, Mifflin.

Emerson Speaks: McGiffert, Arthur C., ed. 1968. *Young Emerson Speaks: Unpublished Discourses on Many Subjects by Ralph Waldo Emerson*. Port Washington, New York: Kennikat.

Journals: Gilman, William H., and Ralph H. Orth, eds. 1960–82. *The Journals and Miscellaneous Notebooks of Ralph Waldo Emerson*. 16 vols. Cambridge, Massachusetts: Harvard University Press.

Letters: Rusk, Ralph L., ed. 1939. *The Letters of Ralph Waldo Emerson*. 6 vols. New York: Columbia University Press.

Poems: Emerson, Ralph Waldo. 1869. *Poems*. Boston, Massachusetts: Fields, Osgood.

Poetry: Orth, Ralph H., ed. 1986. *The Poetry Notebooks of Ralph Waldo Emerson*. Columbia, Missouri: University of Missouri Press.

SECONDARY LITERATURE

Abrahams, Roger, and Barbara Babcock. 1977. "The Literary Use of Proverbs." *Journal of American Folklore* 90: 414–29; also in Mieder 1994, 415–37.

Anderson, John Q. 1953. "Emerson and the Language of the Folk." *Folk Travelers: Ballads, Tales, and Talk*. Mody C. Boatright, Wilson M. Hudson, and Allen Maxwell, eds. Dallas, Texas: Southern Methodist University Press. 152–59.

Arora, Shirley L. 1984. "The Perception of Proverbiality." *Proverbium* 1: 1–38; also in Mieder 1994, 3–29.

Barbour, Frances M. 1974. *A Concordance to the Sayings in Franklin's "Poor Richard."* Detroit, Michigan: Gale Research.

Burke, Kenneth. 1941. "Literature [i.e., proverbs] as Equipment for Living." In Kenneth Burke, *The Philosophy of Literary Form: Studies in Symbolic Action*. Baton Rouge, Louisiana: Louisiana University Press. 253–62.

Cameron, Kenneth W. 1957. "Emerson, Thoreau, *Elegant Extracts*, and Proverb Lore." *Emerson Society Quarterly* 6: 28–39.

——. 1958. "Emerson's Arabian Proverbs." *Emerson Society Quarterly* 13: 50.

D'Avanzo, Mario L. 1969. "Emerson's 'Days' and Proverbs." *American Transcendental Quarterly* 1: 83–85.

Grzybek, Peter. 1987. "Foundations of Semiotic Proverb Study." *Proverbium* 4: 398S.

——. 1991. "Das Sprichwort im literarischen Text." *Sprichwörter und Redensarten im interkulturellen Vergleich*. Annette Sabban and Jan Wirrer, eds. Opladen: Westdeutscher Verlag. 187–205.

La Rosa, Ralph C. 1969. *Emerson's Proverbial Rhetoric: 1818–1838*. Diss., University of Wisconsin.

——. 1970. "Emerson's 'Sententiae' in *Nature*." *Emerson Society Quarterly* 58: 153–57.

——. 1972. "Invention and Imitation in Emerson's Early Lectures." *American Literature* 44: 13–30.

——. 1976. "Necessary Truths: The Poetics of Emerson's Proverbs." *Mid-nineteenth Century Writers: Eliot, De Quincey, Emerson*. Eric Rothstein and Joseph A. Wittreich, eds. Madison, Wisconsin: University of Wisconsin Press. 129–92, 210–16 (notes).

Loomis, C. Grant. 1957. "Henry David Thoreau as Folklorist." *Western Folklore* 16: 90–106.

——. 1958. "Emerson's Proverbs." *Western Folklore* 17: 257–62.

Mieder, Wolfgang. 1974a. "The Essence of Literary Proverb Studies." *Proverbium* 23: 888–94.

——. 1974b. "The Proverb and Anglo-American Literature." *Southern Folklore Quarterly* 38: 49–62.

——. 1989a. "Benjamin Franklin's 'Proverbs.'" In Wolfgang Mieder, *American Proverbs: A Study of Texts and Contexts*. Bern: Peter Lang. 129–42.

——. 1989b. "Proverbs in Prose Literature [Ralph Waldo Emerson]." In Wolfgang Mieder, *American Proverbs: A Study of Texts and Contexts*. Bern: Peter Lang. 143–69.

——. 1993. "'The Apple Doesn't Fall Far From the Tree': History of a German Proverb in the Anglo-American World." *Midwestern Folklore* 19: 69–98; also in Mieder 2000, 109–44.

——, ed. 1994. *Wise Words: Essays on the Proverb*. New York: Garland.

——. 2000. *Strategies of Wisdom: Anglo-American and German Proverb Studies*. Baltmannsweiler: Schneider Verlag Hohengehren.

——. 2002. *"Call a Spade a Spade": From Classical Phrase to Racial Slur*. New York: Peter Lang.

Mieder, Wolfgang, and George B. Bryan. 1996. *Proverbs in World Literature: A Bibliography*. New York: Peter Lang.

Mieder, Wolfgang, Stewart A. Kingsbury, and Kelsie B. Harder, eds. 1992. *A Dictionary of American Proverbs*. New York: Oxford University Press.

Moldenhauer, Joseph J. 1967. "The Rhetorical Function of Proverbs in *Walden*." *Journal of American Folklore* 80: 151–59.

Newcomb, Robert. 1957. *The Sources of Benjamin Franklin's Sayings of Poor Richard.* Diss., University of Maryland.

Norrick, Neal R. 1985. *How Proverbs Mean: Semantic Studies in English Proverbs.* Amsterdam: Mouton.

Reaver, J. Russell. 1963. "Emerson's Use of Proverbs." *Southern Folklore Quarterly* 28: 280–99.

———. 1967. "Thoreau's Ways with Proverbs." *American Transcendental Quarterly* 1: 2–7.

Taylor, Archer. 1931. *The Proverb.* Cambridge, Massachusetts: Harvard University Press. Rpt. as *The Proverb and An Index to The Proverb.* Hatboro, Pennsylvania: Folklore Associates, 1962. Rpt. again with an introduction and bibliography by Wolfgang Mieder. Bern: Peter Lang, 1985.

Taylor, Archer, and Bartell Jere Whiting. 1958. *A Dictionary of American Proverbs and Proverbial Phrases, 1820–1880.* Cambridge, Massachusetts: Harvard University Press (cites proverbs from Emerson's works).

Templeton, John Marks. 1997. *Worldwide Laws of Life.* Philadelphia, Pennsylvania: Templeton Foundation Press.

Willis, Lonnie Leon. 1966. *Folklore in the Published Writings of Henry David Thoreau: A Study and a Compendium-Index.* Diss., University of Colorado.

9. "PROVERBS AND POETRY ARE LIKE TWO PEAS IN A POD"
The Proverbial Language of Modern Mini-Poems

The study of the use, function, and meaning of proverbs in literature is a well-established sub-field of paremiology with a plethora of publications that range from massive dictionaries of the proverbial language in the collected works of major literary figures, to interpretive monographs, and on to small notes investigating but a few or a single proverbial text in a literary work (see Mieder 2009). A special bibliography for *Proverbs in World Literature* (Mieder and Bryan 1996) lists 2,654 studies, with the majority dealing with the appearance of proverbs, proverbial expressions, proverbial comparisons, twin formulas, wellerisms, and other types of phraseologisms in novels and dramas.

There is at least some scholarship on the utilization of proverbial language in poems and songs, but, as holds true for the entire phenomenon of proverbs in literature, most investigations have concentrated on the literary works of the Middle Ages and later centuries, with much less attention being paid to the occurrence of proverbial metaphors in modern literature (see Sackett 1964; Mieder 1974a; Airmet 1985; Lakoff and Turner 1989).

Proverbs in Lyric Poetry

This is not the place to review the entire field of proverbs in lyric poetry and songs throughout the world. But regarding the Anglo-American scene, it can actually be stated that considerable progress has been made in this fascinating area (Mieder 1974b). A short note on "Some Paremiological Verses" (1975) was published by Charles C. Doyle in the old *Proverbium*, thereby drawing the attention of the international community of paremiologists to the appearance of proverbial language in lyrics. There is also the seminal paper on "The Literary Use of Proverbs" (1977) by Roger D. Abrahams and Barbara Babcock, which includes sections on the proverbial epigrams of John Heywood (1497–1580) and the ever popular lyrics of Sir William

Gilbert (1836–1911) and Sir Albert Sullivan (1842–1900), for whose songs a complete list of proverbial references has been put together (Bryan 1999). Early in my own paremiological career, a few years before the just-mentioned papers, I became interested in proverbs and poetry, and my very first publication in English was in fact a study entitled "'Behold the Proverbs of a People': A Florilegium of Proverbs in Carl Sandburg's Poem *Good Morning, America*" (1971; see also Mieder 1973). My friend George B. Bryan and I subsequently published an entire index of the proverbial folk speech in Carl Sandburg's (1878–1967) poetic works (Bryan and Mieder 2003). But to prove the point that there exists a tradition of Anglo-American poetry, I published two articles in 1980 that surveyed this type of poems by such British, Canadian, and American poets as John Heywood, (1497–1580), Nicolas Breton (1545–1626), John Gay (1685–1732), Samuel Taylor Coleridge (1772–1834), Eliza Cook (1818–1889), Alice Cary (1820–1871), Arthur Guiterman (1871–1943), Ambrose Bierce (1842–1914), Robert Frost (1874–1963), W. H. Auden (1907–1973), Vincent Godfrey Burns (1893–1979), Robert Colombo (1936–), and others (Mieder 1980a, 1980b; see also Mieder 1989a, 2004b). Some years later I also looked at "Proverbs in American Popular Songs" (1988), including anonymous folksongs and songs by Lee Brown (1893–1958), Pearl Bailey (1918–1990), the Beatles (John Lennon [1940–1980], Paul McCartney [1942–], George Harrison [1943–2001], and Ringo Starr [1940–]), Bob Dylan (1941–), Elvis Presley (1935–1977), Cher (born Cherilyn Sarkisian, 1946–), and others (Mieder 1988; see also Mieder 1989b, 2004b). But there is considerably more scholarship on this, with my former student Steven Folsom having looked at "Proverbs in Recent American Country Music" (1993), Michael Taft providing an analysis of "Proverbs in the Blues" (1994), and my German student Florian Gutmann having investigated the proverbial language of Johnny Cash (1932–2003). And finally, there is also the magisterial study by Sw. Anand Prahlad, *Reggae Wisdom: Proverbs in Jamaican Music* (2001; see Cooper 1984).

Returning to poetry as such, Janet Sobieski and I have put together the only extant anthology of proverb poems and some songs under the title of *"So Many Heads, So Many Wits": An Anthology of English Proverb Poetry* (2005), which includes 200 texts by 174 authors, among them those already mentioned but also John Lydgate (1370–1451), Michael Drayton (1563–1631), John Mennes (1599–1671), William Blake (1757–1827), Emily Dickinson (1830–1886), Ralph Waldo Emerson (1803–1882), John Godfrey Saxe (1816–1887), William Makepeace Thackeray (1811–1863), Julia Alvarez (1950–), David Budbill (1940–), Branch Cabell (1879–1958), David Citino (1947–), Sheena

Easton (1959–), Robert Eberhart (1904–2005), Robert Frost (1875–1963), Arthur Gillespie (1868–1914), Lisel Mueller (1924–), Paul Muldoon (1951–), Susan Fromberg Schaefer (1941–), David R. Slavitt (1935–), Raymond Souster (1921–), Miriam Waddington (1917–2004), Franz Wright (1953–), and others (Mieder and Sobieski 2005).

We chose as the book title the first line of a proverbial couplet by John Heywood, since it summarizes the diversity of literary minds represented in the anthology with poems written in the many "Englishes" of the world, including texts from Australia, Canada, Great Britain, and the United States:

Of Wits (ca. 1560)
    So many heads, so many wits: nay, nay!
    We see many heads and no wits, some day.
    (Sobieski and Mieder 2005: 11)

The actual couplet also sets the tone for many of the poems and songs included in this book. Whether the proverbs and proverbial expressions appear in the titles, are used as leitmotifs, are amassed into proverbial collages, are changed into anti-proverbs, or are cited as mere allusions, the proverbial language adds much metaphorical expressiveness to these texts that are also filled with humor, irony, and satire. The anthology is based on my forty years of collecting proverbial poetry in English (also in German and other languages), and my International Proverb Archives at the University of Vermont hold several hundred additional poems and songs that await analysis.

Having dealt in my work mostly with English and German texts, it should not be surprising that I have also put together several German anthologies of proverb poems and songs that show how widespread this type of poetry is in cultures other than English (Mieder 1990, 1992, 2001, 2004a). In addition, however, I also had the opportunity a few years ago to take a closer look at the smallest or shortest of these poems with an emphasis on modern poetry (Mieder 2006). I referred to them in German as "Mini-Lyrik," and I see no reason why this term might not be equally appropriate for the following "little" poems (ten lines or less) that in English might best be called "mini-poems." The ensuing discussion will survey the well-established tradition of these texts from the sixteenth through the nineteenth centuries, but the majority of the examples will come from the twentieth and twenty-first centuries, showing once and for all that proverbial mini-poems are very much part of the modern poetic scene in the English language.

Epigrammatic Proverb Poems from the Sixteenth to Nineteenth Centuries

Beginning with the first half of the sixteenth century, it was Sir Thomas Wyatt (1503–1542) who integrated plenty of proverbial materials into his poetry before John Heywood (see Mauch 1963; Daalder 1986; Ross 1987; Crane 1986, 1993; Ward 2000). In one of his epigrammatic poems, he employed the archaic proverbial expression "to claw one by the back" in the meaning of "to falsely flatter someone", using it in fact in the form of a cautionary proverb (Tilley 1950: 26) that adds a colloquial flavor to the didactic message of his short poem:

> Right true it is, and said full yore ago:
> 'Take heed of him that by thy back thee claweth,'
> For none is worse than is a friendly foe.
> Though they seem good, all things that thee delighteth,
> Yet know it well, that in thy bosom creepeth:
> For many a man such fire oft kindleth,
> That with the blaze his beard singeth.
>
> (Wyatt 1975: 41)

John Heywood, the true master of dozens of such short proverbial epigrams in his *Epigrams upon Proverbs* (1556/62), at times alludes to the proverb that he wishes to discuss in a title, quoting the proverb in its precise wording within the poem (Manley 1985; Crane 1986, 1993). In the following text, he has a bit of punning fun with the proverb while also teasingly poking fun at a drinking buddy:

> *Praise of a Man above a Horse* (ca. 1560)
>   A man may well lead a horse to the water
>   But he cannot make him drink, without he list.
>   I praise thee above the horse, in this matter;
>   For I, leading thee to drink, thou hast not missed
>   Always to be ready, without resistance,
>   Both to drink, and be drunk, ere thou were led thence.
>
> (Sobieski and Mieder 2005: 11)

While this poem proves a particular proverb true, there are also epigrams that argue against the implied truth claim of proverbs. John Davies (1565–1618) does this in his *Scourge of Folly* (1611) in one of his 418 epigrams by picking on a proverb that had already been questioned by John Heywood several decades before him (Manley 1985):

> "So many heads, so many witts:" Fy, fy:
> It is a shame for proverbs so to lye;
> For I (though mine acquaintance be but small)
> Know many heads that haue no witt at all.
> (Davies 1878: II, 44)

Such "fun" with proverbs continued well into the seventeenth century, as can be seen from a multitude of epigrams by various authors, mostly attributed, in the very popular (and ever-expanding) anthology *Wit's Recreations* (1640 et seq.), possibly compiled by John Mennes, with the title clearly indicating that the witty little poems are written for recreation (fun) but that they are in part also re-created (changed). Some of these playful texts take on a rather misogynistic tone, but it should be stated that humor or satire is also directed at the male gender:

> *A Disparity*
> Children fondly blab truth,
> and fools their brothers;
> Women have learn'd more wisdome
> of their mothers.
> (Robert Hayman [1628], cited from Mennes 1874: II, 109)

> *On Marriage*
> Wedding and hanging the Destinies dispatch,
> But hanging seems to some the better match.
> (author unknown [seventeenth century], cited from Mennes 1874: II, 134)

It should be noted that the proverbs "Children and fools tell the truth" and "Hanging and wedding (wiving) go by destiny" are only quoted in part or altered for the sake of rhyme, but the readers catch the satirical drift, as it were. For the modern readers, the epigrammatic poems by the authors mentioned here but also by others like John Skelton (1460–1529), Edmund Spenser (1552–1599), John Donne (1572–1631), Ben Jonson (1572–1637), Henry

Peacham (1576–1643), and Robert Herrick (1591–1674) still have much to offer regarding basic insights into human behavior and social mores, and for the literary paremiologists there remains much work to be done (see Mauch 1963; Pitts 1966; Welsh 1978; Manley 1985; Crane 1986; Doyle 2007).

The eighteenth century continued the practice of composing proverbial couplets and quatrains, with John Gay composing an entire "New Song of New Similes" (ca. 1715) of twenty stanzas amorously addressed by a lover to his beloved, of which the eighteenth verse might serve as an example here:

> Till you grow tender as a Chick,
> I'm dull as any Post;
> Let us, like Burs, together stick,
> And warm as any Toast.
> (Sobieski and Mieder 2005: 28)

As will be shown, modern poets also enjoy writing poems based on such proverbial comparisons, but for now here is an all-too-true reaction by John Gay to the proverb "Life is a jest":

> *My Own Epitaph* (after 1720)
>   Life is a jest; and all things show it:
>   I thought so once; but now I know it.
>   (Smith 1957: 236)

Later in that century, there is a poem by William Blake, who is well known to literary paremiologists for his infamous lengthy free-verse poem *Proverbs of Hell* (1790), made up of a string of anti-proverbs and his own proverb-like creations (see Sobieski and Mieder 2005: 21–23; see also Lansverk 1994; Villalobos 1990). In his short poem he expands the old proverb "Love is blind" in order to consider the difference between love and deceit:

> [*How to know Love from Deceit*] (ca. 1780)
>   Love to faults is always blind
>   Always is to joy inclind
>   Lawless wingd & unconfind
>   And breaks all chains from every mind
>
>   Deceit to secresy confind
>   Lawful cautious & refind

To every thing but interest blind
And forges fetters for the mind
(Blake 1982: 472)

About three decades later, Samuel Taylor Coleridge as a romantic poet presents a much more positive view of the proverb "Love is blind," arguing that with a true feeling heart the visual manifestation of physical attraction is not necessary. While the proverb is commonly employed to refer to a relationship that perhaps needs a reality check, Coleridge is quite capable of putting a positive twist on the old wisdom by changing it into an imperative for love itself:

Reason for Love's Blindness (1811)
I have heard of reasons manifold
Why Love must needs be blind,
But this the best of all I hold—
His eyes are in his hand.

What outward form and feature are
He guesseth but in part;
But that within is good and fair
He seeth with the heart.
(Sobieski and Mieder 2005: 45)

But since, proverbially speaking, all good things come in three, here is yet a third "love" poem, this time playing off the proverb "Love creeps where it cannot go." It is an epigram by the transcendentalist Ralph Waldo Emerson from circa 1841 that lacks any special lyrical value (Reaver 1967; La Rosa 1969; Mieder 2007). However, Emerson expands the idea of love conquering everything that may hinder lovers from getting together to include love of the world:

Love creeps where else it cannot go
And eats its way thro Alps of wo
Where way is none twill creep & wind
And eat thro Alps its home to find.
(Emerson 1986: 265)

The following two anonymous epigrams from around the middle of the nineteenth century seem a bit mundane perhaps, but they are clear indications that poets of every ilk do enjoy creating anti-proverbs in verse or making short poems out of contrasting proverb pairs.

> *A Maxim Revisited* (nineteenth century)
> Ladies, to this advice give heed—
> In controlling men:
> If at first you don't succeed,
> Why, cry, cry again.
> (Sobieski and Mieder 2005: 32)

> *& Vice Versa* (nineteenth century)
> If you're inclined
> to think that "Out of sight is out of mind"
> I recommend you ponder
> "Absence makes the heart grow fonder."
> (Sobieski and Mieder 2005: 38)

Perhaps the best short proverb poem in my large collection that belongs to the pre-modern era is Emily Dickinson's poetic deliberation on the vexing nature of the proverb "A bird in the hand is worth two in the bush," which, once it is intellectually analyzed, proves to be a metaphorical statement dealing with the complexity of having to make choices:

> [*Which is best?*] (1865)
> Which is best? Heaven—
> Or only Heaven to come
> With that old Codicil of Doubt?
> I cannot help esteem
>
> The "Bird within the Hand"
> Superior to the one
> The "Bush" may yield me
> Or may not
> Too late to choose again.
> (Sobieski and Mieder 2005: 52)

Interestingly enough, Dickinson actually reduces the proverbial "two birds in the bush" to but one, making the choice almost even between the bird in the hand and the other choice. And yet, the poet sticks to the underlying meaning of the proverb when she too opts for the certainty of the bird already in her hand. She rejects uncertainty but—and this appears to be the major point of the poem—is perfectly happy with the bird she has. Heaven is right here on earth, or the world of reality is better than any heavenly dreams (Barnes 1979). She and Ralph Waldo Emerson appear to be in agreement that proverbs can indeed help us cope with reality.

But be that as it may, the reactions to proverbs, their meanings being very much dependent on particular contexts, will continue to be ambivalent, and this will become perfectly obvious in the following florilegium of modern mini-poems. In all of their conciseness they will exemplify the polyfunctionality, polysituativity, and polysemanticity of proverbs (see Mieder 2004b: 9). In order to give some order to the revealing examples, they will be presented in five groups: 1. poems with proverb titles; 2. poems with unchanged proverbs; 3. poems containing personalized proverbs; 4. poems with proverb allusions; and 5. poems with proverbs changed into anti-proverbs. As in the examples of poems from earlier centuries, there will be some here as well that in addition to using proverbs also include proverbial expressions or proverbial comparisons.

1. Poems with Proverb Titles

Modern poems that carry a proverb or proverbial expression as their title usually also contain the text at the beginning or within as a clear message. This is certainly the case with Raymond Souster's (1921–) poem about the proverb "Money talks" in which he tries to negate the alleged social power of money. Souster employs the introductory formula "so they say" together with the proverb in order to stress the common notion that money is all-powerful when it actually does very little to improve the human lot:

> *Money Talks* (ca. 1960)
>   Money talks
>   so they say;
>
>   [...]
>   but more often than not
>   when it's finally finished,

it really hasn't said
anything at all.
(Sobieski and Mieder 2005: 212)

Souster also takes a pessimistic view of the modern proverbs "Don't (Never) look back; something (someone, they) might be gaining on you" which often occurs in its truncated form of "Never look back." In this poem he deals with old school days that cannot be brought back, reminding his readers (by also alluding to the nursery rhyme "Humpty Dumpty") that such memories of times gone by might lead to a state of depression about the way life has sneaked by and changed everything:

Never Look Back (1975)
Never look back—the danger's
always lurking.

Something or someone
wants me to end like Humpty,
swaying first, then sliding off, to fall
so finally, shatteringly down!
(Sobieski and Mieder 2005: 213)

But there is also Robert Flanagan's (1946–) poem based on the proverb "Do or die," encouraging modern humankind to carry on against all odds. Here the succinct proverb, somewhat reminiscent of the modern scatological wisdom "Shit or get off the pot," tells the reader that life must go on, and the best thing to do is to plow ahead by accepting one's fate:

Do or Die (2000)
Do or die.

[. . .]

Against informal dirt
sky washes chair, table, floor.

Do what you can do.
Nod before heavenly freeze frame.
(Sobieski and Mieder 2005: 250)

Glen Sorestad (1937–) expresses similar thoughts in his poem that is based on the proverbial expression "to turn over a new leaf." He too feels that life is full of chances, and rather than taking the negative view, it might be well to give life and its multifaceted challenges another try. Above all, the speaker in the poem offers another person (or the reader) a helping hand, offering a new leaf of life as encouragement, as it were (reinterpreting the *leaf* in the proverb—a pair of pages in a book—as the green appendage on a tree):

> *Turning a New Leaf* (1998)
>   Would you see this leaf I hold
>   as green, pale as the first flush
>
>   of spring? Or would you say again
>   that this is death I hand you
>
>   [...]
>
>   May I offer you this leaf again?
> (Sobieski and Mieder 2005: 211)

The proverbial symbolism of this poem is clear: the time of spring signifies the opportunity of a new beginning, another chance at the mysteries of life if one is willing to turn over a new leaf!

2. Poems with Unchanged Proverbs

It is interesting to note that quite a few of the mini-poems concern themselves with the anxieties of modern life. Here, for example, is a poem by Linda Stitt (1932–) that is a positive reaction to life on her sixty-third birthday. Obviously in her case it has been a rather positive journey, since she wholeheartedly agrees with the saying "Life just doesn't get better than this":

> *Ancient Wisdom* (1995)
>   Here's sixty-three years of wisdom revealed
>   In a statement succinct and terse,—
>   Life just doesn't get any better than this.
>   Just be glad if it doesn't get worse.
> (Sobieski and Mieder 2005: 218)

In her poem "Seeds," Javaka Steptoe (1971–) clearly also has had a positive experience, with her father having planted in her the seeds for a successful life. That her mentor in this poem is in fact her father is revealed in the title of her book of poems: *In Daddy's Arms I Am Tall: African Americans Celebrating Fathers* (New York: Lee & Low, 1997). She might have concluded her poem with the altered proverb "Like father, like daughter (son)," but instead she chose the more metaphorical proverb "The apple doesn't fall far from the tree," which originated in Germany and has gained much currency in the English language since the nineteenth century (see Mieder 2000):

Seeds (1997)
    You drew pictures of life
    with your words.

    [...]

    I became the words I ate in you.
    For better or worse
    the apple doesn't fall far from the tree.
    (Sobieski and Mieder 2005: 217)

Another female author, Gladys Nolan (1908–), remembers that parents used to instill the proverbial lesson "Waste not, want not" in children, but in her case this wisdom meant eventually sticking it out with a bad marriage. The message of the poem might well be in part that it is not best to adhere to proverbs just because of their claim to ultimate truths. After all, it is well known that proverbs have their contradictions:

When Love Was Not Free (1972)
    When we were young we were taught
    waste not want not
    so when our marriage failed
    we did the best we could
    with what was left of it.

    [...]

    (Sobieski and Mieder 2005: 177)

And yet, the happiness of home life is beautifully expressed in Robert Creeley's (1926–2005) poem "Coming Home," which has as its ultimate wisdom
the proverb "Home is where the heart is," showing with deep emotion the
warmth of home after a walk with the dogs on a snowy winter's day:

> *Coming Home* (1983)
> Saturday late afternoon
>
> [...]
> coming up the path
> with the dogs barking
>
> *home is where the heart is*
> this small house stays put.
> (Sobieski and Mieder 2005: 99)

Of course, not all proverbial mini-poems are this lyrical and positive, stressing as in this case the simple and calm life in rural Vermont. It would be
difficult even there to escape the hustle and bustle of the mercantile life of
modernity, as can be seen from a poetic epigram by Lola Sneyd (1926–), who
puts a personal twist to the proverb "Money talks":

> *Money Talk* (1984)
> I've heard it said that money talks,
> The very thought intrigues me,
> Mine never stops to have a chat
> So hastily it leaves me.
> (Sobieski and Mieder 2005: 210)

And there is also a small quatrain by Shel Silverstein (1932–1999) with its
questioning title "Fish?" The last line with its question transposes the animal proverb "Big fish eat little fish" onto the human world, where greed and
rapacity are just as vicious. This "fish" proverb has served as a metaphor for
the animal-like behavior of humankind for centuries, making it one of the
proverbial leitmotifs in sociopolitical history (see Mieder 1987):

> *Fish?* (1974)
> The little fish eats the tiny fish,
> The big fish eats the little fish–

So only the biggest fish get fat.
Do you know any folks like that?
(Sobieski and Mieder 2005: 208)

It is, of course, easier to integrate proverbial expressions other than full proverbs into the verses of poems, since they are not as fixed in their structure as actual proverbs. Some poets are quite skillful in getting deep meanings out of phraseologisms in but three lines, as is the case in Joe Wallace's (1890–1975) mini-poem:

Verse (1956)
  The American way of life:
  You can get away with murder
  If you use a golden knife.
  (Sobieski and Mieder 2005: 234)

Another minimal text by Elaine Equi (1953–), just like the previous poem, uses a proverbial expression to comment on some of the imperfections of modern life with its superficial behavioral tactics:

To Do
  Never finish everything
  on your to do list.

  It will look as if you have nothing
  better to do.
  (Equi 2007: 35)

Even love appears at times to be not at all serious but rather money-driven, as an intriguing mini-poem by Adrian Henri (1932–2000) indicates by way of the British phraseologism "cupboard love" (i.e., self-interested affection; see also the proverb "A cupboard love is seldom true") that is brought into connection with the more positive phrase "love at first sight." The result is a precise condemnation of insincere love based merely on the bank account of someone else:

Across a Crowded Room (ca. 1980)
  as he glimpsed her
  bank-book

it was
cupboard-love
at first sight.
(Henri 1986: 229)

Finally, from many more mini-poems that could be cited for this section, let me quote a *tour de force* quatrain by Richard Armour (1906–1989) in which the poet successfully uses two proverbial comparisons plus the proverbial phrase "to pat someone on the back" to satirize the tough if not aggressive character of another person:

Iron Constitution (1964)
   He's as hard as nails, I have heard it said,
   And also as sharp as a tack.
   I'm tempted to use a hammer when next
   I give him a pat on the back.
   (Sobieski and Mieder 2005: 70)

It should be noted how throughout these poems it is the indirection of the proverbs, proverbial expressions, and proverbial comparisons that makes them, despite their laconic nature, emotive and valuable statements about modern existence. The proverbial metaphors add much expressiveness to these short poetic statements, making them effective commentaries on the human condition with all its frailties and frustrations. And yet, as has been shown, there are at least some mini-poems that look at modern life with the hope that some of the old proverbial wisdom might help deal with everyday occurrences of existence.

3. Poems Containing Personalized Proverbs

It should not be surprising then that some of today's poets have a tendency to personalize old proverbs by surrounding them with personal pronouns. This gives their mini-poems a certain subjective immediacy, showing how traditional wisdom based on the experiences and observations of many previous generations tends at least at times to still carry important messages for the present. This can be seen from a poem by Alan Riddell (1927–1977) who entitles his incredibly short text "Old Adage" and then proceeds to take the traditional proverb "You have to crawl before you can walk" (variant: "Learn to creep before you run"; see Mieder et al. 1992: 125–26) one important step further, namely to that of old age, where people no longer can take care of themselves and must, figuratively or even literally, regress to the unfortunate state of "creeping" or "crawling" again like a child:

Old Adage (ca. 1965)
   crawl before you
   walk before you
   run before you
   creep
   (Sobieski and Mieder 2005: 189)

The following poem by John Betjeman (1906–1984) is perhaps not quite as morbid in thinking about old age with such debilitating diseases as Alzheimer's or Parkinson's. After all, the poet did, proverbially speaking, "Make hay while the sun shines," and as he reflects on his life in his advanced age, he can with some satisfaction state that, as the proverbial title suggests, he might well have a happy last laugh, hoping that his friends will join in by acknowledging his fulfilled life. Usually the proverbial expression "to have the last laugh" is used with irony or even cynicism, but this is not the case in this poem. On the contrary, Betjeman changes the metaphor into a positive statement:

The Last Laugh (1974)
   I made hay while the sun shone.
   […]
   Now, if the harvest is over
   […]
   Give me the bonus of laughter
   As I lose hold.
   (Sobieski and Mieder 2005: 76)

Two poems by Edna St. Vincent Millay (1892–1950) are of special interest. They were written in 1920, the time of the "Roaring Twenties" with excitement and lust for life. The word "fig" in both titles conjures up all kinds of semantic shades. It might simply refer to the fruit, but there are also such proverbial phrases as "to not care (give, worth) a fig," "to feel in fine fig" (i.e., feel splendidly), and also the obscene "to give someone the fig" (to reproach someone in a sexually explicit way) with its attached gesture of sticking the thumb out at someone between the index finger and middle finger while the hand is closed into a fist (see Leite de Vasconcellos 1925; Rettenbeck 1953; Wilkinson 1992: 344). To a certain degree, all of these meanings enter into a possible interpretation of the two mini-poems that contain the proverbial expressions "to burn the candle at both ends" and "to build on sand" as metaphors for going beyond the normal and expected in a fun-loving and risk-taking approach to life:

> *First Fig (1920)*
> My candle burns at both ends;
> It will not last the night;
> But ah, my foes, and oh, my friends—
> It gives a lovely light!

> *Second Fig* (1920)
> Safe upon the solid rock the ugly houses stand:
> Come and see my shining palace built upon the sand!
> (Sobieski and Mieder 2005: 166)

One thing is for certain: the author is a free spirit and tells others to back off with old-fashioned proverbial advice and antiquated morality. She wants to be free, mindful perhaps of the ancient proverb "Suum quique" (To each his own) or the modern American proverb "Different strokes for different folks." Be that as it may, the two poems are meant to be an expression of liberation together with a vigorous claim for a certain joie de vivre.

4. Poems with Proverb Allusions

Although it has repeatedly been claimed by scholars that proverbs in particular are characterized by a rigid fixity in word and structure, this is in fact far from the truth once proverbs are studied in context. Even though they are more often than not cited in their traditional wording and form, they have always also been varied or reduced to mere fragments. Such allusions are perfectly fine when one considers that proverbs by definition are usually well known to speakers. It therefore might suffice to only allude to their wisdom, as long as the underlying proverb is still recognizable. Poets— restricted by rhyme, rhythm, and structure of their poetic creations, and also wanting to express their thoughts in innovative fashion—are therefore keen to experiment with traditional wisdom by reducing them to still (hopefully) recognizable allusions. A good example is the poem "I built myself a house of glass" by Edward Thomas (1849–1924) that with this title as its first line and the verse "No neighbor casts a stone" of the second stanza appears to be alluding to the proverb "People who live in glass houses shouldn't throw stones." The poem seems to carry the message that glass houses, here perhaps a sign of wealth, isolate the dweller to such a degree that there is no communication left by him or people on the outside. Instead everybody, poor (in tenement) or rich (in a palace of glass), exists in absolute isolation, a fitting metaphor for the impersonal nature of modern life:

I built myself a house of glass (ca. 1910)
    I built myself a house of glass:
    It took me years to make it:
    And I was proud. But now, alas!
    Would God someone would break it.

    But it looks too magnificent.
    No neighbour casts a stone
    From where he dwells, in tenement
    Or palace of glass, alone.
    (Sobieski and Mieder 2005: 222)

With the next poem, by Raymond Souster, who, as has been shown above, is quite adapt at this type of proverbial mini-poetry, it takes a considerable amount of imagination or proverbial literacy to realize that it is in fact a statement about the American proverb "Good fences make good neighbors," which stems from the early nineteenth century and gained considerable literary fame when Robert Frost used it as a leitmotif in his famous poem "Mending Wall" (1914; see Sobieski and Mieder 2005: 128–29; Mieder 2005). But there is definitely an allusion to the proverb, once again raising Frost's earlier question of what the actual use of a fence between neighbors might be, and wondering what is being fenced in and what out:

The New Fence (1955)
    Take my next-door neighbor and I,
    waiting eight years to put one up,
    and now that we've actually done it
    wondering why we bothered in the first place.
    (Sobieski and Mieder 2005: 212)

Another proverb quatrain by Silverstein is a bit easier to figure out, since its title of "Early Bird" conjures up the underlying proverb "The early bird catches the worm." It is not a particularly challenging text, with the author seemingly just having a bit of fun with the traditional "bird" proverb:

> *Early Bird* (1974)
> Oh, if you're a bird, be an early bird
> And catch the worm for your breakfast plate.
> If you're a bird, be an early early bird—
> But if you're a worm, sleep late.
> (Sobieski and Mieder 2005: 208)

Things are not quite as simple with a two-line mini-poem by Seymour Mayne (1944–), with its half carnivorous and half poetic title "Cutlet Couplet." It alludes to the modern American proverb "No matter how (thin) you slice (cut) it, it's still baloney" from the late 1920s, but it is not necessarily known by all English speakers, and most likely not by non-native speakers, begging the question of when such allusions go beyond general comprehensibility. Be that as it may, it is nothing more than a bit of linguistic play with a piece of meat instead of a slice of baloney and a relatively new proverb:

> *Cutlet Couplet* (2000)
> Whatever way you bread or spice it,
> What's the difference how you slice it?
> (Sobieski and Mieder 2005: 255)

This kind of verbal game is also played with proverbial expressions in the shortest of mini-poems. The first by Nina Cassian (1924–) plays off the common phrase "to speak with a forked tongue" (i.e., to speak deceitfully). But rather than maintaining its negative connotation, the poet uses it in a positive sense to allude to her bilingualism:

> *Language* (1998)
> My tongue—forked like a snake's
> but without deadly intentions:
> just a bilingual hissing.
> (Sobieski and Mieder 2005: 89)

Adrian Henri, a virtuoso in the formulation of this type of reductionist mini-poem, changed the proverbial expression "to say something tongue in cheek" (i.e., insincerely, jokingly) from its metaphorical meaning to a literal and sexual interpretation by adding a couple of pronouns to the phrase. For readers not acquainted with the metaphor, this poem could simply be a straightforward if somewhat bizarre declaration of love, missing the insincerity of the somatic poem that enters into it because of the traditional meaning of the underlying proverbial phrase:

Love Poem (ca. 1970)
  "I love you" he said
  With his tongue in her cheek
  (Sobieski and Mieder 2005: 142)

As a last example of such mini-poems, this time somewhat in the traditional haiku form, let me cite the poem "Gossip" by Don Raye (1909–1985, actually Donald MacRae Wilhoite). He takes the proverbial expression "to make a mountain out of a molehill," equates the mountain with the social problems of gossip, uses the adjective *lowly* together with the molehill to designate the negative aspects of the beginning of gossip, and then refers to the fuel that is added to the circulating gossip as dirt. The result is a fascinating metaphorical definition or description of how gossip gets started and is spread:

Gossip (1971)
  The mountain is made
  Out of the lowly molehill
  When dirt is added.
  (Sobieski and Mieder 2005: 187)

It is truly amazing to see how much can be done in one single sentence (!) with a traditional proverbial expression by putting but a small twist to it. The general meaning of exaggeration of the metaphorical phrase becomes a definition of sorts of gossip in this case. It helps, of course, that the author has supplied the "gossip" title, otherwise his poem might say nothing more than that a small molehill can be made into a mountain if dirt is added—not much of an insight, after all.

5. Poems with Proverbs Changed into Anti-Proverbs

From what has been shown, it should not be surprising that modern poets also delight in intentionally varying or parodying proverbs and making so-called anti-proverbs out of them. By deliberately changing traditional proverbs, they are able to put a new light on the old folk wisdom and thus offer new insights into the human condition. Such poems often carry the anti-proverb in their titles, with the ensuing poems becoming exemplifications of the new insight. This is certainly the case with Judith Viorst's (1931–) poem "Familiarity Breeds Content," whose innovative title changes the negative meaning of the proverb "Familiarity breeds contempt" by the mere exchange of two letters to a positive description of a marriage that for once has worked out (rather rare in modern poetry!):

> *Familiarity Breeds Content*
> *(Song of the Long-Married Woman)* (1987)
> Although our married life is full of strife, if you
> proposed again I'd grab it.
> And while it's sometimes hard to be your wife, it's also
> quite a lovely habit.
>
> [...]
> (Sobieski and Mieder 2005: 231)

It might be assumed that this married couple, after all the years of living together, would relate well to the anti-proverb "Where There's Smoke, There's Dinner," which Edmund Conti (1935–) formulated by changing the word "fire," which concludes the traditional proverb on which it is based:

> *Where There's Smoke, There's Dinner* (2003)
> Modern day cooking
> Is easy and fun.
> When the smoke alarm
> Goes off, it's done.
> (Sobieski and Mieder 2005: 248)

For whatever it is worth, let me add here that my dear wife Barbara and I have experienced the smoke alarm going off in the kitchen on various occasions in our many decades of a good marriage. Burnt meat and smoke alarms have not been able to keep us from enjoying our daily evening meals together!

Sometimes the poets state in their titles that their mini-poems are in fact exemplifications of proverbial wisdom, but what follows such classificatory designations are in fact anti-proverbs. Among several short poems under the title "Certain Maxims of Archy," Don Marquis (1878–1937) includes the following text that begins with the quotation of a well-known proverb, whose truth is then questioned by adding a contradictory "but" clause to it. This structure of "proverb, but . . ." is a commonly used procedure for creating anti-proverbs, as can be seen from a large collection of such texts (see Litovkina and Mieder 2006). But here is the poem to illustrate all of this:

certain maxims of archy (ca. 1930)
    every cloud
    has its silver
    lining but it is
    sometimes a little
    difficult to get it to
    the mint
    (Sobieski and Mieder 2005: 161)

Jan Struther (1901–1953) also makes quite sure that his readers are aware of the fact that he is altering a proverb by entitling his proverbial quatrain "Variation on an Old Proverb," the original proverb being "Soft words will break no bones." Of course, he may also be alluding to the proverb "Sticks and stones may break my bones, but words can never hurt me." In any case, he changes the words from soft to hard and claims that they still don't cause as much harm as the "fond words" that are never uttered. In other words, kindness will still go a long way in human relations:

Variation on an Old Proverb (1941)
    Hard words will break no bones:
    But more than bones are broken
    By the inescapable stones
    Of fond words left unspoken.
    (Sobieski and Mieder 2005: 219)

Such substitutions of single words are a most effective way of creating anti-proverbs. Souster takes a slightly different yet equally popular approach to changing proverbs into anti-proverbs, namely by citing the first half of the traditional proverb and then adding a new conclusion to it. Within two years of each other he took the twentieth-century proverb "Old soldiers never die, they just fade away" (going back to a song from World War I) and added new and revealing endings to it. I might point out here that Anna T. Litovkina and I entitled our compilation of such texts *Old Proverbs Never Die, They Just Diversify: A Collection of Anti-Proverbs* (2006), in part because we had collected dozens of examples based on this "soldier" proverb (Litovkina and Mieder 2006: 244–48). At the time of completing our collection we failed to include the following two mini-poems by Souster, both of them unique in their wording. It is astonishing how many mutations one can create on the second part of a well-known proverb without repeating previous alterations:

> *Old Soldiers* (1977)
> Old soldiers never die—
> they live on to send their sons off
> to other wars.
> (Sobieski and Mieder 2005: 214)

> *Old Soldiers Never Die (2)* (1979)
> Old soldiers never die,
> never, that is,
> as long as their livers
> can float them home
> from Legion halls.
> (Sobieski and Mieder 2005: 214)

The sad part in these poetic anti-proverbs is that Souster has no humorous intent in mind with them, showing that the play with traditional proverbs can take on rather serious meanings, as sending young people off to war or veterans falling prey to alcoholism after the return from war.

Of course, anti-proverbs can also be considerably more "twisted," as can be seen from one more mini-poem of merely three lines by Mark Strand (1934–). It is based on that paradoxical Bible proverb "It is easier for a camel to go through the eye of a needle, than for a rich man to enter into the kingdom of God" (Matthew 19:24) and is the first in a series of "Some Last Words" (1998):

> It is easier for a needle to pass through a camel
> Than for a poor man to enter a woman of means.
> Just go to the graveyard and ask around.
> (Strand 1998: 30)

But to end this florilegium of proverbial mini-poems on a subjective note, let me state that for me personally the proverbial glass is always half full and not half empty. I thoroughly believe in the principle or audacity of hope. So let me cite one more two-line poem by Philip Hobsbaum (1932–) with its hopeful title of "The Pursuit of Happiness." The poem is based on the proverbial expression "to turn back the clock" that at times is also cited as the proverb "You can't put (turn) back the clock." The meaning usually is that we cannot or should not go backwards, but that is not to say that the wisdom of the proverb at times cannot be false and need to be adjusted to a particular situation. Especially in human relations, there might be hope to rectify the past by adhering to such proverbs as "Where there is a will, there is a way" or "Hope springs eternal." That is what this last mini-poem appears to be saying:

> *The Pursuit of Happiness* (1969)
>   "You can't put back the clock"—and your commands
>   Are sacred. But, dear, clocks, like us, have hands.
>   (Sobieski and Mieder 2005: 144)

Even in the modern age of stressful and hectic lifestyles, we might not always be controlled by the clock, and with a bit of luck, time might still heal most wounds and give us the proverbial chance to pursue life, liberty, and happiness. Proverbs or anti-proverbs might help us in this worthy pursuit, negating Idries Shah's (1924–1996) absurd claim in one of his aphoristic reflections: "Few things are more absurd than wise saws originally designed to inculcate or maintain the social needs of a society long past—when they are applied to today" (Shah 1971: 123). Life is never that simple nor that black or white, and proverbs as "monumenta humana" (Kuusi 1957: 52) will surely continue to play an effective role in human communication around the world. Proverbs are as imperfect as life itself, but as these mini-poems by numerous literary authors have shown, they continue to be effective metaphors for describing the human condition in the modern age.

BIBLIOGRAPHY

This chapter was first published with the same title in *Proceedings of the Third Interdisciplinary Collo-quium on Proverbs, 8th to 15th November 2009, at Tavira, Portugal*. Rui J. B. Soares and Outi Lauhakangas, eds. Tavira, Portugal: Tipografia Tavirense, 2010. 263–89.

Abrahams, Roger D., and Barbara A. Babcock. 1977. "The Literary Use of Proverbs." *Journal of American Folklore* 90: 414–29. Also in *Wise Words: Essays on the Proverb*. Wolfgang Mieder, ed. New York: Garland, 1994. 415–37.

Airmet, Douglas Elliot. 1985. *The Saying: Snatches for a Poetic.* Diss., University of Iowa.

Barnes, Daniel R. 1979. "Telling It Slant: Emily Dickinson and the Proverb." *Genre* 12: 219–41. Also in *Wise Words: Essays on the Proverb.* Wolfgang Mieder, ed. New York: Garland, 1994. 439–65.

Blake, William. 1982. *The Complete Poetry and Prose.* David V. Erdman, ed. Garden City, New York: Anchor.

Bryan, George B. 1999. "The Proverbial W. S. Gilbert: An Index to Proverbs in the Works of Gilbert and Sullivan." *Proverbium* 16: 21–35.

Bryan, George B., and Wolfgang Mieder. 2003. "The Proverbial Carl Sandburg (1878–1967): An Index of Folk Speech in his American Poetry." *Proverbium* 20: 15–49.

Cooper, Carolyn. 1984. "Proverb as Metaphor in the Poetry of Louise Bennett." *Jamaica Journal* 17, no. 2: 21–24.

Crane, Mary Thomas. 1986. *Proverbial and Aphoristic Sayings: Sources of Authority in the English Renaissance.* Diss., Harvard University.

———. 1993. "'In a Net to Hold the Wind': Gathering, Framing, and Lyric Subjectivity, 1520–1540 [esp. Sir Thomas Wyatt]." In Mary Thomas Crane, *Framing Authority: Sayings, Self, and Society in Sixteenth-Century England.* Princeton, New Jersey: Princeton University Press. 136–61, 244–54 (notes).

Daalder, Joost. 1986. "Wyatt's Proverbial 'Though the Wound Be Healed, Yet a Scar Remains.'" *Archiv für das Studium der neueren Sprachen und Literaturen* 138: 354–56.

Davies, John. 1878. *The Complete Works.* Alexander B. Grosart, ed. Edinburgh: Constable; rpt. Hildesheim: Georg Olms, 1968.

Doyle, Charles Clay. 1975. "On Some Paremiological Verses." *Proverbium* 25: 979–82.

———. 2007. "Proverbs in the Works of Edmund Spenser." *Phraseology: An International Handbook of Contemporary Research.* Harald Burger, Dmitrij Dobrovol'skij, Peter Kühn, and Neal R. Norrick, eds. Berlin: Walter de Gruyter. I, 330–37.

Emerson, Ralph Waldo. 1986. *The Poetry Notebooks.* Ralph H. Orth et al., eds. New York: Columbia University Press.

Equi, Elaine. 2007. *Ripple Effect: New and Selected Poems.* Minneapolis, Minnesota: Coffee House Press.

Folsom, Steven. 1993. "Proverbs in Recent American Country Music: Form and Function in the Hits of 1986–87." *Proverbium* 10: 65–88.

Gutmann, Florian. 2007. "'Because You're Mine, I Walk the Line': Sprichwörtliches in ausgewählten Liedern von Johnny Cash." *"Sprichwörter sind Goldes wert": Parömiologische Studien zu Kultur, Literatur und Medien.* Wolfgang Mieder, ed. Burlington, Vermont: University of Vermont. 177–94.

Henri, Adrian. 1986. *Collected Poems 1967–85.* London: Allison & Busby.

Kuusi, Matti. 1957. *Parömiologische Betrachtungen.* Helsinki: Suomalainen Tiedeakatemia.

Lakoff, George, and Mark Turner. 1989. "The Great Chain of Being." In George Lakoff and Mark Turner, *More than Cool Reason: A Field Guide to Poetic Metaphor.* Chicago: University of Chicago Press. 160–213.

Lansverk, Marvin Duane. 1994. *The Wisdom of Many, the Vision of One: The Proverbs of William Blake.* New York: Peter Lang.

La Rosa, Ralph Charles. 1969. *Emerson's Proverbial Rhetoric: 1818–1838.* Diss., University of Wisconsin.

Leite de Vasconcellos, José. 1925. *A Figa: Estudios de etnografia comparativa.* Porto: Araujo & Sobrinho.

Litovkina, Anna T., and Wolfgang Mieder, eds. 2006. *Old Proverbs Never Die, They Just Diversify: A Collection of Anti-Proverbs.* Burlington, Vermont: University of Vermont. Veszprém, Hungary: Pannonian University of Veszprém.

Manley, Lawrence. 1985. "Proverbs, Epigrams, and Urbanity in Renaissance London." *English Literary Renaissance* 15: 247–76.

Mauch, Thomas Karl. 1963. *The Role of the Proverb in Early Tudor Literature.* Diss., University of California at Los Angeles.

Mennes, Sir John, ed. 1874. *Facetiae. Masarum Deliciae: or The Muses Recreation, Conteining Severall Pieces of Poetique Wit.* 2 vols. London: John Camden Hotten.

Mieder, Wolfgang. 1971. "'Behold the Proverbs of a People': A Florilegium of Proverbs in Carl Sandburg's Poem *Good Morning, America.*" *Southern Folklore Quarterly* 35: 160–68.

———. 1973. "Proverbs in Carl Sandburg's [Epic] Poem *The People, Yes.*" *Southern Folklore Quarterly* 37: 15–36.

———. 1974a. "The Essence of Literary Proverb Studies." *Proverbium* 23: 888–94.

———. 1974b. "The Proverb and Anglo-American Literature." *Southern Folklore Quarterly* 38 : 49–62.

———. 1980a. "A Sampler of Anglo-American Proverb Poetry." *Folklore Forum* 13: 39–53.

———. 1980b. "Traditional and Innovative Proverb Use in Lyric Poetry." *Proverbium Paratum* 1: 16–27.

———. 1987. "'Big Fish Eat Little Fish': History and Interpretation of a Proverb about Human Nature." In Wolfgang Mieder, *Tradition and Innovation in Folk Literature.* Hanover, New Hampshire: University Press of New England. 178–228, 259–68 (notes).

———. 1988. "Proverbs in American Popular Songs." *Proverbium* 5: 85–101.

———. 1989a. "Proverb Poems." In Wolfgang Mieder, *American Proverbs: A Study of Texts and Contexts.* Bern: Peter Lang. 171–93.

———. 1989b. "Proverbs in Popular Songs." In Wolfgang Mieder, *American Proverbs: A Study of Texts and Contexts.* Bern: Peter Lang. 195–221.

———, ed. 1990. *"Kommt Zeit—kommt Rat!?" Moderne Sprichwortgedichte von Erich Fried bis Ulla Hahn.* Frankfurt am Main: Rita G. Fischer.

———, ed. 1992. *"Deutsch reden": Moderne Redensartengedichte von Rose Ausländer bis Yaak Karsunke.* Frankfurt am Main: Rita G. Fischer.

———. 2000. "'The Apple Doesn't Fall Far From the Tree': History of a German Proverb in the Anglo-American World." In Wolfgang Mieder, *Strategies of Wisdom: Anglo-American and German Proverb Studies.* Baltmannsweiler: Schneider Verlag Hohengehren. 109–44.

———, ed. 2001. *"Geht einmal euren Phrasen nach": Sprachkritische Lyrik und Kurzprosa zur deutschen Vergangenheit.* Burlington, Vermont: University of Vermont.

———, ed. 2004a. *"Liebe macht blind": Sprichwörtliche Lyrik und Kurzprosa zum Thema der Liebe.* Burlington, Vermont: University of Vermont.

———. 2004b. "Proverb Poems and Popular Songs." In Wolfgang Mieder, *Proverbs: A Handbook.* Westport, Connecticut: Greenwood. 224–36.

———. 2005. "'Good Fences Make Good Neighbors': History and Significance of an Ambiguous Proverb." In Wolfgang Mieder, *Proverbs Are the Best Policy: Folk Wisdom and American Politics.* Logan, Utah: Utah State University Press. 210–43, 287–96 (notes).

———. 2006. "'In der Kürze liegt die Würze': Zur sprichwörtlichen Sprache moderner Mini-Lyrik." *Nauchnyi vestnik.* Seriia: *Sovremennye lingvisticheskie i metodiko-didakticheskie issledovaniia* no. 5: 7–26.

———. 2007. "Proverbs in the Works of Ralph Waldo Emerson." *Phraseology: An International Handbook of Contemporary Research.* Harald Burger, Dmitrij Dobrovol'skij, Peter Kühn, and Neal R. Norrick, eds. Berlin: Walter de Gruyter. I, 337–48.

———. 2009. *International Bibliography of Paremiology and Phraseology.* 2 vols. Berlin: Walter de Gruyter.

Mieder, Wolfgang, and George B. Bryan. 1996. *Proverbs in World Literature: A Bibliography.* New York: Peter Lang.

Mieder, Wolfgang, Stewart A. Kingsbury, and Kelsie B. Harder. 1992. *A Dictionary of American Proverbs.* New York: Oxford University Press.

Pitts, Arthur William. 1966. *John Donne's Use of Proverbs in His Poetry.* Diss., Louisiana State University.

Prahlad, Sw. Anand. 2001. *Reggae Wisdom: Proverbs in Jamaican Music.* Jackson, Mississippi: University Press of Mississippi.

Reaver, J. Russell. 1963. "Emerson's Use of Proverbs." *Southern Folklore Quarterly* 28: 280–99.

Rettenbeck, Lenz. 1953. *"Feige": Wort, Gebärde, Amulett. Ein volkskundlicher Beitrag zur Amulettforschung.* Diss., University of Munich.

Ross, Diane M. 1987. "Sir Thomas Wyatt: Proverbs and the Poetics of Scorn." *Sixteenth Century Journal* 18: 201–12.

Sackett, S. J. 1964. "Poetry and Folklore [Proverbs]: Some Points of Affinity." *Journal of American Folklore* 77: 143–53.

Shah, Idries. 1971. *Reflections.* Baltimore, Maryland: Penguin.

Smith, A. J. M. 1957. *Seven Centuries of Verse: English & American.* New York: Charles Scribner's Sons.

Sobieski, Janet, and Wolfgang Mieder, eds. 2005. *"So Many Heads, So Many Wits": An Anthology of English Proverb Poetry.* Burlington, Vermont: University of Vermont.

Strand, Mark. 1998. *Blizzard of One: Poems.* New York: Alfred A. Knopf.

Taft, Michael. 1994. "Proverbs in the Blues: How Frequent is Frequent?" *Proverbium* 11: 227–58.

Tilley, Morris Palmer. 1950. *A Dictionary of the Proverbs in England in the Sixteenth and Seventeenth Centuries.* Ann Arbor, Michigan: University of Michigan Press.

Villalobos, John. 1990. "William Blake's *Proverbs of Hell* and the Tradition of Wisdom Literature." *Studies in Philology* 87: 246–59.

Ward, Adrian O. 2000. "Proverbs and Political Anxiety in the Poetry of Sir Thomas Wyatt and the Earl of Surrey." *English Studies* 81: 456–71.

Welsh, Andrew. 1978. "[John Skelton and the Proverb]." In Andrew Welsh, *Roots of Lyric: Primitive Poetry and Modern Poetics.* Princeton, New Jersey: Princeton University Press. 208–15, 217–19.

Wilkinson, P. R. 1992. *Thesaurus of Traditional English Metaphors.* London: Routledge.

Wyatt, Sir Thomas. 1975. *Collected Poems.* Joost Daalder, ed. London: Oxford University Press.

10. "MY TONGUE—IS OF THE PEOPLE"
Friedrich Nietzsche's Proverbial Philosophy in *Thus Spoke Zarathustra*

In the lyrical prelude to Friedrich Nietzsche's *Die fröhliche Wissenschaft* (1882, *The Gay [or: Merry] Science*) appears a short verse whose title serves as an indication that proverbial matters play an important role in this early work and also in his entire writings. Typically for Nietzsche's proverbial and Biblical language and style, its five lines allude to the two Bible proverbs "Be wise as serpents and harmless as doves" / "Seid klug wie die Schlangen und ohne Falsch wie die Tauben" (Matthew 10:16) and "Unto the pure (clean) all things are pure" / "Den Reinen ist alles rein" (Titus 1:15):

The Proverb Speaks
Sharp and mild, rough and fine,
Strange and familiar, impure and clean,
A place where fool and sage convene:
All this I am and wish to mean,
Dove as well as snake and swine.
(Kaufmann 1974: 45)

Das Sprüchwort spricht.
Scharf und milde, grob und fein,
Vertraut und seltsam, schmutzig und rein,
Der Narren und Weisen Stelldichein:
Dieses Alles bin ich, will ich sein,
Taube zugleich, Schlange und Schwein! (KSA3: 355)

This could well be considered as a poetic proverb definition, but Nietzsche hardly had a theoretical deliberation about folk and Bible proverbs in mind. To be sure, it is the proverb that is speaking, but one would hardly be wrong to take the lyrical "I" to be Nietzsche himself, whose differentiated linguistic nuances and stylistic levels contain all the aspects referred to in the poem. That this interpretation is somewhat justified can be seen from a verse of three rhymed lines that Nietzsche had deleted from *The Gay Science* before its publication. Here it is clearly Nietzsche who is speaking:

> Wise and foolish, rough and fine,
> Sharp and mild, water and wine:
> All of this my proverb shall be.
> (translations without references are my own)

> Weis und närrisch, grob und fein,
> Scharf und milde, Wasser und Wein:
> Dies alles soll mein Sprüchwort sein! (KSA14: 234)

Here Nietzsche summarizes quite clearly what his proverbial intention will be, namely to appear intermittently as a sage, fool, ruffian, or gentleman, and to pour questionable water (nonsense) or pure wine (wisdom) into his readers' glasses. Nietzsche speaks indirectly of his linguistic and philosophical desire to express his cultural and moralistic criticism by way of all registers of language available to him. He is concerned about a philosophical and poetic penetration of human, all-too-human conditions. Wordplay with traditional formulas is part of this very conscious linguistic and stylistic endeavor, and it is part of Nietzsche's image as a magisterial "linguistic innovator" / "Sprachschöpfer" (Linden 1933: 65) "linguistic imagination" / "Sprachphantasie" (Kaulhausen 1977: 106), and "linguistic potency" / "Sprachmächtigkeit" (Guager 1984: 335). The at times somewhat colloquial metaphors of folk speech are most certainly part of Nietzsche's creative thoughts and linguistic formulations. A quotation from *Also sprach Zarathustra* (1883–85; *Thus spoke Zarathustra*), written about two years later, makes all of this quite clear and is most likely an allusion to the animal reference of the poem brought about by the rhyme "rein/Schwein": "'To the clean all is clean,' the people say. But I say unto you, 'To the mean [swine] all becomes mean'" (204) / "'Dem [*sic*] Reinen ist alles rein'—so spricht das Volk. Ich aber sage euch: den Schweinen wird Alles Schwein" (KSA4: 256; see Röhrich 1991–92: 3, 1444). Since the construction of the world includes the clean (pure) that has been drawn into the mire, Nietzsche feels compelled to expose antiquated moral attitudes and human falsehoods. It follows that Nietzsche's argumentative leitmotif of the revaluation of all values also confronts so-called virtuous and timeless Bible and folk proverbs that rather appropriately play a considerable role not only in his prophetic masterwork *Thus spoke Zarathustra* but also in his literary, philosophical, and epistolary oeuvre as such.

Little Previous Scholarship on Nietzsche's Proverbiality

It is then surprising that the considerable secondary literature on *Thus Spoke Zarathustra* has been almost completely silent on its obvious proverbiality, and this even though Nietzsche occasionally refers with distinct introductory formulas to Bible and folk proverbs employed by him. To be sure, Hans Morowa deals with Biblical archaisms that Nietzsche took over from Luther's Bible language, but he fails to recognize the many phraseological units in his study on the language and style of *Thus Spoke Zarathustra* (see Morowa 1958: 65–67). Joachim Goth and Marie Hed Kaulhausen mention at least a few proverbial expressions and proverbs from this work, but say nothing about their rhetorical and semantic significance (see Goth 1970: 97–98; Kaulhausen 1977: 122). However, Siegfried Vitens's comments are noteworthy; he refers to Nietzsche's inclination of parodistically negating and reversing fixed formulas, quotations, and proverbs while also citing the altered Biblical expression "Not a few who wanted to drive out their devil have themselves entered into swine" (55) / "Nicht wenige, die ihren Teufel austreiben wollten, fuhren dabei selber in die Säue" (KSA4: 70; see Matthew 8:31) as well as the secularized anti-proverb "The prince proposes, but the shopkeeper disposes" (177) / "Der Fürst denkt, aber der Krämer—lenkt!" (KSA4: 223) as examples from *Zarathustra* (Vitens 1951: 80). Mention should also be made of Ludger Lütkehaus's anthology *"Stehlen ist oft seliger als nehmen": Nietzsche zum Vergnügen* (2000), the title of which cites Nietzsche's shocking perversion of the Bible proverb "It is more blessed to give than to receive" / "Geben ist seliger als nehmen" (Acts 20:25; see Lütkehaus 2000: 79, 82, 87). In the short formulation "Stealing is often more blessed than receiving" / "Stehlen ist oft seliger als nehmen" (KSA10: 395), this anti-proverb is included in a collection of aphoristic fragments entitled by Nietzsche as *"Böse Weisheit." Sprüche und Sprüchwörtliches* (1883; KSA10: 383–413), but in a slightly expanded form this "new" piece of wisdom appears twice in the second and third part of *Zarathustra* (1883 and 1884): "I do not know the happiness of those who receive; and I have often dreamed that even stealing must be more blessed than receiving" (106) / "Ich kenne das Glück des Nehmenden nicht; und oft träumte mir davon, dass Stehlen noch seliger sein müsse, als Nehmen" (KSA4: 136) and "until finally you [Zarathustra] sat thirsty among drunks and complained by night, 'Is it not more blessed to receive than to give, and to steal still more blessed than to receive?'—then you were forsaken!" (184) / "—bis du [Zarathustra] endlich durstig und allein unter Trunkenen sassest und nächtlich klagtest 'ist Nehmen nicht seliger als Geben? Und Stehlen noch seliger als Nehmen?'—Das war Verlassenheit!" (KSA4: 232).

These texts and more than five thousand other proverbial references are cited in their contexts in the index of proverbs and proverbial expressions in Andreas Nolte's and my book *"Zu meiner Hölle will ich den Weg mit guten Sprüchen pflastern": Friedrich Nietzsches sprichwörtliche Sprache* (2012). This voluminous study includes several chapters about the differentiated use and function of proverbial materials in Nietzsche's works. It is shown how he repeatedly relies on elements of preformulated folk speech to add a certain metaphorical expressiveness to his thoughts and arguments, no matter whether they appear in aphorisms, fragments, poems, letters, essays, or entire books (Nolte and Mieder 2012). Quite appropriately, if perhaps a bit surprisingly for many Nietzsche scholars, the following programmatic statement appears in *Zarathustra*: "My tongue—is of the people: I speak too crudely and heartily for Angora rabbits. And my speech sounds even stranger to all inkfish and pen-hacks" (191) / "Mein Mundwerk—ist des Volks: zu grob und herzlich rede ich für die Seidenhasen. Und noch fremder klingt mein Wort allen Tinten-Fischen und Feder-Füchsen" (KSA4: 241). The many variants of the German proverbial expression "to have an evil (quick, audacious, ungodly, rough, big, good, loose, unwashed) glib tongue" / "ein böses [flinkes, freches, gottloses, grobes, großes, gutes, loses, ungewaschenes] Mundwerk haben" (Schemann 1993: 557) might well be looked at as a colloquial self-characterization of Nietzsche's multifaceted use of language. It must, however, be said that our study does not include a detailed interpretation of the proverbiality of individual books by Nietzsche. This essay represents an attempt to show how Nietzsche's major work *Thus Spoke Zarathustra* is informed to a considerable extent by the innovative use of proverbial language that adds much to his powerful style and his intended message.

The Pseudo-Proverb "Man Is Something That Must Be Overcome"

Even though *Zarathustra* is generally considered to be Nietzsche's most prominent work, there is still much uncertainty about what exactly this controversial philosopher or literary author had wanted to say with it. Partially at fault about this open question is his aphoristic, esoteric, and poetic style that often is based on analogies and metaphors. The result are opaque and contradictory proclamations that are immediately put into question in an equally encoded way (see Perkins 1983: 321–23). Thus readers are often not sure whether the prophet Zarathustra speaks for Nietzsche, whether either one envisions a clear goal for humanity, and what the call for a new and elevated humankind actually entails. The seemingly unconnected short chapters with their own open questions are part of this mystification, but altogether Nietzsche is expressing his idea of the revaluation of all values beyond the old concepts of good and evil that will lead to an acceptance of human life as an eternal return (repetition) without any definite goal. This process demands that humankind abolish God and religion as well as antiquated concepts of morality, thus going beyond Christian limitations. All of this entails a destruction of the traditional world order and a change or overcoming of humankind as it exists. In this regard Nietzsche's at times rather elitist and provocative concept of the overman must therefore be understood as a call for human beings to go beyond their present limited state. This has nothing to do with a pathological overhuman will to power, as all of this was manipulatively interpreted by Adolf Hitler and other National Socialists (see Ziolkowski 2012: 214–16).

There is a sententious leitmotif in *Zarathustra* that summarizes all of this, taking on, as do other such formulaic statements, "the character of true proverbs" / "das Gepräge von echten Sprichwörtern" (Vitens 1951: 82). A better term would probably be "pseudo-proverb," and as such it appears for the first time right at the beginning of *Zarathustra* as an incredibly informative statement revealing the intended meaning and purpose of the entire book:

> I teach you the overman. Man is something that must be overcome. What have you done to overcome him? (12)
> Ich lehre euch den Übermenschen. Der Mensch ist Etwas, das überwunden werden soll. Was habt ihr gethan, ihn zu überwinden? (KSA4: 14)

When the pseudo-proverb "Man is something that must be overcome" is quoted for a second time some thirty pages later, it appears in a typically contradictory context of which the meaning becomes clear only after careful deliberation. Apparently humankind must sink very low, symbolically perish or "die," so that a liberating renunciation of traditional concepts of virtue can take place:

> Alas, my brother, have you never yet seen a virtue deny and stab herself?
> Man is something that must be overcome; and therefore you shall love your virtues, for you will perish of them. (37)

Ach, mein Bruder, sahst du noch nie eine Tugend sich selber verleumden und erstechen?
Der Mensch ist Etwas, das überwunden werden muss: und darum sollst du deine Tugenden lieben,—denn du wirst an ihnen zu Grunde gehn. (KSA4: 44)

It takes this symbolic death in order to bring about the rebirth of a new and liberated humankind as argued by Zarathustra and Nietzsche. This basic idea reappears numerous times as a pseudo-proverbial leitmotif in *Zarathustra*, providing this complex work with its philosophical red thread (roter Faden):

Your highest thought, however, you should receive as a command from me—and it is: man is something that shall be overcome. (48)
Euren höchsten Gedanken aber sollt ihr euch von mir befehlen lassen—und er lautet: der Mensch ist Etwas, das überwunden werden soll. (KSA4: 60)

O my friend, man is something that must be overcome. (57)
Oh, mein Freund, der Mensch ist Etwas, das überwunden werden muss. (KSA4: 72)

There it was too that I picked up the word "overman" by the way, and that man is something that must be overcome. (198)
Dort war's auch, wo ich das Wort "Übermensch" vom Wege auflas, und dass der Mensch Etwas sei, das überwunden werden müsse. (KSA4: 248)

Thus my great love of the farthest demands it: do not spare your neighbor! Man is something that must be overcome. (199)
Also heischt es meine grosse Liebe zu den Fernsten: schone deinen Nächsten nicht! Der Mensch ist Etwas, das überwunden werden muss. (KSA4: 249)

"I love the great despisers. Man, however, is something that must be overcome." (267)
"Ich liebe die grossen Verachtenden. Der Mensch aber ist Etwas, das überwunden werden muss." (KSA4: 332)

In the fourth part of *Zarathustra* (1885) this pseudo-proverb is used one more time, albeit in dissolved form, in the chapter "On the Higher Man," who is well on his way to the new but not clearly definable overman:

The most concerned ask today: "How is man to be preserved?" But Zarathustra is the first and only one to ask: "How is man to be overcome?"
I have the overman at heart, that is my first and only concern—and not man: not the neighbor, not the poorest, not the most ailing, not the best. [...]
You higher men, overcome the small virtues, the small prudences, the grain-of-sand consideration, the ants' riff-raff, the wretched contentment, the "happiness of the greatest number"! And rather despair than surrender. And verily, I love you for not knowing how to live today, you higher men! For thus you live best. (287–88)
Die Sorglichsten fragen heute: "wie bleibt der Mensch erhalten?" Zarathustra aber fragt als der Einzige und Ernste: "wie wird der Mensch überwunden?"
Der Übermensch liegt mir am Herzen, der ist mein Erstes und Einziges,— und nicht der Mensch: nicht der Nächste, nicht der Ärmste, nicht der Leidendste, nicht der Beste.— [...]
Überwindet mir, ihr höheren Menschen, die kleinen Tugenden, die kleinen Klugheiten, die Sandkorn-Rücksichten, den Ameisen-Kribbelkram, das erbärmliche Behagen, das "Glück der Meisten"—!
Und lieber verzweifelt, als dass ihr euch ergebt. Und, wahrlich, ich liebe euch dafür, dass ihr heute nicht zu leben wisst, ihr höheren Menschen! So nämlich lebt ihr—am Besten! (KSA4, 357–58)

That is no plan or prescription but "a reflective process [...] of free play, of oscillation between the text-immanent and text-external aspect" that includes "the irrational, the indecipherable and the arbitrarily interpretable" / "ein Reflexionsprozeß [...] des freien Spiels, des Oszillierens zwischen textimmanenter und texttäußerer Seite," der "Irrationales, Unentzifferbares oder beliebig zu Intepretierendes" einschließt" (Naumann 1985: 126, 162–63). Even "Zarathustra does not reach a final state of wisdom" or "a resting place" (Higgins 1987: 231), but by serious struggle he reaches the conviction, perhaps somewhat surprising for the alleged naysayer Nietzsche, the "world-affirming ideal that expresses itself in self-affirmation" and "the celebration of life in eternal return [repetition]" (Lampert 1986: 308). Thus one finds right at the beginning of *Zarathustra* the affirmative declaration:

Behold, I teach you the overman. The overman is the meaning of the earth. Let your will say: the overman shall be the meaning of the earth! (13)
Seht, ich lehre euch den Übermenschen!
Der Übermensch ist der Sinn der Erde. Euer Wille sage: der Übermensch sei der Sinn der Erde! (KSA4: 14)

The same thought reappears more poetically expressed a few pages later, where Nietzsche once again leaves his idea of a new humankind somewhat in the dark:

> I will teach men the meaning of their existence—the overman, the lightning out of the dark cloud of man. But I am still far from them, and my sense does not speak to their senses. To men I am still the mean between a fool and a corpse.
> Dark is the night, dark are Zarathustra's ways. (20–21)
> Ich will die Menschen den Sinn ihres Seins lehren: welcher ist der Über-mensch, der Blitz aus der dunklen Wolke Mensch.
> Aber noch bin ich ihnen ferne, und mein Sinn redet nicht zu ihren Sinnen. Eine Mitte bin ich noch den Menschen zwischen einem Narren und einem Leichnam.
> Dunkel ist die Nacht, dunkel sind die Wege Zarathustra's. (KSA4: 23)

Overcoming Old Values by Not Sticking One's Head in the Sand

There is no doubt that Nietzsche walks on dark and challenging paths to convince humankind "To assume the right to new values" (27) / "Recht sich nehmen [sollen] zu neuen Werthen" (KSA4: 30), because "Around the inventors of new values the world revolves" (52) / "um die Erfinder von neuen Werthen dreht sich die Welt" (KSA4: 65). Humankind lies, as Nietzsche expresses it proverbially, "in fetters of false values and delusive words" (91) / "in Banden falscher Werthe und Wahn-Worte!" (KSA4: 117). Nietzsche also employs the somatic expression "to have one's hands free" / "die Hände frei haben" in order to emphasize the messianic task of his Zarathustra as a life-confirming prophet: "I have become one who blesses and says Yes; and I fought long for that and was a fighter that I might one day get my hands free to bless" (165) / "Zum Segnenden bin ich [Zarathustra] worden und zum Ja-sagenden: und dazu rang ich lange und war ein Ringer, dass ich einst die Hände frei bekäme zum Segnen" (KSA4: 209). But even if life is likened to a wrestling match, Zarathustra freely admits that "life was dearer to me than all my wisdom ever was" (227) / "war mir das Leben lieber, als je alle meine Weisheit" (KSA4: 285). But the problem remains, of course, that even Nietzsche's chosen fellow human beings are not yet ready to follow Zarathustra on his novel path:

Well then, they still sleep, these higher men, while I [Zarathustra] am awake; these are not my proper companions. It is not for them that I wait here in my mountains. I want to go to my work, to my day; but they do not understand the signs of my morning; my stride is for them no summons to awaken. (325) Wohlan! sie schlafen noch, diese höheren Menschen, während ich [Zarathustra] wach bin: das sind nicht meine rechten Gefährten! Nicht auf sie warte ich hier in meinen Bergen.

Zu meinem Werke will ich, zu meinem Tage: aber sie verstehen nicht, was die Zeichen meines Morgens sind, mein Schritt—ist für sie kein Weckruf. (KSA4: 405)

One could certainly observe that Zarathustra has given a hopeful wake-up call, making it possible for him to leave his spiritual mountaintop and make his way confidently to the people at the end of this semiotic work. From darkness to light, from divine disempowerment to free development, as Markus Meckel has expressed it so well in his anthropologically oriented essay "Der Weg Zarathustras als der Weg des Menschen" (1980, "Zarathustra's Path as the Path of Humankind"):

God is dead. Man alone is the topic. [. . .] "Death of God" is thought of as the task of man to comply with his manhood. The talk about God thus becomes the talk about man. In this way the differentiated use of the word "God" by Nietzsche always reveals anthropological statements. But the background for all statements is the turning away for God, the rejection of the Christian, metaphysical God. [. . .] Man for Nietzsche is body and belongs to this earth; he cannot free himself for that. Man and world [that is, the here and not the beyond] belong closely together. [. . .] Thus the turn to the earth as the place for man and the death of God depend on each other.

Gott ist tot. Der Mensch allein ist Thema. [. . .] "Tod Gottes" wird gedacht als die Aufgabe des Menschen, seinem Mensch-Sein zu entsprechen. Rede von Gott wird damit Rede vom Menschen. So eröffnet der recht unterschiedliche Gebrauch des Wortes "Gott" bei Nietzsche immer anthropologische Aussagen. Hintergrund aller Aussagen aber ist die Abwendung von Gott, die Ablehnung des christlichen, des metaphysischen Gottes. [. . .] Der Mensch ist für Nietzsche Leib und gehört zu dieser Erde; davon kann er sich nicht freimachen. Mensch und Welt [also das Diesseits und nicht das Jenseits] gehören eng zusammen. [. . .] So gehört Hinwendung zur Welt (=Erde) zum Grundbestand der Lehre Zarathustras. [. . .] Hinwendung zur Erde als Ort des Menschen und Tod Gottes bedingen einander. (Meckel 1980: 174–75)

After this intriguing analysis, Meckel cites the following reference from *Zarathustra*; but it is surprising that, even as an anthropologist, he ignores the ancient proverbial expression originating from the ostrich sticking his head into the sand. After all, this traditional phrase is a clear indication for the fact that Nietzsche relies on folk language for some of his most fundamental statements:

> It learns to speak ever more honestly, this ego: and the more it learns, the more words and honors it finds for body and earth.
> A new pride my ego taught me, and this I teach men: no longer to bury one's head in the sand of heavenly things, but to bear it freely, an earthly head, which creates a meaning for the earth. (32)
> Immer redlicher lernt es reden, das Ich: und je mehr es lernt, um so mehr findet es Worte und Ehren für Leib und Erde.
> Einen neuen Stolz lehrte mich mein Ich, den lehre ich die Menschen: nicht mehr den Kopf in den Sand der himmlichen Dinge zu stecken, sondern frei ihn zu tragen, einen Erden-Kopf, der der Erde Sinn schafft!
> Einen neuen Willen lehre ich die Menschen. [KSA4: 36–37; see Meckel 1980: 176)

Many pages later Nietzsche returns one more time to this proverbial expression in order to emphasize metaphorically that man has to liberate himself from his ostrich perspective:

> He who will one day teach men to fly will have moved all boundary stones; the boundary stones themselves will fly into the air before him, and he will rebaptize the earth—"the light one."
> The ostrich runs faster than the fastest horse, but even he buries his head gravely in the grave earth; even so, the man who has not yet learned to fly. Earth and life seem grave to him; and thus the spirit of gravity wants it. But whoever would become light and a bird must love himself: thus I teach. (192)
> Wer die Menschen einst fliegen lehrt, der hat alle Grenzsteine verrückt; alle Grenzsteine selber werden ihm in die Luft fliegen, die Erde wird er neu taufen—als "die Leichte."
> Der Vogel Strauß läuft schneller als das schnellste Pferd, aber auch er steckt noch den Kopf schwer in schwere Erde: also der Mensch, der noch nicht fliegen kann.
> Schwer heisst ihm Erde und Leben; und so will es der Geist der Schwere! Wer aber leicht werden will und ein Vogel, der muss sich selber lieben:—also lehre ich. (KSA4: 242)

"Hitting in Front of the Head" and other Somatic Expressions

An explosive, winged self-liberation is necessary so that people can find their preordained purpose for a secular life. That liberating path, however, is filled with contradictions, and they hit a person in a proverbial way "in front of the head" in the sense of being stunned or dumbfounded: "They contradict each other, these paths; they offend each other face to face [hit each other in front of the head]; and it is here at this gateway that they come together. The name of the gateway is inscribed above: 'Moment'" (157–58) / "Sie widersprechen sich, diese Wege; sie stossen sich gerade vor den Kopf:—und hier, an diesem Thorwege, ist es, wo sie zusammen kommen. Der Name des Thorwegs steht oben geschrieben: 'Augenblick'" (KSA4: 199–200). Nietzsche as the "player" with thoughts is quick to rely on at times difficult-to-translate somatic expressions based on "head" / "Kopf" in order to show how momentary insights hit people into the head and how concepts literally need to be turned on their head so that new truths can come to light:

> Too often, verily, did I follow close on the heels of truth: so she kicked me in the face [kicked me in the head]. Sometimes I thought I was lying, and behold, only then did I hit the truth. (274)
> Zu oft, wahrlich, folgte ich der Wahrheit dicht auf dem Fusse: da trat sie mir vor den Kopf. Manchmal meinte ich zu lügen, und siehe! da erst traf ich—die Wahrheit. (KSA4: 340)

> Lift up your hearts, my brothers, high, higher! And do not forget your legs either. Lift up your legs too, you good dancers; and better yet, stand on your heads! (294)
> Erhebt eure Herzen, meine Brüder, hoch! höher! Und vergesst mir auch die Beine nicht! Erhebt auch eure Beine, ihr guten Tänzer, und besser noch: ihr steht auch auf dem Kopf! (KSA4: 366)

> What? he [Zarathustra] cried. What did I hear just now? Verily, it seems to me that you [a scientist] are a fool, or that I am one myself; and your "truth" I simply reverse [stand on its head]. (302–3)
> Wie! rief er [Zarathustra], was hörte ich da eben? Wahrlich, mich dünkt, du [ein Wissenschaftler] bist ein Narr oder ich selber bin's: und deine "Wahrheit" stelle ich rucks und flugs auf den Kopf. (KSA4: 377)

Such somatic expressions appear again and again in *Zarathustra* and add to its emotionally charged metaphorical expressiveness.

Even though such textual references are normally intended seriously, a few humorous observations appear as well. This play between seriousness and humor is yet another example of Nietzsche's contradictory thought and work process, as can be seen from the following somatic examples:

I have long known that the devil would trip me [by putting his leg in my way]. (20)
Ich wusste es lange, dass mir der Teufel ein Bein stellen werde. (KSA4: 22)

You shall build over and beyond yourself, but first you must be built yourself, perpendicular in body and soul. (69)
Über dich sollst du hinausbauen. Aber erst musst du mir selber gebaut sein, rechtwinklig an Leib und Seele. (KSA4: 90)

And when I talked in confidence [under four eyes] with my wisdom she said to me in anger [...]. (108)
Und als ich unter vier Augen mit meiner wilden Weisheit redete, sagte sie mir zornig [...]. (KSA4: 140)

And even if you are right—should that be said to my face? (109)
Und wenn du Recht hättest,—sagt man das mir so in's Gesicht! (KSA4: 141)

They watch each other closely [look each other on the fingers] and mistrust-fully. (125)
Sie sehen einander gut auf die Finger und trauen sich nicht zum Besten. (KSA4: 161)

Eventually his own tongue was loosened as he listened, and the ice of his heart broke. (155)
Zuletzt wurde ihm im Zuhören die eigne Zunge gelöst, und das Eis seines Herzens brach. (KSA4: 197)

I walk among this people and I keep my eyes open. (168, 169)
Ich gehe durch diess Volk und halte meine (die) Augen offen. (KSA4: 212, 213)

You know it well: your cowardly devil within you, who would like to fold his hands and rest his hands in his lap and be more comfortable [...]. (180)

Du weißt es wohl: dein feiger Teufel in dir, der gerne Hände-falten und Hände-in-den-Schoss-legen und es bequemer haben möchte [. . .]. (KSA4: 227–28)

With lashes one should make your legs sprightly again. (207)
Mit Ruthenstreichen soll man euch wieder muntre Beine machen. (KSA4: 259)

Verily, you will yet have to drag him by the hair into his heaven. (207–8)
Wahrlich, ihr werdet ihn an den Haaren in seinen Himmel ziehen müssen. (KSA4: 260)

With his tongue hanging from lasciviousness [out of his throat]. But he calls it his "pity." (218)
Die Zunge hängt ihm aus dem Halse vor Lüsternheit. Er aber heisst es sein "Mitleiden." (KSA4: 273)

Immediately Zarathustra, who had opened his ears and eyes wide at this talk, rose from his hiding-place. (246)
Sofort erhob sich Zarathustra, der zu diesen Reden Ohren und Augen aufgesperrt hatte, aus seinem Schlupfwinkel. (KSA4: 306)

"Speaking in the confidence of three eyes," the old pope said cheerfully (for he was blind in one eye), "in what pertains to God, I am—and have the right to be—more enlightened than Zarathustra himself." (260–61)
"Unter drei Augen gesprochen, sagte erheitert der alte Papst (denn er war auf Einem Auge blind), in Dingen Gottes bin ich aufgeklärter als Zarathustra selber—und darf es sein." (KSA4: 323)

They unburden their hearts, good hours come back to them, they celebrate and chew the cud: they become grateful. (311)
Sie schütten ihr Herz aus, gute Stunden kehren ihnen zurück, sie feiern und käuen wieder,—sie werden dankbar. (KSA4: 387)

Of interest is also how Nietzsche connects the somatic expression "to have a cloven foot" / "einen Pferdefuß haben" with two twin formulas and an additional "devil" / "Teufel" phrase: "My foot is a cloven foot; with it I trample and trot over sticks and stones, crisscross, and I am happy as the devil while running so fast" (192) / "Mein Fuss—ist ein Pferdefuss; damit trapple und trabe ich über Stock und Stein, kreuz- und querfeld-ein und bin des Teufels vor Lust bei allem schnellen Laufen" (KSA4: 241).

Forty pages later Nietzsche returns to the medieval twin formula "over sticks and stones" / "über Stock und Stein" in his prophetic description of the path to enlightenment: "That is a dance up high and down low [over sticks and stones]: I am the hunter; would you be my dog or my doe?" (225) / "Das ist ein Tanz über Stock und Stein: ich bin der Jäger,—willst du mein Hund oder meine Gemse sein?" (KSA4: 283). In his letter of November 19, 1886, to his friend Heinrich Köselitz, Nietzsche mentions that in *Zarathustra* he uses "folk speech with all sincerity and delight just like a mother tongue" / "mit aller Herzlichkeit und Lust die 'Volkssprache', ganz wie eine Muttersprache" (KSB7: 284). Precisely, because elements of folk speech, even the simplest twin formulas, can be found everywhere. But Nietzsche, of course, integrates them in innovative ways into his philosophical context where they add much to a metaphorical expressiveness.

And here is yet another somatic reference in which Zarathustra without any doubt employs an enlightening allusion to the proverb "If you offer someone the little finger, he will take the whole hand" / "Wenn man einem den kleinen Finger bietet (reicht), so nimmt er die ganze Hand." Zarathustra uses this wisdom not as a reproach but rather as an offer to help the "higher" men on their path: "[The offer], however, is my little finger. And once you have that, by all means take the whole hand; well, and my heart too!" (280) / "[Das Angebot] aber ist: mein kleiner Finger. Und habt ihr den erst, so nehmt nur noch die ganze Hand, wohlan! und das Herz dazu!" (KSA4: 348). What becomes clear here is that Nietzsche usually does not use folk proverbs in their known wording to be followed as pieces of wisdom.

Dissolved Proverbs as Expressive Metaphors without Didacticism

Indeed, Nietzsche varies the proverbs' vocabulary and breaks up their original structure so that they take on new semantic functions. Often such proverb alterations are mere generalized observations without any intended didacticism. In fact, one could say that such dissolved proverbs are to be understood merely as expressive metaphors, showing Nietzsche's keen interest in the images of folk speech. The following examples, first citing the original proverb in italics in each case, are ample proof of this:

> *The drowning man will clutch at a straw.*
> *Der Ertrinkende klammert sich an einen Strohhalm (jeden Strohhalm ergreifen).*

They [the preachers of death] reach for sweets while mocking their own childishness; they clutch the straw of their life and mock that they still clutch a straw. Their wisdom says, "A fool who stays alive—but such fools are we. And this is surely the most foolish thing about life." (45)

Sie [Prediger des Todes] greifen nach Zuckerwerk und spotten ihrer Kinderei dabei: sie hängen an ihrem Strohhalm Leben und spotten, dass sie noch an einem Strohhalm hängen.

Ihre Weisheit lautet: "ein Thor, der leben bleibt, aber so sehr sind wir Thoren! Und das eben ist das Thörichste am Leben!"— (KSA4: 56)

A steady drop makes a hole in the stone.
Steter Tropfen höhlt den Stein.

You are no stone, but you have already become hollow from many drops. You will yet burst from many drops. (53)

Du bist kein Stein, aber schon wurdest du hohl von vielen Tropfen. Zerbrechen und zerbersten wirst du mir noch von vielen Tropfen. (KSA4: 66–67)

When the eating tastes the best, one should stop.
Wenn das Essen am besten schmeckt, soll man aufhören.

One must cease letting oneself be eaten when one tastes best: that is known to those who want to be loved long. (72)

Man muss aufhören, sich essen zu lassen, wenn man am besten schmeckt: das wissen Die, welche lange geliebt werden wollen. (KSA4: 94)

Virtue is its own reward.
Tugend ist selbst ihr bester Lohn.

You who are virtuous still want to be paid! Do you want rewards for virtue, and heaven for earth, and the eternal for your today?
And now you are angry with me because I teach that there is no reward and paymaster? And verily, I do not even teach that virtue is its own reward. (93)

Ihr wollt noch bezahlt sein, ihr Tugendhaften! Wollt Lohn für Tugend und Himmel für Erden und Ewiges für euer Heute haben?
Und nun zürnt ihr mir, dass ich lehre, es giebt keinen Lohn- und Zahlmeister? Und wahrlich, ich lehre nicht einmal, dass Tugend ihr eigener Lohn ist. (KSA4: 120)

Fools' hands scribble on tables and walls.
Narrenhände beschmieren Tisch und Wände.

My hand is a fool's hand: beware, all tables and walls and whatever else still offer room for foolish frill or scribbling skill. (192)
Meine Hand—ist eine Narrenhand: wehe allen Tischen und Wänden, und was noch Platz hat für Narren-Zierath, Narren-Schmierath! (KSA 4: 241)

Water has no planks.
Wasser hat keine Balken.

When the water is spanned by planks, when bridges and railings leap over the river, verily, those are not believed who say, "Everything is in flux." (201)
Wenn das Wasser Balken hat, wenn Stege und Geländer über den Fluss springen: wahrlich, da findet Keiner Glauben, der da spricht: "Alles ist im Fluss." (KSA 4: 252; see Paronis 1976: 31)

All that glitters is not gold.
Es ist nicht alles Gold, was glänzt.

Let the shopkeeper rule where all that still glitters is—shopkeepers' gold. The time of kings is past: what calls itself a people today deserves no kings. (210)
Mag da der Krämer herrschen, wo Alles, was noch glänzt—Krämer-Gold ist! Es ist die Zeit der Könige nicht mehr: was sich heute Volk heisst, verdient keine Könige. (KSA 4: 262–63)

The mountain labored and brought forth a mouse.
Der Berg kreißte und gebar ein Mäuslein.

Well then, you higher men! Only now is the mountain of man's future in labor. God died: now we want the overman to live. (287)
Wohlan! Wohlauf! Ihr höheren Menschen! Nun erst kreisst der Berg der Menschen-Zukunft. Gott starb: nun wollen wir,—dass der Übermensch lebe. (KSA 4: 357)

The last reference by the classical philologist Friedrich Nietzsche is a colossal and semantically significant variation of the Latin proverbs "Parturiunt montes, nascetur ridiculus mus" (see Harder 1925–26), where the mountain is now bringing forth the overman instead of the mouse and God as the creator is no longer of any import. It is utterly surprising that the secondary literature has not commented on this blasphemous reference and other such proverb manipulations in that they so obviously are key statements for the meaning and understanding of *Zarathustra*.

"God Is Dead": The Proverbialization of a Quotation

The declaration of the death of God and the turning of man to the world doubtlessly comprise the basis of the lyrical and yet proverbial philosophical treatise, as one might call Nietzsche's *Zarathustra*. Of course, Nietzsche's blasphemous claim that "God is dead" / "Gott ist tot" was at first neither poetic nor proverbial, but as a sententious remark it has long taken on a proverbial nature (albeit with the distinct loss of Nietzsche's philosophically founded reasoning).

Actually Nietzsche already had declared God dead one year earlier in *Die fröhliche Wissenschaft* (1882, *The Gay Science*), and it is this first reference that remains the best known: "God is dead. God remains dead. And we have killed him" (Kaufmann 1974: 181) / "Gott ist todt! Gott bleibt todt! Und wir haben ihn getötet" (KSA3: 481). Other occurrences from this book are above all "The greatest recent event—that 'God is dead,' that the belief in the Christian god has become unbelievable—is already beginning to cast its first shadows over Europe" (Kaufmann 1974: 279) / "Das grösste neuere Ereignis,—dass 'Gott todt ist,' dass der Glaube an den christlichen Gott unglaubwürdig geworden ist—beginnt bereits seine ersten Schatten über Europa zu werfen" (KSA3: 573); and "Indeed, we philosophers and 'free spirits' feel, when we hear the news that 'the old God is dead,' as if a new dawn shone on us" (Kaufmann 1974: 280) / "In der That, wir Philosophen und 'freien Geister' fühlen uns bei der Nachricht, dass der 'alte Gott todt' ist, wie von einer neuen Morgenröthe angestrahlt" (KSA3: 574). Of greatest interest, however, is what Nietzsche expresses shortly afterwards with seemingly considerable more humility in the second part of his *Zarathustra* (1883). But here again it is of utmost importance, as always with Nietzsche, that one considers the context carefully, for it is not Zarathustra who is speaking in this case but rather the devil: "Thus spoke the devil to me once: 'God too has his hell: that is his love of man.' And most recently I heard him say this: 'God is dead; God died of his pity for man.'" (90) / "Also sprach der Teufel einst zu mir: 'auch Gott hat seine Hölle: das ist seine Liebe zu den Menschen.' Und jüngst hörte ich ihn diess Wort sagen: 'Gott ist todt; an seinem Mitleiden mit den Menschen ist Gott gestorben'—" (KSA4: 115). That is for Nietzsche himself a devilish interpretation in contrast to his own liberating deed of annihilating the Biblical God, something that he later in *Zarathustra* repeats very directly in all its shortness and without any compassion: "For this old God lives no more: he is thoroughly dead. Thus spoke Zarathustra" (263) / "Dieser alte Gott nämlich lebt nicht mehr: der ist gründlich todt.—Also sprach Zarathustra" (KSA 4: 326). Nietzsche's claim caught on, and here are at least two of the numerous aphoristic reactions to Nietzsche's infamous declaration of God's death that refer directly to Nietzsche's proverbial slogan:

> God is dead, Nietzsche is dead—and I feel also pretty bad already.
> Gott ist tot, Nietzsche ist tot—und mir ist auch schon ganz schlecht.
> Anonymous (1982; Domzalski 2006: no pp.; Mieder 1997: 115)

> *Short Sunday Sermon*
>   God has—according to Nietzsche—died,
>   but as a multi-purpose weapon
>   is still useful
>   and traded worldwide
>   because not protected by copyright.

> *Kurze Sonntagspredigt*
>   Gott ist—laut Nietzsche—verstorben,
>   doch als Mehrzweckwaffe
>   immer noch tauglich
>   und weltweit im Handel,
>   weil urheberrechtlich nicht geschützt.
>   Günter Grass (1997: 111)

One wonders how Nietzsche might have reacted to such modern reactions to his claim that "God is dead" / "Gott ist tot"? He would hardly have been pleased to learn that his entire oeuvre prevails primarily in folk parlance by way of the three (un)winged words "God is dead!" (Büchmann 1995: 222; Prossliner 2001: 25; 134–35, 137, 229).

The Overman Negating the Proverb "All Men Are Equal"

The higher men, who possess the courageous insight that God would stand in their way to new values and a life-confirming existence, could very well have been labeled as exceptional human beings by Nietzsche. They are those who will not submit to the will of God: "Against this submission, against this God stands the 'I will' of Zarathustra, the creating and loving one, who constructs himself and his living space by going beyond himself. In this going beyond oneself that is the essence of man is implied that men are different, differently advanced on their path to the overman" / "Gegen diese Ergebung, gegen diesen Gott steht das 'ich will' Zarathustras, des Schaffenden und Liebenden, der sich selbst und seinen Lebensraum im Über-sich-hinaus-gehen schafft. In diesem Über-sich-hinaus-gehen, das das Wesen des Menschen ausmacht, ist impliziert, daß die Menschen verschieden sind, verschieden weit auf ihrem Wege zum Übermenschen" (Meckel 1980: 192). It is then no surprise that Nietzsche had to deal quite critically with the two related democratic proverbs "All men are equal" / "Alle Menschen sind gleich" and "Before God all men are equal" / "Vor Gott sind alle Menschen gleich." After all, his "higher men" / "höhere Menschen" are unique and elitist individuals, as is repeatedly pointed out: "I am Zarathustra the godless: where shall I find my equal? And all those are my equals who give themselves their own will and reject all resignation" (171) / "Ich bin Zarathustra, der Gottlose: wo finde ich Meines-Gleichen? Und alle Die sind Meines-Gleichen, die sich selber ihren Willen geben und alle Ergebung von sich abthun" (KSA4: 215). Consequently Zarathustra repeatedly contradicts the proverbial claim that all men are equal:

> I do not wish to be mixed up and confused with these preachers of equality. For, to me justice speaks thus: "Men are not equal." (101)
> Mit diesen Predigern der Gleichheit will ich nicht vermischt und verwechselt sein. Denn so redet mir die Gerechtigkeit: "die Menschen sind nicht gleich." (KSA4: 130)

> For men are not equal: thus speaks justice. And what I want, they would have no right to want!
> Thus spoke Zarathustra. (126)
> Denn die Menschen sind nicht gleich: so spricht die Gerechtigkeit. Und was ich will, dürften sie nicht wollen!
> Also sprach Zarathustra. (KSA4: 162)

> You higher men, learn this from me: in the market place nobody believes the higher men. And if you want to speak there, very well! But the mob blinks: "We are all equal."
> "You higher men"—thus blinks the mob—"there are no higher men, we are all equal, man is man; before God we are all equal."

Before God! But now this God has died. And before the mob we do not want
to be equal. You higher men, go away from the market place!
Before God! But now this God has died. You higher men, this God was your
greatest danger. It is only since he lies in his tomb that you have been resur-
rected. Only now the great noon comes; only now the higher man becomes—
lord. (286)
Ihr höheren Menschen. Diess lernt von mir: auf dem Markt glaubt Niemand
an höhere Menschen. Und wollt ihr dort reden, wohlan! Der Pöbel aber blinzelt "wir sind Alle gleich."
"Ihr höheren Menschen,—so blinzelt der Pöbel—es giebt keine höheren
Menschen, wir sind Alle gleich, Mensch ist Mensch, vor Gott—sind wir Alle
gleich!" [see Meckel 1980: 192]
Vor Gott!—Nun aber starb dieser Gott. Vor dem Pöbel aber wollen wir nicht
gleich sein. Ihr höheren Menschen, geht weg vom Markt!
Vor Gott!—Nun aber starb dieser Gott! Ihr höheren Menschen, dieser Gott
war eure grösste Gefahr.
Seit er im Grabe liegt, seid ihr erst wieder auferstanden. Nun erst kommt der
grosse Mittag, nun erst wird der höhere Mensch—Herr! (KSA4: 356–57)

Additional arguments also employ proverbs against the claimed equality
of men, as for example in the case of the restricted behavior "of the little
people: there one says 'birds of a feather' and 'one hand washes the other.'
They have neither the right nor the strength for your egoism." (291) / "der
kleinen Leute: da heisst es 'gleich und gleich' und 'Hand wäscht Hand':—sie
haben nicht das Recht noch Kraft zu eurem Eigennutz!" (KSA4: 362). Obviously Zarathustra is well aware of the extensive general knowledge of these
two folk proverbs so that he does not need to cite them in their entirety.
Egotistical or elitist is of course also his employment of the cautionary proverb "Trust, watch, whom" / "Trau, schau, wem" that is quickly changed into
an aggressive anti-proverb in regard to the courageous higher men: "I love
the valiant; but it is not enough to wield a broadsword, one must also know
against whom [strike, watch, whom]." (209) / "Ich liebe die Tapferen: aber es
ist nicht genug, Hau-Degen sein,—man muss auch wissen Hau-schau-Wen!"
(KSA4: 262; see Meyer 1914: 142–43). At least Zarathustra accepts a quotation by Pindar long turned proverb in the following self-characterization:

For that is what I am through and through: reeling, reeling in, raising up, raising, a raiser, cultivator, and disciplinarian, who once counseled himself, not
for nothing: Become who you are! (239)

Der nämlich bin ich von Grund und Anbeginn, ziehend, heranziehend, hin-
aufziehend, aufziehend, ein Zieher, Züchter und Zuchtmeister, der sich nicht
umsonst einstmals zusprach: "Werde, der du bist!" (KSA4: 297)

In this case Nietzsche shows himself as so often as a true philologist in his
convincing and skillful use of various terms belonging to the word-field of
"pull" / "ziehen." They enable him to express Zarathustra's difficult task to
educate (pull along) at least some chosen people on their path from an expanded self-knowledge to a free life.

Nietzsche's Discrediting of the Morality of Bible Proverbs

Part of this process, as has already been mentioned, is a definitive rejection
of Christianity with its virtuous lessons of morality that are current among
the folk in the form of uncritically accepted Bible proverbs. In the revealing
chapter of *Zarathustra* "On Old and New Tablets" / "Von alten und neuen
Tafeln," Nietzsche's anti-Christian prophet thus demands very blatantly:
"Break, break, O my brothers, these old tablets of the pious. Break the maxims of those who slander the world" (205) / "Zerbrecht, zerbrecht mir, oh
meine Brüder, diese alten Tafeln der Frommen! Zersprecht mir die Sprüche
der Welt-Verleumder!" (KSA4: 257). From a paremiological point of view,
the word invention "zersprechen" / "to break by speaking" could be regarded
a linguistic description of the alienation of Biblical proverbs into secularized anti-proverbs. The language of the Bible forms the poetic-prophetic basis of this book, not the least because Nietzsche—as the son of a minister
and former student of theology—had a special predilection for the powerful
language of Luther's Bible translation (see Baumgartner 1912). The fact that
Nietzsche succeeds with this consciously employed religious and yet secularized style is in part at least due to the fact that he usually limits himself to
well-known Bible references, with proverbs and proverbial expressions from
the Bible long ago having been accepted into colloquial speech (see Schulze
1860; Grünberg 1888; Krauss 1993; Steger 1998; Schmidt 2002). In this regard it even happens once that Nietzsche cites a Bible proverb with just a
small shortening as a repeated leitmotif. It is the proverb "He that has ears to
hear, let him hear" / "Wer Ohren hat zu hören, der höre" (Matthew 11:15; see
Paronis 1976: 59) that Zarathustra takes almost verbatim from Jesus in order
to convince his fellow human beings to listen to his message concerning the
path to a higher existence:

Courage, however, is the best slayer [. . .]. In such words, however, there is much playing and brass. He that has ears to hear, let him hear! (157)
Muth aber ist der beste Todtschläger [. . .]. In solchem Spruche aber ist viel klingendes Spiel. Wer Ohren hat, der höre.— (KSA4: 199)

And then all the gods laughed and rocked on their chairs and cried, "Is not just this godlike that there are gods but no God?"
He that has ears to hear, let him hear! (182)
Und alle Götter lachten damals und wackelten auf ihren Stühlen und riefen: "Ist das nicht eben Göttlichkeit, dass es Götter, aber keinen Gott giebt?"
Wer Ohren hat, der höre.— (KSA4: 230)

And you shall first learn from me how to learn—how to learn well. He that has ears to hear, let him hear! (206)
Und auch das Lernen sollt ihr erst von mir lernen, das Gut-Lernen!—Wer Ohren hat, der höre! (KSA4: 258)

To this are added proverbial expressions that relate to the topic of listening well, as for example "Open your ears to me, for now I shall speak to you about the death of peoples" (48) / "Jetzt thut mir die Ohren auf, denn jetzt sage ich euch mein Wort vom Tode der Völker" (KSA4: 61); "that whoever pricks up his ears as he lies in the grass or on lonely slopes will find out something about those things that are between heaven and earth" (127) / "dass wer im Grase oder an einsamen Gehängen liegend die Ohren spitze, Etwas von den Dingen erfahre, die zwischen Himmel und Erde sind" (KSA4: 164); and "but it is precisely into their ears that I like to shout, 'Yes, I am Zarathustra the godless!'" (171) / "aber gerade ihnen liebe ich's, in das Ohr zu schreien: Ja! Ich bin Zarathustra, der Gottlose!" (KSA4: 215).

To be sure, Zarathustra, this new type of prophet, always has to be conscious of whether people are hearing and understanding him properly: "As yet my words have not moved mountains, and what I said did not reach men. Indeed, I have gone to men, but as yet I have not arrived" (146) / "Noch versetzte mein Wort keine Berge, und was ich redete, erreichte die Menschen nicht. Ich gieng wohl zu den Menschen, aber noch langte ich nicht bei ihnen an" (KSA4: 188). No wonder then that Zarathustra even picks up the folk expression "to speak German with someone" / "deutsch mit jdm. reden" in order to get the proper attention by speaking very directly (in German!) to them: "My guests, you higher men, let me speak to you in plain and clear German" (282) / "Meine Gäste, ihr höheren Menschen, ich will deutsch und deutlich mit euch reden" (KSA4: 350).

Zarathustra's presumptuous claim that his words might someday move mountains is clearly an allusion to the Bible proverb "Faith can remove mountains" / "Der Glaube kann Berge versetzen" (1 Corinthians 13:2). But when he next uses the Bible proverb "Faith makes blessed" / "Der Glaube macht selig" (Mark 16:16), there is no arrogance involved. He simply wants to point out to his "disciples" / "Jüngern" that he is no fanatical leader but rather someone who explains and interprets and who points out a better way for life without any presumptuous didacticism:

> The disciple answered, "I believe in Zarathustra." But Zarathustra shook his head and smiled.
> Faith does not make me blessed, he said, especially not faith in me. (127)
> Der Jünger antwortete: "ich glaube an Zarathustra." Aber Zarathustra schüttelte den Kopf und lächelte.
> Der Glaube macht mich nicht selig, zumal nicht der Glaube an mich. (KSA4: 163–64)

As the possible founder of a new religion he would most likely be very interested in this faith, but Zarathustra has no ready solutions at hand, as the negated proverb points out. He only wants to point out constellations and possibilities in an often symbolic and contradictory fashion that just might lead to a life-affirming existence without God and religion. But as an existentialist atheist, he most certainly does not want to be the founder of a new religion!

Doubtlessly Nietzsche has a predilection for Bible references that have entered folk speech, but he cites such proverbs and proverbial expressions in his own free way and interprets them in an innovative fashion. They are rarely quoted in their original wording but are instead distorted or negated in ever-changing mutations. Sometimes it suffices simply to allude to a Bible reference with the original piece of wisdom adding much to the intended intertextual irony. The following chronologically arranged examples from *Zarathustra* should show with what virtuosity Nietzsche is able to deal with proverbs from the Old and New Testaments:

> *Proverbs 3:12; Hebrews 12:6:* "Whom the Lord (God) loves he chastises" / "Wen der Herr (Gott) lieb hat, den züchtigt er."
> I love him who chastises his God because he loves his God: for he must perish of the wrath of his God. (16)
> Ich liebe Den, welcher seinen Gott züchtigt, weil er seinen Gott liebt: denn er muss am Zorne seines Gottes zu Grunde gehen. (KSA4: 18)

3 Moses 19:18; Galatians 5:14: "Love your neighbor as yourself" / "Liebe deinen Nächsten wie dich selbst."
My brothers, love of the neighbor I do not recommend to you: I recommend to you love of the farthest.
Thus spoke Zarathustra. (62)
Meine Brüder, zur Nächstenliebe rathe ich euch nicht: ich rathe euch zur Fernsten-Liebe. Also sprach Zarathustra. (KSA4: 79)
"Do love your neighbor as yourself, but first be such as love themselves." (172)
"Liebt immerhin euren Nächsten gleich euch,—aber seid mir erst Solche, die sich selber lieben." (KSA4: 216)

Matthew 7:7: "Seek, and you shall find" / "Suchet, so werdet ihr finden."
Is it your wish, my brother, to go into solitude? Is it your wish to seek the way to yourself? Then linger a moment, and listen to me.
"He who seeks, easily gets lost. All Loneliness is guilt"—thus speaks the herd. And you have long belonged to the herd. (62)
Willst du, mein Bruder, in die Vereinsamung gehen? Willst du den Weg zu dir selber suchen? Zaudere noch ein Wenig und höre mich.
"Wer sucht, der geht leicht selber verloren. Alle Vereinsamung ist Schuld": also spricht die Heerde. Und du gehörtest lange zur Heerde." (KSA4: 80)

Matthew 12:34: "Out of the abundance the mouth speaketh" / "Wes das Herz voll ist, des geht der Mund über"; i.e., Whose heart is full will have his mouth overflow (see Kunstmann 1952; Nelson 1986; Mieder 1995).
Verily, you fill your mouth with noble words; and are we to believe that your heart is overflowing, you liars? (123)
Wahrlich, ihr nehmt den Mund voll mit edlen Worten: und wir sollen glauben, dass euch das Herz übergehe, ihr Lügenbolde? (KSA4: 158)

2 Moses 3:8: "Land flowing with milk and honey" / "Land, darin Milch und Honig fließt."
He who has always spared himself much will in the end become sickly of so much consideration. Praised be what hardens! I do not praise the land where butter and honey flow. (153)
Wer sich stets viel geschont hat, der kränkelt zuletzt an seiner vielen Schonung. Gelobt sei, was hart macht! Ich lobe das Land nicht, wo Butter und Honig—fliesst! (KSA4: 194)

Mark 16:16: "Faith makes blessed" / "Der Glaube macht selig."
"Sure! Sure! Faith makes him blessed, faith in him. That is the way of old people. We are no different ourselves." (182)
"Ja! Ja! Der Glaube macht ihn selig, der Glaube an ihn. Das ist so die Art alter Leute! So geht's uns auch!"— (KSA4: 229)

Ecclesiastes 1:2: "All is vanity (vain)" / "Es ist alles ganz eitel."
It [self-enjoyment] also despises all wisdom that wallows in grief; for verily, there is also wisdom that blooms in the dark, a nightshade wisdom, which always sighs: all is vain. (190)
Sie [Selbstsucht] verachtet auch alle wehselige Weisheit: denn, wahrlich, es giebt auch eine Weisheit, die im Dunklen blüht, eine Nachtschatten-Weisheit: als welche immer seufzt: "Alles ist eitel!" (KSA4: 239)

Revelation 1:8: "I am the alpha and omega, saith the Lord" / "Ich bin das A und das O, spricht Gott der Herr."
And if this is my alpha and omega, that all that is heavy and grave should become light; all that is body, dancer; all that is spirit, bird—and verily, that is my alpha and omega. (230)
Und wenn Das mein A und O ist, dass alles Schwere leicht, aller Leib Tänzer, aller Geist Vogel werde: und wahrlich, Das ist mein A und O!— (KSA4: 290)

5 Moses 8:3; Matthew 4:4: "Man does not live by bread alone" / "Der Mensch lebt nicht vom Brot allein" [see Mieder 2010].
"Bread?" countered Zarathustra, and he laughed. "Bread is one thing hermits do not have. But man does not live by bread alone, but also of the meat of good lambs, of which I have two. (284–85)
"Brod? entgegnete Zarathustra und lachte dazu. Nur gerade Brod haben Einsiedler nicht. Aber der Mensch lebt nicht vom Brod allein, sondern auch vom Fleische guter Lämmer, deren ich zwei habe." (KSA4: 354)

From these very truncated contexts it becomes clear that these more or less independently appearing texts reflect Nietzsche's preoccupation with the revaluation of all values and his definite break with Christianity (see Vitens 1951: 34–40). In order to illustrate this in a bit more detail, the following longer text from the chapter "On New and Old Tablets" / "Von alten und neuen Tafeln" is cited where Nietzsche proves his fascination with Bible and folk proverbs in a unique collage:

"Why live? All is vanity! Living—that is threshing straw; living—that is consuming oneself in flames without becoming warm." Such antiquarian babbling is still considered "wisdom"; it is honored all the more for being old and musty. Mustiness too ennobles.

Children might speak thus: they fear the fire before [i.e., because] it burned them. There is much childishness in the old books of wisdom. And why should those who always "thresh straw" be allowed to blaspheme threshing? Such oxen [i.e., fools] should be muzzled after all.

Such men sit down to the table and bring nothing along, not even a good appetite; and then they blaspheme: "All is vanity." But eating and drinking well, O my brothers, is verily no vain art. Break, break the old tablets of the never gay! (204)

"Wozu leben? Alles ist eitel! Leben—das ist Stroh dreschen; Leben—das ist sich verbrennen und doch nicht warm werden."—

Solch alterthümliches Geschwätz gilt immer noch als "Weisheit"; dass es aber alt ist und dumpfig riecht, darum wird es besser geehrt. Auch der Moder adelt.—

Kinder durften so reden: die scheuen das Feuer, weil es sie brannte! Es ist viel Kinderei in den alten Büchern der Weisheit.

Und wer immer "Stroh drischt," wie sollte der auf das Dreschen lästern dürfen! Solchen Narren müsste man doch das Maul verbinden!

Solche setzen sich zu Tisch und bringen Nichts mit, selbst den guten Hunger nicht:—und nun lästern sie "Alles ist eitel!"

Aber gut essen und trinken, oh meine Brüder, ist wahrlich keine eitle Kunst! Zerbrecht, zerbrecht mir die Tafeln der Nimmer-Frohen! (KSA4: 256)

That is most certainly not idle proverbial gibberish! This passage could hardly be more proverbial, and yet, it is just possible that Nietzsche has Karl Simrock's (since 1846 repeatedly reissued) proverb collection *Die deutschen Sprichwörter* with its 12,396 proverbs in mind, when he observes that "There is much childishness in the old books of wisdom" / "Es ist viel Kinderei in den alten Büchern der Weisheit" (see Simrock 1988: 7–18). Be that as it may, the Bible proverbs "All is vanity"/ "Es ist alles ganz eitel" (Ecclesiastes 1:2) and "You shall not muzzle the ox when he treads out the corn" / "Du sollst dem Ochsen, der da drischt, nicht das Maul verbinden" (5 Moses 25:4) as well as the folk proverbs "Work (also: virtue) ennobles" / "Arbeit [auch: Tugend] adelt" and "A burnt child dreads the fire" / "Gebranntes Kind scheut das Feuer" are mixed together in the form of repetitions, allusions, and anti-proverbs. The result is a passage that contains an important basic idea of

Zarathustra, namely that it is "high time" / "höchste Zeit" that stone tablets with antiquated wisdom chiseled onto them must finally be broken so that the path for a new type of existence beyond old moral rules becomes free.

"It Is High Time" as a Phraseologism Calling for Change

No wonder that the phraseologism "It is high time" (see 130, 162, 242) / "Es ist höchste Zeit" (see KSA4: 167, 204, 301) reappears as a verbal sign for the extreme urgency of this fundamental change. However, typical for Nietzsche in the case of such calls for radical change, a precise description of the path is lacking. Thus all that remains is a questioning scream for certainty:

> "What shall I think of that?" said Zarathustra; "am I a ghost then? But it must have been my shadow. [...]
> And once more Zarathustra shook his head and wondered. "What shall I think of that?" he said once more. "Why did the ghost cry, 'It is time! It is high time!' High time for what?"
> Thus spoke Zarathustra. (133)
> "Was soll ich davon denken! sagte Zarathustra. Bin ich denn ein Gespenst? Aber es wird mein Schatten gewesen sein." [...]
> Und nochmals schüttelte Zarathustra den Kopf und wunderte sich. "Was soll ich davon denken!" sagte er nochmals.
> "Warum schrie denn das Gespenst: es ist Zeit! Es ist die höchste Zeit! Wozu ist es denn—höchste Zeit?"—
> Also sprach Zarathustra. (KSA4: 171)

But does Zarathustra really not know the answer? Or does he not want to elevate his own thoughts or his individual path to the sole way of life for all? A hidden proverbial statement offers a helpful hint: "And if a man goes through fire for his doctrine—what does that prove? Verily, it is more if your own doctrine comes out of your own fire!" (93) / "Und wenn Einer durch's Feuer geht für seine Lehre,—was beweist diess! Mehr ist's wahrlich, dass aus eignem Brande die eigne Lehre kommt!" (KSA4: 119). This appears to say that Zarathustra (as the spokesperson for Nietzsche) does not want to offer a definitive doctrine. After all, human existence in a modern world without God depends on individuals who know how to find their own path after they have demolished the old world. Seen in this way, Nietzsche's obscure use of the classical proverb "To each his own" / "Jeden das Seine," so problematical today in light of its use on the gates of concentration camps, starts making sense: "But how could I think of being just through and through? How can I give each his own? Let this be sufficient for me: I give each my own" (69) / "Aber wie wollte ich gerecht sein von Grund aus! Wie kann ich Jedem das Seine geben! Diess sei mir genug: ich gebe Jedem das Meine" (KSA4: 88; see Doerr 2000). Thus Zarathustra shows himself not as a prophet of established doctrines but rather as a companion and an adviser to equally free spirits on their path to earthly self-fulfillment.

There are then no ready-made lessons or directions given by Zarathustra since he himself is learning and developing. Certain insights come to him only by and by that lighten up his own path to liberation from old moral concepts: "The annihilator of morals, the good and just call me: my story is immoral" (68) / "Den Vernichter der Moral heissen mich die Guten und Gerechten: meine Geschichte ist unmoralisch" (KSA4: 87). When Nietzsche at the beginning of the book describes how Zarathustra wakes up from a long sleep and how his prophetic task takes on a clearer meaning, he couches this new insight in an illuminating way into a twofold use of the proverbial expression "a light (insight) comes to someone" / "jdm. geht ein Licht auf":

> For a long time Zarathustra slept, and not only dawn passed over his face but the morning too. At last, however, his eyes opened: amazed, Zarathustra looked into the woods and the silence; amazed, he looked into himself. Then he rose quickly, like a seafarer who suddenly sees land, and jubilated, for he saw a new truth. And thus he spoke to his heart:
> An insight has come to me: companions I need, living ones—not dead companions and corpses whom I carry with myself wherever I want to. Living companions I need, who follow me because they want to follow themselves—wherever I want.
> An insight has come to me: let Zarathustra speak not to the people but to companions. Zarathustra shall not become the shepherd and dog of a herd. (23)
> Lange schlief Zarathustra, und nicht nur die Morgenröthe gieng über sein Antlitz, sondern auch der Vormittag. Endlich aber that sein Auge sich auf: verwundert sah Zarathustra in den Wald und die Stille, verwundert sah er in sich hinein. Dann erhob er sich schnell, wie ein Seefahrer, der mit Einem Male Land sieht, und jauchzte: denn er sah eine neue Wahrheit. Und also redete er dann zu seinem Herzen:
> Ein Licht gieng mir auf: Gefährten brauche ich und lebendige,—nicht todte Gefährten und Leichname, die ich mit mir trage, wohin ich will.
> Sondern lebendige Gefährten brauche ich, die mir folgen, weil sie sich selber folgen wollen—und dorthin, wo ich will.

Ein Licht gieng mir auf: nicht zum Volk rede Zarathustra, sondern zu Gefährten! Nicht soll Zarathustra einer Heerde Hirt und Hund werden! (KSA4: 25)

In addition to repeating that an "insight had come to him" (30) / "ihm war
ein Licht aufgegangen" KSA4: 34), Zarathustra also repeatedly employs the
expression "to bring something to light" / "etwas ans Licht bringen" in order
to allude to the fact that all inadequacies and mendacities of life must be put
under a scrutinizing light if a break with Christian morality is truly to take
place:

But like the boar's snout, my words shall tear open the foundation of your
souls [of the supposedly virtuous ones]: a plowshare will I be to you. All the
secrets of your foundation shall come to light; and when you lie uprooted and
broken in the sun, then will your lies also be separated from your truths. (94)
Aber dem Rüssel des Ebers gleich soll mein Wort den Grund eurer Seelen [der
angeblich Tugendhaften] aufreissen; Pflugschar will ich euch heissen.
Alle Heimlichkeiten eures Grundes sollen an's Licht; und wenn ihr auf-
gewühlt und zerbrochen in der Sonne liegt, wird auch eure Lüge von eurer
Wahrheit ausgeschieden sein. (KSA4: 120)

Thus I speak to you in a parable—you who make souls whirl, you preachers
of equality. To me you are tarantulas, and secretly vengeful. But I shall bring
your secrets to light; therefore I laugh to your faces with my laughter of the
heights. (99)
Also rede ich zu euch im Gleichniss, die ihr die Seelen drehend macht, ihr
Prediger der Gleichheit! Taranteln seid ihr mir und versteckte Rachsüchtige!
Aber ich will eure Verstecke schon an's Licht bringen: darum lache ich euch
in's Antlitz mein Gelächter der Höhe. (KSA4: 128)

For earthquakes bury many wells and leave many languishing, but they also
bring to light inner powers and secrets. Earthquakes reveal new wells. In
earthquakes that strike ancient peoples, new wells break open. (211)
Das Erdbeben nämlich—das verschüttet viel [*sic*] Brunnen, das schafft viel
Verschmachten: das hebt auch innre Kräfte und Heimlichkeiten an's Licht.
Das Erdbeben macht neue Quellen offenbar. Im Erdbeben alter Völker bre-
chen neue Quellen aus. (KSA4: 265)

Proverbial Misogyny in Nietzsche's Revaluation of All Values

Despite such sources of light, there are also dark spots in *Zarathustra*, especially in regard to Nietzsche's obvious misogyny. Such proverbial statements as "I should sooner believe in the man in the moon than in the woman" (121) / "eher noch will ich an den Mann im Monde glauben als an das Weib" (KSA4: 156) and "even the most cunning still buys his wife in a poke" (70) / "seine Frau kauft auch der Listigste noch im Sack" (KSA4: 91) are anti-feministic tirades that beg for justified criticism to this day. And surely criticism would also be leveled against Nietzsche by both genders regarding the following statement where Nietzsche, by way of a degrading allusion to the proverb "Marriages are made in heaven" / "Ehen werden im Himmel geschlossen," labels this institution as worthless:

> That which the all-too-many, the superfluous, call marriage—alas, what shall I name that? Alas, this poverty of the soul in pair! Alas, this filth of the soul in pair! Alas, this wretched contentment in pair! Marriage they call this; and they say that their marriages are made in heaven. Well, I do not like it, this heaven of the superfluous. No, I do not like them—these animals entangled in the heavenly net. And let the God who limps near to bless what he never joined keep his distance from me! (70)
>
> Das, was die Viel-zu-Vielen Ehe nennnen, diese Überflüssigen,—ach, wie nenne ich das?
>
> Ach, diese Armuth der Seele zu Zweien! Ach, dieser Schmutz der Seele zu Zweien! Ach, diess erbärmliche Behagen zu Zweien!
>
> Ehe nennen sie diess Alles; und sie sagen, ihre Ehen seien im Himmel geschlossen.
>
> Nun, ich mag ihn nicht, diesen Himmel der Überflüssigen! Nein, ich mag sie nicht, diese im himmlischen Netz verschlungenen Thiere!
>
> Ferne bleibe mir auch der Gott, der heranhinkt, zu segnen, was er nicht zusammenfügte! (see Matthew 19:6; KSA4: 90–91)

A philosopher or writer who gets carried away to the extent that he refers to married people as animals also would not shy away from the declaration "For man is the cruelest animal" (218) / "Der Mensch nämlich ist das grausamste Thier" (KSA4: 273). People also appear to be proverbial "dumme Esel" / "dumb asses" at times, as can be seen by the comment added to a pseudo-proverb about the challenges of life: "Life is hard to bear; but do not act so tenderly! We are all of us fair beasts of burden, male and female asses" (41)

/ "Das Leben ist schwer zu tragen: aber so thut mir doch nicht so zärtlich! Wir sind allesammt hübsche lastbare Esel und Eselinnen" (KSA4: 49). The animal world, seen as representing human existence, appears as eagles, snakes, lions, camels, asses, monkeys, dogs, sheep, etc. throughout *Zarathustra* (see Thatcher 1977), with corresponding animal expressions referring more or less indirectly to human behavioral patterns (see Carl 1962; Meisser 1969; Schmidt 1972; Sternkopf 1993; Dobrovol'skij and Piirainen 1996), as for example:

When the fire hound heard this he could no longer bear listening to him [i.e., me]. Shamed, he drew in his tail, in a cowed manner said "bow-wow," and crawled down into his cave. (132)
Als diess der Feuerhund vernahm, hielt er's nicht mehr aus, mir zuzuhören. Beschämt zog er seinen Schwanz ein, sagte auf eine kleinlaute Weise Wau! Wau! und kroch hinab in seine Höhle.— (KSA4: 170)

Stop splashing about that, you raincloud in the morning! Do I not stand here even now, wet from your melancholy and drenched like a dog? (243)
Höre davon auf zu plätschern, du Regenwolke am Vormittag! Stehe ich denn nicht schon da, nass von deiner Trübsal und begossen wie ein Hund? (KSA4: 303)

In the end, a frog which has puffed itself up too long will burst: the wind comes out. To stab a swollen man in the belly, I call that a fine pastime. (258)
Zuletzt platzt ein Frosch, der sich zu lange aufblies: da fährt der Wind heraus. Einem Geschwollnen in den Bauch stechen, das heisse ich eine brave Kurzweil. (KSA4: 320)

And verily, he is the strangest sage who is also clever and no ass. (285)
Und wahrlich, das ist das Seltsamste an einem Weisen, wenn er zu alledem auch noch klug und kein Esel ist. (KSA4: 355)

Has there been anything filthier on earth so far than desert saints? Around them not only was the devil loose, but also the swine. (292)
Gab es Schmutzigeres bisher auf Erden als Wüsten-Heilige? Um die herum war nicht nur der Teufel los,—sondern auch das Schwein. (KSA4: 363)

Women might not be "filthy like desert saints" for Nietzsche, but they certainly are bad as far as he is concerned, to wit his infamous *Zarathustra*

quotation that has become current in folk speech as "When you go to a woman, don't forget the whip" / "Wenn du zum Weibe gehst, vergiß die Peitsche
nicht" (see Thomas 1980). By summer/fall 1882 Nietzsche already had written down the following note: "You go to women? Don't forget the whip!
In the way how and what one honors, one always draws a distance around
oneself" / "Du gehst zu Frauen? Vergiß die Peitsche nicht! In der Art, wie
und was man ehrt, zieht man immer eine Distanz um sich" (KSA10: 97–98).
This anti-feministic statement then appears in 1883 in the first part of *Zarathustra* in a varied form in the chapter "On Little Old and Young Women"
/ "Von alten und jungen Weiblein," but it should be noted that it is actually
uttered by a woman:

> Then the little old woman answered me [Zarathustra]: "Many fine things has
> Zarathustra said, especially for those who are young enough for them. It is
> strange: Zarathustra knows women little, and yet he is right about them. Is
> this because nothing is impossible with woman? And now, as a token of gra-
> titude, accept a little truth. After all, I am old enough for it. Wrap it up and
> hold your hand over its mouth: else it will cry overloudly, this little truth."
> Then I said: "Woman, give me your little truth." And thus spoke the little old
> woman:
> "You are going to women? Do not forget the whip!" (67)
> Da entgegnete mir [Zarathustra] das alte Weiblein: "Vieles Artige sagte Zara-
> thustra und sonderlich für Die, welche jung genug dazu sind.
> "Seltsam ist's, Zarathustra kennt wenig die Weiber, und doch hat er über sie
> Recht! Geschieht diess desshalb, weil beim Weibe kein Ding unmöglich ist?
> "Und nimm zum Danke eine kleine Wahrheit! Bin ich doch alt genug für sie!
> „Wickle sie ein und halte ihr den Mund: sonst schreit sie überlaut, diese kleine
> Wahrheit."
> "Gieb mir, Weib, deine kleine Wahrheit!" sagte ich. Und also sprach das alte
> Weiblein:
> "Du gehst zu Frauen? Vergiss die Peitsche nicht!"— (KSA4: 86)

As usually happens with a well-known quotation, people have reacted to this
quotation in parodistic aphorisms and verses. Jürgen Christen even edited a
book with the title *Vergiß die Peitsche nicht. Frauenfeindliche Sprüche* (1991;
see Spicker 2010). Here are at least a few examples of such anti-quotations
with some of them referring directly to Nietzsche:

As is well known, Nietzsche says: When you go to a woman, don't forget the whip.—Only a hopeless and revengeful weakling could have made such an utterance.

Nietzsche sagt bekanntlich: Wenn du zum Weibe gehst, vergiß die Peitsche nicht.—Nur ein hoffnungsloser und rachsüchtiger Schwächling konnte einen solchen Ausspruch tun.

Erich Brock (1975)

Love advice freely adapted from Nietzsche
You go to women?
Don't forget the flowers!
You go to men?
Don't forget the pill!
Liebestip frei nach Nietzsche
Du geht zu Frauen?
Vergiß die Blumen nicht!
Du gehst zu Männern?
Vergiß die Pille nicht!
Heinrich Schröter (1977)

When you go to a woman, don't forget the dough [money].
Wenn du zum Weibe gehst, vergiß die Piepen nicht.
Anonym (1981)

If you go to a woman, don't forget to really whip yourself up beforehand.
(Nietzsche the Elder)
Gehst du zur Frau, vergiß nicht, dich vorher tüchtig aufzupeitschen. (Nietzsche der Ältere)
Winfried Bornemann (1983)

You go to women? Don't forget the rubber [condom]!
Du gehst zu Frauen? Vergiß das Gummi nicht!
Ulrich Erckenbrecht (1991; for references see Mieder 1997: 333–35)

Nietzsche advised men to take the whip along when they go to a woman. Did he not trust the intellectual supremacy of man?
Nietzsche riet den Männern, die Peitsche mitzunehmen, wenn sie zum Weibe gehen. Traute er der geistigen Überlegenheit des Mannes nicht?
Walter Rupp (2010: 50)

It must also be stated in addition that, in the "whip" / "Peitsche" reference in *Zarathustra*, yet another anti-feministic proverb comes into play. It is the Bible proverb "With God all things are possible" / "Bei Gott sind alle Ding möglich" (Matthew 19:26), which Nietzsche had already mutated twice in 1882/1883 into the questionable anti-proverb "With women no thing is impossible" / "Bei Weibern ist kein Ding unmöglich" before it appeared in the singular form of "woman" / "Weib" in *Zarathustra*. The two earlier variants show how such fragmentary texts serve Nietzsche as "preliminary studies" / "Vorstudien" to his larger works.

> You do not know the women: how come that occasionally you are right about them?—With women no thing is impossible.
> Du kennst die W<eiber> nicht: wie kommt es, daß du bisweilen über sie recht hast?—Bei den W<eibern> ist kein Ding unmöglich. (KSA10: 89)

> It is difficult to say something false about a woman: with women no thing is impossible—answered Zarathustra.
> Es ist schwer, über das Weib etwas Falsches zu sagen: bei den Weibern ist kein Ding unmöglich—antwortete Zarathustra. (KSA10: 160)

Perhaps Nietzsche also included positive abilities of women here, but more likely these are ironic statements that originate from his blatant anti-feminism. In his defense it might be said that Nietzsche otherwise does not cite traditional proverbs against women in his voluminous writings. He certainly would have had plenty of anti-feministic proverbs at his disposal, since such unfortunate texts are current throughout the world (see Schipper 2003; Rittersbacher 2002).

Nietzsche's Anti-Proverbs and Pseudo-Proverbs as Philosophical Signs

The formulation of shocking anti-proverbs is part and parcel of Nietzsche's consciously employed style with elements from folk speech. In his fragments from 1882 the short anti-proverb "A wrong shared is half right" / "Getheiltes Unrecht ist halbes Recht," i.e., Shared injustice is half justice (KSA10: 49, 78) is listed twice, and probably is based on the proverb "Shared suffering is half joy" / "Geteiltes Leid ist halbe Freud." Half a year later this longer and challenging variant found its way into his *Zarathustra*: "Did you already know this? A wrong shared is half right. And he who is able to bear it should take the wrong upon himself" (68) / "Wusstet ihr diess schon? Getheiltes

Unrecht ist halbes Recht. Und der soll das Unrecht auf sich nehmen, der es tragen kann!" (KSA4: 88). Also of interest is Nietzsche's change of the proverb "What does not exist can still be [happen, take place]" / "Was nicht ist, das kann noch werden" into the anti-proverb "For, what does not exist cannot will [want]; but what is in existence, how could that still want existence?" (115) / "Denn: was nicht ist, das kann nicht wollen; was aber im Dasein ist, wie könnte das noch zum Dasein wollen?" (KSA4: 149). And the proverb "Everything has two sides" / "Jedes Ding hat zwei Seiten" ist quickly changed into the life-affirming anti-proverb "That you would learn my wisdom from me: even the worst thing has two good reverse sides" (295) / "So lernt mir doch meine Weisheit ab: auch das schlimmste Ding hat zwei gute Kehrseiten" (KSA4: 367).

Of course, Nietzsche also simply creates his own pseudo-proverbs when he appears to have no traditional proverb at hand to "play" with. But no matter how poetic and even mystical his style in *Zarathustra* might be, he is forever keen to include formulaic structures that add a colloquial and authoritative flavor, as for example:

> But even the superfluous still make a fuss about their dying; and even the hollowest nut still wants to be cracked. (71)
> Aber auch die Überflüssigen thun noch wichtig mit ihrem Sterben, und auch die hohlste Nuss will noch geknackt sein. (KSA4: 93)

> In some, the heart grows old first; in others, the spirit. And some are old in their youth: but late youth preserves long youth. (72)
> Andern altert das Herz zuerst und Andern der Geist. Und Einige sind greis in der Jugend: aber spät jung erhält lang jung. (KSA4: 94)

> Or they spend long evenings watching a cunning, ambushing, cross-marked spider, which preaches cleverness to the other spiders and teaches thus: "Under crosses one can spin well." (181)
> Oder sie sehen lange Abende einer listigen lauernden Kreuzspinne zu, welche den Spinnen selber Klugheit predigt und also lehrt: "unter Kreuzen ist gut spinnen!" (KSA4: 228)

> And should we sweat, we are told: "Yes, life is a grave burden [hard to bear]." (193; see also 41: "Life is hard to bear")
> Und schwitzen wir, so sagt man uns: "Ja, das Leben ist schwer zu tragen!" (KSA4: 243; see also KSA4: 49, "Das Leben ist schwer zu tragen")

There is much filth in the world; that much is true. But that does not make the world itself a filthy monster. (205)

Es giebt in der Welt viel Koth: so Viel ist wahr! Aber darum ist die Welt selber noch kein kothiges Ungeheuer! (KSA4: 256)

The higher its type, the more rarely a thing succeeds. You higher men here, have you not all failed? (292)

Je höher von Art, je seltener gerät ein Ding. Ihr höheren Menschen hier, seid ihr nicht alle—missgerathen? (KSA4: 364)

Taking the popular proverbial structure "Rather (better) X than Y" / "Lieber (besser) X als Y" as a basis (see Peukes 1977: 145–46), Nietzsche creates the following proverb-like statement: "Rather know nothing than half-know much! Rather be a fool on one's own than a sage according to the opinion of others!" (250) / "Lieber Nichts wissen, als Vieles halb wissen! Lieber ein Narr sein auf eigne Faust, als ein Weiser nach fremdem Gedünken!" (KSA4: 311). The somatic expression "to do something on one's own (with one's own fist)" / "etwas auf eigene Faust machen" is also included, and it is also present in the following text, albeit without the "than" / "als" comparison: "Rather no God, rather make destiny on one's own, rather be a fool, rather be a God oneself!" (262) / "Lieber keinen Gott, lieber auf eigne Faust Schicksal machen, lieber Narr sein, lieber selber Gott sein!" (KSA4: 325). Both statements are of considerable importance for the actual message of *Zarathustra*, since the overman is supposed to manage his own affairs even if at times he feels like a fool in his affirmation of life. The key issue for Zarathustra is always that man must accept his existential fate without God.

This requires man, according to Nietzsche, to be "hard" / "hart" in committing himself to the revaluation of all values and in standing firm in the eternal struggle against antiquated moral concepts. Regarding this necessary liberation from God and Christianity, Nietzsche has formulated a prophetic declaration that he repeated four years later at the end of *Götzen-Dämmerung* (1888, *The Demise of the Gods*) with the title "The Hammer Speaks" / "Der Hammer redet." But who would have expected him to start this key passage about "become hard!" / "werdet hart!" with the pseudo-wellerism "Why so hard? the kitchen coal once said to the diamond. After all, are we not close kin?" / "Warum so hart!—sprach zum Diamanten einst die Küchen-Kohle; sind wir denn nicht Nah-Verwandte?" (see Hoefer 1855; Mieder 2000). This is yet another example that Nietzsche cannot make do without proverbial elements:

"Why so hard?" the kitchen coal once said to the diamond. "After all, are we not close kin?"

Why so soft? O my brothers, thus I ask you: are you not after all my brothers?

Why so soft, so pliant and yielding? Why is there so much denial, self-denial, in your heads? So little destiny in your eyes?

And if you do not want to be destinies and inexorable ones, how can you triumph with me?

And if your hardness does not wish to flash and cut and cut through, how can you one day create with me?

For creators are hard. And it must seem blessedness to you to impress your hand on millennia as on wax.

Blessedness to write on the will of millennia as on bronze—harder than bronze, nobler than bronze. Only the noblest is altogether hard.

This new tablet, O my brothers, I place over you: become hard! (214)

"Warum so hart!—sprach zum Diamanten einst die Küchen-Kohle; sind wir denn nicht Nah-Verwandte?"—

Warum so weich? Oh meine Brüder, also frage ich euch: seid ihr denn nicht— meine Brüder?

Warum so weich, so weichend und nachgebend? Warum ist so viel Leugnung, Verleugnung in eurem Herzen? So wenig Schicksal in eurem Blicke?

Und wollt ihr nicht Schicksale sein und Unerbittliche: wie könntet ihr mit mir—siegen?

Und wenn eure Härte nicht blitzen und scheiden und zerschneiden will: wie könntet ihr einst mit mir—schaffen?

Die Schaffenden nämlich sind hart. Und Seligkeit muss es euch dünken, eure Hand auf Jahrtausende zu drücken wie auf Wachs,—

—Seligkeit, auf dem Willen von Jahrtausenden zu schreiben wie auf Erz,— härter als Erz, edler als Erz. Ganz hart ist allein das Edelste.

Diese neue Tafel, oh meine Brüder, stelle ich über euch: werdet hart!— (KSA4: 268; KSA6: 161)

Since Nietzsche is full of contradictions, it should not be surprising to find a textual reference in *Zarathustra* where hardness is replaced by something pleasant. After all, fate offers many possibilities and man has a free choice! And it is in this regard that Nietzsche's very own formulation "One thing is more necessary than another" / "Eins ist notwendiger als das andere," identified by him as a proverb, is of special interest (see Higgins 1987: 241–41). It appears first as an aphorism in the fall of 1881 as "One thing is always more necessary then another" / "Eins ist immer nöthiger als das Andre" (KSA9:

584). Four years later it is presented in *Zarathustra* without the word "always" / "immer" as Zarathustra's proverbial wisdom:

> But around the hour of noon, when the sun stood straight over Zarathustra's head, he came to an old crooked and knotty tree that was embraced, and hidden from itself, by the rich love of a grapevine; and yellow grapes hung from it in abundance, inviting the wanderer. Then he felt the desire to quench a slight thirst and to break off a grape; but even as he was stretching out his arm to do so, he felt a still greater desire for something else: namely, to lie down beside the tree at the perfect noon hour, and to sleep.
> This Zarathustra did; and as soon as he lay on the ground in the stillness and secrecy of the many-hued grass, he forgot his slight thirst and fell asleep. For, as Zarathustra's proverb says, one thing is more necessary than another. Only his eyes remained open: for they did not tire of seeing and praising the tree and the love of the grapevine. (275–76)
> Um die Stunde des Mittags aber, als die Sonne gerade über Zarathustra's Haupte stand, kam er an einem alten krummen und knorrichten Baume vorbei, der von der reichen Liebe eines Weinstocks rings umarmt und vor sich selber verborgen war: von dem hiengen gelbe Trauben in Fülle dem Wandernden entgegen. Da gelüstete ihn, einen kleinen Durst zu löschen und sich eine Traube abzubrechen; als er aber schon den Arm dazu ausstreckte, da gelüstete ihn etwas Anderes noch mehr: nämlich sich neben den Baum niederzulegen, um die Stunde des vollkommenen Mittags, und zu schlafen.
> Diess that Zarathustra; und sobald er auf dem Boden lag, in der Stille und Heimlichkeit des bunten Grases, hatte er auch schon seinen kleinen Durst vergessen und schlief ein. Denn, wie das Sprichwort [*sic*] Zarathustra's sagt: Eins ist nothwendiger als das Andre. Nur das seine Augen offen blieben—sie wurden nämlich nicht satt, den Baum und die Liebe des Weinstocks zu sehn und zu preisen. (KSA4: 342)

Without a reference to the alleged proverbiality of this formulaic statement, it reappears twice about ten pages later, and the only half-cited proverb "A word at the right time is better than ten at the wrong time" / "Ein Wort zur rechten Zeit ist besser als zehn zur Unzeit" as well as the proverbial expression "not to have time to lose" / "keine Zeit zu verlieren haben" are added to boot:

> For it was at this point that the soothsayer interrupted the welcome, pushed forward like one who has no time to lose, seized Zarathustra's hand,

and shouted: "But Zarathustra! One thing is more necessary than another: thus you say yourself. Well then, one thing is more necessary to me now than anything else. A word at the right time: did you not invite me to supper? And here are many who have come a long way. Surely, you would not feed us speeches alone? [...]" (284)

An dieser Stelle nämlich unterbrach der Wahrsager die Begrüssung Zarathustra's und seiner Gäste: er drängte sich vor, wie Einer, der keine Zeit zu verlieren hat, fasste die Hand Zarathustra's und rief: "aber Zarathustra! Eins ist nothwendiger als das Andre, so redest du selber: wohlan, Eins ist mir jetzt nothwendiger als alles Andere.

Ein Wort zur rechten Zeit: hast du mich nicht zum Mahle eingeladen? Und hier sind Viele, die lange Wege machten. Du willst uns doch nicht mit Reden abspeisen? [...]" (KSA4: 353)

After this not at all uncommon accumulation of proverbial texts, Nietzsche's invented proverb appears one more time in a letter of August 8, 1887, to his composer friend Heinrich Köselitz, where he cites it as a little explanatory justification:

But it is to be self-understood a hundred times over that "One thing is more necessary than the other"; and lastly I would not know any more pleasant events for myself than a timely performance of your splendid work: even supposing, which unfortunately has to be supposed, that I am not present at it. Aber es versteht sich hundert Mal von selbst, daß "Eins nothwendiger ist als das Andre"; und zuletzt wüßte ich für mich selbst wenig angenehmere Ereignisse als eine baldige Aufführung Ihres herrlichen Werks: selbst angenommen, was leider angenommen werden muß, daß ich bei ihr nicht zugegen bin. (KSB8: 121)

Since Nietzsche places his own proverb into quotation marks, he points to its apparent currency as a formulaic statement, even though it has not been registered in any reference works, not even in Werner Ross's *Lexikon der Nietzsche-Zitate* (2001). Regarding the comprehensive meaning of *Zarathustra*, Nietzsche's intent with his pseudo-proverb appears to be that in view of the eternal return (repetition) of life it makes not much difference what appears to be more necessary or more pleasant at a certain point in time. The missed opportunity will reappear sometime as long as life itself will be affirmed and returning opportunities will be taken by the forelock.

"As the Proverb of Zarathustra Says: 'What Does It Matter'?"

As an anti-absolutist, for whom everything is something becoming and not an end, Nietzsche developed a "linguistic relativity principle" / "sprachliches Relativitätsprinzip" (Albrecht 1979: 226) that makes the description of an open and free worldview possible. The conspicuous contradictoriness of *Zarathustra* is a result of this, for Nietzsche wants to show that the positive struggle with fate has to be undertaken in eternal return (repetition) without "straight" / "gerade" guidelines. Zarathustra says as much in the following comment by way of his semantic alteration of the proverbial expression "to go crooked paths" / "krumme Wege gehen," where the adjective "crooked" / "krumm" is not to be understood as "bad" / "schlecht" but rather as "bent, imprecise, complicated, etc." / "verbogen, ungenau, kompliziert, etc.": "That I must be struggle and a becoming and an end and an opposition to ends— alas, whoever guesses what is my will should also guess on what crooked paths it must proceed" (115) / "Dass ich Kampf sein muss und Werden und Zweck und der Zwecke Widerspruch: ach, wer meinen Willen erräth, erräth wohl auch, auf welchen krummen Wegen er gehen muss!" (KSA4: 148). Later on there is also this additional reference: "Is not the perfect sage fond of walking on the most crooked ways? The evidence shows this, O Zarathustra—and you are the evidence" (315) / "Geht nicht ein vollkommener Weiser gern auf den krümmsten Wegen? Der Augenschein lehrt es, oh Zarathustra,—dein Augenschein" (KSA4: 392). There is then no prescribed goal in Nietzsche's worldview but always only repetitive possibilities and situations to be confronted by man as an individual (see Allison 2001: 120). For this idea Nietzsche has coined yet another pseudo-proverb at the end of the long and hard Zarathustra-path. But it took Nietzsche more than two years until he declared his leitmotif based on the phraseologism "what does it (really) matter" / "was liegt (schon) daran" in the general meaning of "much, little, nothing of avail" / "viel, wenig, nichts auf sich haben" (Schemann 1993: 491) as Zarathustra's ultimate "proverb" / "Sprichwort" (see the second to the last reference in the following list). One gets the impression from these references from between 1883 until 1885 that Nietzsche himself only slowly but surely advanced to this insightful point:

> Then it spoke to me [Zarathustra] again without voice: "What do you matter? You are not yet humble enough for me. Humility has the toughest hide."
> (146)

Da sprach es wieder ohne Stimme zu mir [Zarathustra]: "Was liegt an dir? Du bist mir noch nicht demüthig genug. Die Demuth hat das härteste Fell."— (KSA4: 188)

But what could we do? Again and again you [Zarathustra] pierced our ears and hearts with your maxims. So we said at last: what difference does it make [what does it matter] how he looks? (247)

Aber was half's! Immer wieder stachst du [Zarathustra] uns in Ohr und Herz mit deinen Sprüchen. Da sprachen wir endlich: was liegt daran, wie er aussieht! (KSA4: 307)

—what does it matter whether it [a reason] be great or small? whether it be called swamp or sky? A hand's breadth of ground suffices me [a scientist], provided it is really ground and foundation. (250)

—was liegt daran, ob er [ein Grund] gross oder klein ist? Ob er Sumpf oder Himmel heisst? Eine Hand breit Grund ist mir [einem Wissenschaftler] genung [*sic*]: wenn er nur wirklich Grund und Boden ist! (KSA4: 311)

A throw had failed you. But, you dice-throwers, what does it matter? You have not learned to gamble and jest as one must gamble and jest. Do we not always sit at a big jesting-and-gaming table? (292)

Ein Wurf missrieth euch. Aber, ihr Würfelspieler, was liegt daran! Ihr lerntet nicht spielen und spotten, wie man spielen und spotten muss! Sitzen wir nicht immer an einem grossen Spott- und Spieltische? (KSA4: 363–64)

Be of good cheer, what does it matter? How much is still possible! Learn to laugh at yourselves as one must laugh! (292)

Seid guten Muths, was liegt daran! Wie Vieles ist noch möglich! Lernt über euch selber lachen, wie man lachen muss! (KSA4: 364)

You higher men, the worst about you is that all of you have not learned to dance as one must dance—dancing away over yourselves! What does it matter that you are failures? How much is still possible! So learn to laugh away over yourselves! Lift up your hearts, you good dancers, high, higher! And do not forget good laughter. [...] Laughter I have pronounced holy; you higher men, learn to laugh! (295–96)

Ihr höheren Menschen, euer Schlimmstes ist: ihr lerntet alle nicht tanzen, wie man tanzen muss—über euch hinweg tanzen! Was liegt daran, dass ihr missriethet!

Wie Vieles ist noch möglich! So lernt doch über euch hinweg lachen! Erhebt eure Herzen, ihr guten Tänzer, hoch! höher! Und vergesst mir auch das gute Lachen nicht!
[...] Das Lachen sprach ich heilig; ihr höheren Menschen, lernt mir—lachen! (KSA4: 367–68)

They [Zarathustra's guests] are merry, he began again, and, who knows? perhaps at their host's expense. And if they learned to laugh from me, it is still my laughter that they have learned. But what does it matter? They are old people, convalescing in their own way, laughing in their own way; my ears have suffered worse things without becoming grumpy. (310)
Sie [Zarathustras Gäste] sind lustig, begann er wieder, und wer weiss? vielleicht auf ihres Wirthes Unkosten; und lernten sie von mir lachen, so ist es doch nicht mein Lachen, das sie lernten.
Aber was liegt dran! Es sind alte Leute: sie genesen auf ihre Art, sie lachen auf ihre Art; meine Ohren haben schon Schlimmeres erduldet und wurden nicht unwirsch. (KSA4: 386)

There are even some who relate that the ass danced too, and that it had not been for nothing that the ugliest man had given him wine to drink before. Now it may have been so otherwise; and if the ass really did not dance that night, yet greater and stranger wonders occurred than the dancing of an ass would have been. In short, as the proverb of Zarathustra says: "What does it matter?" (318)
Es giebt sogar Solche, die erzählen, das damals der Esel getanzt habe: nicht umsonst nämlich habe ihm der hässlichste Mensch vorher Wein zu trinken gegeben. Diess mag sich nun so verhalten oder auch anders; und wenn in Wahrheit an jenem Abende der Esel nicht getanzt hat, so geschahen doch damals grössere und seltsamere Wunderdinge als es das Tanzen eines Esels wäre. Kurz, wie das Sprichwort Zarathustra's lautet: "was liegt daran!" (KSA4: 396)

"My suffering and my pity for suffering—what does it matter? Am I concerned with happiness? I am concerned with my work. [...]
This is my morning, my day is breaking: rise now, rise, thou great noon!"
Thus spoke Zarathustra, and he left his cave [on the mountain], glowing and strong as a morning sun that comes out of dark mountains. (327)
"Mein Leid und mein Mitleiden—was liegt daran! Trachte ich denn nach Glücke? Ich trachte nach meinem Werke! [...] [see Higgins 1987: 216, 236]

Dies ist mein Morgen, mein Tag hebt an: herauf nun, herauf, du grosser Mittag!"—

Also sprach Zarathustra und verliess seine Höhle [auf dem Berg], glühend und stark, wie eine Morgensonne, die aus dunklen Bergen kommt. (KSA4: 408)

With this last excerpt *Thus Spoke Zarathustra* comes to its conclusion, and hopefully the case has been made that Zarathustra's "proverb" / "Sprichwort" should no longer be ignored in the interpretation and comprehension of this work of world literature. But it also needs to be emphasized that Nietzsche would have done better to have labeled his "What does it matter!" / "Was liegt daran!" as a proverbial expression instead of a proverb. Regarding this matter, the following two English translations are quite informative:

In short, as the proverb of Zarathustra says: "What does it matter?" (318; see Common 1967: 355)

In short, as Zarathustra's saying has it: "What does it matter!" (Parkes 2005: 278; see Del Caro 2006: 259)

In the first translation the question mark is inappropriate because Nietzsche does not mean it as an interrogative but rather as an indicative, as is common with proverbs altogether. The second translator did well by employing the term "saying" which carries with it the connotation of proverbial expression. But be that as it may, Nietzsche has no intention to express a piece of proverbial wisdom but rather the conviction that there are many possibilities and paths to master life. Men are "dice throwers" (292) / "Würfelspieler" (KSA4: 363), who can deal with their fate by dancing and laughing, and the one who can do exactly that will, proverbially speaking, "jump over his shadow—and verily, into his sun" (117) / "über seinen eignen Schatten springen—und, wahrlich! hinein in seine Sonne" (KSA4: 151). One might even venture the guess that Nietzsche thought of his earlier proverbial statement "They (men) simply want to be the smiths [architects] of their own fortunes and misfortunes" (Faber 1984: 210) / "Sie [die Menschen] wollen nun einmal ihres Glückes und Unglückes eigene Schmiede sein" (KSA2: 285) from his *Menschliches, Allzumenschliches* (1878, *Human, All Too Human*). Surely all of this is part of Nietzsche's thought, but Zarathustra is not searching for fortune as such. He understands his calling as worthwhile work toward the renewal of humankind and the world as such. That means struggle, as it is announced proverbially at the beginning of *Zarathustra*: "to crash through these ultimate walls with its [i.e., the] head, and not only with its [i.e., the] head—over there to 'that world'" (31–32) / "mit dem Kopfe durch die letzten Wände, und nicht nur mit dem Kopfe—hinüber zu 'jener Welt'" (KSA4: 36).

Zarathustra's Proverbial Stone of Sisyphus and the Eternal Repetition of Life

To be sure, Sisyphus does not appear in this work, but some of this conjures up the existentialist philosophy of Albert Camus, who knew and treasured his Nietzsche well. In his book *Le mythe de Sisyphe* (1942) Camus states existentially and life-confirmingly: "La lutte elle-même vers les summets suffit à remplir un cœur d'homme. Il faut imaginer Sisyphe heureux" / "The struggle itself toward the heights is enough to fill a man's heart. One must imagine Sisyphus happy" (Camus 1942: 166; see Rosenthal 1977: 50). And there is a passage in *Zarathustra* that permits the assumption that Nietzsche and Camus had similar thoughts, even though Camus is less elitist and more humane. And sure enough, there is a significant "stone image" / "Steinbild" passage in *Zarathustra* that is reminiscent of the myth of Sisyphus. As is typical for such key statements in Nietzsche's works, it is based on the leitmotif-like allusions to the proverb "Who throws the stone (high) above himself will have it fall on his head" / "Wer den Stein [hoch] über sich wirft, dem fällt er auf den Kopf" and the proverbial expression "to search for the philosophers' stone (stone of the wise)" / "den Stein der Weisen suchen." But, as expected, the proverb is negated by Nietzsche, because the falling stone most certainly will not rob Zarathustra of his courage to confront the struggle of life:

> A path that ascended defiantly through stones, malicious, lonely, not cheered by herb or shrub—a mountain path crunched under the defiance of my foot. Striding silently over the mocking clatter of pebbles, crushing the rock that made it slip, my foot forced its way upward. Upward—defying the spirit that drew it downward toward the abyss, the spirit of gravity, my devil and archenemy. Upward—although he sat on me, half dwarf, half mole, lame, making lame, dripping lead into my ear, leaden thoughts into my brain.
> "O Zarathustra," he [a dwarf] whispered mockingly, syllable by syllable; "you philosopher's stone [stone of the wise], you slingstone, you star-crusher! You threw yourself up high; but every stone that is thrown must fall. Sentenced to yourself and to your own stoning—O Zarathustra, far indeed have you thrown the stone, but it will fall back on yourself."

Then the dwarf fell silent, and that lasted a long time. His silence, however, oppressed me; and such twosomeness is surely more lonesome than being alone. I climbed, I climbed, I dreamed, I thought; but everything oppressed me. I was like one sick whom his wicked torture makes weary, and who as he falls asleep is awakened by a still more wicked dream. But there is something in me that I call courage; that has so far slain my every discouragement. This courage finally bade me stand still and speak: "Dwarf! It is you or I!"

For courage is the best slayer, courage which attacks; for in every attack there is playing and brass. [. . .]

Courage, however, is the best slayer—courage which attacks: which slays even death itself, for it says, "Was that life? Well then! Once more!"

In such words, however, there is much playing and brass. He that has ears to hear, let him hear! (156–57)

Ein Pfad, der trotzig durch Geröll stieg, ein boshafter, einsamer, dem nicht Kraut, nicht Strauch mehr zusprach: ein Berg-Pfad knirschte unter dem Trotz meines Fusses.

Stumm über höhnischem Geklirr von Kieseln schreitend, den Stein zertretend, der ihn gleiten liess: also zwang mein Fuss sich aufwärts.

Aufwärts:—dem Geiste zum Trotz, der ihn abwärts zog, abgrundwärts zog, dem Geiste der Schwere, meinem Teufel und Erzfeinde.

Aufwärts:—obwohl er auf mir sass, halb Zwerg, halb Maulwurf; lahm; lähmend; Blei durch mein Ohr, Bleitropfen-Gedanken in mein Hirn träufelnd.

"Oh Zarathustra, raunte er [ein Zwerg] höhnisch Silb' um Silbe, du Stein der Weisheit! Du warfst dich hoch, aber jeder geworfene Stein muss—fallen!

Oh Zarathustra, du Stein der Weisheit, du Schleuderstein, du Stern-Zertrümmerer! Dich selber warfst du so hoch,—aber jeder geworfene Stein—muss fallen!

Verurtheilt zu dir selber und zur eignen Steinigung: oh Zarathustra, weit warfst du ja den Stein,—aber auf dich wird er zurückfallen!"

Drauf schwieg der Zwerg; und das währte lange. Sein Schweigen aber drückte mich; und solchermassen zu Zwein ist man wahrlich einsamer als zu Einem!

Ich stieg, ich stieg, ich träumte, ich dachte,—aber Alles drückte mich. Einem Kranken glich ich, den seine schlimme Marter müde macht, und den wieder ein schlimmerer Traum aus dem Einschlafen weckt.—

Aber es giebt Etwas in mir, das ich Muth heisse: das schlug bisher mir jeden Unmuth todt. Dieser Muth hiess mich endlich stille stehn und sprechen: "Zwerg! Du! Oder ich!"—

Muth nämlich ist der beste Todtschläger,—Muth, welcher angreift: denn in jedem Angriffe ist klingendes Spiel. [. . .]

> Muth aber ist der beste Todtschläger, Muth, der angreift: der schlägt noch
> den Tod todt, denn er spricht: "War das das Leben? Wohlan! Noch Ein Mal!"
> In solchem Spruche aber ist viel klingendes Spiel. Wer Ohren hat, der höre.—
> (KSA4: 198–99)

Zarathustra, like Sisyphus condemned to himself, carries on by accepting
and confirming the eternal repetition (return) of life. At the end Zarathustra
dances, sings, and laughs, and despite his hard existence is happy like Sisyphus. With enthusiastic joy he steps toward the morning sun, ready to accept
the dynamics of life anew every day:

> All anew, all eternally, all entangled, ensnared, enamored—oh, then you loved
> the world. Eternal ones, love it eternally and evermore; and to woe too, you
> say: go, but return! For all joy wants—eternity. (323)
> —Alles von neuem, Alles ewig, Alles verkettet, verfädelt, verliebt, oh so liebtet
> ihr die Welt,—
> —ihr Ewigen, liebt sie ewig und allezeit: und auch zum Weh sprecht ihr: ver-
> geh, aber komm zurück! Denn alle Lust will—Ewigkeit! (KSA4: 402)

Proverbial matters have accompanied Zarathustra on his path toward self-
recognition and the acceptance of life. The numerous proverbial expressions
with their metaphors add much to the poetic style of *Thus Spoke Zarathustra*, while the usually varied Bible and folk proverbs are used to underscore
Nietzsche's break with God and Christianity. Anti-proverbs and pseudo-
proverbs also do their part to emphasize Nietzsche's call for the revaluation
of all values. Liberated men need no proverbial rule system and do not "run
against open doors" / "offene Türen einrennen," as a proverbial expression
would have it. Zarathustra's higher men (overmen) maintain self-assured
and anti-proverbially: "We do not question each other, we do not complain
to each other, we often [i.e., openly] walk together through open doors"
(184) / "Wir fragen einander nicht, wir klagen einander nicht, wir gehen
offen mit einander durch offne Türen" (KSA4: 232). Naturally the often
repeated phrase "Thus spoke Zarathustra" / "Also sprach Zarathustra" has
long become proverbial, but it would certainly be of great benefit, if modern
people in their ever more absurd world would occasionally remind themselves what Friedrich Nietzsche actually said and meant with his not at all
didactic *Zarathustra*.

BIBLIOGRAPHY

This chapter appeared with the slightly different title "My Tongue—Is of the People: The Proverbial Language of Friedrich Nietzsche's *Thus Spoke Zarathustra*" in *Proverbium* 30 (2013), 171–226.

NIETZSCHE EDITIONS

KSA: Friedrich Nietzsche, *Kritische Studienausgabe in 15 Bänden*. Giorgio Colli and Mazzino Montinari, eds. München: Deutscher Taschenbuch Verlag, 1999.
KSB: Friedrich Nietzsche, *Sämtliche Briefe. Kritische Studienausgabe in 8 Bänden*. Giorgio Colli and Mazzino Montinari, eds. München: Deutscher Taschenbuch Verlag, 2003.

TRANSLATIONS

Friedrich Nietzsche. 1978 (first published 1954). *Thus Spoke Zarathustra*. Translated by Walter Kaufmann. New York: Penguin. Page numbers in parentheses refer to this English translation.
Friedrich Nietzsche. 1967 (first published 1909). *Thus Spake Zarathustra: A Book for All and None*. Translated by Thomas Common. London: George Allen & Unwin. Cited as Common 1967.
Friedrich Nietzsche. 2005. *Thus Spoke Zarathustra: A Book for Everyone and Nobody*. Translated with an Introduction by Graham Parkes. Oxford: Oxford University Press. Cited as Parkes 2005.
Friedrich Nietzsche. 2006. *Thus Spoke Zarathustra: A Book for All and None*. Translated by Adrian Del Caro. Cambridge: Cambridge University Press. Cited as Del Caro 2006.
Friedrich Nietzsche. 1974. *The Gay Science*. Translated by Walter Kaufmann. New York: Vintage. Cited as Kaufmann 1974.
Friedrich Nietzsche. 1984. *Human, All Too Human: A Book for Free Spirits*. Translated by Marion Faber. Lincoln: University of Nebraska Press. Cited as Faber 1984.

A NOTE ON TRANSLATIONS

Where possible, I have relied on published translations of Nietzsche's works, slightly altering them at times when the translators did not translate the proverbs effectively.
All translations of primary (especially posthumously published fragments) and secondary sources that are not otherwise identified are my own.

Albrecht, Jörn. 1979. "Friedrich Nietzsche und das 'sprachliche Relativitätsprinzip.'" *Nietzsche-Studien* 8: 225–44.
Allison, David B. 2001. *Reading the New Nietzsche*. Lanham, Maryland: Rowman & Littlefield.
Baumgartner, Oskar. 1912. "Nietzsche und die Bibel." *Wissen und Leben* 5: 526–31.
Büchmann, Georg. 1995. *Geflügelte Worte. Der klassische Zitatenschatz*. 40th ed. Winfried Hofmann, ed. Berlin: Ullstein.
Camus, Albert. 1942. *Le mythe de Sisyphe. Essai sur l'absurde*. Paris: Gallimard.
Carl, Helmut. 1962. "Unsere Haustiere in sprichwörtlichen Redensarten." *Muttersprache* 72: 333–39.
Christen, Jürgen. 1991. *Vergiß die Peitsche nicht. Frauenfeindliche Sprüche*. Frankfurt am Main: Eichborn.
Dobrovol'skij, Dmitrij, and Elisabeth Piirainen. 1996. *Symbole in Sprache und Kultur. Studien zur Phraseologie aus kultursemiotischer Perspektive*. Bochum: Norbert Brockmeyer.
Doerr, Karin. 2000. "'To Each His Own' (Jedem das Seine): The Mis-(Use) of German Proverbs in Concentration Camps and Beyond." *Proverbium* 17: 71–90.

Domzalski, Oliver Thomas, ed. 2006. *Das goldene Album der Sponti-Sprüche.* Frankfurt am Main: Eichborn.

Gauger, Hans-Martin. 1984. "Nietzsches Stil am Beispiel von *Ecce homo.*" *Nietzsche-Studien* 13: 332–55.

Goth, Joachim. 1970. *Nietzsche und die Rhetorik.* Tübingen: Max Niemeyer.

Grass, Günter. 1997. *Fundsachen für Nichtleser.* Göttingen: Steidl.

Grünberg, Paul. 1888. *Biblische Redensarten. Eine Studie über den Gebrauch und Missbrauch der Bibel in der deutschen Volks- und Umgangssprache.* Heilbronn: Henninger.

Harder, Franz. 1925–26. "'Parturient [*sic*] montes, nascetur ridiculus mus.'" *Zeitschrift des Vereins für Volkskunde* 35/36: 278–80.

Higgins, Kathleen Marie. 1987. *Nietzsche's "Zarathustra."* Philadelphia: Temple University Press.

Hoefer, Edmund. 1855. *Wie das Volk spricht. Deutsche Sagwörter.* Stuttgart: Adolph Krabbe; rpt. of much expanded 9th ed. of 1885, Wolfgang Mieder, ed. Hildesheim: Georg Olms, 1995.

Kaulhausen, Marie Hed. 1977. *Nietzsches Sprachspiel gedeutet aus seinem Lebensgefühl und Weltverhältnis.* München: R. Oldenbourg.

Krauss, Heinrich. 1993. *Geflügelte Bibelworte. Das Lexikon biblischer Redensarten.* München: C.H. Beck.

Kunstmann, John G. 1952. "And Yet Again: 'Wes des Herz voll ist, des geht der Mund über.'" *Concordia Theological Monthly* 23: 509–27.

Lampert, Laurence. 1986. *Nietzsche's Teaching: An Interpretation of "Thus Spoke Zarathustra."* New Haven, Connecticut: Yale University Press.

Linden, Walter. "Friedrich Nietzsche als Meister der deutschen Sprache." *Muttersprache* 28: 65–71.

Lütkehaus, Ludger, ed. 2000. *"Stehlen ist oft seliger als nehmen": Nietzsche zum Vergnügen.* Stuttgart: Philipp Reclam.

Meckel, Markus. 1980. "Der Weg Zarathustras als der Weg des Menschen. Zur Anthropologie Nietzsches im Kontext der Rede von Gott im *Zarathustra.*" *Nietzsche-Studien* 9: 174–208.

Meisser, Ulrich M. 1969. "Tiersprichwörter und Verhaltensforschung. Zur gegenseitigen Erhellung von didaktischer Literatur und Naturwissenschaft." *Studium Generale* 22: 861–89.

Meyer, Richard M. 1914. "Nietzsches Wortbildungen." *Zeitschrift für Deutssche Wortforschung* 15: 98–146.

Mieder, Wolfgang. 1995. "Martin Luther und die Geschichte des Sprichwortes 'Wes das Herz voll ist, des geht der Mund über.'" In Wolfgang Mieder, *Sprichwörtliches und Geflügeltes. Sprachstudien von Martin Luther bis Karl Marx.* Bochum: Norbert Brockmeyer. 13–22.

———, ed. 1997. *Ver-kehrte Worte. Antizitate aus Literatur und Medien.* Wiesbaden: Quelle & Meyer.

———. "'Irren ist menschlich, sagte der Igel': Aphoristische Sagwörter aus Literatur und Medien." In Wolfgang Mieder, *Aphorismen, Sprichwörter, Zitate. Von Goethe und Schiller bis Victor Klemperer.* Bern: Peter Lang. 127–58.

———. 2010. "'Der Mensch lebt nicht vom Brot allein': Vom Bibelsprichwort über das Volkssprichwort zum Antisprichwort." *Slowo, tekst, czas. Jednostka frazeologiczna w tradycyjnych i nowych paradygmatach naukowych.* Michaił Aleksiejenko and Harry Walter, eds. Szczecin: Wydawca Print Group. 279–300.

Morowa, Hans. 1958. *Sprache und Stil von Nietzsches "Zarathustra." Ein Beitrag zur Erkenntnis seines geistig-seelischen Ausdrucksgehalts.* Diss., Free University of Berlin.

Naumann, Barbara. 1985. "Nietzsches Sprache 'Aus der Natur.' Ansätze zu einer Sprachtheorie in den frühen Schriften und ihre metaphorische Einlösung in *Also sprach Zarathustra.*" *Nietzsche-Studien* 14: 126–63.

Nelson, Timothy C. 1986. "'Ex abundantia cordis os loquitur': Ein Beittrag zur Rezeptionsgeschichte eines umstrittenen Sprichworts." *Proverbium* 3: 101–23.

Nolte, Andreas, and Wolfgang Mieder. 2012. *"Zu meiner Hölle will ich den Weg mit guten Sprüchen pflastern." Friedrich Nietzsches sprichwörtliche Sprache.* Hildesheim: Georg Olms.

Paronis, Margot. 1976. *"Also sprach Zarathustra." Die Ironie Nietzsches als Gestaltungsprinzip*. Bonn: Bouvier.

Perkins, Richard. 1983. "Analogistic Strategies in *Zarathustra*." *The Great Year of Zarathustra (1881–1981)*. David Goicoechea, ed. Lanham, Maryland: University Press of America. 316–38.

Peukes, Gerhard. 1977. *Untersuchungen zum Sprichwort im Deutschen. Semantik, Syntax, Typen*. Berlin: Erich Schmidt.

Prossliner, Johann. 2001. *Licht wird alles, was ich fasse. Das Lexikon der Nietzsche-Zitate*. München: Deutscher Taschenbuch Verlag.

Rittersbacher, Christa. 2002. *Frau und Mann im Sprichwort. Einblicke in die sprichwörtliche Weltanschauung Großbritanniens und Amerikas*. Heidelberg: Wunderhorn.

Röhrich, Lutz. 1991–92. *Das große Lexikon der sprichwörtlichen Redensarten*, 3 vols. Freiburg: Herder.

Rosenthal, Bianca. 1977. *Die Idee des Absurden. Friedrich Nietzsche und Albert Camus*. Bonn: Bouvier.

Rupp, Walter. 2010. *Hieb- und Stichelsätze. Aphorismen*. Neckenmarkt: Novum Publishing.

Schemann, Hans. 1993. *Deutsche Idiomatik. Die deutschen Redewendungen im Kontext*. Stuttgart: Ernst Klett.

Schipper, Mineke. 2003. *"Never Marry a Woman with Big Feet": Women in Proverbs from Around the World*. New Haven, Connecticut: Yale University Press.

Schmidt, Rudolf. 1972. *Tierisches in unserer Muttersprache*. Gerabronn-Crailsheim: Hohenloher Druck- und Verlagshaus.

Schmoldt, Hans. *Reclams Lexikon der Bibelzitate*. Stuttgart: Philipp Reclam.

Schulze, Carl. 1860. *Die biblischen Sprichwörter der deutschen Sprache*. Göttingen: Vandenhoeck & Ruprecht, 1860; rpt. Wolfgang Mieder, ed. Bern: Peter Lang, 1987.

Simrock, Karl. 1988. *Die deutschen Sprichwörter*. Wolfgang Mieder, ed. Stuttgart: Philipp Reclam (reprint of 1846 edition).

Spicker, Friedemann. 2010. "Der mit der Peitsche geht: Friedrich Nietzsche." In Friedemann Spicker, *Die Welt ist voller Sprüche. Große Aphoristiker im Porträt*. Bochum: Norbert Brockmeyer. 88–93.

Steger, Heribert. 1998. *333 biblische Redensarten*. Augsburg: Pattloch.

Sternkopf, Jochen. 1993. "Tierbezeichnungen in phraseologischen Einheiten." *Muttersprache* 103: 324–31.

Thatcher, David S. 1977. "Eagle and Serpent in *Zarathustra*." *Nietzsche-Studien* 6: 240–60.

Thomas, R. Hinton. 1980. "Nietzsche, Women and the Whip." *German Life and Letters* 34: 117–25.

Vitens, Siegfried. 1951. *Die Sprachkunst Friedrich Nietzsches in "Also sprach Zarathustra."* Bremen-Horn: Walter Dorn.

Ziolkowski, Theodore. 2012. "Zarathustra's Reincarnations: Literary Responses to Nietzsche's Work." *Modern Language Review* 107: 211–29.

Proverbs in Culture

11. "THE DOG IN THE MANGER"

The Rise and Decline in Popularity of a Proverb and a Fable

Much has been written on the interrelationship of various types of folk narratives with proverbs, proverbial expressions, and wellerisms, with many such diachronic and often comparative studies reaching the conclusion that it is not always absolutely clear which came first—the longer narrative or the shorter proverbial text (Mieder 2009). This folkloric conundrum is especially vexing when dealing with fables and proverbs, where it is indeed difficult or near impossible to ascertain whether a particular fable was reduced to a proverbial remnant or whether the wisdom of a proverb was explicated by way of a prose or rhymed fable. Even in those cases where the fable is summarized by a proverb to start with, it is usually not clear which text gave rise to the other (Carnes 1988). It is the old story of what came first: the chicken or the egg? Regarding the fable or proverb (perhaps more precisely proverbial expression) of "The dog in the manger," Archer Taylor, the doyen of international proverb studies and also keen narrative scholar, made up his mind about the primary text in his succinct but revealing chapter on "Proverbs Based on Narratives" in his classic study on *The Proverb*: "The Aesopic fable, for example, stands godfather to many a proverb: *Sour grapes*; *A dog in the manger*; *Don't kill the goose that lays the golden egg*; *Don't count your chickens before they are hatched* (which belongs in the modern Aesopic tradition, although it is not part of the original stock of fables)" (Taylor 1931: 28). In fact, Taylor is so convinced that "The dog in the manger" goes back to Aesop that he reiterates his assertion in his final sentence of the chapter: "The fable which can be positively recognized as the source of a proverb appears in its proverbial dress as an allusion, intelligible to those familiar with the story, and not a summary, e.g. *Sour grapes*; *Dog in the manger*; *Ass in a lion's skin*" (32). Taylor had not undertaken one of his comprehensive studies for the examples cited, and in the case of "The dog in the manger" he too quickly jumped to the conclusion that it was a proverbial allusion to an old Aesopic fable. In this case he ignored the possibility that a fable might well have been invented in order to explain a proverbial utterance that to later generations makes little sense without an explanatory narrative.

The Proverb and Cultural Literacy

With this short introductory paragraph serving as a backdrop, let me mention why I am taking a look at "The dog in the manger" at all. Certainly not because I want to do my mentor Archer Taylor one better—nothing could be further from the truth! My interest in this phrase—and I don't look at it as a proverb but rather as a proverbial expression—"To be a dog in the manger" or a proverbial comparison "To be like a dog in the manger" stems from a twofold experience that I have had during the past two academic years with the students of a large lecture course on "'Big Fish Eat Little Fish': The Nature and Politics of Proverbs" at the University of Vermont. In both instances I discussed the following proverbial remarks that President Franklin Delano Roosevelt made during his fourth Inaugural Address on January 20, 1945:

> Today, in this year of war, 1945, we have learned lessons—at a fearful cost— and we shall profit from them. We have learned that we cannot live alone, at peace; that our own well-being is dependent on the well-being of other nations far away. We have learned that we must live as men, not as ostriches, nor as dogs in the manger. We have learned the simple truth, as Emerson said, that "the only way to have a friend is to be one." We can gain no lasting peace if we approach it with suspicion and mistrust or with fear. We can gain it only if we proceed with the understanding, the confidence, and the courage which flow from conviction. (Hunt 1997: 396; Mieder 2005: 168–69)

As I explained to the students the first time around in 2009 that this paragraph is a fine example of Roosevelt's proverbial rhetoric, I noticed their blank faces and learned that except for one student, a retired gentleman auditing the course, not a single student had ever heard of a "dog in the manger," while the ostrich allusion was known to a considerable number of them. I quickly explained that the proverbial phrase goes back to an Aesopic fable, recalling that I had read about this in Taylor and elsewhere. After this event I was better prepared when I faced my 75 proverb students in the fall of 2010, and sure enough, not one of my young students had any idea what Roosevelt was talking about. Having done a bit of homework on the phrase, I did not mention Aesop any longer but stuck to the fable connection. To show the students that there must have been a time at least during the first half of the twentieth century that politicians could count on citizens knowing the meaning of the phrase, I brought in the following statements by none less than the masterful wordsmith Winston S. Churchill. After all, my deceased colleague and dear friend George B. Bryan and I had found eight references of the proverbial expression in Churchill's massive published works:

I will deal with only two aspects, with only two functions, of the House of Lords—their function as the spoke in the wheel and their function as a dog in the manger. (Laughter.) I only use those expressions metaphorically; there is not intended to be any disrespect in the use of them. (February 4, 1907)

Yes, in this land of England [. . .] you find that even those few persons [of the landed aristocracy] to whom the whole advantage and richness of the soil has been accorded are themselves but little better for the great possessions with which they have been endowed, and like the dog in the manger, they only stand in the way of those [landless peasantry] who would seek to put them to a better use. (loud cheers.) (February 7, 1907)

They [the conservatives] speak of the profits of the land monopolists as if they were the fruits of thrift and industry and a pleasing example for the poorer classes to imitate.—(Laughter.) We don't take that view of the process.—(Hear, hear.) We think it is a dog-in-the-manger game.—(Hear, hear.) (July 17, 1909)

[. . .] I am distinctly of opinion that their [the Tory Party] refusal of such an offer would tend very greatly to isolate them and show very clearly to the English electorate what a "dog in the manger" policy they are pursuing. (September 8, 1912)

Of course we are disappointed here at the turn events have taken, but we shall do our best to help the French in their feeble secondary "dog-in-the-manger" attack on the left flank. (December 14, 1914)

The newspapers no longer report public speeches. They only go about dogging your steps from place to place to see if you say something that, clipped from its context, can be made into a headline. They only go prowling about looking for the wrong tit-bits. (Laughter.) Well, if they don't wish to report political speeches, why should they act a dog-in-the-manger part and stand in the path of this great and wonderful new invention [the radio]. (February 10, 1928)

Greater populations are necessary, not only for defence—which ultimately rests upon man-power—but also for proper development. We cannot let ourselves be represented as "dogs in the manger." We put ourselves in an entirely false position when we say to the nations of the earth: "Here are fertile territories which we cannot, or will not, develop, but which no one else must touch." (May 22, 1938)

The arts are essential to any national life. The nation owes it to itself to sustain and encourage them. The country possesses in the Royal Academy an institution of power and reputation for the purpose of encouraging the arts of painting and sculpture. It would be disastrous if the control of this machine fell into the hands of any particular school of artistic thought, which like a dog in a manger would have little pleasure itself but would exclude al others. (April 30, 1953)

Churchill pulls all linguistic registers in his effective and often ironic or satirical employment of the dog metaphor, using it as a proverbial expression, a proverbial comparison, and a hyphenated adjective to boot (for the precise references in Churchill's works, see Mieder and Bryan 1995: 199–200). Had people of his time not understood this proverbial rhetoric, surely much of what made Churchill such a unique communicator would have been lost!

Be that as it may, what would my dear students do with the following absurd editorial by the conservative columnist Kelly O'Connell of June 20, 2010:

Dog in the Manger Presidency
Obama's Character Described 2,500 Years Ago by Aesop

Is it possible to base an entire presidency on venal acts of jealousy and illicit confiscation? This essay argues such is currently the case. If one accepts that Obama has socialist/Marxist values, then he seeks by definition, an economy based upon a shattering of the 10th Commandment... "Thous [*sic*] Shalt Not Covet Thy Neighbor's House..." But the Greek pagan moralist writer Aesop had Obama's character pegged in his Dog in the Manger fable 2,500 years ago. (O'Connell 2010)

The ridiculous claims and examples of President Obama's alleged selfish and covetous behavior aside, the students might get an inkling of what the phrase could perhaps mean, albeit with the false attribution to the ancient Aesop. What this headline and first paragraph show—and I will return to the very modern use of the proverbial phrase at the end—is that E. D. Hirsch and his co-authors were most likely correct in including the following entry in *The Dictionary of Cultural Literacy* (1988), which has, to be sure, its own problems (with its controversial lists of what people should know):

> *dog in the manger* a person who spitefully refuses to let someone else benefit from something for which he or she has no personal use: "We asked our neighbor for the fence posts he had left over, but, like a dog in the manger, he threw them out rather than give them to us." The PHRASE comes from one of AESOP'S FABLES, about a dog lying in a manger full of hay. When an ox tries to eat some hay, the dog bites him, despite the fact that the hay is of no use to the dog. (Hirsch et al. 1988: 64)

Altogether a succinct and useful definition and description, and my students would at least have a pretty good idea what "The dog in the manger" is all about. But knowing my young friends, they would now go to the internet and in a split second find a much more satisfactory treatise on the issue at hand at Wikipedia. While the first paragraph has its problems, the next four pages together with significant references and two illustrations are quite impressive, and it would be dishonest if I were not to admit that I learned about a couple of sources by way of this entry:

> *The Dog in the Manger*
> The story and metaphor *The Dog in the Manger* derives from an old Greek fable which has been transmitted in several different versions. Interpreted variously over the centuries, it is used now of those who spitefully prevent others from having something that they themselves have no use for. Although the story was ascribed to Aesop's Fables in the 15th century, there is no ancient source that does so. (en.wikipedia.org/wiki/The_Dog_in_the_Manger: 20.04.2011)

In any case, I like the introductory description of "The dog in the manger" as a "story and metaphor," and it is exactly this binary genre designation that will play a considerable role in my ensuing attempt to make sense out of this metaphorical dog. As I do so, I will fluctuate in my referring to the dog-metaphor as a proverb, proverbial expression, and proverbial comparison, since all three specific genre designations can be appropriate depending on how the phrase is being used in any given context. Following others who have commented on this proverbial metaphor, I will quite often employ "proverb" as a generic term.

Greek and Other Early Proverbs, but No Fable

More than thirty years ago I came across Gyula Moravcsik's article "'Hund in der Krippe' Zur Geschichte eines griechischen Sprichwortes" and I. Trencsényi-Waldapfel's equally informative reaction to it entitled "Sprichwort oder geflügeltes Wort?" Both papers by the two Hungarian scholars were published in 1964 in *Acta Antiqua Academiae Scientiarum Hungaricae* (Mieder 1982: 313, 478). In fact, the latter had already published two smaller papers a few years earlier in the *Acta Orientalia Academiae Scientiarum Hungaricae* on the dog metaphor, which I have located only recently. As can be seen from the titles of the two major studies, both authors speak of proverbs rather than fables, with Trencsényi-Waldapfel making the point that the earliest references under discussion, from the second century A.D., could be literary quotations and not yet proverbs. Neither scholar was able to discover any ancient Greek fable from Aesop or another author that might have led to the phrase. This is also true for John F. Priest's article "The Dog in the Manger: In Quest of a Fable" (1985), which summarizes much of the earlier findings in English and could also not find a fable in antiquity. As is the case with classically trained philologists, the Hungarian scholars cite their references in Greek or German and without translations, and as I cite those important references given by them, I have located them in their original publications and list them here in English.

Interestingly, the four major contenders for the earliest reference thus far all stem from that second century A.D., and there is then the possibility that they might be variants of yet an earlier source, perhaps a proverb or a fable after all. I personally definitely lean against the fable possibility, as will become clear later. Here then are the four key references cited from their originals and not from the three scholars just mentioned—three by the Greek authors Lucian and Strato, and the fourth from the apocryphal Gospel of Thomas:

Lucian, *The Ignorant Book Collector*
You might, to be sure, lend your books to someone else who wants them, but you cannot use them yourself. But you never lent a book to anyone; you act

like the dog in the manger, who neither eats the grain herself nor lets the horse eat it, who can. (Harmon 1960: III, 211, 30)

Lucian, *Timon, or the Misanthrope*
As a matter of fact, you used to say that they acted absurdly in that they loved you to excess, yet did not dare to enjoy you when they might, and instead of giving free rein to their passion when it lay in their power to do so, they kept watch and ward, looking fixedly at the seal and the bolt; for they thought it enjoyment enough. Not that they were able to enjoy you themselves, but that they were shutting out everyone else from a share in the enjoyment, like the dog in the manger that neither ate the barley herself nor permitted the hungry horse to eat it. (Harmon 1919: II, 341–42, 14)

Strato, [epigram]
A certain eunuch has good-looking servant-boys—for what use?—and he does them abominable injury. Truly, like the dog in the manger with the roses, and stupidly barking, he neither gives the good thing to himself nor to anyone else. (Paton 1956: IV, 401, 236)

Gospel of Thomas
Jesus said: Woe to them, the Pharisees, for they are like a dog sleeping in the manger of oxen, for neither does he eat nor does he allow the oxen to eat. (Guillaumont et al. 1959: 51–52, 102)

The closest parallel to this last Biblical text is Matthew 23:13, but it does not include the dog metaphor in its description of covetousness: "But woe unto you, scribes and Pharisees, hypocrites! for ye shut up the kingdom of heaven against men: for ye neither go in yourselves, neither suffer ye them that are entering to go in." A similar reference appears in Luke 11:52, this time accusing lawyers of this selfish behavior: "Woe unto you, lawyers! for ye have taken away the key of knowledge; ye entered not in yourselves, and them that were entering in ye hindered." Since Thomas employs the considerably different animal image in his text, he might well have been influenced especially by Lucian or by a yet not located phrase from their native land of Syria. This possible Near Eastern connection has led to speculation that an earlier common phrase might have been current in that general area. Sure enough, while such a related phrase is not listed among the Aramaic proverbs contained in the so-called *Ahiqar* (see Lindenberger 1983), a tale and wisdom book from the fifth century B.C., it appears in Syriac, Arabic, and Armenian versions of

Ahiqar, showing that the general idea of an envious dog was quite prevalent (cited from Priest 1985: 55):

> Syriac: My son, thou has been to me like the dog that came to the potter's oven to warm himself, and after he was warm rose up to bark at them.

> Arabic: O my son, thou hast been to me like the dog that was cold and it went into the potter's house to get warm. And when it had got warm, it began to bark at them, and they chased it out and beat it, that it might not bite them.

> Armenian: Son, thou hast been to me like the dog which went into the oven of the potter. When he was warm, he began to bark at them.

But this particular proverb variant is older yet, for I found the following entry in H. F. Lutz's "Babylonian Proverbs" (1933: 41):

> *When the dog of the potter had entered the oven, he barked at the potter.*
> This proverb was widely used in Assyria, according to the statement of the writer of a letter, and indicated as well by the fact that it found a place among other proverbs in the story of Ahiqar. In its Aramaic garb it becomes more intelligent: "You have been, my son, like the dog, who, in order to warm himself, entered the oven of the potters, and after he had become warm, arose, and barked at them." "Undank ist der Welt Lohn" (Ingratitude is the reward of the world).

Not quite three decades later the proverb also appears with additional notes in W. G. Lambert's more extensive *Babylonian Wisdom Literature* (1960: 281), who cites it with an introductory formula from the letter mentioned by Lutz that identifies it clearly as a "popular proverb" to boot:

> The popular proverb says: "When the potter's dog enters the kiln it will bark at the potter."
> This is from a letter by a Late Assyrian king, almost certainly Esarhaddon. He addresses some "pseudo-Babylonians," and this proverb commences his communication to them. The point of the proverb seems to be that the dog inside the kiln is really in a very vulnerable position to bark at its master. The letter goes on to explain that these pseudo-Babylonians have been complaining against the king's servants. The king probably used the proverb with the implication that the people were in danger of receiving much harm at his

hands, and were in no position to raise complaints against trusted servants. This proverb is also known from the Syriac and Arabic versions of the Ahiqar saying [. . .; quoted from Priest above].

From what has been said, it appears to me that Lambert is not quite correct in his interpretation of the proverb by missing its basic meaning of covetousness. But be that as it may, there is finally the most ancient reference, which the Danish scholar Bendt Alster deciphered from a Sumerian cuneiform tablet dating from the third millenium B.C. in his two-volume *Proverbs of Ancient Sumer: The World's Earliest Proverb Collections* (1997: vol. I: 136, tablet 5, text no. 81):

A dog knows "Take it!"
It does not know "Put it down!"

Having written to my friend Bendt Alster about the possibility of a Sumerian proverb or even fable that might mark the beginning of all of this, he wrote back that there appears to be no direct precursor or parallel. He checked with the German scholar Kai Laemmerhirt as well, and both of them agree that the Sumerian text could be a vague antecedent. It certainly expresses a similar idea to the "dog in the manger" metaphor, but that is not to say that these texts might not have been created independently from one another. But while polygenesis is a possibility, it can certainly be stated now that the idea of an envious dog begrudging someone else something of no use to him was in the ancient air and current in proverbial form without having found expression in a fable.

Early European Dissemination up to Erasmus of Rotterdam

One thing is for certain: the "dog in the manger" proverb or proverbial expression was in existence by the second century A.D. in the Greek language, and it should not be surprising that early Greek paremiographers registered it in their collections afterwards. It is interesting to note that in both of the following references the "dog in the manger" is cited as the phrasal metaphor as such, with the ensuing text serving as its explication. Both texts appear in the invaluable *Corpus Paroemiographorum Graecorum* (1839 and 1851) in Greek, and I thank my colleague and friend Jacques Bailly from our Classics Department for providing the translations:

Diogenianus 83

LITERALLY: The dog in the manger: concerning those who neither themselves use nor allow others to use: insofar as the dog neither itself eats the barleycorns nor allows the horse to.

BETTER ENGLISH: The dog in the manger is about those who neither use a thing themselves nor allow others to use it: insofar as the dog does not eat the barley and does not allow the horse to either. (Leutsch and Schneidewin 1839 and 1851: II, 32, 83)

Gregorius Cyprus 61

LITERALLY: The dog in the manger: concerning those neither using themselves nor allowing others: insofar as the dog does not eat the barley while it stays in the manger and does not allow the horse.

BETTER ENGLISH: same as above. (Leutsch and Schneidewin 1839 and 1851: I, 363, 61)

The proverbial expression subsequently entered medieval Latin, with the fact that it is not to be found in classical Latin serving as additional proof that it was not known in the "dog in the manger" formulation during ancient times. Of course, once it was translated from the Greek of Lucian, Strato, and others into Latin as the lingua franca for the emerging vernacular languages of Europe, it subsequently was able to gain much ground in the form of loan translations throughout that area. Here are but three Latin variants from the Middle Ages out of Hans Walther's massive nine-volume collection *Proverbia sententiaeque latinitatis medii aevi* (1963–86):

Bos presepis eget, canis hunc abstemius arcet.
(Walther 1963: I, 246, 2159)

In presepe canis femo non vescitur ipse,
Nec sinit fenum qui cupit equus edat.
(Walther 1964: II, 468, 11938)

Avarus idem cum cane in presepio.
(Walther 1982: VII, 259, 35091q)

The third definitional text is of special interest, since it contains the proverbial idea in its shortest from of "Cane in presepio" (Dog in the manger), which gained great currency in Latin and other languages including English, of course.

This is not the place to review all the variants from numerous European languages, but I would like to cite a few from some of the standard comparative proverb collections as an indication that proverbs as a verbal form of folklore live in variants, the history of each of which deserves its own investigation. In 1872 Ida von Düringsfeld and Otto von Reinsberg-Düringsfeld included almost thirty texts from a number of Germanic and Romance languages in their two-volume collection *Sprichwörter der germanischen und romanischen Sprachen* (1872–75: I, 396–97, 756), among them:

German: Er gleicht dem Hunde, der auf dem Heu [hay] lag: er mocht' es selbst nicht und wollte nicht zugeben, dass der Ochs es frässe.

English: A dog in the manger, that neither eats, nor lets others eat.

Danish: Han sidder derpaa, som Hunden paa Høet.

French: Comme le chien du jardinier, qui ne mange pas de choux [cabbage] et ne veut pas que personne en mange.

Italian: E' fa com' can che guarda l'aglio [garlic], che non ne mangia egli, ne lascia mangiarne altrui.

Spanish: El perro del hortelano, que ni cime las berzas [cabbage], ni las dexa comer.

As can be seen, the variants are by no means restricted to hay or barley as food and the ox or horse who are prevented from eating it. In fact, at times the dog of the gardener is not at all in a manger but simply guards cabbage, garlic, salad, or other vegetables without naming anybody in particular who desires to eat from his meaningless treasure. The Danish variant "He sits on it like the dog on the hay" is a mere remnant and hard to understand without knowledge of a more detailed rendering. The most prevalent variant is clearly the one with cabbages, an image that everybody can relate to easily. Most of the texts also take on the form of a proverbial comparison with the particle "like" being part of it. These variants do not contain the wisdom of a proverb but rather describe fellow human beings by comparing their greed and envy with that of a dog.

Samuel Singer, in his three-volume *Sprichwörter des Mittelalters* (1943–47), also included a number of Germanic and Romance texts, wondering whether the phrase might not have originated in the Near East: "Ob das Gleichnis [proverbial comparison] ursprünglich aus dem Orient kommt? Lukian, bei dem wir es zuerst finden, ist ein Syrer, und auch die Araber kennen es: 'Wie der Hund in der Krippe, der nicht frißt und den andern nicht fressen läßt'" (III, 98–99; Ecker 1934: 26). I have checked his Arabic reference, but unfortunately could not find any additional references in my various Arabic proverb collections, not even in Johann Ludwig Burckhardt's *Arabische Sprüchwörter* (1834). But I would not be surprised if some day more Arabic variants will still be found. In the meantime we have even more Germanic and Romance parallels that have been edited from Singer's manuscripts in the magisterial thirteen-volume *Thesaurus proverbiorum medii aevi. Lexikon der Sprichwörter des romanisch-germanischen Mittelalters* (1995–2002). Since variety is the proverbial spice of life (and scholarship), let me cite but a few more variants (VI, 231–32, 286 [Middle Greek texts]). The first text in Latin is of special interest, since it states that the folk says that the dog defends the hay that he himself does not eat. In other words, the proverbial expressions are very much current in the Middle Ages:

Latin: Sic canis, ut vulgo aiunt, defendit fenum quod non comedit.

French: Tez est li chiens Ke ne lairoit mangier por riens La vace qui a moult grant fain [hunger] Et si ne puet mangier del fain [hay].

Italian: Si come el cane in guarda posto a lo orto, Che non mangia e proponi [melons], e non consente Che altri ne mangi.

English: Thogh it be noght the houndes kinde To ete chaf, yit wol he werne [prevents] An Oxe which comth to the berne, Therof to taken eny fode.

German: Der hunt enizzet höuwes niht Und grînt [growls] doch, so êrz ezzen siht.

This time we can add the cow who is prevented from eating, as well as melons the dog is holding on to, another food that does not do him any good. After this plethora of medieval texts, who will be surprised to find Erasmus of Rotterdam chime in on all of this in his massive compendium of *Adagia* (1500ff.)? He does indeed have a short entry with the "Dog in the manger" in Latin as title, and I cite the relevant first part of it in its English translation here:

Canis in praesepi
Dog in the manger
[Greek equivalent], The dog in the manger, is said of those who neither enjoy something themselves nor allow other people to get any benefit from it; for instance if a man were to keep valuable manuscripts tightly locked up, which he never opens himself nor allows anyone to read them, just like a dog in the manger that does not eat the barley itself and prevents the horse from eating it. Lucian *Against an Ignoramus*: "But you behave like the dog that lies in the manger, neither eating the barley itself nor making way for the horse that could eat it." He uses it again in his *Timon*. (Mynors 1989: XXXII, 240)

Clearly the bookish scholar Erasmus enjoyed his reference to Lucian's comment that someone who is unwilling to lend a book (manuscript) to someone, especially if he cannot read it himself, is like a dog in the manger. In any case, as usual Erasmus has done his homework, and his celebrated *Adagia* in Latin or its various translations did their part in spreading this proverbial metaphor all over Europe, including Finland, where it is known as well, as my friend Jarmo Korhonen informed me from Helsinki in 2011, containing several variants, among them: "On kun koira heinäkuorman päällä: ei syö itse eikä anna toiselle" ([He] is like the dog on a bale of hay: [He] doesn't eat himself and also doesn't give to another) (Kuusi 1982: 469). The Swedish proverb scholar Reinhold Strömberg is thus absolutely correct with his observation in a footnote that "the common proverb about a dog's envy [. . .] in later times gained almost universal currency" (1954: 49). But regarding Erasmus's entry, and this is extremely important, he mentions nothing about a possible fable! Nor has anybody else thus far in this discussion alluded to such a narrative, and this fact adds to the informed conclusion that we are dealing with proverbial matters until the fifteenth century and not with an Aesopic fable.

The Big Surprise: Enter the Fable

Renowned fable scholars like Hermann Österley, Ben Edwin Perry, Pierre Ruelle, as well as Gerd Dicke and Klaus Grubmüller (1987: 350–52) agree with this conclusion, for they too have not been able to find an Aesopic source for the proverb. However, they have discovered a "modern" fable

from an anonymous Latin manuscript *Fabvlae extravagantes* of the fifteenth
century that the German author Heinrich Steinhöwel included in Latin together with his own German translation in his important compilation *Buch
und Leben des Fabeldichters Esopi* (1475/77):

> *Fabula xi de cane invide.*
> Sunt plures, qui hoc invident aliis, quod ipsi habere nequeunt, et quamvis ipsis
> non prosit, tamen alios impediunt. De hoc audi fabulam. Canis impius iace-
> bat in presepe, quod erat plenum feno. Et venientes boves ut comederent, non
> sinebat ore patulos suos dentes ostendens. Tunc boves dixerunt ei: Inique agis,
> naturam invidens in nobis, quam tu non habes. Non enim tua est natura, ut
> comedas fenum, et vetas tarnen nobis illud comedere. Similiter cum teneret os
> in suo ore non valens illud rodere, non tarnen dimittebat alteri cani, ut illud
> roderet. Monstrat hec fabula non facile posse vitari invidiam, cum difficultate
> tamen vitatur, sed quiescere nescit.

> *Die xi fabel von dem nydigen hund.*
> Vil sint der menschen, die den andern engundent, das inen nit werden mag
> und villycht inen nit nücz wäre, ob sy es hetten, dannocht irrent sy die an-
> dern daran. Darvon hör ain fabel. Ain ungütiger hund lag in ainer krippen
> vol höws, der wolt die komenden ochsen von der waid nit eßen laßen, und
> bleket über sie die zend und gruwet. Da sprachen die ochsen zuo im: Du tuost
> unrecht, du bist unserer natur nydig, darumb das dir dyn natur dir nit gyt,
> daz du höw eßest, und wilt uns verbieten, daz wir das ouch nicht eßen sollen.
> Des gelychen hete er ouch ain bain in synem mul, daz er selber nicht nagen
> mocht. Aber dannocht wolt er es kainem andern hund vergünden ze nagen.
> Dise fabel zaiget, daz der nyd nit wol noch lychtiglich ist ze vermyden, und ob
> er wol mit arbait vermitten würt, so ruowet er doch nit lang.
> (Österley 1873: 91, 217–18)

The Latin text above is also included in Ben Edwin Perry's *Aesopica* (1952:
696, 702), for which he subsequently provided the following English translation in his *Babrius and Phaedrus* (1965: 597, 702):

> The Dog in the Manger: A dog without conscience lay in a manger full of hay.
> When the cattle came to eat of the hay he would not let them, but showed his
> teeth in ugly mood. The oxen protested: "It is not right for you to begrudge
> us the satisfaction of indulging our natural appetite when you yourself have
> no such appetite. It is not your nature to eat hay, and yet you prevent us from

eating it." And so it was when this dog had a bone in his mouth; he couldn't gnaw it any more himself, but he wouldn't let another dog gnaw it.

It should be pointed out here that Steinhöwel's fable includes a second proverbial expression with basically the same meaning, i.e. a dog that will not let another dog have a bone that he was not gnawing any longer. The *Thesaurus proverbiorum medii aevi* (Singer and Liver 1998: VI, 255) cites medieval Latin, French, Italian, and German references for it.

Barely a few years later, Julien Macho translated Steinhöwel's fable into French in his *L'Esope* (1480), thus entering it into the fable tradition of France. In his moralizing at the end, he goes so far as to compare such envious behavior with the devil himself:

> *La .xi. fable si est du chien maulvais et envieux.*
> Nul ne doit avoir envie du bien d'aultruy ne du bien lequel ne luy peut proffiter, ainsi que appert par ceste fable d'ung chien envieux qui jadis estoit en l'estable des beufz, laquelle estoit plaine de fain. Lequel chien gardoit les beufz de entrer en l'estable pour les garder de non menger de cestuy fain. Et, adoncques, les beufz luy dysrent: "Tu es bien parvers et inique de avoyr envye de avoyr du bien lequel nous est necessaire, et toy, tu n'en as que faire, car ta nature n'est pas de menger de fain." Et ainsi faisoit d'ung os qu'il tenoit en sa bouche, lequel il ne vouloit laisser a ung aultre chien. Et, pour ce, garde toy de la compaignie d'ung envieux, car avoir a besoigner a luy est chose perilleuse et difficille, ainsi que nous est demonstré par Lucifer. (Ruelle 1982: III, 174)

About three years later William Caxton translated Macho's rendition into English and included it together with a splendid woodcut in his frequently reprinted *Aesop's Fables* (1484), thus starting an impressive tradition of the fable in the English-speaking world with the fable being retold in slight variants:

> *The xi fable is of the enuyous dogge*
> None ought not to haue enuye of the good of other/ As it iappiereth by this fable/ Of a dogge whiche was enuyous/ and that somtyme was within a stable of oxen/ the whiche was ful of heye/ This dogge kept the oxen that they shold not entre in to theyr stable/ and that they shold not ete of the sayd hey/ And thenne the oxen sayd to hym/ Thow arte wel peruers and euylle to haue enuye of the good/ the whiche is to vs nedefull and prouffitable/ And thow hast of hit nought to doo/ for thy kynde is not to ete no hey/ And thus he dyd of a

grete bone/ the whiche he held at his mouthe/ and wold not leue hit by cause
and for enuye of another dogge/ whiche was therby/ And therfore kepe the
wel fro the company or felaushshp of an enuyous body/ For to haue to doo with
hym hit is moche peryllous and dyffycyle/ As to vs is wel shewen by Lucyfer.
(Lenaghan 1967: 153; with the woodcut and modernized text in Gascoigne
1984: unpaginated)

With these four texts in Latin, German, French, and English, the proverb
turned into a fable could conquer Europe and other parts of the world. As
my colleague and friend Dennis Mahoney mentioned to me quite spontaneously over a cup of coffee when hearing about my interest in the "Dog in the
manger" proverb, "it literally begs to be placed into a narrative to make sense
of its metaphor" (March 2011). In 2011 Charles Doyle from the University
of Georgia, another dear friend and co-paremiologist, sent me this exciting
e-mail message: "Dear Wolfgang, In an interesting turn of phrase, the English translation of Francisco Rodríguez Adrados's *History of the Graeco-Latin
Fable* (2003, III: 614) says that 'the dog in the manger' is a proverb that was
'fabulized into a fable.' (That's probably redundant; what else could 'fabu-
lize' mean?!)." My immediate answer was: "Dear Charlie, What a super reference!!! I'll hunt it down tomorrow—UVM has the three volumes. Many,
many thanks." What would scholarship be without such great friends! And
what a mistake it would be if we scholars did not communicate with each
other about our projects.

The Aesopization of an Anonymous Fable and its English Tradition

Since the Latin fable from the anonymous Latin manuscript appeared in collections of fables that included ancient Aesopic fables and which had the
name of Aesop in their titles, it should not be surprising that the fifteenth-
century fable "The Dog in the Manger" is usually considered an Aesopic
fable by scholars and laypersons alike. It is far beyond the scope of this work
to trace the polyglot history of this fable from different countries, but let
me present at least a representative diachronic list of texts for the English-
language tradition. Because the fable is actually quite short, I will register at
least thirteen texts of many more that I have located. They all tell the basic
narrative in succinct fashion, with the animals being mistreated always being
oxen. Only the variant from 1984 contains the more generic term "beasts"
(also "corn" and not "hay"). It should also be noted that all fables carry the
title "The Dog in the Manger," with only the variant from 1666 having the

perhaps more telling different designation of "The Dog and the Ox." As expected, there are obvious repetitions, with editors copying from previous collections. Thus the short and precise variant from 1868 is cited identically in books from 1909 and 1968. These are also the texts that have no short statement that summarizes the fable's content (the 1984 text also lacks such a statement). There is a major exception: the early fable rendition from 1842 contains a rather lengthy discussion of its possible "application" in life. All together, these texts build on William Caxton's first English publication of the fable in 1484 and as such they are nothing more and nothing less than short explications of the much older proverbial metaphor:

1666: *The Dog and the Ox*
The envious dog that brooding lay,
Upon a crib replete with hay,
Snarls at the ox that thither came,
An eager appetite to tame.
And forced him back, incensed, whereat
He on the dog invokes this fate:
May the just gods so punish thee
As thy rude spleen hath injured me
Who does prohibit me the meat
Whereon thyself disdains to eat.

SOME WITH KEEN ENVY WOULD THEMSELVES ANNOY,
SO THOSE THEY EMULATE THEY MIGHT DESTROY.

(McKendry 1964, 46)

1842: *The Dog in the Manger.*
A dog was lying upon a manger full of hay. An Ox, being hungry, came near, and offered to eat of the hay; but the envious ill-natured Cur, getting up and snarling at him, would not suffer him to touch it. Upon which, the Ox, in the bitterness of his heart, said, "A curse light on thee for a malicious wretch, who wilt neither eat hay thyself, nor suffer others to do it."

APPLICATION.
Envy is the most unnatural and unaccountable of all the passions. There is scarce any other emotion of the mind, however unreasonable, but may have something said in excuse for it; and there are many of these weaknesses of the soul, which, notwithstanding the wrongness and irregularity of them, swell the heart, while they last, with pleasure and

gladness. But the envious man has no such apology as this to make; the stronger the passion is, the greater torment he endures; and subjects himself to a continual real pain, by only wishing ill to others. Revenge is sweet, though cruel and inhuman; and though it sometimes thirsts even for blood, yet may be glutted and satiated. Avarice is something highly monstrous and absurd; yet, as it is a desire after riches, every little acquisition gives it pleasure; and to behold and feel the hoarded treasure, to a covetous man, is a constant uncloying enjoyment. But envy, which is an anxiety arising in our minds, upon our observing accomplishments in others which we want ourselves, can never receive any true comfort, unless in a deluge, a conflagration, a plague, or some general calamity that should befall mankind: for, as long as there is a creature living, that enjoys its being happily within the envious man's sphere, it will afford nourishment to his distempered mind; but such nourishment as will make him pine, and fret, and emaciate hinuelf to nothing.

(Anonymous 1842: 60–61)

1868: *The Dog in the Manger.*
A dog lay in a manger, and by the growling and snapping prevented the oxen from eating the hay which had been placed for them. "What a selfish Dog!" said one of them to his companions; "he cannot eat the hay himself, and yet refuses to allow those to eat who can."

(Townsend 1887: 25)

1909: *The Dog in the Manger*
identical with 1868
(Anonymous 1985: 16)

1909: *The Dog in the Manger*
A dog looking out for its afternoon nap jumped into the Manger of an Ox and lay there cosily upon the straw. But soon the Ox, returning from its afternoon work, came up to the Manger and wanted to eat some of the straw. The Dog in a rage, being awakened from its slumber, stood up and barked at the Ox, and whenever it came near attempted to bite it. At last the Ox had to give up the hope of getting at the straw, and went away muttering:
"AH, PEOPLE OFTEN GRUDGE OTHERS WHAT THEY CANNOT ENJOY THEMSELVES."

(Anonymous 1909: 27)

1947: *The Dog in the Manger*
A dog looking for a quiet and comfortable place to take a nap jumped into the manger of the ox and lay there on the hay.

Some time later the ox, returning hungry from his day's work, entered his stall and found the dog in his manger. The dog, in a rage because he had been awakened from his nap, stood up and barked and snapped whenever the ox came near his hay.

The ox is a patient beast, but finally he protested: "Dog, if you wanted to eat my dinner I would have no objection. But you will neither eat it yourself nor let me enjoy it, which strikes me as a very churlish way to act."

Application: SOME BEGRUDGE OTHERS WHAT
THEY CANNOT ENJOY THEMSELVES.
(Anonymous 1947: 1)

1968: *The Dog in the Manger*
identical with 1868 and 1909
(Anonymous 1968: 57)

1984: *The Dog in the Manger*
A Dog made his bed in a manger, and lay snarling and growling to keep the beasts from their provender. "See," said one of them, "what a miserable cur, who neither can eat corn himself, nor will allow those to eat it who can."
(Anonymous 1984: 60)

1988: *The Dog in the Manger*
Once a mean Old Dog who was tired of yipping and yapping and chasing the chickens around, decided to take a rest. Looking for a quiet spot, he came across a manger and jumped into it. As he did, he got some hay in his mouth and had to spit it out.

"Phooey!" he said. "I don't see how any animal could eat this. It's dry and tasteless." Then, the Dog settled down and went to sleep. He would have been better off without the scratchy hay beneath him, but he was too lazy to get rid of it.

Later, after a long day's work, three Oxen came to the manger to eat some of the hay that had been put there for them. The Old Dog was awakened by the sound of their approaching hoofs and began to bark angrily, "Go away! Can't you see I'm sleeping?"

"But we're hungry," said the first Ox.

"Get up and let us have our supper," begged the second.

The Dog stayed where he was and went on barking.

"Why, you don't even want to eat that hay," said the third tired Ox. "And it can't be very comfortable. But still you won't let us near it. You're just mean."

To show how mean he was, the Dog barked one last time at the Oxen, then went right back to sleep on their supper.

ONLY THE MEANEST CREATURES WOULD KEEP FROM OTHERS
THINGS THEY CANNOT EVEN USE THEMSELVES.

(Calmenson 1988: 55)

1994: *The Dog in the Manger*

One day, a dog was wandering through the countryside. He hadn't eaten for a whole day, and he was very hungry.

When he came to a farm, the dog went into the stable. "Perhaps I will find some food in here," he thought.

But all the dog found was a manger filled with hay. "Well," he thought, "I can't eat this, but at least it will make a nice, warm bed. And he jumped into the manger and went to sleep.

Sometime later, the dog felt something soft nuzzling him. It was the nose of one of the horses who lived in the stable. He was standing over the manger, and another horse was behind him.

"Sorry to disturb you," said the horse, "but we'd like our dinner now. Would you please get out of the manger so that we can eat our hay?"

"No, I will not!" barked the dog.

"Why?" asked the surprised horse. "You can't eat this hay, can you?"

"No, of course not," said the dog.

"Then why not let us have it?" asked the horse.

"Because if I can't eat, I don't want anyone else to eat, either!" said the dog. "Now go away!"

So the poor horses went hungry, all because of a selfish dog.

Moral: DON'T KEEP OTHERS FROM HAVING WHAT YOU CAN'T USE.

(Randall and Barbato 1994: 45–47)

1997: *The Dog in the Manger*

At the end of the day's work, the ox went to her manger to get some hay for dinner. She found the dog there and politely asked him to move so she could get to the hay. But the dog snapped, "Leave me alone, you old ox!"

The ox tried to eat the hay several more times. But each time the dog growled and snapped at her. Finally the ox said, "You cannot eat the hay or use it for a bed, but still you will not let me enjoy it. You're mean and selfish."

SOME WILL NOT LET OTHERS HAVE WHAT THEY CANNOT ENJOY THEMSELVES.

(Leach 1997: 16)

2000: *The Dog in the Manger*
A dog found a cozy spot to sleep, curled up in the soft hay of the oxen's manger. When the oxen came into the stables, tired from plowing the field and eager for their supper, the dog bared his teeth and growled at them, as if the manger were filled with the best of meat and bones all for himself.

"Selfish beast!" one of them exclaimed, not daring to come near. "He can't eat the hay himself, yet he still won't give any to us who are so hungry for it!"

DON'T GRUDGE OTHERS WHAT YOU CANNOT ENJOY YOURSELF.

(Pinkney 2000: 44)

2002: *The Dog in the Manger*
There was a wicked dog lying in a manger full of hay. When the cattle came and wanted to eat, the dog barred their way, baring his teeth. The cattle said to the dog, "You are being very unfair by begrudging us something we need which is useless to you. Dogs don't eat hay, but you will not let us near it." The same thing happened when a dog was holding a bone in his mouth: the dog couldn't chew on the bone that way, but no other dog was able to chew on it either.

THE FABLE SHOWS THAT IT IS NOT EASY TO AVOID ENVY: WITH SOME EFFORT YOU CAN TRY TO ESCAPE ITS EFFORTS, BUT IT NEVER GOES AWAY ENTIRELY.

(Gibbs 2002: 84)

The four variants before the last one are from editions for children, with the 1988 retelling by Stephanie Calmenson most likely being especially appealing to children because of the expanded dialogue between the dog and the three oxen. But regarding the fable retold by Andrea Stacy Leach in 1997, I cannot for the life of me figure out why she would refer to the male ox by the pronouns "she" and "her." Is the odd mixture of genders driven by some hypersensitive and politically correct obsession? If Andrea Leach wanted to stress feminist issues, she could easily have changed "ox" to "cow." As it is now, I am convinced that most children would be quick in noticing that an "ox" is not a "she"—and right they are!

One more point needs to be made here that is of significance for the widespread misconception that the proverb "The dog in the manger" is a summation of an Aesopic fable. This started with Heinrich Steinhöwel, Julien Macho, and William Caxton, who included the fable in their books with authentic fables going back at least as far as Aesop. English-language editors and retellers of the fifteenth-century fable of "The Dog in the Manger" simply ignored all of this and mixed fables from a wide variety of sources and times together under the label of "Aesop." It is then no surprise that all thirteen fables cited above come from books that somewhat misleadingly carry the name of Aesop in their titles. But, to be sure, this has been done with fables and Aesop for a long time, and only scholars interested in such details would and can delight in pointing such matters out. For the paremiologist, of course, it is also of interest that the title "The Dog in the Manger" of these fable variants has done its part in keeping the proverb alive! However, there is today a definite decline in the interest in fables with the ever-increasing volume of new children's books entering the market. In fact, most children will not be introduced to fables at all any longer, and this decline of cultural literacy regarding fables has its effect on the survival chances of the proverbial phrase "to be a dog in the manger" as well. But this matter will be discussed at the end of these deliberations.

The English History of the Original Proverb

Not even well-established scholars can escape the problem just mentioned, thus doing their part in spreading the false supposition of an Aesopic fable origin of "The dog in the manger." A case in point is Burton Stevenson's short statement in his massive and still extremely useful *The Home Book of Proverbs, Maxims and Familiar Phrases* (1948: 601):

> A dog in the manger. (Greek text.)
> AESOP, *Fables: The Dog and the Horses.* (ca. 570 B.C.) From the well known fable of the dog which growled and snarled to prevent the horses from eating their corn, although the dog itself had no use for it. The form of the proverb usually found in the collections is (Greek text), a bitch. Another Greek proverb of a dog where it doesn't belong is "A dog among roses" (Greek text), applied to a person living more luxuriously than he deserves.

It is not clear where Stevenson got the name of the fable from, and I have also not come across the female dog. But this by no means is to say that the actual references that Stevenson lists from Lucian, John Gower, John Lyly, Robert Burton, and others for the proverb in literary contexts are not invaluable for a diachronic survey of the proverb in the English language. Other historical proverb dictionaries for the English language obviously add considerable references, among them those of G. L. Apperson (1929: 160–61, 68), Morris Palmer Tilley (1950: 167–68, D513, and 252, G38), Sanki Ichikawa et al. (1964: 176, with a reference to Aesop), Archer Taylor and Bartlett Jere Whiting (1958: 106, 28), Bartlett Jere Whiting (1968: 295: H565), F. P. Wilson (1970: 195), Bartlett Jere Whiting (1977: 114–15, D233; 1989: 174, D217), Robert W. Dent (1984: 299, D513), John A. Simpson and E. S. C. Weiner (1989: IV, 929), Robert A. Nowlan and Gwendolyn L. Nowlan (2000: 41–42, 85), George B. Bryan and Wolfgang Mieder (2005: 216–17), and, to be sure, also the impressive online 3rd edition of the *Oxford English Dictionary*. These crucial historical collections have been of great value in assembling the following list of proverbial references from the fourteenth century to today. While I obviously also found additional diachronic English texts on my own, I want to acknowledge my debt to these fellow paremiologists from times gone by. Their work was executed without the possibility of computer searches and digitalized books, and it is truly amazing what these paremiographers were able to locate without the assistance of modern technology. I have located all their references and I am glad to add my own finds to them with more textual information than would be possible in the proverb dictionaries by the scholars just mentioned. The result of our collective labors is the following list of 44 references from 1390 to 1972. In order to make their sources more immediately recognizable and also by way of reducing the length of my list of scholarly references, I have decided to add the bibliographical information for each text right here. This will doubtlessly make for interesting reading, and my short comments (added where appropriate) will also help realize the value of these revealing texts of "The dog in the manger" proverb in context over several centuries.

Let me start with three appearances of the proverb prior to the publication of the anonymous Latin fable and its translation into German, French, and English in the last quarter of the fifteenth century. These references could thus not possibly have been influenced by the fable and definitely show that the proverb was established in the English language prior to William Caxton's fable collection of 1484:

1390: Mi Sone, er I axe eny more,
I thenke somdiel for thi lore
Telle an ensample of this matiere
Touchende Envie, as thou schalt hiere.
Write in Civile this I finde:
Thogh it be noght the houndes kinde
To ete chaf, yit wol he werne
An Oxe which comth to the berne,
Therof to taken eny fode.
And thus, who that it understode,
It stant of love in many place:
Who that is out of loves grace
And mai himselven noght availe,
He wolde an other scholde faile;
And if he may put eny lette,
He doth al that he mai to lette.
John Gower, *Confessio Amantis*, in *The Complete Works of John Gower*. G. C.
Macaulay, ed. Oxford: Clarenden, 1899–1902. I, 132, 79-94.

1426: Whyl I may walken on the ground;
ffor I resemble vn-to that hound
Wych lyggeth in a stak off hay,
Groynynge al the longë day,
Wyl suffre no beste ther-to to gon,
And het hym sylff wyl etë noon.
John Lydgate, *The Pilgrimage of the Life of Man, Englisht by John Lydgate,
A.D. 1426, from the French of Guillaume de Deguileville, A.D. 1330, 1355*. F. J.
Furnivall, ed. London: Kegan Paul, Trench, Trübner, 1899. 468, 17473–78.

1450: But I am lich the hound that lyth on the hep of hey to which if any sette
hand he abayeth and berketh and cryeth, albeit that he ete noon therof.
The Pilgrimage of the Lyfe of the Manhode. Translated anonymously into prose
from The First Recension of Guillaume de Deguileville's Poem *Le Pèlerinage
de la vie humaine*. Avril Henry, ed. 2 vols. Oxford: Oxford University Press,
1985. I, 120, 5027–29.

Since John Gower was fluent in French and since the other two references by
John Lydgate and an anonymous author are both translations from the same
French original *Le Pèlerinage de la vie humaine* (mid-fourteenth century) by

Guillaume de Deguileville, it is fair to assume that the proverbial metaphor jumped across the Channel from France to England. Of course, that does not mean that Erasmus of Rotterdam and his fellow humanists did not have any influence on the spread of the proverb in Great Britain. This can be seen from a Latin epigram by Thomas More, a close friend of Erasmus who doubtlessly knew the Latin "Canis in praesepi" from the *Adagia* cited above. He most likely was aware of the three references just cited, and Caxton's English fable rendition by 1518 as well, when he published his Latin epigram. But since Gower, Lydgate, and Caxton have an ox for the animal wanting the hay, the Erasmus source with its reference to a horse is much more likely:

1518: CANIS IN PRAESEPI.

AVARVS HOMO.

In praesepe canis foeno nec uescitur ipse,
Ne sinit ut foenum qui cupit indat equus.
Seruat auarus opes, opibus non utitur ipse,
Atque alios uti qui cupiunt, prohibet.

THE MISER IS A DOG IN THE MANGER
The dog in the manger does not himself eat the hay,
nor does he let the horse, who wants hay, take any.
The miser guards his wealth, does not use it himself,
And those who want to put it to some use he keeps at a distance.
Thomas More, *Latin Poems*, ed. Clarence H. Miller. New Haven, Connecticut: Yale University Press, 1984. Vol. 3, part II: 176–77.

Thomas More's Latin epigram is not referred to in any of the historical proverb dictionaries mentioned above, and I wish to acknowledge that my friend Charles Doyle drew my attention to it 2011 along with his short remarks on the epigram in *Moreana* (1977: 62–63). More's humanistic text is clearly an important link in the developmental chain for the proverb from its Greek original via Latin into the English tongue. There is, in fact, one more late humanistic text that was informed by Erasmus of Rotterdam's *Adagia*. Johannes Ferrarius published his *De republica bene instituenda, paraenesis* in 1556, which contains, in its 1559 English translation, the following reference mentioning Lucian and horses just as Erasmus did:

1559: Not muche vnlike to Lucians Dogge, whiche liyng in the maunger, neither would eate oates hymself, ne yet suffer the horses ones to laie their lippes
on them.
*A VVorke of Ioannes Ferrarius Montanus, Touchynge the Good Orderynge of a
Common Weale* . . . Englished by William Bauande. London: Ihon Kingston,
1559, fol. 17.

With this we can leave the humanistic tradition, for by the time of the
mid-sixteenth century, the English language has gained dominance in literary works, a development that will become clear from the treasure trove of
chronologically arranged texts in contexts that follows:

1546: And why do these [rich] men disable them [the poor] for readers of the
Scriptures, that are not indued with the possessions of this worlde? Vndoutely
because they are the very same that shut yp the kyngdome of God before men;
thei enter not them selues, nother suffre thei them to entre that wolde. They
are lyke a curre dogge liyng in a cocke of haye. For he wyll eate none of the
heye hym selfe, nother suffer any other beast that commeth to eate therof.
Simon Fish, *A Supplication of the Poore Commons*, in S. Fish, *A Supplication for
the Beggars*, ed. J. Meadows Cowper. London: N. Trübner, 1871. 65.

1564: And like vnto greate stinkyng mucle medin hilles, whiche neuer doe
pleasure vnto the lande or grounde, vntill their heapes are caste abrode to
the profites of many, whiche are kepte neither to their owne comfortes, nor
others, but enely in behadyng them; like vnto cruell dogges, liyng in a Maunger, neither eatyng the heye themselues, ne suffering the horse to feede thereof
hymself.
William Bullein, *A Dialogve bothe Pleasaunte and Pietifull, Wherein is a Goo-
dly Regimente against the Feuer Pestilence with a Consolacion and Comfort
against Death*. London: Ihon Kingston, 1964, fol. 4; and William Bullein, *A
Dialogue against the Feuer Pestilence*. Mark W. Bullen and A. H. Bullen, eds.
London: N. Trübner, 1888. 9, 11–17.

1573: And as for the Syr Lowte
That playdst inne and owte;
A dogg in ye maunger,
A very ranke raunger;
A squrvy knave skratch the,
Ann all ye divells go with the.

Gabriel Harvey, *Letter-Book*. Edward John Long Scott, ed. Westminster, UK: Camden Society, 1884. 114.

1573: AGAINST FANTASTICAL SCRUPLENESS
At this time and that time, some make a great matter;
Some help not, but hinder the poor with their clatter.
Take custom from feasting, what cometh then last?
Where one hath a dinner, a hundred shall fast.

To dog in the manger, some liken I could,
That hay will eat none, nor let other that would.
Some scarce, in a year, give a dinner or two,
No well can abide nay other to do.
Thomas Tusser, *Five Hundred Points of Husbandry together with A Book of Huswifery*. William Mavor, ed. London: Lackington, Allen, 1812. 72, chap. XXIX.

1578: Thou livest in Athens as the wasp doth among bees, rather to sting than to gain honey, and thou dealest with most of thy acquaintance as the dog in the manger, who neither suffereth the horse to eat hay nor will himself; for thou being idle, wilt not permit any (as far as in thee lieth) to be well employed.
John Lyly, *Euphues: The Anatomy of Wit. Euphues & His England*. Morris William Croll and Harry Clemons, ed. London: George Routledge, 1916. 177. See also Tilley 1926: 125–26, 159.

The following citation from Edmund Spenser is of special interest, since he refers to an Aesop's fable just prior to citing the "Dog in the manger" proverb. Could it be that he had not yet come across Caxton's fable edition? In any case, if he had been aware of the fable, he would most likely have mentioned it as well:

1579: The second shame [of people arguing against the use of certain old words in English] no less than the first [of those not wanting to accept foreign words in English], that what so they understand not, they straightway deem to be senseless, and not at all to be understood. Much like to the mole in Aesop's fable, that, being blind herself, would in no wise be persuaded that any beast could see. The last, more shameful than both, that of their own country and natural speech, which together with their nurse's milk they sucked, they

have so base regard and bastard judgment, that they will not only themselves
not labour to garnish and beautify it, but also repine, that of other it should
not be embellished. Like to the dog in the manger, that himself can eat no hay,
and yet barketh at the hungry bullock, that so fain would feed: whose currish
kind, though it cannot be kept from barking, yet I conne them thank that
they refrain from biting.
Edmund Spenser, *The Shepherd's Calendar Containing Twelve Eclogues, Pro-*
portionable to the Twelve Months, in *The Poetical Works of Edmund Spenser.*
George Gilfillan, ed. Edinburgh: James Nichol, 1859. IV, 215. See Doyle 1990:
311.

It took almost another three decades until a British author cited the proverb
together with a reference to a fable by Aesop, clearly showing that William
Caxton's fable collection had succeeded in bringing about this association.
Of course, the proverb was long established by then, often being used as a
proverbial comparison:

> 1604: Ile not budge: ile lie like a dog in a manger.
> Thomas Dekker, *The Honest Whore*, in *The Dramatic Works of Thomas Dekker.*
> Fredson Bowers, ed. Cambridge: Cambridge University Press, 1955. II, 79, Act
> IV, scene 2.

But here is Thomas Dekker again, together with John Webster in their joint-
ly authored play *Westward Hoe* (1607), where it comes to that first coupling
of the fable and the proverb in a literary reference:

> 1607: And like Esop's Dog, vnlesse himselfe might eate hay, wil lie in the man-
> ger and starue; but heele hinder the horse from eating any.
> Thomas Dekker and John Webster, *Westward Hoe*. John S. Farmer, ed. Lon-
> don: Tudor Facsimile Texts, 1914. Act V, scene 1.

The explicit association with the fable is a rare exception in the literary references I present here. Clearly the authors feel that their readers know the
metaphor in its various formulations as a proverb, a proverbial expression, or
a proverbial comparison. It should be noted that they also tend to vary the
type of animal, if it is mentioned at all, among ox, horse, bullock, and beast.
In the first text of the following list, the skilled Robert Burton augments the
fixed reference to the dog for once by a hog that obviously can also not benefit from the hay as nourishment:

1621: For what greater folly can there be, or madness, than to macerate himself when he need not? and when, as Cyprian notes, *he may be freed from his burden, and eased of his pains, will go on still, his wealth increasing, when he hath enough, to get more, to live besides himself,* to starve his *Genius,* keep back from his wife and children, neither letting them nor other friends use or enjoy that which is theirs by right, and which they much need perhaps; like a hog, or dog in the manger, he doth only keep it, because it shall do nobody else good, hurting himself and others; and, for a little momentary pelf, damn his own soul? Robert Burton, *Anatomy of Melancholy.* Floyd Bell and Paul Jordan-Smith, eds. New York: Farrar & Rinehart, 1927. 246, part 1, section 2.

1639: Nor here may we overpasse, how Boemund Prince of Antioch with a great navie spoiled the harbours of Grecia, to be revenged of treacherous Alexius the Emperor. Voluntaries for this service he had enough, all desiring to have a lash at the dog in the manger, and every mans hand itching to throw a cudgel at him, who like a nut-tree must be manured by beating, or else would never bear fruit: yet on some conditions an agreement at last was made betwixt them. Thomas Fuller, *The Historie of the Holy VVarre.* Cambridge: Thomas Buck, 1639. 59, book II, chapter 11.

1663: And when I talked that I would go about doing something of the Controllers work when I had time, and that I thought the Controller would not take it ill, he wittily replied that there was nothing in the world so hateful as a dog in a manger. Samuel Pepys, *The Diary of Samuel Pepys.* Robert Latham and William Matthews, eds. Berkeley, California: University of California Press, 1971. IV, 397–98.

1674: Yet have the English no maw to open any of them [silver mines in New England], whether out of ignorance or of fear for bringing a foreign Enemy upon them, or (like the dog in the manger) to keep their Sovereign from partaking of the benefits, who certainly may claim an interest in them as his due, being eminently a gift proceeding from divine bounty to him. John Josselyn, *An Account of Two Voyages to New-England.* London: Giles Widdows, 1674. 45.

1709: And if *Horses* could tell *Stories,* they would certainly complain to their *Masters,* either of their own *Servants,* or of the *Livery-Stables* in LONDON, or

of *both* in Combination to defraud those poor dumb Creatures of their *Due*, and their just *Allowances* of *Hay* and *Straw*, or of *Oats* and *Beans*. The lazy *Dog* in the *Manger*, deserv'd *hanging* for serving the weary'd *Ox* so barbarously, and keeping him from his *Crib*, after the laborious *Toil* of the Day.
Oswald Dykes, *English Proverbs with Moral Reflexions*. London: G. Sawbridge, 1709. 282. (This is part of an essay and not a proverb entry.)

1729: It will be thought not a little extraordinary at Court That any Servant of his Majesty should be found fault with for rebuilding the Kings Fortifications by a people who have often disobeyed Orders for soe doeing, it looks like ye dog in ye Manger (I beg pardon for the Comparison) that would not let the Horse eat hay or eat it himself.
Letter by David Dunbar of December 4, 1729 (Boston), in *Documentary History of the State of Maine. The Baxter Manuscripts*. James Phinney Baxter, ed. Portland, Maine: Lefavor-Tower, 1907. X, 452–53.

1760: What have I to do with fathers and guardians! a parcel of preaching, prudent, careful, curmudgeonly—dead to pleasures themselves, and the blasters of it in others—mere dogs in a manger—no, no, I'll veer, tack about, open my budget to the boy, and join in a counter-plot.
Samuel Foote, *The Minor, A Comedy*. New York: D. Longworth, 1813. 19, Act I.

1775: *Willing*. The Gents. favorite Plan is to induce foreigners to come here. Shall We act like the Dog in the Manger, not suffer N.Y. and the lower Counties and N. Carolina to export because We cant. We may get Salt and Ammunition by those Ports.
From a debate in the Continental Congress of October 3, 1775, in *Diary and Autobiography of John Adams*. L. H. Butterfield, ed. Cambridge, Massachusetts: Harvard University Press, 1961. II, 190.

1779: Ballendine has got Possession of the Key to the Navigation of James River, & is acting exactly the Part of the Dog in the Manger. I am very uneasy about it, & fearful nothing decisive will be done, & the Gentlemen left in Doubt, & Disgust.
Letter by George Mason to Richard Henry Less of June 19, 1779 (Williamsburg), in *The Papers of George Mason, 1725–1792*. Robert A. Rutland, ed. Chapel Hill, North Carolina: University of North Carolina Press, 1970. II, 524.

1792: "Your Equal-Right gentry I ne'er could abide
That all are born equal, by Me is denied:
And Barlow and Paine shall preach it in vain;
Look even at brutes, and you'll see it confest
That some are intended to manage the rest;
Yon' dog of the manger, how stately he struts!
You may swear him well-born, from the size of his guts;
Not a better-born whelp ever snapped at his foes,
All he wants is a Glass to be stuck on his Nose:
And then, my dear Sue, between me and you,
He would look like the gemman whose name I forget,
Who lives in a castle and never pays debt."
Philip Freneau, "A Matrimonial Dialogue," in *The Poems of Philip Freneau,*
Poet of the American Revolution. Fred Lewis Pattee, ed. New York: Russell &
Russell, 1963. III, 105.

As can be seen from this poetic stanza, Philip Freneau could clearly count
on the fact that his readers would understand the mere "dog of the manger"
allusion. But this popular poet of American revolutionary times also appears
to know that they are aware of the fable that had gained considerable currency by the end of the eighteenth century. He says as much in the following
stanza from a long ode "To Peter Pindar":

1801: Like fabl'd dog, who in the manger lay,
Because his maw could not digest the hay,
Would not permit the honest, delving ox,
To chew his prickly quid in quiet;
But he must bite his nose and pull his locks,
And raise around his horns and tail a riot.
Philip Freneau, "To Peter Pindar," in *The Poems of Philip Freneau, Poet of the*
American Revolution. Fred Lewis Pattee, ed. New York: Russell & Russell,
1963. III, 110.

But again, it is much more prevalent to cite simply the proverbial expression
or the proverbial comparison, as did James Fenimore Cooper early in the
nineteenth century as he tried to liberate the American artistic and literary
scene from its European dependence. The more modern employments of the
"dog" metaphor also use it as a mere proverbial utterance without any reference to the fable tradition:

1829: We must break the chain of mental dependance [*sic*] which enslaves us, and having so long acted, begin to think, for ourselves. Three fourths of the opinions of Europe are perfectly conventional, and are adopted to suit circumstances that they cannot change, however they may wish it, and yet our puritans in politics and religion stand ready to swallow all they say, provided they are left free from tythes and kings themselves. Now there is a good deal of this empyricism [*sic*] in their taste as well as in their other theories, and, in every case it is quite intolerable that a set of second rate men, at home, should pretend to keep down the feeling of the nation, merely because the dolts, having run over a few countries, wish to be exclusive. There is nothing exclusive in true talent. It comes from nature and it appeals to nature. Any man whose knowledge can compass the medium through which talent communicates its gifts can feel its power, and convention seldom begins to create beauties in any of the arts until genius is exhausted. These rogues are like a dog(s) in the manger, unable to do any thing themselves, they take a pleasure in frightening the young and timid from the field.
James Fenimore Cooper in a letter to Horatio Greenough of November 5, 1829 (Sorrento), in *The Letters and Journals of James Fenimore Cooper*. James Franklin Beard, ed. Cambridge, Massachusetts: Harvard University Press, 1960. I, 395–96.

1830: It is enough to do anybody's heart good to see how kind and obliging these Democratic Republikans and National Republikans are to each other, and how each party tries to help the other along; and it's enough to make anybody's blood boil to see the Jacksonites and the Huntonites, jest [*sic*] like the dog in the manger, because they can't eat the hay themselves, snap at these two clever parties the moment either of 'em sets out to take a mouthful.
Jack Downing (pseud. Seba Smith), *My Thirty Years Out of the Senate*. New York: Oaksmith, 1859. 64.

1836: "Why, what a dog in the manger you must be—you can't marry them both. Still, under the circumstances, I can analyze the feeling—it's natural, but all that is natural is not always creditable to human nature."
Frederick Marryat, *Japhet in Search of a Father*. New York: Wallis & Newell, 1836. 197.

1868: "Oh, that's the trouble, is it? I thought there was something in the dimple that didn't suit you. Not being a dog in the manger, but the happiest fellow

alive, I assure you I can dance at Jo's wedding with a heart as light as my heels. Do you doubt it, *ma amie?*"
Louisa M. Alcott, *Little Women*. New York: Modern Library, 1983. 562, chapter XXI.

1905: I have never made any claims on her since she found out that she didnt care for me; and she might have known from that that I was not the man to keep her against her will and play dog in the manger with a fellow like Douglas. However, thats past praying for now. She has had enough of me; and I have had more than enough of her set and her family, except that I should like to remain good friends with you. You are the only one of the whole lot worth your salt.
[George] Bernard Shaw, *The Irrational Knot*. New York: Brentano's, 1926. 337. See Bryan and Mieder 1994: 111.

1911: Are you so much wiser than I? Am I so stupid, so vilely rotten, that I cannot have some hand in forming my children's minds and souls? Let me warn you that you are playing the part of a dog-in-the-manger when you insist by your past and present attitude in dwarfing my children through their lack of me—and all because Charmian has proven herself a better wife and mate for me than you proved yourself.
Letter by Jack London to Bessie London of January 8, 1911 (Los Angeles), in *Letters from Jack London*. King Hendricks and Irving Shepard, eds. New York: Odyssey, 1965. 330.

1923: "I felt a little like that myself," he said. "But we mustn't be dogs in the manger: old men like us."
E. V. Lucas, *Advisory Ben: A Story*. London: Methuen, 1913. 179.

1925: "There you are; the dog in the manger! You won't let him discuss your affairs, and you are annoyed when he talks about his own."
Willa Cather, *The Professor's House*. James Woodress and Frederick M. Link, eds. Lincoln, Nebraska: University of Nebraska Press, 2002. 48.

1928: Sneaking and mean, Irene prevented June from getting her lover. Sneaking and mean, she prevents Fleur. She is the bitch in the manger. She is the sneaking *anti*. Irene, the most beautiful woman on earth!
D. H. Lawrence, "John Galsworthy," in D. H. Lawrence, *Selected Literary Criticism*. Anthony Beal, ed. New York: Viking, 1966. 130.

1928: "And that was the weak joint that Maurice saw and went for—damn him! He took it upon himself to tell me that I was here more or less on sufferance. He'd been generous in the past—he actually reminded me of that!—but he didn't see how he was to continue to subsidize me indefinitely. You see his game? If he couldn't have Una himself, he'd take care that I shouldn't have her either. Damned dog-in-the-manger! That's a nice sort of brother for you! I wonder what his father would think about him if he knew of this trick."
J. J. Connington, *Tragedy at Ravensthorpe*. Boston: Little, Brown, 1928. 22.

1930: "I shouldn't have asked you, but you told me the other day that you weren't going to write anything about him yourself. It would be rather like a dog in the manger to keep yourself a whole lot of materials that you have no intention of using."
W. Somerset Maugham, *Cakes and Ale*. New York: Triangle, 1930. 162.

1930: "This is where the unfairness of the sex comes in. I was ready to let her go out or stay in, just as she pleased. But what about her? Had she the same fair-minded attitude, the same broad principles?" Mr. Benenden here removed his pipe to make room for a short bitter laugh. "When she wanted to go out, I'd to go out too, and when she wanted to stay in, I'd to stay in as well. That was her idear [*sic*]. Dog in the manger, she was, all the time, and specially on Saturdays and Sundays, just when you wanted a bit of give and take. We didn't get on. Why, some men like to tell you they get on well with women's [*sic*, women is] a mystery to me. I never did get on with 'em, and I don't care who knows it."
John B. Priestley, *Angel Pavement*. New York: Harper & Brothers, 1930. 230.

1932: "As for Charles—my son—and his wife, they have no thought for anything but a career. They wouldn't, of course, have agreed to anything being sold that might some day belong to them, simply from the point of view of the dog in the manger."
Henry Wade, *No Friendly Drop*. New York: Brewer Warren & Putnam, 1932. 313–14.

It is interesting at this point to note that none of the last citations include any explanatory comments about an ox or horse being prevented by a dog from getting to its hay. The authors simply and appropriately assume that their readers can manage the proverbial metaphor without explication. But how about these concluding lines from the second stanza of the poem "Home

Thoughts from Little Mouse" (1933) by the popular Ogden Nash? I wonder what my good students would do with that today. I have the feeling that they might have to respond to Nash's rhetorical question "You know the Manger and the Terrier?" in a negative way:

> 1933:
> A double joy, a double pride,
> Is that which others are denied.
> You know the Manger and the Terrier?—
> In other words, the less the merrier.
> Ogden Nash, *The Face Is Familiar: The Selected Verse of Ogden Nash*. Boston: Little, Brown, 1940. 158.

And how about these proverbial lyrics from the considerably older musical *H.M.S. Pinafore* (1878), by the ever-popular William S. Gilbert and Arthur Sullivan, who amassed proverbs and anti-proverbs alike in their works (Bryan 1999)?

> 1878: Wink is often good as nod;
> Spoils the child who spares the rod;
> Thirsty lambs run foxy dangers;
> Dogs are found in many mangers.
> W. S. Gilbert and Arthur Sullivan, *The Complete Plays of Gilbert and Sullivan*. New York: Cerf, 1936. 123.

Gilbert and Sullivan continue to delight audiences; can these audiences in fact understand their proverb songs? Of course, the question of meaningful communication via this proverbial metaphor does not only pertain to students of today. When I delivered a lecture in 2011 on the proverbial rhetoric of Martin Luther King (Mieder 2010) at the public library of my village of Williston in Vermont, I asked the audience of mixed age whether they had ever heard of "The dog in the manger"; not a single hand went up! What then would these neighbors and friends do with these last four short references from popular Anglo-American literature?

> 1942: UNCLE HARRY: What do you think?
> LUCY: You mustn't be a dog in the manger.
> UNCLE HARRY: Having a hell of a good time, aren't you?

Thomas Job, *Uncle Harry: A Play in Three Acts*. New York: Samuel French, 1942. 26, Act II.

1959: "It would be all the same if I did believe you had killed her. She was playing dog-in-the-manger and deserved it. I hated her."
Roy Vickers, "Wife Missing," in *Best Detective Stories of the Year (14th Annual Collection)*. David Cooke, ed. New York: E.P. Dutton, 1959. 150.

1964: "I guess she had a little [counseling], and of course it did her good to get into town every Saturday. She wanted to move into town but there was no money for it. She left McGee and moved in with me instead. That took some of the strain off her. He couldn't stand to see that. He couldn't stand to see her getting her dignity back. He killed her like a dog in the manger."
Ross Macdonald, *The Chill*. New York: Alfred A. Knopf, 1964. 109.

1972: "When I answered no, I meant it. I'm not polyandrous by nature, Kit. And no woman in my position could be a dog in the manger. I might say bitch in the manger if it weren't open to the wrong interpretation."
John Dickson Carr, *The Hungry Goblin: A Victorian Detective Novel*. New York: Harper & Row, 1972. 199.

But let me conclude this florilegium of "Dog in the manger" references from seven centuries with the proverb poem "A Fool in Sheep's Clothing is Soon Parted" (1957) by G. S. Galbraith, which Janet Sobieski and I did not know about when we published our *"So Many Heads, So Many Wits": An Anthology of English Proverb Poetry* (2005). It is a fine example of creating humorous anti-proverbs out of mixing up halves of proverbs that actually once in a while make some innovative sense (Litovkina and Mieder 2006):

> 1957: I dote on her mixed green metaphors,
> Her minced clichés, and her scrambled saws.
> [...]
>
> A rolling stone, she is prone to muse,
> Is worth two in the bush, and (even stranger)
> If the shoe fits, then what can you lose?
> But don't put all your dogs in one manger.

[...]
G. S. Galbraith, "A Fool in Sheep's Clothing is Soon Parted," *Punch* 233 (September 4, 1957): 259.

Does the innovative anti-proverb "Don't put all your dogs in one manger" make any sense? I think so, but admittedly only, if one recalls the traditional proverb "A dog in the manger." The ancient original text simply describes an envious dog or, metaphorically speaking, a person, while the anti-proverb argues against overemphasizing one's envious hang-ups. Of course, the proverb "Don't put all your eggs into one basket" enters into this as well. The playful or serious juxtaposition of proverbs and anti-proverbs is part of the delight of using clichés, as the poet seems to tell us. But this is what proverbial literacy in a narrow sense and cultural literacy in general are all about, and it might well be worthwhile to pay more attention to this linguistic and communicative phenomenon.

The History of the Proverb in Anglo-American Proverb Collections

The significance of several major proverb collections of the twentieth century has already been discussed at the beginning of the section on literary references. Here I wish to present how the proverb, proverbial expression, or proverbial comparison was recorded in English-language collections from the sixteenth century until the modern collections of today that list the "dog in the manger" metaphor with a clearly necessary explanation. This was originally not necessary, because people knew the image as a proverb and slowly but surely also from William Caxton's fable and its later renditions. Let me start with Francis Bacon's *Promus of Fourmes and Elegancyes* that he assembled between 1594 and 1596, which consists of fifty folios containing English, French, Greek, and Latin sententiae, proverbs, and proverbial expressions. As its editor explains, "'Promus' means larder or storehouse, and these 'Fourmes, Formularies and Elegancyes' appear to have been intended as a storehouse of words and phrases to be employed in the production of subsequent literary works" (Bacon 1594/96: 189). Be that as it may, discovering this compilation has been a most exciting by-product of my work on "The dog in the manger," and I have all intentions to study this fascinating collection in more detail in the future. For now, here are just a few texts that lead up to the proverb under discussion:

1594/96: It smelleth of the lampe
You are in the same shippe
Between the hamer and the Andville
Res est in cardine
Vndarum in vinis
Lepus pro carnibus (of a man persecuted for profite and not for malice)
Corpore effugere
Nunquid es saul inter prophetas
A dog in the manger
(Bacon 1594/96: 230)

The next appearance of the proverb, in John Clarke's collection of *Paroemio-logia Anglo-Latina* (1639), is of special interest. The Latin texts come primarily from Erasmus of Rotterdam's *Adagia* (1500ff.), but clearly the translator was not aware of the currency of "The dog in the manger" equivalent in the English language. The result is a rather mundane translation without the animal metaphor:

1639: He neither will doe, not let doe. / Canis in praesepi. (Clarke 1639: 96)

The following reference from James Howell's polyglot *Paroimiographia* (1659) is also quite interesting in this regard, since the English text is obviously a translation of the Italian variant cited together with it. The reference to a "gardener's dog" and a cabbage is otherwise not known in English, yet another sign that such bilingual proverb dictionaries have definite problems by not differentiating among true equivalents and literal translations:

1659: As the Gardeners dog, who would not eat cabbage himself, nor suffer others to do it. /
Come il can dell' ortoldano che non mangia de cavoli & non ne lascia mangiar altri. (Howell 1659: 16)

About a decade later John Ray, in his invaluable *Compleat Collection of English Proverbs; Also the Most Celebrated Proverbs of the Scotch, Italian, French, Spanish, and Other Languages* (1670), did a splendid job in registering the metaphor as a proverbial expression. Not only does he include the verb "to play," but he also cites Lucian in Greek and the Latin text from Erasmus of Rotterdam. But there is also the Italian variant with its English translation to boot, borrowed without doubt from James Howell:

1670: To play the dog in the manger, not eat yourself nor let any body else. (Greek text.) Lucian. *Canis in praesepi.* E come il cane del ortolano, che non mangia de cauoli egli & non ne lascia mangiar altri. *Ital.* Like the gardener's dog who cannot eat the coleworts himself, noir will suffer others. (Ray 1670: 171–72, 16)

In yet another bilingual *Paroemiologia Anglo-Latina* (1672), William Walker appears to have copied from John Ray's collection, doing well however to add the name of Erasmus of Rotterdam to his entry:

1672: To play the dog in the manger; not eat your self, nor let any body else. / Canis in praesepi. Eras. (Walker 1672: 50, 15)

By the eighteenth century, English paremiographers no longer see any reason to list the Latin text or those of other languages. They simply cite the proverb and its explanatory comment in slight variants, doubtlessly considering it to be part of the mainstay of English proverbial language. It should be noted that the hay and the horse or the ox are now becoming part of the variants, taking the lead most likely from the fable that contains these details:

1721: Like a Dog in a Manger; neither eat Hay, nor suffer the Horse to eat it. (Kelly 1721: 242, 98)

1732: Like a dog in a manger, you'll not eat yourself, nor let the horse eat. Like the gardener's dog, that neither eats cabbage himself, nor lets any body else. (Fuller 1732: 98, 3222, 3235)

1832: Like the cur in the crib, neither do nor let do. (Henderson 1881: 18)

This last Scottish reference is once again quite interesting with the alliterative "cur" and "crib," but it did not gain general currency. The standard text in its shortest form of "The dog in the manger" is well established by the nineteenth century, with Anglo-American speakers seemingly having no problem understanding and using it. However, as has been mentioned already, the familiarity with this ancient proverb has definitely declined, and it should not be surprising that modern paremiographers have felt compelled to explain its origin, metaphor, and meaning together with other traditional expressions in such need. What follows are a few of these explanatory comments from some of these useful books. It will, of course, be noted that there is considerable misinformation, especially regarding the connection between the proverb and the fable. So keep in mind that Aesop had nothing to do with all of this as you peruse the following paragraphs, which are nevertheless quite useful and informative:

1948: *A dog in the manger*
Aesop, back about 600 B.C., is said to have told his master about a dog which went to sleep in a manger full of hay. According to the fable, the ox, for whom the manger had been filled, came up to it for his rations, whereupon the dog, roused from his slumbers, snapped at the ox and drove him away. The ox, annoyed by this behavior, accused the dog of being churlish, because, he said, "You are unable to eat the hay yourself but will not leave it for those who can." Or, in the quaint words of John Gower, in *Confessio Amantis*, written about 1390, "Thogh it be noght the houndes kinde To ete chaf, yit wol he werne (prevent) An oxe which comth to the berne (barn), Therof to taken eny fode. (Funk 1948: 41)

1970: *A dog in the manger*
A mean-spirited individual who will not use what is wanted by another, nor yet let the other have it to use; one who prevents another enjoying something without any benefit to himself. The allusion is to the fable of the dog that fixed his place in a manger and would not allow the ox to come near the hay but would not eat it himself. (Brewer 1970: 330)

1980: *Dog in the manger*
A person who out of pure spite prevents others from using or enjoying something that he himself does not need or want. The allusion is to the fable of a dog who situated himself in a manger and selfishly would not allow the ox or horse to feed on the hay it contained. This expression has been in use since at least the late 1500s. (Urdang and LaRoche 1980: 294)

1983: *Dog in the manger*
In one of Aesop's fables, a dog fell asleep on the hay in the manger of an ox. Later the hungry ox entered the stall and tried to eat. But the dog, angry because it had been awakened, barked and snapped and would not let the ox eat the hay. Finally the ox said, "Dog, if you wanted to eat my dinner, I would have no objection. But you will neither eat it yourself nor let me enjoy it." Today anyone who neither enjoys a thing nor allows others to enjoy it is called a *dog in the manger*. (Lyman 1983: 61)

1985: *Dog in the Manger, A.*
Someone who is not capable of using something or not entitled to use it but is denying the use of it to someone who is. The saying comes from an Aesop fable of the same title, which reads: "A Dog was lying in a Manger full of hay. An Ox, being hungry, came near and was going to eat of the hay. The Dog, getting up and snarling at him, would not let him touch it. 'Surly creature,' said the Ox, 'you cannot eat the hay yourself, and yet you will let no one else have any.'" (Rogers 1985: 68–69)

1988: *Dog in the manger.*
Another of Aesop's contributions to the language; his fable concerned a dog who lay in an ox's manger, preventing the animal from eating the hay—which, of course, the dog itself couldn't eat. In the words of a fourteenth-century English poet [John Gower], which I've translated rather freely:

> Though it is not the way of dogs
> To feed on hay, he would prevent
> The ox that came into the barn
> From eating what *he* did not want.

Whence the human dog in the manger, who operates on the principle of "I don't want it but you can't have it." (Claiborne 1988: 89)

1989: *Dog in the manger*
Even older is the proverbial *dog in the manger*, from Aesop's fable (ca. 570 B.C.) about a snarling dog who prevents the horses from eating their corn, even though the dog himself does not want it. The term is still used for an individual who, out of sheer meanness, takes or keeps something desired by another. (Ammer 1989: 21)

1992: *Dog in the manger.*
A person who takes or keeps something wanted by another out of sheer meanness. The expression comes from one of Aesop's fables about a snarling dog who prevents the horses from eating their fodder even though the dog himself does not want it. It was probably a cliché by the time Frederick Marryat wrote (*Japhet*, 1836), "What a dog in the manger you must be—you can't marry them both." (Ammer 1992: 88–89)

Of special value among these explanation attempts is that by Linda and Roger Flavell in their *Dictionary of Idioms and Their Origins* (1992). To be sure, they attribute the origin of the proverbial expression to Aesop as well, but then they point out correctly that the phrase can also be used as a noun or adjective, as will be discussed in the following and last section of this chapter. In addition, they list two literary references from Willa Cather and W. Somerset Maugham that have already been cited above and thus need not be repeated here:

> 1992: *dog in a manger*
> Unwilling to let others benefit from things one cannot use oneself; spoiling. One of Aesop's fables tells of a dog which sat in a manger full of hay and snapped at a hungry ox to prevent it from eating. The dog had no use for the hay but begrudged the ox its fodder. The application is to someone who holds on to things he cannot use in order to deprive someone else of having use of them.
> [references from Cather and Maugham]
> *usage:* The phrase can be used as a noun but today is much more commonly found adjectivally e.g. *a dog-in-the-manger attitude.* It is then often hyphenated. (Flavell and Flavell 1992: 71)

My findings would not necessarily agree with the statement that the proverb is used that frequently as an hyphenated adjective, but the hyphenated noun-phrase "dog-in-the-manger" is indeed very prevalent. And from what has been shown in this chapter, there is no way that P. R. Wilkinson's claim, in his otherwise valuable *Thesaurus of Traditional English Metaphors* (1993), that the proverbial metaphor comes from a fable by Lucian can have any authenticity:

> 1993: *Dog in the manger*
> A type of selfishness where someone prevents another having what he needs, although he does not want it himself. (From Lucian's fable of the dog who kept an ox away from the manger of hay, although he would not eat it himself.) (Wilkinson 1993: 392)

Of particular interest is also the unique variant "dogs in the manger" that Robert A. Palmatier has included in his *Speaking of Animals: A Dictionary of Animal Metaphors* (1995). A Google search undertaken in 2011 lists but five references, of which Palmatier's citation is one! We can safely assume that the plural use of "dogs" with this proverbial allusion is extremely rare, although it most certainly makes a lot of sense in regard to party politics:

1995: *Dog in the manger*
A mean-spirited person who denies access by others to something that he/she has no need or use for. The allusion is to an Aesop fable in which a snarling dog moves into a manger and refuses to allow an ox to eat the hay that the dog itself has no appetite for. A modern *dog in the manger* is a person who maintains an "attractive nuisance" but denies use of it to others. In government, when "the dogs are in the manger," there is strong opposition to a proposal. (Palmatier 1995: 116)

But here then are two final paragraphs from recent idiom and proverb collections that show once and for all that lexicographers and paremiographers of collections for the popular market insist on the association of the proverbial metaphor with a fable from the ancient Aesop; the last text repeats the apocryphal title of "The Dog and the Horses" that Burton Stevenson had given to it in *The Home Book of Proverbs, Maxims and Familiar Phrases* (1948: 601), already cited above:

1997: *Dog in the manger*
One who prevents others from enjoying something despite having no use for it. For example, *Why be a dog in the manger? If you aren't going to use those tikkets, let someone else have them.* This expression alludes to Aesop's fable about a snarling dog that prevents horses from eating fodder that is unpalatable to the dog itself. [Mid-1500s] (Ammer 1997: 166)

2000: *Dog in the Manger*
A dog in the manger.
Aesop; Fables "The Dog and the Horses," c. 570 B.C.
[In this fable a dog growled and snarled to prevent the horses from eating the corn, although the dog itself had no use for it.] (Nowlan and Nowlan 2000: 41, 85; with 8 literary references)

Together these statements add up to useful information for the general reader. As has always been the case with proverb collections and dictionaries, their compilers inform each other or even copy more or less from each other. This is not to say that their compilations and explanatory comments are not useful for quick and ready reference. They do contain viable information, usually referring to an ox or horse(s) and hay, fodder, or corn, variants that exist in the long versions of the proverb as well. It would, of course, be appropriate to drop the reference to the classical Aesop form these entries, and yet, since the original proverb was turned into a fable narrative in the fifteenth century, with its own impressive tradition, it is absolutely appropriate to continue to mention this fascinating connection.

"The Dog in the Manger" Proverb Is Alive Today

There are clearly those among us who rightfully or wrongfully think that the "dog" proverb is still somewhat known today. Obviously I believe so as well, although I more often than not have to explain its meaning (and if time permits, its origin) after having cited it. Just imagine how ridiculous the following list of book titles would be if nobody understood the metaphor. Actually, if asked, I would have advised the authors to add an explanatory subtitle that would flag the basic content of the book. From what I know from my ad hoc surveys among various groups of people during the past few years, the proverb is no longer known well enough to assure meaningful communication by itself and without any explanatory context. In passing, let me at least mention here that the Spanish dramatist Lope de Vega entitled one of his plays *El perro del hortelano* (1618), not surprisingly indicating that the proverb was well established in Spain at the beginning of the seventeenth century. The translators over the years have been more than correct in translating the title as *The Dog in the Manger* rather than as *The Dog in the Garden*, since that variant is barely known in the English language. But here then are some titles that mean not much, even if the reader knows the message of the proverb:

Brown, Edward. *The Dog in the Manger*. Newcastle-upon-Tyne: no publisher given, 1877 (political satire).

Moss, Hugh. *P.U.P., or, The Dog in the Manger: An Original Farce in One Act*. London: S. French, 1883.

Spaulding, George L. *The Dog in the Manger*. London: M. Witmark, 1910 (musical score).

Lee, Joseph. *Hot Dog in the Manger*. Boston: Massachusetts Civic League, 1928 (about hot dog stands).

Miller, Harold D. "Is Australia 'A Dog in the Manger'?" *Hibbert Journal* 32 (1934): 609–16 (article on economics).

Reason, Joyce. *The Dog in the Manger: A Story of the Christ-Child*. London: Independent Press, 1934 (originally published as *The Christian World*).

Bacon, N. H. *Dog in the Manger*. Sheffield: Gladwin & Bacon, 1942 (on the problem of unemployment and methods of solving it).

Law, William Templeton. *Dog in the Manger: A Christmas Play*, in Winfried Bannister et al., *North Light: Ten New One-Act Plays from the North*. Glasgow: William McLellan, 1947.

Procter, Marjorie. *Dog in a Manger*. Poole, UK: Blandford, 1963 (juvenile book).

Randell, Beverly. *The Dog in the Manger*. London: Methuen, 1976 (children's book).

Curtiss, Ursula Reilly. *Dog in the Manger: A Novel of Suspense*. New York: Dodd, Mead, 1982.

Resnick, Michael D. *Dog in the Manger*. Alexander, North Carolina: Alexander, 1995 (fiction).

Lancaster, Katherine. *Dog in a Manger*. Bloomington, Indiana: 1st Books, 2003 (fiction).

Grobbo, A. R. *Dog in a Manger*. Oakville, Ontario: LTD, 2005 (mystery).

It is to be assumed that these publications somehow deal with envy of some type, except for the two titles relating to Christmas. Here the "manger" might simply refer to the one in the Christmas story itself that is visited by a dog. In those two titles we might not have the proverb at all!

But speaking of comprehensibility, what do people nowadays do with the hyphenated adjective "dog-in-the-manger" that does appear in *The Oxford English Dictionary* (Simpson and Weiner 1989: 929)? At times the context will help, as when James Fenimore Cooper adds "Neither eat, nor let eat" in the earliest and first of the following examples, but usually modern readers might be rather perplexed by these adjective-noun constructions of the proverbial metaphor, unless, of course, they know the proverb:

1833: I am nearly half through my last romance, for the pen and I have quarreled. The country is getting to be too big for men of my calibre. I must give way to my betters, of which it would seem to be full, by their *talk*. I once met a Sir William Abdy, who would sit an hour listening to the nothings of a set of jabbering Frenchmen[,] shrug his shoulder, and say—"There is a great deal of *ta-a-lk*." If our Homers would do something themselves, their talk would be more respectable—As it is, there is a good deal of the Dog-in-the-manger spirit about them—Neither eat, nor let eat. Thank God, I am nearly done with them. You must not be surprised if you hear of my sailing a sloop between Cape Cod and New-York ere long. Let it pass.
Letter of James Fenimore Cooper to Horatio Greenough of January 19, 1833 (Paris), in *The Letters of James Fenimore Cooper*. James Franklin Beard, ed. Cambridge, Massachusetts: Harvard University Press, 1960. II, 368–69.

1912: "But your thanks are due to Captain Robert Burgoyne, for 't is he, under heaven, has saved your son's life. He has done a miracle, and that's the word for it, and when the chance comes—which may not be yet awhile—'t is him you'll have to thank. A man in a thousand—a marvel! It makes me mad to think he's not an Englishman; and yet not that neither, for 't would be a dog-in-the-manger deed for us in this great country to grudge the man to his own land. I lay we have a few as good; but I swear we have none better."
Eden Phillpotts, *The Lovers: A Romance*. New York: Rand McNally, 1912. 372.

1939: "She got after Lawrence and scared the life out of him by saying she was going to tell his wife about his 'goings on.' It was her duty. Duty be damned! She was just a self-righteous old busybody with so much time on her hands, she made trouble for everybody else. What if Lawrence Carter did come to me a couple of times a month? It wasn't doing his wife any harm as long as she didn't know about it, was it?" Lucile asked indignantly with a hardy indifference to morals. "Of course as soon as Lawrence Carter thought his wife was going to be wised up he dropped me like a hot potato. I don't blame him. But what did make me mad was his dog-in-the-manger attitude after Pete and I started going together."
Inez Oellrichs, *The Man Who Didn't Answer*. New York: Doubleday, Doran, 1939. 96.

1941: "Now, who hates Vivian enough to try to pin a murder on her?"

"Nearly everyone but you."

"I'd give my right arm for a cigarette ... I think you're mistaken about that, Sandy. You just don't understand her sharp way of talking; the rest of us are used to it. But Henry, now ... He's jealous of her, of course, but that may be dog-in-the-manger stuff. 'I don't want her but you can't have her,' that sort of thing, rather than love. Don't you think so?"

"Perhaps."

Richard Shattuck, *The Snark Was a Boojum* ... New York: William Morrow, 1941, 131.

1965: But he did not leave the premises. No; this irascible bachelor took up quarters beside my wren box, sitting all day on the perch outside and chirruping in his best whisky baritone in the hopes of attracting a nonaligned she. The fact that no sparrow could have kept house in the box did not deter him from his sparrow-in-the-manger procedure. The result was that, when my wrens returned from points south and started to unpack in their summer cottage, they were viciously assailed by the ragamuffin and put to rout.

R. D. Symons, *Silton Seasons: From the Diary of a Countryman.* New York: Doubleday, 1965. 28.

This last example is unique, since its aviary context quite naturally brings about the new variant "sparrow-in-the-manger," but who will understand this without recall of the "dog-in-the-manger" precursor?

And who would have thought that the adjectival form of "dog-in-the-mangerish" exists as well (Simpson and Weiner 1989: IV, 929), as can be seen from the following example of an open letter entitled "On St. Patrick's Cathedral" published by no other than George Bernard Shaw in the *East Anglican Daily Times* of January 23, 1935?

1935: My own family and antecedents are ultra-Protestant, and I am a bit to the left of Protestantism myself; but when there are two cathedrals available within a stone's-throw of one another, it seems rather dog-in-the-mangerish to deny its use to the catholic majority, in whose hands no visitor could at any hour find it completely deserted, as I did.

[George] Bernard Shaw, *The Matter with Ireland.* Dan H. Laurence and David H. Greene, eds. Gainesville, Florida: University of Florida, 2001. 280. See Bryan and Mieder 1994: 111.

It should be noted in any case that the hyphenated adjectival use of the proverbial metaphor is rather rare, with Google yielding but 11,700 hits in 2011. As I checked the first ten pages of this internet yield for "dog-in-the-manger-ish," it once again became obvious that there are many repetitions, making such frequency hits quite inaccurate.

But, finally then, what are we to make of the 6,030,000 results that I obtained from Google for "dog in the manger" in general? Even allowing for about 20 percent duplications, there would be almost five million hits. And now comes the $64,000 question: What does this seemingly impressive number mean in light of what has been said thus far? Does this impressive number mean anything at all? Does it reflect actual currency, frequency, and above all familiarity and understanding of this not quite two-thousand-year-old proverbial metaphor? From what has been presented in the preceding pages, I would have to conclude that the several million occurrences have relatively little to do with the reality of modernity. Having done my own impromptu field research among numerous people of varied age, education, and background, I have to conclude that by far the majority of them do not know it or even recall ever having heard of it. This result seems strange perhaps, especially since there are those Aesop's fable books that continue to be published for children and adults alike. But I have the feeling that they do not belong to the most popular reading materials any longer, especially since there exists such an overabundance of exciting children's books. Books with fables don't reach a large audience today, and this in turn has its effect on what belongs to the cultural literacy of people today when it comes to those only too-human animal fables of olden times. And since it is the fable that contextualizes and thus explains the proverb, it should not be surprising that this piece of folk wisdom is also much less current and known today than in days gone by. For now, as can be seen from the contextualized references cited here and ample more found in the internet, the proverb is not yet dead. It is still alive, and since humankind will surely be plagued by envy, selfishness, and meanness for ages to come, it would be my educated prophecy that it will remain alive, albeit with much reduced frequency of use, in times to come. After all, it is a most fitting animal metaphor for human behavior that unfortunately is too often far from being humane. It is certainly doubtful that the awareness and employment of proverb and fable have been substantially reduced because the human condition and behavior have much improved. In other words, there is considerable reason and justification for keeping this proverbial wisdom alive as a verbal and metaphorical sign and warning against ill treatment of others. We are all dogs in the manger from time to time, but by calling our unfair behavior by its proverbial name, we might just get beyond our shortcomings. So let's try to keep the fable as a narrative and the proverb as a piece of wisdom alive by citing them when the occasions arise—and knowing human nature, they most certainly will appear as time goes on.

BIBLIOGRAPHY

This chapter was first published with this title in *Midwestern Folklore* 37 (2011): 3–44. It was dedicated in memoriam to my friend Pack Carnes (1939–2000).

Adrados, Francisco Rodríguez. 2003. *History of the Graeco-Latin Fable.* 3 vols. Leiden: E.J. Brill.

Alster, Bendt. 1997. *Proverbs of Ancient Sumer: The World's Earliest Proverb Collections.* 2 vols. Bethesda, Maryland: CDL Press.

Ammer, Christine. 1989. *It's Raining Cats and Dogs . . . And Other Beastly Expressions.* New York: Paragon House.

———. 1992. *Have a Nice Day—No Problem! A Dictionary of Clichés.* New York: Dutton.

———. 1997. *The American Heritage Dictionary of Idioms.* Boston: Houghton Mifflin.

Anonymous. 1842. *Aesop's Fables, with Upwards of One Hundred and Fifty Emblematical Devices.* Philadelphia: John Locken.

———. 1909. *Folk-Lore and Fable: Aesop, Grimm, Andersen.* New York: P.F. Collier.

———. 1947. *Aesop's Fables.* With Drawings by Fritz Kredel. New York: Grosset & Dunlap.

———. 1968. *Aesop's Fables.* Based on the Translation of George Fyler Townsend. Illustrated by Murray Tinkelman. Garden City, New York: International Collections Library,

———. 1984. *Aesop Fables.* From Translations of Thomas James and George Tyler [*sic*] Townsend. With Illustrations by Charles H. Bennett. Franklin Center, Pennsylvania: Franklin Library.

———. 1985. *The Fables of Aesop.* Illustrated by Edward J. Detmold. New York: Weathervane.

Apperson, G. L. 1929. *English Proverbs and Proverbial Phrases: A Historical Dictionary.* London: J.M. Dent, 1929; rpt. Detroit: Gale Research, 1969.

Bacon, Francis. 1594/96. *Promus of Fourmes and Elegancyes.* In *Bacon is Shake-Speare.* Edwin Durning-Lawrence, ed. New York: John McBride, 1910. 185–86.

Brewer, Ebenezer Cobham. 1970. *Dictionary of Phrase and Fable.* Ivor H. Evans, ed. New York: Harper & Row.

Bryan, George B. 1999. "The Proverbial W. S. Gilbert: An Index to Proverbs in the Works of Gilbert and Sullivan." *Proverbium* 16: 21–35.

Bryan, George B., and Wolfgang Mieder. 1994. *The Proverbial Bernard Shaw: An Index to Proverbs in the Works of George Bernard Shaw.* Westport, Connecticut: Greenwood.

———. 2005. *A Dictionary of Anglo-American Proverbs and Proverbial Phrases Found in Literary Sources of the Nineteenth and Twentieth Centuries.* New York: Peter Lang.

Burckhardt, Johann Ludwig. 1834. *Arabische Sprüchwörter oder die Sitten und Gebräuche der neueren Aegyptier.* Weimar: Verlag des Landes-Industrie-Comptoirs. Rpt. with an introduction and bibliography by Wolfgang Mieder. Hildesheim: Georg Olms, 2012.

Calmenson, Stephanie, ed. 1988. *The Children's Aesop: Selected Fables.* Illustrated by Robert Byrd. New York: Doubleday Book & Music Clubs.

Carnes, Pack, ed. 1988. *Proverbia in Fabula: Essays on the Relationship of the Fable and the Proverb.* Bern: Peter Lang.

Clairborne, Robert. 1988. *Loose Cannons & Red Herrings: A Book of Lost Metaphors*. New York: W.W. Norton.

Clarke, John. 1639. *Paroemiologia Anglo-Latina in usum scholarum concinnata. Or Proverbs English, and Latine*. London: Felix Kyngston.

Dent, Robert W. 1984. *Proverbial Language in English Drama Exclusive of Shakespeare, 1495–1616: An Index*. Berkeley, California: University of California Press.

Dicke, Gerd, and Klaus Grubmüller. 1987. *Die Fabeln des Mittelalters in der frühen Neuzeit. Ein Katalog der deutschen Versionen und ihrer lateinischen Entsprechungen*. München: Wilhelm Fink.

Doyle, Charles Clay. 1977. "The Background of More's Epigrams." *Moreana* 55/56: 62–63.

———. 1990. "Folklore," in *Spenser Encyclopedia*. A. C. Hamilton et al., eds. Toronto: University of Toronto Press. 311–12.

Düringsfeld, Ida von, and Otto von Reinsberg-Düringsfeld. 1872–75. *Sprichwörter der germanischen und romanischen Sprachen*. 2 vols. Leipzig: Hermann Fries; rpt. Hildesheim: Georg Olms, 1973.

Dykes, Oswald. 1709. *English Proverbs with Moral Reflections*. London: G. Sawbridge.

Ecker, Lawrence. 1934. *Arabischer, provenzalischer und deutscher Minnesang. Eine motivgeschichtliche Untersuchung*. Bern: P. Haupt.

Flavell, Linda, and Roger Flavell. 1992. *Dictionary of Idioms and Their Origins*. London: Kyle Cathie.

Fuller, Thomas. 1732. *Gnomologia; Adagies and Proverbs; Wise Sentences and Witty Sayings, Ancient and Modern, Foreign and British*. London: B. Barker.

Funk, Charles Earle. 1948. *A Hog on Ice and Other Curious Expressions*. New York: Harper & Row.

Gascoigne, Bamber, and Christina Gascoigne. 1984. *Aesop's Fables of William Caxton's Original Illustrated Edition*. London: Hamish Hamilton.

Gibbs, Laura, ed. 2002. *Aesop's Fables*. Oxford: Oxford University Press.

Guillaumont, A., H.-Ch. Puech, G. Quispel, W. Till, and Yassah 'Abd Al Masih, eds. 1959. *The Gospel According to Thomas: Coptic Text Established and Translated*. Leiden: E.J. Brill.

Harmon, A. M., ed. 1919. *Lucian: With an English Translation*. 7 vols. London: William Heinemann.

———, ed. 1960. *Lucian: With an English Translation*. 8 vols. Cambridge, Massachusetts: Harvard University Press.

Henderson, Andrew. 1881. *Scottish Proverbs Collected and Arranged by Andrew Henderson with Explanatory Notes and a Glossary*. James Donald, ed. Glasgow: Thomas D. Morison; rpt. Detroit: Gale Research, 1969.

Hirsch, E. D., Joseph F. Kett, and James Trefil. 1988. *The Dictionary of Cultural Literacy*. Boston: Houghton Mifflin.

Howell, James. 1659. *Paroimiographia. Proverbs, or, Old Sayed Savves & Adages in English (or the Saxon Toung) Italian, French and Spanish whereunto the British, for their great Antiquity, and weight are added*. London: J.G.

Hunt, John Gabriel, ed. 1997. *The Inaugural Addresses of the Presidents*. New York: Gramercy.

Ichikawa, Sanki, Takuji Mine, Ryoichi Inui, Kenzo Kihara, and Shiro Takaha, eds. 1964. *The Kenkyusha Dictionary of Current English Idioms*. Tokyo: Kenkyusha.

Kelly, James. 1721. *A Complete Collection of Scotish [sic] Proverbs. Explained and Made Intelligible to the English Reader*. London: William and John Innys.

Kuusi, Matti. 1982. *Suomen kansan vertauksia*. Helsinki: Suomalainen Kirjallisuuden Seura.

Lambert, W. G. 1960. *Babylonian Wisdom Literature*. Oxford: Clarendon.

Leach, Andrea Stacy, ed. 1997. *Aesop's Fables: The Lion and the Mouse & Other Fables*. Illustrated by Holly Hannon. Plantation, Florida: Paradise Press.

Lenaghan, R. T., ed. 1967. *Caxton's Aesop*. Cambridge, Massachusetts: Harvard University Press.

Leutsch, Ernst Ludwig, and Friedrich Wilhelm Schneidewin, eds. 1839 and 1851. *Corpus Paroemiographorum Graecorum.* 2 vols. Göttingen: Vandenhoeck & Ruprecht; rpt. Hildesheim: Georg Olms, 1965.

Lindenberger, James Miller. 1983. *The Aramaic Proverbs of Ahiqar.* Baltimore, Maryland: Johns Hopkins University Press.

Litovkina, Anna T., and Wolfgang Mieder. 2006. *Old Proverbs Never Die, They Just Diversify: A Collection of Anti-Proverbs.* Burlington, Vermont: University of Vermont; Veszprém, Hungary: Pannonian University.

Lutz, H. F. 1933. "Babylonian Proverbs." *University of California Chronicle* 35: 38–54.

Lyman, Darryl. 1983. *The Animal Things We Say.* Middle Village, New York: Jonathan David.

McKendry, John J., ed. 1964. *Aesop: Five Centuries of Illustrated Fables.* New York: Metropolitan Museum of Art.

Mieder, Wolfgang. 1982. *International Proverb Scholarship: An Annotated Bibliography.* New York: Garland.

———. 2005. *Proverbs Are the Best Policy: Folk Wisdom and American Politics.* Logan, Utah: Utah State University Press.

———. 2009. *International Bibliography of Paremiology and Phraseology.* 2 vols. Berlin: Walther de Gruyter.

———. 2010. *"Making a Way Out of No Way"" Martin Luther King's Sermonic Proverbial Rhetoric.* New York: Peter Lang.

Mieder, Wolfgang, and George B. Bryan. 1995. *The Proverbial Winston S. Churchill: An Index to Proverbs in the Works of Sir Winston Churchill.* Westport, Connecticut: Greenwood.

Moravcsik, Gyula. 1964."'Hund in der Krippe.' Zur Geschichte eines griechischen Sprichwortes." *Acta Antiqua Academiae Scientiarum Hungaricae* 12: 78–86.

Mynors, R. A. B., ed. 1989. *Collected Works of Erasmus. Adages* (Vol. 32). Toronto: University of Toronto Press.

Nowlan, Robert A., and Gwendolyn L. Nowlan. 2001. *A Dictionary of Quotations and Proverbs about Cats and Dogs.* Jefferson, North Carolina: McFarland.

O'Connell, Kelly. 2010. www.canadafreepress.com/index.php/article/24469 (05.04.2011).

Österley, Hermann, ed. 1873. *Steinhöwels Äsop.* Tübingen: Literarischer Verein in Stuttgart.

Oxford English Dictionary. 3rd ed. (online). www.oed.com/view/Entry/56467?redirectedFrom=dog+in +the+manger& (20.04.2011).

Palmatier, Robert A. 1995. *Speaking of Animals: A Dictionary of Animal Metaphors.* Westport, Connecticut: Greenwood.

Paton, W. R., ed. 1956. *The Greek Anthology: With an English Translation.* 5 vols. Cambridge, Massachusetts: Harvard University Press.

Perry, Ben Edwin. 1952. *Aesopica: A Series of Texts Relating to Aesop or Ascribed to Him or Closely Connected with the Literary Tradition that Bears His Name.* Urbana, Illinois: University of Illinois Press.

———. 1965. *Babrius and Phaedrus: Newly Edited and Translated into English, Together with an Historical Introduction and Comprehensive Survey of Greek and Latin Fables in the Aesopic Tradition.* Cambridge, Massachusetts: Harvard University Press.

Pinkney, Jerry. 2000. *Aesop's Fables.* New York: SeaStar.

Priest, John F. 1985. "The Dog in the Manger: In Quest of a Fable." *Classical Journal* 81: 49–58.

Randall, Ronne, and Juli Barbato, eds. 1994. *Aesop's Fables.* New York: Ladybird (children's book).

Ray, John. 1670. *A Compleat Collection of English Proverbs; Also the Most Celebrated Proverbs of the Scotch, Italian, French, Spanish, and other Languages.* Cambridge: W. Morden.

Rogers, James. 1985. *The Dictionary of Clichés.* New York: Facts on File.

Ruelle, Pierre. 1982. *Recueil général des Isopets.* 3 vols. Paris: Société des Anciens Textes Français.

Simpson, John A., and E. S. C. Weiner. 1989. *The Oxford English Dictionary.* 2nd ed. Vol. 4. Oxford: Clarendon.

Singer, Samuel. 1943–47. *Sprichwörter des Mittelalters.* Bern: Herbert Lang.

Singer, Samuel, and Ricarda Liver, eds. 1995–2002. *Thesaurus proverbiorum medii aevi. Lexikon der Sprichwörter des romanisch-germanischen Mittelalters.* 13 vols. Berlin: Walther de Gruyter.

Sobieski, Janet, and Wolfgang Mieder, eds. 2005. *"So Many Heads, So Many Wits": An Anthology of English Proverb Poetry.* Burlington, Vermont: University of Vermont.

Stevenson, Burton Egbert. 1948. *The Home Book of Proverbs, Maxims and Familiar Phrases.* New York: Macmillan.

Strömberg, Reinhold. 1954. *Greek Proverbs: A Collection of Proverbs and Proverbial Phrases which Are Not Listed by the Ancient and Byzantine Paroemiographers.* Göteborg: Wettergren & Kerbers Förlag.

Taylor, Archer. 1931. *The Proverb.* Cambridge, Massachusetts: Harvard University Press; rpt. as *The Proverb and An Index to "The Proverb".* Wolfgang Mieder, ed. Bern: Peter Lang, 1985.

Taylor, Archer, and Bartlett Jere Whiting. 1958. *A Dictionary of American Proverbs and Proverbial Phrases, 1820–1880.* Cambridge, Massachusetts: Harvard University Press.

Tilley, Morris Palmer. 1926. *Elizabethan Proverb Lore in Lyly's "Euphues" and in Pettie's "Petite Pallace" with Parallels from Shakespeare.* New York: Macmillan.

———. 1950. *A Dictionary of the Proverbs in England in the Sixteenth and Seventeenth Centuries.* Ann Arbor, Michigan: University of Michigan Press.

Townsend, Rev. Geo. Fyler. 1887. *Three Hundred Aesop's Fables. Literally Translated from the Greek.* With One Hundred and Fourteen Illustrations Designed by Harrison Weir and Engraved by J. Greenaway. London: George Routledge.

Trencsényi-Waldapfel, I. 1961. "Das Thomas-Evangelium aus Nag Hammâdi und Lukian von Samosata." *Acta Orientalia Academiae Scientiarum Hungaricae* 13: 131–33.

———. 1962. "'Der Hund in der Krippe.'" *Acta Orientalia Academiae Scientiarum Hungaricae* 14: 139–43.

———. 1964. "Sprichwort oder geflügeltes Wort? *Acta Antiqua Academiae Scientiarum Hungaricae* 12: 365–71.

Urdang, Laurence, and Nancy La Roche. 1980. *Picturesque Expressions: A Thematic Dictionary.* Detroit, Michigan: Gale Research.

Walker, William. 1672. *Paroemiologia Anglo-Latina or, English and Latin Proverbs, and Proverbial Sentences and Sayings.* London: R. Royston.

Walther, Hans. 1963–86. *Proverbia sententiaeque latinitatis medii aevi. Lateinische Sprichwörter und Sentenzen des Mittelalters in alphabetischer Anordnung.* 9 vols. Göttingen: Vandenhoeck & Ruprecht.

Whiting, Bartlett Jere. 1968. *Proverbs, Sentences, and Proverbial Phrases from English Writings Mainly Before 1500.* Cambridge, Massachusetts: Harvard University Press.

———. 1977. *Early American Proverbs and Proverbial Phrases.* Cambridge, Massachusetts: Harvard University Press.

———. 1989. *Modern Proverbs and Proverbial Sayings.* Cambridge, Massachusetts: Harvard University Press.

Wilkinson, P. R. 1993. *Thesaurus of Traditional English Metaphors.* London: Routledge.

Wilson, F. P. 1970. *The Oxford Dictionary of English Proverbs.* 3rd ed. Oxford: Clarendon.

12. "TO BUILD CASTLES IN SPAIN"

The Story of an English Proverbial Expression

The proverbial expression "to build castles in Spain" is known in a number of variants in numerous European languages, and as such it clearly belongs to the group of so-called "widespread idioms" (Piirainen 2012). The idea or concept of building an imagined structure in the form of a house or castle in Spain, or more generally in the air, clouds or sky, might well go back to the church-father Augustine (354–430) whose sermons contain two early Latin references: "Ne subtracto fundamento rei gestae, quasi in aere quaeratis aedificare" and "Ne subtracto fundamento, in aere velle aedificare videamur" (Röhrich 1991–92: 2, 979; Singer and Liver 1995–2002: 8, 54). Perhaps these texts are nothing more than variants of the Biblical proverbial expression "to build on sand" (Matthew 7:26). But be that as it may, Augustine's non-metaphorical phrase "to build in the air" (Wilkinson 1993: 105) appears since the Middle Ages in numerous more imaginative loan translations in European languages primarily as "to build castles in the air" (for the German tradition, see Mieder 2010b: 341–62). The meaning of the popular phrase is always that of making impracticable or unrealizable plans, of imagining unrealistic hopes, or of dreaming wishful thoughts without any chance that these pipe dreams might ever become a reality.

Early French Sources of "Faire des châteaux en Espagne"

The origin of the expression "to build castles in Spain" dates back to French literature of the Middle Ages (Morel-Fatio 1925: 119–30), with the earliest reference thus far having been located in the medieval epic *Roman de la Rose* 1225/30) by Guillaume de Lorris, in the wording of "faire des châteaux en Espagne":

> Tel foiz sera qu'il t'iert avis
> Que tu tendras cele au cler vis

Entre tes braz trestoute nue,
Ausi con s'el fust devenue
Dou tot t'amie e ta compaigne;
Lors feras chastiaus en Espaigne
E avras joie de neient,
Tout con tu iras foleiant
En la pensee delitable
Ou il n'a que mençonge e fable
Mais poi i porras demorer.

(Langlois 1920: 124–25; see also Larsen 1978)

From approximately the same time there is also this only recently registered reference that clearly contains the same phrase with its connection to Spain. It appears in an anonymous medieval French adaptation of Bishop Martin of Braga's Latin *Formula Honestae Vitae* of sixth-century Portugal:

Faus pensers est samblans a songe,
qui trestous est plains de mençoigne:
souvent fait castiaus en Espaigne,
mais en fin merit n'i gaaigne;
il ne t'en puet nus bien venir.

(Irmer 1890: 18; Singer and Liver 1995–2002: 2, 146)

Since the original Latin text does not even contain the proverbial expression in the medieval Latin wording of "castra in spera aeris" (Singer and Liver 1995–2002: 8, 54), one would have to conclude that the phrase "faire des châteaux en Espagne" and its more appropriate variant "bâtir des châteaux en Espagne" must have been established in French by the middle of the twelfth century. Of interest, of course, is that such variants as "faire (bâtir) des châteaux en Brie (en Asie, en Albanye [Albion=England])" also gained currency in France during the following decades (Långfors 1914; see the fifteen references in Singer and Liver 1995–2002: 2, 146–47). In fact, the French "Espagne" variant was even loan translated into Latin by Albertus Magnus in his popular *Philosophia pauperum* of the thirteenth century: "Hec enim virtus facit castra in Hispania, et fingit chimeras et hircocervos." However, in later editions of the *Philosophia pauperum* from the fifteenth century, "Spain" is replaced by the more general word "air": "Hec enim virtus facit castra in spera aeris & fingit chimeran & in lupo cornua" (Nelson 1951: 167–68). Quite naturally, perhaps, later editors simply questioned the whole idea why someone would want to build castles in Spain or anywhere else, when in fact the building of fantastic dreams might be better done in the open air.

But this in turn begs the question why the idea of building castles in Spain in the first place? Some years ago, my beloved mentor Stuart A. Gallacher, trying to find an answer to this conundrum, came up with a most convincing solution. Of course, there were fortifications in the Middle Ages between Spain and France that separated the Muslim from the Christian world, and some of these might well have appeared to be rather fancy or extravagant to the French imagination. But based on some earlier scholarship, supplemented with his own discoveries, Gallacher proved beyond the shadow of a doubt that in fact the idea of "Spain" was most likely nothing more than that the French poets of the time needed a poetic rhyme where the noun refers to a distant or even imagined land. This is evident from all the literary texts in which the proverbial phrase appears with the mention of Brie, Asie, or Albanye (Gallacher 1963). But be that as it may, the variant "bâtir des châteaux en Espagne" established itself in the French language and culture as the dominant variant, and it has a long and distinguished history through the centuries, with the phrase remaining very popular even though it really does not make particular sense any longer (Hassell 1982: 67; Di Stefano 1991: 148–49; Rey and Chantreau 1993: 156–57). This is most likely the reason why the French phrase with the "Spain" reference never really caught on in other languages. Elisabeth Piirainen informed me of two rare exceptions, namely the Romanian "a cladi / construi castele în Spania / pe nisip / în aer" (to build castles in Spain / in the sand / in air) and the Turkish "Ispanaya'da satolar kurmak" (to build castles in Spain). I can add the extremely rare German "spanische Schlösser bauen" (Wander 1867–80: 4, 247), but all of this is rather inconsequential as far as the European dissemination of the French "bâtir des châteaux en Espagne" is concerned.

The English Loan Translation "To Build Castles in Spain"

Does this mean that the important French language and culture of the Middle Ages and of later centuries had basically no significant influence on other languages when it comes to building castles in Spain as a metaphorical expression of dreams and fantasies that will never come true? Absolutely not! For while late medieval Latin and the European vernacular languages took over the variant "to build castles in the air" that lacked the almost nonsensical "Espagne" reference, it was the English language that embraced the French original. In fact, the English loan translation "to build castles in

Spain" continues to compete well in the Englishes of the world together with
the later variants of "to build castles in the air/clouds/sky" (Stevenson 1948:
292–93; Tilley 1950: 84–85; Taylor and Whiting 1958: 57; Wilson 1970: 107;
Whiting 1977: 59–60; Whiting 1989: 94; Bryan and Mieder 2005: 133–34).

But how and why did all of this come about? That is what the following contextualized texts from the latter part of the fourteenth century to the
present day will abundantly illustrate. Many more historical references could
be cited, but here are the most representative examples in the fascinating
spread of this proverbial expression in the English-speaking world. Before
turning to the chain of English references, the by now obvious fact of the
nonexistence of the "Espagne" variant in Spain should be emphasized, with
the Spanish language going along with the dominant variants of the rest of
Europe: "hacer / construir / forjar castillos en el aire / de naipes" (Buitrago
Jiménez 1995: 197; Martín Sánchez 1997: 86).

The first English reference of any variant of the proverbial expression is
found in what is believed to be Geoffrey Chaucer's translation of the French
Roman de la Rose during the last quarter of the fourteenth century. The fact
that he maintained the country designation of Spain was surely the key factor in establishing the phrase in the English language:

> And wite thou wel, withoute were,
> That thee shal seme, somtyme that nyght,
> That thou hast hir, that is so bright,
> Naked bitwene thyne armes there,
> All sothfastnesse as though it were.
> Thou shalt make castels thanne in Spayne,
> And dreme of joye, all but in vayne,
> And thee deliten of right nought,
> While thou so slombrest in that thought,
> That is so swete and delitable,
> The which, in soth, nys but a fable;
> For it ne shall no while laste.
>
> (Robinson 1933: 689; Smith 1945)

It is impossible to know whether he kept "Spayne" for the sake of rhyming
with "vayne," or whether he simply translated verbatim. The latter appears
to be the case, and no matter what, this translation marks the beginning of
the English proverbial expression "to build castles in Spain" that clearly was
taken over from the French. And this wording certainly stuck, as is especially
the case in later literary works that were translated from French into English.

About one hundred years after Chaucer's translation, William Caxton kept the "Spain" reference in *The History of Jason* (1475), his translation of Raoul Le Fèvre's French original: "He [Jason] began than first to thenke on the fayt of his lady [Mirro]. And after he began to make castellis in Spaygne as louers doo" (Caxton 1913: 25). Not quite another hundred years later, Geoffrey Fenton translated a French version of Matteo Bandello's originally Italian *Tragical Tales* (1567) by also maintaining the "Spain" reference: "[. . .] in place of sleep, and to restore his weary body with the course of natural rest, he began to sigh and build castles in Spain; preferring in his mind the images of a thousand fancies and follies such as are appointed to appear and torment them as have their brain weakened with vain cogitations" (Fenton 1923: 502). It should be noted that in these prose works there is no rhyme that could have dictated the maintenance of the "Spain" designation.

The reason for sticking so closely to this rather obscure formulation in the English language is probably quite simply that the common variant "to build castles in the air" of mainland Europe had not yet established itself in the British Isles. In fact, the earliest reference of the "air" variant appears only four decades later in Randle Cotgrave's comparative *A Dictionarie of the French and English Tongues* (1611) with a splendid explanatory note:

> *Faire des chasteaux en Espaigne.* To build castles in the aire (say we;) to muse he knowes not what about; to bestow the time in friuolous contemplations; to bee full of wandering, and vain imaginations; to propound vnto himselfe, or others, most idle, or impossible, exploits; (for there are but few Castles in the main land of Spain; or if more were to be built, who hath to do withall but the Spaniard?) (Cotgrave 1611: no pp.)

The remark "say we" appears to be signaling that the phrase "to build castles in the air" had become current by Cotgrave's time to such an extent that he did not find it necessary to cite the already established English phrase "to build castles in Spain." And Cotgrave is correct, for the earliest registered "air" variant in English comes from the year 1566 (Tilley 1950: 84–85; Wilson 1970: 107).

Two English Variants: "To Build Castles in Spain / in the Air"

Later translators of French works into English differed in their choice between the "Spain" and "air" variants in their English translations, owing to the fact that both had become current as popular phrases. Thus Montaigne's reference "Que je me jette à faire des chasteaux en Espaigne, mon imagination m'y forge des commoditez et des plaisirs desquels mon ame est reellement chatouillée et resjouye" (Villey 1965: 839), in his essay "De la diversion" (1595), was translated some 370 years later as "If I take to building castles in Spain, my imagination fabricates comforts and pleasures there by which my soul is really tickled and rejoiced" (Frame 1965: 637). Of special interest in this regard is Alain René Le Sage's sentence "Tant de bien peu à peu m'assoupit et je m'endormis en bâtissant des châteaux en Espagne" in his *Historie de Gil Blas de Santillane* (1715–35), which was translated in 1759 by Thomas Smollett as "I was gradually lulled by so much wealth, and fell asleep in the very act of building castles in Spain" (Smollett 1840: 66) and in 1887 by Henri van Laun as "So much wealth gradually made me drowsy, and I fell asleep building castles in the air" (Laun 1887: 371). The later translator feels obliged to add the following footnote: "*Des châteaux en Espagne*, in the original; an expression the more suitable, as the action takes place in Spain." But why? Did Laun not know the older English equivalent "to build castles in Spain" any longer, or was he already aware of the fact that it was ever more replaced by the less specific "to build castles in the air"?

This type of vacillation between two variants of the same expression can best be shown by the way a number of translators have dealt with La Fontaine's famous fable "La laitière et le pot au lait" (1678). The rhymed fable contains the following dual questions in the French original: "Quel esprit ne bat la campagne? / Qui ne fait châteaux en Espagne?" (La Fontaine 1958: 264). And here are several English translations of the past fifty years:

> Whom does a daydream not entrance?
> Have castles in air no romance?
> (Moore 1954: 155)

> Who doesn't build castles in Spain?
> Which of us isn't mildly insane?
> (Michie 1979: 171)

> Who doesn't roam off to Cockaigne?
> Who doesn't build castles in Spain?
> (Spector 1988: 319)

> All dreamers like to build castles in Spain,
> From Antiquity to our Milkmaid, wise and foolish dreamers both.
> (Christofides 2006: 76; a rather free translation)

Many will go woolgathering, fore and aft:
Castles in Spain are nothing new.
(Shapiro 2007: 170)

Whose thoughts don't run in the same vein?
Who doesn't build castles, off in Spain?
(Hill 2008: 163)

With one exception, all translations maintain the "Spain" variant, but not always because of an attempt to maintain the rhyme. The modern translators seem to prefer to stick as close as possible to the French original, and since it has its perfect English equivalent, their choice is not surprising. However, when I tried this on my modern American students who claim not to know the phrase "to build castles in Spain," I could not help but think that it would perhaps be better today to choose the more generally known variant "to build castles in the air." I might even argue that it fits better into the context of the fable, avoiding the confusion that a less figuratively inclined reader might experience by reading the metaphor literally.

Of course, a wordsmith and proverbial genius like Charles Dickens avoided such possible confusion by simply citing both variants in the same context in a letter to Thomas Baylis of July 2, 1862: "I am quite confident that the constancy of the young person [Dickens's daughter] is not to be trusted, and that she had best attach her [idea of having a] Fernery to one of her chateaux in Spain, or one of her English castles in the Air" (Storey 1998: 10, 98). Nevertheless, the other four times that Dickens uses the proverbial expression in his writings (Bryan and Mieder 1997: 80–81), he decides on the "air" variant, as for example in this passages from his novel *Bleak House* (1852): "So Richard [. . .] immediately began, on no other foundation, to build as many castles in the air as would man the great wall of China. He went away in high spirits" (Dickens 1948: 183). The American author Louisa M. Alcott proceeds in similar fashion in her well-known novel *Little Women* (1886), where she first uses the English "air" variant and then follows it up with the "Spain" variant in its original French wording:

The dream of filling home with comforts, giving Beth everything she wanted, from strawberries in winter to an organ for her bedroom; going abroad herself, and always having more than enough, so that she might indulge in the luxury of charity, had been for years Jo's most cherished castle in the air. The prize-story experience had seemed to open a way which might, after long travelling and much up-hill work lead to this delightful *châteaux en Espagne*. (Alcott 1886: 376–77)

As with Dickens, this is but a unique double employment of the phrase, and as would be expected, earlier in the novel she had used only the common English "air" variant: "'Would n't it be fun if all the castles in the air which we make could come true, and we could live in them?' said Jo, after a little pause" (Alcott 1886: 159). And this should not come as a surprise, for by the end of the nineteenth century the older proverbial expression "to build castles in Spain" was losing ground among American speakers, who most likely saw no reason to refer to Spain in particular when the popular "air" variant appeared to be a more universal statement. But the literary world is full of surprises, as can be seen from Bertram Atkey's modern novel *The Pyramid of Lead* (1925) with its marvelous juxtaposition of a real castle and a double allusion to imaginary castles:

> "Do you think it grasping and avaricious of me to feel rather sorry because now Lord Kern is coming back I shall never have Kern Castle after all?"
> Prosper shook his head—carefully, for he ached everywhere.
> "Why, of course not. They have let you believe for years that it would be yours. And you were meant for a castle. . . . Who knows? Perhaps some day you may yet have one of your own!"
> Marjorie May laughed rather ruefully.
> "Oh, I have several of those already—some in Spain, and some in the air!"
> (Atkey 1925: 207–8)

What a delightfully poetic statement about having lost the chance of obtaining a real castle by somewhat ironically alluding to the two proverbial phrases as an expression of hope springing eternal, as the proverb claims.

"To Build Castles in the Clouds / in the Air / in the Sky"

But before tracing the tenacious "Spain" variant in the English language to the present day, it is well to say a few words about the three more general variants that do not mention Spain. This is not the place to delineate their respective histories, but let it be said that a Google search undertaken in 2012 yielded the following results: 87,500 hits for "to build castles in the clouds"; 139,000 hits for "to build castles in Spain"; 1,090,000 hits for "to build castles in the air"; and the surprisingly high number of 1,270,000 hits

for "to build castles in the sky." The high yield on Google for the "sky" variant is something of a riddle, especially since the standard Anglo-American
proverb collections as well as my own textual archive have but very few references, and the same is true for the "clouds" variant, which appears not to
have caught on much at all (Stevenson 1948: 293; Tilley 1950: 85; Whiting
1977: 60; Whiting 1989: 94). One of the most interesting references I can
cite is from Martin Luther King's celebrated book *Strength to Love* (1963):

> In any realistic doctrine of man we must be forever concerned about his
> physical and material well-being. When Jesus said that man cannot live by
> bread alone [Deut. 8:3; Matt. 4:4], he did not imply that men can live with-
> out bread. As Christians we must think not only about "mansions in the sky,"
> but also about the slums and ghettos that cripple the human soul, not merely
> about streets in heaven "flowing with milk and honey" [Exodus 3:8], but also
> about the millions of people in this world who go to bed hungry at night.
> Any religion that professes concern regarding the souls of men and fails to be
> concerned by social conditions that corrupt and economic conditions that
> cripple the soul, is a do-nothing religion, in need of new blood. Such a reli-
> gion fails to realize that man is an animal having physical and material needs.
> (King 1963: 89; Mieder 2010a)

There is no doubt that the "air" variant has been the most prevalent formulation, and it has given the original English loan translation "to build castles in
Spain" a run for its money, to put it proverbially. Since it appears to be the
dominant variant despite the Google calculations, which are to be enjoyed
with a grain of salt due to the uncontrollable counting of duplicates, at least a
few examples of a plethora of references will be mentioned here before turning to the "Spain" variant that keeps hanging on despite an obvious decline
in instances. Here then are at least a few chronologically arranged references
from some well-known authors:

> 1628—Robert Burton
> When I go musing all alone,
> Thinking of divers things fore-known
> When I build castles in the air,
> Void of sorrow and void of fear,
> Pleasing myself with phantasms sweet,
> Methinks the time runs very fleet.
> All my joys to this are folly,

Naught so sweet as melancholy.
(Burton 1972: 11)

1728—Alexander Pope
Hence the Fool's paradise, the Statesman's scheme,
The air-built Castle, and the golden Dream
(Pope 1928: 36)

1773—James Boswell
There have been many people who built castles in the air, but I [James Boswell] believe I am the first that ever attempted to live in them. (Rogers 1876: 225)

1854—Henry David Thoreau
If you have built castles in the air, your work need not be lost; that is where they should be. Now put the foundation under them. (Thoreau 2000: 257)

1857—Charles Dickens
The Storming of the Castle in the Air (chapter title in *Little Dorrit*) (Dickens 1953: 637)

1860—Ralph Waldo Emerson
I know how easy it is to men of the world to look grave and sneer at your sanguine youth, its glittering dreams. But I find the gayest castles in the air that were ever piled, far better for comfort and for use, than the dungeons in the air that are daily dug and caverned out by grumbling, discontented people. (Emerson 1861: 233)

1872—Mark Twain
I went to bed all on fire with excitement [...]. I could not sleep, my fancy so rioted through its castles in the air. (Twain 1996: 402)

1916—Eugene O'Neill
I am sorry, Tom. I would not hurt you for anything in the world, but this—must be! My highest duty is toward myself, and my ego demands freedom, wide horizons to develope in (*she [Lucy] makes a sweeping gesture*) Castles in the air, not homes for human beings! (*tenderly*) You understand, don't you Tom? (O'Neill 1988: 1, 416; Bryan and Mieder 1995)

1924—Arthur Guiterman
'Tis Cheap to build a Castle in the Air,
But Costly keeping up a Dwelling there.
(Guiterman 1924: 58)

1936—P. G. Wodehouse
In the first numbing shock of a great disappointment, when all the castles he
had been building in the air have come tumbling about his ears and his soul
seems to have been tied in knots and passed through the wringer, a man's in-
stinct is for solitude.
(Wodehouse 1936: 223)

1944—George Bernard Shaw
Now your castle in the air is growing at such a rate that I must knock it down
with an almighty kick or it will be your ruin. It will do you no harm to have
a hobby; but having a hobby is one thing & earning a living another. (Shaw
1988: 4, 734; Bryan and Mieder 1994)

1978—Hugh Fleetwood
And sometimes, when he sat with them and started to tell his stories, build
his marvelous gothic castles in the air that were—or had been—so real that
one could stretch out one's fingers and touch the stones, could walk down
cold flagged corridors, could stand on the parapet and catch sight of the most
breathtaking views, or open great heavy doors and suddenly find oneself in
the most splendid, painted ballroom, blazing with candles and alive with cha-
racters in masks, he became terribly aware that now not only had he failed to
conjure up even the flimsiest wall, but was doing nothing but repeat tales he'd
already told—and repeat them, inexcusably, without the slightest variation.
(Fleetwood 1978: 81)

These references are ample proof that the general phrase "to build castles in
the air" had become the dominant variant over time as a metaphor for all-
too-human fantasies and dreams.

The Steadfastness of the Variant "To Build Castles in Spain"

However, the more exotic "Spain" variant persisted and can most certainly
be found to the present day, albeit with considerably less frequency. And as
can be seen from a letter of December 9, 1920, by Eugene O'Neill to George

C. Tyler, the same author might well employ both variants. While he had used the "air" variant four years earlier (see above), he now prefers its more exotic variant:

> He [O'Neill's father] was leaving my Mother with the barest sufficiency. Even now, she is having difficulty in getting his messed-up estate into a sane condition where it can maintain her with a fair degree of comfort. The treasures of *Monte Cristo* [O'Neill's plan of adapting the plot of Dumas's novel for a play] are buried deep again—in prairie dog cold mines, in unlubricated oil wells, in fuelless coal lands—the modern Castles in Spain of pure romance. (Bogard and Bryer 1988: 143)

Here are a few additional references of the proverbial expression "to build castles in Spain" from the past two centuries that illustrate its continued application as a far-reaching metaphor for all types of wishful thinking—or, to use a phraseologism often employed by Eugene O'Neill, of the "pipe dreams" of humankind (Bryan and Mieder 1995: 270–73). In fact, the phrase "to be a pipe dream" might also have something to do with the decreased popularity of the old French phrase that was loan translated hundreds of years ago into the English language. In the following list, Mark Twain's hopeful message to his mother is of particular interest by couching his future success as a writer into the "castles in Spain" metaphor:

> 1868—Mark Twain
> Dear Mother: Don't worry—I'm all right. [. . .] Some few castles in Spain going up. (Wecter 1949: 47)

> 1872—Oliver Wendell Holmes
> He is a dreamer, almost poet. [. . .] In his chest is a castle of Spain, a real one, and not only in Spain, but anywhere he will choose to have it. (Holmes 1872: 256)

> 1898—William Black
> "And I am less hopeful now; the three places we have looked at were clearly out of the question; and my Highland mansion may prove to be a castle in Spain after all." (Black 1898: 455)

> 1909—Elinore Pruitt Stewart
> Like all the kindergartners, she depended upon others to amuse her. I was very sorry about it, for my castles in Spain have been real homes to me. But there is no fear. (Stewart 1989: 13)

1925—J. S. Fletcher
Left alone to her own reflections, and with the sure consciousness that the castle in Spain which she had recently been building had fallen into dust and fragments about her ears, Mrs. Walsingham, on Carsdale's departure, immediately set to work to consider her position. She knew everything had gone wrong, that the pleasant and easy-going present had vanished like a morning's dream. (Fletcher 1925: 205)

1928—John Esteven
As I studied every sharply formed character on the page [of a letter], something struck me at the end. She had hesitated once before the conclusion, had started a sentence beginning "I long—" and had scratched it out, signing herself, "Sincerely yours." It illustrates clearly enough what state of mind I was in that castles in Spain should rise out of two canceled words. I was absurd enough to complete that sentence in a hundred ways, all flattering, until the hour of our interview. (Esteven 1928: 223)

1934—Aldous Huxley
The Indians must have worked very hard to make and keep the church of Sacapulas so splendid; but at least it was *their* church, and the gilded idols on the altars, *their* saints. They themselves lived in huts; but the rich and glittering temple in the plaza was their spiritual home. A spiritual home, moreover, having the additional merit of being physically there; a castle in Spain that was visibly present in Sacapulas. (Huxley 1960: 154–55)

1938—W. Somerset Maugham
The images, free ideas that throng his [a writer's] mind, are not guides but materials for action. They have all the vividness of sensation. His day-dreams are so significant to him that it is the world of sense that is shadowy and he has to reach out for it by an effort of will. His castles in Spain are no baseless fabric, but real castles that he lives in. (Maugham 1938: 230)

1958—H. F. M. Prescott
To her, rishaws had brought back the brief hours of that happy night when her castle in Spain had been a house in London with a kitchen in which she herself would make rishaws for him. (Prescott 1958: 362)

1974—Emma Lathen
They both took a sip to celebrate this beautiful thought. But Gene Orcutt was not building castles in Spain. (Lathen 1974: 101)

It should be noted that many of these literary references put a rather pessimistic spell on those wishful castles in Spain that in earlier times had a much more romantic vision to them. This is also the case in Eugene O'Neill's play *More Stately Mansions* (1939) where Sara wants to gain her very own "castle in Spain" in Ireland by means of any devices possible. The three references to the greedy and manipulative behavior of Sara by way of the "castle in Spain" metaphor are void of any legitimate dream world:

> The ambitious Sara who used to long to own an Irish-castle-in-Spain, gentleman's estate!—who was willing to use any means or to pay any price— even her beautiful body—to get what she wanted. (O'Neill 1988: 3, 394)

> I'm merely pointing out that you [Sara] had been swindled. But you would realize it if you spent more time examining the true values of his [Simon's] gifts and less in designing your impossible Irish-Castle-in-Spain! (O'Neill 1988: 480)

> You [Sara] are welcome to the farm. I am glad you at last realize what you are and where you belong. A stupid peasant tilling the soil, her bare feet in the earth, her gross body stinking of sweat, a dumb brainless, begetting female animal with her dirty brats around her! But what becomes of your grand estate, and the ridiculous Irish dream castle in Spain? (O'Neill 1988: 541)

While such references take the fanciful and romantic aspect out of the wishful "castles in Spain" metaphor, there is a poetic medium that does maintain its dreamy world of romance and fairy tale.

"To Build Castles in Spain" in Poems and Songs

Poems and the lyrics of songs are perfect environments for the more traditional meaning of the proverbial expression. John Godfrey Saxe, a nineteenth-century poet from my agricultural state of Vermont in the United States, was quite capable of employing "my Spanish Chateau" as a leitmotif at the end of each stanza in his poem "My Castle in Spain" (1855) that describes a wholesome family with its castle-like homestead:

> There's a castle in Spain, very charming to see,
> Though built without money or toil;
> Of this handsome estate I am owner in fee,

And paramount lord of the soil;
And oft as I may I'm accustomed to go
And live, like a king, in my Spanish Chateau!

There's a dame most bewitchingly rounded and ripe,
Whose wishes are never absurd;
Who doesn't object to my smoking a pipe,
Nor insist on the ultimate word;
In short, she's the pink of perfection, you know;
And she lives, like a queen, in my Spanish Chateau!

I've a family too; the delightfulest girls,
And a bevy of beautiful boys;
All quite the reverse of those juvenile churls
Whose pleasure is mischief and noise;
No modern *Cornelia* might venture to show
Such jewels as those in my Spanish Chateau!

I have servants who seek their contentment in mine,
And always mind what they are at;
Who never embezzle the sugar and wine,
And slander the innocent cat;
Neither saucy, nor careless, nor stupidly slow
Are the servants who wait in my Spanish Chateau!

I have pleasant companions; most affable folk;
And each with the heart of a brother;
Keen wits, who enjoy an antagonist's joke,
And beauties who're fond of each other;
Such people, indeed, as you never may know,
Unless you should come to my Spanish Chateau!

I have friends, whose commission for wearing the name
In kindness unfailing is shown;
Who pay to another the duty they claim,
And deem his successes their own;
Who joy in his gladness, and weep at his woe;
You'll find them (where else?) in my Spanish Chateau!

"O si sic semper!" I oftentimes say,
(Though 't is idle, I know, to complain,)
To think that again I must force me away
From my beautiful castle in Spain!
Ah! would that my stars had determined it so
I might live the year round in my Spanish Chateau!
(Saxe 1868: 9–10; Mieder 1989: 181–82)

About a dozen years later, the American poet James Russell Lowell wrote "Aladdin" (1868), which takes the proverbial phrase from the more realistic interpretation by Saxe to a romantic level, where a man is willing to give up everything to get his departed love back:

When I was a beggarly boy,
And lived in a cellar damp,
I had not a friend nor a toy,
But I had Aladdin's lamp;
When I could not sleep for the cold,
I had fire enough in my brain,
And builded, with roofs of gold,
My beautiful castles in Spain!

Since then I have toiled day and night,
I have money and power good store,
But I'd give all my lamps of silver bright
For the one that is mine no more;
Take, Fortune, whatever you choose,
You gave, and may snatch again;
I have nothing 't would pain me to lose,
For I own no more castles in Spain!
(Lowell 1897: 300)

Some fifty years later, Florence Earle Coates wrote the love poem "An Idle Ditty" (1916), in which a woman longs for changing her relationship with her beloved from the state of unrealistic "castles in Spain" to true married bliss:

'T is I have been waiting to know, dear,
The day that ye'r ship would come in,

For if I'm to love ye at all, dear,
I'm thinking it's time to begin.

    \

The mavis is singing hard by, dear,
The hedges are white wi' the may,
And there's never a cloud i' the sky, dear,
To hinder a ship on its way.

Ye've told me o' castles a many,
And though they're but *castles in Spain*,
I surely were better in any
Wi' you, than alone wi' my pain!

The mavis that's close to her mate, dear,
For no castle would part wi' her nest,
And the ship that brings you, though it's late, dear,
Brings me what is worth all the rest!

(Coates 1916: 117)

And in the musical *Face the Music* (1932), with lyrics by the renowned Irving Berlin, appears the short song "On a Roof in Manhattan (Castles in Spain)" (1931), which speaks of love in New York with the romantic dream of castles in Spain:

[…]
We'll be so close to the moon,
I'll reach up and pluck you a star,
And through the night we'll remain,
Wrapped in velvet and satin,
And dream of castles in Spain
On a roof in Manhattan.

(Kimball and Emmet 2001: 275)

But speaking of New York, there is also the song "Autumn in New York" (1934) by Vernon Duke (recorded in 1949 by Frank Sinatra) with a verse claiming that at this beautiful time of the year the big city is the perfect place for lovers: "This autumn in New York / Transforms the slums into Mayfair / Autumn in New York / You'll need no castles in Spain" (www.risa.co.uk/sla/song.php?songid=16995).

Apparently lovers don't necessarily need castles in Spain, as yet another song, "My Romance" by Lorenz Hart from the musical *Jumbo* (1935), claims:

> My romance
> Doesn't need a blue lagoon standing by.
> No month of May,
> No twinkling stars.
> [...]
> My romance
> Doesn't need a castle rising in Spain.
> (Hart and Kimball 1986: 216–17)

Other lyrics could be cited (Bryan 2001: 21, 38) to show the popularity of the "castles in Spain" metaphor in modern songs, but it must suffice to cite one last, truly unique example. Jimi Hendrix's song "Spanish Castle Magic" (1967; with Hendrix recalling "The Spanish Castle," a dance hall in Seattle) takes the romantic dream world of the medieval "châteaux en Espagne" into the world of lovers high on hallucinatory drugs:

> Hang on my darling, yeah
> Hang on if you wanna go
> Get on top, really let me groove baby with uh
> Just a little bit of Spanish Castle Magic.
> Yeah baby,
> Here's some
> Yeah, ok babe, ok
> It's all in your mind babe
> [...]
> (www.lyricsfreak.com/j/jimi+hendrix/spanish+castle+magic_20071567.html)

Considering the long history of the proverbial expression "to build castles in Spain" and its "air," "clouds," and "sky" variants—from the French Middle Ages and on through the English-speaking world with its global influence as the lingua franca of the world—it is amazing to see the ever new interpretive possibilities of this old proverbial motif. From the dreams of lovers to the desires and wishes for a better existence and on to the highs of psychedelic hallucinogenic drugs, the phrase has served humanity as a metaphorical sign for the wonders of human existence. People will always have their fantasies and dreams, and there is certainly nothing wrong with building imaginary castles in Spain or elsewhere. A life without wishful aspirations would be mundane indeed, so let's continue building all kinds of "castles in Spain" with the eternal hope that some of them might just become reality not just for ourselves but for humanity in general.

BIBLIOGRAPHY

This chapter will be published with the same title in *Festschrift for Antonio Pamies Bertrán*. Rosemeire Monteiro, ed. Fortaleza, Brazil: Ceará Federal University, 2014.

Alcott, Louisa M. 1886. *Little Women; or Meg, Jo, Beth, and Amy*. Boston: Roberts Brothers.

Atkey, Bertram. 1925. *The Pyramid of Lead*. New York: D. Appleton.

Black, William. 1898. *White Heather*. New York: Harper & Brothers.

Bogard, Travis, and Jackson R. Bryer, eds. 1988. *Selected Letters of Eugene O'Neill*. New Haven, Connecticut: Yale University Press.

Bryan, George B. 2001. "An Unfinished List of Anglo-American Proverb Songs." *Proverbium* 18: 15–56.

Bryan, George B., and Wolfgang Mieder. 1994. *The Proverbial Bernard Shaw: An Index to Proverbs in the Works of George Bernard Shaw*. Westport, Connecticut: Greenwood.

———. 1995. *The Proverbial Eugene O'Neill: An Index to Proverbs in the Works of Eugene Gladstone O'Neill*. Westport, Connecticut: Greenwood.

———. 1997. *The Proverbial Charles Dickens: An Index to Proverbs in the Works of Charles Dickens*. New York: Peter Lang.

———. 2005. *Anglo-American Proverbs and Proverbial Phrases Found in Literary Sources of the Nineteenth and Twentieth Centuries*. New York: Peter Lang.

Buitrago Jiménez, A. 1995. *Diccionario de dichos y frases hechas*. Madrid: Espasa Calpe.

Burton, Robert. 1972. *The Anatomy of Melancholy*. Holbrook Jackson, ed. London. J.M. Dent.

Caxton, William. 1913. *The History of Jason: Translated from the French of Raoul Le Fèvre*. John Murro, ed. London: Kegan Paul, Trench, Trübner.

Christofides, Koren, ed., and C. Christofides, transl. 2006. *Fables of La Fontaine*. Seattle, Washington: University of Washington Press.

Coates, Florence E. 1916. *Poems*. Boston: Houghton Mifflin.

Cotgrave, Randle. 1611. *A Dictionarie of the French and English Tongues*. London: Adam Islip; rpt. Hildesheim: Georg Olms, 1970.

Di Stefano, Giuseppe. 1991. *Dictionnaire des locutions en moyen français*. Montréal: Editions CERES.

Dickens, Charles. 1948. *Bleak House*. Oxford: Oxford University Press.

———. 1953. *Little Dorrit*. Oxford: Oxford University Press.

Emerson, Ralph Waldo. 1861. *The Conduct of Life*. Boston: Ticknor and Fields.

Esteven, John. 1928. *The Door of Death*. New York: Century.

Fenton, Geoffrey. 1923. *Bandello: Tragical Tales. The Complete Novels translated*. H. Harris, ed. London: George Routledge.

Fleetwood, Hugh. 1978. *Roman Magic*. New York: Atheneum.

Fletcher, J. S. 1925. *The Wolves and the Lamb*. New York: Alfred A. Knopf.

Frame, Donald M., transl. 1965. *The Complete Essays of Montaigne*. Stanford, California: Stanford University Press.

Gallacher, Stuart A. 1963. "'Castles in Spain.'" *Journal of American Folklore* 76: 324–29.

Guiterman, A. 1924. *A Poet's Proverbs*. New York: E.P. Dutton.

Hart, Dorothy, and Robert Kimball, eds. 1986. *The Complete Lyrics of Lorenz Hart*. New York: Alfred A. Knopf.

Hassell, James Woodrow. 1982. *Middle French Proverbs, Sentences, and Proverbial Phrases*. Toronto: Pontifical Institute of Mediaeval Studies.

Hill, Craig, transl. 2008. *The Complete Fables of La Fontaine*. New York: Arcade.

Holmes, Oliver Wendell. 1872. *The Poet at the Breakfast-Table*. Boston: Houghton Mifflin.

Huxley, Aldous. 1960. *Beyond the Mexique Bay*. New York: Vintage.

Irmer, Eugen. 1890. *Die altfranzösische Bearbeitung der "Formula Honestae Vitae" des Martin von Braga*. Halle: E. Krebs.

Kimball Robert, and Linda Emmet, eds. 2001. *The Complete Lyrics of Irving Berlin*. New York: Alfred A. Knopf.

King, Martin Luther. 1963. *Strength to Love*. New York: Harper & Row.

La Fontaine, Jean de. 1958. *Fables*. Paris: Robert Laffont.

Långfors, Arthur. 1914. "Châteaux en Brie et—en Espagne." *Neuphilologische Mitteilungen* 16: 107–10.

Langlois, Ernest, ed. 1920. *Le Roman de la Rose*. Paris: Firmin-Didot.

Larsen, J. C. 1978. *Proverbial Material in the "Roman de la Rose."* Diss., University of Georgia.

Lathen, Emma. 1974. *Sweet and Low*. New York: Simon & Schuster.

Laun, Henri van, transl. 1887. *The Adventures of Gil Blas of Santillana*. Edinburgh: William Paterson.

Lowell, James Russell. 1897. *The Complete Poetical Works*. Boston: Houghton Mifflin.

Martín Sánchez, Manuel. 1997. *Diccionario del español coloquial (Dichos, modismos y locuciones populares)*. Madrid: Tellus.

Maugham, W. Somerset. 1938. *The Summing Up*. New York: Literary Guild of America.

Michie. James, transl. 1979. *La Fontaine: Selected Fables*. New York: Viking.

Mieder, Wolfgang. 1989. *American Proverbs: A Study of Texts and Contexts*. Bern: Peter Lang.

———. 2010a. *"Making a Way Out of No Way": Martin Luther King's Sermonic Proverbial Rhetoric*. New York: Peter Lang.

———. 2010b. *"Spruchschlösser (ab)bauen": Sprichwörter, Antisprichwörter und Lehnsprichwörter in Literatur und Medien*. Wien: Praesens.

Moore, Marianne, transl. 1954. *The Fables of La Fontaine*. New York: Viking.

Morel-Fatio, Alfred. 1925. *Etudes sur l'Espagne*. Paris: Edouard Champion.

Nelson, Axel. 1951. "'Châteaux en Espagne' dans le latin médiéval." *Eranos* 49: 159–69.

O'Neill, E. 1988. *Complete Plays*. 3 vols. New York: Library of America.

Piirainen, Elisabeth. 2012: *Widespread Idioms in Europe and Beyond: Phraseology in a Eurolinguistic Framework*. New York: Peter Lang.

Pope, Alexander. 1928. *The Dunciad: An Heroic Poem*. Oxford: Clarendon.

Prescott, H. F. M. 1958. *The Man on a Donkey*. New York: Macmillan.

Rey, Alain, and Sophie Chantreau. 1993. *Dictionnaire des expressions et locutions*. Paris: Dictionnaires Le Robert.

Robinson, F. N., ed. 1933. *The Complete Works of Geoffrey Chaucer*. Boston: Houghton Mifflin.

Rogers, Charles, ed. 1876. *Boswelliana: The Common Place Book of James Boswell*. London: Houlston.

Röhrich, Lutz. 1991–92. *Das große Lexikon der sprichwörtlichen Redensarten*. 3 vols. Freiburg: Herder.

Saxe, John Godfrey. 1868. *The Poems*. Boston: Ticknor and Fields.

Shapiro, Norman R., transl. 2007. *The Complete Fables of Jean de La Fontaine*. Urbana, Illinois: University of Illinois Press.

Shaw, George Bernard. 1988. *Collected Letters*. Dan H. Laurence, ed. New York: Viking.

Singer, Samuel, and Ricarda Liver, eds. 1995–2002. *Thesaurus proverbiorum medii aevi. Lexikon der Sprichwörter des romanisch-germanischen Mittelalters*. 13 vols. Berlin: Walter de Gruyter.

Smith, Roland M. 1945. "Chaucer's 'Castles in Spain.'" *Modern Language Notes* 60: 39–40.

Smollett, Tobias, transl. 1840. *The Adventures of Gil Blas of Santillane*. Exeter: J. and B. Williams.

Spector, Norman B., transl. 1988. *The Complete Fables of Jean de la Fontaine*. Evanston, IL: Northwestern University Press.

Stevenson, Burton, ed. 1948. *The Home Book of Proverbs, Maxims and Familiar Phrases*. New York: Macmillan.

Stewart, Elinore P. 1989. *Letters of a Woman Homesteader*. Lincoln, Nebraska: University of Nebraska Press.

Storey, Graham, ed. 1998. *The Letters of Charles Dickens*. 10 vols. Oxford: Clarendon.

Taylor, Archer, and Bartlett Jere Whiting. 1958. *A Dictionary of American Proverbs and Proverbial Phrases, 1820–1880*. Cambridge, Massachusetts: Harvard University Press.

Thoreau, Henry David. 2000. *Walden and Civil Disobedience*. P. Lauter, ed. Boston: Houghton Mifflin.

Tilley, Morris Palmer. 1950. *A Dictionary of the Proverbs in England in the Sixteenth and Seventeenth Centuries*. Ann Arbor, Michigan: University of Michigan Press.

Twain, Mark. 1996. *Roughing It*. George Plimpton, ed. New York: Oxford University Press.

Villey, Pierre, ed. 1965. *Les essais de Michel de Montaigne*. Paris: Presse Universitaries de France.

Wander, Karl Friedrich Wilhelm. 1867–80. *Deutsches Sprichwörterlexikon*. 5 vols. Leipzig: F.A. Brockhaus; rpt. Darmstadt: Wissenschaftliche Buchgesellschaft, 1964.

Wecter, Dixon, ed. 1949. *Mark Twain to Mrs. Fairbanks*. San Marino, California: Huntington Library.

Whiting, Bartlett Jere. 1977. *Early American Proverbs and Proverbial Phrases*. Cambridge, Massachusetts: Harvard University Press.

——. 1989. *Modern Proverbs and Proverbial Sayings*. Cambridge, Massachusetts: Harvard University Press.

Wilkinson, P. R. 1993. *Thesaurus of Traditional English Metaphors*. London: Routledge.

Wilson, F. P. 1970. *The Oxford Dictionary of English Proverbs*. Oxford: Oxford University Press.

Wodehouse, P. G. 1936. *The Luck of the Bodkins*. Boston: Little, Brown.

13. "LET GEORGE DO IT"
The Disturbing Origin and Cultural History of an American Proverb

Whenever the question of the origin of a particular proverb arises, pare-miologists or proverb scholars are confronted with the vexing task of finding a multitude of references in the hope of tracing the proverb back to what is hoped to be its first occurrence. The impressive proverb collections with historical data are of much help in this regard, with additional contextualized references being found by much study of primary documents ranging from literary works to the mass media. Of course, nowadays such searches are greatly enhanced by way of new and ever expanding electronic databases. The search possibilities have increased tremendously for the pare-miological sleuth, and it should come as no surprise that the previously established dates of the first occurrences of certain proverbs have been pushed back. This is also true for proverbs of newer coinage, with texts that were believed to be from the second half of the twentieth century actually being considerably older and dating back to at least the previous century. Modern internet searches are indeed revolutionizing the paremiographical work of proverb scholars; we are able by way of ever more historical references to update all extant proverb collections.

Before the "miracle" of the internet with its well-known imperfections, scholars depended on the more or less isolated work of individuals who plow-ed along by culling through vast amounts of reading materials to establish the origin and historical dissemination of individual proverbs. This resulted in a considerable number of impressive monographs and articles that show by way of many examples, often including variants from other languages, how one particular proverb gained regional, national, and even internatio-nal prominence over time (Mieder 1977). But there were and continue to be such journals as the British *Notes and Queries*, which since 1849 has gi-ven scholars the opportunity to post various types of queries in the hope that short notes providing the answer might be published. At times an entire series of responses appeared, quite similar to the way scholars communicate via various listserves today.

Early Comments on "Let George Do It"

In any case, I remember well the summer of 1983, when with my two students Nancy Magnuson and John Hermanski, I worked through that British gold mine of thousands of notes, looking for those that deal with proverbial matters. The result was a book, with about 10,000 such notes, entitled *Investigations of Proverbs, Proverbial Expressions, Quotations and Clichés: A Bibliography of Explanatory Essays which Appeared in "Notes and Queries" (1849–1983)* (1984), with one of them from June 23, 1923, being the following well-informed question by R. E. Gossage from the New York Public Library:

> "Let George do it."—The expression "Let George do it" has in the last ten or dozen years become current in America. Especially during the war was it in common use. The phrase meaning, of course, "Let the other fellow do it." We are interested to learn if there is any foundation to the statement that this phrase is of English origin. We know that the French have employed for several centuries a very similar expression, "Laissez faire a George, il est homme d'age [*sic*; the spelling of French *à*, *Georges*, and *âge* varies in both my French and English sources and will be cited as given throughout]," which they trace back to the time of Louis XII. Has such an expression been used in England, and if so, is there any explanation of its origin known to you or your readers. (Gossage 1923: 492; Mieder 1984: 148)

Unfortunately, there was no response, but mindful of my colleague and friend George B. Bryan, my American brother George Schumm, and a number of other Georges dear to me, I started a folder on the proverb, adding references to it that I came across serendipitously during the past three decades. But now the time is ripe to deal with that ninety-year-old query in earnest.

I assume that R. E. Gossage found the possible French connection in H. L. Mencken's celebrated *The American Language* (1921):

> ["Let George do it"] originated in France, as "laissez faire à Georges," during the fifteenth century, and at the start had satirical reference to the multiform activities of Cardinal Georges d'Amboise, prime minister to Louis XII. [In note 11 Mencken adds where he probably found this information:] *Cf. Two*

Children in Old Paris, by Gertrude Slaughter, New York, 1918, p. 233. (Mencken 1921: 364)

The reference cited by Mencken is of utmost importance, because it represents the earliest literary text found thus far that links the French and English proverbs. The passage is especially fascinating, since the English proverb placed in quotation marks takes on an intriguing sexual meaning:

> "I wonder what Marguerite [of Angouleme, later queen of Navarre] did when they were gone hunting," mused Trudion.
>
> "I imagine she was not always at her embroidery frame," I said, "because I have heard that she read the legends of King Arthur and Greek stories and the Imitation of Christ when she was a little girl. I wonder if she loved the story of Cupid and Psyche, too. She even read Greek philosophy with her teacher, the wonderful Cardinal, Georges d'Amboise."
>
> "I wonder if she 'let George do it,'" laughed Elizabeth.
>
> "Sister, you got that out of a book," Trudion made an effort not to smile. We had just learned the day before that the august Cardinal and Marechal de France was the origin of the phrase, "Laissez faire a Georges." "I wonder if she could play tennis," Trudion added. (Slaughter 1918: 233)

A few years later in 1931, Archer Taylor, the renowned American folklorist and paremiologist and obviously a reader of Mencken's classic work, considers this connection of the two proverbs a possibility and adds some important information to it:

> *Let George do it*, which is perhaps a vaudeville phrase, is now less frequently heard than formerly and is perhaps on its way to extinction. [in note 2 Taylor adds:] Possibly we can see a connection with *Laissez faire à George, il est homme d'âge*, a historical proverb. We are told that Louis XII expressed his confidence in his minister, George d'Amboise, in these words. The traditional explanation in America is based on "George" as a name used in addressing Pullman porters. (Taylor 1931: 9)

Taylor's careful and speculative wording makes it abundantly clear that he was not entirely convinced that there is in fact a connection with the two "George" proverbs, although the possibility cannot be dismissed. Separate origins of such minimalistic texts as proverbs can occur, after all, as Alan Dundes has pointed out: "If one is engaged in citing cognates of a particular proverb, one should be careful to distinguish actual cognates, that is, versions and variants of the proverb in question, assumed to be historically/genetically related to that proverb, from mere structural parallels which may well have arisen independently, that is, through polygenesis" (2000: 298). The issue of monogenesis vs. polygenesis has been discussed in folklore circles since the Brothers Grimm, and it remains a perplexing scholarly problem to this day (Chesnutt 2002).

Letting the proverbial cat ever so slightly out of the bag for a moment, let me state here that I lean toward the polygenetic argument regarding the two "George" proverbs, with not even the internet being able to present an entirely satisfactory solution. But before delving deeper into this complex conundrum, I would like to refer to an internet exchange that doubtlessly would have delighted E. R. Gossage. In 2005 Robert Whealey, professor of history at Ohio University, posted the following query under the heading of "Pop Culture":

> I'm now seventy-five. Sometime in the 1940-1948 era, I used to hear on radio a cliche [sic]—"Let George do it." After the World Trade tower disaster in September 2001, I expected to hear again among critics of President George W. Bush the slogan, "Let George do it." The atmosphere of fear in 2001 is beginning to fade.
>
> Question: Where did the phrase "Let George do it" originate? A play? a movie?
> (H-Net Discussion Networks—Re: Pop Culture)

A number of responses referred Whealey to the British film *Let George Do It* (1940), starring George Formby in one of his best roles. But there was also this somewhat smart-aleck response of October 11 by Matt Clark: "Do a Google search. You can spend the day going from site to site, including movies, plays, etc. I didn't have the time to find the ultimate source of the phrase, but maybe you do." Well, Prof. Douglas Deal from the History Department of the State University of New York at Oswego did take the time, and his comments of October 15 deserve to be repeated, as they refer to modern research questions as such:

> The advice given by Matt Clark to Robert Whealey—use "Google" to find the answer to your question about the origins [sic] of the expression "let George do it" . . . if you have all day to look—set me to thinking. How has the computer—in particular, its "search engines"—transformed the way we ask

and answer simple questions? And what about not so simple questions? Is it reshaping the ways in which we academic types (not to mention the general public) do "research"?

My first impulse, when I saw professor Whealey's question, was to check in a reference work I have at my personal library, Mitford M. Mathews, *A Dictionary of Americanisms* [1951]. There under "George," I found the answer to his question. It took me about 30 seconds.

Now I have also spent a lot of time "googling" for answers to questions. Sometimes, I'm lucky (or I use a well chosen array of search terms) and I discover what I'm looking for fairly quickly. But usually I have to "search within results" or pore over dozens of useless entries to get what I want.

So I wonder: as we get into the habit of looking for everything (or almost everything) on the Web, will we forget—or just neglect—our older research skills (knowing the right place to look in the books on hand, for instance) and end up spending lots more time "searching" than we really need to? So much time, in fact, that we can't be bothered to find answers to other people's questions, because it takes too long!

[plus two references from 1910 and 1912 of the proverb found in Mathews]

This is a point well taken! Dictionaries, collections, and printed books in general remain important resources for scholarly work. As they continue to be consulted, they quite often can provide reliable answers to short queries. However, it would be foolish not to augment these traditional publications with the vast and ever-increasing possibilities of searching on the internet. Printed and online sources do not form a dichotomy but rather present complementary research strategies that feed and inform on each other. This is most certainly true for this case study of "Let George do it." The investigation would be much less complete if only printed sources or only internet sources would have been used. Employing both of them as widely as possible, this search for the origin of the proverb "Let George do it" has hopefully proceeded as far as is possible at this moment.

The French Connection: "Laissez faire à Georges"

The origin of the French proverb, reduced from the longer quotation "Laissez faire à Georges, il est homme d'âge" is well established. In fact, Louis-Pierre Anquetil in his fourteen-volume *Histoire de France depuis les Gaulois jusqu'à la fin de la monarchie* (1805) cites its start in the year 1498, when Cardinal Georges d'Amboise (1460–1510) became the minister of state under King Louis XII, who had been impressed with his administrative abilities:

1498 [in the margin]. Il (Louis XII] avoit une telle confiance en lui que, dans les circonstances embarrassantes, sa solution ordinaire aux difficultés qu'on lui présentoit, étoit, *laissez faire à Georges*, et il se tranquillisoit sur l'événement. Cette sécurité a été souvent funeste. (Anquetil 1805: V, 375–76)

The long version of the proverb appears for the first time in Fleury de Bellingen's early collection *L'Etymologie ou Explication des Proverbes Francois* (1656):

Le Roy se confioit entierement en sa [Georges d'Amboise] sagesse pour la conduite des affaires de son Royaume, disoit ordinairement en prenant resolution de bien servir le Roy & l'Estat dans les occasions, qui se presentoient, & [l]es choses dont il s'agissoit: *Laissez faire à George, il est homme d'age.* Donnant à entendre par là qu'il se comporteroit prudemment, sagement, & avec toute la consideration, & circonspection necessaire en ce qui concernoit le service de sa Majesté, la gloire de sa coronne, & le bien de ses Peuples; car c'est là agir en homme d'age; comme au contraire proceder inconsiderement, hastivement, & sans meure deliberation, c'est agir temerairement & en jeune estourdi. (1656: 37)

Antoine Oudin also registers the proverb in 1656 with a short explanatory comment, as one would expect it from a dictionary entry: "Laissez faire à George, il est homme d'aage, ne [d]outez point, ne vous mettez point au peine, nous viendrons bien à bout de nos desseins" (Oudin 1656: 194).

The proverb clearly has the meaning of not having any doubts or worries, because everything will work out if that George [d'Amboise] is in charge. It is interesting to note here that the minister is actually not mentioned, showing that the proverb has taken on a meaning of its own. In references from proverb collections of later times, the editors have found it necessary to give a more precise historical explanation:

1690: *George.*—est un nom propre qui est venu en usage en ce proverbe, Laissez faire à *George*, c'est un homme d'âge. Il s'est fait du temps du Cardinal *George* d'Amboise Ministre d'Estat: quand on parloit des affaires publiques, on disoit, Laissez faire à *George*, il est homme d'âge, pour dire, qu'il s'en falloit rapporter à sa bonne conduitte & à sa grande intelligence. (Furetière 1690: R[3])

1771: *George.* Ce nom propre, *George*, est venu en usage en ce proverbe. Laissez faire à *George*, c'est un homme d'âge. Il s'est fait du temps du Cardinal *George* d'Amboise, Ministre d'Estat de François Premier. Et parce-que ce Ministre étoit extrêmement habile, on disoit, en parlant des affaires publiques: laissez faire à *George*, il est homme d'âge, pour dire, qu'il s'en falloit rapporter à sa bonne conduitte, & à sa grande intelligence. (Furetière et al. 1771: IV, 483)

1821: *George, (laissez faire à) il est homme d'âge.*
On a tort de dire que ce proverbe a été fait pour le cardinal George d'Amboise, ministre d'état sous Louis XII. A la vérité ce prince lui est redevable du glorieux titre de *Père du peuple*. Le cardinal d'Amboise retrancha le dixième de tous les impôts, et les réduisit aux deux tiers. Sa prudence dans dispensation des derniers publics était si grande, que jamais il ne rétablit ce qu'il avait supprimé; mais comment trouver un homme d'âge dans George d'Amboise qui ne vécut que cinquante ans? (La Mesangère 1821: 207)

1826: *George*: *laissez faire à George, il est homme d'âge.* Ce proverbe est du temps du cardinal George d'Amboise, ministre d'état de Louis XII. Comme ce ministre était extrèmement habile, on disait en parlant des affaires publiques: *laissez faire à George, il est homme d'âge,* pour dire qu'il s'en fallait rapporter à sa bonne conduite et à sa grande intelligence. (Caillot 1826: 333)

1842: *Laissez faire à George, il est homme d'âge.*
Le cardinal Georges d'Amboise, ministre du roi Louis XII, avoit une grande autorité sur l'esprit de son maître. Lorsque l'on estoit embarassé sur quelques affaires importantes, ce cardinal avoit coutume de dire, parlant de luy-mesme: *laissez faire Georges, il est homme d'aage*; comme s'il eust voulu dire qu'il avoit assez d'expérience pour s'en tirer, parce que l'expérience est le fruit de l'aage. (Le Roux de Lincy 1842 [1996]: 471)

1842: *George.—Laissez faire à George, il est homme d'âge.*
On croit que ce proverbe est un mot que répétait souvent Louis XII, pour exprimer sa confiance dans l'habileté du cardinal George d'Amboise son ministre; non que ce ministre fût réellement un homme d'âge, puisqu'il mourut à cinquante ans, mais parce qu'il déployait dans l'administration des affaires publiques une expérience comparable à celle des plus sages vieillards. *Être homme d'âge* signifiait alors, être homme d'expérience. (Quitard 1842 [1968]: 423)

Basically all of the explanations of the proverb say the same, namely that Georges d'Amboise was indeed a very experienced administrator and that the reference to his age does not refer to longevity (he died at the age of fifty) but rather to his skills based on much experience. Of much interest and importance is the fact that French lexicographers and paremiographers stopped registering the proverb by the middle of the nineteenth century. I know of but one exception, namely Claude Duneton's massive *Le Bouquet des expressions imagées* (1990) that registers it as an historical proverb from the seventeenth century but says nothing about its survival in the modern age:

> XVII^c 1640 *laissez faire à Georges, c'est un homme d'âge*—proverbe fait du temps du cardinal "George" d'Amboise, ministre d'Etat: quand on parlait des affaires publiques, on disait: "laissez faire à George, c'est un homme d'âge": il s'en fallait rapporter à sa bonne conduite et à sa grande intelligence. (Duneton 1990: 228)

Besides this one reference, the proverb is absent from modern French proverb collections as well as mono- and bilingual (French and English) dictionaries. It also cannot be found in written or oral communication any longer, and it would appear that it never gained much currency in earlier times either—certainly nothing in comparison to the English "Let George do it" once it begins to appear at the end of the nineteenth century. This leads me to the informed conclusion that the French proverb had fallen out of use by the middle of the nineteenth century and most likely even earlier, with the paremiographers merely registering it as an historically interesting proverb but not one in actual use. I have also not found any sign of it in Quebecois or Louisiana French proverb collections or dictionaries, and so I doubt very much that it was brought to North America by immigrants.

I am also quite convinced that the French proverb did not make it to Great Britain. My major reasons for arguing against a loan translation into English are: 1. the French proverb had currency primarily in its long version of "Laissez faire à Georges, c'est un homme d'âge," with its specific reference to the experienced d'Amboise, and as such would have made little sense to someone outside of France; 2. the meaning of the French proverb is quite different from the English "Let George do it"—the French text suggests that one should or could hand over a difficult task to a more experienced person, and the English text refers to a situation where someone unwilling to take on a task is pushing it off to another person; and 3. the English proverb appears only around 1900, when the French proverb is long out of currency. There is then a definite historical, linguistic (long and short texts), and semantic difference that appears to support the argument for polygenesis.

Lexicographical and Paremiographical Insistence on a French-English Relationship

While my findings lead me to the likelihood of polygenesis—something that will become much clearer later on—numerous Anglo-American lexicographers and paremiographers cling to the idea that monogenesis is at play. They argue that the English proverb was translated from the French original, with W. Gurney Benham taking the lead in 1926, most likely taking his cue from H. L. Mencken's claim five years earlier in *The American Language*. Note, by the way, that Benham refers to the English text as an American proverb, thereby leaving out the possibility that the French proverb came to North America via Great Britain—something that would perhaps make some sense:

> *Let George do it.*—American saying, specially current during the war, 1914–1918. It means "Let the other fellow do it," and comes from the French.
> Laissez faire à George, il est l'homme d'âge.—Leave it to George, he is the man of years.—(Old Fr. saying, said to have been traced to the time of Louis XII (1498–1515.) (Benham 1926: 800b)

What follows is a florilegium of similar references with insistence on a French-English connection. This does not necessarily devalue such entries, which often include additional information of much use to the development of the English language proverb. All of this textual material and many other print and internet references will be of help in determining whether the proverb is, if not of French, then of British or American origin. Some of the following chronologically arranged paragraphs prove to be a bit repetitive, pointing to the lamentable fact that dictionary makers not only copy a lot from each other but also ignore new findings or neglect to do additional research. This is something that is changing; such modern quotation sleuths as Nigel Rees from Great Britain and Fred R. Shapiro from the United States make heavy use of the internet to verify and often correct dates of first occurrences of quotations and proverbs alike. But here now the revue of claims for the French origin of the proverb "Let George do it," with the first reference also bringing the significant variant "Leave it to George" into play. Some of them include references to contextualized citations I will not include here. They were all located in their original sources and will be presented in the next section:

1936: "*Let George do it*," or "*Leave it to George*" is another way of expressing buckpassing ["To pass the buck"]. A translation of *Laissez faire à Georges* (Georges d'Amboise, prime minister to Louis XII, c. 1500), the saying was revived in England in reference to [David] Lloyd George. At William College it was a venerable motto of an enterprising pants-presser. (Holt 1936: 47)

1947: *Let George do it.* (Laissez faire à Georges, il est l'homme d'âge.)
Louis XII of France. A satirical reference to his prime minister, Cardinal Georges d'Amboise. (c. 1500). Translated into modern slang as meaning, "Let the other fellow do it." (Stevenson 1947: 766)

1948: *Let George do it, he is the man of years.* (Laissez faire à George, il est l'homme d'âge.)
Louis XII of France, referring satirically to his prime minister, Cardinal Georges d'Amboise. (c. 1500). Translated into modern slang as meaning "Let the other fellow do it." [And quoting Archer Taylor from 1931, see above:] The traditional explanation in America is based on "George" as a name used in addressing Pullman porters. (Stevenson 1948: 946)

1949: *Let George do it, he is the man of the time.*
Louis XII of France (1462–1515)
[note 2:] *Laissez faire à Georges, il est homme d'âge.*—Referring to his prime minister, Cardinal Georges d'Amboise.
George McManus, American cartoonist, in his comic series, *Let George Do It*, popularized the saying in the early 1900s. (Bartlett 1949: 1218)

1968: *Let George do it.* [Louis XII of France (1462–1515)].
George = Georges d'Amboise (1460–1510), Cardinal, First Minister of State and Lieutenant-General of the Army, one of those incredible Renaissance figures who seemed able to do everything and to do it well.
Louis admired the Cardinal and trusted him, and he was well and faithfully served. But perfection is always slightly annoying and Louis's "Let George do it" was satirically intended. In its original form, it was: "Let George do it; he's the man of the Age." (Evans 1968: 268)

1970: *Let George do it.* Let someone else do it. Derived from Louis XII of France who, when an unpleasant task arose, was apt to say "Let George do it", referring to his minister, Cardinal Georges. (Brewer 1970: 457)

1970: *let George do it*! A journalistic catch phrase, dating from ca. 1910 and applied to the calling-in of an unnamed expert and putting the writer's own words into his mouth. Perhaps ex Fr. *Laissez faire à Georges*. (Partridge 1970: 1250)

1977: *let George do it*!—roughly. Let someone else do it! A journalistic catch phrase dating from c. 1910 and applied to the enlistment of an unnamed expert or authority and the putting of the writer's own words into his mouth, and probably, as HLM[encken] pointed out in 1922 [*sic*, 1921], deriving from the synonymous Fr. *laissez faire à Georges*, which goes back a long way, had an historical source, but 'later became common slang, was translated into English, had a revival during the early days of David Lloyd George's career, was adopted into American without any comprehension of either its first or its latest significance, and enjoyed the brief popularity of a year'. W[entworth] & F[lexner] pinpoint it to c. 1920 and note that it was popular during WW2, when it 'implied a lack of responsibility in helping the war effort': clearly the phrase was general enough during all the intervening US years. Moreover, as Professor John T. Fain wrote to me, on 25 April 1969, it 'can still be heard' in the US. In Britain, it had, by 1950, become very obsolete—and by 1970, I'd say, obsolete. (Partridge 1977: 135)

1985: *Let George Do It*. Who is the "George" of the expression "let George do it"?
This expression is believed to have originated in France in the fifteenth century in a satirical reference—*laissez faire à Georges*—to the many activities of Cardinal Georges d'Amboise, Archbishop of Rouen and Prime Minister of Louis XII. (Almond 1985: 151)

1994: *Let George do it*: Let someone—anyone—take the responsibility.
Coined at the French court as a derisory remark aimed at Louis XII who was given to passing the buck to Cardinal George, George d'Amboise (1460–1510). The original French "*Laissez faire à George*" became popular throughout France and eventually crossed the channel, reaching peak popularity at the beginning of this century, boosted by the advent of the automatic pilot which was nicknamed "George." (Donald 1994: 205)

2000: *Let George do it*. Let someone else do the work or take the responsibility. The expression is of US origin and dates from the turn of the 20th century. The source of the phrase is uncertain but it is possibly a learned adoption of the French *Laissez faire à Georges* in the same sense, where the reference is to Cardinal Georges d'Amboise (1460–1510), a church and government official under Louis XII responsible for major tax and judicial reforms. It was the English phrase that gave "George" as the colloquial term for an automatic pilot in an aircraft. (Brewer 2000: 397)

2001: *Let George Do It.*
If you want to push an unpleasant task upon somebody else, you might say, "Let George do it." The first to use this expression was no less than a king—Louis XII of France.

Louis XII's prime minister was Georges d'Amboise. He was both prime minister and the king's closest confidant, which gave him as much power as the king himself. Louis would not make a move unless it was approved of or urged by d'Amboise. Whenever the king was asked to do something, his reply was stock: "*Laissez faire à Georges,*" which roughly translates to "Let George do it."

So frequently did Louis use this phrase that the court attendants picked it up. Jokingly, at first, they would say "*Laissez faire à Georges*" whenever they wanted to shirk their duties. Through the courtiers, "*Laissez faire à Georges*" circulated throughout France. When it crossed the English Channel, it was translated into its English equivalent, "Let George do it." (Korach and Mordock 2001: 91)

Admittedly, there is a lot of valuable material here, and I should point out that it would not have been found by way of the internet! It is, to be sure, still important to go to books to find this type of information. The various references show how lexicographers and paremiographers cling to the idea that the French proverb "Laissez faire à Georges" must be the legitimate antecedent to the English proverb "Let George do it." To a certain degree these explanations follow or copy each other, but there is some new information mentioned, to wit the cartoonist George McManus's comic strip *Let George Do It*, the association of the proverb with the British statesman and prime minister David Lloyd George, the association of the proverb with African American Pullman train porters, and the fact that the proverb was used to refer to the automatic pilot of an airplane. All of these early-twentieth-century matters will be dealt with, but for now it must be observed that none of the informative paragraphs just cited explain how a French proverb that had long dropped out of use—if in fact it ever was very popular in France at all—crossed the English Channel at about the turn of the twentieth century? It would have had no associative meaning to English speakers, i.e., why George and how about this George being a man "of age" (experience) or of "the Age"? The French proverb had long become obsolete, and apparently it is Anglo-American lexicography and paremiography that is keeping the questionable connection alive. How "dead" the French proverb is can well be seen from a bilingual *Dictionary of French and American Slang* (1965), whose editors know the English proverb but have no idea of the old French version: "George—to let George do it.—laisser à un autre le soin d'accomplir une tâche ou une corvée" (Leitner and Landen 1965: 60). All of this strengthens my conjecture that the English proverb had its own origin, and that it was coined in the United States, from where it crossed the ocean to become current in England as well.

Lexicographical and Paremiographical Entries without a French Reference

With the prevalence of associating the English proverb with a French origin, one is surprised that some truly major dictionaries and proverb collections make no mention of this assumed French-English connection! After all, lexicographers and paremiographers do build on earlier reference works, and they must for the most part have been aware of this stubborn claim. Could one not have expected a statement to the effect that the supposed French source of the English proverb "Let George do it" is no longer viable? By not stating explicitly that they reject any French claim, I have no definite idea whether these colleagues agree with my conclusion of a separate origin of the English proverb. In any case, by only consulting the following publications, the serious scholar would remain utterly uninformed of an important part of the whole story, as it were. Of course, the major dictionaries and collections listed below—among them the print editions of the *Oxford English Dictionary*—include invaluable contextualized references from the twentieth century, starting with the year 1910, for the English proverb "Let George do it." Again I have located all of them, and since they will be dealt with in another section of this chapter, I shall not include them here. Instead, I will cite only the information that deals with the proverb in and of itself:

> 1951: *Let George do it*, let someone (or something) else do the work or take the responsibility. *Colloq.* or *slang*. (Mathews 1951: 690)

1970: Colloq. phr. *let George do it*: let someone else do the work or take the responsibility. orig. *U.S.* (Burchfield 1972: I, 1218; identical in Simpson and Weiner 1989: VI, 464)

1975: *let George do it* v. phr., informal. To expect someone else to do the work or take the responsibility.—A cliché. Compare "Pass the buck." (Boatner and Gates 1975: 203)

1975: *George do it, let*—Let someone else do it. Said in avoiding responsibility. Common c1920 and during W.W. II when the term implied a lack of responsibility in helping the war effort. (Wentworth and Flexner 1975: 212)

1980: *let George do it* Let someone else do the work or assume the responsibility; pass the buck. This American colloquial expression dates from the turn of the [19th/20th] century. *George* is a male generic term which derives from the Greek word for husbandman or farmer. By the 1920s this term was used by the British to refer to an airman, corresponding to *Jack* for a sailor (bluejacket) and *Tommy* for a soldier. *George* is also a British slang term for an automatic pilot in an aircraft or ship. (Urdang and LaRoche 1980: 202)

1989: Let *George* do it
[no explanation, just several historical references] (Whiting 1989: 250–51)

1993: *Let George do it* Find someone else do it; I won't. (Wilkinson 1993: 279)

1994: *let George do it* let someone else do the task. (Lighter 1994: I, 879)

1995: *let George do it!* meaning, 'let someone else do it, or take the responsibility,' this catchphrase was in use by 1910 and is probably of American origin. (Rees 1995: 121)

1997: *Let George do it.* Archer Taylor ([1931] p. 9) suggests that this expression may have originated as a vaudeville phrase. He notes that Pullman porters were frequently addressed as George. (Berman 1997: 157)

1997: *let George do it* let someone else do the work or take the responsibility. (Knowles 1997: 353)

2006: *Let George do it*. Anon. referring to the universal nickname of Pullman attendants, who attended to the passengers' every wish; probably from the name of the founder of the company, George Mortimer Pullman. Eric Partridge, in his *Dictionary of Catchphrases*, does not make the connection with Pullman. One wonders if the expression led to the adoption of "George" as the nickname for automatic aircraft pilots. (Dow 2006: 168)

2012: *let George do it!* on the railways, used as a humorous attempt to delegate an unpleasant task *US*. Pullman porters, low men on the food chain for railway workers, were known as George. (Dalzell and Victor 2012: 1201)

2012: Let *George* do it.
[no explanation, but we included it in a list of proverbs that we judged (erroneously?) as being older than the year 1900] (Doyle, Mieder, and Shapiro 2012: 288)

All of these references imply or state directly that the proverb "Let George do it" is of English or more likely of American origin. This is also true for my friend Nigel Rees, the ingenious phraseological sleuth from London. In one of his more recent comprehensive volumes on phrase origins, he does come in on an American origin of the phrase, even though he mentions the French-origin argument once again:

2006: *let George do it!* Meaning 'let someone else do it, or take the responsibility', this catchphrase was in use by the 1900s and is probably of American origin. It appears on a screen title in *Gertie the Dinosaur*, one of the first movie cartoons (US 1909). A bet is placed in an archaeological museum that a dinosaur cannot be made to move. When it does so, a celebratory dinner is held. The question then is, who will pay? 'Let George do it' is the reply. It seems unlikely that this was the origin of the phrase—merely one of the uses that popularized it. Indeed, H. L. Mencken, *The American Language* (1922 [i.e., 1921]), traces it back to the French *laissez faire à Georges*. The phrase received a new lease of life with the invention of the autopilot in the Second World War. Inevitably, the autopilot was dubbed 'George'. (Rees 2006: 407)

And this almost definitely American origin is now being upheld by the up-to-date electronic version of the *Oxford English Dictionary* as accessed on November 29, 2012:

N. Amer. colloq. *let George do it*: let someone else do the work or take the responsibility.

[Origin unknown.

It has frequently been suggested (e.g. by H. L. Mencken *Amer. Lang.* (1921) xi.) that the phrase is after French *laissez faire à Georges*, said to have been used by King Louis XII (1462–1515, king from 1498) with reference to his prime minister Cardinal Georges d'Amboise (1460–1510), to whom he entrusted much of the day-to-day running of the country. However, this French phrase is apparently not attested before 1805 (in L.-P. Anquetil *Hist. de France* V. 376, which may have been the first source to attribute its use to King Louis XII), although a variant *laisser faire à George, c'est un homme d'âge* is found earlier (1690; apparently last recorded in *Dict. de Trevoux* (1771)). Regardless of the origin of the French phrase, it is very uncertain whether there is any link with the English phrase, since the French phrase (in any form) appears to have been very rare by the date of the first attestation of the English phrase.] (www.oed.com)

This incredibly valuable explanatory discussion precedes the earliest reference dated 1909 found by the staff of the *Oxford English Dictionary* thus far. As will become obvious shortly, I can say with a bit of scholarly delight that I cannot only push this date back by seven years to 1902, and I have already shown in a previous section of this chapter that the registration of the French proverb begins at least in 1656 (thirty-four years earlier than 1690) and was recorded at least until 1842 (seventy-one years later than what the OED has found). But never mind this expansion of dates! The key issue is that the editors of the *Oxford English Dictionary* agree with me that the proverb "Let George do it" is most likely and perhaps definitely of American origin and is not related historically to the French proverb. This does indeed strengthen my claim that all of this is a case of polygenesis, as will now become ever more clear by way of my discussion of numerous contextualized examples.

The Pullman Porters and the Beginnings of the American Proverb "Let George do it"

It is my belief that it is appropriate for a scholar to stick out his proverbial neck on certain occasions. This is one of those cases, for I am convinced that the proverb "let George do it" must have been current before 1900. Sure enough, the earliest printed reference thus far (that my friend Charles C. Doyle found) stems from 1902, but that basically presupposes that the proverb was in oral use before then. This up-to-now earliest reference from an anonymous superintendent on the "Characteristics of Superintendents and Workmen" makes it clear that the proverb must have been known, for otherwise the occurrence of the name "George" would be senseless:

> I believe about the most aggravating person to come in contact with is the one who, when asked to do a certain kind of work, to which he is not used, will say, "Well, I've never done that before, hadn't you better let George do it!" About this time you want to get out your lecture on self-reliance and con- fidence and deliver it to that man in such a way that he will not only do the work, but later, in thinking it over, will really feel proud of the fact that he can do something new. (Superintendent 1902: 15–16)

In fact, Doyle also drew my attention to the fact that the variant "Leave it to George," with the same meaning of pushing a job off to someone else, was current in the latter part of the nineteenth century, referring me to a short article about the early Quaker George Fox (1624–1691) published anony- mously by the "London Society" on September 26, 1886, in the *New York Times*: "Although he [George Fox] was so highly esteemed that when dif- ficult matters arose at the general meetings of the [Quaker] society they were usually shelved with the remark they 'would leave it to George,' individual members who thought he erred did not scruple to tell him so to his face" (London Society 1886: 11). Yes, Mr. Fox does have "George" as his first name, but I agree with Doyle's comment to me in a letter of November 27, 2012, that included this important reference: "'I believe 'Leave it to George' is an authentic variant (I have a clear instance from 1915). In the 1886 article at- tached, the subject is the early Quaker George Fox—but what's interesting is the enclosure of the phrase 'would leave it to George' in quotation marks, as if the writer is playfully adapting the proverb to the account of the historical figure." In any case, the lexicographer Alfred Holt, it will be recalled from an earlier section of this chapter, also felt that "Let George do it" and "Leave it to George" are two sides of the same proverbial coin (Holt 1936: 47).

And now comes the $64,000 question, to put it proverbially: Who is this George of the English proverb if not Georges d'Amboise of the much earlier French text? The answer has actually already been alluded to by a number of the lexicographical and paremiographical references cited above. The "George" of the American proverb is the generic name that was given to African American men who were hired by George Pullman after the Civil War as cheap porters in his famous Pullman sleeping cars. There is plenty of documentation to this stereotypical and degrading name calling, and it took courageous and powerful labor leaders like Phillip Randolph, the African American founder of the Brotherhood of Sleeping Car Porters, to overcome this infuriating and un-called-for custom. All of this has been brought to life by the film *10,000 Black Men Named George* (2001) that documents how Randolph formed the first black-controlled union in support of the black porters who summarily were called "George" after George Pullman, the railroad entrepreneur who decided to employ emancipated slaves:

> At one time traveling salesmen considered it the acme of wit to call Pullman porters "George," presumably after the paternal founder himself. No one knows precisely when or why Pullman decided that porters must be men of the Negro race; but, for close to a century all porters in the United States have been Negroes. The first was probably a well-trained ex-slave, hired about 1867. Nameless in history, he filled his positions so capably that he established an exclusive field of employment for thousands of other black men, who gained education, mobility, and social status by working for the railroad. (Reinhardt 1970: 298)

True, African American porters were able to carve out a livelihood for themselves and their families, but they were clearly exploited by demanding travel schedules and low pay, resulting in the eventual formation of the "Brotherhood" union. But travelers clearly depended on the services of the porters, and one wonders why they would have been so condescending as to de-individualize the porters into anonymous Georges! After all, the porters performed a multitude of services to assure a pleasant trip for the Pullman passengers, performing their tasks to such perfection that "In the Pullman Parlor Car of the 1880s, the saying was: 'Let George do it'" (Reinhardt 1970: 304). This statement appears as the caption of a picture of the exquisite interior of one of these Pullman cars, but alas, I have not been able to locate any instances of the proverb in the impressive literature dealing with the Pullman porters that actually quote the proverb from the last quarter of the nineteenth century! Most of the extant literature deals only with the name "George." In fact, Jervis Anderson entitles an entire chapter "George" in his book *A. Philip Randolph: A Biographical Portrait* (1972), indicating how insulting this generalized naming was to the porters:

> "Then, too," a porter from Jacksonville recalls, "there was this thing of 'George.' No matter who you were, or how old, most everybody wanted to call you

'George.' It meant that you were just George Pullman's boy, same as in slave days when if the owner was called Jones the slave was called Jones. It got so you were scared to go into the office to pick up your check, for fear some little sixteen-year-old office boy would yell out 'George.'" (Anderson 1972: 163)

This obsession with "George"-calling went so far that, irony of irony, white men with the name George felt insulted by this widespread use of the name for black porters! And here is the result of their frustration, as it has been described in a number of accounts:

"This thing of 'George,'" however, infuriated quite a few passengers—mainly those who answered, legitimately, to the name George. They were tired of looking up suddenly from their newspapers or cups of coffee only to find that it was not *they* whom their neighbors wanted, but "George." One of them, a Chicago lumber merchant named George W. Delaney, decided to do something about it—though apparently more in fun than anger. In 1916, he launched an anti-"George" campaign by forming the Society for the Prevention of Calling Sleeping Car Porters George. In later years, the society's letterhead would carry such names as Senator [Walter] George, of Georgia; George Arliss; George Ade; George M. Cohan; George Cardinal Mundelein; King George V; Georges Carpentier; George B. Cortelyou; King George of Greece; and the "Babe," of the New York Yankees. The society's patron saints were the first president of the United States and the builder of the "Pioneer" [a newspaper founded by George Allen in 1865]. By 1941, George Delaney claimed a membership of 33,000 Georges, after which nothing more was heard of his society. It probably exploded from an excess of frivolity. (Anderson 1972: 163–64; see also Harshberger 1932: 70; Kersten 2007: 28)

But enough of this absurdity! Jack Santino, in his richly documented book *Miles of Smiles, Years of Struggle: Stories of Black Pullman Porters* (1989), cites a drama-like song from 1923 that testifies to the demands that were incessantly placed on the porters:

> Porter, come here, sir,
> Porter, stay there,
> Porter, the pillow is as hard as a rock,
> Porter, please give me more air.
> Porter, come here, sir,
> Porter, stay there.

All night the people complain.
We is porters, dandy porters,
and we ride on the vestibule train.
(Santino 1989: 120)

Santino's book contains numerous interviews with former black porters that illustrate how the generic name "George" rendered them anonymous and subservient to the white passengers. He summarizes his findings in a powerful statement:

> The epithet "George," by which they [the porters] were known generally, did much to create and maintain the stereotypes. The term was associated with the days of slavery, because it identified porters as the property of George Pullman, with all the associated ramifications of inferiority and childlike dependency. As such, A. Philip Randolph insisted there be porters' name cards in each Pullman car, and he recognized that this symbolic change altering the term of address was as important as the more tangible improvements that increased pay and lessened hours. "George" is in many ways the sum total of the stereotype, and porters tried their best to ignore it. (Santino 1989: 125–26)

This change took effect on October 19, 1926, when the Pullman Company officially "announced that thereafter all Pullman cars would have the active porter's name displayed in a prominent place so that the passengers would know how to address him when he was needed. The company instructed porters that they were to answer only to their own names, and that Pullman would take no disciplinary actions against them for refusing to respond to "George" (Harris 1977: 83–84).

The African American labor leader and civil rights champion A. Philip Randolph deserves most of the credit for having freed the large number of black porters from their modern enslavement. He brought an end to "the time when all Pullman porters were indiscriminately called 'George,' [and] he brought them the respect of the traveling public and confidence in themselves. The value of the union, in Randolph's opinion, lay in its demonstration that blacks indeed possessed a 'spirit of self-help, self-initiative, and self-reliance'" (Pfeffer 1990: 31). It took decades to bring this change about, and with all the "George" name-calling that went on it should not be surprising that the proverb "Let George do it" sprang up in the last decades of the nineteenth century. Clearly Patricia and Fredrick McKissack must agree with this conjecture, since they employed the proverb as a chapter heading in their book *A Long Hard Journey: The Story of the Pullman Porter* (1989). The time was ripe for it, and I am thoroughly convinced that the proverb "Let George do it" was current in the United States before 1900 and that it came from the questionable treatment that the black Pullman porters received from their white passengers. It is almost inconceivable to me that I have not been able to find it in the many printed and online accounts that I have checked in this regard, but, as the proverb states, "Hope springs eternal!"

From a Stereotypical Phrase to a General Proverb

While the stereotypical comment "Let George do it" had its inauspicious beginnings on the Pullman trains, it soon became a generally accepted proverb without being directed in a racially malevolent way against black porters. In other words, the name "George" lost its unfortunate association with George Pullman and his African American porters and took on the meaning of any male person at all. This is already the case in the reference from 1902 cited in the previous section, and it is certainly also true for the proverb's appearance in Frank C. Hasse's short pro-union article "Think It Over" from 1909:

> Be a union man by name and action. Join hands with your neighbor. Go to the meetings; take an active part as you do in your home; pay your dues and don't be a mollycoddle and think: "Oh, well, let George do it." Nothing can be gained in that manner. Put your shoulder to the wheel. It may be hard to start, but if we have enough [union members] how easy it will be, and so easy to keep rolling that it will be a pride to think: "I helped do it." Therefore I say: If a union man, remain one; if not, become one. (Hasse 1909: 476)

By the year 1909 the generalized and innocuous proverb "Let George do it" appears to be well established in American parlance and the print media, which is not to say that it dropped out of use as a stereotypical and condescending phrase toward the black Pullman porters. In any case, in 2005 my friend Fred R. Shapiro supplied me with what seems to be the first occurrence of the early comic strip *Let George Do It*, by the American cartoonist George McManus (1884–1954), that appeared on the "Amusements" page of the *Columbus Evening Dispatch* of June 29, 1909. In three frames a fellow asks other men to lend him five dollars, but they all put him off by saying he should come back in an hour. In the fourth frame our fellow confronts all three of them together, but they respond by saying "Oh! Let George do it!" That "George" actually is a kind little man standing next to them who simply responds with a perplexed "Hum?" The final frame shows this man handing the fellow a five-dollar bill with the statement "And George did" accompanying his generous action (Newspaperarchive.com). McManus published a series of *Let George Do It* comics during the following two to three years, and it is to be assumed that his own first name "George" had something to do with the proverbial title. Commenting on the good humor of these comic strips (including an example on 292), Amos Stote states in 1910:

> McManus has succeeded in creating a clever burlesque on conditions and traits with which we are all familiar, and giving us plenty of fun with it all. It goes to show that he can pick a droll situation out of any hour of the day and make us good natured during those which are left. There are so many things we want to let George do—and that we should do ourselves, that the knowledge of George doing it for some one else helps to lighten the burden along the way—though we really would like to know the address of the obliging young man. (Stote 1910: 293)

George McManus's *Let George Do It* comics are dealing in good humor with all-too-human everyday trials and tribulations, and there are no racial undertones to be found in them. This is also the case with one of the first animated cartoon films ,created by Winsor McCay in 1909 after having made a bet with his friend McManus that he could bring a dinosaur alive on the screen by a multitude of rapidly shown drawings. The film's first version of 1909, with the title *Gertie the Dinosaur* (Davenport, Iowa: Blackhawk Films), was a major success, with another release following in 1914. The silent films contain a number of written screen titles, and when at the end a celebratory dinner for having brought Gertie to life is to be held, the question "Who pays for the dinner?" with the answer "Let George do it!" appears on the screen. Clearly this was an ingenious allusion to the bet McCay had made with McManus, but it also indicates how well known the proverb "Let George do it" had become, with the extremely popular twelve-minute film doing its part to spread it around.

But there is yet a third item from 1909 that helped to popularize the proverb nationwide without any disrespect for the Pullman porters. It is the vaudeville song "Let George Do It" with words by Ray Zirkel and music by Bill Carney:

> Some folks are born to do great things and some to do the small,
> But I get done by ev'ry one, it don't seem right at all.

If some one's got a job that's good I'm forty miles away,
But find a job that no one wants, I'm always in the way.

Let George do it! I hear somebody say
Let George do it! That's always the way.
When some one's it, you'll always note,
it's "give it to George, for he's the goat."

There's no one gets the worst of it like Georgie.

I used to be a single man, as happy as could be,
I always told my married friends "no wedding bells for me."
I went to see a wedding once, they said the Bridegroom fled,
His cross-eyed bride then cried aloud: Who'll marry me instead?

Let George do it! I heard somebody say
Let George do it! That always is the way.
When wed your trouble just begins
and mine came double for we got twins.

There's no one gets the worst of it like Georgie.
(Zirkel and Carney 1909: 2–4)

With vaudeville songs like this (there is also Edgar Leslie and Al. Piantidosi's song "Let Georgie Do It" from 1910), the comic strips by George McManus, and Winsor McCay's film, everything was set for the proverb to conquer the American stage without any association to the Pullman porters, unless this little piece from a list of "Railway Paint Shop Gossip" from June 1913 is a slanderous allusion to their enforced subservience: "Master Painter John D. Wright is 'coming back' with a sort of 'let George do it' smile in anticipation of an order for seventy-two passenger cars, which his company has arranged to place" (*Painters Magazine* 40: 464). After 1909 the proverb appears with considerable frequency in various literary and media contexts, of which the following references might serve as examples:

1910: Were I a member of the legislature in this state [Oregon] and some kind friend should come out of a corporation law office and request me to father any of these schemes, I should gently request him to "Let George do it" especially if I were enamoured of a public career. (King 1910: 15)

1911: Our political acrobat [William Randolph Hearst] has sought to be a Mayor, Governor and President. Occasionally, when utterly worn out running for office, he mutters "Let George do it," and produces a city editor as candidate for Sheriff, or a private counsel for Governor or Judge. (*New York Times*, November 11: 9)

This early motivational text, from George Matthew Adams's self-help book *You Can: A Collection of Brief Talks on [. . .] Your Success* (1913), shows the inappropiateness of the "Let George do it" philosophy of pushing tasks off on others and avoiding responsible action oneself:

1913: *The "George" Habit*
If you only realized how much you miss Pleasure, Growth and increased Power every time you push Responsibility upon someone else, you would never again let a chance pass to do what comes to you to do.

Once for all, break the "Let George Do It" habit. When a task steps up before you—take hold of it and do it Yourself.

In every community—in this community—there are always big, ready, generous, willing people quick to respond to any call for Service at the moment someone else shirks. They are the "Georges." And if you will let them perform your work, they will do it. But when they do—you move backward. YOU—be a "George."

Work that should be done by Yourself is never done so well when shifted to someone else.

You are either a Do or a Let Do. It is a personal matter of Success or Failure as to which you are.

The "Let George Do It" folks are easily spotted. They line the sidewalks of very busy streets. They do the "easy" jobs in the Stores and Factories. They are the fellows that board at Jails and Alms Houses and keep the Lawyers busy. They are the men and women that are "too busy" to do what is asked and required of them to do.

Don't "Let George Do It." Do it YOURSELF.
(Adams 1913: 109)

And here is a little satirical story about "Poor Little Eddie" (1916) by William McNutt that also points out that the wisdom of "Let George do it" is flawed if one wants to get ahead in life. This negative reaction to the proverb makes sense once it is realized that one must face one's own tasks and that there will not always be Pullman porters around to do the chores:

1916: Be helpless—that's what wins. Be a harmless, wide-eyed boob, and you won't have to rise early to get the money. No! All you have to do is lie in bed and wait for some sympathetic money person to bring you plenty on a tray.

Let George do it—that's the idea. If you can't, there's always some George that will. Sure!

Of course, helpless stupidity is like every other accomplishment—you've got to be perfect to get the best results. You can't expect to have a silver spoon rammed down your throat if you're capable of guiding it to your lips by your own efforts. Oh, no! Nobody drops pennies into a cup held by a man owning one perfectly good eye. A blind man must be totally so to go into business for himself. (McNutt 1916: 37)

It is impossible to comment on every revealing use of the proverb, but let it be said summarily that most of the following references question the wisdom of the proverb "Let George do it," albeit with the understanding that the attitude of pushing tasks and responsibilities off on others does, unfortunately, prevail in human interactions:

1918: *Let the Government Do It*
Under their new national impulse Americans must not lose consciousness of community responsibility. State rights may well go by the board; but state, city and village duties must not be forgotten. "Let the Government do it," must not be the excuse for communities to shirk the performance of functions which are clearly theirs. "Let the Government do it," must not become synonymous with the slacker's willingness to "let George do it." (*Rotarian* 13, no. 5 [November]: 209)

1919: *"Let George Do It"*
Under the subject of "Let George Do It" I wish to say that an executive is a man who obtains results through efforts of others. Your job is, then, in a sense, to "let George do it." Every once in a while something goes wrong and some fellow will come to me and say, "If I am to get that thing done right I have got to do it myself." That idea is contrary to the principles of executive work. When a man gets an idea that, in order to get something done right, he has to do it himself, he is a long way off the road leading to his success as an executive.

Your principal business is to so control the work of others as to get equally as good results as you would if you yourselves were doing the work. That is why we employ you as executives, because we believe you have the ability to get work out of others, the ability to "let George do it." (Anonymous 1919: 397–98)

1920: *"Let George Do It"*
"Let George do it." We are all familiar with the phrase. It's another way of saying: "Let someone else do it," or "I hope someone else will do it."

It's another way of shirking duty, a responsibility, or any act which we should do ourselves. "Let George do it" is a sort of hopeless hope, because we know down in our hearts that George isn't going to do it well, if at all.

This principle is detrimental to a business, and ofttimes letting "George do it" spells ruin to it.

It's all right to "Let George do it" if he is the right sort of a George. But be sure he is. The wrong sort is going to hurt you. You had better do the job yourself.

[...]

Don't have any careless "Georges" in your shop, office, or in any department. They are building ill will. (Sills 1920: 25)

1921: *The Art of Getting Out of It*
"Let George do it" is another bit of slang invented by this [alimentative] type. He seldom does anything he really hates to do. He is so likable he either induces you to let him out of it or gets somebody to do it for him. He just naturally avoids everything that is intense, difficult or strenuous. (Benedict and Benedict 1921: 69–70)

1921: *"Let George Do It."*
There is an old theory that a large part of our leadership consists of getting other people to work. That may be sound, but it does not mean that other people can do my work without loss to me. [. . .] It is the willing and able person who pulls the load in every community. There is not a church, lodge or other community enterprise that would be worth attending if five per cent of its aggressive membership were removed. We let George do it and criticize him because he tries to run things. (Carothers 1921: 15–16)

1927: Dr. Ella A. Boole, National President of the Women's Christian Temperance Union, speaking at the annual Tristate Conference of the organization here today, said that the enforcement of the prohibition law was being retarded by a spirit of "let George do it." (*New York Times*, July 20: 26)

1931: "That's right," said Asey contemptuously. "Pass the buck. Let George do it."
(Taylor 1931: 276)

Do note the use of the equivalent phrase "pass the buck" in this last example. By this time the use of the proverb "Let George do it" had become so prevalent that the linguist Josephine Burnham registered the neologism "let-George-do-it-itis" (1927: 245), referring to the proverb's excessive employment. Little wonder that Ogden Nash wrote his lengthy satirical poem about that proverbial George in 1935 with such lines as:

> *Let George Do It, If You Can Find Him*
> [...]
> George! George! Where are you, George?
> Come out from under the sofa, George!
> I thought you were braver, George!
> I'm doing you a favor, George!
> You can use my desk,
> And sit in my chair,
> Snugly away
> From the nasty air.
> [...]
> George! You softie, where are you?
> (Nash 1981: 21–22)

Two very widely seen British movies, *Let George Do It* (1938 by British Empire Films), starring the stage comedian George Wallace, and *Let George Do It* (1940 by EMI), with famed stars George Formby and Phyllis Calvert, helped establish the proverb in Great Britain as well, although it was already in use earlier in the twentieth century with reference to David Lloyd George. Mention should also be made of the *Let George Do It* radio drama series that was produced from 1946 to 1954.

No surprise, then, that the proverb also began to appear in advertisements, as for example: "It is a duty to trap Beetles. Where would our gardens be today if ye [*sic*] all said "let George do it"? You can buy the G&O new patented Japanese Beetle Trap in practically every town" (*New York Times*, July 14, 1940: 42) and "Let George Do It—Saving and the future are two words that Charlie has forgotten all about. Don't forget, though, it's the Georges who are saving money now who'll be in the driver's seat when it's all over" (Savings Bank of New York; *New York Times*, August 5, 1943: 10). This reminds me of my undergraduate alma mater, Olivet College in Michigan, which tried to lure alumni into donating money with the fact that the philosophy of "Let George do it" will not do because "George can't do it alone any more" (brochure from spring 1976). And of course, if you happen to be the president of the First New York Option Advisors with the name George M. Spadaro, it makes perfect sense to publish a large ad with the proverbial slogan: "You Don't Have to Be an Expert to Take Advantage of Options. Let George Do It" (*New York Times*, May 23, 1976: F11). And finally, who would ever have expected that the English proverb was translated into Latin as "Faciat Georgius" and inscribed as the motto on a 1943 medal commemorating the valiant struggle of U.S. Marines on Guadalcanal (Camp 2002: no pp.)?

Clearly the first half of the twentieth century is replete with various types of occurrences of the proverb "Let George do it" with its meaning being rather ambivalent. On the one hand its wisdom is considered to be ill-advised, and on the other references show that it can be interpreted positively in certain contexts. As is true for most proverbs, their meaning depends on their contextualized use, with this polysituativity resulting in polyfunctionality and polysemanticity (Mieder 2004: 9).

Modern Survival of the Seemingly Dated Proverb "Let George Do It"

With this set of examples from the second half of the twentieth century and beyond, I would like to dispel the notion that the proverb has become obsolete. The linguist Eric Partridge, for one, felt that the proverb has disappeared (see in a previous section), and when I have undertaken my own field research among friends, colleagues, and students, I have often received the answer that they have never heard of "Let George do it." And yet, when I arrived in the United States in 1960 as a high school student in Detroit, I recall vividly that I heard and learned the proverb quite quickly. It often was used jocularly in oral communication in my American home, especially since my wonderful American dad and brother were both called George Schumm! When one checks in Google for "Let George do it" or "Leave it to George" millions of modern hits occur, and the proverb is surely not extinct in the modern age. Fortunately its racial beginnings are gone and forgotten, something that becomes wonderfully clear from the popular African American heavyweight boxer George Foreman's delightful children's book *Let George Do It!* (2005). He certainly would not have given his book this title, if he saw any lingering anti-black stereotype in it, nor would the prestigious Simon & Schuster have published it for children! It is well known that George Foreman (Big George) named all of his five sons "George," and in the humorously illustrated book Foreman offers some funny insights into his family, where the proverb "Let George do it" exhibits a universal applicability. This book remains quite popular, and it surely did its part in keeping the proverb alive. In any case, there is one thing that I have learned over the years when asking native speakers whether they are aware of a certain proverb. They are often surprisingly quick in responding negatively, but upon further probing, it frequently becomes clear that they simply find it difficult to recall proverbs without contexts.

Be that as it may, let me begin a list of modern references with a statement that President Harry S. Truman made at a press conference on August 7, 1952. Being asked by a journalist why there might be such low voter interest in the upcoming national election, Truman recounted what he thought was going through people's minds: "Laziness and indifference. They think 'George' will do it. 'It will be all right, anyway. You don't need me. I would rather go on vacation, if I have the day off, than go and vote'" (Truman 1966: 510; Mieder and Bryan 1997: 133). Here "George" represents a large part of the American electorate, and it is to that portion of the population that John Foster directed his book *Let George Do It!* (1957) with its basic proverbial message: "Politics is your business. Don't Let George Do It" (1957: 185). But here are some additional occurrences in the media and literature of modern times:

1960: Investors are giving increasing evidence of abandoning the motto, "Let George do it," and shifting to a new one, "Do it yourself." (*New York Times*, January 17: F1)

1961: *Letting George Do It*
"Let George do it" may be human nature, but it is scarcely the stuff of patriotism. And if every Reservist or Guardsman were to take this attitude the nation might just as well eliminate the entire Guard and Reserve structure. (*New York Times*, November 30: 36)

1966: What he thinks is wrong he fights to destroy. He can't pass by a wrong or an injustice without fighting it any more than he can pass by the sick, or the wounded, or the helpless without lending an extraordinarily gentle hand. I don't think Jericho has ever heard the phrase, "Let George do it." (Pentecost 1966: 5)

1976: We, and our organizations, tend to settle for less than we are and could be. We deflect, we abrogate, we compromise, we assign to committee, we capitulate, and we "let George do it." Fortunately, just as we've learned these lessons well, so can we unlearn them for better. (Maidment 1976: 14)

1982: *"Let George Do It"*
The saying "let George do it" usually connotes an attitude of negligence and irresponsibility on the part of the speaker. Naturally, I would never be guilty of any such sins. No, the "George" I have in mind is not just "any old George" but an organization [the British Library Lending Division] specifically mandated, designed and stocked to act as an extension or back-up collection of libraries and therefore able to provide the loan service with maximum effectiveness. (Rothstein 1982: 108)

1990: *Let George Do It*
"Let George do it!" they used to say, when I was still little. Anything that really ought to be done, that you didn't have time for, or didn't know how to do, was a candidate for George. He was the one who would pick up the trash on the side of the highway. He would worry about corruption in government and chuck holes in the pavement. Whatever it was, we just said, "let George do it."

Now that I'm grown up, and rapidly approaching my 50s, I realize, more and more, that people are still depending on George. The trouble is, George isn't going to do it today any more than he was going to do it when I was a kid.

I guess that's why I keep writing letters to the editor about water fluoridation, and why others write about things they know ought to be fixed. We know George won't do it for us. (Sherell 1990: no pp.)

1996: Control is essential in the team management environment. An eye must be kept on the bottom line and on project timetables. The tendency to "let George do it" in the team management environment is a real danger. The team leader has a responsibility to ensure that the "it's everybody's responsibility and no one's" mentality does not pervade the team management environment. (Baldwin and Migneault 1996: 43)

2004: There was an old cliche [*sic*] we kids, especially the boys, would always say when asked to do something.

"Let George do it," was always the reply. When George started coming around there was that inevitable remark to a chore. "Let George do it."

George looked around surprised and got up and did it the first time he heard it. We all laughed and explained. But even after our explanation of the meaning, George insisted on doing things. I cautioned him, "You're always going to have to do things for everybody."

George said "I don't mind."

Many times after that initial episode he continued doing things when one of us said, "Let George do it!" This went on for years long after we were married. (Massing 2004: 63)

2006: There are those of us who will do things, so others can benefit and those that benefit the most are usually those who will not do things for others. They are the ones who think, "Let George do it." My theory is if it's left up to George, it will never get done. There is an adage that is something like, "What you do when you don't have to will determine what you will be when you can no longer help it." I do not know who said this originally, but it makes good sense. (Kirkpatrick 2006: 388)

2009: Finally, we may note that people often do understand the logic of collective action, perhaps especially in relatively local contexts in which the cooperative contributions would be costly and readily perceived. The slogan "Let George do it" is grounded in a recognition of the logic. It may have taken a very substantial level of proselytizing to get people not to see that logic in the case of voting, although the proselytizers may themselves have been led to believe in their own preachment. (Hardin 2009: 76)

2010: *Let George Do It*
Coming from the early 1900's, the slogan "Let George Do It" has now been applied to the federal government as well as to the national psyche. Let the government pay for the retirement, let the government pay for health care, let the government feed the poor, let the government pay the unemployed, and let the government keep our food and water safe. And let's not forget highway and transportation safety. Besides the obvious fact of who's going to pay for all of this, there is a more serious issue, one that is deviously dangerous.

There is, it seems to me, to be an inherent danger in excessive reliance upon government authority, upon the government to do everything. When it does, apathy sets in. Apathy is easy, isn't it? Creativity, innovation, and personal ingenuity go out the window. It's so much easier to let George do it. (Wilson 2010: no pp.)

Regarding this last reference, it should be noted that in 1943 Frederick R. Barkley of the *New York Times* had argued against this attitude of letting the government take care of everything: "The only way to avoid the 'let George do it' attitude is to put the equal obligation of service on every one" (*New York Times*, March 19: 1). Employing the proverb as an adjectival phrase preceding the word "attitude" is quite widespread, as can be seen from these citations:

1954: The United States had at last decided not to wait any longer for private industry, with its puzzling "let George do it" attitude, to play its part, but to begin construction of a multi-million dollar nuclear reactor for the large-scale generation of electricity. (*New York Times*, January 4: 49)

1970: He said the main trouble with our society was the let-George-do-it attitude. If more people acted like him, then we'd have a better society. No incompetence, no indifference, no crime in the streets. (Lathen 1970: 161)

1989: Policymakers worry about how to stretch the public dollar as far as they can before resorting to unpopular increases in taxes. But social analysts worry about the potentially deeper problem—the "let George do it" attitude that comes with big government. (Wuthnow 1989: xiii)

But speaking of government, here are three final adjectival uses of the proverb relating to politics in Canada and the United States, where too many citizens want government to take care of matters for them:

1998: The referendum scare jolted the English [speaking] community [of Quebec] out of what he [Keith Henderson] calls the ingrained "let-George-do-it" political culture. (Bauch 1998: B2)

2002: Today, having watched my country [Canada] slowly but steadily change from a pre–Second World War frontier mentality with "cando" attitude into what can only be called a "let George do it" nation in visible decline, I can readily understand the unease felt by these Montana farm folk transplanted to pogey-land. (Sangster 2002: 9)

2009: The need for aggressive marketing by interest groups suggests that getting people who sympathize with a group's goals to support the group with contributions is difficult. Economists call this difficulty the *free-rider problem*, but we might call it, more colloquially, the "let-George-do-it" problem. (Janda, Berry, and Goldman 2009: 195)

All of these references leave no doubt that the proverb "Let George do it" is alive and well today, even if there are voices that claim never to have come across it. The last example even illustrates how three university professors look at the proverb as a colloquial phrase that might add some clarity to their explanation of economic issues. Clearly they assume that their readers will be acquainted with the proverb's meaning, and since it expresses the widespread no-caring and irresponsible attitudes of unconcerned and uninvolved citizens so well, it is cited as a most fitting metaphor. What is needed are clearly "let-George-do-it-himselfers" (Anonymous 1954: 7), as an editorial states it with a fitting mutation of the old proverb.

"Let George Do It" and Its Connections with Various Georges

This last section—on numerous well-known persons named George and their almost expected association with the "Let George do it" proverb—will quite unexpectedly begin with two machines. With a bit of scholarly pride I can report a reference that connects the name "George" and the proverb with the operation of a motor-driven movie projector. What is fascinating is that the citation is from 1912, indicating that the proverb was already well known:

> Motor driven machines are allowed in some cities, under certain restrictions, and are not allowed at all in others. The objection to the motor-drive is the temptation for the operator to "let George do it," the motor representing "George." The place for the operator is beside the machine, with his eye glued to the picture on the screen every instant the machine is running. The argument for compelling the operator to run his projector by hand is that he is obliged to remain right there, where he belongs. With a motor drive he usually does not remain constantly beside the machine, ready for instant action should anything in the way of film or machine trouble occur. (Richardson 1912: 366)

But there is a much more important and internationally used machine or instrument called "George," namely the automatic pilot of ships and airplanes that was developed as early as 1913 (Urdang and LaRoche 1980: 202; Donald 1994: 143; Rees 2006: 407). Here is what Jefferson M. Koonce has to say in his *Human Factors in the Training of Pilots* (2002) about this important invention:

Let George do it
Pilots often refer to the autopilot as "George" and one often hears the saying of "Let George do it," when engaging the autopilot. How did the term "George" get applied to the autopilot? Early autopilots, like the current autopilots, utilized gyroscopes to provide stable reference inputs to the system. Thus they were called gyroscopic systems and abbreviated as "G-systems." In those early days, the phonetic alphabet term for the letter G was "George" (today it is golf), and the autopilots became known as George. (Koonce 2002: 286)

The following passage out of Bobbie Ann Mason's novel *The Girl in the Blue Beret* (2011) provides a recent occurrence of the use of the proverb as it relates quite specifically to a specialized aeronautical device:

> Later, as he was walking through the parc Montsouris, he looked up to see a 747 [Boeing] above the city, on its way out of De Gaulle [airport]. The gear was up, the wings clean, the nose jacked high. Things would be quieting down in the cockpit, the crew squaring things away, getting ready to hand control over to the autopilot. "Let George do it," they used to say. (Mason 2011: 129)

But turning now to human Georges, it seems appropriate to begin with America's famous first president George Washington. I have discovered the very early statement of May 30, 1898, in *The San Francisco Call* that might just be an allusion to the "Let George do it" proverb. If so, it would be a rare pre-1900 occurrence: "America must no longer let George Washington do its thinking for it" (Anonymous 1898: 3). I know that I am overzealously clutching at straws, but I cannot resist including this sentence, even if it only serves as an example that database searches can lead scholars down the proverbial garden path.

But allusions to grand George do occur in connection with the proverb, to wit an ad from 1944 of a machine tool maker:

Let (George) Washington Do It
If one thing more than any other has made America great, has given us the highest standard of living in the world, it is the grand American custom of "paddling your own canoe." It is that manly habit that has led millions of Americans to launch their own business, creating millions of better jobs for others.
(www.industryweek.com/companies-amp-executives/rebuilding/)

With the name George Washington, the idea of the capital Washington, D.C., and consequently the government also come into play, which leads me to stating that Charles Doyle pointed out to me that by 1911 the variant "Let Sam do it" starts popping up:

1911: *The Monroe Doctrine—Let Sam Do It*
[Cartoon caption by Udo J. Keppler showing Uncle Sam as a soldier with a gun on a pile of money bags with the label "Financial Interests in South & Central America"]. (*Puck*, April 5: no pp.)

1915: "Let George do it" in England may refer to King George or to Lloyd George, but more especially to the latter gentleman if the public wants to do something to or for the doctors. But in the United States we say "Let Sam do it," and Uncle Sam does. (Anonymous 1915: 260a)

1918: *Let Sam Do It! A Spineless Cry*
Among quite a lot of N.Z. farmers the idea is prevalent that New Zealand should not strike another blow for freedom. A representative farmer put it this way: "We've only got a million people in N.Z. and have sent 100,000 men to the war. America has a hundred million people—why can't she finish the war?" (*Observer*, September 28: 2)

1931: *"Let Sam Do It"*
[Cartoon by Winsor McCay showing Uncle Sam confronting the League of Nations and the conflict between Japan and China] (unpublished, <www.corbisimages.com>)

But let us return from Uncle Sam to George Washington, who also is a representative figure of the American government, as can be seen from this short unsigned editorial:

Let George do it
With the copper being taken out of the American penny, would you like to offer us a silver half dollar for our thoughts? Thank you. The half dollar we have in mind is a proposed commemorative coin for next year's 250th birthday of George Washington. The idea, already ratified by the House of Representatives, is to sell the coin for more than its silver content is worth and use the profits to pay off debts of the federal government.

Didn't Washington virtually ask for something like this when he declared in his farewell address that "towards the payment of debts there must be Revenue"? Very sound.

But the father of his country also sagely told his offspring to "cherish public credit" and "one method of preserving it is to use it as sparingly as possible." This, you might say, is the other side of the coin. And Congress is trying this way, too—isn't it? (Though you don't hear much about legislators refusing their official pay as Washington did in his first inaugural address.)

Now you get one more thought for your half dollar, which is more than we paid the friend who inspired it. If thrifty Washington threw a silver dollar across the Potomac, would he throw a half dollar half way across? Or twice across? Or simply all the way to the bank? (*Christian Science Monitor*, June 2, 1981: 24)

Speaking of money, here is a more recent passage linking the proverb with the government in Washington:

And we also think that all of us need to reorder our priorities in caring for the neediest among us. The "Let George (Washington) do it" mentality of shoving the burden away from our communities and onto the governments in Harrisburg and Washington breeds these abuses. Cut the federal taxes, leave the money closer to home, and administer welfare, not according to abstruse formulae, but according to actual needs. (*McLean*, December 8, 2011: no pp.)

While the United States has its famous early political George, Great Britain can bring up its great statesman David Lloyd George, who was an effective and popular prime minister from 1916 to 1922. The fact that his last name was George (even though, more properly, the surname was "Lloyd George") did much to spread the American proverb in his country, where it most likely had taken a foothold in the beginning of the twentieth century due to the close ties of the two nations. In any case, in the middle of World War I there appeared an advertisement in *Everybody's Magazine* in 1916 with a large picture of David Lloyd George and the following short text:

"Let George Do It!"
This has been England's answer in times of crisis since the war began. How David Lloyd George has "done" it, will be told by Isaac F. Marcosson, just back from England, in a brilliant character study. Also, Mr. Marcosson brings

a direct message to the American people from England's "man of the hour." (*Everybody's Magazine* 35, no. 6 (December 1916): 23)

Here is an admiring statement from a wartime article in *Boy's Life—The Boy Scout's Magazine*: "'Let George do it,' is now the cry of all England in her hour of need—and George is doing it. He has organized the factories, marshalled the manhood, and welded together all the resources and power of the Empire" (Rigney 1917: 14). And a third telling reference shows that the proverb had gotten a hold in Great Britain and that it was being used in connection with the admired wartime prime minister:

> *Just a Tip! "Let George Do It"*
> In England the people are forming a habit of saying, whenever they run against a hard problem or public task, "Let George do it." The expression has two meanings: First, it shows unlimited confidence in the prime minister— the little Welshman, David Lloyd George; second, to have the job done by the public officials instead of by profit-seeking private "grab-alls." (Holder 1917: 172)

But there are, of course, many other well-known Georges, and whenever they do appear, it seems that the proverb finds another spike in popularity—at times so much so that it is a riddle to me that so many people whom I have asked about the proverb maintain a complete ignorance of it! Let me present a small selection of such "George" finds here without further ado, but drawing attention to the fact that some people named George also use the proverb self-referentially:

> 1942: George Moon (character in a novel)
> He looked deeply pained. "That's right—blame me. George can take it—let George do it. I was racin' up here with my hair flyin' in the wind, and they go and grab me off for another job. I try tellin' them I'm needed here, but nobody gives a damn." (Little 1942: 221)

> 1962: George Romney
> *Let George Do It?*
> As far as Michigan Republicans were concerned, it was a famous victory last week—it catapulted their man, George Romney, former president of American Motors Comp., into the first rank of Republican contenders for the Presidential nomination in 1964. (*Newsweek*, August 20: 22)

1965: George Price
Let George Do It
George Price, who was resoundingly re-elected Premier of British Hondu-
ras last week, is probably his country's greatest asset. But he is also a liability.
(*Newsweek*, March 15: 65)

1966: George Brown
Let George Do It
The visitor was British Foreign Secretary George Brown, 52, making his first
trip to the Soviet Union to discuss with Premier Aleksei Kosygin and Foreign
Minister Andrei Gromyko a peace plan for Viet Nam and the problems of
nuclear proliferation. (*Time*, December 2: 33)

1971: George McGovern
"We have a slogan we want to check out for George McGovern," we said.
"How does *Let George Do It* grab you?"

"As *laissez-faire à Georges*," said Catchphrase, displacing some erudition,
"that was originally applied to Cardinal Georges d'Amboise, who dominated
the reign of Louis XII in the early sixteenth century. It worked for him, but it
didn't work for Romney in New Hampshire in 1968. We can do better. How
about a punning slogan you can tie to a campaign song?"

We nodded, and the computer printed out *George Is On My Mind*. "Keep
playing on McGovern's name. Something to appeal to the urban vote."

Cities Are Not UnMcGovernable was the first output, than an easier-to-pro-
nounce *Clean McGovernment*. With a last gasp, the computer tried *Govern for
McPresident*. (Safire 1971: SM8)

1988: George Shultz
Let George Do It
If the Reagan administration is going to help pull the Palestinians and Israelis
back from each other's throats, George Shultz will have to do it. (*Christian
Science Monitor*, February 12: no pp.)

1991: George Steinbrenner
Bring Back George
Baseball Commissioner Fay Vincent should reinstate Steinbrenner immediately. Vincent can say whatever he wants to say. He can claim that Steinbrenner has paid his debt to society. He can say he is doing it for the good of the

Yankees fans. Whatever. Let George do it. In public. (*New York Times*, December 7: 37)

2002: George Stephanopoulos
Let George Do It
After weeks of speculation, it's official. Bill Clinton's former aide, George Stephanopoulos, will take over the helm of ABC's "This Week" in its post-Sam and Cokie remake. The shake-up should come shortly after Labor Day. (*Milwaukee Journal Sentinel*, June 19: 10B)

Finally the time has come to see what our two George Bush presidents have done for keeping the proverb "Let George do it" alive and well. There certainly has been an overuse of the name "George" because of this presidential father and son tandem, to wit such book titles as Donald Miller's *From George . . . to George: 200 Years of Presidential Quotations* (1989). From the dozens of references let me just select a few for both former presidents. First George Herbert Walker Bush:

1986: *Should the GOP Let George Do It?*
Come on, George, do your stuff. You've got class, style, smarts, and dignity, plus experience and know-how that none of these yo-yos come close to having. Be nice to them, but please don't lower yourself to their level. (Kimmel 1986: 25E)

1988: *Let George Do It*
Let George Do It
Vote George Bush
President 1988
(campaign button; private collection)

1990: *Let George Do It*
While all these elites now claim to "support" George Bush, do they really? They're now all positioned to jump on board and be seen as backing any successful mission Mr. Bush decides to launch. But if the going gets tough, they're also positioned to get going. Either way, they'd all rather let George do it. (*Wall Street Journal*, September 11, 1990: A22)

1992: *Congress Can't Just Let George Do It*
It's not enough for the United Nations to authorize peace enforcement in Somalia, as it did yesterday, or for President Bush to provide U.S. troops for that

worthy purpose. The Constitution, the law and prudent politics require Congress also take responsibility for dispatching American troops abroad. (*New York Times*, December 4: A30)

And what is good for father George is also good for the son. Clearly George Walker Bush could not escape having his first name be linked to the buck-passing wisdom of the proverb "Let George do it." In the first reference the proverb is even linked to two Georges, as the plural form of the name in the title makes clear:

1999: *Let Georges Do It*
Gail Collins Op-Ed column on favorable signs that New York may be able to hoist its governor, George Pataki, onto Republican ticket as running mate for George W. Bush; lists advantages of ticket on which everyone shares the same name, sex, age, schooling and current job; adds that no other governor can match Pataki's desire to become Vice President, possibly because no one else has to deal with New York Legislature. (*New York Times*, October 8: no pp.)

2003: What if President Bush surprises the world and puts off a war against Iraq? [. . .] An improbable scenario? Certainly. But if it happens, nations around the world would suddenly be faced with a new reality: They could not achieve regime change in Iraq—a goal most countries favor—simply by relying on the United States to get the job done. "Let George do it," would no longer be a policy option. (*Pittsburgh Post-Gazette*, March 16: B3)

2003: Iraq's nervous neighbors are hoping that we will remove the Saddam-shaped thorn from their side. [. . .] "Let George do it! Let's you [George W. Bush] and him [Saddam] fight!," say the encouragers, "We're right behind you 1,000 percent!" (*St. Louis Post-Dispatch*, February 2: B3)

2007: *Let George Do It*
Nancy Pelosi and George W. Bush have something dangerous in common: they both ignore the voice of the American people. In November 2006 the people voted for change. Both Pelosi and Bush responded by not changing at all: she kept impeachment off the table; he sent more troops to Iraq. (*Huntington Post*, December 6, 2007)

This proverbial name-calling went so far that people seemingly thought that the proverb belongs to the Bushes, to wit this fascinating start of a blog posted on June 6, 2009:

Let George Do It

No. Not George W. Bush. The "George" here refers to an old idiom which was common in the US until about a half century ago. The phrase, "Let George do it," meant quite simply, let someone else do the job; it's not our department.

In this case the "George" in question is the Peoples Republic of China. And, the "it" in question is North Korea. (historygeeksblog.blogspot.com/2009/06)

Was the proverb "Let George do it" really common in the United States only until about the 1950s? All of the occurrences registered here—as well as dozens more—make it perfectly clear that this American expression has by no means gone underground or died out. While it might be less frequently heard or read in Great Britain (which might change with the birth of Prince George [Alexander Louis] of Cambridge on July 22, 2013), it is solidly established in the American media and mind. Its racially motivated beginning during the last quarter of the nineteenth century is absent from its use and meaning today, but it should not be forgotten that the proverb originated as an insensitive slogan for getting black Pullman porters to be at the beck and call of their white passengers. Today the proverb is thankfully free of this shameful stereotype against African Americans, and as far as I can tell, it has not been employed as a racially motivated proverb for many decades. By now the proverb is indeed an innocuous statement that can stand next to "Pass the buck" in expressing the unfortunately only too human tendency of avoiding action or passing responsibility to others. But that is the nature of proverbs in general—they reflect human nature and are used when a ready-made metaphor can hit the proverbial nail on the head better than lengthy prose could. As this discussion with its numerous contextualized references has shown, the proverb "Let George do it" remains well suited as a concise traditional piece of wisdom to deal with the complexities and ambiguities of modernity.

Acknowledgment

Tracing the origin, history, use, and meaning of a proverb requires the location of as many significant references as possible. The following colleagues and friends have been of invaluable help in this regard, and I would like to thank them for their much appreciated efforts. Charles Clay Doyle and Fred R. Shapiro have been of special importance in locating a number of the earliest references by way of database searches, but I also received useful information and leads from Mabel Agozzino, Jake Barickman, Catherine Blanchoud, Carl Bridges, Hope Greenberg, Barbara Lamonda, Douglas Lehman, Nigel Rees, Erin Regin, John Robinson, Jack Santino, and Doug Wilson.

BIBLIOGRAPHY

A much shorter version of this chapter will appear as "'Laissez faire à Georges' and 'Let George do it'" in *Paremia* 22 (2013). This chapter is dedicated to George B. Bryan, George Schumm, and all my other friends called George.

Adams, George Matthew. 1913. *You Can: A Collection of Brief Talks on the Most Important Topic in the World—Your Success*. New York: Frederick A. Stokes.

Almond, Jordan. 1985. *Why Do We Say It? The Stories Behind the Words, Expressions and Clichés We Use*. Secaucus, New Jersey: Castle.

Anderson, Jervis. 1972. *A. Philip Randolph: A Biographical Portrait*. New York: Harcourt, Brace, Jovanovich.

Anonymous. 1898. "Three Spanish Spies Make Their Escape." *San Francisco Call* (May 30): 3.

———. 1915. "How Federal Licensure May Be Brought to Pass." *Maryland Medical Journal* 58, no. 10: 260a-e.

———. 1919. *Packard Advanced Training School: Lecture Course 1919*. Detroit, Michigan: Packard Motor Car Company.

———. 1954. "Could George Do It Better?" *Life* 37, no. 9 (August 30): 7.

Anquetil, Louis-Pierre. 1805. *Histoire de France depuis les Gaulois jusqu'à la fin de la monarchie*. 14 vols. Paris: Garnery.

Baldwin, David A., and Robert L. Migneault. 1996. *Humanistic Management by Teamwork*. Englewood, Colorado: Libraries Unlimited.

Barkley, Frederick R. 1943. "Patterson Backs Manpower Bill As an Essential Step to Victory." *New York Times* (March 19): 1.

Bartlett, John. 1949. *Familiar Quotations*. 12th ed. Christopher Morley, ed. Boston: Little, Brown.

Bauch, Hubert. 1998. "Struggle for the Soul of Alliance Quebec." *Gazette* (May 23): B2.

Benedict, Elsie Lincoln, and Ralph Paine Benedict. 1921. *How to Analyze People on Sight Through the Science of Human Analysis*. East Aurora, New York: Roycrofter.

Benham, W. Gurney. 1926. *Putnam's Complete Book of Quotations, Proverbs and Household Words*. New York: G.P. Putnam's Sons.

Berman, Louis A. 1997. *Proverb Wit & Wisdom: A Treasury of Proverbs, Parodies, Quips, Quotes, Clichés, Catchwords, Epigrams and Aphorisms*. New York: Perigee.

Boatner, Maxine Tull, and John Edward Gates. 1975. *A Dictionary of American Idioms*. Woodbury, New York: Barron's Educational Series.

Brewer, Ebenezar Cobham. 1970. *Dictionary of Phrase and Fable*. Revised Centenary Edition by Ivor H. Evans. New York: Harper & Row.

Brewer, Ebenezar Cobham. 2000. *Dictionary of Phrase and Fable*. Adrian Room, ed. London: Cassell.

Burchfield, R. W. 1972. *A Supplement to the Oxford English Dictionary*. Oxford: Clarendon.

Burnham, Josephine. 1927. "Three Hard-Worked Suffixes." *American Speech* 2: 244–46.

Caillot, A. 1826. *Nouveau Dictionnaire Proverbial, satirique et burlesque*. Paris: Dauvin.

Camp, Dick. 2002. "The George Medal." *Leatherneck: Magazine of the Marines* (August): no pp.

Carothers, Willis H. "Leadership." *Teaching* 6, no. 2 (December): 10–17.

Chesnutt, Michael. 2002. "Polygenese." *Enzyklopädie des Märchens.* Kurt Ranke et al., eds. Berlin: Walter de Gruyter. 10, 1161–64.

Dalzell, Tom, and Terry Victor. 2012. *The New Partridge Dictionary of Slang and Unconventional English.* 2 vols. New York: Routledge.

Donald, Graeme. 1994. *The Dictionary of Modern Phrase.* New York: Simon & Schuster.

Dow, Andrew. 2006. *Dictionary of Railway Quotations.* Baltimore, Maryland: Johns Hopkins University Press.

Doyle, Charles Clay, Wolfgang Mieder, and Fred R. Shapiro. 2012. *The Dictionary of Modern Proverbs.* New Haven, Connecticut: Yale University Press.

Dundes, Alan. 2000. "Paremiological Pet Peeves." *Folklore in 2000. Voces amicorum Guilhelmo Voigt sexagenario.* Ilona Nagy and Kincső Verebélyi, eds. Budapest: Universitas Scientarium de Rolando Eötvös nominata. 291–99.

Duneton, Claude. 1990. *Le Bouquet des expressions imagées. Encyclopédie thématqiue des locutions figurées de la langue française.* Paris: Éditions du Seuil.

Evans, Bergen. 1969. *Dictionary of Quotations.* New York: Avenel.

Fleury de Bellingen. 1656. *L'Etymologie ou Explication Des Proverbes Francois.* Paris: Adrian Vlaco.

Foreman, George. 2005. *Let George Do It!* New York: Simon & Schuster.

Foster, John. 1957. *Let George Do It!* New York: Harcourt, Brace.

Furetière, Antoine. 1690. *Dictionnaire universel, Contenant generalement tous les mots françois tant vieux que modernes.* La Haye: Arnout & Reinier Leers; rpt. Paris: Le Robert, 1978.

Furetière, Antoine et al. 1771. *Dictionnaire universel françois et latin: vulgairement appelé dictionnaire de Trévoux, contenant la signification & la définition des mots de l'une & de l'autre langue, avec leurs différens usages* [...]. 8 vols. Paris: Avec Appropriation et Privilege du Roi, 1771.

Gossage, R. E. 1923. "Let George Do It." *Notes and Queries,* 12th series, 12 (June 23): 492.

Hardin, Russell. 2009. *How Do You Know? The Economics of Ordinary Knowledge.* Princeton, New Jersey: Princeton University Press.

Harris, William H. 1977. *Keeping the Faith: A. Philip Randolph, Milton P. Webster, and the Brotherhood of Sleeping Car Porters, 1925–37.* Urbana, Illinois: University of Illinois Press.

Harshberger, Billie. 1932. "Don't Call the Porter 'George'!" *American Magazine* 113: 70.

Hasse, Frank C. 1909. "Think It Over." *Journal of the International Brotherhood of Boilermakers, Iron Ship Builders and Helpers of America* 21, no. 8 (August 1): 476.

Holder, Arthur E. 1917. "Just a Tip! 'Let George Do It.'" *Machinist's Monthly Journal* 29, no. 2: 172–73.

Holt, Alfred H. 1936. *Phrase Origins: A Study of Familiar Expressions.* New York: Thomas Y. Crowell.

Janda, Kenneth, Jeffrey M. Berry, and Jerry Goldman. 2009. *The Challenge of Democracy: American Government in a Global World.* Boston: Wadsworth.

Kersten, Andrew E. 2007. *A. Philip Randolph: A Life in the Vanguard.* Lanham, Maryland: Rowman & Littlefield.

Kimmel, Joseph W. 1986. "Should the GOP Let George Do It?" *Wall Street Journal* (February 26): 25E.

King, George Judson. 1910. "Oregon Makes Answer." *La Follette's* 2, no. 52: 5, 15.

Kirkpatrick, Garland P. 2006. *Doing All Right Is Not Hard to Beat: A Memoir.* Bloomington, Indiana: Author House.

Knowles, Elizabeth. 1997. *The Oxford Dictionary of Phrase, Saying, and Quotation.* Oxford: Oxford University Press.

Koonce, Jefferson M. 2002. *Human Factors in the Training of Pilots.* London: Taylor & Francis.

Korach, Myron, and John B. Mordock. 2001. *Common Phrases and Where They Come From.* Guilford, Connecticut: Lyons.

La Mesangère, Pierre de. 1821. *Dictionnaire des proverbes français*. Paris: Treuttel et Würtz.

Lathen, Emma. 1970. *Pick Up Sticks*. New York: Simon & Schuster.

Le Roux de Lincy, Adrien Jean Victor. 1842. *Le livre des proverbes français*. 2 vols. Paris: Paulin; rpt. Paris: Hachette Livre, 1996.

Leitner, M. J., and J. R. Lanen. 1965. *Dictionary of French and American Slang*. New York: Crown.

Leslie, Edgar, and Al. Piantidosi. 1910. *Let Georgie Do It*. New York: Leo Feist.

Lighter, J. E. 1994. *Random House Historical Dictionary of American Slang*. 2 vols. New York: Random House.

Little, Constance, and Gwenyth Little. 1942. *The Black Thumb*. Garden City, New York: Doubleday, Doran.

London Society. 1886. "George Fox." *New York Times* (September 26): 11.

Maidment, Robert. 1976. *Robert's Rules of Disorder: A Guide to Mismanagement*. Gretna, Louisiana: Pelican.

Mason, Bobbie Ann. 2011. *The Girl in the Blue Beret*. New York: Random House.

Massing, Kathryn Busby. 2004. *Then and Now: A Grain of Salt*. Bloomington, Indiana: Author House.

Mathews, Mitford M. 1951. *Dictionary of Americanisms on Historical Principles*. Chicago: University of Chicago Press.

McKissack, Patricia, and Fredrick McKissack. 1989. *A Long Hard Journey: The Story of the Pullman Porter*. New York: Walker.

McNutt. William Slavens. 1916. "Poor Little Eddie." *Munsey's Magazine* 59 (October): 37–47.

Mencken, H. L. 1921. *The American Language*. New York: Alfred A. Knopf.

Mieder, Wolfgang. 1977. *International Bibliography of Explanatory Essays on Individual Proverbs and Proverbial Expressions*. Bern: Herbert Lang.

———. 1984. *Investigations of Proverbs, Proverbial Expressions, Quotations and Clichés: A Bibliography of Explanatory Essays which Appeared in "Notes and Queries" (1849–1983)*. Bern: Peter Lang.

———. 2004. *Proverbs: A Handbook*. Westport, Connecticut: Greenwood.

Mieder, Wolfgang, and George B. Bryan. 1997. *The Proverbial Harry S. Truman: An Index to Proverbs in the Works of Harry S. Truman*. New York: Peter Lang.

Miller, Donald L. 1989. *From George . . . to George: 200 Years of Presidential Quotations*. Washington, DC: Braddock Communications.

Nash, Ogden. 1981. *A Penny Saved Is Impossible*. Boston: Little, Brown.

Oudin, Antoine. 1656. *Curiositez Francoises, pour Supplément aux Dictionnaires ou Recueil de plusieurs belles proprietez, avec une infinité de Proverbes & Quolibets*. Paris: Antoine Sommaville.

Partridge, Eric. 1970. *A Dictionary of Slang and Unconventional English*. 7th ed. New York: Macmillan.

———. 1977. *A Dictionary of Catch Phrases, British and American, from the Sixteenth Century to the Present Day*. New York: Stein and Day.

Pentecost, Hugh. 1966. *Hide Her from Every Eye*. New York: Dodd, Mead.

Pfeffer, Paula F. 1990. *A. Philip Randolph: Pioneer of the Civil Rights Movement*. Baton Rouge, Louisiana: Louisiana State University Press.

Quitard, Pierre-Marie. 1842. *Dictionnaire étymologique, historique et anecdotique des proverbes et des locutions proverbiales de la langue française*. Paris: P. Bertrand; rpt. Genève: Slatkine Reprints, 1968.

Rees, Nigel. 1995. *Dictionary of Catchphrases*. London: Cassell.

———. 2006. *A Word in Your Shell-like: 6,000 Curious & Everyday Phrases Explained*. London: HarperCollins.

Reinhardt, Richard. 1970. *Workin' on the Railroad: Reminiscences from the Age of Steam*. Palo Alto, California: American West.

Richardson, F. H. 1912. *Motion Picture Handbook: A Guide for Managers and Operators of Motion Picture Theaters*. New York: Moving Picture World.

Rigney, Frank J. 1917. "More Powerful Than a King: What David Lloyd George, a Poor Boy, Did for Himself and His Country." *Boy's Life—The Boy Scout's Magazine* 6, no. 10: 14, 48.

Rothstein, Samuel. 1982. "The Extended Library and the Dedicated Library: A Sceptical Outsider Looks at Union Catalogues and Bibliographic Networks." *The Future of the Union Catalogue*. C. Donald Cook, ed. New York: Haworth. 103–20.

Safire, William. 1971. "It's Time for a Change of Political Slogans." *New York Times* (December 26): SM8.

Sangster, John T. 2002. "A Better Place?" *Maclean's* (November 18): 9.

Santino, Jack. 1989. *Miles of Smiles, Years of Struggle: Stories of Black Pullman Porters*. Urbana, Illinois: University of Illinois Press.

Shapiro, Fred R. 2006. *The Yale Book of Quotations*. New Haven, Connecticut: Yale University Press.

Sherell, Darlene. 1990. "Let George Do It: Fluoride Poisoning." www.rvi.net/~fluoride/george.htm.

Sills, W. C. 1920. *Sales Talks: Being a Series of Man-to-Man Articles, Instructive and Inspirational*. New York: Chevrolet Motor Company.

Simpson, J. A., and E. S. C. Weiner. 1989. *The Oxford English Dictionary*. Oxford: Clarendon.

Slaughter, Gertrude. 1918. *Two Children in Old Paris: From the Notes of a Journal by Their Mother*. New York: Macmillan.

Stevenson, Burton. 1947. *The Home Book of Quotations, Classical and Modern*. New York: Dodd, Mead.

———. 1948. *The Home Book of Proverbs, Maxims, and Familiar Phrases*. New York: Macmillan.

Stote, Amos. 1910. "Some Figures in the New Humour." *The Bookman: A Magazine of Literature and Life* 31, no. 3: 286–93.

Superintendent. 1902. "Characteristic of Superintendents and Workmen." *Wood-Worker* 211 (March): 15–16.

Taylor, Archer. 1931. *The Proverb*. Cambridge, Massachusetts: Harvard University Press; rpt. with an introduction and bibliography by Wolfgang Mieder as *The Proverb and An Index to "The Proverb."* Bern: Peter Lang, 1985.

Taylor, Phoebe Atwood. 1931. *The Cape Cod Mystery*. Woodstock, Vermont: Countryman.

Truman, Harry S. 1966. *Public Papers of the Presidents of the United States. Harry S. Truman. 1952–1953*. Washington, DC: United States Government Printing Office.

Urdang, Laurence, and Nancy La Roche. 1980. *Picturesque Expressions: A Thematic Dictionary*. Detroit, Michigan: Gale Research.

Wentworth, Harold, and Stuart Berg Flexner. 1975. *Dictionary of American Slang*. New York: Thomas Y. Crowell.

Whiting, Bartlett Jere. 1989. *Modern Proverbs and Proverbial Sayings*. Cambridge, Massachusetts: Harvard University Press.

Wilkinson, P. R. 1993. *Thesaurus of Traditional English Metaphors*. London: Routledge.

Wilson, Norman W. 2010. "Let George Do It." camanocommunity.net/2010/04/29/norman-w-wilson-let-george-do-it/.

Wuthnow, Robert. 1989. *The Struggle for America's Soul: Evangelicals, Liberals, and Secularism*. Grand Rapids, Michigan: William B. Eerdman.

Zirkel, Ray, and Bill Carney. 1909. *Let George Do It*. Columbus, Ohio: Carney and Zirkel.

Proverb Index

www.ingramcontent.com/pod-product-compliance
Lightning Source LLC
Chambersburg PA
CBHW030633270326
41929CB00007B/55

9 781496 814654